PART A: PROTOSTOME ANIMALS

A Comprehensive Guide to Animal Development, Body Plans, Simple Invertebrates, Ecdysozoans, and Lophotrochozoans

PROTOSTOME OUTLINE TABLE OF CONTENTS

PART A:

Animal Traits & Protostome Animals

SECTION 1: Animal Traits and Development

A) General Animal Traits

1. Now we ask the question 'What is an animal'? Animals are **multi-celled heterotrophic eukaryotes** that seemed to have a direct line of evolution tracing back to **protozoans**.
2. Protozoans are a fairly obvious direct line of ancestry, due to the fact that the structure of many animal cells strongly resembles those of protozoans. Many cytoskeletal and membrane components are shared.
3. For instance, the **choanocytes**, used to filter feed by sponges, look nearly identical to a group of protozoans known as the **choanoflagellates**. Both use a collar-shaped membrane and flagella to funnel plankton in to feed.
4. Likewise, the **amoebocytes** of sponges also bear a strong resemblance to the cells of amoebas. Both types of cells look like amorphous blobs. Both use **endocytosis** to bring food particles in to be digested by lysosomes.
5. For this reason, some biologists still hold that sponges should be classified as colonial protozoans, rather than animals. However, most believe them to be animals, due to the undifferentiated and mobile larval stage.
6. It is the designation as a multi-celled mobile organism that graduates sponges to animal status. A second common feature true to all animals, is that at some point in their life cycles, they are **mobile**.
7. Some animals, like sponges, barnacles, or scale insects are **sessile** (stay fixed in place during their adult lives), but their larval stages are still mobile.
8. A deeper look across the animal kingdom reveals many common forms and functions at the cell level.
9. Flagellated **sperm cells** of all animals also closely resemble the structure of other **zooflagellates**.
10. Ciliated cells in the respiratory tract and female reproductive tract resemble the structure of **ciliate** protozoans.
11. Now let's move on to more complex animals that clearly make the cut as members of **kingdom animalia**. A second commonality, with the exception of sponges, is that all animals have cells organized into **tissues.**
12. **Tissues** are groups of **differentiated cells** with similar functions, that work together for a common purpose.
13. For instance, **cnidarians**, which include corals and jellyfish, have true dermal, muscular, and digestive tissues.
14. Cnidarians are stuck somewhere in the middle of tissues and organs, developmentally speaking. They lack true organs, due to their primitive body design, but they have much greater adaptability, thanks to true tissues.
15. With the exceptions of sponges and cnidarians, all other more advanced animals have **tissues** organized into specific **organs** and **organ systems**. Organs are composed of multiple tissue types working together.
16. Reproductively, all animals use **sexual reproduction** at some stage in their lives (except for rare instances where this has de-evolved).
17. With the exception of certain colonial insects like bees and wasps, and a few other oddballs, almost all animals are **diploid** (2n) with two copies of each chromosome, one from mom and one from dad.
18. Animal **gametes** (sperm and eggs) are **haploid**, with each sperm and egg contributing one half of the new animal's genome. After fertilization, the developing **zygote** will have two full sets of chromosomes.

19. The presence of **dominant** and **recessive genes** on these chromosomes, along with the contributions of **independent assortment** and **independent segregation** created by meiosis during gamete development, ensures genetic diversity in offspring.
20. With that said, some groups of primitive animals, such as corals and starfish, have retained the ability use **asexual reproduction**, cloning themselves by either **budding** or **fragmentation**.
21. However, these abilities disappears with increasing complexity in higher animals. Even the ability to clone certain tissues, such as tail regeneration in certain lizards, disappears in highly evolved mammals and birds.
22. Before we can discuss the differences in classification in the animal kingdom, it is vital to examine the developmental stages of animals that beget those differences. Read on for a discussion of embryology.
23. The picture below summarizes some of the major features that qualify an organism to be classified as an animal.

CHARACTERISTICS OF ANIMALS

MOTILE

SEXUAL REPRODUCTION

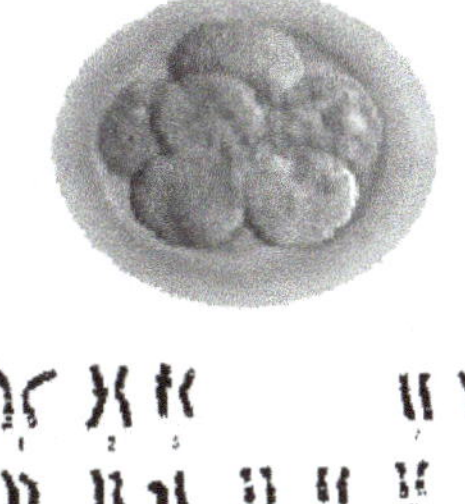

DIPLOID CELLS

HETEROTROPHIC

B) Animal Development

1. Animal life begins at conception, when a **haploid sperm** fertilizes a **haploid egg cell**, producing a **diploid zygote**.
2. The sperm cell penetrates the egg by chewing a hole in its membrane with an enzyme known as **hyalurodinase**. This enzyme is stored in a modified **lysosome** at the front of the sperm called an **acrosome**.
3. Only one **sperm** can penetrate the prospective egg cell. As soon as its **antigen** meets the **receptor** on the egg, this triggers a cascade of signaling events that causes the membrane of the egg cell to **depolarize**.
4. Once the surface of the egg cell reverses polarity, the charge reversal blocks the entry of any other sperm.
5. Only the nucleus of the sperm makes it past the cell membrane and into the egg. The flagella and any residual organelles are left behind. Eventually, the two nuclei fuse together, resulting in a **diploid zygote** (fertilized egg).
6. **Ion channel proteins** in the egg cell trigger **G proteins** in the membrane to signal **kinase enzymes** inside of the cell to activate **cyclins**. These cyclins trigger a surge in **mitosis**, leading to many cycles of cell division.
7. In addition to the obvious reason of the zygote developing and differentiating into a baby, mitosis is also necessary to get the surface area to volume ratio of the zygote down as rapidly as possible.
8. Cell division causes a huge spike in **metabolism**, leading to the rapid consumption of food reserves in the egg, combined with an exponentially accelerated respiration rate and generation of waste.

9. Cells must get smaller or risk losing control of their **homeostasis** and dying.
10. These divisions of the zygote into smaller cells, via mitosis, are called **cleavage.** Like the folding of a piece of paper in half, the egg cell divides in half again-and-again in rapid succession.
11. **Cleavage** continually until individual cells become so small that they are hard to distinguish.
12. At this point, the embryo becomes more compact and starts to give rise to **germ layers**, that will eventually **differentiate** into different types of cells that are fated for different organs.
13. The developmental pattern is based on the pattern of **homeotic genes** switching on and off, and for how long each gene remains active. These genes determine the difference between a fin, flipper, or hand in vertebrates.
14. Eventually, a hollow ball of cells called a **blastula** will form as cells repeatedly divide. The space in the middle is called the **blastocoel**, while the layer of cells is called the **blastoderm**.
15. The diagram below shows the opening sequence of animal development, up to the blastula stage.

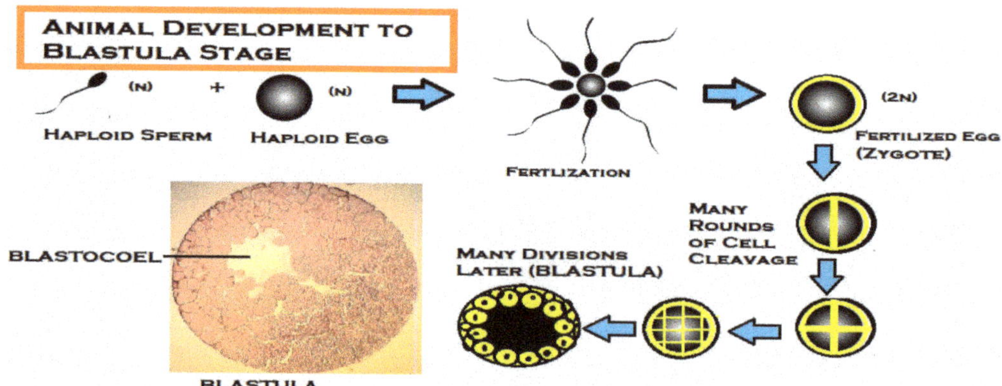

16. It is at this stage of development that the simplest animals, the sponges, stop developing.
17. Hence, sponges become the hollow blob-shaped mass of cells. Since development stops before germ layers can form, their cells are not differentiated into tissues. The **blastocoel** eventually fills with the **yolk sac**.
18. The blastocoel is not perfectly centered. The majority of the cells in the blastula migrate to one side and become the **embryoblast**, which will become the embryo. The other remaining cells become a **trophoblast**.
19. The **trophoblast** nourishes the blastula until it finds the placenta, or until the **yolk sac** has finished developing.
20. The trophoblast is contiguous with the outer layer of the embryo, which will become the future **endoderm**.
21. In more advanced vertebrates (reptiles, birds, and mammals), a water-filled pouch called the **amnion** will form around the cells of the **endoderm**, providing a 'pond inside the egg'.
22. At this point, cells begin to **differentiate** and an opening called the **blastopore** forms.
23. The **blastopore** will become the mouth of **protostome animals** (most groups of invertebrates) or it will become the anus of **deuterostome animals** (vertebrates, primitive chordates, and echinoderms).
24. The embryo then moves on to the **gastrula stage**. The **blastopore** essentially punches one end of the hollow ball of cells in the embryoblast, forming a vase-like structure called the gastrula.
25. The **blastopore** continues to punch in, forming a cavity through the embryo known as an **archenteron**.
26. It is at this point that tissue differentiation begins, thanks to numerous factors, such as hormonal signals, the position of the cells in the embryo, and genetic switching.
27. In **diploblastic animals**, such as jellyfish and corals, only two tissue layers will form. The outer **ectoderm layer** will become the skin and nervous system, while the inner **endoderm** will form the

gut cavity and gonads.

28. The space in the middle of the two layers will become the **mesoglea**, and it fills with a jelly-like protein matrix.
29. Three layers of tissues form in **triploblastic animals.** Triploblastic animals include flatworms and essentially every other classification of animals with a more complicated body plan.
30. Triploblastic embryos have an **ectoderm**, **mesoderm**, and **endoderm**. The **mesoderm** becomes a layer of connective tissue, muscle, blood, bone, and lymphatic ducts in triploblastic animals. The mesoglea is absent.
31. As differentiation continues, a second opening called the **gastrocoel** develops when the **archenteron** connects the other end of the digestive system to the outside of the body.
32. In **protostomes**, this opening becomes the anus. In **deuterostomes**, this second opening forms the mouth.
33. Up to this point, the embryo (and all primitive animals that stop developing at early points) had either **asymmetry** or **radial symmetry**. Once the animal becomes a tube-shape, **cephalization** begins.
34. **Cephalization** implies the presence of a head (and also a tail). At this point of development, symmetry becomes **bilateral**, as only the medial plane of the animal can be bisected into two equal halves.
35. The diagram below shows the developmental stages associated with the gastrula in animal embryos.

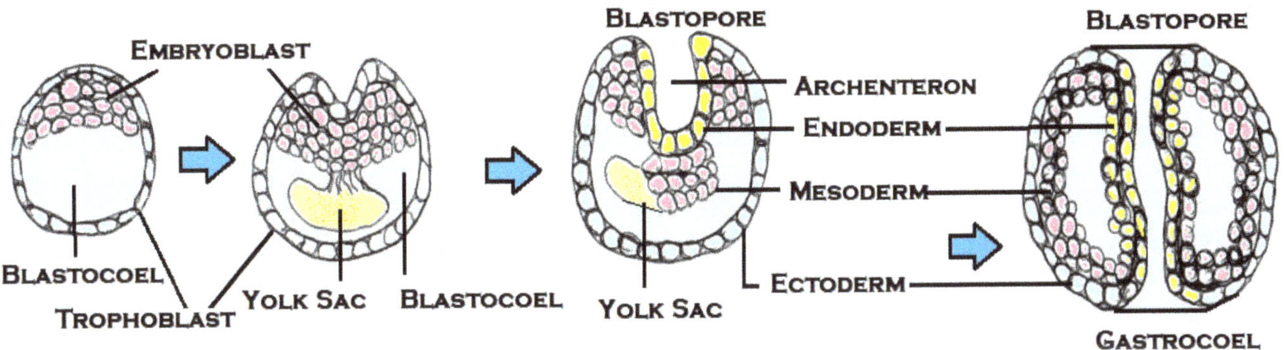

36. At this point, we will digress from getting into too many details in our short lesson in embryology, due to the highly varied patterns of development among various taxa of animals.
37. In the next section, we will discuss patterns of development in embryos, with regard to the different germ layers of embryonic tissues. This will be related back to animal body plans and evolution.

C) Developmental Patterns and Body Plans

1. Before discussing the various developmental patterns taken by different phyla of animals, let's review the fate of each set of tissues in the embryo.
2. The outermost set of cells, the **ectoderm**, is fated to become dermal and nervous tissues as they develop.
3. If present, the middle layer of cells, the **mesoderm**, will become connective tissues, such as muscles, blood, fat tissue, bone, cartilage, and connective tissue. It also is the origin of the kidneys and excretory system.
4. The innermost layer of cells, the **endoderm**, will develop into the organs of the digestive, respiratory, and reproductive systems. Many of the glands in the endocrine system also have their ancestry in the endoderm.
5. The diagram below summarizes the embryonic origins of various organs.

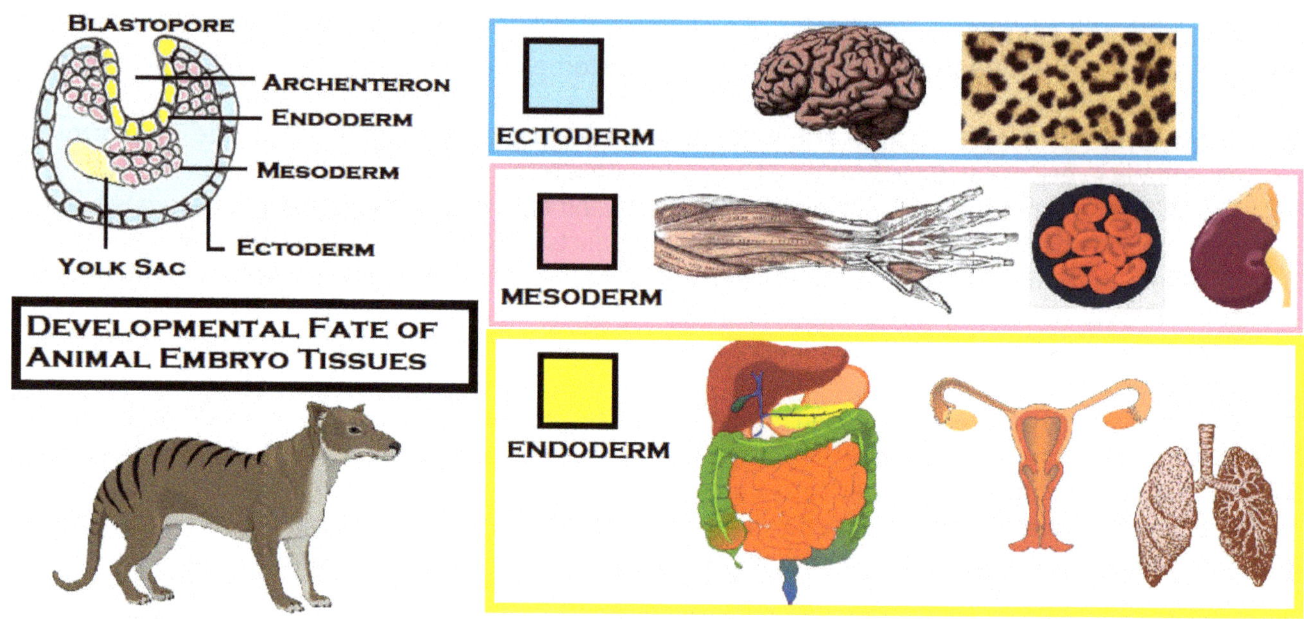

6. Almost from the gastrula stage forward, animal embryo development differs markedly between phyla, growing in complexity as groups advance, due to evolutionary changes and additional effects of **homeobox genes.**
7. As previously mentioned, sponges stop developing before they get to the **gastrula stage.**
8. **Sponges** are classified by themselves as **parazoan animals.** They diverged from **colonial flagellate protozoans**, but took a different developmental route than all the other animals, since they never organized into tissues.
9. They remain the only group of extant animals that have no defined tissues or organs.
10. All other animals are considered to be **eumetazoans** or 'true animals'. Eumetazoans have true tissues with differentiated cells and a definite body plan. Every animal that isn't a sponge is a eumetazoan.
11. The simplest of the **eumetozoans** are the **cnidarians** (jellyfish and allies) and **ctenophores** (comb jellies).
12. **Cnidarians**, which include jellyfish, hydroids, corals, and anemones are little more than a living **gastrula** that didn't quite make it all the way to more advanced stages of organ differentiation.
13. This is why their body is a cup shape. The 'mouth' or **gastrovascular cavity** of jellyfish is derived directly from the **blastopore**. Since the **archenteron** doesn't reach the far side of the embryo at this stage, they have no anus.
14. The diagram below shows a schematic of the tissue layers of a jellyfish.

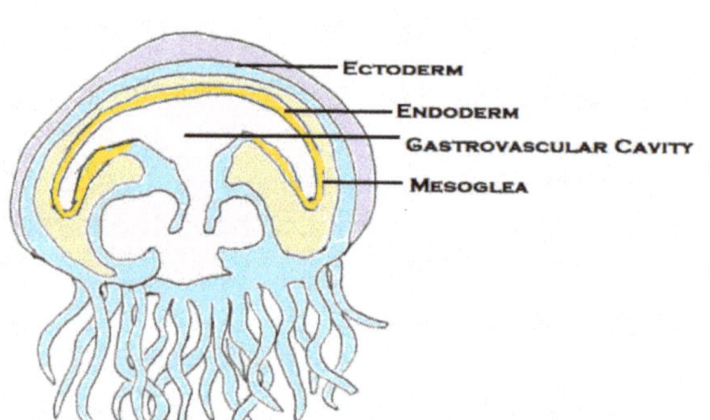

What kind of sandwiches do mermaids eat?
Peanut butter and jellyfish
Who is the leader of the Undersea Communist party?
Coral Marx
Why won't army recruiters call sponges?
Because they've got no guts.
Why won't TV stations hire flatworms as reporters?
Because they can't even talk you or hold a microphone you moron! They are worms for crying out loud!

15. Since jellyfish stop developing before a rudimentary layer of cells known as the **mesenchyme** can fully differentiate into connective tissue, they are called **diploblastic animals.**
16. They have an **ectoderm** and **endoderm**, but they lack a true **mesoderm**. Instead, this part of the embryo becomes a **mesoglea**, filling in with water and secreted jelly-like proteins called **collagen** and **proteoglycans.**
17. There are only two living phyla of animals that are **diploblastic**. The aforementioned cnidarians are joined by the ctenophores, which are known more commonly as comb jellyfish, though they are not related to true jellies.
18. Instead of stinging large prey animals, comb jellies are filter feeders that eat plankton. Their body designs are fundamentally different. We will discuss both phyla of animals shortly in the pages ahead.
19. The diagram below shows a flowchart of primitive animal evolution of what we have discussed so far.

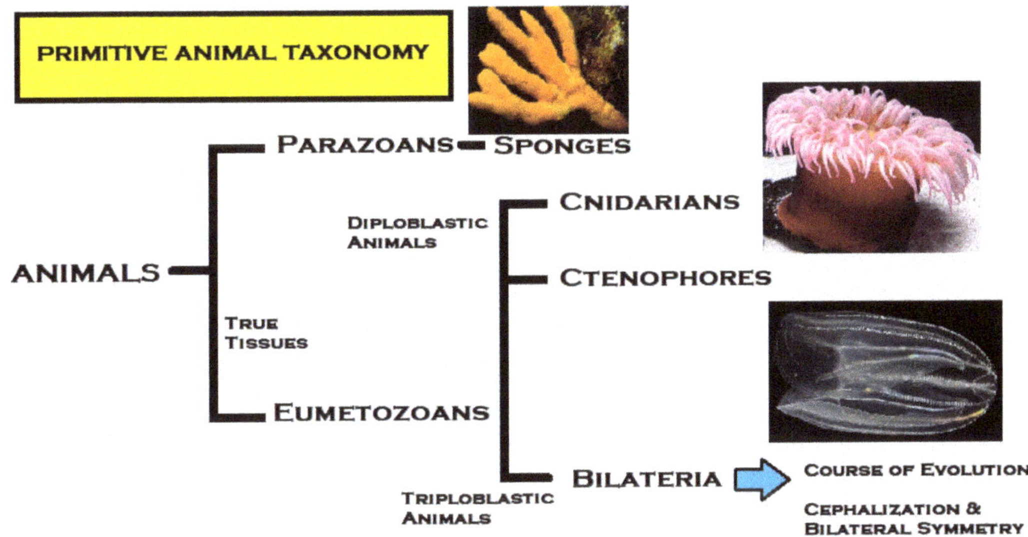

20. As animals continued to evolve and advance, the **mesenchyme cells** at the center of the embryo eventually differentiated into the entire **mesoderm layer**, which then differentiated into all the connective tissue organs.
21. We are now at the point that **triploblastic animals** evolved. Triploblastic animals have three tissue layers, including a true layer of mesoderm.
22. The great majority of all triploblastic animals show **cephalization** (have a head) and **bilateral symmetry**.
23. The most primitive **triploblastic animals** (which have all three tissue layers) are the **platyhelminthes**, more commonly known as the flatworms. They retain many other primitive traits, but gain true organs.
24. Flatworms are considered to be **acoelomate animals**. All three layers of tissue are tightly sandwiched together.
25. **Acoelomate animals** have no body cavity. When their gastrula is finished developing, there is no remaining **blastocoel** space between the mesoderm tissues and the endoderm. This limits mobility greatly.
26. Flatworms are limited to 'doing the worm' in an up-and-down plane of movement. Flatworms are basically the Shabba Doo of the animal kingdom. Like the 1980s breakdance group, they can really only do one thing well.
27. For the uninitiated, in 1982 or so, you were no one if you weren't carrying an 80 pound boom-box inches from your face, while it blasted synthesizer music (such as Shabba Doo) at a decibel level on par with a Boeing 747.

28. Groups of cool people would gather at public parks and 'jam'. For fun, they would repeatedly slam their bodies into the ground in convulsions, as they did 'the worm' across asphalt parking lots to Grandmaster Flash music.
29. In order to gain full credibility, the requisite uniform was high-top Adidas with Velcro straps, parachute pants, an airbrushed T-shirt, and a flap-cap. A mullet with parallel-lines carved into the sides only enhanced the look.
30. The most primitive groups of **triploblastic animals** improved on the flattened **acoelomate** design by adding a body cavity called a **pseudocoelem**. The drawback of this design is that the organs float in the body cavity.
31. There are only two kingdoms of **pseudocoelomates. Phylum nematode** includes the roundworms, which are almost entirely parasitic in their lifestyle. **Phylum rotifera** is the rotifers, which are small planktonic animals.
32. While being a **pseudocoelomate** allows you to have 360 degree mobility, it comes with a drawback. The organs slosh around inside your body cavity like someone shaking up a bowl of Jello. The potential for damage is great.
33. Roundworms get around this problem by living inside the soft tissues of other animals as parasites. Rotifers are so small, that at their miniscule size, water flow behaves more like honey, so they are cushioned from impacts.
34. **True coelomate animals** have a true **coelom** or body cavity. Their internal organs from the endoderm are tethered to the mesoderm at points, but there is still a gap between them, allowing 360 degree mobility.
35. This design combined the best of both worlds, allowing mobility and a degree of shock-absorbing protection.
36. With the aforementioned exceptions, all other living animals are **true coelomates**.
37. The body design of all three types of **triploblastic animals** is shown below.

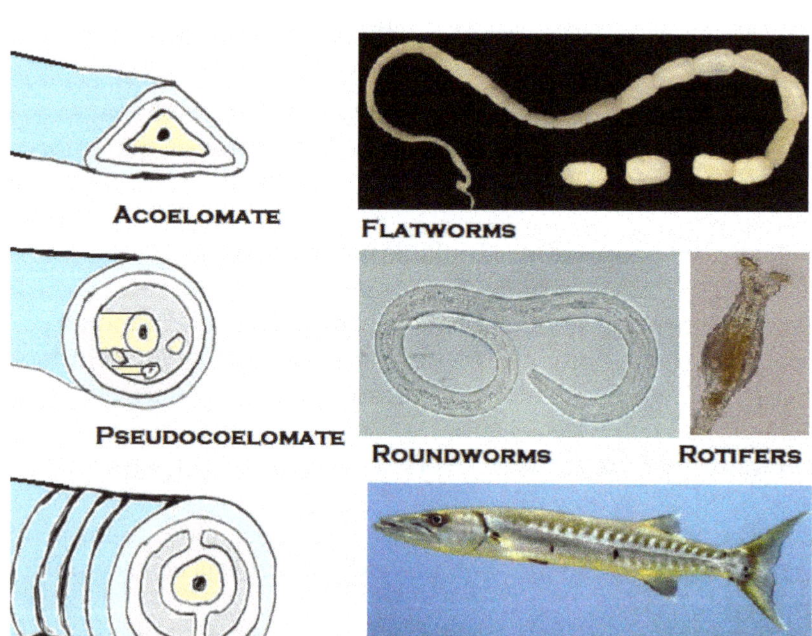

What Roman Emperor was the only lobster ever to hold political power? Clawdius

Why was Clawdius considered to be ineffective at relating to the common citizens of Rome? He could never really come out of his shell.

How was Clawdius commemorated after his death? He was broiled at 475 and served with melted butter.

Why was fish Emperor, Ichthyus, his successor, also gill-ty of poor leadership? He saw things on small scales and floundered on decisions.

38. **True coelomate animals** are then classified again as either **protostomes** or **deuterostomes**, depending on which end of the body develops from the **blastopore** and resultant **archenteron**.
39. As important as body cavity was to the evolutionary success of triploblastic animals, it is of secondary importance to animal classification. Other factors are considered to be more predictive of evolutionary history.
40. One of these factors is the developmental pattern an animal embryo takes, with regard to body openings.
41. **Protostome coelomates** develop mouth first. The original blastopore turns into the mouth, and the anus develops later from the **gastrocoel**. The majority of invertebrates develop with this body plan.
42. During early development, **protostomes blastulas** exhibit **spiral cleavage**. Their embryonic cells divide in a DIAGONAL pattern. The layer of cells above the previous layer is always staggered like bricks in a brick wall.
43. **Protostomes** also show **determinate cleavage**. After the first 4 cells have formed, they are already genetically marked to develop into a certain section of the body.
44. For these reasons, it is NOT POSSIBLE for ANY protostome to have identical twins. The spiral pattern of cells will not allow the egg to split, nor can the early cells clone themselves and double up potential organs.
45. **Deuterostome coelomates**, on the other hand, develop anus first. Their **blastopore** and **archenteron** become the back end of the digestive tract, while the second opening becomes the mouth.
46. **Deuterostomes** exhibit **radial cleavage**, with cells stacking directly on top of one another on even planes.
47. Their embryonic cells also wait much longer to **differentiate**. **Vertebrate stem cells** can develop into virtually any type of tissue, as their genes are switched on or off according to need.
48. Because of their embryonic geometry and delayed differentiation, it is possible for egg cells in **deuterostomes** to split and develop into identical twins or to give rise to multiple births of clones.
49. The **cleavage patterns** difference between **protostomes** and **deuterostomes** is shown below, along with the differences in blastopore and gastrocoel fate between the two sub-divisions of animals.

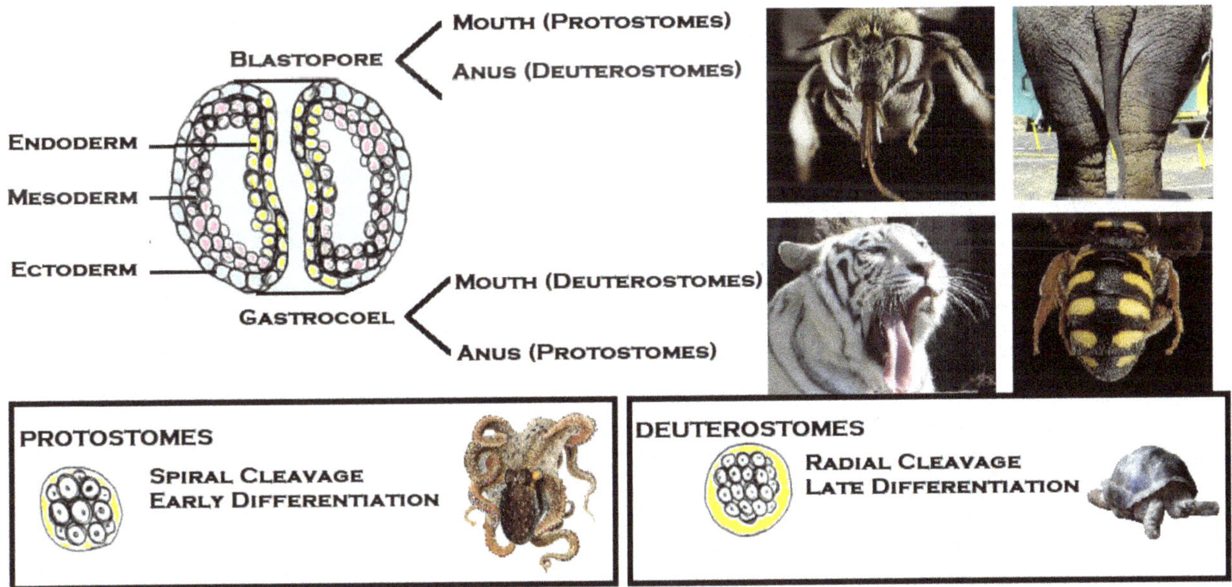

50. It is worth noting that all animals can be described as having one of three definite types of **symmetery**.
51. Sponges, the only members of the **parazoan animal** classification have **asymmetry**. Since they are an amorphous blob of cells, they cannot be cut into two equal halves on any plane.

52. In unusual cases, some more advanced animals show asymmetry. For instance, **bivalves** (clams and oysters) are **asymmetric** since they lack a definite head and their shells are jointed on one side or the other.
53. Flounder, soles, and halibut are all asymmetric fish, since their eyes and skin chromatophores migrate to the dorsal surface of their body early in their larval development.
54. All **diploblastic animals**, such as jellyfish and comb jellyfish, show **radial symmetry**. Like a pizza, they can be cut in equal halves along any circular diameter of the organism.
55. A few **triploblastic animals**, such as **echinoderms** (starfish and sea cucumbers) also have radial bodies.
56. The great majority of **triploblastic animals** show **cephalization**, with a definite head and tail. They show **bilateral symmetry** along the left and right planes of their bodies, divided by a nerve cord.
57. The diagram below depicts the three general types of animal symmetry.

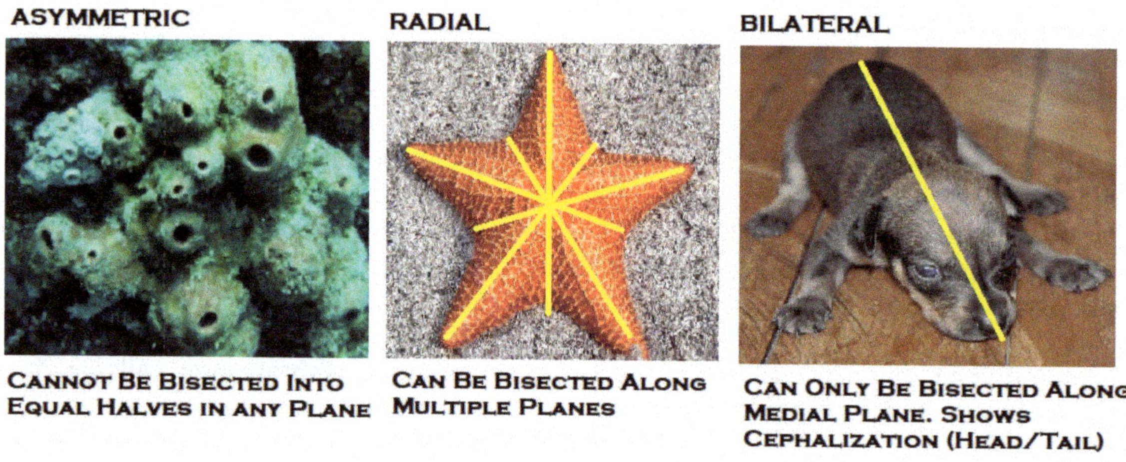

58. **Bilateral animal** anatomy is also described with **directional planes**. We will go ahead and review this terminology, because it will come up with some frequency as we discuss anatomical features of animals.
59. The diagram at the top of the next page illustrates directional planes and provides descriptions of their relative positions on the body.

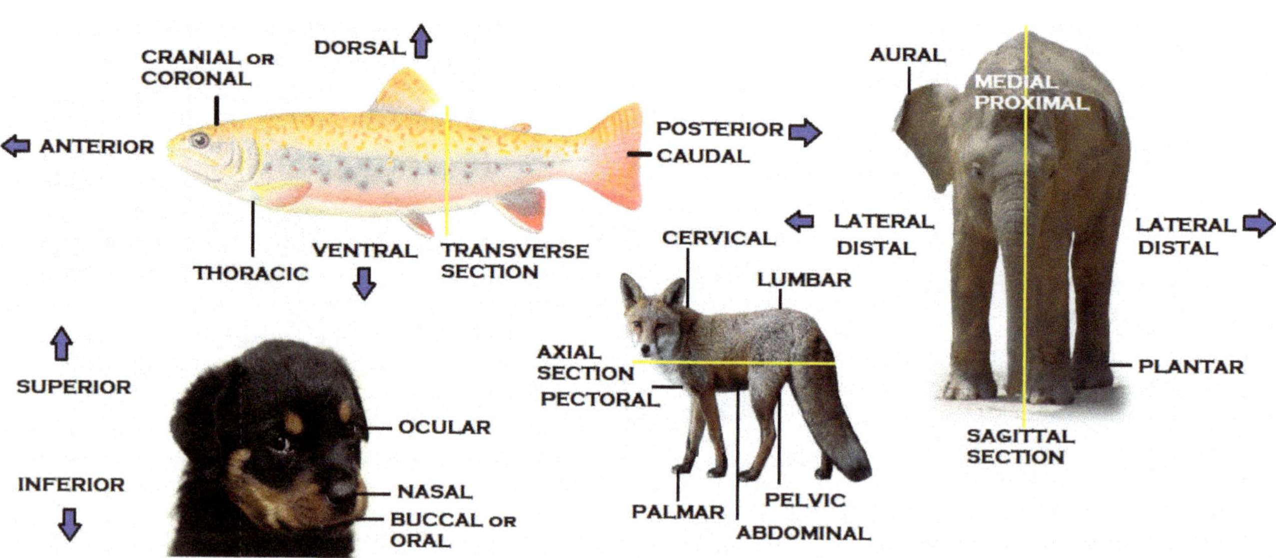

ANATOMICAL TERM	DESCRIPTION	ANATOMICAL TERM	DESCRIPTION
Anterior	Toward the Front of Body	**Posterior**	Toward the Back of Body
Lateral	Toward the Outside of Body	**Medial**	Toward the Inside of Body
Proximal	Close to Reference Structure	**Distal**	Far from Reference Structure
Sagittal	Sections Left & Right Sides of Body	**Axial**	Sections Top and Bottom of Body
Transverse	Sections Front & Back of Body	**What Fox Says**	Ring-Ding-Ding-Ding-Ringeringeding
Superior	Above a Reference Structure	**Inferior**	Below a Reference Structure
Cranial or Coronal	Refers to the Head	**Caudal**	Refers to the Tail
Ventral	Refers to Belly Region of the Body	**Dorsal**	Refers to the Back of the Body
Thoracic	Refers to Front Segment of Torso	**Abdominal**	Refers to Back Segment of Torso
Pelvic	Refers to Groin Region of Body	**Pectoral**	Refers to Chest Region of the Body
Plantar	Refers to Food Region of Body	**Palmar**	Refers to Hand Region of Body
Ocular	Refers to Eye Region of Body	**Aural**	Refers to Ear Region of Body
Buccal or Oral	Refers to Mouth Region of Body	**Nasal**	Refers to Nose Region of Body

60. Now that we have opened up discussion on animals with bilateral symmetry, we must consider other factors that are considered to be more predictive of the evolutionary history of specific groups.
61. To do so, let's review where we are, with regard to the present discussion of primitive bilateral animals.
62. We know that bilateral animals can have **acoelomate**, **pseudocoelomate**, or **true coelomate** body cavity plans.
63. Let's begin with classification criteria for **protostome animals**. We will come back to **deuterostomes** shortly.
64. There are factors that carry more weight than body cavity design in the classification of **protostomes**.
65. These factors are the structure of the animal's **Integumentary layer** and mouth. These two factors seem to denote a major evolutionary **divergence** that divided the invertebrates permanently into two camps.
66. **Ecdysozoan invertebrates** have hard protective **cuticles** that are secreted over the skin. It is a non-living protein or glycoprotein matrix. In roundworms, it is made of **keratin**, while arthropods primarily use **chitin**.
67. This protective shell may also extend to the mouth, allowing hard specialized appendages to develop.
68. Unrelated to the shell, most ecdysozoans tend to have evolved to have separate sexes.
69. **Lophotrochozoan invertebrates** have soft bodies and **tentacles** around the mouth. Their bodies are usually supported by hydraulic pressure in **hydrostatic skeletons**. Like worms and mollusks, they are slimy and squishy.
70. Some **lophotrochozoans** lose their tentacles as adults, but their presence in larvae, still indicate where they should be classified. Some animals in the group DO make shells, but they are calcified, rather than proteins.
71. **Hermaphroditism** is common among lophotrochozoan taxa, though some exceptions do have separate sexes.
72. Most criteria for classification are now molecular, but it is also still possible that this classification scheme could change as taxonomists find more information down the road. Right now, this is everyone's best guess.

73. Phylogenetic trees for protostome animal evolution are shown below. Notice that some groups of animals can be advanced in one way, but primitive in others. Let's begin with **Ecdysozoan** classification in the first diagram.

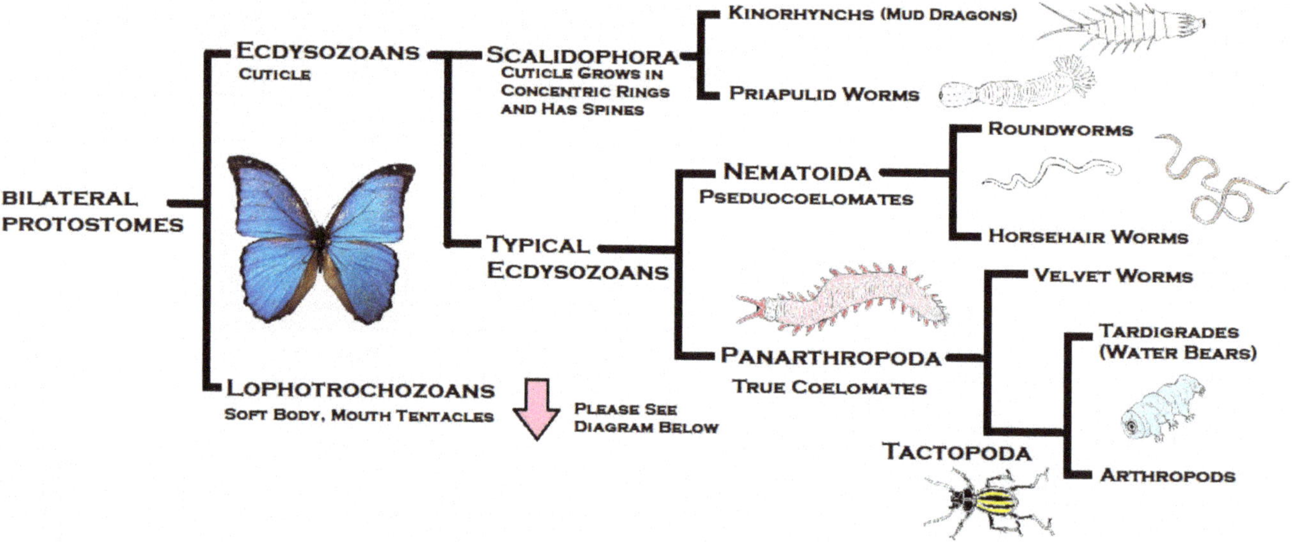

74. The **Ecdysozoan** branch of the bilateral protostomes is split into a group of typical members and a separate branch called **Scalidophora**. The two phyla in this branch are basically evolutionary dead ends.

75. **Kinorynchs** and **Priapulid worms** both have a cuticle that forms concentric rings around their bodies.

76. Both groups live in ocean sediment and haven't evolved much in millions of years. Neither has any limbs, both groups have **pseudocoelomate** body plans, and both have separate sexes.

77. Kinorynchs don't get much bigger than a pencil lead. They Zamboni the bottom for algae or suck in diatoms.

78. **Priapulid worms** are ringed with circles of spines and the cuticle is shed and grown in rings. They eat other burrowing animals like segmented worms and can live in highly anoxic silt, unlike most animals.

79. Some species of **priapulid worms** can get to be the size of a banana. They have separate sexes and lay eggs.

80. The typical ecdysozoans are split into the **nematoidia**, which includes pseudocoelomate parasitic worms and the **panarthropodia**, which groups together true coelomates with legs.

81. From there, the **velvet worms** are thought to have diverged from the **tactopods**, which then evolved into **tardigrade water bears** and into **arthropods**, the most successful group of all invertebrates.

82. The **arthropods** include the insects, crustaceans, arachnids, and several other classes of invertebrates with segmented bodies, exoskeletons, jointed appendages, and relatively advanced organ systems.

83. We will cover each of these phyla in their own individual sections.

84. Now we turn our attention to the phylogeny of **lophotrochozoan** invertebrates. The members of this classification all have soft bodies and lack cuticles or exoskeletons.

85. True lophotrochozoans also have tentacles around the mouth in at least one of their life stages.

86. This branch is regarded as **paraphyletic** by many biologists, in that some of the groupings in this taxa don't necessarily indicate close evolutionary relationships.

87. For instance, no one really knows for sure what to do with the flatworms. They are the only large group of acoelomate animals and they lack tentacles around the mouth, but they do have soft bodies.

88. The diagram below, like the one of the ecdysozoans, represents everyone's best guess at the moment. Molecular evidence will probably end up leading to further classification refinement as time goes on.

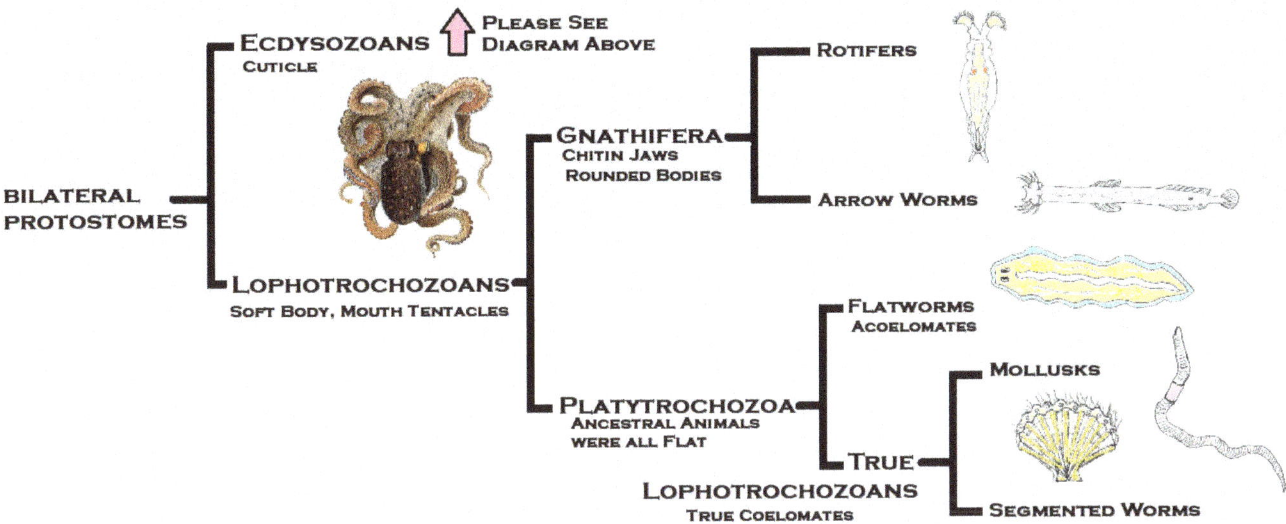

89. The **lophotrochozoans** had their first evolutionary split a very long time ago in the ancient oceans more than 500 million years back when they diverged into the **gnathiferans** and the **platytrochozoans**.

90. **Rotifers** and **arrow worms** still exist in the oceans today. Both have chitin jaws and soft rounded bodies like their ancestors. However, both groups show some surprising complexity.

91. Members of both phyla have ciliated feeding structures in the mouth and pharynx. Rotifers use these for filter feeding, but arrow worms use them to detect vibrations from prey animals like fish larvae and crustaceans.

92. In spite of being about the size of a period on a page, **rotifers** have a full digestive tract and ganglion that functions like a primitive brain. They cruise along in the plankton and filter feed algae, largely unnoticed.

93. Rotifers also show a weird set of evolutionary turns, with regard to gender.

94. Some species are solely female and use **parthenogenesis** to auto-fertilize their own eggs, while other types are **sexually dimorphic**, with large females and smaller males.

95. While rotifers are **pseudocoelomates**, the larger arrow worms needed to keep their organs in place, so they evolved into **true coelomates**, albeit independently of the other lophotrochozoans.

96. **Arrow worms**, like the majority of lophotrochozoan animals, are **hermaphrodites**. In spite of their primitive origins, they have eyes and a full digestive tract.

97. Arrow worms also show **convergent evolution** with fish, since they possess paired fins on their body and a caudal fin. Their fins even have ray-like gradations to allow them to be retracted and fanned.

98. On the other branch of the **lophotrochozoan** evolutionary tree, the original **platytrochozoan animals** diverged about the same time as the early gnathiferans. They appear to have had flat soft bodies.

99. This early group then diverged into two very different branches of animals. The **flatworms** are **acoelomates** with a number of primitive features, while the **true lophotrochozoans** are relatively advanced **true coelomates**.

100. The true lophotrochozoans can be further sub-divided into the **mollusks** and the **segmented worms**.

101. We will cover each of these phyla in detail in the sections ahead.

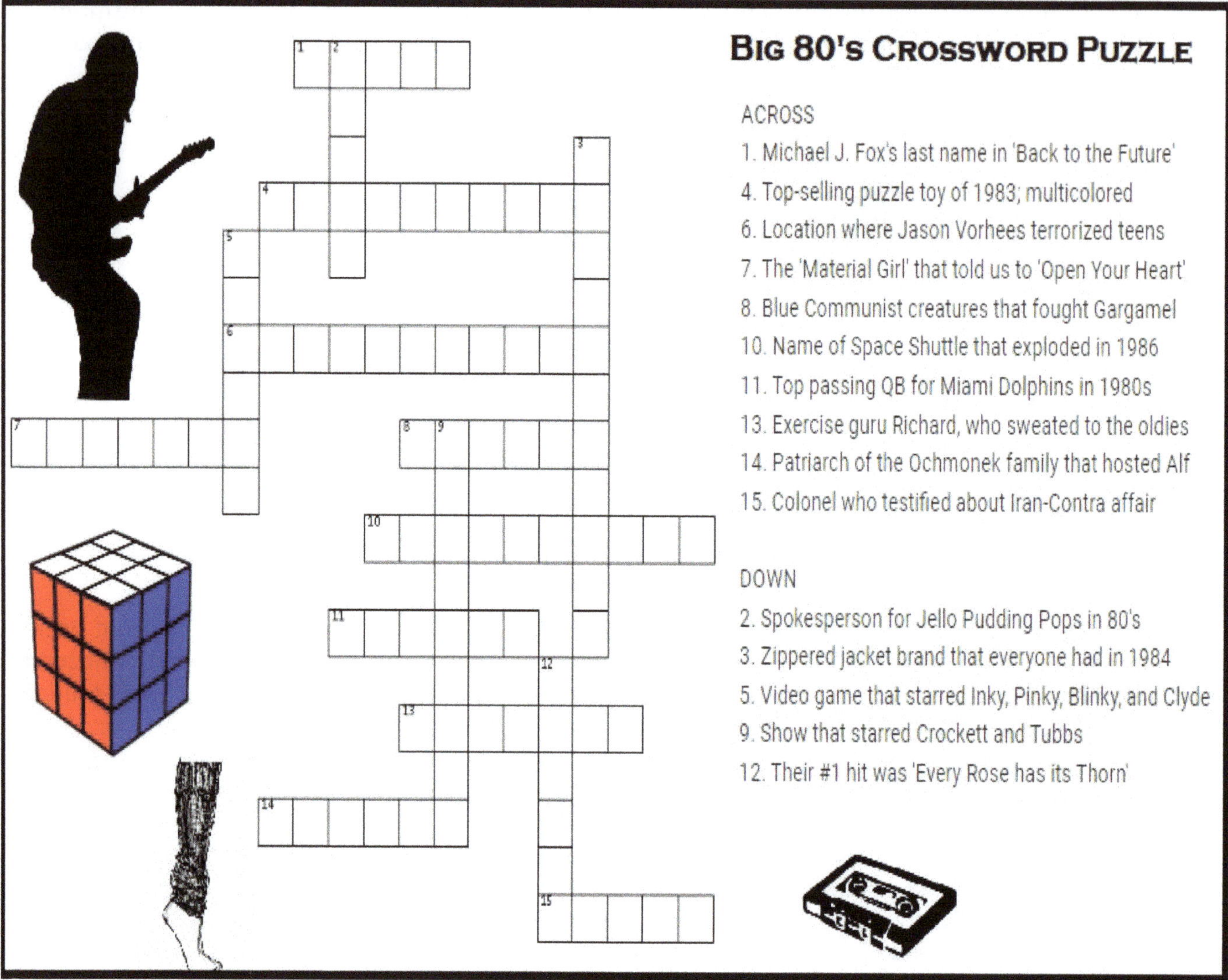

In the spirit of the 1980's reference above, we now present DUMB THINGS FROM THE 80's TRIVIA

1) A kid named 'Mikey' was the spokesperson for 'Life' cereal in the 1980s. According to unsubstantiated rumors, how did Mikey die (surprise....it turned out to be false)?
2) Name the 1980's workout guru who sold more than 65 million videotapes, helped millions of overweight women 'sweat to the oldies' and had a public feud with David Letterman.
3) Name the wife of this former Tennessee senator (and later presidential candidate) who battled the likes of Twisted Sister in the senate to try to stop kids from getting their albums.

ANSWERS ON PAGE 17

SECTION 2: Primitive Protostome Phyla

A) Phylum Porifera: Sponges

1. **Sponges**, as previously mentioned, are lowest on the evolutionary tree of animals.
2. Members of the **phylum porifera** are stuck somewhere in the middle of protozoans and animals, with their mobile larval stage really being the only criteria that gains them admission into the animal club.
3. Colonial **Choanoflagellate** protozoans are the direct ancestors of sponges.
4. Like protozoans, sponges lack defined **tissues**, instead relying on several repeating types of individual cells that are embedded in a secreted **matrix**. These cells work cooperatively to help the sponge feed and reproduce.
5. Randomly peppered through their matrices are individual **choanocytes** (collar cells) that resemble **zooflagellates, amoebocytes** that resemble **amoebas**, and **porocytes**.
6. **Choanocytes**, known informally as **collar cells**, whip their flagella and create water flow that drags plankton in through donut-shaped **porocyte cells** and through gaps in the **matrix** of the sponge.
7. Some sponges have a mouth-like opening called an **osculum** that aids in water flow.
8. As water flows through the sponge, they **filter feed** on whatever algae or zooplankton gets trapped in the sponge and taken up by **endocytosis**. Most of the digestion of the food is done in vacuoles of **amoebocytes**.
9. **Amoebocytes** are the cells that also undergo **meiosis** to produce **gametes** for sexual reproduction. Like most primitive animals, sponges are **hermaphrodites** that use **external fertilization**.
10. All sponges release clouds of sperm into the water, and all sponges undergo **oogenesis** to produce eggs.
11. The flagellated sperm swim into other sponges and fertilize eggs that are embedded in the protein component of the sponge's matrix. After **fertilization** and **embryogenesis**, free-swimming larvae called **planulae** hatch.
12. **Planulae** are ciliated and free-swimming. They swim out of their parent sponge and find another place on the reef that seems favorable. After finding a good place, they glue themselves down and become **sessile**.
13. Adult sponges remain in the same location for life, feeding on whatever comes by, being couch potatoes.
14. In addition to sexual reproduction, sponges can also reproduce asexually by **budding** miniature clones of themselves, or via **fragmentation**. Many species of sponges form colonies on reefs via these methods.
15. The types of cells and skeletal elements of sponges are described and shown below.

ANSWERS TO DUMB THINGS FROM THE 80's

1) He ate dozens of packets of pop rocks and drank an entire 6 pack of coke and his stomach exploded, at least the rumors said so....
2) Richard Simmons
3) Tipper Gore

Cell Type/ Part	Description
Choanocytes	'Collar cells' found around 'mouth' and inside surface, which whip and draw in water current. Work cooperatively with amoebocytes.
Osculum	The circular opening that forms the 'mouth' of the sponge. Derived from the blastopore. Allows water flow in filter-feeding.
Amoebocytes	Most of the cells in the sponge. They feed by endocytosis, secrete the spicules and skeletal material, and divide by meiosis to produce gametes. Can also regenerate a new sponge asexually.
Inner and Outer Epidermis	Layers of amoebocytes embedded in the 'skeleton' on the outside and inside surfaces. Conduct many different functions.
Mesohyl (Matrix)	A jelly-like matrix of proteins that forms between the inner and outer epidermis. Provides support and place for eggs to embed.
Spicules	Crystals of spongin protein, calcium salts, and/or silica, which forms the protective matrix the amoebocytes live inside of. The 'skeleton' of the sponge. Differences in these are the basis for sponge classification. Openings in scaffold allow water flow in feeding.
Porocytes	Modified amoebocytes that form tunnels to allow water flow into the sponge. Critical to suction that allows filter-feeding.

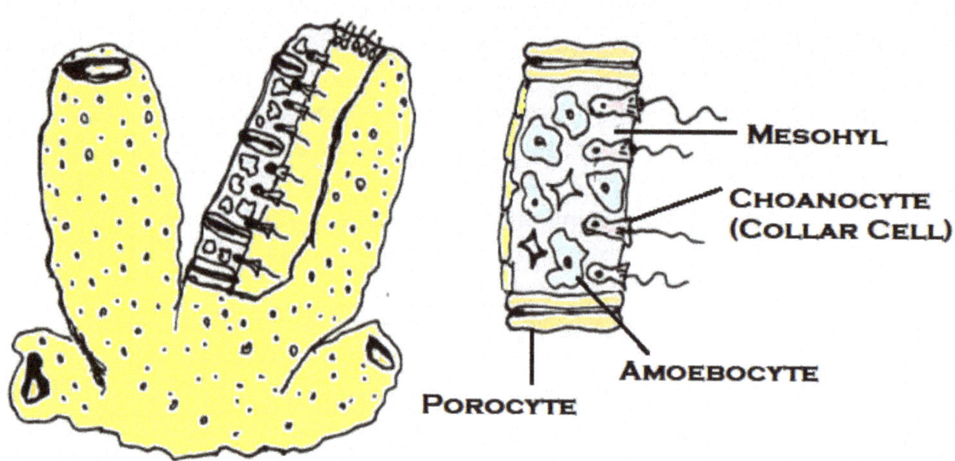

16. As you can see, there's not a lot of substance to sponges. The life of the adult basically consists of **filter-feeding** and **reproducing**, working in underwater fast-food restaurants, and hanging out with idiot starfish.
17. Since sponges can't exactly get up and move around, many of them concentrate powerful toxins from the **dinoflagellates** they eat, to deter grazing animals from eating them.
18. Sponges are also full of the anti-bacterial compound, **triclosan**, which prevents bacterial rotting.
19. In spite of these defenses, a number of animals seem to be unfazed by the toxins. Hawksbill sea turtles, pufferfish, wrasses, and boxfishes seem to enjoy eating slimy little glass shards spiked with poison.
20. **On the flipside, some sponge toxins are now promising candidates for new pharmaceutical drugs.**
21. Several anti-cancer drugs and anti-viral drugs, such as manzamine A (leukemia treatment) and remdisivir (used to treat COVID and Ebola) were derived from compounds made by sponges.
22. Many sponges are brightly-colored. While some of this may be the evolution of warning coloration, it seems that the primary purpose of the pigments is to absorb sunlight and protect sponges from

baking in UV rays.

23. Sponges are classified into 3 classes, based on what they use for **spicules** in their **mesohyl matrix**.

24. Sponges in **Class Demospongae** use soft **spongin proteins**, while members of **Class Calcarea** and **Class Hexactinellida** are rock-like, using limestone and silica, respectively, to strengthen their bodies.

25. The table below shows example specimens from each class of sponge.

Hexactinellida: Glass sponges	**Calcarea: Hard Sponges**	**Demospongae: Soft Sponges**
Hard silica spicules. Usually found in deep ocean below the photic zone.	Spicules are made out of calcium carbonate like coral. Common on most coral reefs worldwide.	Spicules made of soft spongin protein. Used commercially. Also very common.

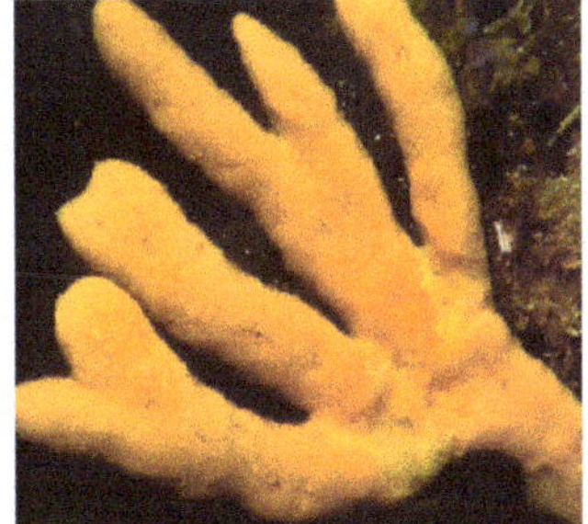

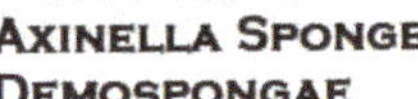
AXINELLA SPONGE
DEMOSPONGAE

YELLOW RUFFLE SPONGE
DEMOSPONGAE

BLUE REEF SPONGE
CALCAREA

VENUS FLOWER BASKET SPONGE
HEXACTINELLIDA

i) Budding: **Sponges may also produce 'mini-me' copies of themselves by mitosis.**

B) Phylum Cnidaria: Jellyfish, Corals, and Allies

1. **Cnidarians** are an evolutionary step up from sponges. As the most primitive members of the **eumetazoan animal** clade, they have definite **tissues** organized by function.
2. The **cniarians** include jellyfish, box jellyfish, corals, anemones, hydroids, and other similar relatives.
3. Cnidarians are **diploblastic** with just the two layers of the **endoderm** and **ectoderm**, with a jelly-like protein matrix, the **mesoglea**, serving as a cushion between the two tissue layers.
4. The name of the phylum is derived from stinging cells called **cnidocytes** that line the **tentacles** that are also ubiquitous to all cnidarians. The tentacles, themselves, are extensions of the **ectoderm**.
5. **Cnidocytes** have a stinging organelle in the center called a **nematocyst**, which resembles a tiny harpoon. Osmotically triggered, if something brushes against the cell, it fires off and injects neurotoxic **venom**.
6. Most cnidarians can't sting people, because their nematocysts aren't rigid enough to penetrate the tough layers of dead epidermal cells on your skin, but there are many notable exceptions that can put you in a world of hurt.
7. With that said, with a few oddball exceptions, almost all cnidarians are predators that can sting SOMEBODY, even if that somebody happens to be a shrimp. There are millions of **cnidocytes** on every tentacle.
8. And yes, the old rumor about using your tee-tee to treat a jellyfish sting is actually true. The venom is a protein, so the high pH of urine denatures the protein and inactivates the toxin...or you can just use ammonia....
9. After a fishy victim has been stung, the **tentacles** sweep the prey into the **gastrovascular cavity**. Tentacles are innervated and connected to the **nerve net** in the ectoderm layer of the body.

10. Like pulling your hand off a hot stove or kicking when the doctor taps your knee, the tentacles and nerve net behave as **reflex nerves** that contract the muscles on contact.
11. The **gastrovascular cavity** is a two-way pouch derived from **endoderm**. This primitive belly contains cells that secrete digestive enzymes and absorb nutrients. Indigestible trash is spat back out of the mouth.
12. Besides the feeding reflex, the **nerve net** controls the relaxation and contraction of crude muscle cells that are responsible for the swimming motions that jet propel jellyfish through the water.
13. Anemones and corals use the nerve net to shape-shift, so that they can reach prey items and force them down their **pharynx** and into the **gastrovascular cavity**.
14. Now let's talk about the classification scheme of **cnidarians**. Cnidarians are divided into classes based on a combination of reproductive life history and, secondarily, slight anatomical differences.
15. **Cnidarians** have two life stages known as **polyps** and **medusas**. **Polyps** are cup-shaped, mostly **sessile**, and sit on the bottom as ambush predators. **Medusas** are bell-shaped free-swimming pelagic predators.
16. The biggest anatomical differences between polyps and medusas are the length of the tentacles, the shape of the body, and the function of their rudimentary **mesenchyme muscles**.
17. While cnidarians are **diploblastic**, they still develop crude muscle tissues from **mesenchyme** cells that border the **endoderm**. However, they never fully expand into a **mesoderm** and the **mesoglea** fills in the gap instead.
18. The illustrations below depict the differences in anatomical layout between polyps and medusas.

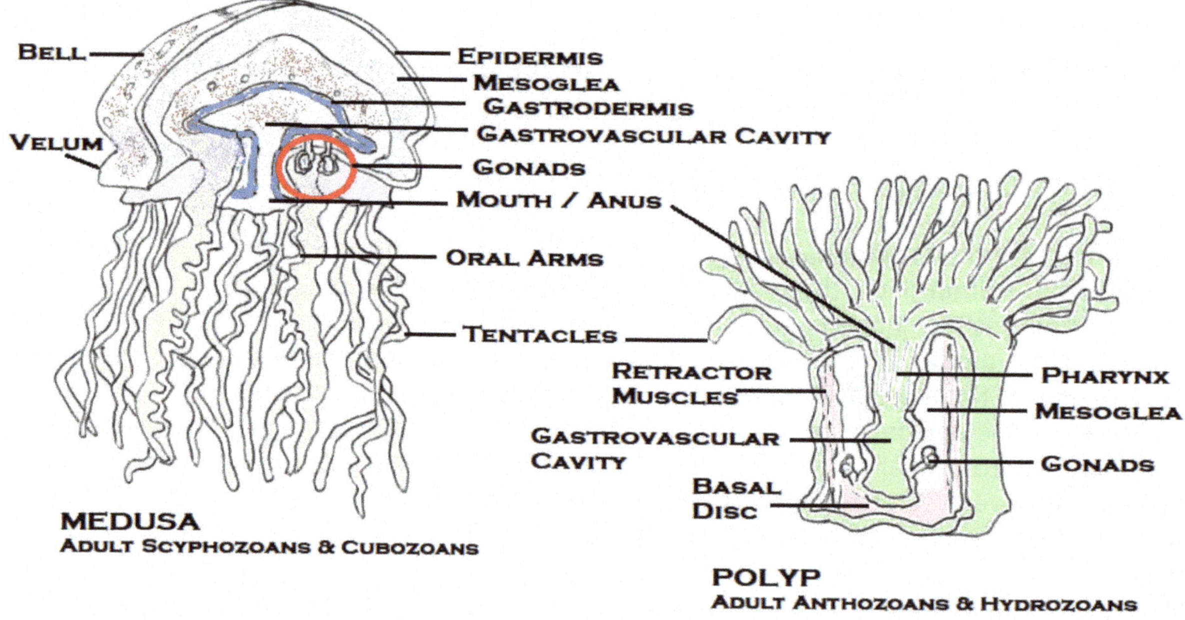

19. With a few notable exceptions, ALL cnidarians pass through BOTH of these stages in their life history, but which of these are the juvenile stages and which are the adult stages vary by classification.
20. Members of **Class Scyphozoa** (jellyfish) and **Class Cubozoa** (box jellyfish) are medusas during their adult reproductive stage. Their zygotes develop into **sessile** polyps that pass through stages of development.
21. Members of **Class Hydrozoa** (hydroids) and most members of **Class Anthozoa** (corals and anemones) are polyps during their adult stages, while their zygotes develop into microscopic juvenile medusa.
22. At this point, it is helpful to divide the cnidarians into their constitutive classes and discuss the anatomical, reproductive, and behavioral differences unique to each group.

23. **Class Schyphozoa** includes around 25,000 species of true jellyfish. Medusas as adults, jellyfish generally have four-part symmetry, with the gastrovascular cavity extending into four pouches called **ring canals**.
24. Jellyfish, in spite of their simplicity, have a couple of sensory organs. They have a balancing organ called a **statocyst** that keeps them flipped upright, and they also have very primitive light-sensing organs.
25. These crude light-detecting organs, called **ocelli**, allow jellyfish to distinguish the outlines of their prey, and to stay swimming in the photic zone where their prey will be.
26. With a few exceptions, jellyfish are predators, using numerous **cnidocyte** covered tentacles to sting prey and sweep it into the **gastrovascular cavity**. Each individual cnidocyte fires like a venom-tipped harpoon.
27. A few jellyfish, however, host **dinoflagellate zooxanthella**e and primarily feed off of the photosynthetic products of their symbionts. The upside-down jellyfish is one of these, laying upside down to collect sunlight.
28. Reproductively, most jellyfish species are separate sexes. The gonads are located at the base of the **oral arms**, emerging from the **endoderm layer**. Eggs and sperm are expelled into the water from the gastrovascular cavity.
29. From there, **external fertilization** occurs in the plankton and the **zygote** develops into a larval **planula**.
30. The planula swims to the bottom and implants itself. Once glued to the bottom, it transforms into a miniscule polyp or group of branched polyps called a **scyphistoma**. The scyphistoma is the first of several juvenile stages.
31. As scyphistomas grow larger, they bud asexually and rise up a growing tree-like column of polyps called a **strobili**. Eventually, at a critical size, the mature polyp at the end of the branch transforms into a tiny medusa.
32. This medusa, called an **ephyra**, breaks off and re-enters the water column, eventually maturing into an adult.
33. The diagram below shows the reproductive scheme used by jellyfish.

AURELIA MOON JELLYFISH

CHRYSAORA SEA NETTLE

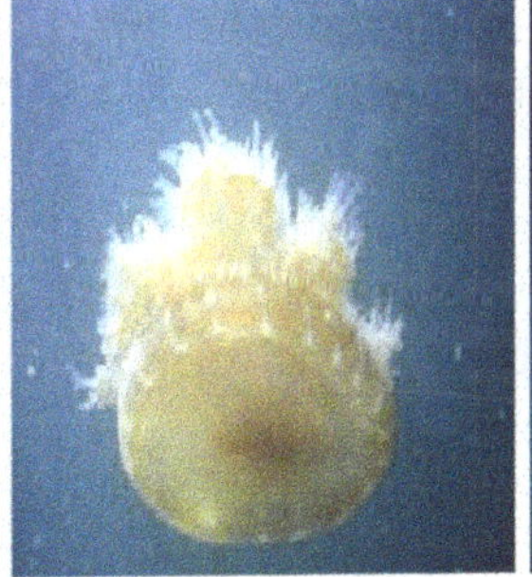
CASSIOPEA UPSIDE DOWN JELLYFISH

CROSSOTA JELLYFISH

34. The next diagram shows a handful of the 25,000 plus species of jellyfish found on the planet.
35. **Class Cubozoa** includes around 50 species box jellyfish, which have been sub-divided into a different class from the true jellyfish, because of several distinct features that differ from between the groups.
36. Interestingly, box jellyfish have 4 eyes with retinas and lenses that can detect shapes, as opposed to the simple **ocelli** found in jellyfish that only detect light or dark. Box jellies also have an additional 20 simple ocelli.
37. As opposed to most true jellyfish, the **nerve net** of box jellies makes a concentric ring around the bottom of the ectoderm that directly innervates the tentacles and oral arms, controlling swimming.

38. Another distinguishing feature of box jellyfish is that they have unbelievably toxic venom. Getting stung by a box jellyfish is apparently like being lashed with barbed wire....barbed wire dipped in acid and set on fire.

39. As you might expect, the most threatening species of box jellyfish are found off of the Great Barrier Reef in Australia, the continent where everything except kangaroos seem to be highly venomous.

40. In the graphic below, the worst of the worst of box jellyfish is shown on the left. This species is *Chironex fleckeri*.

41. The rest of the graphic sort of gives you the hint that most of Australia's wildlife would rather not have you around....and we aren't even getting to deadly sharks or that the world's most venomous PLANT also lives there.

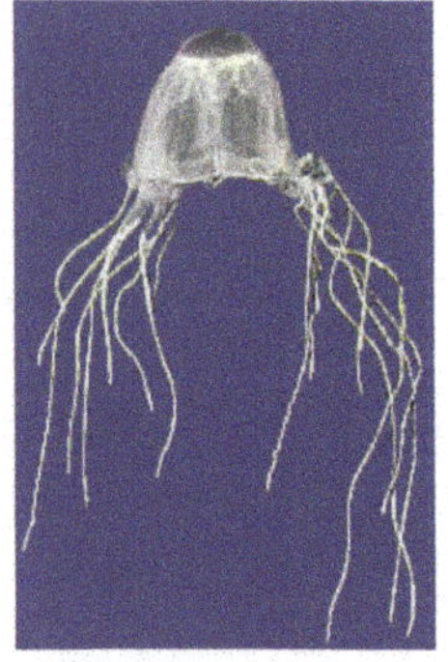

SEA WASP
BOX JELLYFISH

G'DAY MATE! I'M HERE TO KILL YOU! CUTE CUDDLY VENOMOUS AUSSIE ANIMALS

1) INLAND TAIPAN: WORLD'S MOST VENOMOUS LAND SNAKE
2) COASTAL TAIPAN: 2ND MOST VENOMOUS LAND SNAKE
3) EASTERN BROWN SNAKE: BAD TEMPER. TOP 10 VENOMOUS
4) WESTERN BROWN SNAKE: BAD TEMPER. ALSO IN TOP 10
5) BELCHER'S SEA SNAKE: MORE VENOMOUS THAN A COBRA.
6) DUBOIS SEA SNAKE: EVEN MORE VENOMOUS THAN BELCHER'S
7) MULTIPLE SPECIES OF BOX JELLYFISH: SCARRING AT BEST....
8) BLUE-RINGED OCTOPUS: ONE BITE CAN KILL 26 PEOPLE....NO ANTIVENOM!
9) MULTIPLE SPECIES OF CONE SHELL SNAIL: INNOCENT LOOKING AND DEADLY....
10) AUSTRALIAN FUNNEL WEB SPIDER: NERVE TOXIN CAN KILL WITHIN 30 MINUTES
11) REDBACK SPIDER: VENOM LIQUIFIES TISSUES & ALSO HAS NEUROTOXINS.
12) ESTUARINE STONEFISH: VENOM CAN SHUT DOWN RESPIRATION & HEARTBEAT.
13) PLATYPUS: YEAH YOU READ THAT RIGHT. MALE PLATYPI HAVE VENOMOUS SPINES.
14) GIANT AUSTRALIAN CENTIPEDE: MAY NOT KILL YOU, BUT UNBELIEVABLY CREEPY.
15) SALTWATER CROCODILE: OKAY....NOT VENOMOUS, BUT DOES IT REALLY MATTER?

CUTE, BUT NASTY!

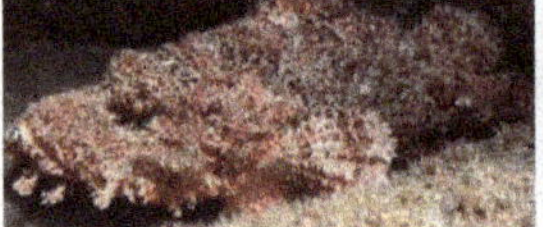

42. Reproductively, box jellyfish are much like true jellyfish. They are larger medusas as adults, fertilization of eggs occurs in the plankton, and the larvae (planulae) swim to the bottom and become self-cloning juvenile polyps.

43. The diagram below depicts the life cycle used by **scyphozoans**.

44. Now let's turn our attention to another group of cnidarians that are strongly-identified with Australia. **Corals** are responsible for forming the Great Barrier Reef, home to many of the aforementioned venomous animals.

45. **Class Anthozoa** includes two major **sub-classes. Sub-class Hexacorallia** includes **hard corals**, **anemones**, and **zooanthid polyps**. Their polyp radial symmetry includes six body segments and dozens of tentacles.

46. The diagram below shows a sampling of some of the 4,300 plus species of the sub-class Hexacorallia.

SHORT LIST OF FAMOUS CORALS....I MEAN CARLS....OR IT COULD BE KARL.....

1)	Malone	NBA Hall of Famer	No one ever hit the baseline fadeaway like him...
2)	Sagan	Astrophysicist	Probably the smartest person to ever be on TV
3)	Marx	Father of Communism	Yeah Karl....everyone works and pulls their weight....
4)	Lewis	Olympic Sprinter	Won 9 gold medals. One of greatest athletes EVER.
5)	Sandburg	Poet and Writer	Wrote lots of stuff about Chicago and Abe Lincoln

ACROPORA GLAUCA CORAL | ACROPORA SECALE CORAL | DIPLORIA BRAIN CORAL | FAVITES BRAIN CORAL

CHRISTMAS ANEMONE | BUBBLE ANEMONE WITH CLOWNFISH | GREEN PLATY ZOOANTHIDS | PINK TUBE ANEMONE

47. **Sub-class Octocorallia** includes **soft corals**, **sea pens**, and **gorgonians**.
48. Their polyp radial symmetry includes eight body segments. Amoeba-like cells inside their mesoglea secrete internal skeletons that may join other polyps to form colonies.
49. The diagram below shows some members of the 3000 plus members of sub-class Octocorallia.

EGYPTIAN FLOWER CORAL | XENIA CORAL | LEATHER CORAL | LEPTOGORGIA GORGONIAN

50. Members of **Class Anthozoa** have a completely different life history than either group of jellyfish. Anthozoans remain polyps for their entire lives, skipping the medusa stage altogether.
51. Gender determination varies widely across different orders of anthozoans. About 2/3rd of coral species, such as brain corals and acroporans are **hermaphrodites**, while the other 1/3rd, like elkhorn corals, are separate sexes.
52. While some species anemones are separate sexes, there are others that are **sequential hermaphrodites** that change sexes during their life cycles due to hormone levels and other cues.
53. **Anthozoans** can reproduce sexually by **external** or **internal fertilization**, but they are also capable of cloning themselves **asexually** through **budding** and sending out new clone colonies, or by **fragmentation** if damaged.
54. Anthozoans that reproduce via **external fertilization** are known as **broadcast reproducers**. Water

temperature and moon phases are cues that cause corals to release eggs and sperm into the water column.

55. When the sperm and egg meet, the zygote develops into a **larval planula** in the plankton. The planula then makes a break for the bottom, attaches itself, and goes through several juvenile stages to get to maturity.
56. **Brooders** use internal fertilization, with sperm entering the gastrovascular cavity of the recipient and fertilizing eggs embedded in the endoderm. Brooders release the **planula** after they develop from the zygote.
57. From there, the concept is the same. Planulae pass through a juvenile polyp stage, another stage where symbiotic **zooxanthellae** algal species move in (if applicable), and a stage where their skeleton develops.
58. Eventually, the maturing polyp clones itself by budding and the species slowly adds structure to the reef.
59. The diagram below summarizes the reproductive strategies used by anthozoans.

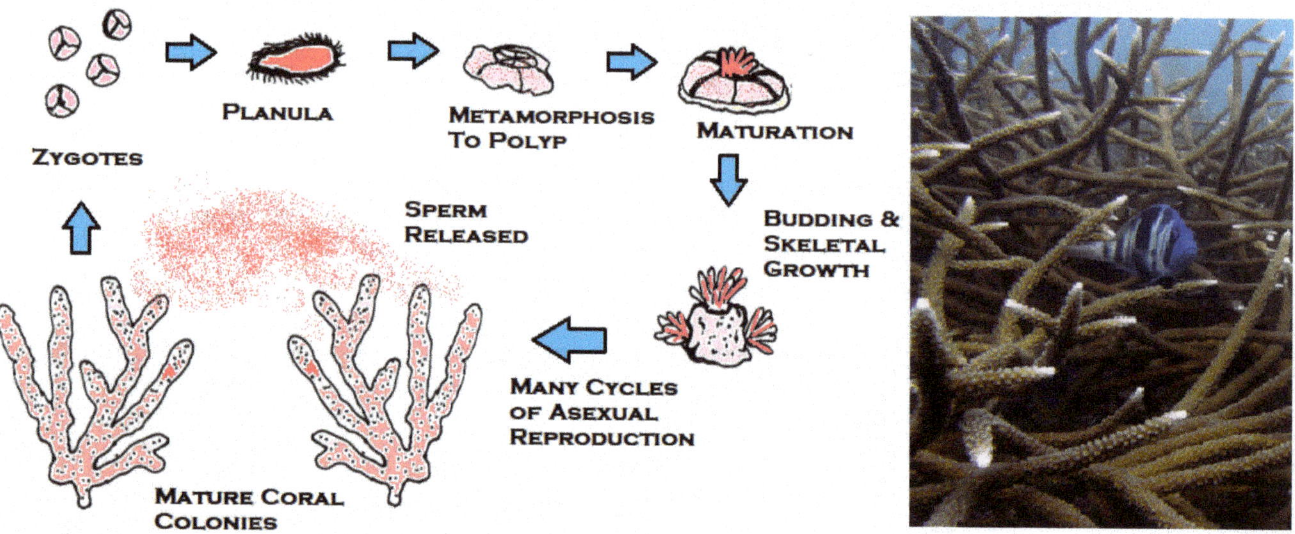

60. Anthozoan feeding strategies run the gamut from strictly carnivorous ambush predators (such as anemones) to complete dependence on **photosynthesis** products from their resident algae (such as acroporan corals).
61. **Zooxanthellae** algae are species of single-celled **dinoflagellates**. In addition to gaining pigmentation from the algae that help shield them from UV, many dinoflagellates also produce toxins that protect the coral.
62. While coral-eating fish like parrotfish seem to be immune to these toxins, **biomagnification** up the levels of the food chain can cause the coral toxin **ciguatera** to accumulate in large predatory fish like amberjacks.
63. If you dine on a large barracuda or an amberjack that lives on certain coral reefs, you will experience the misery of ciguatera poisoning, which includes projectile vomiting, sweating, and reversal of hot and cold sensations.
64. Like all cnidarians, corals and anemones also have venomous stinging **cnidocytes** for disabling prey.
65. Clownfish take advantage of this anemone defense. They condition themselves to the venom by taking a few stings, cover their skin with thick mucus, and use the host's tentacles to evade predators.

66. It is probably fair to say that the majority of corals are somewhere in between, capable of feeding on zooplankton, but also getting a boost from resident algae embedded in their ectoderm.
67. The ecological importance of this group of cnidarians can't be undersold. Coral reefs cover less than 1% of the ocean's territory, almost exclusively found near shorelines in the **photic zone**, but house 25% of marine species.
68. Huge numbers of fish, mollusk, and crustacean species are completely dependent upon the reefs to complete their life cycles. **Primary productivity** of coral reefs is, on average, around 50 times higher than open ocean.
69. Presently, rising ocean temperatures and silt in the water are leading to a global **coral bleaching** epidemic. **Bleaching** occurs when the algae get annoyed with water conditions and move out.
70. When the dinoflagellates move out, the animal turns white and slowly starves, since most corals are not very good at feeding themselves (though most will eat plankton, given the chance).
71. The coral can't possibly filter enough plankton to survive (and some can't even do that), and the reef dies.
72. Corals also have huge economic impacts on people, since they support seafood production, sport fishing, and scuba diving. Reefs also form the islands that the very resorts sit on.
73. Indeed, with no corals, Florida would not be there.
74. Without Florida, you wouldn't have the privilege of paying $3000 to stand in line for hours behind other tourists, while your kids throw up cotton candy and creepy adults dressed as cartoon animals get handsy and try to get you to take a picture with them for $25. Thanks corals.
75. Now let's move on to a lesser well-known group.
76. The last major classification of anthozoans belong to **Class Hydrozoa**. This group includes the namesake **hydroids** and number of floating colonial animals, such as **Portuguese man-of-war** that resemble jellyfish.
77. Most hydrozoans have an adult **polyp** stage and a juvenile **medusa** stage, but there are individual taxa that lack one life stage or the other.
78. With a few exceptions, such as **hydras**, most hydrozoans look plant-like. This is because multiple polyps remain attached as they clone, growing a **chitin** covered sheath around the connecting **stolons** (branches).
79. Typically, the colony will contain hundreds of tiny polyps that poke their tentacles out of the protective covering.
80. Imagine a bunch of prairie dogs, all clones of each other joined by their tails, popping their heads out of a huge network of pipes with peep-holes for each animal. This is essentially the way most hydroids form colonies.
81. There are two types of polyps in the colonies. **Gastrozoids** have stinging tentacles and gather food. **Gonozoids** lack tentacles and are specialized for **sexual reproduction**. They must be fed by the rest of the colony.
82. Gastrozoids work together, feeding every animal in the colony. Gonozoids get fed, but so do young gonozoids and gonozoids who are having bad fishing days.
83. In most cases, reproductive polyps are separate sexes, but both occur in the same colony. This is the animal equivalent of a **dioecious plant** like pine tree with separate male and female gametophytes on the same tree.
84. During reproduction, tiny **medusas** are budded off of the **gonozoids**. From there, the medusas produce and release eggs or sperm, depending on their sex. **External fertilization** occurs in the plankton.
85. From there, a larval **planula** swims to the bottom, grows into a polyp, and starts another colony elsewhere.

86. The pictures below show several representative members of **Class Hydrozoa**.

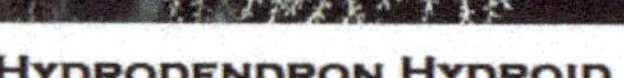

HYDRODENDRON HYDROID

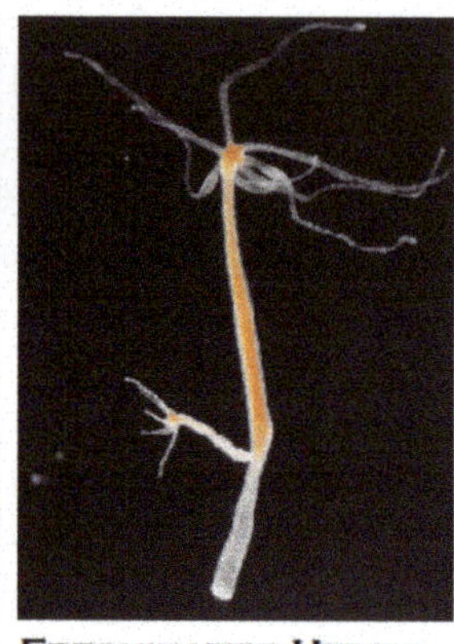

FRESHWATER HYDRA

OBELIA HYDROID

C) Phylum Ctenophora: Comb Jellies

1. **Ctenophores** (comb jellies) resemble jellyfish, in that they are **diploblastic** and also fill the space between their ectoderm and their endoderm with a jelly-like **mesoglea**. They also have a **gastrovascular cavity.**
2. Some people argue that ctenophores should be re-classified as **triploblastic** because they have a significant amount of muscle tissue in the space between their ectoderm and endoderm.
3. However, because there is still a large quantity of space-filling protein gel, the majority still say diploblastic.
4. Comb jellies have a different feeding strategy than true jellyfish. While they do have tentacles, they are not designed the same way. Instead of **cnidocytes**, they have structures called **colloblasts**.
5. When a tentacle contacts objects in the plankton, cells on the colloblasts secrete sticky substances to trap the algae, zooplankton, or particles like a mouse getting hung up on a glue trap.
6. Lacking **cnidocyotes** (and thus any stinging ability), comb jellies, instead are filter-feeding **planktivores**. Their comb-like tentacles are covered with **cilia** that strain the water for plankton.
7. Another way that comb jellies are more advanced than cnidarians, is that they route the waste from their feeding out of extensions of the **gastrovascular cavity** known as **anal pores**, rather than back out the mouth.
8. An organ at the top of the comb jelly called a **statocyst** acts like a little gyroscope, keeping the comb jelly oriented right-side up in the water as they feed or swim around.
9. Comb jellies use flap like organs called **auricles** like rudders to push water over their combs. A series of canals
10. Many comb jellies appear bioluminescent because of the dinoflagellates that they filter.
11. Some comb jelly species have become a major nuisance as **invasive species**. For instance, the warty comb jelly invaded the Black Sea along shipping channels from New England.

My Favorite Type of Jelly is Comb Jelly!

Believe it or not, some people eat comb jellies, even though they are basically a tube of gelatinous goo. To cook one, you soak them in vinegar and salt to get the collagen to stiffen. Then you simply fry them in hot peanut oil and add some garlic and chili flakes. Apparently, it's like eating spicy rubber cement!

12. Now, certain shipping channels are crammed up with goo. Billions of comb jellies are now stealing plankton from local fish larvae that need to feed on zooplankton to grow up.

13. There really isn't a whole lot more to say about comb jellies that is likely to make any sort of big impact on your life unless you are a Turkish boat captain . Sea turtles and other jellyfish love to eat them. Next.

14. The diagram below shows some pictures of comb jellies, along with a layout of their basic anatomy.

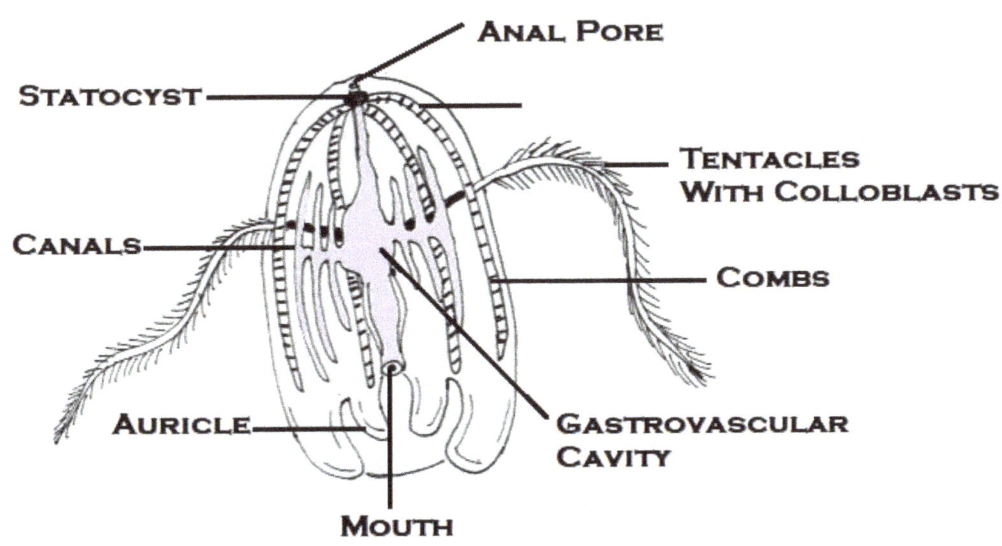

The Great Barrier Reef: The largest assemblage of cnidarians in the world

The largest coral reef in the world spans 1429 miles of Australian coast. It is critical to the ecology of the Indo-Pacific Ocean. Here is just how much influence trillions of tiny simple animals have on the ocean's ecology....

* Over 10% of the bony fish species on earth make the reef their home.
* There are more than 3000 individual reefs and 900 coral islands there.
* It is estimated that the reef began more than 20 million years ago.
* In just 2 generations, people have managed to destroy about 50% of it.
* Australia has made protecting the reef one of its top national priorities.
* Seafood and tourism from the reef are worth $7 billion each year.
* More than 600 species of corals contribute to building the reef.

SECTION 3: Triploblastic Protostome Ectodysozoan Invertebrates

A) Ecydosozoan Traits

1. **Ecdysozoan invertebrates** have a hard protective **cuticle** that is secreted over the skin. It is a non-living protein or glycoprotein matrix. In roundworms, it is made of **keratin**, while arthropods primarily use **chitin**.
2. This hard protective shell may also extend to the mouth, allowing hard specialized appendages to develop.
3. Unrelated to the shell, most ecdysozoans tend to have evolved to have separate sexes.
4. The **Ecdysozoan** branch of the bilateral protostomes is split into a group of typical members and a separate branch called **Scalidophora**. The two phyla in this branch are basically evolutionary dead ends.
5. Let's look at the Scalidophorans first.

B) Scalidophoran Invertebrates

1. **Scalidophorans** are invertebrate **ecydsozoans** that have concentric cuticle rings around the body, spines called scalids between the segments, and a retractable head.
2. There are two extant groups of these animals called **Kinorhynchs** and **priapulid worms**.
3. Chances are that you have probably heard of neither, since both groups include obscure burrowing ocean animals that hit evolutionary dead ends.
4. **Phylum Kinorhyncha** includes strange little animals called **kinorhynchs**, which are also called **mud dragons**.
5. Barely noticeable, with a clear concentric exoskeleton lined with spines, they are only around a millimeter long.
6. Like a tiny turtle, mud dragons can completely retract their head into their body if threatened.
7. Mud dragon exoskeletons are made of 11 concentric plates of **chitin**. Little spines emerge from the borders of the plates. In place of legs, cilia, or flagella, they are used like legs to push the animal along the substrate.
8. Mud dragon mouths opens into a **pharynx**. The head has a **basal ganglion** that functions like a puny little brain. A **ventral nerve cord** branches off of this ganglion. Each segment also has a pair of ganglia that controls it.
9. Kinorynchs are **pseudocoelomates** with a relatively complex gut, considering their diminutive size.
10. The digestive system is aided by **salivary glands** and **pancreatic glands** that dump enzymes into a **midgut** that acts like a funnel-shaped intestine. After the food is absorbed, waste passes out via a **hindgut**.
11. As small as they are, diffusion takes care of gas exchange, so they don't have circulatory or respiratory systems.
12. Like most **ecdysozoans**, mud dragons have two distinct sexes. Females are egg layers, while males produce gigantic sperm cells that are nearly ¼ of their body length.
13. Probably because they are difficult to find and study, and because almost no one cares about kinorhynchs, only basic information is known about their reproduction, while nearly nothing is known about larval stages.
14. **Priapulid worms**, the other major group in the **Scalidophora** clade are members of **Phylum Priapulida**.
15. Like kinoryhnchs, their body is covered with concentric rings of chitin, which are periodically molted and replaced as the worm grows bigger. Some priapulids can get to be over a foot long.

16. **Priapulids** are burrowing worm-like animals that live in deep anoxic mud near ocean shores. They have a retractable **proboscis** that is used to snatch up soft-bodied invertebrates like worms and sea cucumbers.
17. The **pharynx** is located on the inside of the proboscis and is rooted to two retractor muscles that push and pull the proboscis into shape. There are chitin teeth inside the throat.
18. The pharynx flows into **intestine**, which terminates into the anus. There are no accessory digestive organs.
19. On either side of the gut are a pair of **urogenital organs** that seem to serve both functions.
20. Certain cells in the organs act like the **flame cells** of flatworms, filtering waste, while others develop into **speramatogonia** or **oogonia**, depending on their sex.
21. A bizarre set of brush-like organs called **caudal appendages** line the area around the worm's anus. These seem to serve dual purposes of pushing the worm through the mud and for excreting nitrogenous wastes.
22. The diagram below shows a sketches of a kinorhynch and a priapulid worm.

C) Phyla Nematoda and Nematomorpha: Roundworms and Horsehair Worms

1. **Roundworms** and **horsehair worms** are **ecdysozoans**, with an acellular chitin cuticle around their body. At first glance, this can be deceptive, because the cuticle is so thin and tightly bound to the body, it is easy to miss.
2. Members of both groups are all **pseudocoelomates**, with floating digestive and reproductive tracts (the endoderm). The muscles of the body wall remain tethered to the skin of the ectoderm.
3. On one hand, the **pseudocoelom** gives these groups the 360 degree flexibility that flatworms lack. On the other hand, their guts slosh around like a bowl of jello. This vulnerability seems to have driven their evolution.
4. The safest and most convenient place, where most roundworms live, is the gut of animals. Guts are padded, squishy environments where food is constantly available. Moving little, they are not in danger of being crushed.
5. Some roundworms, however, such as soil **nematodes** are parasites of root vegetables, rather than animals.
6. However, one nematode, *Caenorhabditis elegans*, has been a major study of subject in DNA sequencing and genetics, since they have relatively complex genomes, but reproduce very rapidly.
7. Let's discuss the anatomy of **roundworms** and **horsehair worms** consecutively, as there are a few differences that cause them to be grouped into separate phyla. Let's begin with **roundworm** anatomy.
8. As compared to horsehair worms, **nematode roundworms** have a wider body girth relative to their length.

9. The **digestive tract** of roundworms is one way, with food passing through the mouth, on into the **pharynx** and finally into a very long linear **intestine**, which is necessary due to the lack of folded surface area.
10. Nematode roundworms have distinct **separate sexes** with very large internal gonads.
11. Males fertilize females via their **sperm ducts**, while females deposit thousands of eggs from their **oviducts**. Both organs exit via a **reproductive duct** on the ventral surface of the worm in front of a separate **terminal anus**.
12. **Horsehair worms** are grouped into a different phyla, primarily because of their different reproductive anatomy.
13. Instead of having a separate reproductive pore and anus, horsehair worms have a one-thing-does-it-all opening for both waste and reproductive cells known as a **cloaca**. It is in a terminal position on the body.
14. While **roundworms** tend to victimize vertebrate animals and root crops, parasitic **horsehair worms** almost exclusively attack insects like grasshoppers and mantises. They area also capable of free-living in water.
15. Sometimes horsehair worms will wait for their insect host to drink. Sensing the end is near for their beleaguered host, they will then make a horrifying exit out of their anus, revealing a foot-long worm.
16. From there, they will scavenge food underwater until they lay eggs or find another victim.
17. Both groups of worms have a **cerebral ganglion** and **ventral nerve cords**. Both groups lack eyes.
18. Both groups also lack circulatory, respiratory, or excretory systems. Diffusion takes care of everything.
19. The diagram below shows the anatomy of a typical nematode roundworm. Horsehair worms are similar, as previously mentioned, with the exception of the exit strategies of the reproductive and digestive tracts.

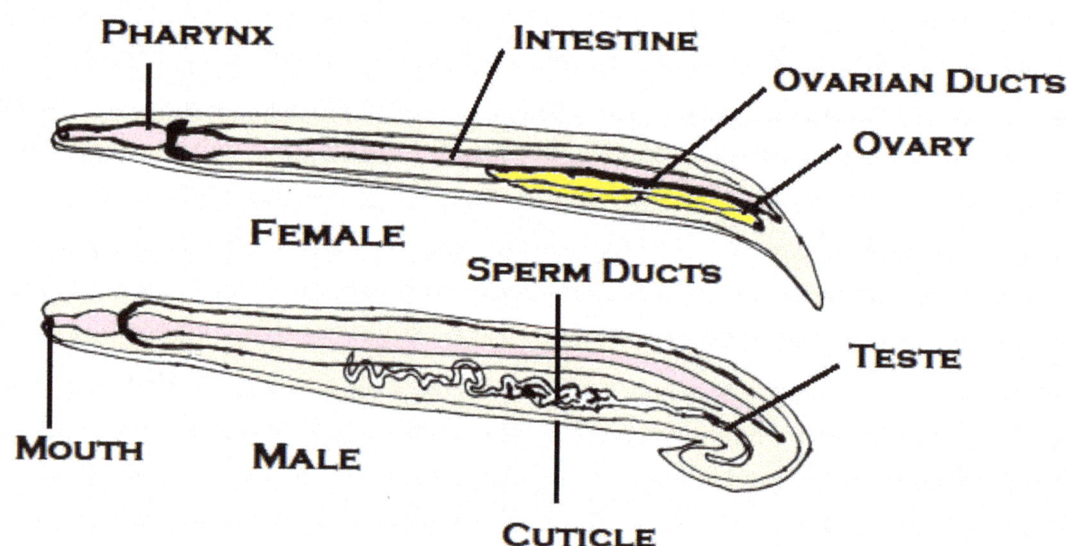

20. Roundworms are the stuff of nightmares for many people (and animals), so we would be remiss not to discuss a few of the more common offenders. The diagram below briefly describes some of these. Discussion follows.

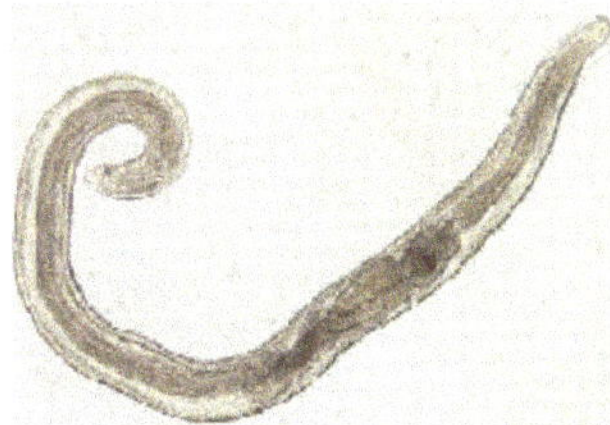

Pinworms
Intestinal; Eggs Spread among Dogs by Sniff Greetings.

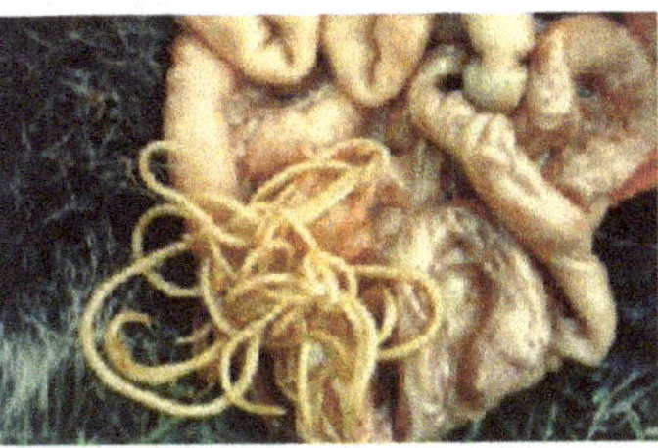

Raccoon Roundworm
Intestinal; Cysts Shed into Water by Host and Picked up by Drinking.

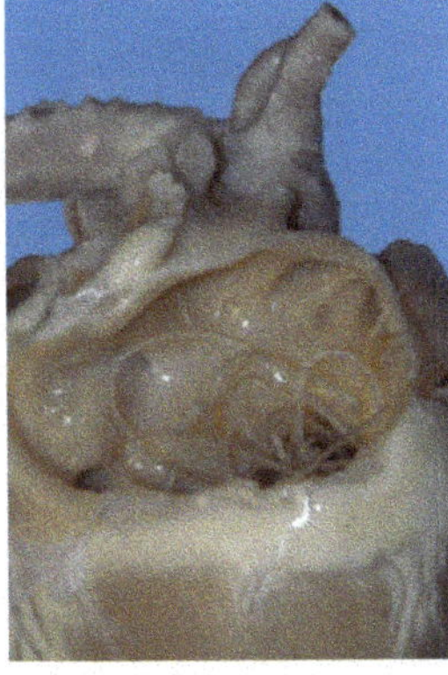

Dog Heartworm
Cardiac; spread by Mosquito Bites

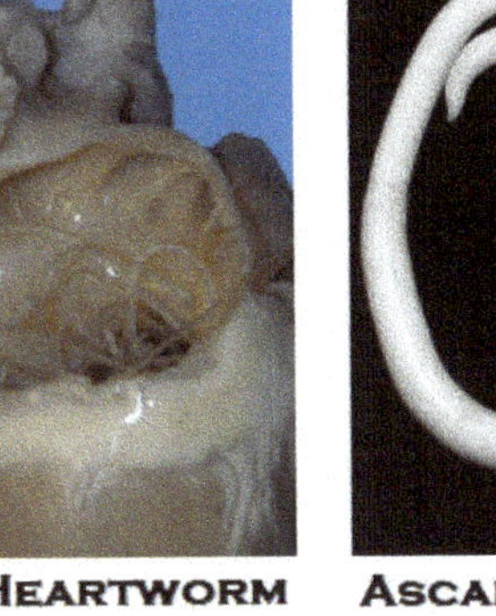

Ascaris Hookworm
Intestinal; Cysts Spread By Polluted Water

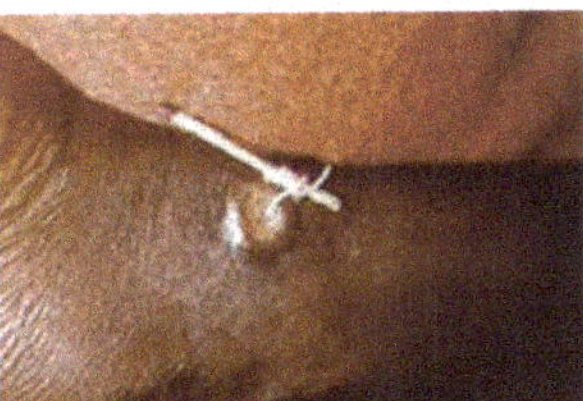

Guinea Worm
Dermal; Cysts Hatch and Worms Burrow Between Skin & Muscle

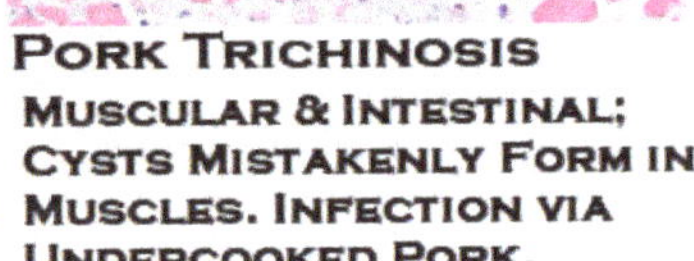

Pork Trichinosis
Muscular & Intestinal; Cysts Mistakenly Form in Muscles. Infection via Undercooked Pork.

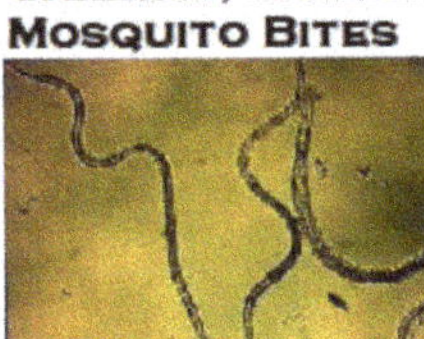

Soil Nematodes
Parasitize Root Vegetable Crops.

Cricket Horsehair Worm
Digestive; Live inside Insects or in Water.

21. Roundworms are a big problem in areas of poor sanitation and/or in areas with lots of vectors to spread them.

22. Probably the most common roundworms you might encounter are the somewhat innocuous **pinworms** that dogs and cats can easily pick up from each other by sniffing each other or eating poo.

23. Pinworms aren't really that dangerous, but can cause malnourishment, because they live in the intestines and steal semi-digested food. When it is time to lay eggs, the female crawls to the surface of the anus.

24. Once at the anus, the female glues her eggs onto the outside surface with a sticky glue that is highly irritating to the host. This can be why dogs skid across the grass butt first. Other dogs then come along and sniff up eggs.

25. In the old days, when people got pinworms, the standard treatment was to seal their anus with tape, thereby trapping the female worms when they came up to lay their eggs. Thankfully, we now have de-wormers.

26. Pet de-wormers are important for stopping other more sinister roundworms. The **raccoon roundworm** is much larger and nastier than a pinworm. Pets and people can pick them up by drinking **cysts** found in creek water.

27. Think twice before drinking from a 'crystal clear mountain stream' when hiking, because if a raccoon took a dump in that creek, you are taking a risk. In worst case scenarios, raccoon roundworms can enter the brain.

28. Requiring a different preventive medicine is the infamous **dog heartworm**. Dog heartworm infestations can block heart valves, lower blood oxygen, heavily fatigue the poor canine, and slowly kill them.

29. Heartworm **cysts** are released into the blood and picked up when the infected dog is bitten by a mosquito. The next dog bitten by the mosquito starts the infection cycle again.

30. The diagram below shows the life cycle of the dog heartworm.

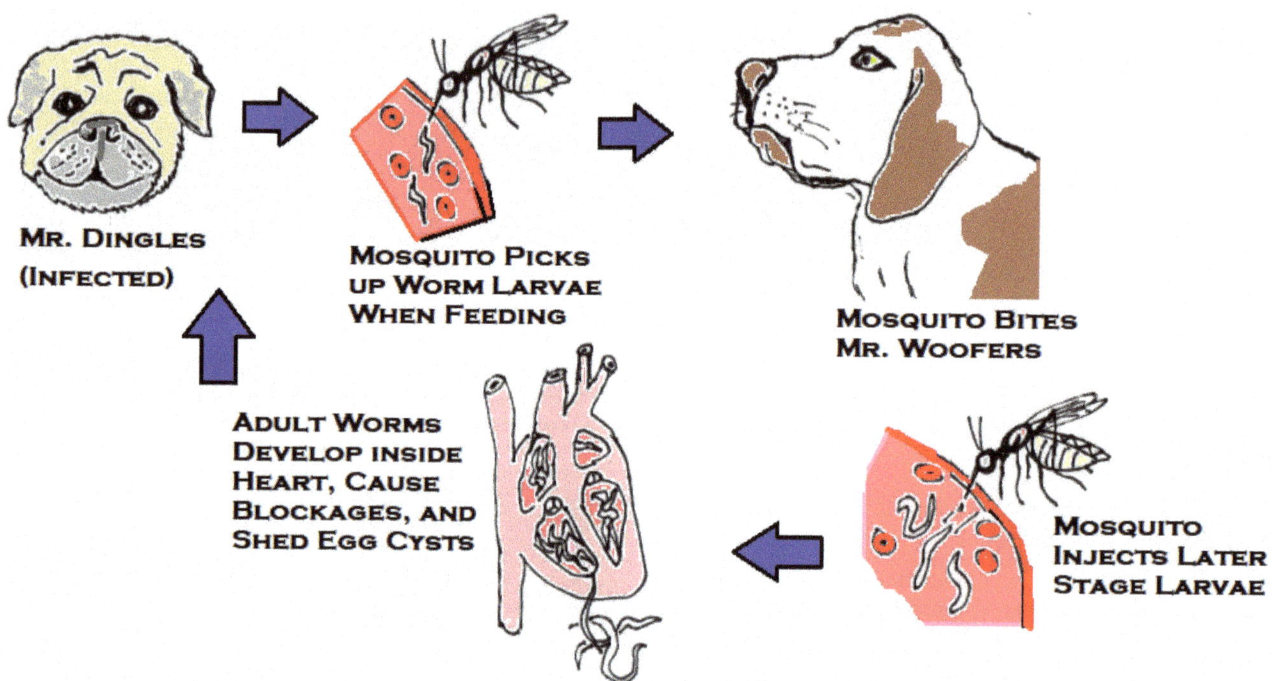

31. **Ascaris hookworms** are the largest intestinal roundworm parasites of warm-blooded vertebrates, getting more than a foot long. They can cause a major infestation that leads to intestinal blockages.
32. En route to becoming an adult, the worm passes through nasty little larval stages in the liver and the lungs.
33. During the lung phase, an ascaris infection causes the victim to cough up bloody sputum (which is also infectious). The presence of worms in the lungs can also trigger a major allergic reaction.
34. Eventually, the victim coughs up (and swallows) hatching cysts, allowing the worm to establish in the intestinal tract. Mature females can release nearly a quarter of a million egg cysts during their lifetime in the intestine.
35. A stat you might not want to know.....though rare (but not absent) in the United States, it is estimated that one in six people (1.2 billion), worldwide, have at least one ascaris hookworm in their intestines.
36. Hey all you cool cats and kittens, with Carol Baskin's help, the diagram below shows the ascaris life cycle.

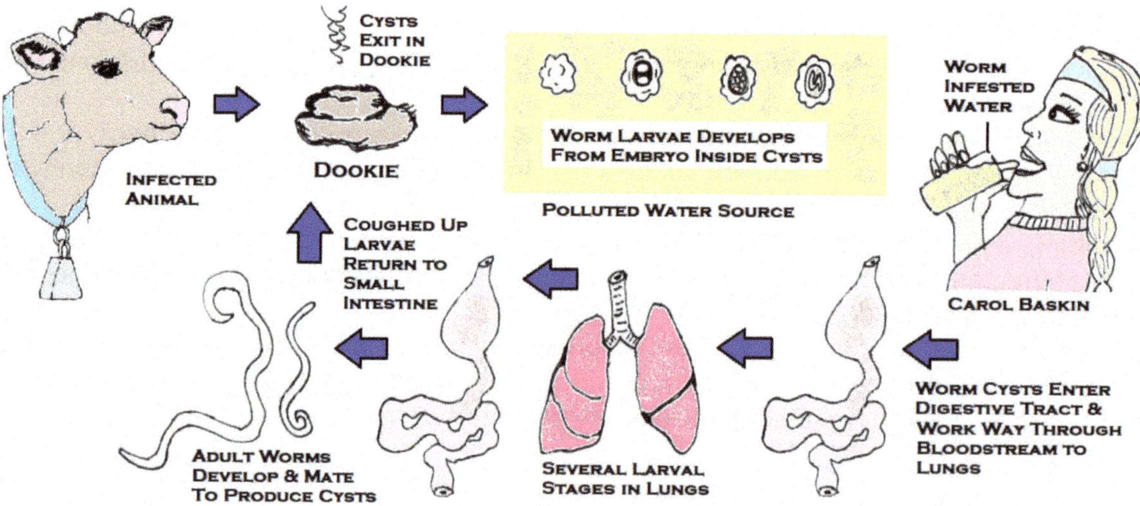

37. Another horrifying roundworm is African guinea worm. The cysts of guinea worm are spread in polluted water.
38. Early larval guinea worms are microscopic are ingested through drinking polluted water.
39. From there, the worm grows into an adult and can be seen wiggling between the skin and muscles, living off of nutrients in the blood and lymphatic system. Worse, you can't just yank them out quickly.
40. If a guinea worm breaks off, the bacteria in their gut can cause life-threatening sepsis in the bloodstream.
41. Victims have to slowly pull the worm out by spooling it around a stick, stopping when the worm resists. It can take the better part of a day or two to get the disgusting wriggling nightmare out of the skin.
42. Happily, the guinea worm has nearly been eradicated over the last three decades. In 1986, there were nearly 3.5 million cases in Africa, with around 80% of those occurring in Sudan, Mali, Chad, Ethiopia and Ghana.
43. By 2020, there were only 27 total cases in Africa. The eradication happened mostly as a result of distribution of water filters that sieve out the cysts. All other methods also involved hygiene, and not any sort of drugs.
44. In most places, infected people are now forbidden from bathing in rivers until their worms are gone. Likewise, people stopped feeding dogs fish scraps from infected rivers, which prevents canines from spreading the cysts.
45. **Trichuris** is another animal-borne roundworm that can infect people. In **trichinosis**, some of the worm cysts in the original host lose their way in the bloodstream. Rather than ending up in the intestine, they go to muscles.
46. **Cysts** trapped in muscle tissue can then be ingested by other animals that eat the meat, spreading the worm. Pork is particularly bad about spreading trichinosis, which is why you shouldn't eat undercooked pork.
47. While trichinosis has mostly been eradicated from domesticated pigs with de-wormers, the same can't be said for wild boars or farm pigs. It's always a good idea to clean and process either with rubber gloves.
48. Vertebrates, as attractive as they are to roundworms, aren't always the only victims or roundworms.
49. For instance, there are hundreds of species of **soil nematodes** that attack root crops and vegetables. Some are marginally destructive, while others can be devastating.
50. Oddly, some of these nematodes are ecologically important in aerating the soil as they move.
51. One example of a **nematode worm** that is actually used commercially overseas is the **vinegar eel worm**, *Turbatrix aceti*, which can be found in cultures of pickled foods, feeding on bacteria and yeasts.
52. Since they tunnel through vegetables in the pickling brine to seek out the microbes they eat, they help the acetic acid fermentation process speed up by providing extra surface area for microbe growth.
53. The **horsehair worms** are much thinner than regular **nematode roundworms**, and differ anatomically. They also differ from vertebrate roundworms in their choice of victims. Most horsehair worms attack insects.
54. Mantises, cockroaches, grasshoppers, and crickets can be hosts to some truly horrifying foot-long horsehair worms. They are also able to release hormones that affect their host's behavior.
55. When the horsehair worm has grown too large for its victim, it will send out biochemical signals that will cause the insect to enter water and drown itself. From there, the horsehair worm tunnels out and swims away.
56. Once in the water, the adult worms are free-living, eventually laying egg cysts that are picked up by the next insect victim. Once again, the cysts hatch and undergo several larval stages before killing their hosts.

D) Phylum Onychophora: Velvet Worms

1. The phylum **Onchyophora** is probably the leading candidate for 'cute' if a worm could ever be described that way. Velvet worms superficially resemble giant fuzzy caterpillars. They have many legs and a pair of antennae.
2. However, **velvet worms** have their own phylum for obvious anatomical reasons.
3. Velvet worms don't fit with other groups of worms because of the presence of legs, but they don't fit with arthropods because they lack joints. Additionally, **velvet worms** are **pseudocoelomates** with floating organs.
4. These organs float in a space called the **homocoel**, which is filled with a thick clear fluid. Inside the fluid are **amoebocyte cells** that act like a crude immune system and also **nephrocytes** that trap and filter waste.
5. The digestive tracts and reproductive tracts float in the **pseudocoelom**. Circulatory and respiratory systems are absent. There is a combination of reliance on diffusion through the skin and fluid flow through the body.
6. The **digestive tract** is rather simple, with the pharynx and esophagus giving way to a ribbed **midgut** the shape of a crinkle French fry. The **hindgut** evacuates waste.
7. Velvet worms have two separate sexes, with female worms receiving sperm through a vagina-like opening, rather than a cloaca. Fertilized eggs develop into offspring inside of a **uterus**.
8. Male worms have testes that extend into **seminiferous tubules** that exit through an **ejaculatory duct**.
9. Oddly, in spite of their relatively simple anatomy, most velvet worms are **ovoviviparous** and give live birth. An advantage of letting the eggs hatch inside the body, is that better-developed offspring survive at higher rates.
10. Velvet worms have cone-shaped legs that are inflated by **hydrostatic pressure** from body fluids. Each leg can be controlled and wiggled by muscles inside the body wall. They have anywhere from 13 to 43 pairs of these legs.
11. Each leg is tipped by a pair of claws that are extensions of the **exoskeleton**. The claws are molted each time the exoskeleton is shed, but they are replaced immediately, since the claws grow in stacked rows like shark teeth.
12. While velvet worms are segmented, this isn't obvious, other than the fact that legs and bodily openings occur at regular intervals. When the **chitin exoskeleton** is molted, the segments are also visible.
13. There are two sets of openings under each leg. The **crural glands** open behind each leg and secrete **sex pheromones**, while the **coxal vesicles** seem to be involved in absorbing and drinking water droplets.
14. The digestive system of velvet worms begins at the mouth with a pair of lip-like structures derived from the **pharynx** called the **labrum**. The labrum extends into a pair of **antennae** that are used for tasting.
15. Deeper inside the pharynx are a pair of crushing jaws that are pretty much like the claws at the tips of their feet.
16. Behind the mouth in the third segment are a pair of **slime glands** that produce a goopy substance that looks like school glue. This traps prey animals and it also is used to slow down predators that might try to eat them.
17. Velvet worms are one of the only phyla of animals that are strictly terrestrial. All species are found in moist leaf litter and mossy forest floor areas. There are zero species that live in water.

18. The diagrams below show a couple of species of velvet worms. These are followed by anatomy diagrams.

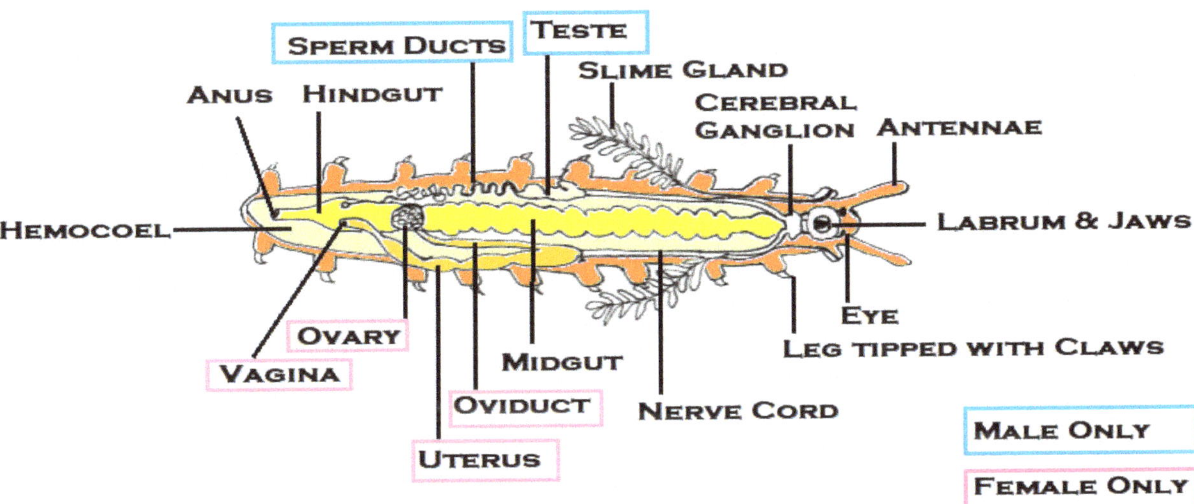

E) Phylum Tardigrada: Water Bears

1. Members of **Phylum Tardigrada**, informally called water bears, are among the strangest animals you could ever hope to find. Measuring less than a millimeter long, they are very complex for something so small.
2. **Water bears** are like the Rasputins of the animal kingdom. You practically can't kill them. They can be irradiated, frozen, boiled, pressurized, dehydrated, starved, and deprived of air and stay alive.
3. They manage do to this by shutting down all their genes for **metabolism** and existing in a sort of suspended animation. Some tardigrades have been revived after 2 or 3 decades in this condition.
4. In case you've forgotten about Rasputin, he was stabbed in the stomach, poisoned with cyanide-laced cake, shot three times in the head at close range, and was finally dispatched by being drowned in an icy river.
5. **Water bears** have a head, three thoracic segments with a pair of legs on each, and a single pair of legs at the end of the abdomen. Their legs are somewhat like those of a velvet worm, with claws on each tip.
6. An odd thing about tardigrades is that they are the only phylum of animals with a hybrid body plan. While their gut floats in a **pseudocoelem**, there gonads are tethered by muscles and closed in a true **coelem**.
7. Water bears have a syringe-like organ inside their mouth called a **stylet** that is used like a syringe. They use the stylet to pierce plant cells or unlucky little invertebrates and they suck their juices like little vampires.

8. Water bears somewhat resemble bandleader Max Rebo of the namesake band, entertainers in the palace of Jabba the Hutt in Return of the Jedi. In spite of his cute appearance, Max Rebo was a terrible person.
9. You might recall that he laughed sadistically during a band intermission when Jabba put on the moves, got rejected, and subsequently threw Oola the go-go dancer into the rancor pit, where she was devoured alive.
10. Honestly, the Max Rebo band sucked anyway. They couldn't hold a candle to the Star Wars cantina band in the first movie. This band consisted of woolwith horn-playing Bith aliens who had obvious butts for heads.
11. No word on whether or not water bears enjoy alien music or have no regard for the personal safety of others.
12. Similar to velvet worms, they have a pharynx that gives way to a **midgut** and **hindgut**. Unlike velvet worms, they use a **large salivary** gland that empties enzymes into the **midgut** to aid the digestive process.
13. A pair of insect-like **Malphigian tubules** filter the waste in the **hindgut**. These tubules extract water out of the waste and move materials on toward the anus.
14. Some species of water bears have separate genders, while others are strictly **parthenogenic** females.
15. Among species with two sexes, individuals have one large gonad that is sandwiched between the gut and the muscles in the body wall. Females are **oviparous** egg-layers, unlike the live-bearing velvet worms.
16. Typically, **external fertilization** occurs, with male water bears depositing sperm over the eggs outside the body of the female. The female presents the eggs for fertilization inside of a package of shed cuticle.
17. **Parthenogenic** all-female species self-fertilize their eggs. In parthenogenesis, the **oogenesis** process occurs normally until the end of **meiosis I**, with all prior genetic recombinations being allowed to happen.
18. At this point, after **crossing-over** and **independent assortment** have been allowed to occur, the two resultant cells are fused together again to create another **tetraploid** cell.
19. After **meiosis II**, the cells divide again and become **diploid** cells with new genetic combinations different than their mother. At this point, biochemical cues cause the diploid **zygote** to develop, as if fertilized.
20. The diagram below covers the anatomy of a water bear and shows pictures of two extant species.

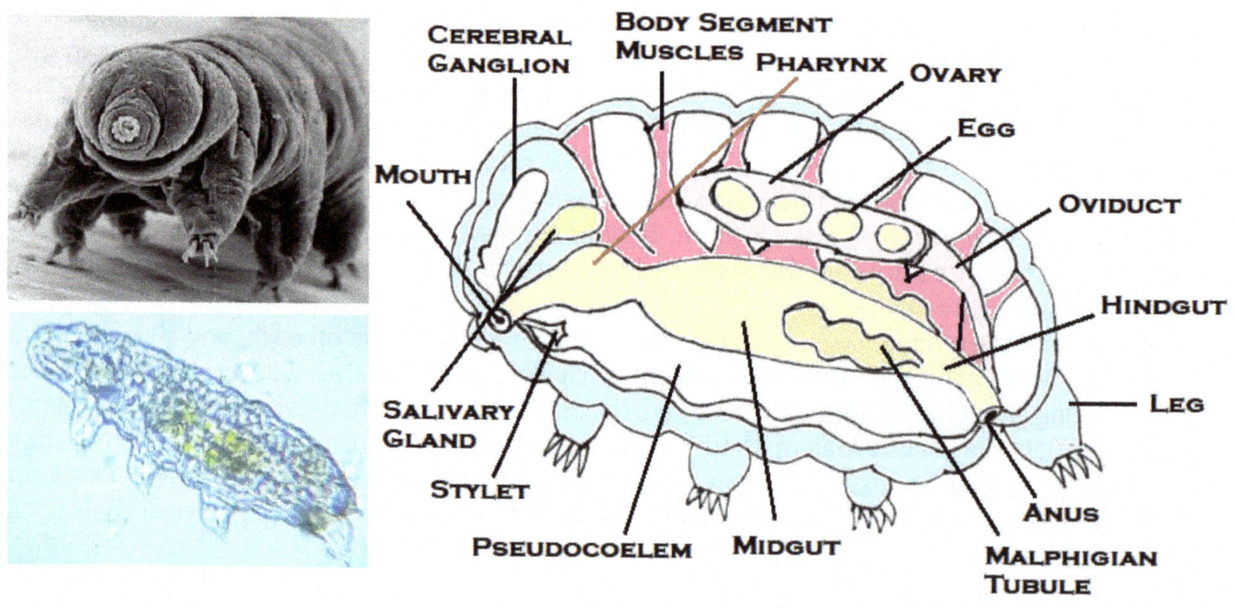

F) Phylum Arthropoda: General Characteristics

1. **Phylum Arthropoda**, in terms of sheer number of species, is almost the unquestioned king of the animal phyla.
2. So far, more than a million species of arthropods have been scientifically catalogued, representing 3 sub-phyla and 8 different classes of invertebrates. By way of comparison, there are only 40,000 known vertebrates.
3. The **arthropods** have evolved and adapted to almost every conceivable habitat and lifestyle. There are species present in every ecosystem on earth and on every continent, some in places you would never guess.
4. In spite of their large diversity in form, all **arthropods** share a number of common morphological features.
5. **Segmentation** into a head, thorax, and abdomen is a common feature of all arthropods.
6. In some arthropods, such as crustaceans and arachnids, the head and thorax are fused into a **cephalothorax**. In some insects like stinkbugs, it is the abdomen and thorax that are fused together into a **propodeum**.
7. One defining characteristic common to all arthropods is a **chitin exoskeleton** that is **molted** and replaced as the animal grows. The molting cycle is controlled by growth hormones secreted by the posterior part of the brain.
8. Forming first-class levers that allow great feats of physical strength relative to their size, abdominal and thoracic muscles are anchored to the exoskeleton. Thanks to this design, ants can lift 5,000 times their own body weight.
9. To put this in perspective, this is the equivalent of a person lifting a Boeing 747.
10. The **exoskeleton** extends into segmented **paired jointed appendages** that are almost always specialized and evolutionarily adapted and modified to suit their lifestyle.
11. Since all arthropods have a head segment, they show **cephalization**. A brain-like **cerebral ganglion** in their head attaches to a **ventral nerve cord**. Many large **reflex arcs** branch off of the nerve cord.
12. **Arthropods**, in spite of their small cerebral capabilities, have highly evolved and impressive components of the nervous system. **Reflex arcs** allow gnats and midges to beat their wings more than 60,000 times per minute.
13. Additionally, all **arthropods** have compound eyes. Each of the dozens or hundreds of **lenses** of the eye sits atop **pigment cells** and **retinula cells** that trigger impulses in **optic nerves**.
14. The **axons** of these nerves **synapse** back to the **cerebral ganglion**.
15. Contrary to what you may have seen in movies or been told by your Uncle Billy, flies do NOT see hundreds of images. All of the images from each lens are integrated into one pixeled image by the brain.
16. **Arthropods** have an **open circulatory system**, with a **heart** that sits in a collecting basin known as a **hemocoel**. This basin collects **hemolymph** and/or **blood**. The heart then sucks this up and pumps it into the body cavity.
17. When a big beetle splatters yellow goo on your windshield, it is hemolymph you are removing with washer fluid.
18. The **respiratory system** is always present, but varies by, and even within, the class of arthropods. Crustaceans and horse-shoe crabs have varied gill designs, insects have gills or tracheal systems, and arachnids have lungs.
19. Arthropod digestive systems are all segmented into specialized organs. An enzyme-secreting **digestive gland** sits atop the stomach and intestine, releasing their products into ducts to aid digestions.
20. All arthropods also have **excretory systems**, but this design also varies by class. Crustaceans have kidney-like **green glands**, while insects and arachnids make use of **Malphigian tubules**.

21. Reproductively, like the great majority of **ecdysozoans**, the arthropods are separate sexes. The great majority of arthropods are egg-laying **R-strategists** that maximize their number of offspring and offer little parental care.
22. The lobster below depicts the basic external anatomical features of an arthropod. A recipe is included.
23. We will wait to detail internal anatomy until we discuss each class, since each group usually has detailed specializations that require further explanations.

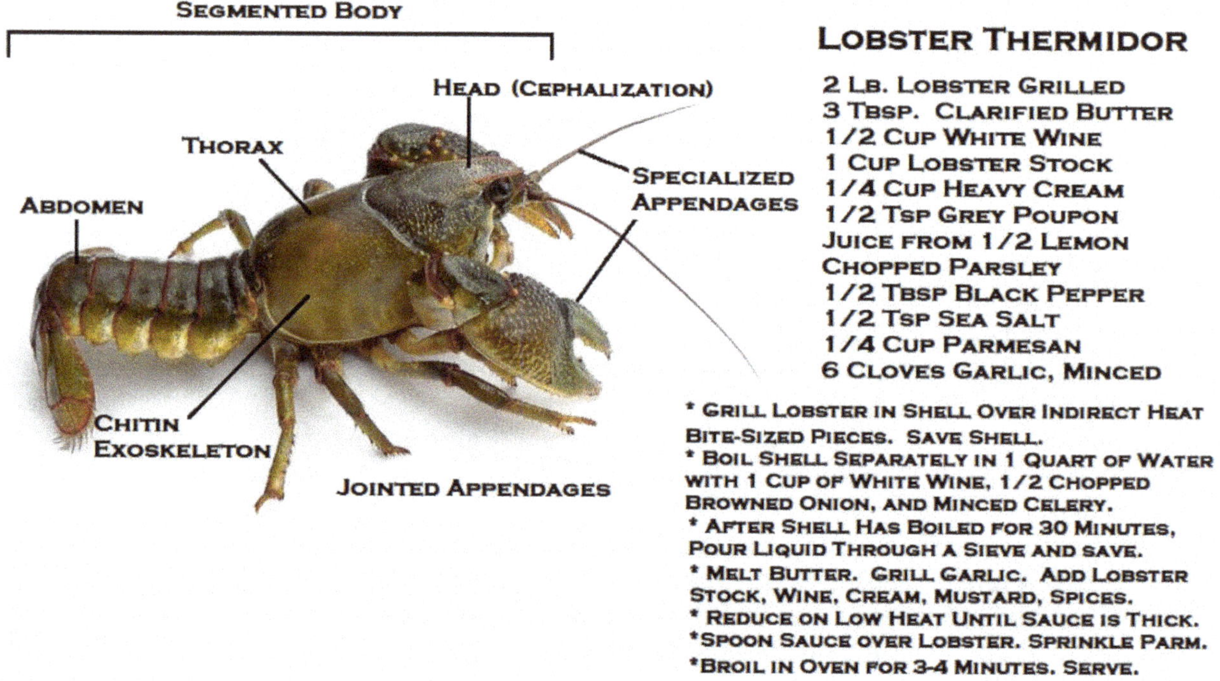

24. We now turn our attention to the evolutionary history of arthropods. The first known arthropod fossils found in the Cambrian era (500 plus million years ago) look like primitive shrimp or sow-bug like trilobites.
25. Modern arthropods can be divided up into two major groups called the **chelicerate** or the **mandibulata** according to their mouthparts. The former group have fangs, while the latter have mandibles.
26. Modern chelicerates include two classes. These are **Class Arachnida** (spiders, scorpions, harvestmen, and others) and the **Class Xiphosura** (horseshoe crabs).
27. Using the simplest classification system, the modern groups of mandibulates belong to **Class Crustacea** (crustaceans), **Class Insecta** (insects), or to **Class Myriapoda** (centipedes and millipedes).
28. However, many evolutionary biologists are now arguing that a combination of molecular and morphological evidence would suggest that the crustaceans be further sub-divided into several classes.
29. We now turn to a discussion the two main divisions of arthropods, the chelicerates and mandibulates.

G) The Chelicerate Arthropods: Arachnids, Horseshoe Crabs, and Sea Spiders

1. The **Chelicerate Arthropods** have several distinct features that serve as criteria for a common grouping.
2. The most distinctive feature of chelicerates is that members of these groups only have a single pair of appendages in from of the mouth. These **chelicerae** are usually highly modified to suit a specific purpose.

3. **Chelicerates** have tube-shaped **hearts** that connect to open blood vessels. The fluids pumped by the heart in t their **open circulatory systems** trickle back into a **hemocoel**, where they are picked up again.
4. Most chelicerates have a fused **cephalothorax** and a large protruding abdomen called an **ophistoma** that houses both the circulatory and respiratory systems.
5. It is more useful to discuss individual classifications to delineate other distinguishing anatomical features.
6. **Class Arachnida** is, by far, the largest group of chelicerates. Nearly 100,000 species of arachnids are known to science, with estimates that the actual number of arachnids is several times higher.
7. Three quarters of these species are either spiders (40,000) or mites (32,000). There are another 12,000 species of ticks, and more than 6,000 types of daddy longlegs. There are a number of relatively obscure arachnids.
8. The taxonomy of arachnids is still being worked out. There are multiple conflicting classification schemes right now, based on different morphological criteria and genetic studies.
9. The arachnid classification scheme below is only one of several alternate phylogenetic schemes. With that said, this system represents one possible evolutionary history of this group of arthropods.

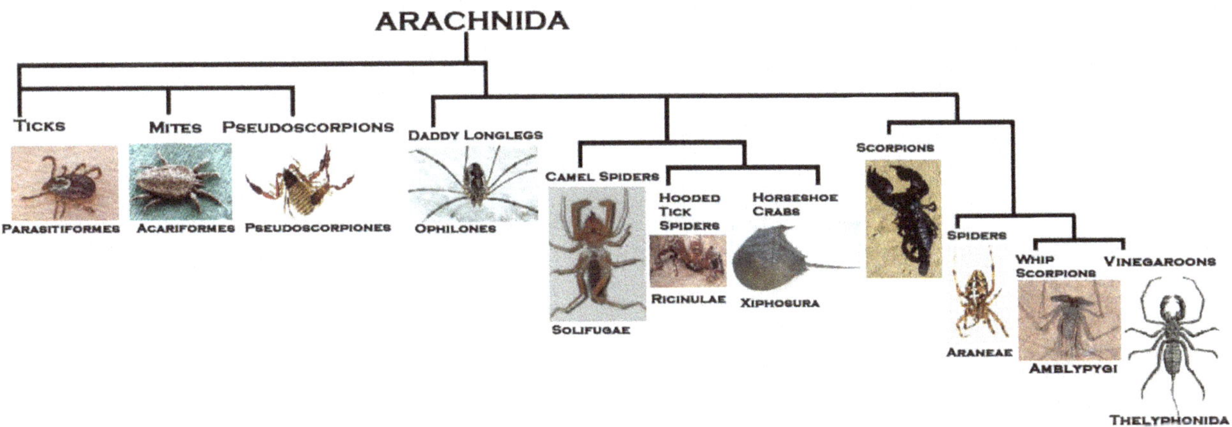

10. **Order Parasitiformes** includes **ticks** and **bird mites**, which don't seem to have any biological purpose other than being disgusting disease-spreading parasites that cost you lots of extra money at the vet's office.
11. Anatomically, ticks are distinctly different than most other arachnids because all three of their body segments (head, thorax, and abdomen) are fused into one.
12. **Hard ticks** have a hard shell on their backs, extending into a piercing mouthpart in the front. **Soft ticks** have mouthparts on the ventral surface of their heads.
13. Ticks find their hosts by following the infrared from their body heat, sensing moisture, or detecting carbon dioxide or odors emanating from the host. Once they find a nice tender spot to feed, they bite down.
14. Ticks use a **serrated** needle-like mouth part called a **hypostome** to suck the blood of their host.
15. Huge **salivary glands** inject **anticoagulants** to thin the blood. Ticks also inject other proteins that tamp down the host immune system, buying them time to feed before an inflammatory response attacks them.
16. Because of their limited diets (blood only), ticks have evolved **symbioses** with many different gut bacteria that help them supplement nutritional deficiencies. Some of these bacteria are harmful to humans.
17. For instance, *Coxiella burneti* causes Q-fever, while *Borrelia burgdorferi* is the causative agent of Lyme disease.

18. Like all other arachnids, ticks have a gut with attached waste-filtering **Malphigian tubules**.
19. Ticks have a respiratory system more reminiscent of insect tracheal tunnels, rather than the enlarged book lungs found in many larger-bodied arachnids. Respiratory **spiracles** open on the **ventral** side of the body.
20. Reproductively, ticks have up to seven life stages and as many as three hosts, depending on the species.
21. Ticks show **incomplete metamorphosis**, in that their juvenile stages look like miniature adults. They progress from egg to larvae to **nymph** stages. The **nymph stage** may require several **molts** to complete.
22. Each increasingly larger **nymph** is known as an **instar**. Instar nymphs may switch hosts after each molt.
23. The pictures below depict several species of ticks.

Dog Tick

Deer Tick

Rocky Mountain Wood Tick

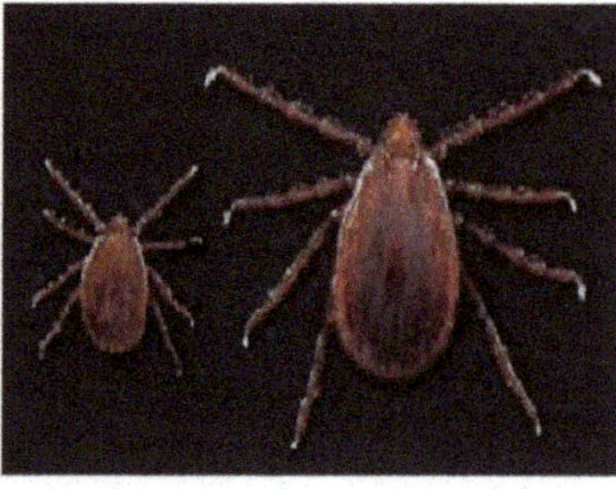
Asian Longhorned Tick

African Bont Tick

24. Most **mites** (other than bird mites) belong to **Superorder Acariformes**. Their classification is surprisingly complex, but since odds are that you aren't an aspiring mite taxonomist, we will keep it simple here.
25. **Superorder Acariformes** is divided into two orders called the **Trombid mites** and the **Sarcoptid mites**. Trombid mites tend to be parasites that suck on living hosts, while sarcoptid mites tend to have chewing mouthparts.
26. Anatomically, most mites are built similarly to ticks. Their chitin exoskeleton is divided into hard protective plates. The **sternal plate** and **abdominal plate** protect the ventral nerve cord under the body.
27. A third plate protects the gonads and contains openings for sperm ducts or ovarian ducts.
28. Internally, like ticks, their digestive tract is divided into a **midgut** and a **hindgut**, with waste-filtering **Malphigian tubules** emerging from the hindgut and wrapping back toward the front of the body under the legs.
29. Like ticks, the **spiracles** of the respiratory system open underneath the back legs.
30. There are a number of **Trombid mites** that cause agricultural problems. These include plant spider mites, peacock mites, gall mites, and red-legged earth mites. All of these pests suck juices from their plant hosts.
31. Spider mites are a scourge to greenhouses everywhere. Like spiders, they spin webs around their host plant. They move down their silk ziplines and can drain a plant of chlorophyll, leaving them ghostly white.
32. Peacock mites have bristles on their backs called **setae** that discourage predators from eating them. They emerge from their backs like the plumes of a peacock. They are hated parasites of citrus trees.
33. Gall mites have devolved all but two pairs of legs. The back halves of their bodies are elongated like worms. A number of tree species, such as maples and ashes are attacked by species of gall mites.
34. Secretions in the saliva of gall mites causes damaged cells to form galls in the areas where the mites feed.

35. Red-legged earth mites prey on herbaceous agricultural crops like brassicas, peas, and beans. They crawl up plants from the soil and congregate on leaves, feeding like a little herd of cattle, sucking all the juices out.
36. The pictures below show representatives of these agricultural pests.

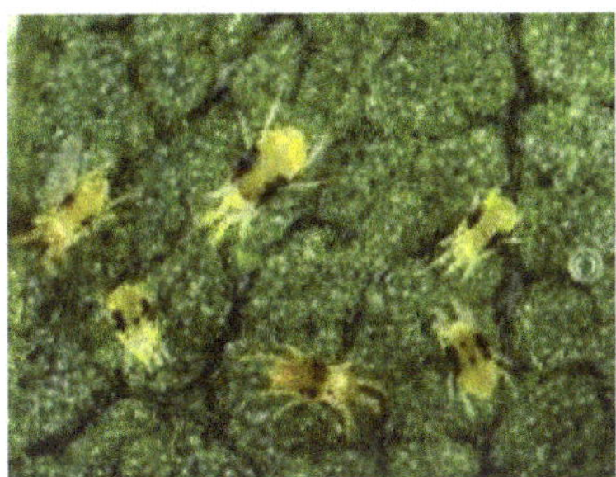
SPIDER MITES

PEACOCK MITE

GALL MITE

RED-LEGGED EARTH MITE

37. In addition to agricultural pests, the trombid mite classification also includes animal ectoparasites.
38. The universally-hated chigger is a trombid mite that feeds on the blood of just about any vertebrate host during its **nymph** stage. As adults, they are free-living predators of other small arthropods.
39. Other trombid mites are predators. Snout mites and velvet mites live in leaf litter and prey on arthropods and worms. Velvet mites can even take down large insects like a pack of wolves. Water mites feed on zooplankton.
40. The infamous hair follicle mites that inhabit almost every human on earth, snacking on our dead skin flakes and body oils, are really just harmless trash-eating commensals. Like gall mites, they have devolved their back legs.
41. The **Sarcoptid mites** have chewing mouthparts. They include beetle mites, armored mites, dust mites, feather mites, and the parasitic itch mites that cause mange in dogs and scabies in humans.
42. The beetle mites and armored mites live in leaf litter and soil, and like earthworms, are important to the carbon cycle, since they are often among the first animals to start breaking down organic matter.
43. Dust mites are also detritivores, feeding on skin flakes, body oils, and other organic trash.
44. Mange and scabies are both caused by *Sarcoptes* or *Dermodex* mite species. In both conditions, mites burrow into hair follicles and feed on blood and tissue. Their feces cause an intense immune reaction.
45. As the mites infest their host, they cause a scaly, crusty, weeping rash. Scabies and mange are very similar.
46. Mange causes dogs to scratch to the point that they lose their hair. Sarcoptic mange is tranmissable between species, while dermodectic mange is specific to species.
47. It would be entirely possible to go on for another 30 or 40 pages and keep describing different types of mites. Mites are kings of the micro-kingdom and there are THAT many species. But guess what? We won't. NEXT!
48. **Order Pseudoscorpiones** includes the **pseudoscorpions**, which are much more closely related to mites than they are to actual scorpions. Other than pincher-like **pedipalps**, they really aren't much like scorpions at all.
49. Hidden in plain sight, most people never actually notice a pseudoscorpion, because they are so small. The largest species on earth is no more than half an inch long, while most species are a fraction of that size.
50. Pseudoscorpions are 'good bugs' that you would want to have around, because they eat mites, lice, moth larvae, beetle larvae, maggots, small flies, and other small household pests.

51. Unlike scorpions, it is the **pedipalp** itself that is venomous, injecting venom as the pseudoscorpion grabs its prey. This is no threat to humans, because they are way too small to be able to penetrate your skin.
52. Like spiders, they expel digestive enzymes onto their prey and begin to liquefy them before they feed.
53. The **thorax** of the pseudoscorpion articulates with the legs, while the **abdomen** is divided into 12 segments covered with armored plates. The rear four segments contain **spiracles** that open to **trachea**.
54. True scorpions have **book lungs**, rather than tracheal tunnels. True scorpions also have a tail that extends into a stinger, while the abdomen of pseudoscorpions is rounded and ends abruptly.
55. Pseudoscorpions have silk glands in their jaws. They spin cocoons around themselves to hibernate during winter, to protect themselves when they are molting their **exoskeletons**, and when they mate.
56. Pseudoscorpions have several spider-like behaviors when they reproduce. Males produce **spermatophores** which are wrapped packets of sperm. This is transferred to females, fertilizing their eggs.
57. Once the eggs have been fertilized, the female carries them on her back until they hatch. Like spiders, hatchlings may also remain under their mother's care for a short period of time.
58. The images below show a few species of pseudoscorpions.

59. **Order Opiolones** includes the daddy longlegs or harvestmen, which are frequently mistaken for spiders for some reason. They also supposedly have super-deadly venom that can melt your face. They don't.
60. **Daddy longlegs** are not close relatives of spiders. Unlike spiders, all three body segments are fused and there is not an hourglass restriction that divides the abdomen. They lack venom glands and spinnerets.
61. Their abdomen has 10 segments, with the first five segments fused into a hard protective plate on their back.
62. To protect themselves from predators, **harvestmen** have a pair of glands that secrete foul-smelling compounds. Any kid who has ever picked one of these guys up and smelled their hands afterward knows that stank.
63. While they have eight legs like any other arachnid, the second pair of legs is longer and is used for probing their environment, because their eyes are simple and are really just light sensors that don't do well with detail.
64. Most members of the opiolones are omnivores that feed on a combination of small insects, fungi, plant scraps, and manure. Unlike most other arachnids, their mouth is not straw-like, so they can swallow large solid bites.
65. Their digestive system contains a **midgut, hindgut**, and **Malphigian tubules**, like other simple arachnids.
66. Like pseudoscorpions, **harvestmen** have **spiracles** on the abdomen that open into **tracheal tubes**.

67. Male daddy longlegs have a copulatory penis for **internal fertilization** rather than using sperm packets. In many species, the male remains with female until the eggs hatch to guard the eggs from oophagus predators.
68. The pictures below show several types of harvestmen.

69. Now we get to the group of arachnids that can purportedly bring down a grown camel, run as fast as a Jeep, jump six feet straight up in the air, kill a grown man in their sleep, and steal your credit cards.
70. We are, of course, talking about camel spiders or solpugids, which belong to **Order Solfugidae**.
71. **Solpugids** are mostly native to deserts and arid scrubland. They are fierce predators with large biting **chelicerae** that can run down and devour rodents, snakes, scorpions, lizards, beetles and locusts. They do NOT eat people.
72. After running down their prey, they grab them with their **pedipalps**, bite down with their chelicerae, and rip off pieces. From their, they secrete digestive enzymes and suck up the juices through a straw-like **pharynx**.
73. The **pedipalps** of camel spiders are so long that they look like a fifth pair of legs. They also contain **adhesive glands** that help them hold on to their prey, as well as assisting them in climbing surfaces.
74. **Solpugids** are often mistaken for spiders, but they have no venom, no spinnerets, an inflexible abdomen, tracheal tubes instead of book lungs, and a number of other features that spiders do not share.
75. Camel spiders usually follow a mating routine that involves the male body-slamming the female onto her back and transferring a **spermatophore** packet into the female's oviduct.
76. From there, the female digs a burrow, lays a couple of hundred eggs, and then stands guard until they hatch.
77. Camel spiders got their fearsome reputations mostly from soldiers stationed in the Middle East, where they are abundant. They would stage solpugid fights and bet on the winner.
78. In spite of the rumors, the biggest sopulgids are less than 6 inches long. So yeah...they DO get 5 inches long.....
79. The pictures below show species of the notorious camel spider.

80. **Hooded tick spiders** are neither ticks nor spiders, but instead belong to their own classification, the **Order Ricinulae**. They have several odd features that are not shared by any other type of arachnid.
81. Members of this group are small and inconspicuous and feed on small arthropods.
82. Their **exoskeleton** is very thick and armor-like, extending into a hood that can lowered to protect the head. Unlike spiders, they are eyeless and rely solely on tactile senses, using their legs and pedipalps.
83. Internally, hooded tick spiders have anatomy similar to mites, which are considered to be their closest relatives by some. They have tracheal tubes for respiration and they have a midgut, hindgut, and Malphigian tubules.
84. A number of features differ from true spiders. While they have a narrow waist like a spider, their **ophistoma** (abdomen) has a locking mechanism that hooks to the **prosoma** (thorax), protecting their soft underbelly.
85. Their sperm ducts and oviducts are located on the **prosoma**, rather than the abdomen (also not common in arachnids), so they must unlock their two rear segments in order to mate.
86. Like most arachnids, male transfer sperm packets to the female. Females carry their eggs under their hood until they hatch. Oddly, they have six legs until their first molt. The second **instar** then has eight legs.
87. While one school of arachnid biologists believe mites to be the closest relatives to hooded tick spiders, recent DNA evidence suggests that **horseshoe crabs** may actually share the closest common ancestry.
88. The same study also definitively concluded that horseshoe crabs actually ARE marine **arachnids** that diverged long ago when they made the ocean their habitat. **Order Xiphosura** has since been moved into the arachnids.
89. **Horseshoe crabs** are living fossil relics, largely unchanged from fossils that date to the Jurassic era. However, because of their numerous anatomical differences from most arachnids, we're going to go old school.
90. Until there is more evidence other than some DNA sequences that horseshoe crabs should be classified as arachnids, we will stick with the concept that they are a sister group of the arachnids. You will see why shortly.
91. **Scorpions** are designated as members of **Order Scorpiones**, due to their unique combination of traits. They are the only arachnids with a **prosoma** tipped by a venomous stinger.
92. Additionally, the **pedipalps** of scorpions are highly modified into cutting pinchers that can be used for grabbing prey, fighting rivals, gripping and climbing, or for fending off predators.
93. Scorpions have two eyes on top of the **cephalothorax** and five pairs that line the edges of the segment. They cannot form sharp images, but they are extremely sensitive to light.
94. The **cerebral ganglion** of scorpions is located in the middle of the **cephalothorax**, further back than the puny little invertebrate brains of other arachnids. The **nerve cord** is ventral and divided into segments with the body.
95. The back of the **cephalothorax** is segmented and has thick chitin armor. It is called the **mesosoma**, while the abdomen is divided into tightly segmented muscular bundles known as a **metastoma**.
96. Segments 3,4,5,and 6 of the mesosoma each have **spiracles** that open up into **book lungs**, which each have over 100 'sheets' of respiratory blood vessels. Since scorpions are fat-bodied, they can't get away with just **trachea**.
97. The **gonads** of both genders are located in the rear of the **mesosoma**. They are tube-shaped with with spermatic or ovarian ducts running between the testes or ovaries.
98. Males produce **spermatophores** that are transferred to females during fertilization. Most species of scorpions are **ovoviviparous**, giving live birth to young. During their nymph stage, they ride on the back of their mother.

99. The tail segment (the metastoma) is mostly muscle. The end of the intestine runs through the middle, terminating in the anus at the next-to-last segment. The final segment contains a pair of **venom glands**.

100. The diagrams below depict the external and internal anatomy of a scorpion.

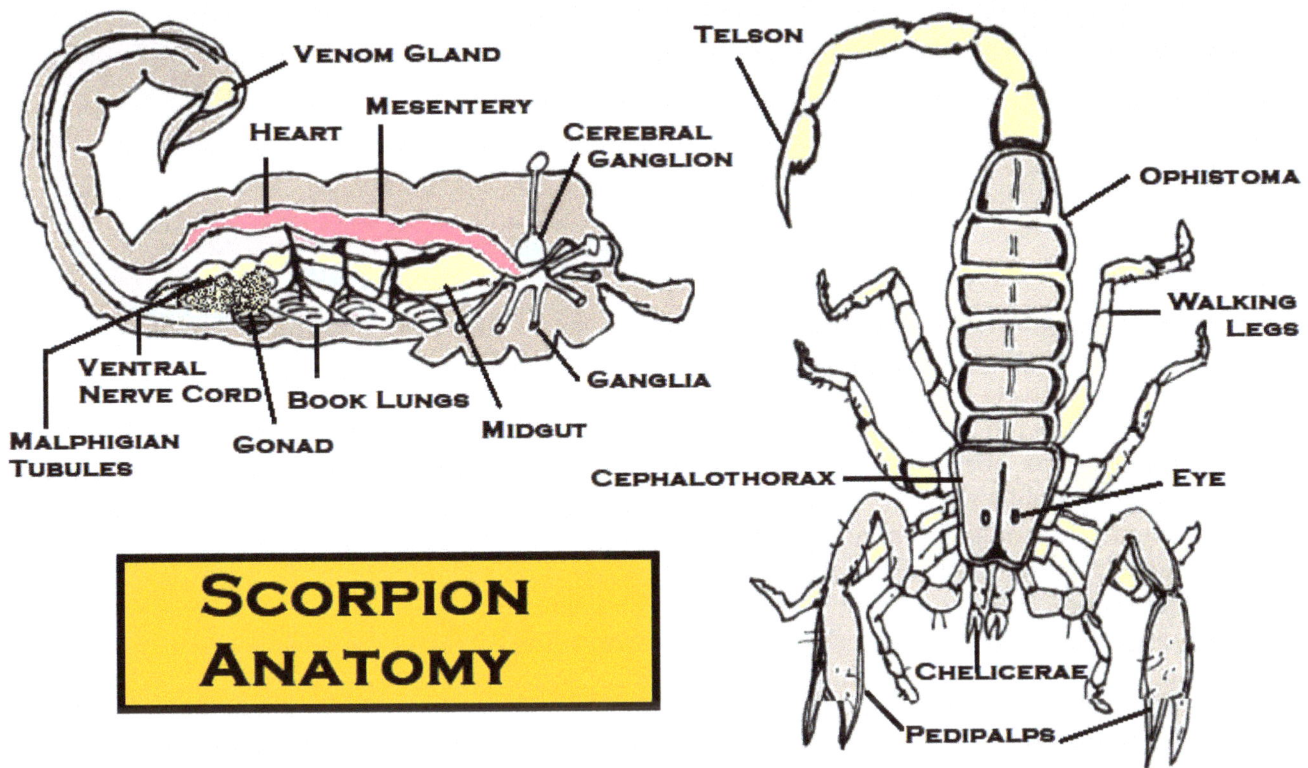

101. Scorpions classification divides these arachnids into one large ancient family called **Buthidae**, whose fossils date back to Pangea, and 18 other smaller families, such as **Scorpionidae**, which are more recently evolved.

102. Scorpion classification mostly uses exoskeletal features and genetic sequencing to determine evolutionary relationships. Classification is still under debate and confusing to anyone who isn't a scorpion expert by trade.

103. Scorpion **venom** varies by family, but is almost always a complicated cocktail of toxic substances. Prominent ingredients include toxins that block **potassium channels** and **sodium channels** of neurons.

104. Certain scorpions have venoms that can throw the **parasympathetic nervous system** into overdrive, resulting in muscle spasms, sweating, salivation, cardiac palpitations, blurred vision, fluid on the lungs, and seizures.

105. While most scorpions just cause severe localized pain, swelling, and spasms, there are a few species that are anything but child's play. The deathstalker scorpion has extremely powerful neurotoxins and other protein toxins that can cause seizures and anaphylactic shock. They can kill children and elderly victims.

106. Scorpion venoms are currently under research for the variety of potentially useful medical effects that they might have if separated and given at lower doses.

107. For instance, in clinical trials, brain tumors and diabetes seem to respond to certain scorpion toxins.

108. The pictures below show several species of scorpions from around the world.

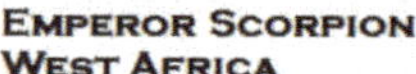

Emperor Scorpion
West Africa

Arizona Bark Scorpion
Southwestern USA

Spider-Hunting Scorpion
Western Australia

Deathstalker Scorpion
Sahara & Middle East

109. **Spiders** belong to **Order Araneae**. Hey arachnophobes......there are about 48,000 different species of spiders belonging to 117 families, and there are MILLIONS of each species. Think about that at 2 AM as you lie awake.

110. **Spiders** are unique among arachnids for their body plans. Their head and thorax are fused into a **cephalothorax**, that gives way to an hourglass shaped narrow waist, and an enlarged abdomen known as an **ophisthoma**.

111. While many arachnids have venom glands and silk glands, independently, spiders are the only group of arachnids with BOTH venomous fang-like **chelicerae** and **spinnerets** and **silk glands** at the end of the abdomen.

112. Only nervous system **ganglia** and the beginning of the digestive tract can be found in the **cephalothorax**.

113. Spiders also lack many of the muscles found in other arachnids, relying solely on pressure in hydraulic sacs to move and flex their legs. They do not have muscles in any of their appendages.

114. This is why spiders curl up into a ball when they are squished. As fluid seeps out of the hydraulic system, dropping internal pressure in the gut cavity causes the legs to collapse inward.

115. Since the abdomens of most spiders are so voluminous and fat, as compared to the body plans of most arachnids, adaptations had had to be made to deal with potentially slower transport of materials.

116. Internally, spiders have a unique internal layout, with the **heart,** large **book lungs**, **digestive tube**, and **gonads** all restricted to the abdominal **ophisthosoma** segment.

117. Spider hearts are tube-like, giving way to a network of blood vessels that terminate into the **hemoceol** after distributing **hemolymph** over the organs. While somewhat sophisticated, it is still an **open circulatory system**.

118. A **pulmonary blood vessel** articulates to the underside of the heart, opening up into numerous sheet-like beds of blood vessels that resemble pages in a book. For this reason, spider respiratory organs are called **book lungs.**

119. The **digestive system** begins with the **venom glands**, **chelicerae**, and **pedipalps**, since spiders use these mouthparts to subdue and paralyze prey. Digestive enzymes are secreted with the bite, slowly liquefying prey.

120. After the spider has mummified its victim in a wrapping of silk, they begin sucking up their gooey juices through their tiny mouth, up to their **espophagus**, and into their **sucking stomach.** They basically feed on bug gravy.

121. The sucking stomach connects to canals at the base of each leg called **digestive cecae** that continue to secrete enzymes and digest any remaining solids or goo into protein-packed liquidy goodness.

122. Eventually the bug slurry makes its way into the large **digestive tube** in the abdomen. Hundreds of tracks branch off of this tube, providing more surface area for digestion.

123. At the end of the digestive tube is a pouch called a **sterocecal pocket** that, along with the **Malphigian tubules**, extracts remaining water and nutrients, and squeezes out paste-like spider dookie. It leaves via the anus.

124. Unlike some invertebrates that use a single **cloaca** to plumb all exiting materials, spiders have three separate openings. In addition to the anus, they have **reproductive ducts** and **spinnerets**.

125. **Gonads** take up a large part of the ventral side of the abdomen in both sexes. Female spiders lay dozens to hundreds of eggs from a single ovary, while males produce sacs full of sperm called **spermathecae**.

126. It is beyond the scope of this book to detail the complexity of all of the different spider mating rituals in nature, as they run the gamut of dances, displays, and males' life-threatening attempts at mating with larger females.

127. Spiders, as was previously mentioned, are classified into 117 separate families. However, the classification scheme can be simplified by considering the traits of the 3 major superorders.

128. **Superorder Mesothelae** have several distinct traits that set them apart from the other superorders. Their **chelicerae** are positioned at the sides of their head, rather than directly in front, for one.

129. Spiders in this order have 8 eyes in a cluster, two sets of book lungs, a pair of urine secreting **coxal glands** under each leg, and 8 spinnerets at the end of their abdomens. They have segmented **tergite plates** on their backs.

130. An ancient taxa, this group of spiders are relatively obscure, as there are only around 100 species in existence, most don't have common names, and all live in the jungles of Southeast Asia.

131. **Superorder Opisthothelae** is a much larger group that appears to have evolved from the Mesothelae.

132. Anatomically, they are very similar to their ancestors, but they have devolved the chitin tergite plates on their backs. They only have 1 or 2 pairs of spinnerets. They are medial on the abdomen and much further forward.

133. There are nearly 3000 extant species of spiders in **Superorder Opisthothelae.** They are found worldwide.

134. The remaining 45,000 or so species of spiders belong to **Superorder Araneomorphae**.

135. As compared to the latter two groups, their mouthparts function differently. Instead of stabbing down like an excavator, their **chelicerae** close side-to-side like a pair of pincers in the same orientation as the **pedipalps**.

136. This simple re-design of the jaws made them much more efficient predators. With the exception of some of the large tarantula families, the majority of spider families in existence today belong to this group.

137. Differences in eye number and placement, spinneret number and placement, numbers of sets of book lungs, reproductive strategy, and other physical characteristics are criteria for classifying this group into families.

138. The pictures on the next page show representatives from each group of spiders and facts about each.

139. A good secondary purpose for this chart is to open your book to this page at 3 AM, wake someone you love from a deep sleep, and shine a powerful flashlight onto this page as they open their eyes.

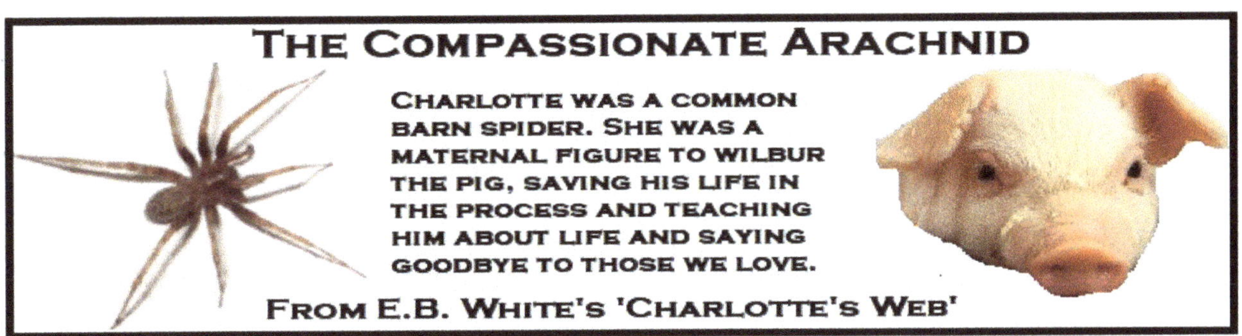

Funnel Webs
* Spin funnel-shaped webs across burrow
*Highly venomous
*Oval-shaped abdomen
*Extremely fast afoot

House Spiders
*Long elaborate mating ritual with hour-long mating dance & male reels in female with web.
*Web not sticky, but velcro-like

Pholcus Spiders
*Live mostly in houses.
*Legs are 5-6 times as long as their body.
*Prey on other spiders.

Jumping Spiders
*Flat face and forward facing eyes.
*Longer front legs for jumping leverage
*Largest spider family

Recluses
*Fiddle-shaped body
*3 pairs of eyes
*Furry abdomen
*Will discard a leg to escape predators

Black Widows
*Potent venom affects smooth muscle tissues
*Hang upside down from sporadic webs in dark holes
*Female consumes male after mating if he doesn't escape

Crab Spiders
*Don't spin webs. Only use silk for droplines.
*Ambush predators of aphids, other insects.
*Camouflaged to blend in with leaves, flowers.

Wolf Spiders
*Solitary hunting spiders; ambush predators
*Carry egg cases on abdomen glued buy webs
* 2 large eyes with sharp vision; 6 smaller eyes

Orb Weavers
*Have 3 claws on legs for weaving webs...Y-shaped scaffold supports sticky web.
*Dramatically larger females cannibalize males.

Tarantulas
*Many species have irritating bristles to discourage predators
*Most live in burrows
*Includes largest spider in world (Bird Eating Goliath) with 12 inch legspan

140. Perhaps the most dangerous species of spider, notwithstanding the deadly Brazilian wandering spider that likes to hide in bunches of bananas that end up in grocery aisles, is the Calaveras County barking spider.

141. Barking spiders are different from most species of spider, in that instead of injecting their toxins with their fangs, they distribute noxious fumes in brown clouds throughout their environment.

142. The most dangerous species of barking spiders are misnomers, as they are silent, but quite deadly.

143. You would think that we would be to the end of this eight-legged nightmare, but you would be wrong. There are several other groups of arachnids that also max out the creepy factor coming up.

144. **Whip scorpions** look incredibly menacing, yet they are actually relatively harmless. They are neither scorpions, nor spiders, but they combine the leggy creepiness of both. They belong to **order Thelyphonida**.

145. **Whip scorpions** have incredibly large curving **pedipalps** on their head, but unlike scorpions, they inside of these appendages are ridged, rather than hinged into claws. They use these to crush prey.

146. As if their appearances weren't creepy enough, so are their diets. Their favorite food is large cockroaches, but they also eat slugs, centipedes, beetles, roly-polies, grasshoppers, spiders, tree frogs,and avocado toast.

147. The fuzzy legs of whip scorpions have a wide breadth, like a tarantula. While some whip scorpions can have bodies up to 3 inches long, their legs spread to a much wider breadth. They can detect vibrations with these.

148. Like true scorpions, whip scorpions have two eyes at the front of the **cephalothorax**, with three other pairs of simpler eyes along the edges of the front segment.

149. While their abdominal segment resembles that of a scorpion, with segmented armored plates, the anatomy at the end of the tail differs. Rather than a stinger, there is a whip-like appendage.

150. The whip is actually used as a distributor of nastiness. When threatened, a special gland under the whip releases extremely concentrated acetic acid, which is fanned into the faces of predators of whip scorpions.
151. Since vinegar is acetic acid, some people refer to whip scorpions as **vinegaroons**.
152. Reproductively, whip scorpions are similar to spiders, in that males produce **spermatophores** that are then transferred to the female's oviducts with his **pedipalps**.
153. The last monstrous looking group of arachnids belong to the **order Amblypgyi** and they look like mutated aliens from someone's worst nightmare. Whoever named the order also seemed to have a problem with vowels.
154. Common names for this order of arachnids are the **tailless whip scorpions, whip spiders,** or **worky-daddies.**
155. The image on the left shows a member of the aforementioned **order Thelyphonida** (whip scorpions) while the image on the right shows an example from the **order Amblypygi** (whip spiders).

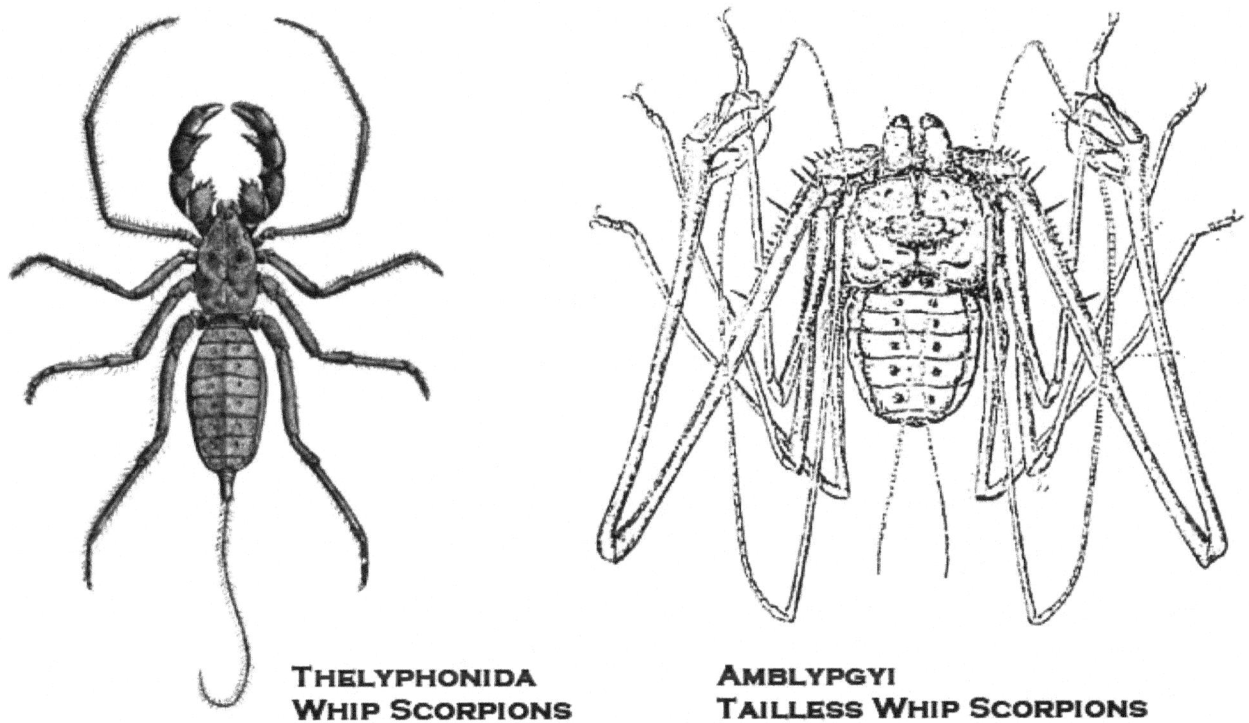

156. Anatomically, the first thing one would notice about members of **order Amblypgyi** are that their legs are astonishingly long when unfolded. Some of the gigantic species have legspans of over two feet.
157. The bodies of whip spiders can be several inches long. Unlike scorpions, the **pedipalps** are lined with rows of spikes that are used to impale prey. From there, the pincher-like **chelicerae** crush them.
158. The front pair of legs are especially long, but are used like antennae as feelers. Since they often live in caves and dark areas, they often locate their prey by feel, rather than by sight.
159. The back three pairs of legs are still very long, but not as long as their feelers. This makes functional sense, since whip spiders spend a lot of time hanging vertically on cave walls or above your bed watching you sleep.
160. The eyes of worky-daddies are laid out in pretty much the same orientation as vinegaroons, with two eyes on the front and top of the **cephalothorax** and the other three pairs lining the edges of the carapace.

161. Whip spiders reproduce much like all the other arachnids, with the male transferring **spermatophores** with their **pedipalps** to the **oviducts** of the female.
162. Oddly, whip spiders show a relatively high degree of parental care. Females keep track of their disgusting little progeny and even communicate with them by doing some weird handshake with their front feeler legs.
163. To this point, everything we have covered in the clade of **chelicerate arthropods** has been an **arachnid**. The classification of the last two chelicerates groups are under debate.
164. In both cases, some of the DNA evidence seems to point to common ancestry with arachnids.
165. However, what has not been resolved so far, is just how far back this common ancestry goes, and why their physical characteristics are so different than other extant arachnids.
166. These two debated groups are the **sea spiders** and the **horseshoe crabs**. Let's begin with the former.
167. **Sea spiders** of the **Order Pantopoda,** are truly bizarre animals. The body of a sea spider is so small and skinny that some of their organ systems must be extended into the legs in order to have a functional fit.
168. It appears from DNA and fossil evidence that the **sea spiders** were the first group of arthropods to diverge off of the mainline group that went on to become arachnids. Therefore, some shared features appear to be archaic.
169. For instance, sea spiders, like most arachnids, have a straw-like sucking mouth called a **proboscis**. Like spiders, they suck the juices out of their prey. While not present in all species, many groups have accessory mouth parts.
170. Some sea spiders have manipulative hand-like **palps** and biting **chelifores** that seem to show **convergent evolution** with the **pedipalps** and **chelicerae** of true terrestrial spiders.
171. Sea spiders prey on or parasitize cnidarians, sponges, marine worms, and other slow soft-bodied animals.
172. Once the food enters the gut from the mouth, it enters a very narrow passage through the head, thorax, and abdomen. These segments are virtually indistinguishable, since sea spiders are so skinny.
173. Several hundred miniscule **salivary glands** empty their juices into the **foregut**. The **midgut** diverges into tracts called **diverticula.** Each of the 8 to 12 legs houses a tunnel of the midgut. Digestion and absorption occur here.
174. The **hindgut** terminates in the anus at the end of the **abdomen.**
175. **Sea spiders** have no respiratory system, since they are skinny enough to allow diffusion to take care of gas exchange. However, they do have an **open circulatory system** that pumps **hemolymph** through the segments.
176. The heart, however, doesn't seem to pump juices into the legs. The combined motions of walking and digestive processes seem to sufficiently pump fluids through the legs.
177. Waste is evacuated through the anus, but also seems to be secreted, so that it accumulates under the **exoskeleton** of the legs. When the sea spider undergoes **molting**, the waste is discarded.
178. Sea spiders are almost exclusively separate sexes. The use **external fertilization**, with the male collecting eggs from the female, fertilizing them, and then caring for them until they hatch.
179. There are at least four different ways that larvae of various species develop, some of them a relative mystery.
180. Some species seem to gradually **metamorphose** into their adult form, adding legs and anatomical complexity. Other species seem to have a cyst-covered parasitic larvae that feeds on coral polyps.

THE ANCESTORS OF ARACHNIDS: THE ULTIMATE SEA SPIDER

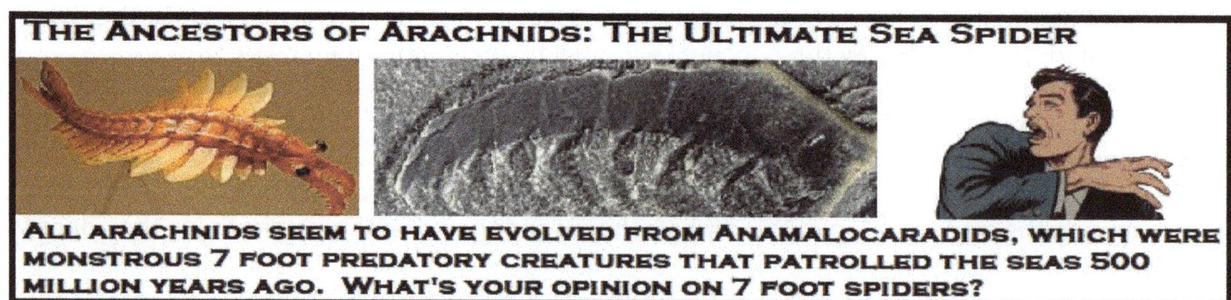

ALL ARACHNIDS SEEM TO HAVE EVOLVED FROM ANAMALOCARADIDS, WHICH WERE MONSTROUS 7 FOOT PREDATORY CREATURES THAT PATROLLED THE SEAS 500 MILLION YEARS AGO. WHAT'S YOUR OPINION ON 7 FOOT SPIDERS?

181. Pictures of sea spiders are shown below.

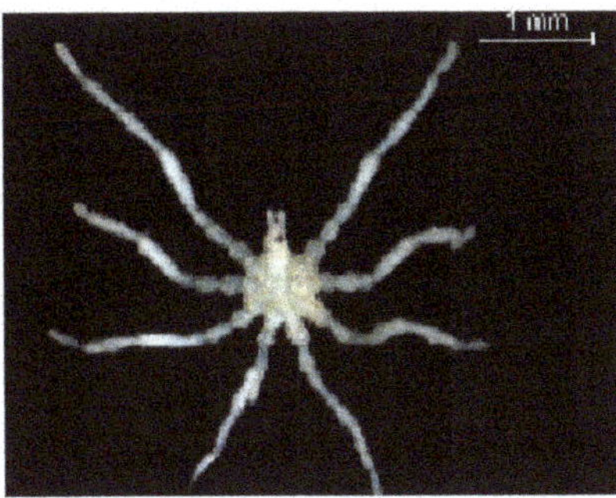

182. **Horseshoe crabs** are now considered to be true arachnids by some taxonomists. However, there are some dramatic differences in gross anatomy that make this seem like a molecular oversimplification.
183. For instance, with the exception of the modified pincers of scorpions and whip scorpions, all arachnid appendages are **uniramous**, coming to a single point, whereas all the legs of a horseshoe crab are **biramous.**
184. **Horseshoe crabs** belong to the **Order Xiphosura**. They are one of the best examples of a living fossil you can find, having been around for nearly a quarter of a billion years. There are only four living species remaining.
185. The entire body of a horseshoe crab is covered with a chitin **carapace**. Two large **compound eyes** emerge toward the front of the carapace, each with about 1000 lenses. Like insects, they can detect UV light.
186. In addition to these complex eyes, there are also smaller light-sensitive photoreceptors along the spike-shaped **telson** (tail) at the posterior of the body. Their brain sits in the center of the eyes under the **prosoma.**
187. The **prosoma** is the curved front part of the shell, while the tapered segment at the back of the shell is known as the **ophistoma**. Six pairs of appendages are rooted under the ventral surface of the shell.
188. The first pair of appendages are the **chelicerae**, the second pair are the **pedipalps**, while the remaining four pairs of legs are **walking legs**. The pedipalps and walking legs are all **biramous** and tipped with a pair of claws.
189. Things get weird when horseshoe crabs eat. The mouth of a horseshoe crab emerges from the middle of the legs. The lower joints of each leg are used to crush food, which is essentially crammed directly into the belly.
190. Imagine if you had several pairs of hands around your naval that crushed food and crammed it directly into your belly button and into your stomach. That's how horseshoe crabs actually eat.
191. Once they have shoved clams, oysters, worms, dead fish, tater tots, or hot pockets into their mouth, it is held in a chamber called the **crop**, ground up inside the muscular **gizzard**, and passed on to the **midgut** and **hindgut**.
192. The respiratory system of horseshoe crabs looks similar to the design of spiders, in that they have stacked membranes full of blood vessels to maximize respiratory surface area.
193. The **book gills** are under the back of the carapace and can be unfolded like louvers to get more oxygen.
194. The blood supply from the gills passes through an **open circulatory system**, where a powerful heart sprays blood over the organs. Horseshoe crabs are among the largest of all animals with this circulatory design.
195. The blood of horseshoe crabs is the color of rockin blue radberry Kool-Aid because it contains the copper-based **hemocyanin** pigment as an oxygen carrier, rather than red hemoglobin.
196. Horseshoe crab blood is harvested for use in medical applications, because it contains **amoebocytes** that function like the white blood cells of vertebrates.

197. Because the cells contain enzymes that react with bacterial proteins, these cells are sought out for medical test kits. However, the crabs probably don't enjoy this too much, as they frequently get juiced and thrown back.
198. Bleeding usually doesn't kill the horseshoe crab, but it does put them under a lot of stress....probably the same way it would stress you out if a creature the size of Godzilla picked you up and jammed a needle into you.....
199. When it comes time to make baby horseshoe crabs, everybody migrates to a sandy beach and males play piggy-back on a female of their choice. When the female releases her eggs, they are fertilized by **external fertilization**.
200. From there, the eggs are buried up in the sand. Most of them get eaten by fish, birds, crabs, and other opportunists, but a few of the thousands hatch and swim away.
201. From there, the larvae molt multiple times and undergo incomplete metamorphosis through several different juvenile stages before attaining their adult form. From there, adults molt infrequently.
202. The picture below shows representative horseshoe crabs and external anatomy.

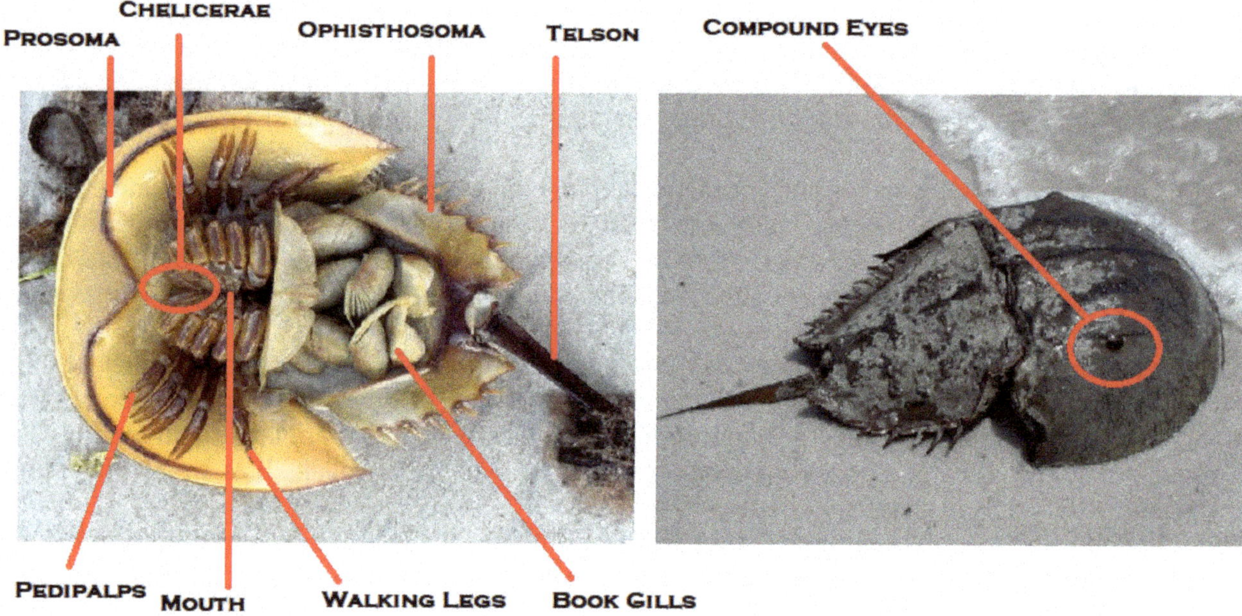

H) Class Insecta: The Insects

1. Insects are almost inarguably the most successful group of terrestrial arthropods, if not THE most successful group of invertebrates in existence. Over a million species have been formally classified.
2. Insects can be found on every continent in virtually every type of habitat. It is estimated that the ACTUAL number of extant insect species is 5 to 10 times greater than the million so far described.
3. If you want to find a new species and name it after yourself to honor your big ego, an insect is probably your best bet of doing so. Just hang out in the tropics under a porch light and you'll eventually succeed.
4. Members of **Class Insecta** have several defining characteristics. As you've known since kindergarten, all insects have six jointed legs, a **chitin exoskeleton**, a segmented body, **compound eyes**, and a lone pair of **antennae**.
5. Internally, insects also have many anatomical commonalities.

6. The nervous system of insects is probably the most impressive example of invertebrate evolution as a result of specialization to their terrestrial niches. In order to accommodate flight and jumping, it had to advance.
7. All insects have a **cerebral ganglion** that serves as sort of a puny little brain. Most of this tissue is dedicated to olfaction, vision processing, and integration of reflexes. Surprisingly, they DO have a little bit of memory.
8. At the rear of the brain are glands that produce **brain hormone** that control **metamorphosis**.
9. Vision is integrated in the cerebral ganglion from many optic nerves from each facet of their **compound eyes**.
10. The eyes, themselves, have hundreds of **lenses** that each form a **crystalline cone** with the nerve body and **bipolar cell** beneath the lens. Contrary to popular belief, insects do NOT see hundreds of images.
11. Instread, the **cerebral ganglion** integrates all the signals from each lens into a single pixelated image like a TV.
12. Nerves run backward from the main body of the cerebral ganglion like a daisy chain of electrical cords through the sub-segments of the thorax.
13. From there, the nerves cluster up again into **thoracic ganglia** that control the movement of the legs, wings, and muscles of the torso. Some insects have as many as six pairs, while some have as few as one large cluster.
14. These ganglia are important for the quick reactions required to turn on a dime in mid-flight or lunge and attack prey. The main brain (cerebral ganglion) doesn't have to get involved. These reactions are on **reflex arcs**.
15. The nervous system of an insect is relatively impressive, giving a lot of 'bang for the buck', considering the incredibly small size of certain insects like gnats and thrips.
16. The diagram below summarizes the wiring of the insect nervous system.

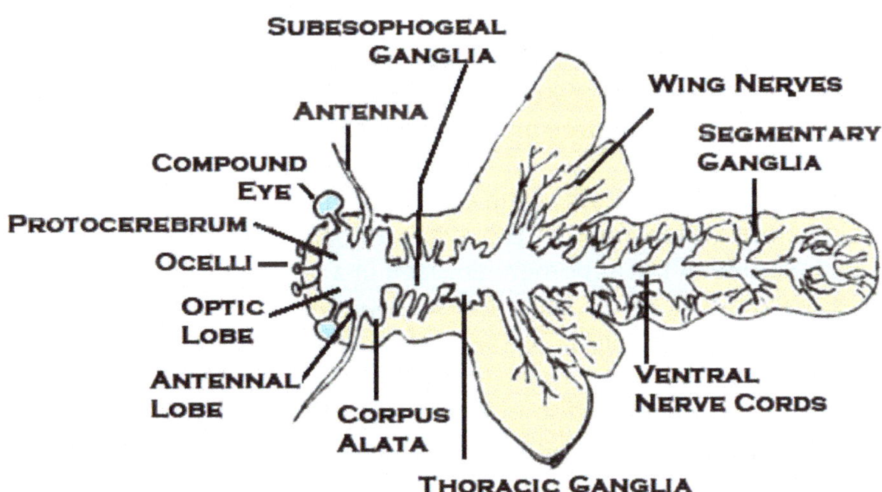

17. Insect taxonomy leans heavily on the modification of the **mouthparts** as a scheme for classification. For now, we will table the discussion on mouthparts, as it will be covered when we discuss classification.
18. Behind the mouth are **salivary glands** that begin the digestive process as food moves into the gut.
19. The digestive system of all insects contains a **foregut**, **midgut**, and **hindgut**. Different orders of insects have specialized modifications to all of these, especially the foregut, which may enlarged into a digestive **crop**.
20. The **foregut** begins digesting food with the help of amylases and other enzymes secreted by the salivary glands.

21. The **midgut** or **digestive gland** dumps digestive enzymes into the midgut via ducts. Peristalsis mixes the slurry of insect food with the enzymes. From there, the midgut and hindgut absorb the nutrients.
22. The midgut shows convergent evolution with the vertebrate digestive tract, in that it has millions of tiny projections called **microvilli** that increase the surface area for digestions.
23. **Malpighian tubules** diverticulate off of the hindgut, extracting water and nutrients from the digested food, until it is released as paste-like dookie from the anus at the terminus of the hindgut.
24. Not only do the tubules remove water and nutrients from the waste, they also pump **uric acid** and other wastes out of the **hemolymph**. This is the gooey yellow liquid that surrounds the organs that splatters on windshields.
25. Hemolymph distributes nutrients to organs and also has crude immune cells, but no red blood cells.
26. The **open circulatory system** is surprisingly simple. There is a tube-like **heart muscle** that sprays the hemolymph over the organs of the torso. It is not connected to any blood vessels at all.
27. So how do insects get away with this? Especially something as large as a praying mantis.....How?
28. The secret is the extensive **respiratory system**. Port-hole like openings on the abdomen called **spiracles** open up into a long and deep network of **tracheal tubes**. These essentially form a ventilation system through the body.
29. Very few cells inside the insect are more than a few cells away from a flow of air.
30. Also located primarily in the abdomen is the **reproductive system**.
31. Insects, like almost all **ecdysozoans**, have two separate genders, with the exception of a handful of all-female species, such as aphids, which use **parthenogenesis** to self-fertilize their own eggs.
32. Female insects have a pair of **ovaries** connected, via ducts to a pair of **spermathecae**. Female insects of many different orders can store sperm after mating, releasing the sperm from the ducts to fertilize their eggs later.
33. For instance, most flies lay eggs with multiple paternities. Female fruit flies can auto-fertilize a clutch of eggs with sperm from many different male parents. Some species can even choose the sperm they will use.
34. This allows species with a short lifespan to maximize the genetic diversity of their offspring.
35. The **oviducts** connect the ovaries to accessory shell glands that cover the eggs with a tough coating, and in some species like praying mantises and cockroaches, they produce a shell around an entire clutch.
36. Eggs exit the oviducts via the **ovipositors** at the end of the abdomen.
37. Male insects have a pair of **testes** made of coiled sperm-producing tubes. They float between the tracheal systems of each side of the abdomen, encased in a layer of fat.
38. A **vas deferens** exits each of the testes. Near the testes, there is a pocket called a **seminal vesicle** that stores back sperm for later matings. The vas deferens continues on to the **ejaculatory duct** at the end of the abdomen.
39. In some species, there is a hard projection of chitin from the exoskeleton at the ejaculatory duct. These structures are called **aedegii** and are used like a penis to deliver sperm to females during mating.

40. The diagram below shows the layout of the internal anatomy of a generic insect.

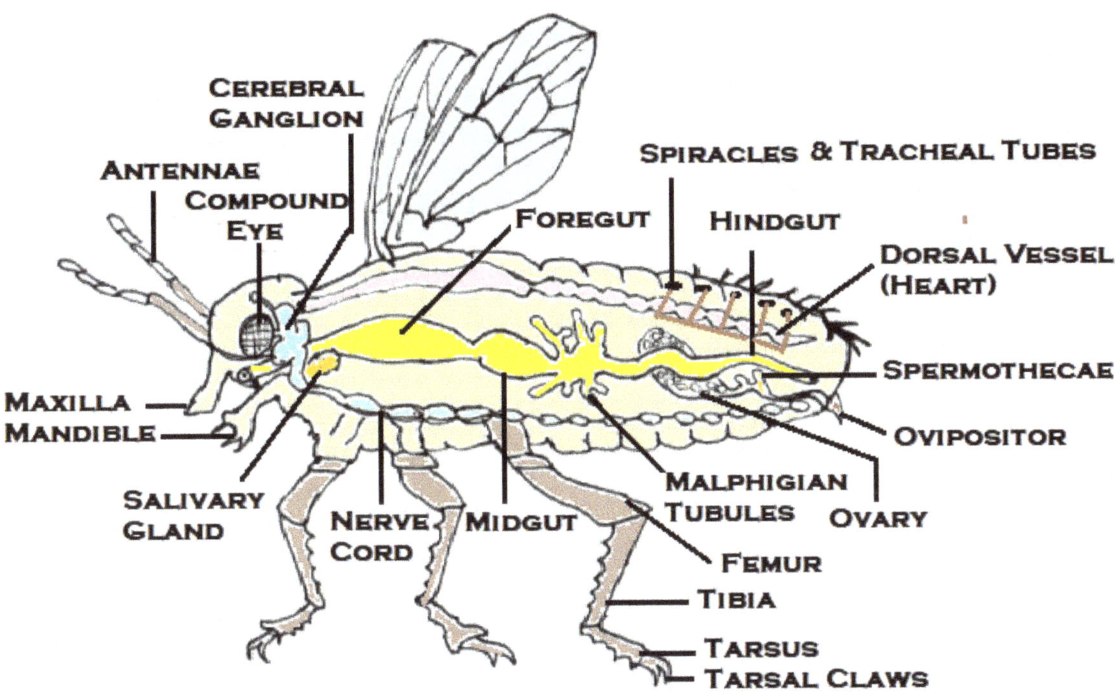

41. The actual process of reproduction is quite variable between different orders of insects. It is beyond the scope of this book to cover all of the detailed variations that exist, but we will provide a brief overview.
42. The majority of insects are **oviparous**, laying eggs with protective **chitin** shells and the insect equivalent of an **amnion** that keeps the developing embryo moist. However, this is not always the case.
43. Members of the **Order Diptera**, which includes flies and mosquitoes, lay their eggs either in water or in rotting fruit or meat, since their eggs lack cuticles.
44. Numerous other insect groups, such as **Order Ephemeroptera** (mayflies), **Order Trichoptera** (caddisflies) and **Order Plecoptera** (stoneflies) also lay their eggs in water, since their larval stages are aquatic.
45. Some species of cockroaches and flesh flies like the African tsetse fly, are **ovoviparous**, with the eggs hatching inside the female. The female then gives live birth to the first larval stage.
46. One rare exception among insects are the fully **viviparous** Diploptera cockroach species, that give birth to miniature versions of themselves, nourishing the young in a womb-like organ.
47. Members of **Order Hymenoptera** (bees and wasps) determine the gender of their offspring by using a system called **haplodiploidy**. Males are given one set of chromosomes, while females receive two.
48. This allows queen honeybees to control the number of individuals of different castes in a hive. For instance, by laying haploid eggs, she can pre-determine the number of new male drones in the hive.
49. Once eggs have been fertilized and hatch, larval insects start undergoing different developmental stages.
50. The process of **metamorphosis** varies greatly between different types of insects. However, as a general rule, all insects can be said to undergo either **incomplete metamorphosis** or true **complete metamorphosis**.
51. Insects that use **incomplete metamorphosis** have larval stages called **nymphs** that look like miniature versions of their adult form. Examples of such insects include mantises, stinkbugs, and grasshoppers.
52. Under the influence of hormones called **ecdysteroids**, as nymphs grow larger, new exoskeleton layers develop under the outer shell. Eventually, the insect grows too large for its exoskeleton and undergoes **molting**.

53. Each time the insect molts, it is a step closer to adult size.

54. Insects, such as flies, butteflies, beetles, and wasps, undergo **complete metamorphosis**.

55. Each stage of metamorphosis is hormonally controlled in response to feeding and environmental cues.

56. One reason that complete metamorphosis may have evolved, is that larval stages usually do not compete with adult stages for food. For instance, adult butterflies are nectar eaters, while caterpillars consume leaves.

57. Larval stages vary according to insect order. Different taxa of insects of have different numbers of larval **instars** (juvenile stages) of different appearances.

58. For instance, flies have anywhere from 5 to 8 **instars**, depending on the family in question.

59. Aquatic beetles, such as riffle beetles usually have wire-like larvae that undergo several molts, while terrestrial beetle larvae are fat **grubs** that live underground or in rotting wood, with a chitin covered head and six legs.

60. While caterpillars have a somewhat similar body design, they usually have bristles or hairs. Like beetle larvae, they rely on hydraulic pressure inside the exoskeleton to inflate and deflate themselves as they move.

61. Eventually, hormonal changes trigger a metabolic shift and quiescent **pupal stage**. Most insects become inactive, hide away in protected locations, and undergo dramatic developmental changes.

62. Under the direction of **homeotic genes**, larval insects develop their adult segmentation, appendages, and body plan. In most species, there is a dramatic morphological shift. Pupation varies by type of insect.

63. **Obtect pupae** like butterflies and moths develop inside of a **cocoon** or **chrysalis**, with their appendages sealed inside their exoskeleton (the chrysalis or cocoon) until they finish development.

64. **Exarate pupae** can extent their appendages through their exoskeleton and move during pupation, but they usually only move as far as they need to go to protect themselves. Flies and many beetles are exarate.

65. **Coarctate pupae** develop inside of the exoskeleton of their last larval instar. Eventually, the adult pushes its way out of the husk and leaves the last exoskeleton behind. Cicadas are a well-known example of this strategy.

66. The diagrams below show examples of different insect developmental strategies.

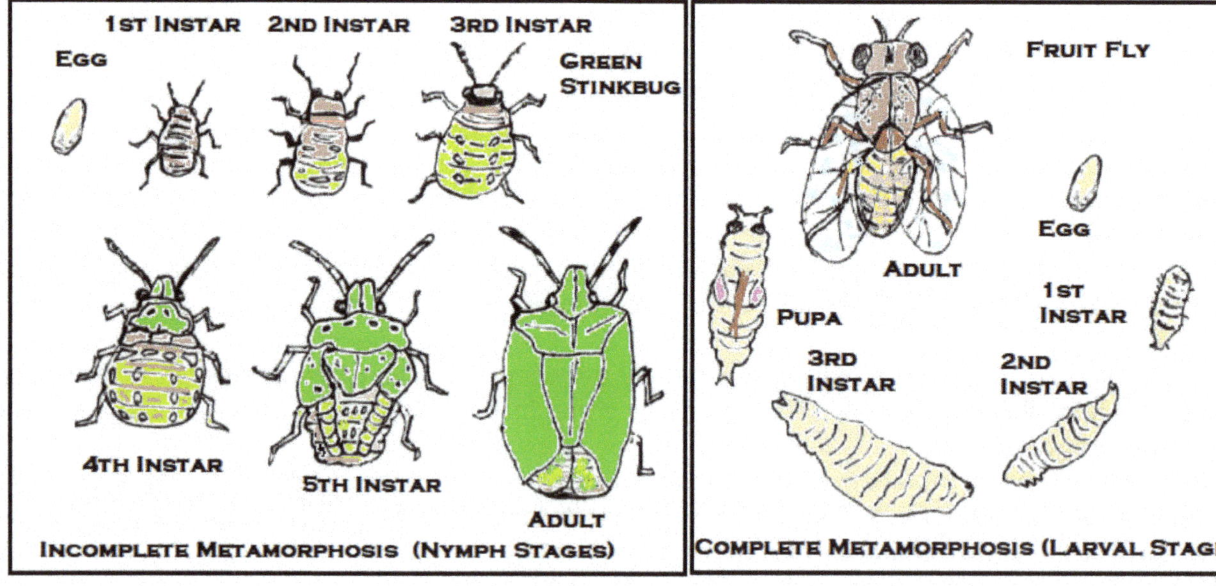

Incomplete Metamorphosis (Nymph Stages)

Complete Metamorphosis (Larval Stages)

67. Now that we have covered the basics of insect anatomy and physiology, let's take a quick walk through some of the most prominent of the 32 orders of extant insects.
68. The charts that follow on the next page briefly summarize characteristics of 21 commonly-encountered orders.

Order Odonata
Dragonflies

*Aquatic Carnivorous Larvae; Adults Prey on Mosquitoes.
*Larvae Have Vestigial Tail Fibers.
*2 Pairs of Membranous Unfolded Wings.

Order Orthoptera
Grasshoppers & Katydids

*Incomplete Metamorphosis
*Two Pairs of Folded Membranous Wings
*Able to Produce Sound By Rubbing Wings Together.
*Hundreds of Species of Agricultural Pests.

Order Phasmotoedea
Walking Sticks

*Longest Insects in Existence (to 2 feet)
*Reduced 1st Wings & Enlarged 2nd Pair.
*Tubercles on Body and Camouflage Coloration
*Spray Foul Secretions As Predator Defense

Order Collembola
Springtails

*Chewing Mouthparts
*Omnivorous
*Abdominal appendage

Order Diplura
Silverfish

*Chewing Mouthparts
*Omnivorous
*3 Abdominal Appendages

Order Ephemeroptera
Larval and Adult Mayflies

* Larval Stage Gilled & 3 Abdominal Appendages
* Larvae are detritivores
* Adults live one day (Breeding)
* 2 pairs Membranous Wings

Order Dermaptera
Earwigs

*Reclusive Omnivores That Emerge To Feed at Night.
*Incomplete Metamorphosis with 5 Nymph Stages.
*Females Care For Young.

Order Plecoptera
Stoneflies

*Aquatic Larvae; Gills & Tail Bristles
*Live Several years as Larvae; May Molt Dozens of Times Before Adulthood
*Wing Fold Flat Over Abdomen in Adults
*Sensitive to Water Pollution; Presence Indicates a Clean Water Body

Order Isoptera
Termites

*Social Insects with Queen & Numerous Castes
*Symbiotic Microbes in Gut Digest Wood Cellulose
*10 Soft Body Segments
*Only Reproductive Castes Have Wings.

69. Among the more primitive insects are the trash-eaters of **Order Collembola** (springtails) and **Order Diplura** (silverfish). They lack wings, retain primitive abdominal appendages, and appear early in the fossil record.
70. The next time you catch a silverfish eating wallpaper glue or old issues of People magazine, you can tell yourself you have basically found the insect version of a dinosaur.
71. **Order Ephemeroptera** (mayflies) and **Order Odonata** (dragonflies) also date back hundreds of millions of years.
72. Mayflies (and the fake tied flies that resemble them) make excellent trout bait.
73. On the flipside, mayflies emerge from their larval stage into their adult stage all at once by the billions. These adults have no feeding mouthparts, live for only a day to mate, and then all die at the same time.
74. Around the Great Lakes, some towns have to employ snow plows to clear the roads of 2 foot mounds of dead rotting insects that reportedly smell like rotten sardines and boo-boo mixed together.
75. Dragonflies and damselflies of **Order Odonata** are well known allies in the timeless fight against mosquitoes.
76. Both the aquatic larval and free-flying adult stages of dragonflies are efficient ambush predators.
77. Prehistoric dragonfly fossils have been found with wingspans of nearly a yard across. Were there more oxygen in the atmosphere to support such large insects now, some birds would probably be crapping a brick.
78. Their smaller cousins, the damselflies, differ in that their larvae have terminal gills on the abdomen.
79. Members of the highly diverse **Order Orthoptera** include grasshoppers, katydids, locusts, and crickets. They are a highly diverse group of insects represented by 20,000 different species.
80. Crickets are capable of generating sound by rubbing notches on their back legs together. In addition to their roles as scavengers and prey insects, they serve an important role in filling the awkward silence after a bad joke.
81. Some species of grasshoppers can morph into locusts under the influence of serotonin, causing them to swarm and go into a feeding frenzy. The largest locust swarms can measured nearly 500 square miles.
82. Given the modern calculation that a swarm of locusts can consume 2 million tons of vegetation, the Egyptians had a big problem in the Exodus, along with dealing with rivers of blood, frogs, dead flies, and other problems.
83. Walking sticks of the **Order Phasmotodea** are among the longest invertebrates in existence. The Giant Chinese Stick Insect can grow as long as 25 inches. A captive-bred specimen is said to want to eat only strawberry jam.
84. Stick insects have some of the most impressive evolved camouflage on any group of invertebrates, blending in seamlessly with various temperate and tropical forest tree branches and leaves.
85. **Order Demoptera** (the earwigs) have two hooked-shaped appendages on the tail and obvious segmentation.
86. Earwigs are purported to crawl into your ear canal as you sleep, and tunnel into your brain. This, of course, is complete bullcrap. They can pinch you with their forceps, but unless you are a rotten turnip, you'll be just fine.
87. The stoneflies belong to **Order Plecoptera**. In addition to serving as a model for effective trout flies, they are valuable to the determination of stream water quality by the EPD, because they disappear in polluted areas.
88. Termites belong to **Order Isoptera**. They are ecologically critical in many habitats as food for foragers.
89. This is especially true in the savannas of Africa and South America, where they are sought out by warthogs, honey badgers, mongooses, anteaters, and armadillos.

90. Termite mounds contain several castes, such as workers, soldiers, drones, and queens. Ploidy and hormones determine the fate of termite larvae into their roles. More than a million individuals can live in a mound.
91. Recent DNA evidence, along with common microbes in their gut cavity, seem to suggest that cockroaches and termites are relatively closely related and diverged into different orders much more recently than thought.
92. Wood-eating termites rely on the cellulose and lignin degrading enzymes produced by **proteobacteria, archaebacteria, firmicutes**, and **ciliate protozoans** housed in their gut.
93. Thanks to these acts of **mutualistic symbiosis**, those little (fill in obscenity of your choice) cause more than $30 billion dollars in damage every year in the USA and make us waste our time crawling under houses to spray.

INSECTS THAT ARE PUNKS....THE DEADLIEST BUGS ON EARTH

MOSQUITOES SUCK LITERALLY & FIGURATIVELY. DISEASES THEY CARRY LIKE MALARIA & DENGUE KILL A MILLION A YEAR!

TSETSE FLIES CARRY AFRICAN SLEEPING SICKNESS PROTOZOANS IN THEIR SALIVA. THANKS TO THESE LITTLE TURDS, ABOUT 500,000 PEOPLE PER YEAR GO INTO COMAS AND DIE. KEEP A FLY SWATTER HANDY!

KISSING BUGS ARE LIKE HORRIFYING GIANT BED BUGS THAT SUCK BLOOD FROM YOUR FACE WHEN YOU ARE SLEEPING. THEY ARE VECTORS FOR PROTOZOANS THAT CAUSE CHAGA'S DISEASE THAT KILLS 12,000 A YEAR.

WHEN YOU PULL SOMETHING LIKE CARRYING A VECTOR THAT KILLS 1/3RD OF EUROPE, YOU DON'T GET TO SAY IT WAS A LONG TIME AGO. YEAH....200 MILLION PEOPLE...JUST NOT MANY RECENTLY.

NO ONE KNOWS EXACTLY HOW MANY PEOPLE DIE FROM THE STINGS OF HYMENOPTERANS (BEES, WASPS, ETC.) WORLDWIDE. IN THE USA, IT'S AROUND 100. A FEW THOUSAND SOUNDS RIGHT.

ORDER MANTODEA
MANTISES

*ENLARGED RAPTORIAL FRONT LEGS FOR AMBUSHING PREY.
*PROTHORAX SEGMENT ARTICULATES HEAD AND FRONT LEGS.
*EXCELLENT 360 DEGREE VISION.
*PAIRED MEMBRANOUS WINGS VARY IN SIZE TO ABSENT AMONG SPECIES.

ORDER BLATTODEA
COCKROACHES

*SYMBIOTIC MICROBES SIMILAR TO TERMITES IN GUT.
*GENERIC INSECT ANATOMY. NOT MANY SPECIALIZATIONS.
*SPECIES FOUND GLOBALLY IN ALMOST EVERY HABITAT.
*PHEROMONES INFLUNCE THE BEHAVIOR OF COLONIES.

ORDER HEMIPTERA
TRUE BUGS

*SUCKING MOUTHPARTS FOR FLUID CONSUMPTION.
*SECRETE CARMINE AND SHELLAC IN SHELLS.
*STINKBUGS, APHIDS, CICADAS, BEDBUGS ALL BELONG TO THIS ORDER.
*MEMBRANOUS FOREWINGS.

ORDER THYSANOPTERA
THRIPS
*ASYMMETRICAL CUTTING & SUCKING MOUTHPARTS.
*AGRICULTURAL PESTS FEED ON PLANT FLUIDS.
*HYDRAULIC CHAMBER IN LEGS ALLOWS FLEXING TO WALK VERTICALLY.
*DON'T FLY, BUT INSTEAD FLEX WINGS TO FLICK THEMSELVES FORWARD.

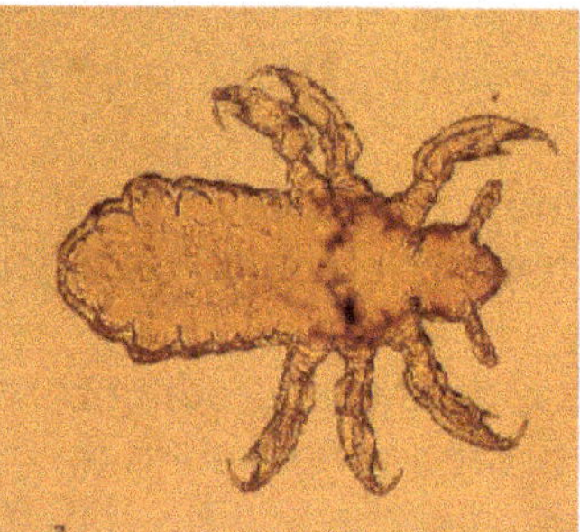

ORDER PHTHIRAPTERA
LICE
*SUCKING LICE FEED PARASITICALLY ON FLUIDS.
*CHEWING LICE ARE DETRITUS SCAVENGERS.
*GLUE-LIKE SALIVA AND HOOKED CLAWS TO REMAIN BOUND TO THEIR HOSTS.
*CAN BE DISEASE VECTORS.
*FUSED THORAX.

ORDER COLEOPTERA
BEETLES
*TOP WINGS HAVE HARD CHITIN SHELL.
*MEMBRANOUS BACK WINGS FOLD UNDERNEATH SHELLED FRONT WINGS.
*HIGHLY EVOLVED AND VARIABLE. MOST NUMEROUS INSECTS (750,000 SPECIES).
* COMPLETE METAMORPHOSIS WITH TRUE LARVAL STAGES.
* PLATED ARMOR-LIKE EXOSKELETON MADE OF FUSED CHITIN SCLERITES.

94. Mantises of the **Order Mantodea** have a well-deserved reputation as voracious ambush predators.
95. Some of the best camouflage in nature belongs to the flower mantises, that lie in wait pretending to be a nectar-filled blossom before slamming their raptorial claws into a shocked victim. They are much like Jennifer Lopez.
96. Formerly classified together, mantises and the cockroaches of **Order Blattoidea** share a lot of common features.
97. Among these are downward facing heads with similar skull-like chitin plates, internal teeth in the digestive system, an enlarged abdominal plate above the genital pores, and chitin-covered egg cases that are glued down.
98. Cockroaches, like termites, have internal **symbionts** that manufacture enzymes capable of digesting cellulose and lignin. If there's nothing available in your trash can, they'll just eat the wallpaper instead.
99. A comforting thought is that if you will never be alone if you have cockroaches. Chances are that if you see one, you probably have around 57 million more that will leave droppings on all of the dishes you eat off of.
100. **Order Hemiptera** are the true bugs. This is such a large order, that it is useful to further discuss its constitutive sub-orders and classes. Cicadas, aphids, leafhoppers, stinkbugs, and bedbugs all belong to this group.
101. Cicadas are unique in many ways. Living underground in their instar stages for up to 17 years, the adults that emerge, like all bugs, have sucking mouthparts. They feed on tree sap and make a lot of racket.
102. Cicadas, unlike other bugs, produce the noise by vibrating a mouthpart known as the **rostrum**.
103. Some species of cicadas can also **thermoregulate** by evaporative cooling. They evaporate the water from sap through specialized pores on their back, generating their own sort of bug sweat.
104. Aphids, also sap-suckers, are no bigger than a pinhead, usually bright green or brown, and soft-bodied. They are an absolute nuisance to fruit orchards and rose growers.
105. As aphids feed, they secrete a layer of protective wax around themselves with a pair of abdominal glands.
106. Many types of aphids are **parthenogenetic** all-female species that auto-fertilize their own eggs.

107. Additionally, aphids can undergo a special adult metamorphic stage where they grow wings in response to overcrowding. This allows them to fly to new plants.
108. Leafhoppers are also sapsuckers. One unique feature is that they have protective hairs on their bodies that also serve as **pheromone** traps. They sometimes gain negative notoriety as vectors for plant diseases.
109. Stinkbugs and potato bugs also feed on plant sap. They are noted for their shield-like protective carapace, foul-smelling secretions, and entertainment value. Chasing younger siblings with a stinkbug is a childhood pastime.
110. Bedbugs, also owners of a sucking proboscis, do not attack plants. They attack YOU. At only a millimeter long, they emerge at night, inject anticoagulants, and eat their blood meal.
111. Bedbugs are nasty in many ways. For one, they release pheromones to attract other bedbugs to their nesting site (your bed). When they reproduce, males stab the female directly into the abdomen to release their sperm.
112. The sperm then make their way through the **hemolymph** to sperm storage receptacles.
113. Nearly as agriculturally annoying as the aphids are the thrips of **Order Thysanoptera**.
114. Thrips also feed on plant fluids by suction. Unique to thrips is their odd method of taking flight. Hydraulic chambers under the wings 'pump up' and deflate the wing bases to keep them in the air.
115. **Order Phthiraptera** are the lice. Many lice features are vestigial or absent, such as the wings and the eyes. Subsisting off of blood and body fluids of their victims, they glue themselves and their eggs to hair and feathers.
116. Nearly every warm-blooded creature is afflicted by at least one type of louse. In addition to being itchy and disgusting, some lice species are also disease vectors for various bacterial diseases and worm infections.
117. The best way elementary schools can avoid lice infestations is by keeping girls and boys separated to deter the spread of cooties. If infected, it is important to quickly administer the circle-circle dot-dot-dot cootie shot.
118. **Order Coleoptera** (the beetles) are the most numerous of the insects. Found worldwide in just about every imaginable habitat, their anatomical design has worked so well that they now number around 750,000 species.
119. There are so many species of beetles with such variety, that it is nearly impossible to make any generalities.
120. From the scarabs of Egyptian lore, to the beneficial ladybugs that prey on aphids, the diversity of beetles is nearly endless. Destructive weevils, wood-scavenging stag beetles, and lightning bugs are all beetles.

INSECTS MENTIONED IN THE BIBLE

DESERT LOCUST
8TH PLAGUE OF THE EXODUS AND FAVORITE PROTEIN SOURCE OF JOHN THE BAPTIST

HORSEFLY
4TH PLAGUE OF THE EXODUS, FOLLOWING A PRIOR DIPTERAN PLAGUE OF GNATS (3RD)

HONEYBEE
THE PROMISED LAND WAS FLOWING WITH MILK AND HONEY, SO BEES WERE THERE FOR CALEB & JOSHUA

ANTS
PROVERBS TELLS LAZY PEOPLE TO TAKE A LESSON FROM THE WORK ETHIC OF ANTS.

ORDER NEUROPTERA
LACEWINGS & ANTLIONS

*ADULTS HAVE FOUR MEMBRANOUS WINGS.
*COMPLETE METAMORPHOSIS.
*LARVAE FEED ON APHIDS.
*ADULTS ARE PREDATORY OR NECTAR FEEDERS.
*POORLY EVOLVED GROUP. GENERIC MORPHOLOGY.
*ADHESIVE DISCS ON ABDOMEN FOR CLINGING.

ORDER HYMENOPTERA
BEES, WASPS, & ANTS

*HIGHLY EVOLVED INSECTS WITH COMPLEX SOCIAL HIERARCHIES.
*CHEWING MOUTHPARTS WITH STRONG MANDIBLES.
*ADVANCED COMPOUND EYES.
*GENDER DETERMINED BY PLOIDY. MALES = HAPLOID; FEMALES = DIPOID
*EVOLVED VENOM GLANDS
*PAIRED MEMBRANOUS WINGS.

ORDER TRICHOPTERA
CADDISFLIES

*AQUATIC GILLED LARVAE LIVE IN SILKEN CASES.
*COMPLETE METAMORPHOSIS; SEVERAL LARVAL INSTARS.
*LARVAE FEED ON LEAVES, ALGAE, PLANKTON.
*ADULTS HAVE LARGE TRIANGULAR MEMBRANOUS WINGS & LONG ANTENNAE.
*ADULTS DO NOT FEED. LIVE ONLY LONG ENOUGH TO BREED.

121. **Order Neuroptera** is comprised of lacewing insects. They are omnivores that feed on aphids, flower nectar, pollen, and sap. Some lacewings are so voracious that they are used for biological pest control.
122. Arguably, the most evolved insects of all belong to **Order Hymenoptera**. Bees, ants, and wasps have not only evolved defensive venom and **warning coloration**, they have extremely complex **social hierarchies**.
123. Honeybees are critical to proper agricultural function in farming countries. The effect of bees and other pollinators is estimated to be worth around $500 billion to the U.S. economy, not counting honey.
124. The bee life cycle begins when eggs are laid in the honeycomb of the hive by the queen.
125. If the haploid egg goes unfertilized, it will become a male **drone**. If fertilized, it will become a diploid female.
126. Females either become **workers** or **queens**. All larvae are fed royal jelly during the early instars.
127. Workers are switched over to honey and pollen, while the hormones in royal jelly will cause a female to become a queen if they continue to be fed royal jelly.
128. A complex set of pheromones and dances allows communication between workers and hive cooperation.
129. Ants also have extremely complex social structures. Ant queens are also responsible for manning the colony with workers. Unlike bees, ant workers are somewhat independent, yet they collaborate cooperatively.
130. Ants can form supercolonies of hundreds of millions of workers. One colony of red wood ants in Japan spans for over 600 acres, has an estimated 45,000 queen-led sub-colonies, and is around 1,000 years old.
131. Several colonies of invasive Argentine ants have since been shown to be larger than the one in Japan. There are populations in Europe, California span lengthwise for hundreds of miles.
132. Wasps are critical as predators and specialty pollinators. For instance, figs are solely wasp-pollinated.
133. **Order Trichoptera** (the caddisflies) are mainstays in streams and rivers worldwide. Their larvae are ecologically important as scavengers, and as prey for fish and crustaceans.
134. Caddisflies, like several other orders of insects, have gills during the larval stage. Caddisfly larvae are distinct, in that they spin silken cocoons around them that trap sediment. This forms a case, within which they reside.

135. Like many strict **R-strategist** insects, caddisfly adults aren't long for this world. Most adult species lack feeding mouthparts altogether, living only long enough to mate and get themselves devoured by a trout.

136. Sorry, I need a moment....that's how Grandma went too....minding her own business, tubing down a quiet river on a Spring Day, only to be violently dragged to a watery grave by an irradiated mutant salmon.....

ORDER LEPIDOPTERA
BUTTERFLIES & MOTHS

*COMPLETE METAMORPHOSIS.
*CATERPILLARS ARE FOLIVORES, ADULTS ARE NECTAR FEEDERS.
*TWO WIDE MEMBRANOUS WINGS COVERED IN IRIDESCENT SCALES.
*COILED STRAW-LIKE MOUTHPARTS.

ORDER DIPTERA
FLIES, GNATS, MOSQUITOS, MIDGES

*COMPLETE METAMORPHOSIS.
*LARVAE MUST REMAIN WET; LACKING HARD CUTICLE.
*SECRETE DIGESTIVE ENZYMES FROM SALIVARY GLANDS AND USE EXTRACELLULAR DIGESTION.
*SCAVENGERS & BLOOD FEEDERS.
*BACK WINGS REDUCED TO TINY GYROSCOPES IN FLIES, GNATS.

ORDER SIPHONAPTERA
FLEAS

*BACK LEGS EXTREMELY ENLARGED FOR JUMPING.
*ECTOPARASITES THAT FEED ON ANIMAL BLOOD.
*WINGS ARE ABSENT.
*LACK COMPOUND EYES.
*BODY IS FLAT AND COVERED WITH HARD CUTICLE (SMUSH-PROOF).
*OFTEN DISEASE VECTORS.

137. Butterflies, moths, and skippers comprise **Order Lepidoptera**. In addition to their scale-covered gigantic membranous wings, their straw-like mouthparts and metamorphic stages define this group.

138. Buteflies differ from moths by undergoing **metamorphosis** inside a **chrysalis** instead of a **cocoon**.

139. Additionally, the **antennae** of moths are feather-like and used to broadcast **pheromones**, while butterflies simply use their antennae as tactile organs. Most butterflies tend to be **diurnal**, while moths are **nocturnal**.

140. Lepidopterans are critical as pollinators to numerous agricultural crops and natural flowers. The **caterpillar** stage of both groups can be agricultural pests, such as the cabbage white butterfly or the gypsy moth.

141. Flies, gnats, and mosquitoes belong to **Order Diptera**, a much-hated group that play out a necessarily evil role as **detritivores**. Dipterans have biting mouthparts that are often accompanied by caustic salivary secretions.

142. The majority of dipterans digest their food outside the body and suck up a slurry of digested juices.

143. Flies, in particular have a checkered reputation. While species of *Drosophila* fruit flies have greatly advanced our understanding of genetic principles and embryo development, others are an ever-present nuisance.

144. Numerous species of botflies infect livestock and humans with screw-worm larvae, particularly in the Tropics.

145. In equatorial Africa, the tsetse fly is a natural vector for the flagellate that causes African sleeping sickness. However, this disease is close to being eradicated, dropping to less than 1000 cases per year.

146. Flies are more significant in spreading bacterial diseases by flying back and forth between sewage, garbage, rotting animals, and food sources. Cholera, dysentery, and typhoid are all worsened by fly infestations.

147. Mosquitoes are also notorious disease vectors, aiding in the spread of yellow fever, dengue fever, and malaria. Millions of people in the Tropics are afflicted by these diseases every year.
148. While male mosquitoes are nectar eaters, females need the protein and iron-rich blood for their egg clutches.
149. While the dipterans are, at best, pollinators (such as the bee fly) and a source of food for birds and other small animals, they mostly have a reputation as filthy disease-ridden pests that deserve death by newspaper on sight.
150. However, the worst disease vectors of all-time belong to **Order Siphonaptera**. Rat fleas, in their quest for a blood meal, helped spread the bubonic plague in the middle ages, ultimately killing 1/3rd of Europe's population.
151. Fleas are among nature's best jumpers. Some species can jump around 200 times the length of their body, which is the equivalent of you jumping ¼ mile. This is about 40 times the current world long jump record.
152. Alright, so now that we've given you a crash course in entomology, it's time to jump to another taxa.

I) Class Crustacea: The Crustaceans

1. Members of **Class Crustacea** are the evolutionary equivalent of insects in the water, especially in marine waters. With very few truly marine insects in existence, crustaceans have filled those ecological niches.
2. There are far fewer known species of crustaceans (about 70,000) than insects, but this is probably because there are thousands of undescribed small species like **copepods, amphipods,** and deep ocean species.
3. Additionally, what they may lack in **biodiversity**, they make up for in **biomass**. For instance, there are around 6 billion tons of krill in the ocean and copepods, individually, are the most numerous animals on earth.
4. Like the rest of their **arthropod** brethren, crustaceans have jointed appendages, a segmented body, compound eyes and a relatively complex nervous system. They are covered in an **exoskeleton** made of chitin.
5. There is so much diversity in lifestyle and body form, that it is hard to make too many anatomical generalizations about the entire group. For that reason, the initial anatomical discussion will be brief.
6. Most crustaceans have a fused **cephalothorax** covered by a protective **carapace**. In some species, this carapace extends into a point in front of the eyes to form a spear-like **rostrum** that protects them from predators.
7. Most crustaceans have two pairs of antennae, with a shorter front pair known as **antennules** and a longer back pair of true **antennae** that can be longer than the body in certain shrimp species.
8. The exoskeleton is segmented into armored plates down the abdomen, typically ending in a flipper like tail with a central rudder known as a **telson**, with flexible **uropods** on each side.
9. However, this exoskeleton plan is not true for copepods or for several other obscure orders of small marine crustaceans. For instance, copepods have barbed tails that end in a point.
10. It is common for many crustaceans to have jointed **walking legs** on the segments of their **thorax**. The motion of walking helps to drive water flow over the feathery **gills** rooted at the base of each leg.
11. The abdominal segments may have **swimmerets**. Sometimes the front swimmeret is modified into a reproductive structure, as in male crawfish that use the front pair of swimmerets to deliver sperm to females.
12. Most crustaceans have **biramous appendages**, which terminate in the two points of a claw. While this is usually true for many walking legs, it is always true for the enlarged **cheliped** pincers of crabs, lobsters, and others.
13. The **mandibles** and **maxillae** are appendages in front of the mouth on the head, which are used to manipulate their food. The first few legs of the thorax are also usually **maxillipeds**, which also help them to feed.

14. The diagram below shows the exoskeletal terminology of a variety of different crustaceans. Notice the diversity of morphological forms between different taxa.

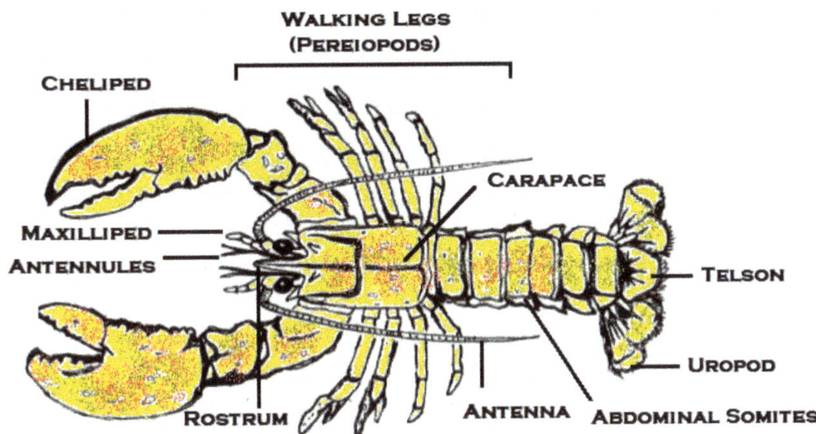

15. Crustaceans, like insects, rely on **reflex arcs** and local **ganglia** in order to generate lightning-fast reflexes without having to process the information all the way back in their puny little brains.
16. Like insects, a large portion of the crustacean brain is dedicated to articulating visual cues from the **compound eyes**, interpreting tactile and chemical information from the **antennae** and controlling the **molting cycle**.
17. Like other arthropods, they have a **ventral nerve cord** with numerous clusters of ganglia for each of the thoracic and abdominal segments.
18. Some of these nerves are particularly large, making crawfish and lobsters good model organisms for studying neurology. A lot has been learned about synapses and anesthesia by studying the tail flick reflex.
19. The crustacean digestive tract has a short **foregut** that enters a **stomach**. The back of the stomach has hard chitin teeth and muscle rings like a **gizzard** in order to grind up the food entering the **intestine**.
20. The intestine is covered by a very large **digestive gland** that connects via ducts, secreting digestive enzymes like lipases and proteases into the lumen. The digestive gland sort of serves as a dual liver and pancreas.
21. **Crustaceans**, unlike insects, do NOT have Malpighian tubules. Instead, they have a pair of kidney-like **green glands** in their head, inferior to the brain that have a filtration network of tubules similar to a kidney nephron.
22. After re-absorbing glucose, amino acids, and needed salt ions, the remaining liquid is sent to a bladder-like pouch. **Excretory pores** next to the mouth expel urinary waste. Yes that's right. Crabs pee out of their face.
23. It's hard to imagine proper urinary etiquette in the crustacean world. Is it rude to pee out of your face when you are talking to others, seated at the dinner table, or in public? Or is it a natural process that everyone just does?
24. Also different from insects are the circulatory and respiratory systems of crustaceans.
25. Most crustaceans have a triangular-shaped **heart** that has openings called **ostia** that suck up pooled **hemolymph** from a sac in the body cavity called a hemocoel where interstitial fluids pool up.
26. A certain number of vessels exit the heart like a sprinkler system, bathing muscles and organs with oxygenated hemolymph. Muscular movements and gravity cause the hemolymph to migrate back to the hemocoel.
27. The respiratory system of crustaceans consists of paired feather-like **gills**. These are usually rooted at the base of the walking legs, extracting oxygen from the motion of the surrounding water.

28. Reproduction in most crustaceans occurs between two sexes via **internal fertilization**. However, there are **ostracods, amphipods**, and other small crustaceans that use **parthenogenesis**.
29. Male crustaceans usually have a single W-shaped **testis** that spans the width of the animal under the posterior part of the thorax. Two **vas deferens** emerge from this laterally on each side of the body.
30. The vas deferens then carries the sperm to **ejaculatory ducts** and out a pair of small penis-like organs located under the last pair of walking legs or plumbed directly through a hardened front pair of swimmerets.
31. Female crustaceans have similarly shaped **ovaries** with two lateral horns that meet in the middle. A **spermathecal** emerges underneath each ovary, allowing the female to store sperm.
32. The vaginal openings of the female crab are also under the back walking legs or in front of the first pair of swimmerets. Since the hard **exoskeleton** normally blocks access to the vagina, mating occurs during a molt.
33. When this occurs, many male crustaceans, especially crabs, straddle the female in a protective posture after they mate, waiting on their exoskeleton to harden.
34. Depending upon the classification, some crustaceans may directly release their eggs and ditch them. However, many crustacean females carry a **clutch** of fertilized eggs under their abdomen until hatching occurs.
35. The diagram below depicts the internal anatomy of a shrimp, a typical decapod crustacean.

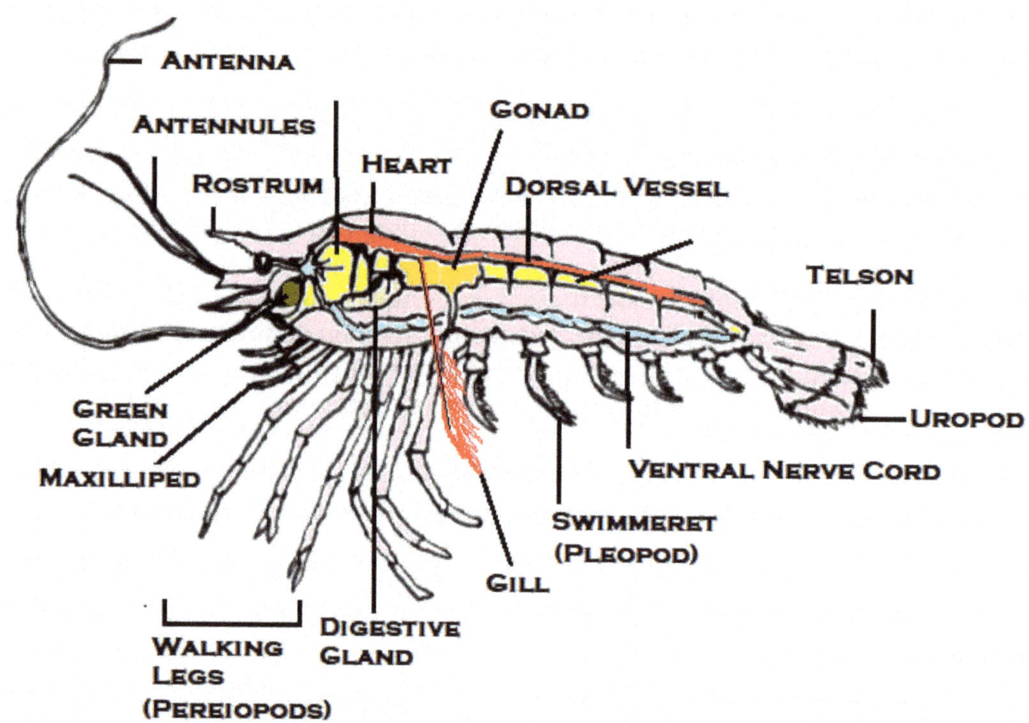

36. Crustaceans show a lot of variation in their larval development between orders. Most commonly, crustacean larvae metamorphose through several stages called **nauplii**.
37. Each stage can look dramatically different, particularly as compared to the adult stage. Many crustacean larvae are planktonic, so they need spines and extensions to stay afloat in the **photic zone** where there is food.
38. Since it is hard to make too many generalizations for every order of crustaceans, the development of two different crustacean orders is shown below.
39. The first diagram depicts copepod metamorphosis, while the second shows a decapod (blue crab).

40. Notice that each has multiple larval stages with major differences in exoskeleton segmentation.

41. Copepods have anywhere from 5 to 7 distinctly different stages of **nauplii** before losing the majority of their appendages during another 5 juvenile **copepodite** stages before attaining their adult morphology.

42. Decapods pass through two developmental periods called the zoea and the megalops, both planktonic and microscopic. There are also several distinctly different stages of both the **zoea** and **megalops** periods.

43. Think of these metamorphic stages like school grades, with the crustacean passing on to the next grade after a molt, where they gradually acquire more adult characteristics, increasing the size of their food as they go.

44. Eventually the crustacean becomes a miniature adult or **juvenile**, and they grow increasingly larger throughout their lives. Size gains cause levels of **ecdysosteroid hormones** to increase, triggering **molting**.

45. Crustaceans can continue molting throughout their adult lives, growing successively larger.

46. In the case of Maine lobsters, this can go on for a 100 year lifespan. Eventually, the size of the animal will kill it, since it takes progressively more energy and nutrients to molt a larger exoskeleton.

47. When this fails, the lobster will pass away from old age, trapped in its own exoskeleton. This is why it's really more humane to euthanize an old lobster and give it a dignified service with drawn butter, lemon, and parsley.

48. The diagrams on the next page show the differences in developmental stages between copepods and crabs. Note that there are numerous juvenile stages in both and that their body plans are dramatically different.

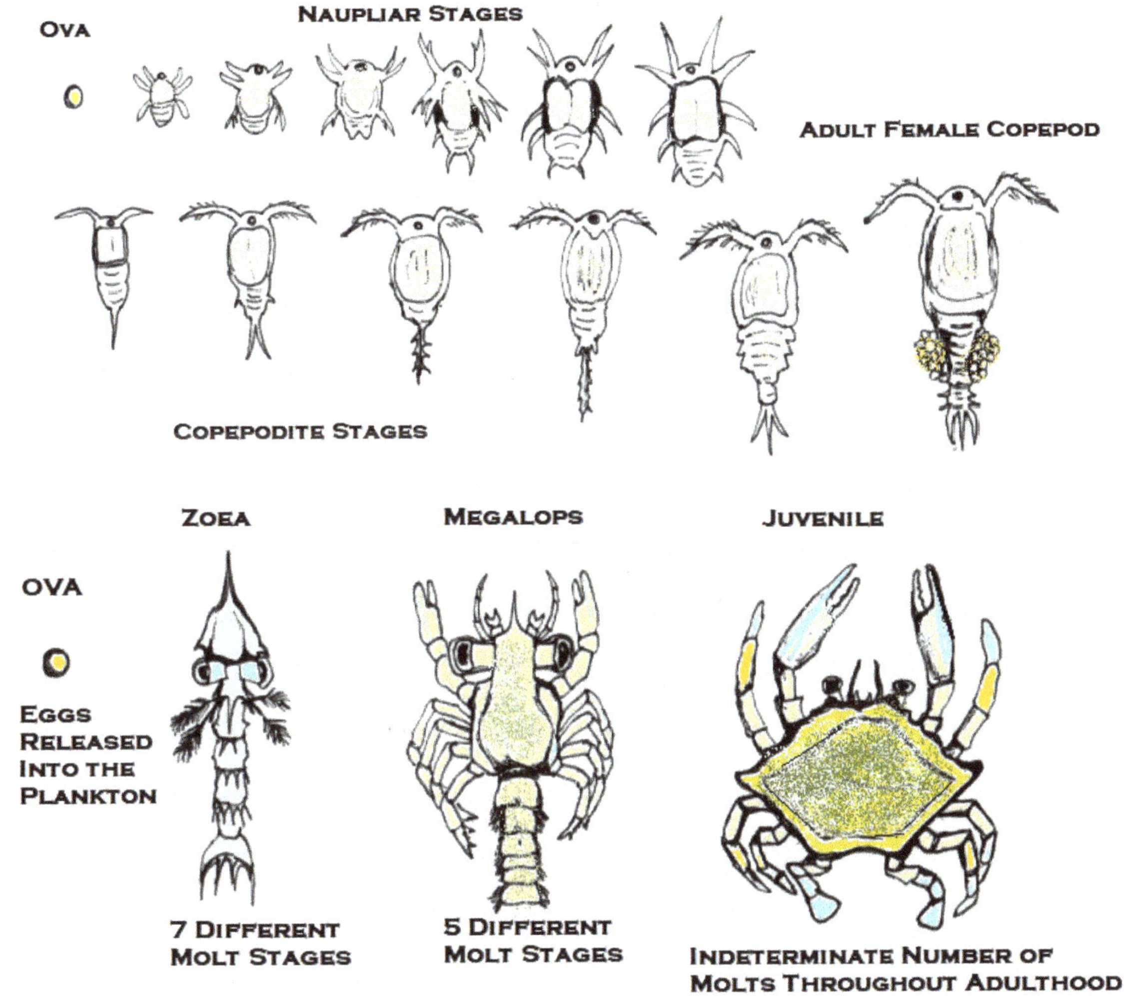

49. Given the large anatomical, developmental, and behavioral disparities between different sub-orders and families of crustaceans, it is now appropriate to turn to the discussion of some of the major taxa.
50. The diagrams below summarize some of the traits and features of the most representative groups.

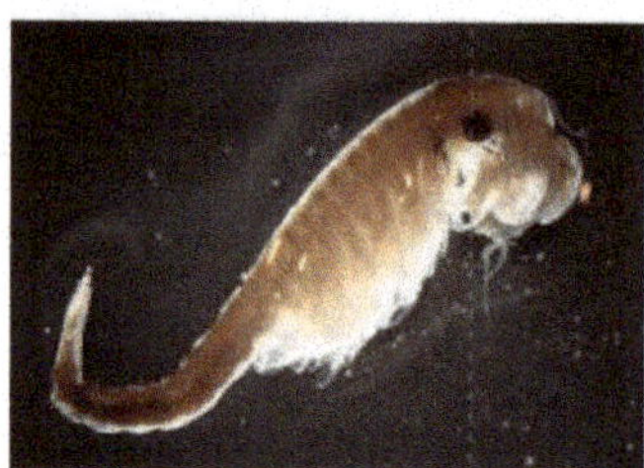

ORDER ANACOSTRACA
FAIRY SHRIMP

*SPECIES FOUND GLOBALLY IN SALINE LAKES, POOLS.
*20 SEGMENTS WITH 11 PAIRS OF LEGS.
*OFTEN SWIM UPSIDE DOWN TO FILTER ALGAE
*TWO PAIRS OF ANTENNAE
*RAISED FOR FISH FOOD FOR AQUACULTURE.

ORDER NOTOSTRACA
TADPOLE SHRIMP

* ONE PAIR OF COMPOUND EYES.
* UNIRAMOUS MANIDBLES WITH NO MAXILLIPEDS AROUND MOUTH.
*HARD SHIELD-LIKE CARAPACE
*EACH OF 11 THORACIC SEGMENTS HAVE A PAIR OF LEGS.
*ESPECIALLY COMMON IN ESTUARIES, BOGS, MARSHES, AND SILTY LAKES.

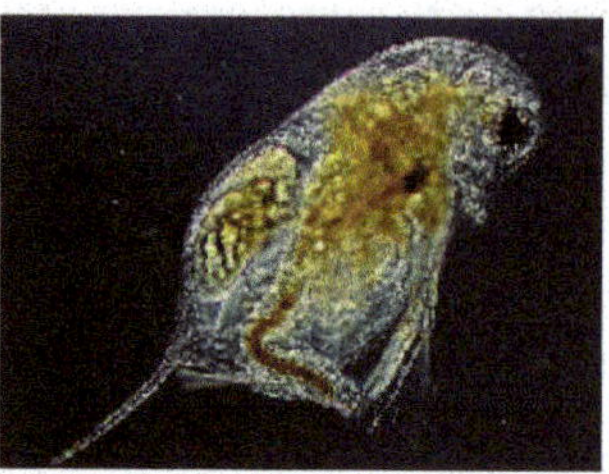

ORDER CLADOCERA
DAPHNIA

*ALSO KNOWN AS WATER FLEAS.
*ESPECIALLY PROMINENT IN FRESHWATER ZOOPLANKTON.
*TWO PAIRS BRANCHED ANTENNAE.
*ABDOMINAL SETAE (SPINE)
*SEGMENTS ARE FUSED.
*5-6 PAIRS OF LEGS.
*IMPORTANT FOOD FOR JUVENILE FISH AND OTHER CRUSTACEANS.

51. **Order Anacostraca** contains the **fairy shrimp**. They are scum feeders who swim upside and use their legs like little brushes to strain algae from the water or scrape algae off of surfaces.
52. Fairy shrimp are probably better know to the general public as brine shrimp or 'sea monkeys'. They are raised on a mass scale for fish food in the aquarium and aquaculture industry....and also by 8 year olds in jars.
53. In nature, brine shrimp make cockroaches look like lightweights. They can osmoregulate just fine in places like the Great Salt Lake and Mono Lake and the Dead Sea. The salinities there are 5 to 10 times that of sea water.
54. Since fish and mollusks would go belly-up in those places, brine shrimp serve an important ecological role, grazing on the archaebacterial that replace algae as photosynthesizers.
55. Additionally, the eggs of brine shrimp can remain viable for hundreds of years. Yes, that's right... hundreds!
56. When their lake beds dry up, they cram their cells full of trehalose sugars, which basically crystalizes all of their embryo parts in place, allowing them to reconstitute when water returns.
57. Tadpole shrimp of order **Notostraca** are sometimes sold as curiosities to aquarists. Befitting their namesake bodies, their front **carapace** is shaped like a rounded-shield, with the abdominal segments trailing like a tail.
58. Tadpole shrimp are oddities among crustaceans, in that the eggs hatch directly into a miniature version of their adult forms, without passing through any oddly shaped nauplius stages.
59. Considered to be living fossils, they date back at least 250 million years.
60. Another primitive trait of tadpole shrimp that is not seen in the closely related copepods and daphnia, is that they have two compound eyes, rather than a single fused eye.
61. **Order Cladocera** contains the **daphnia** or water fleas. A typical daphnia species is about the size of a typed period. They are a huge component of freshwater zooplankton and an important food source for larval fish.
62. Bearing a single fused compound eye and two pairs of antennae, their bodies are strange among crustaceans, in that their bodies have mostly de-evolved segmentation and are covered by a single fused carapace.

63. Reproduction varies greatly among different daphnia species. Some are typical two sex egg layers, others are all-female **parthenogenetic** species, while others give live birth to miniature versions of themselves.
64. Like their relatives, the brine shrimp, daphnia cysts are also incredibly tough, capable of hatching years later.

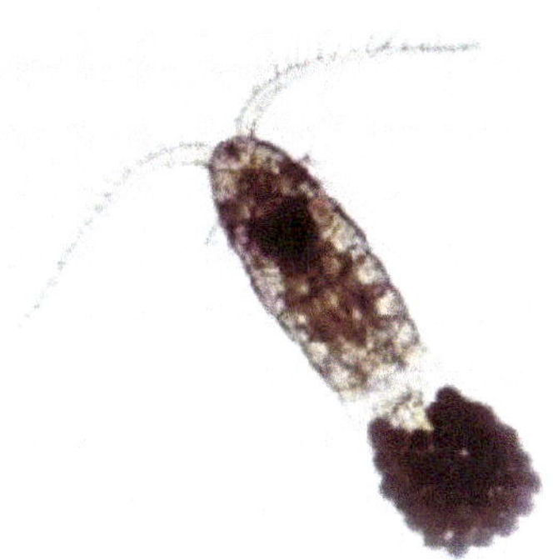

SUBCLASS COPEPODA
MULTIPLE ORDERS
COPEPODS

*UBIQUITOUS IN ALMOST ALL ZOOPLANKTON.
*2 PAIRS OF ANTENNAE; SINGLE COMPOUND EYE.
*METAMORPHOSIS THROUGH THROUGH NUMEROUS ODD LOOKING NAUPLIUS PHASES.
*NO CIRCULATORY OR RESPIRATORY SYSTEM.
*FEMALES CARRY EGG CLUTCHES UNTIL HATCH.

ORDER PEDUNCULATA
GOOSENECK BARNACLES

*SESSILE FILTER FEEDERS ON ROCKY COASTS.
* MUST LIVE IN TIDAL ZONE. RELY ON WAVES TO FEED.
*A GOURMET DELICACY IN MANY PARTS OF EUROPE.
*FLEXIBLE PEDUNCLE ORGAN ATTACHES ANIMAL TO ROCKS.
*ANIMAL 'STANDS ON HEAD' INSIDE SHELL.
*LEGS MODIFIED INTO FEEDING CIRRI ORGANS.

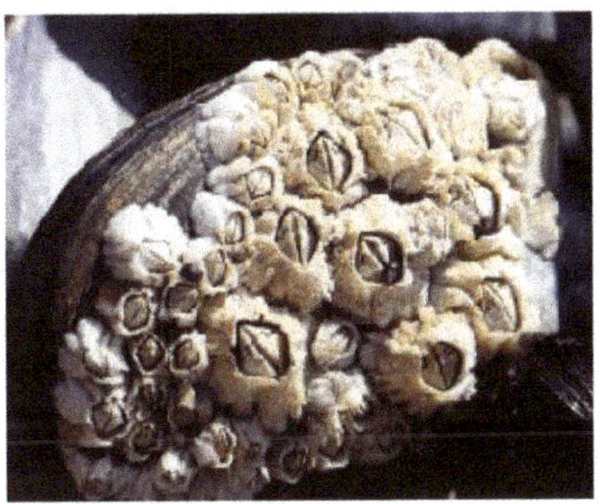

ORDER SESSILIA
ACORN BARNACLES

FEEDERS THAT USE CIRRI. APPENDAGES TO TRAP FOOD.
*CEMENT GLAND NEAR HEAD GLUES BARNACLE TO SURFACE.
*PASS TROUGH NAUPLIUS METAMORPHOSIS STAGE.
*NO GILLS OR HEART
*PHOTORECEPTORS FORM A PRIMITIVE EYE.
*SIX CALCIFIED PLATES AROUND BODY SEGMENTS.

65. **Order Copepoda** contains the **copepods**, which are quite likely the most numerous animals on planet earth.
66. Especially common in the ocean **zooplankton**, there are more than 11,000 known species of copepods.
67. While the majority of copepods are tear-drop shaped phytoplankton feeders, some species are parasites of fish gills and epidermal tissue. By themselves, they don't kill the fish, but they can introduce infections that do.
68. Like the daphnia, copepods have a single fused **compound eye**. They have a pair of horn-like antennae, a tapered carapace with few appendages in the adult stage, and a multi-segmented abdomen terminating in a tail.
69. Most copepod females carry their eggs in a **clutch** underneath the appendages on their abdomen, providing protection from other predators in the plankton, until the first **nauplius larval stage** hatches.
70. Copepods are critical to the ecology of the ocean in many ways. First and foremost, in some places like the Arctic and Antarctic, they can comprise more than ¾ of the **biomass** in the zooplankton.
71. They are basically like microscopic deer or cows in the ocean, present through the entire **photic zone** of the ocean, grazing on diatoms, dinoflagellates, green algae, golden algae, and cyanobacteria.
72. Some biologists think the combined mass of all the copepods in the ocean is greater than every other species of **primary consumer** combined. They represent a huge amount of biomass to feed higher trophic levels.

73. Copepods feed everything from larval fish and crabs to baleen whales in the water column. Their molted exoskeletons, poop, and dead carcasses rain down to the bottom of the ocean, providing nutrients there.
74. **Gooseneck barnacles** of the **Order Pedunculata** are highly modified crustaceans that basically stand on their heads inside their shells, filter feeding plankton from the motion of ocean tides.
75. Chefs esteem gooseneck barnacles as being incredibly delicious in garlic butter, in spite of the fact it takes hundreds of them to make a decent meal.
76. If you are stranded in the wilds of the Pacific Northwest, you can pick them off of rocks and driftwood.
77. You can maybe get a meal that will send you to bed disappointed, rather than hungry enough to eat a dead sun-bloated porcupine covered in maggots....that is unless the 'reality' show compels you to do it for the ratings.
78. Regular old **acorn barnacles** of **Order Sessilia** lack the muscular appendage of gooseneck barnacles. They cement themselves to the surface of a whale, deck pylon, boat, or rock and remain **sessile**.
79. It was not realized that barnacles were crustaceans, rather than mollusks, until some time in the 1800's when someone scraped one off a rock and cut one open, surprised to see the segments and legs inside the shell.
80. Basically, the animal stands on its head and extends filamentous appendages called **cirri**, which trap floating particles in sticky mucus. These are then directed to the mouth of the animal for consumption.
81. Both groups of barnacles are greatly simplified from most other crustaceans, in that their abdominal segments are basically vestigial. They also lack gills and a circulatory system, since diffusion works well for these purposes.
82. In addition to crapping up boats and forcing their owners to scrape them off with a putty knife while cursing, the other main contribution of barnacles to human society is their contribution to the filthy limerick song 'Barnacle Bill the Sailor', a mainstay in fraternity houses across the nation.

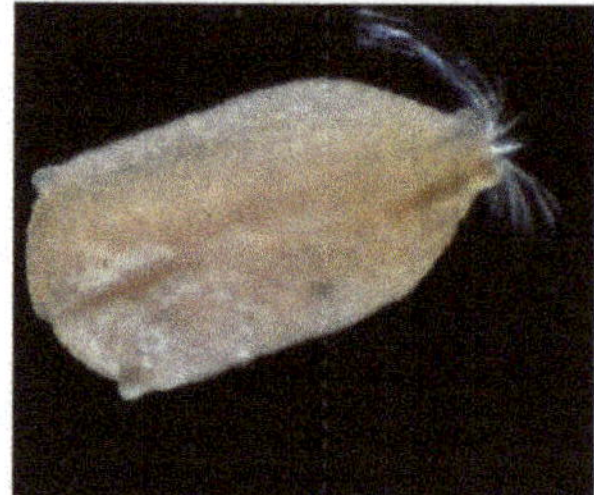

CLASS OSTRACODA
MULTIPLE ORDERS
SEED SHRIMP

*LATERALLY FLATTENED BODIES WITH CHITIN SHELL.
*NO SEGMENTATION. HEAD FUSED WITH THORAX.
*VESTIGIAL ABDOMEN.
*HAVE MANDIBLES AND MAXILLAE FOR FEEDING.
*MOST SPECIES HAVE A SINGLE SIMPLE EYE.
*MANY SPECIES HAVE APPENDAGES AT TAIL.
*BOTH ZOOPLANKTONIC & BENTHIC SPECIES EXIST.

ORDER STOMATOPODA
MANTIS SHRIMP

*CARAPACE ON HEAD & FIRST 4 THORACIC SEGMENTS.
*EXTREMELY AGGRESSIVE BURROWING AMBUSH PREDATORS.
*FRONT APPENDAGES ARE MODIFIED INTO SMASHING CLUBS AND SPEARS.
*STRIKE WITH CLAWS CAN REACH SUPERSONIC SPEEDS & BREAK GLASS.
*EXTREMELY SHARP EYESIGHT WITH ABILITY TO SEE UV AND FAR RED.
*CHANGE COLORS AND FLUORESCE TO COMMUNICATE WITH EACH OTHER.
*MANY SPECIES ARE LONG-LIVED AND MONOGAMOUS WITH PARTNERS.

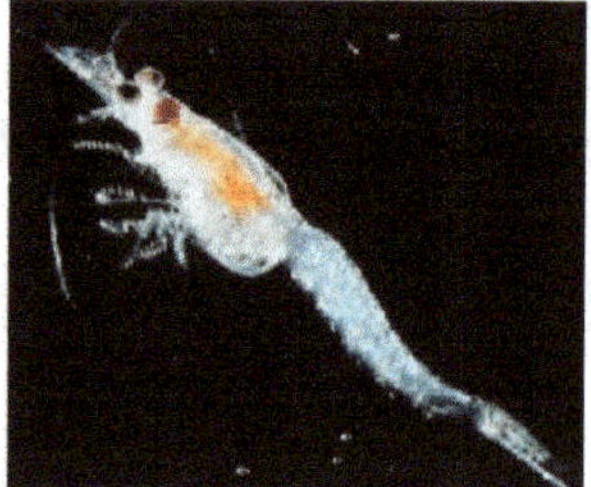

ORDER MYSIDA
OPOSSUM SHRIMP

*EGGS HATCH IN A BROOD POUCH. LARVAE PROTECTED.
*8 BODY SEGMENTS, EYES ON STALKS, 2 PAIRS ANTENNAE.
*8 PAIRS OF WALKING LEGS.
*6 PAIRS OF SWIMMERETS ON ABDOMINAL SEGMENTS.
*USUALLY OMNIVOROUS. SPECIES FOUND WORLDWIDE.
*CULTURED FOR FISH FOOD AND FOR PROTEIN.

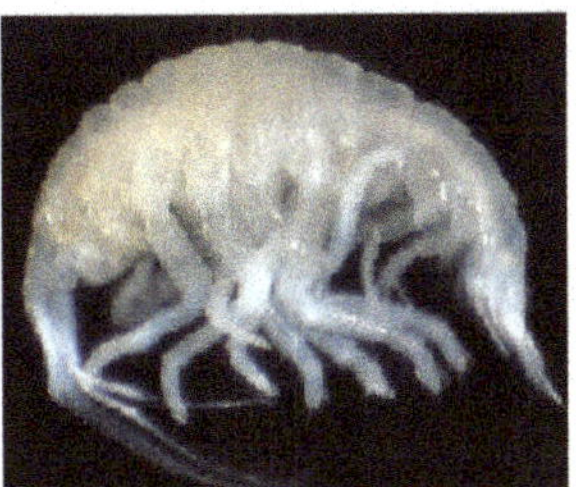

ORDER AMPHIPODA
AMPHIPODS
*MOST SPECIES ARE BENTHIC SCAVENGERS.
*13 BODY SEGMENTS; 2 PAIRS OF ANTENNAE.
*SINGLE PAIR OF EYES
*8 PAIRS OF UNIRAMOUS LEGS UNDER THORAX.
*TAIL HAS A TELSON & 3 PAIRS OF UROPOD FLIPPERS.
*MALES CLUTCH
*EGGS IN BROOD POUCH.

ORDER ISOPODA
ISOPODS
*PILL-SHAPED BODY. 7 THORACIC & 5 ABDOMINAL SEGMENTS.
*LEGS ON THORACIC SEGMENTS AND GILLS ON ABDOMEN.
*USUALLY FLATTENED DORSALLY.
*GREAT VARIABILITY IN SIZE.
*SPECIES FOUND IN OCEANS, FRESHWATER, AND ON LAND.
*ANTENNAE, MAXILLA, AND MANDIBLES ON HEAD.
*ONE PAIR OF COMPOUND EYES.

ORDER EUPHAUSIACEAE
KRILL
*MOSTLY FEED ON PHYTOPLANKTON AS PRIMARY CONSUMERS. INCREDIBLY NUMEROUS.
* FISH, WHALES, PENGUINS, SQUID, SEALS ALL RELY ON KRILL AS MAJOR FOOD SOURCE.
*TRANSPARENT CHITIN EXOSKELETON
*BIRAMOUS LEGS ON THORAX AND SWIMMERETS ON ABDOMEN. TAIL HAS ROSTRUM & UROPODS.
*SPERM ARE TRANSFERRED IN SACS TO FEMALES WHO CARRY THOUSANDS OF EGGS IN ABDOMEN.
*CAPABLE OF GENERATING BIOLUMINESCENSE BY CONCENTRATING DIATOM PIGMENTS.

83. **Seed shrimp** of the **Order Ostracoda** are weird little crustaceans that no one would normally ever notice. They are flat as a pancake in a vertical plane, with the chitin carapace covering their segments almost completely.
84. Like the copepods and daphnia, they usually only have a single fused **compound eye**. Their abdomen is mostly vestigial. Oddly, the carapace is hinged like a bivalve shell, allowing them to open up and extend their legs.
85. Diminutive in size, they have discarded their gills and circulatory system. They do just fine using diffusion for gas exchange, especially since they have a large amount of flat surface area on their bodies.
86. Seed shrimp are residents of ocean sediment, burying up in the sand and feeding on detritus and plankton.
87. Some species of clams rely heavily on seed shrimp for nourishment. Freshwater ostracod species are sought out by hungry salamanders, but also by middle-aged college-educated women with secret addictions to shellfish.
88. Oddly, some species of ostracods are **bioluminescent**, producing bright blue light shows underwater during mating season like millions of tiny police cars.
89. The secret to their bioluminescence is due to enzyme chemistry.Seed shrimp have two pairs of glands in their faces. One set of glands make the protein **luciferin**, while the other pair of glands make **luciferase enzyme**.
90. The enzyme cleaves the luciferin in two, and the resulting chemical reaction generates blue light.
91. As cool as seed shrimp might be, there is almost nothing in nature cooler than **mantis shrimp**. Mantis shrimp belong to the **Order Stomatopoda** and have the temperament and weaponry of Mike Tyson circa 1986.
92. Remember that Mike Tyson once told fight opponent, Lennox Lewis, that he would eat his children. Mantis shrimp would most definitely eat your children if they were about 100 times bigger.
93. Mantis shrimp are well-known for their front claws, which contain hammer-like smashing parts and stabbing parts resembling an ice pick. Combine that with an insatiable appetite and they are basically little dragons.
94. Their claws are essentially spring-loaded, as a specialized saddle-shaped part of their exoskeleton pulls the claws back and locks a muscle underneath. When released, they sling forward with incredible speed.

95. Even if the claws don't penetrate their prey, the shockwave they create stuns or kills them.
96. Mantis shrimp also have some of the most complex compound eyes in the invertebrate world. In addition to having vision in high-definition resolution, they can see everything from far red to ultraviolet.
97. Combine these characteristics with their ability to change colors, and they are **basically** the coolest animals ever.
98. **Opossum shrimp** of the **Order Mysida** are common in estuaries and tropical freshwater ecosystems. In spite of looking like clear miniature true shrimp, their reproductive strategy sets them apart.
99. Like marsupial mammals, they keep their eggs in a brood pouch, protecting the hatched larvae from predators until they advance past the first nauplius stage.
100. Mysid shrimp are important to the aquaculture industry, as they are cultured as a convenient high protein feed.
101. **Amphipods** are sort of the garbage men of the ocean, sifting through the sand and silt for leftovers. They eat dead organic matter that rains to the bottom. They also enjoy Captain D's batter crispies that fall off the fish.
102. Most amphipods are around a millimeter in size, but there are a few whoppers, such as a freshwater species from Lake Baikal in Russia that is the stuff of nightmares. It is covered in spines and can be several inches long.
103. Baikal, for some reason, has hundreds of species of freshwater amphipods. They are a clear case of **adaptive radiation**, where one or a few ancestral species evolved to occupy niches all over the lake.
104. There are around 10,000 known species of amphipods, with about 2,000 of these occurring in freshwater. Nearly 20% of these species are communist crustaceans, solely found in Lake Baikal.
105. Amphipods are unique for several reasons. First, they are very leggy, with 14 total pairs of appendages. Their odd bodies are laterally compressed and they lake a hard **carapace** or any sort of fan-like tail flippers.
106. Male amphipods select a mate and hold them until they molt, at which point they fertilize their eggs.
107. Like the opossum shrimp, the females carry their eggs in a brood pouch until they hatch. Amphipods lack larval nauplius stages and hatch directly into a miniature adult.
108. While **Order Amphipoda** contains laterally-compressed amphipods, **Order Isopoda** comprises the horizontally flattened **isopods**. Isopods include everything from sowbugs and roly-polies to foot-long deep sea monsters.
109. While there around 10,000 species of isopods, it could be argued that they are the best adapted group of terrestrial crustaceans, as fully half of these species are land-dwelling wood lice.
110. Wood lice, like pillbugs, sowbugs, and roly-polies have **symbiotic** gut microbes that secrete cellulase, allowing them to consume things that would otherwise not be food, such as moss, twigs, dead leaves, and so on.
111. Of the marine species, there are more than a few that have evolved freakish parasitic lifestyles.
112. Exhibit A in this category is the tongue-eating isopod that preys on numerous species of reef fish.
113. These filthy little goblins eat the tongue of their host, replace it, and pretend to be their tongue, taking their cut of food as the fish consumes its meals.
114. Other parasitic isopods live inside the carapaces of crabs and shrimp or in the gill filaments of other animals.
115. Krill, members of the **Order Euphausiacea** compete with copepods, in terms of having the largest biomass of any type of animal on earth. Krill school at densities of more than 25,000 animals per cubic meter.
116. Krill schools, on average, are about the size of a football field that extends down to the bottom of the **photic zone**, but they can join to form superschools that go on for many miles.
117. Krill superficially resemble shrimp, but their body segmentation differs. Shrimp have a **cephalothorax**, while the head and thorax are distinct in krill. Likewise, they vary in the number of appendages on each segment.

118. Krill are critical to the ecology of cold water ecosystems, because they are, by far, the largest source of protein available to carnivores. Among the animals that subsist off krill are fish, penguins, seals, squid, and whales.

SUBORDER DENDROBRACHIATA
PRAWNS

*SHORT BIRAMOUS FRONT ANTENNAE, LONG UNIRAMOUS BACK ANTENNAE.
*3 PAIRS OF MAXILLIPEDS AND 5 PAIRS OF WALKING LEGS ON THORAX TIPPED WITH ROSTRUM.
*TAIL HAS 6 SEGMENTS TIPPED WITH UROPODS & TELSON FINS.
*EGGS ARE RELEASED DIRECTLY INTO WATER AT SPAWN.
*NUMEROUS NAUPLIUS AND ZOEAE JUVENILE STAGES.

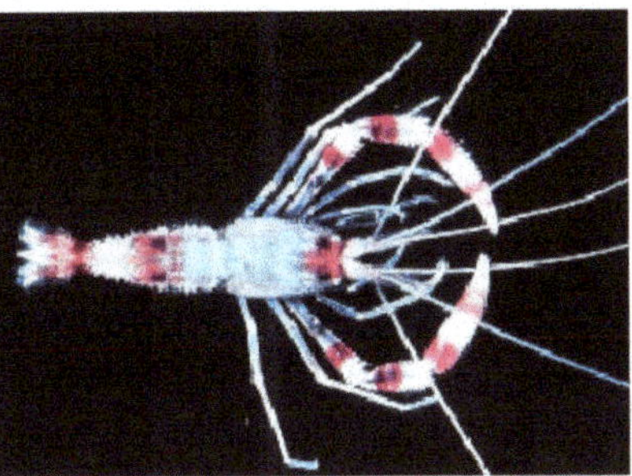

SUBORDER STENOPODIDEA
BOXER SHRIMP

*THIRD PAIR OF LEGS ARE GREATLY ENLARGED INTO CLAWS.
*FEMALES KEEP AND BROOD THEIR EGGS UNDER ABDOMEN.
*DO NOT HAVE BRANCHED GILLS LIKE TRUE SHRIMP.
*USUALLY LIVE IN BURROWS AND ACT AS AMBUSH PREDATORS.
*SEVERAL SPECIES ARE SOLD AND KEPT AS PETS IN SALTWATER AQUARIUM TRADE.

SUBORDER CARIDEA
TRUE SHRIMP

*MAXILLAE AND MAXILLPEDS PUMP WATER OVER BRANCHED GILLS INSIDE THORAX.
*5 PAIRS OF WALKING LEGS ON THORAX AND 5 SWIMMERETS ON ABDOMEN (10 TOTAL PAIRS).
*BACKWARD FLICK OF TAIL IS HARDWIRED ESCAPE RESPONSE.
*FEMALES BROOD CLUTCHES OF THOUSANDS OF EGGS.
*NUMEROUS NAUPLIUS AND ZOEAE JUVENILE STAGES.

119. Now we move on to a number of sub-classifications in the large **Order Decapoda**. These various sub-taxa are unique enough, ecologically and anatomically, and so numerous in species, that they bear coverage.

120. All **decapods**, regardless of their particular arrangement, have 10 pairs of appendages.

121. **Prawns** belong to **Suborder Dendrobrachiata**. Strongly resembling shrimp, the main difference between the two is in reproductive strategies. Prawns release eggs directly into the water, while shrimp have brood **clutches**.

122. It is also a fairly safe bet that you don't care, but the segmentation, number of appendages, and juvenile stages also differ between the two orders. With that said, prawns are just as delicious with butter and garlic.

123. **Boxer shrimp** also look like true shrimp, but there are obvious differences in gill structure and an obvious pair of giant **chelipeds** derived from their third walking legs.

124. Saltwater aquarists keep a number of members of **Suborder Stenopodidea** as interesting and decorative specimens. Probably the most common of these are the coral-banded shrimp and the peppermint shrimp.

125. True **shrimps** belong to **Suborder Caridea**. Unlike the aforementioned groups, they can actively pump water over a set of branched gills, via their walking legs and hydraulic pressure.

126. This comes in handy, since many shrimp species live in estuaries and other relatively low oxygen waters.

127. Shrimp have an especially prominent backflip reflex, snapping a hinge in their tail to propel themselves backward to avoid predators. This reflex is controlled by **ganglia** that don't need the brain's approval.

128. Shrimp are a (mostly) sustainable and incredibly important nutritional source that account for nearly 2 billion tons of seafood production each year, most of it now aquacultured.

129. Shrimp are a very versatile food. You can barbecue it, bake it, boil it, broil it, saute it. There's shrimp kabobs, shrimp creole, shrimp gumbo. Pan fried, deep fried, stir-fried.

130. There's pineapple shrimp, lemon shrimp, coconut shrimp, pepper shrimp, shrimp soup, shrimp stew, shrimp salad, shrimp and potatoes, shrimp burger, shrimp sandwich. Well that's about it.

INFRAORDER ACHELTA
SPINY & SLIPPER LOBSTERS

* LACK CHELIPEDS (PINCERS) & USE THEIR ANTENNAE INSTEAD.
*HAVE A SPIDER-LIKE LARVAL STAGE CALLED A PHYLLOSOMA
*WALKING LEGS ARE BIRAMOUS.
*CAN GENERATE SHRIEKING NOISES FOR SELF-DEFENSE BY RASPING THEIR ANTENNAE.
*LIVE ON CORAL REEFS & MIGRATE IN SINGLE FILE LINES.

INFRAORDER ASTACIDAE
TRUE LOBSTERS & CRAWFISH

*ENLARGED CHELIPEDS (PINCERS) FOR PREDATION & DEFENSE.
*ANTENNAE LONG & THREAD-LIKE
*BLUE BLOOD DUE TO COPPER-BASED HEMOCYANIN PIGMENTS.
*8 PAIRS OF WALKING LEGS WITH SMALL CLAWS ON FIRST 3 PAIR.
*LOBSTERS LACK TAIL JOINT IN ABDOMEN. CRAWFISH CAN FLICK TAIL AT THIS JOINT.

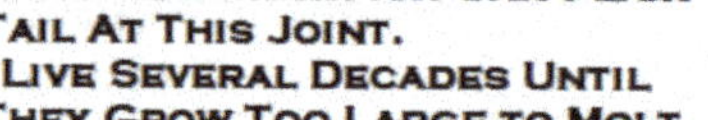

*LIVE SEVERAL DECADES UNTIL THEY GROW TOO LARGE TO MOLT.

INFRAORDER AXIIDEA
GHOST & MUD SHRIMP

*CREATE INTRICATE TUNNELS ON SEA FLOOR. IMPORTANT IN GEOCHEMICAL CYCLING.
*VERY NUMEROUS, BUT HIDE IN BURROWS & RARELY SEEN.
*HOURGLASS SHAPED BODY WITH LARGER ABDOMEN.
*COMPACT FRONT CLAWS FOR TUNNELING AND DIGGING.
*SOME SPECIES HAVE LONG BACK WALKING LEGS TO HELP CLEAR SILT FROM BURROWS.

131. **Spiny lobsters** of the **Infraorder Achelta** are not true lobsters. However, they fill a similar niche as true lobsters in sub-tropical and tropical seas. Most are reef-dwelling scavengers and burrowing ambush predators.

132. Instead of possessing a large pair of **cheliped** pincers like a true lobster, their antennae are greatly enlarged to the diameter of a large pencil or wooden dowel. They can be clenched together like chopsticks for gripping.

133. Spiny lobsters are not particularly threatening, so they have to avoid predators by relying on a combination of shock and flight. If grabbed, they will make loud squealing noises and rapidly retreat by flipping their tails.

134. Spiny lobsters are well known to scientists. Gigantic abdominal nerves are easy to access and manipulate for neurological studies. Their long choo-choo train migrations from reef-to-reef also interest animal behaviorists.

135. **True lobsters** and **crawfish** belong to **Infraorder Astacidae**. Their functional **cheliped** claws are used for predation, defense, and manipulating objects.

136. The main difference between crawfish and lobsters is the presence of a hinge-like snapping joint in the tail of crawfish that is absent in lobsters. Additionally, crawfish are found in freshwater, while lobsters are marine.

137. With a few exceptions, such as a gigantic species from Tasmania, most crawfish are also considerably smaller.

138. Both lobsters and crawfish have 8 pairs of functional walking legs, with **biramous** claws on the first 3 pairs.

139. A number of crustacean features become obvious amongst lobsters, because of their large size. For instance, they have obvious mandibles, maxillae, and maxillipeds that are used to shovel food into their faces.

140. While most crustaceans have blue blood with copper-based **hemocyanin** instead of **hemoglobin** for oxygen transport, this is more obvious in large crustaceans like some of the cat-sized whoppers they catch in Maine.

141. After a complex series of stages during juvenile metamorphosis, lobsters have an indeterminate lifespan that is only limited by hungry groupers and a natural surface-area limit on their ability to undergo **molting**.

142. The hourglass-shaped **ghost shrimp** of **Infraorder Axiidea** are kind of like the flying squirrels of the ocean. Almost no one sees them or realizes that they are there, but in reality, there are gazillions of them hiding.

143. A heavy-duty pair of front claws allows ghost shrimp to tunnel through ocean silt like a prairie dog, building complex tunnels with multiple hallways and chambers.

144. Ghost shrimp are so active that they are critical to nutrient cycling in the ocean, since a colony can repeatedly turn over the local sediment many times, releasing contents back into the water.

145. Many ghost shrimp also have broom-like back walking legs that are used in housekeeping their burrows, scooping fallen sediment back out of their dens.

146. Ghost shrimp can also shoot laser beams out of their heads. Divers have been killed. OK I can't back that up.

INFRAORDER ANOMURA
HERMIT, KING, ROBBER CRABS, SQUAT LOBSTERS

*HAVE A REDUCED OR VESTIGIAL ABDOMEN LACKING SEGMENTATION.
* TEN PAIRS OF WALKING LEGS, BUT BACK TWO PAIR USUALLY TUCKED.
*HERMITS SCAVENGE SHELLS TO PROTECT VULNERABLE ABDOMEN.
*FRONT CHELIPEDS ARE OFTEN VERY LARGE RELATIVE TO BODY SIZE.

INFRAORDER BRACHYURA
TRUE CRABS

*10 OBVIOUS PAIRS OF WALKING LEGS AND A FRONT PAIR OF CHELIPEDS.
*ABDOMEN REDUCED TO AN APRON THAT IS FOLDED UNDERNEATH THORAX.
*SEXUAL DIMORPHISM. MALES WITH POINTED APRON, FEMALES ROUNDED. MALES OF MOST SPECIES HAVE LARGER CLAWS.
*MATING OCCURS AFTER FEMALES HAVE MOLTED. PROTECTED BY MALE UNTIL EXOSKELETON HARDENS AROUND CLUTCH.

147. **Infraorder Anomura** contains an assortment of crustaceans that most people think are crabs, but they really aren't. King crabs, coconut crabs, snow crabs, and hermit crabs.

148. So why aren't these things crabs? It's mostly because taxonomists like to get technical. Mostly it's because their abdomens are almost non-existent or vestigial in nature. In hermits, even segmentation has disappeared.

149. Anatomically, these crustaceans have 8 visible pairs of walking legs, with the back two either tucked into the shells that they stole or underneath their bodies.

150. Some of the largest and most delicious crustaceans belong to this group. King crabs can attain a leg span of over 5 feet across and weigh as much as a small dog. Coconut crabs can be 3 feet long and over 10 pounds.
151. Thanks to their delectability, king and snow crabs also have necessitated some of the most dangerous jobs on the planet, as you probably know from the Discovery channel.
152. In any given year, your chances of plunging into the icy waters of the Bering Strait, never to be heard from again are about 1 in 781. Extrapolate that over a 30 year career, and your odds are nearly 5%.
153. The chances of a secretary finding Davy Jones' locker after leaning back and falling out of her wheelie-chair are pretty close to zero....that is unless she is a secretary aboard a crab boat....then the odds are pretty good.

J) Sub-Phylum Myriapoda: Centipedes and Millipedes

1. We are nearing the end of our Odyssey through the arthropods as we examine a group that is under much debate among taxonomists, the **myriapods**, which are better known as **centipedes** and **millipedes**.
2. Their group is extremely ancient, with some fossils dating back more than 400 million years.
3. Given the fact that a lot can happen in that period of time, including instances of convergent evolution, their classification is under debate. No one has definitively shown any other group to be their closest relatives.
4. Some taxonomists argue that they belong somewhere on the phylogenetic tree between the **hexapods** and **crustaceans**. Others argue that they are closer to the **chelicerates**.
5. We aren't going to settle that debate here, but we will point out the commonalities between sister groups as we progress through the different classes of **myriapods**.
6. In addition to **centipedes** (**Class Chilopoda**) and **millipedes** (**Order Diplopoda**), two other rather obscure groups belong to the myriapods. These belong to **Order Symphlapoda** and **Order Pauropoda.**
7. **Symphlapods** and **pauropods** are small, rarely seen, and anatomically different enough from the other two groups to warrant their own classifications.
8. Let's begin with the **centipedes**. Contrary to their name, centipedes usually have closer to a few dozen legs and segments, rather than the 100 their moniker suggests. However, some species may have over 300.
9. Unlike insects and arachnids, centipedes don't secrete any kind of hard sealant around their cuticles, so they must remain buried up in moist leaf litter or moss to avoid dying from dessication.
10. Centipedes have a single pair of **antennae**, a pair of **mandibles** and two pairs of **maxillae** surrounding the mouth on a flattened, armored head. They are ugly and gross.
11. Their front legs are modified into a pair of pinching **forcipucles**, which have **venom glands** at their base. These are used to subdue prey and to shove the poor victims into their mouths.
12. Cave-dwelling centipede species may lack eyes altogether, some have simple light-sensing **ocelli**, while other diurnal rainforest species have fully functional **compound eyes**.
13. **Centipedes** have a variable number of segments, from a little over a dozen to more than 100, depending on the species. Each segment has a pair of legs, which get progressively longer toward the tail of the animal.
14. The final pair of legs on the last segment are extraordinarily long and stiff, providing balance and climbing grips. Depending on the sex, the **sperm ducts** or **oviducts** are located on the last segment, which ends with a **telson**.
15. Internally, centipedes are laid out much like insects. A long pair of **mandibular glands** extends all the way from the mouth to the end of the foregut, with its ducts feeding into points along the stomach.

16. Like insects, their respiratory tract consists of a long set of **tracheal tubes** that open out of the shell via **spiracles**.
17. Similarly, their circulatory system is centered around a long pumping heart-like tube that forces **hemolymph** over the organs. Muscular motion helps the hemolymph migrate back to the **hemoecoel** to be pumped again.
18. The reproductive glands of centipedes are quite large, extending from the middle of the body all the way to the reproductive ducts at the last segment.
19. Males produce sacs of sperm called **spermatophores**. Males spin webs and suspend these spermatophore packages in the web (hence the theory that chelicerates like spiders might be evolutionarily related).
20. The male centipede then finds a female centipede and keeps tapping her back legs with his antennae until she is sufficiently annoyed and just wants to get the whole thing over with. She inserts the pack into her **oviducts**.
21. The female centipede then buries herself in a brood chamber, cleans the several dozen eggs she lays with regularity, and hangs around until the little bundles of horror pass through the first larval stage.
22. Centipedes can have a significant ecological role as predators of insects, earthworms, small rodents, lizards, and whatever other protein-rich creature that they can run down and jam in their mouths.
23. While some crazy, stupid, and / or stubborn animals like mongooses, kangaroo mice, and snakes will eat centipedes, they have to contend with various gooey toxic secretions to get their reward.
24. Depending on the species, some of these bug goos contain acids, cyanide, or other foul-smelling substances that capture the essence of a Port-a-Potti baking on a sunny Summer's day.
25. Alright, that's enough about centipedes before we all lose sleep. We will leave you with pictures of several different species of centipedes below, along with a basic schematic of their internal anatomy.

House Centipede

Giant Redheaded Centipede

Burmese Centipede

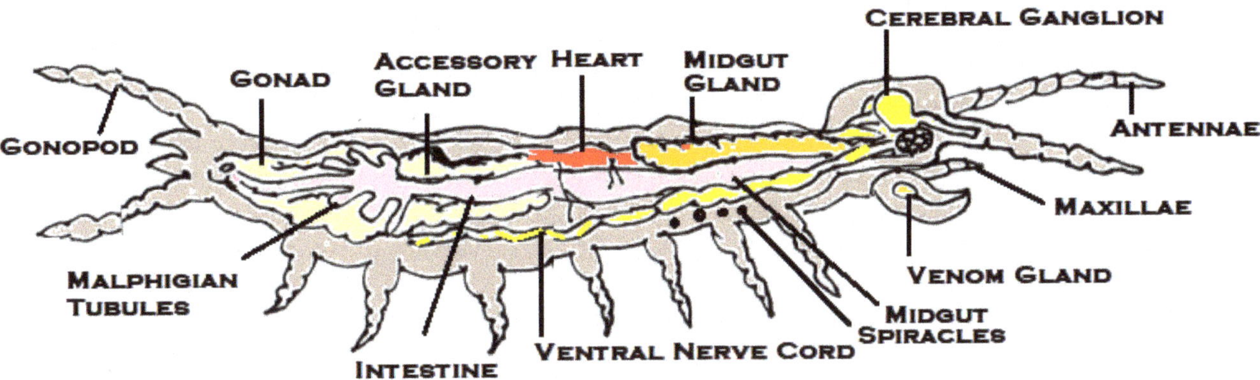

26. **Millipedes** are the kinder and gentler **myriapods**. They are almost exclusively either **herbivorous** or they are harmless trash feeding **detritivores** that enjoy a good salad of dead leaves, humus, and toenail clippings.
27. Genetic studies reveal that millipedes are only distantly related to centipedes, in spite of similar morphology.
28. There are more than 16,000 species of millipedes (about 10,000 more than all the mammals combined) divided into 16 orders and more than 100 families. We will NOT be covering these in detail.
29. While some livings species can grow to the size of a foot-long hot dog, there are extinct millipedes in the fossil record that were the size of a lamp post. At 450 million years old, they were also some of the first land animals.
30. Genetically, millipedes and centipedes are only distantly related. Their body shape and locomotion are mostly cases of **convergent evolution**. However, if one looks past these things, there are major differences.
31. First and foremost, the digestive system, mandibles, legs, and behaviors of centipedes are built for predation, while millipedes are built to be omnivorous or herbivorous.
32. Starting with the head, let's take a quick look at the anatomical layout of millipedes. The **mandibles** of millipedes are shovel-like, rather than pincer-like and they have a ridged lower jaw for grinding food.
33. Instead of pointing outward (as in centipedes), their **antennae** are folded down the sides of their head.
34. There are several simple eyes called **ocelli**, though many cave-dwellings groups of millipedes have lost these through de-evolution. These connect back to a **central ganglion** in the front segment.
35. The first 'neck' segment behind the head is known as the **collum** has no legs, while the next few segments have just one pair of legs, and the remaining segments, known as **metameres** each have two pairs of legs.
36. **Millipedes** have dozens to hundreds of repeating **metameres** with identical calcified **exoskeleton** plates that serve as armor. On their undersides are open **spiracles** for respiration.
37. Since they have no way to close their spiracles (kind of like if you left your mouth hanging open all the time), millipedes are susceptible to drying out. For this reason, they usually are found in moist soil or leaves.
38. The final segment is known as a **telson**, which is where the digestive system terminates in the anus.
39. The internal layout of millipedes is not dramatically different from most other segmented arthropods.
40. For instance, there are a pair of **salivary glands** connected to a simple tube-like gut with a **digestive gland**, followed by a long **intestine** with excretory **Malpighian tubules**.
41. Reproduction varies among different orders of millipedes.
42. Some millipedes spin a web, deposit sperm packets, and let the females pick up the package like they are going to the mailbox. However, this is not a common strategy.
43. Most millipedes mate directly, with the male having a modified back pair of legs known as **gonopores**, which are used like a penis. Male and female millipedes face each other and sperm packets are transferred to the **oviduct**.
44. In some orders, the gonopores are on the very last few segments, but it's the seventh pair of legs in most types of millipedes. Usually, the female opening is located on the third segment.
45. Once the eggs are fertilized, most females lay dozens to hundreds of eggs in wet humus or dirt. Some species spin a silk cocoon around their eggs. Millipede larvae are pretty much on their own, as the parents dash.
46. Millipedes typically undergo several molts over several years, with the last one resulting in the mature reproductive stage. However, some millipedes are **parthenogenetic** (all female) with self-fertilizing eggs.

47. The diagram below shows examples of pill millipedes and worm-like millipedes. There are 3 orders of the former and 13 orders of the latter. Their sub-classification is based mostly on reproduction and anatomical minutiae.

48. So unless you decide that your life's work needs to include millipedes, you are likely done here. Vegas odds say that you probably won't think about millipedes in detail for the rest of your days on this earth.

PILL MILLIPEDES

SUPERCLASS PENTAZONIA

SEGMENTS OVERLAP LIKE PLATES OF ARMOR

WORM-LIKE MILLIPEDES

SUPERCLASS HELMINTHOMORPHA

SEGMENTS ARE FUSED AND CONCENTRIC. SUB-CLASSIFIED BY REPRODUCTION AND BY SELF-DEFENSE COMPOUNDS MADE.

CREEPY ARTHROPOD WORD SEARCH

```
S I I H K W A L K I N G S T I C K D P E
H D E L T E E B B A R A C S F M I O T T
X O E K E O M I R K S J C W B G S A B I
P X R C V I N E G A R O O N L S R A O M
B I O S A L T S M S L Z X U U E R X V R
M M L J E P J K Y H P B P M C C O A N E
G Q E L O S O N N Q V O S I G X D L A T
S H M H B J H D Z A S H L N J K L U R C
W I T C F U K O W U R E I C S D X T E L
P R T V B B G Q E I H K Q P C U Y N T Y
O G E N X L J F M C X D X N B R T A P Y
Y I N Y A Q D P C M R C I G G I M R O Q
Q B I R D M I T E B V A G N P P U A D O
R E T S B O L Y N I P S B E H U F T I I
M I L L I P E D E L W O D I R C I N P S
E T I B O L I R T O M E P J D K A I E O
V V M Y Q T T M D B Q O I C B R G R L P
Z H B Q H J P X U X D X O C S I H V A O
N A R E T P O N E M Y H Z E F L G S A D
P M I R H S S I T N A M R O O L X F R D
```

Amphipod	Arachnid	BirdMite
Centipede	Chelicerate	Decapod
HorseshoeCrab	Hymenopteran	Isopod
KingCrab	Krill	Lepidopteran
Mantis	MantisShrimp	Millipede
Orthopteran	Pillbug	PossumShrimp
ScarabBeetle	Sopulgid	SpinyLobster
Tarantula	Termite	Trilobite
Vinegaroon	WalkingStick	

SECTION 4: Triploblastic Protostome Lophotrochozoan Invertebrates

A) Lophotrochozoan Traits

1. **Lophotrochozoans** represent the other major phylogenetic split in triploblastic invertebrates. Like their ecdysozoan brethren, they are bilaterally symmetrical and the blastopore develops head-first.
2. Lophotrochozoans lack a **cuticle** around their bodies, they are typically supported by a hydrostatic skeleton or the weight of the water around them, and they often have tentacles or soft appendages.
3. Members of this group, at some life stage, also have a **lophophore** around their mouths, which is a crown of cilia that is used for filtering food from the water or sweeping it into the mouth.
4. In many groups of lophotrochozoans, the lophophore is only present during one of the larval stages, such as the trochophore stage of bivalves.
5. The lophotrochozoans include several distinctly different types of worms (arrow worms, spoon worms, sipunculate worms, and annelids), along with colonial animals like bryozoans, and the mollusks.
6. Since it is impossible to make many generalizations past this point, we will begin by working our way through the groups of lophotrochozoan worms.
7. We will begin with flatworms, which don't really fit with this group, because they pre-date the evolutionary advancement up to the point of true lophotrochozoans. However, since they have no cuticle around their bodies, have hydrostatic body support, and seem to have evolved further, they get to be club mascot.
8. The **lophotrochozoans** had their first evolutionary split a very long time ago in the ancient oceans more than 500 million years back when they diverged into the **gnathiferans** and the **platytrochozoans**.
9. **Rotifers** and **arrow worms** still exist in the oceans today. Both have chitin jaws and soft rounded bodies like their ancestors. However, both groups show some surprising complexity.
10. Members of both phyla have ciliated feeding structures in the mouth and pharynx. Rotifers use these for filter feeding, but arrow worms use them to detect vibrations from prey animals like fish larvae and crustaceans.
11. In spite of being about the size of a period on a page, **rotifers** have a full digestive tract and ganglion that functions like a primitive brain. They cruise along in the plankton and filter feed algae, largely unnoticed.
12. Rotifers also show a weird set of evolutionary turns, with regard to gender.
13. Some species are solely female and use **parthenogenesis** to auto-fertilize their own eggs, while other types are **sexually dimorphic**, with large females and smaller males.
14. While rotifers are **pseudocoelomates**, the larger arrow worms needed to keep their organs in place, so they evolved into **true coelomates**, albeit independently of the other lophotrochozoans.
15. **Arrow worms**, like the majority of lophotrochozoan animals, are **hermaphrodites**. In spite of their primitive origins, they have eyes and a full digestive tract.
16. Arrow worms also show **convergent evolution** with fish, since they possess paired fins on their body and a caudal fin. Their fins even have ray-like gradations to allow them to be retracted and fanned.
17. On the other branch of the **lophotrochozoan** evolutionary tree, the original **platytrochozoan animals** diverged about the same time as the early gnathiferans. They appear to have had flat soft bodies.

18. This early group then diverged into two very different branches of animals. The **flatworms** are **acoelomates** with a number of primitive features, while the **true lophotrochozoans** are relatively advanced **true coelomates**.
19. The true lophotrochozoans can be further sub-divided into the **mollusks** and the **segmented worms**.

B) Clade Gnathofera, Phylum Rotifera: The Rotifers

1. **Phylum Rotifera** comprises an odd group of tiny zooplanktonic animals called **rotifers**.
2. Rotifers are one of several related phyla of **gnathferans** that diverged from the most ancestral lophotrochozoans. All the animals in this group have jaws lined with **chitin** teeth, most do not have **complete metamorphosis** with distinguishable life stages, and many have anuses that open on their dorsal surface.
3. Rotifers are extremely small, with no species larger than about the size of a pencil lead and the smaller species being barely visible specks. They have a spittoon shaped body with a mouth that opens at the top.
4. In spite of being extremely tiny, they are surprisingly complex in their anatomy. Externally, unlike other lophotrochozoans, rotifers have retained a cuticle-like protein shell around their bodies.
5. A crown of **coronal cilia** whip and rotate above the vase-shaped **mouth**, drawing in algae and other plankton, where a **mastax pharynx** crushes prey or parasitizes a host with a pair of tooth-like **trophi**.
6. The pharynx opens into a massive **stomach** that floats in a **pseudocoelom**, making rotifers one of the few animal phyla to use this design. The only way they get away with floating organs is the physics of their size.
7. Because rotifers are nearly microscopic, hydrogen-bond forces raise the Reynolds number of the water around them to the point that the surface tension and viscosity of the water shields them from impact damage.
8. A **digestive gland** sits atop the stomach and empties a slurry of digestive enzymes through a duct.
9. The short **intestine** is hard to distinguish from the stomach, ending in a **cloacal opening** near the caudal end of the body. A pair of **protonephridia** (primitive kidneys) filter the body fluids and also terminate at the cloaca.
10. The inferior part of the body terminates into a blunt-ended foot with a pair of appendages called **toes**.
11. **Rotifers**, in spite of their diminutive size, have a surprisingly large **brain** for the size of their body. Nerves lead from this **cerebral ganglion** to five **photoreceptor eyes**, a pair of **antennae**, and to the **cilia**.
12. Rotifers have no circulatory or respiratory system, because they are small enough to get oxygen by diffusion.
13. Rotifer reproduction determines the basis of how they are divided into classes.
14. Members of **Class Seisonidea** dioecious, with females usually being several times larger than the males.
15. Female rotifers have a pair of **ovaries** connected to glands called **vitellarium glands** that supply yolk to developing eggs, which then migrate down a pair of **syncytial oviducts** to the **cloacal opening**.
16. Male rotifers live for one thing....reproduction. They are born without a digestive system, so their time is obviously limited. Males have a **single testis** connected to a **sperm duct** that empties into a **gonopore**.
17. Since males have no digestive tract, they don't need an anus either, so this body opening is different. Usually the gonopore is tube-shaped, so it can act as a functional penis.

18. In species that use sexual reproduction, the male inserts his gonopore into the cloacal opening of the female or stabs it directly into her pseudocoelem and through the body wall.
19. Once fertilized, the eggs develop into a clutch. Depending on the species, the female will either hold the clutch between her toes or deposit the entire batch of eggs onto a nearby surface, where they hatch.
20. Once hatched, males are mature at birth, while females gradually grow into their mature form.
21. Rotifers of **Class Bdelloidea** are strictly reproduce by **parthenogenesis**, producing haploid eggs that they self-fertilize. Every member of these species are female and there are no poor starving males.
22. In **Class Monogonata**, reproduction is usually by parthenogenesis, since it allows for rapid population growth, but occasionally a sexual generation will occur, with males allowing a regeneration of genetic diversity.
23. The diagram below shows the anatomical layout of a rotifer, along with pictures of several species.

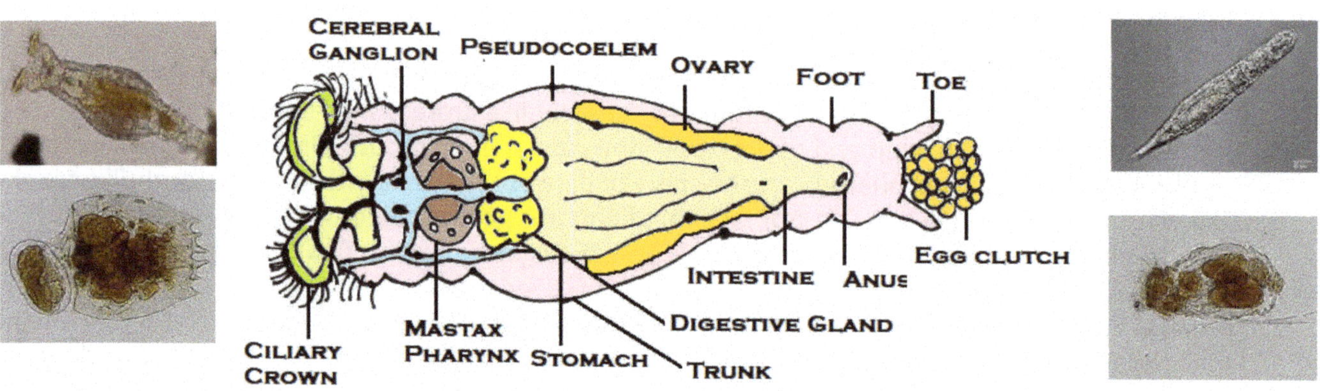

C) Clade Gnathofera, Phylum Chaetognatha: Arrow Worms

1. **Arrow worms**, members of **Phylum Chaetognatha**, are protostomes that don't fit well with either the Ecdysozoans or the Lophotrochozoans, to which they are most similar.
2. Arrow worms are sort of an evolutionary experiment that worked out, but only to an extent. They are only a little over 100 species of them in existence, but they are numerous in the ocean.
3. Like an Ecdysozoan, they have a **cuticle** around the body and distinct head, thorax, and tail segments.
4. However, like Lophotrochozoans, they have a soft, flexible body. They are also **hermaphroditic**.
5. Each side of their mouths have hooked spines like Wolverine's claws, which they use to trap prey, though some scavenging and omnivorous species use them like the bristles of a brush to feed on detritus.
6. Arrow worms show a high degree of **convergent evolution** with fish, as they have paired soft fins with ray-like structures that allow them to be flexed and relaxed. They also have a **caudal fin**.
7. Some arrow worms are venomous or bioluminescent, since these traits assist with hunting prey.
8. The mouth of arrow worms contains chitinous teeth. It opens up into a **pharynx** that lubricates the food with mucus and passes it straight into an **intestine** with a pair of digestive pouches called **diverticula**.
9. They are **true coelomates** with muscles tethering the gut into place. The lining of the gut is covered with **cilia**, which seem to serve the functions of circulatory, respiratory, and excretory systems.
10. As the cilia whip, they oxygenate the tissues and move metabolic wastes out of the body by diffusion.

11. There is a **cerebral ganglion** which is connected to a pair of **compound eyes** and to a **lateral-line organ** down each side of the body (also fish-like) that detects vibrations in the water around them.
12. Since all arrow worms are hermaphroditic, they have both **ovaries** and **testes**. The ovaries are located at the posterior end of the body, while the testes are further back in front of the tail.
13. Tests produce sperm cells, which then pass through the **sperm ducts** to be packaged into **spermatophores**.
14. When arrow worms mate, each worm places its sperm duct onto the neck area (if they had them that's where it would be) of the partner and releases a **spermatophore pouch**.
15. The pouch breaks open and the sperm then crawl down the body and enter pores that open into the **oviducts**.
16. Once fertilized, depending on the species, the eggs are either held in a kangaroo-like pouch or they are deposited onto a surface like sea grass.
17. Once hatched, baby arrow worms look like miniature adults. There is no metamorphosis through stages.
18. The diagram at the top of the next page shows arrow worm anatomy, along with a couple of photographs of the real McCoy. This cliché got me wondering why people say 'the real McCoy'.
19. Apparently, it is named after some guy named Elijah McCoy who had a ton of patents. He was known for doing good quality work and when people bought his stuff, they wanted the real thing and not some knock-off.
20. Among his inventions were the ironing board, the lawn sprinkler, train engine lubricators, the Sham-wow, the Schticky, the Snuggie, the Clapper, and Oxi-Clean.
21.

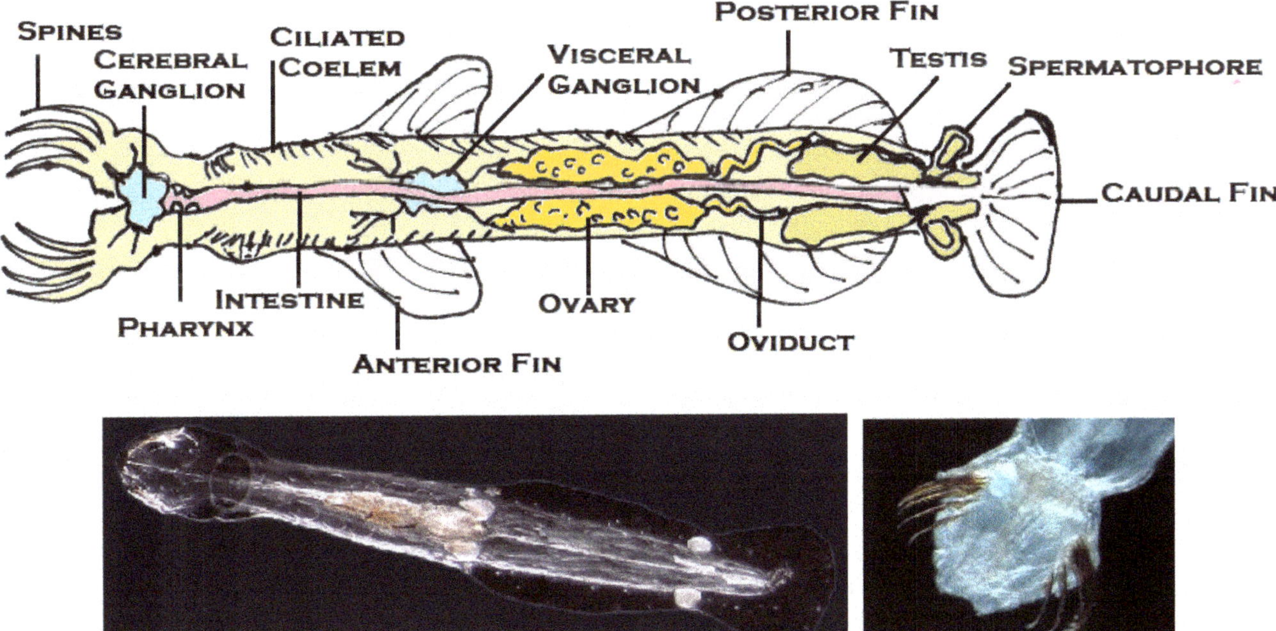

D) Phylum Platyhelminthes: Flatworms

1. Not even PETA cares about **flatworms**. You won't be **seeing** a dying tapeworm flopping around as 'Arms of an Angel' plays. For the most part, they are an icky and problematic group...the veritable 'smelly kids' of nature.
2. Flatworms are a big evolutionary step forward from **diploblastic animals.** Flatworms have a complete **mesoderm** between their ectoderm and endoderm layers, allowing muscles to articulate between layers.
3. However, since they are **acoelomates**, there is no space between the layers, sandwiching everything together severely limits their mobility. They have no body cavity (**coelom**) to allow them any flexibility.
4. Therefore, flatworms must 'do the worm' in order to move. They have almost no lateral flexibility.
5. In addition to being **acoelomate triploblastic animals**, flatworms also show evolutionary advances in body plan, since they have **cephalization** (a clear head) and **bilateral symmetry**.
6. Flatworms also are among the most primitive animals that have evolved **true organs** and **organ systems**. Among the systems that show up in flatworms are true **nervous** and **reproductive** systems.
7. At their most advanced, as in freshwater and marine **planarians**, flatworms have a sad little brain called a **cerebral ganglion**, a pair of **eyes**, and two ladder-like **ventral nerve cords** that articulate to the brain.
8. All flatworms are egg-laying **hermaphrodites** with a pair of **testes** and a pair of **ovaries**. When they mate, they face opposite directions, line up sperm and ovarian ducts, and transfer sperm via **internal fertilization.**
9. Flatworms also have other tissues that don't quite make organ status. For instance, the edges of their body are lined with flagellated **flame cells** that function like primitive kidneys, ridding the body of waste.
10. Flame cells are so-named because they are lined with flagella that look like flames whipping around under a microscope. They are responsible for keeping osmotic balance in the worm, especially the marine species.
11. Since they are **acoelomates** and lack an anus, their digestive system is limited to a **gastrovascular cavity** that exits the body through a tube-like snout called a **pharynx**.
12. The pharynx allows flatworms to feed like the creepy vacuum cleaner on Teletubbies. In case you wanted to know, the sun baby is now a 25 year-old woman named Jessica Smith, and not a demon, as some suggested.
13. The purple Teletubby is Tinky Winky, the yellow one is Laa Laa, the green one is Dipsy, the red one is Po, and the blue one is Richard. Teletubbies eat 'tubby custard', which is a mix of mashed potatoes and acrylic paint.
14. Getting back to anatomical descriptions, there are no **circulatory** or **respiratory systems** in a flatworm. Being so flat, everything is done by diffusion, so they are not needed.

IF YOU SEE ME IN THE USA, KILL ME ON SIGHT!

THE HAMMERHEAD FLATWORM WAS ACCIDENTALLY INTRODUCED TO THE USA THROUGH CONTAMINATED PLANTS AND SOIL FROM SOUTHEAST ASIA. THEY EAT NATIVE EARTHWORMS AND SNAILS AND ARE TOXIC. IF YOU SEE ONE, POUR SALT ON IT TO KILL IT!

15. The anatomical diagrams below depicts the organ systems of a planarian flatworm.

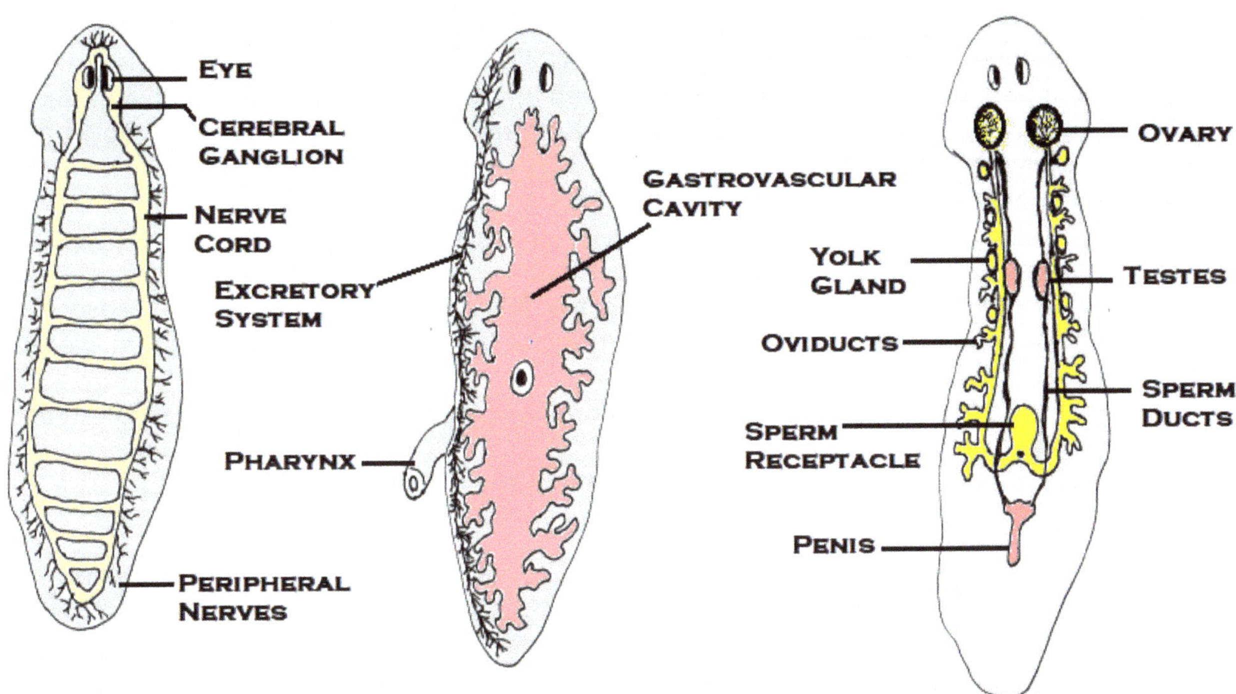

16. The degree of complexity of flatworms depends on their classification.

17. There are four classes of flatworms. **Class Turbelleria** includes free-living freshwater and marine planarian worms. These are the only group of free-living scavengers. All other groups are parasitic.

18. Parasitic fluke worms belong to **Class Tremotoda. Class Monogenea** comprises a group of parasitic worms that live in the gills of fish. Tapeworms belong to **Class Cestodes**.

19. **Planarians** have a full slate of organ systems, but the parasitic members of this phylum have devolved many features that ended up being unnecessary to a parasitic lifestyle.

20. Most freshwater planarians are small peaceful trash-eating scavengers that Zamboni rocks in creeks for algae.

21. Marine flatworms are predators of slow-moving benthic animals, such as starfish, sea squirts, and mollusks.

22. There are also terrestrial planarians that live in places with moist topsoil. One such land planarian, the hammerhead worm, is a predator of earthworms that has become an invasive nuisance in North America.

23. While they anatomically resemble planarians in many ways, **flukes** use a different life strategy altogether, since they pass from host-to-host as parasites of internal organs.

24. All members of **Class Trematoda** are aggressive parasites that attack a host during the adult stage. The cysts they produce develop into larvae, which are spread passively by a second host, which is often a snail.

25. Flukes have devolved their eyes because they live inside of livers, lungs, and other internal organs. Since it is dark up in there, it would be pointless to have eyes, since they wouldn't see anything anyway.

26. Flukes shed their zygotes inside of protective **cysts** via the waste of the host. These mature into developing **embryos** after leaving the body. From there, they hatch into early ciliated larvae called **miracidia**.

27. The **miracidia** then crawl around on wet plants and soil until they find a snail. They then live in the mucus of the snail under the shell and progress to a flagellated larval stage called a **cercaria.**
28. These flagellated larvae then leave the snail and crawl onto wet vegetation, where the next cow, sheep, other horse, or other unlucky herbivore swallows them with their food source.
29. After entering the small intestine, the **cercaria** swim up the bile duct and into the liver, where they set up shop. From there, the worms grow into adults, mate, and release **cysts** back down the bile duct, re-starting the cycle.
30. Any fluke infection is serious business, because they set up shop in internal organs and wreak havoc.
31. For instance, the **liver fluke**, *Fasciola hepatica* can jam up bile ducts, causing extreme nausea and vomiting, jaundice, fever, and scarring of the liver that can possibly lead to liver cancer.
32. A lot of Vietnam veterans became infected with liver flukes from rice paddy snails. Statistically, the vets had higher incidences of liver cancer than normal. No one knows if this was from liver flukes, Agent Orange, or both.
33. These worms like the liver, because it is full of stored nutrients, like glycogen, iron, cholesterol, and vitamins.
34. The life cycle shown below depicts the life cycle of the liver fluke, *Fasciola hepatica*.

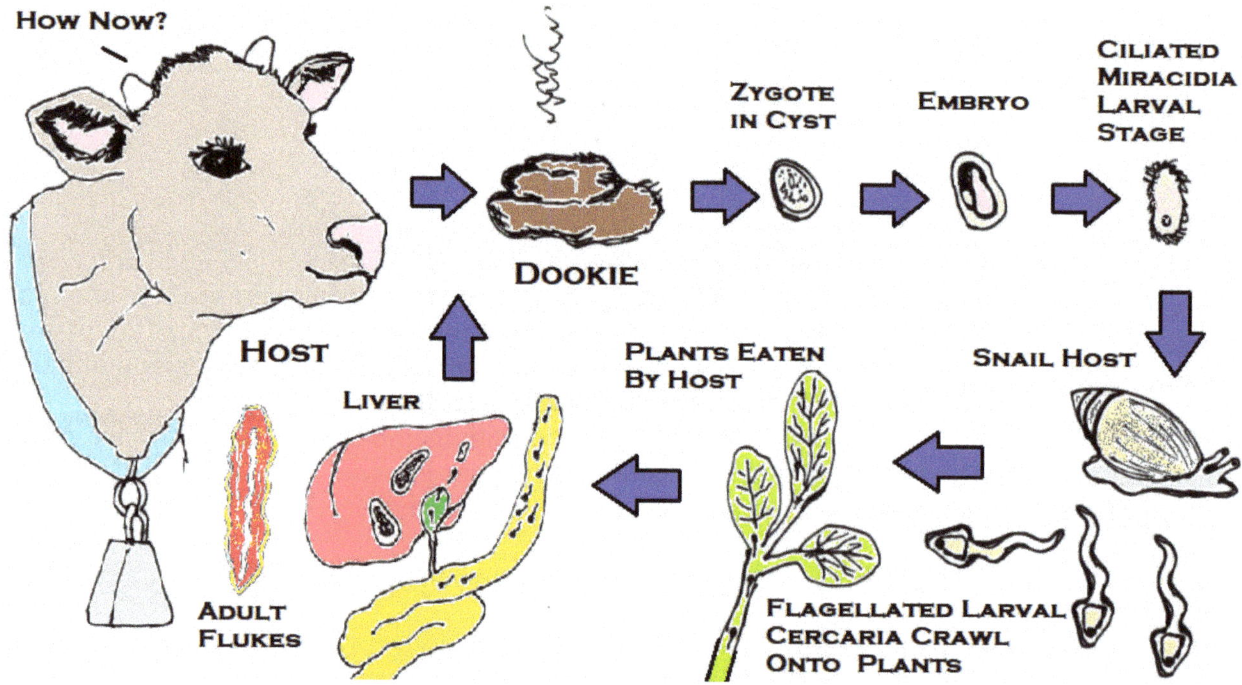

35. **Lung flukes**, *Paragonimus westermani*, invade lungs, rather than the liver. Their larvae pass through two different hosts, with the **miracidia** living in a snail, while the **cercaria** invade the muscles of crustaceans.
36. Lung flukes attack whatever mammal is unlucky enough to ingest undercooked crab, shrimp, or crawfish meat. People and fish-eating carnivores like tigers, otters, and fishing cats are the usual victims.
37. When they stay restricted to the lungs, the symptoms are similar to tuberculosis, with a bloody cough and calcification of cysts inside the lungs. However, if cysts hatch in the spine, heart, or brain, it can be fatal.
38. **Schistosomias**, which is caused by several species of tropical flukes, is the easiest flatworm infection to catch. If you go to the tropics, stay out of polluted and/or slow-moving rivers!

39. Microscopic larvae of these flatworms leave their snail hosts, burrow through the skin of their victim, and work their way through the blood stream until they decide on which internal organ they would like to inhabit.
40. Schistosomiasis causes extreme illness, high fever, and skin lesions where the larvae entered. The worms cause lesions on the spleen, liver, intestine, or spinal cord that can lead to organ failure and death if untreated.
41. Now let's move on to another group of disgusting flatworms and be thankful that we aren't fish.
42. Members of **Class Monogenea** look strongly resemble flukes in appearance and anatomy.
43. However, the life cycle of monogenean worms differs from the flukes. Instead of needing an intermediate host, worms in this group complete their entire life cycle in one place.
44. **Monogenean worms** most commonly attach to the gills and skin of bony fish, the skin of turtles, hippos, stingrays, sharks, or other marine and aquatic animals. Most are **ectoparasites** rather than endoparasites.
45. Since they need to find their hosts, they never devolved eyes like the flukes did.
46. Some monogenean worms are also **viviparous**, given birth to live larvae, rather than laying eggs, which is unusual among invertebrates and unique among flatworms.
47. Now let's move on to the group that can probably be crowned kings of disgusting....namely, the tapeworms.
48. Tapeworms have devolved their eyes and gastrovascular cavity. Since all they do is sit around in digesting food stealing nutrients like a bunch of slobs, they have few needs that the host doesn't take care of.
49. Nearly every warm-blooded animal species in existence have species of tapeworms that infect them.
50. Tapeworms have essentially been reduced to reproductive machines. They are **hermaphrodites**.
51. Segments are known as **proglottids**. Each proglottid is basically an autonomous worm. Each segment has a pair of testes and a pair of ovaries capable of producing and receiving sperm and laying thousands of eggs.
52. In addition to **sexual reproduction**, tapeworms are experts at **asexual reproduction**. Each proglottid can clone itself via **budding**. When segments break off, they become a completely autonomous worm.
53. The front segment of any tapeworm is specialized to become a grappling hook. This segment has a spiky **scolex** that acts like a grappling hook, sticking to the intestinal wall. There are also **suckers** that help the worm cling.
54. From there, they basically just sit in digested food and mooch off the host. One tapeworm is barely noticeable to most hosts, but problems arise when an infestation occurs.
55. An infestation can cause weight loss, malnutrition, intestinal blockage, and in rare cases, death.
56. Deaths from blockages to occur, but usually a more horrifying fate is the cause of mortalities. Sometimes worm cysts lose their way, take a wrong turn, and end up in muscles or in the brain.
57. If they hatch into adults in the brain, you're talking straight horror movie stuff there.

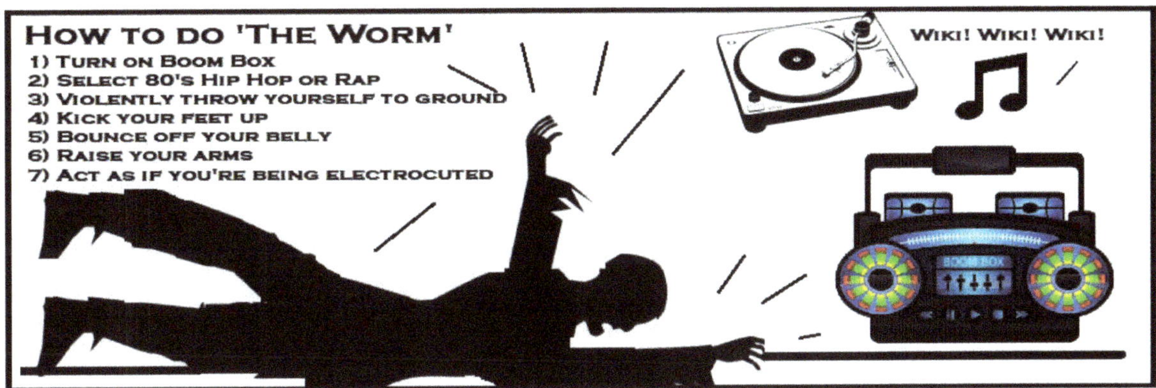

58. The simplicity of tapeworm anatomy is shown below. Essentially they have been reduced to a pair of gonads.

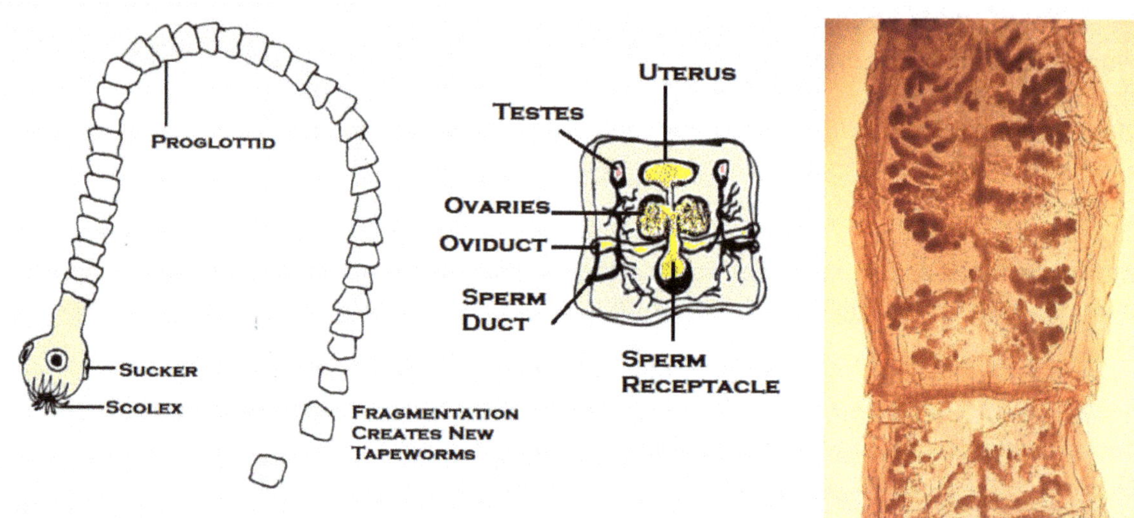

59. Representative members of each group of flatworms are shown in the diagrams below, along with specific facts that are unique to each class.

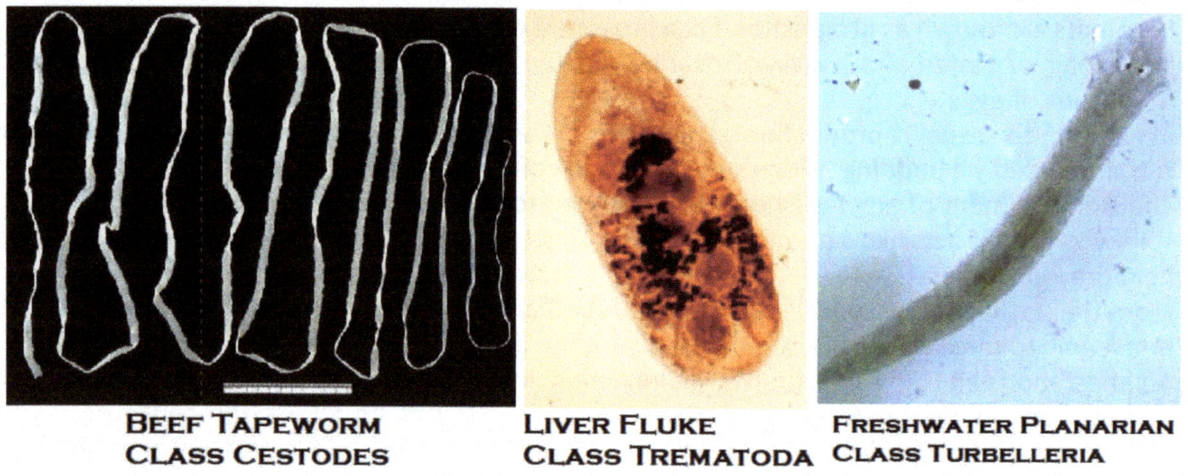

Beef Tapeworm
Class Cestodes

Liver Fluke
Class Trematoda

Freshwater Planarian
Class Turbelleria

E) Phylum Nemertea: Ribbon worms

1. **Nemerteans** (ribbons worms) are long, narrow, brightly colored worms found in the ocean.
2. They are also called **proboscis worms**, since they have a long hollow nose called a **proboscis** they throw at their prey like an elephant's trunk. However, unlike an elephant trunk, it is retractable.
3. The body form of ribbon worms is **acoelomate**. Their organs are squished flat together, but they do have a false body cavity called a **rhynchocoel** that holds a long feeding **proboscis** called a
4. The long sticky proboscis runs almost the entire length of the body and is controlled by a **retractor muscle**. They can extend this proboscis and grab things that they want to shove into their mouths like an elephant.
5. Evolutionarily speaking, some people think that flatworms gave rise to ribbon worms.

6. Other people think that ribbon worms used to be true **coelomates**, but de-evolved their coelom. DNA evidence seems to suggest that the second idea is correct, so they are placed in the lophotrochozoans as a result.
7. However, they have **flame cell nephridia** similar to the waste-filtering cells of planarians. This may be coincidental though, as their similar habits and needs could have caused a case of convergent evolution.
8. Another hint that suggests they were probably former coelomates, is that they have a one-way digestive system, similar to that of a roundworm, with a mouth, a long intestine, and an anus. They don't rely on a gastrovascular cavity like flatworms, which must take up food and expel waste from the same orifice.
9. Ribbon worms have a **closed circulatory system**, but lack a heart, instead relying on muscular contractions and fluid pressure inside the **rhynchocoel** to push blood through the vessels.
10. Ribbon worms have a **brain** that diverges into two ladder-like **nerve cords**, similar to that seen in annelids.
11. They have a pair of **chemosensory papillary organs** in the head that can taste and smell their surroundings, along with simple **ocelli** that can sense light and contrasts. They also have **statocysts** that keep them oriented upright.
12. Marine ribbon worms are usually **dioecious**, while all freshwater ribbon worms are **hermaphrodites**.
13. Their **gonads** are re-generated every time they reproduce and form a long row down the mesenchyme inside the body. Sperm or eggs are produced and pushed through temporary **gonopores** in the body wall.
14. **External fertilization** occurs in most species. Reproductive strategies vary, with some ribbon worms hatching from free-standing eggs. Other species hide their eggs in burrows, and others carry an **egg cocoon** until they hatch.
15. Some species, however, use **internal fertilization** and are even **viviparous,** nourishing hatching larvae from the fluids inside their body walls.
16. The diagrams below show the anatomy of a ribbon worm, along with a few pictures of ribbon worms.

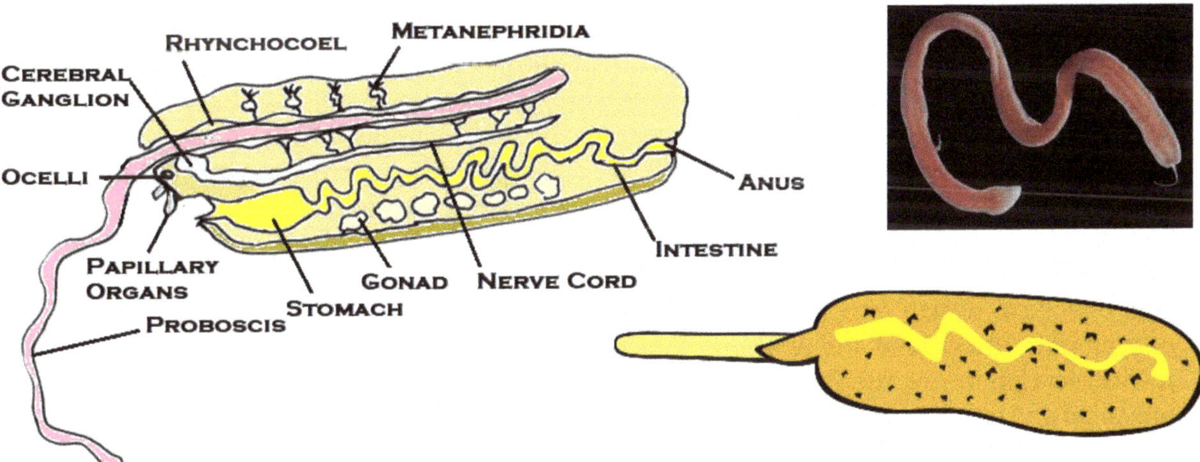

F) Phylum Annelida: Segmented Worms

1. Segmented worms are among the most primitive **triploblastic** true **coelomates**.
2. While we won't get into the debate here, before taxonomists split invertebrates into ecdysozoans and lophotrochozoans, they were the originally placed as the next phylum up the hierarchy from roundworms.

3. Annelid organs are tethered in place to the mesoderm, allowing a full 360 degree range of motion without sloshing the organs around and damaging them. Consequently, annelids are free-living, rather than internal parasites.
4. Annelid bodies are divided into 100 or more ring-like segments that can move independently of each other.
5. The segments are also NOT interchangeable and can't regenerate. What is under segment one is not the same as what's under segment 37. You can't break an earthworm in half to make more. You just kill it.
6. Segmented worms can have a fixed number of segments or they can add segments to their posterior as they grow. It all depends on the genetics of the particular classification.
7. All segmented worms use a hydraulic system of movement created by fluid pressure within the segments. They use **peristaltic movement** created when segments flex and push against each other, propelling the worm forward.
8. A layer of connective tissue called a **mesothelium** lines the interior of each segment. These layers of wrapping abut to vertical walls of muscle called **mesenteries** that form walls between each segment.
9. Consequently, each segment has its own little body cavity, or **coelom**. Each segment is, in essence, its own water balloon. However, there are openings for nerves and digestive organs to pass through these segments.
10. All **annelids** have bristle-like appendages called **setae** on their ventral surface.
11. Each segment has pairs of these. Depending on the type or worm, they can be used for gripping, locomotion, as gill-like respiratory appendages, or to deliver venom.
12. The setae are why the belly of an earthworm feels like sandpaper. These are used to gain leverage against slippery surfaces as the worm or leech propels itself through sticky mud.
13. In the case of **polychaete bristle worms**, these bristles can be quite large. Some of these worms use them for respiration, as leg-like appendages, or to harbor stingers.
14. Now let's look deeper at the anatomy of annelids.
15. Let's start at the front segment and walk back, system-by-system. The first segment is called the **prostomium** and this is where the brain and sensory organs are located. The engine is at the front of the bus, so to speak.
16. The **cerebral ganglion** is a puny, primitive little brain. It wraps around the **pharynx** at the throat and then bifurcates into two lateral ventral **never cords**. These run the length of the body.
17. At each segment, the nerve cord divides off into a ganglion that controls very large ladder-like nerves.
18. The muscles of each segment are controlled by numerous nerves, giving the worm a lot of precise 360-degree control of their musculature. Red wigglers make this known when fishermen try to bait their hooks.
19. This biological design also inspired the timeless and classy 'worm' breakdance. Oddly, throwing oneself onto the ground and writhing along on the belly actually began in the 1920's.
20. It was recycled during the funk period of the 1970s and by Michael Jackson in the 80's. Now it's so universal and ubiquitous that no one would think anything of it, if their grandparents dropped to the floor and did the worm.
21. Some segmented worms have eyes, while others do not. Predatory **polychaete** marine worms usually DO have eyes, while earthworms and leeches don't really need them. It's all a matter of evolution.
22. Large predatory **polychaetes** have complex **compound eyes** that rival those of insects, while others, such as tubeworms have simpler **ocelli** that can sense the shadows of prey items or predators above them.
23. Some **tubeworms** and burrowers like clam worms have **statocyst organs** that are filled with little crystals of calcified material that fall onto pressure nerves and tell them which way is up and which way is down.

24. Many segmented worms also have organs called **nuchae** that are basically clusters of cilia on the segments near their head. These are used as feelers like the antennae of insects.
25. The second segment of an annelid is known as the **peristomium**. The **labia** of the mouth emerge from here. Mouth modifications vary by the lifestyle and the needs of each particular type of worm.
26. **Leeches** can be sub-divided by how they feed. Most leeches have three pairs of calcified blade-like **tooth jaws** inside their mouth, along with a gland that secretes a cocktail of enzymes, anticoagulants, and anesthetic.
27. **Proboscis leeches** don't have these tooth jaws because most of them are predatory. Instead, they protrude the muscles of their pharynx and suck in their prey like a vacuum cleaner.
28. **Earthworms** often have sticky pads in the roof of their mouth. These secrete mucus and grab food like glue traps.
29. **Tubeworms** typically have a crown of cilia that helps them filter feed trash out of the water.
30. **Polychaete bristle worms** can have some truly frightening equipment up in their grill. Depending on the genus and species, these can be anything from small bristles to large razor-sharp blade-like teeth.
31. The material in these jaws has been found to be unique in nature. Basically unbreakable, they are extremely durable and hard proteins built around chelated metal ions like iron and magnesium.
32. Moving past the annelid mouth, the next stop along the digestive tract is the throat-like **pharynx**, which funnels into the blender-jar like **crop**.
33. Instead, the crop feeds food particles through the densely muscular **gizzard**. Much like it does in a bird, the gizzard uses sand grains and tiny pebbles to pulverize the food and increase its surface area for digestion.
34. The gizzard releases food into an extremely long **intestine** that runs the entire length of the remainder of the body.
35. Each segment within an annelid is lined with a layer of connective tissue called the **mesothelium** that is innervated and impregnated with blood vessels. Fluids build up in each segment, allowing their **peristaltic locomotion**.
36. This design makes it difficult or impossible for organs to occupy much space within a segment unless they are running right down the middle of the animal, such as the **endoderm**-derived **intestine**.
37. While he intestine secretes digestive enzymes into the food slurry and extracts nutrients into the bloodstream, it still needs some help. However, you won't find a liver or a pancreas in a dissected worm.
38. Some species compensate for this. They use clusters of specialized **chlorogonen cells** that perform similar functions to many of the tasks of the liver. In addition to making enzymes, they store fat and glycogen in each segment.
39. Since the intestines are not coiled to increase their surface area, as they are in higher organisms, to get enough nutrients out of the food, this necessitates that the digestive tract spans a huge percentage of the body's length
40. If you were a worm, your intestine would start somewhere around your collar bone and you would have to be about 40 feet tall to get enough out of your food. Needless to say, we would all look like freaks.
41. We would all hit our heads on doorways and have to drive school buses laying on our bellies. However, we would be able to get Frisbees off the roof and everyone would be tall enough to 'ride this ride', so there's that....
42. The food that goes INTO the digestive tract varies by the type of segmented worm.
43. **Oligochaete worms** (earthworms) mostly nosh on dead leaves, organic material in soil, and assorted detritus.
44. **Hirudinids** (leeches) enjoy a good blood meal, which is still relatively easy to digest.

45. However, **polychaete worms** (marine worms) are predatory carnivores that subsist on seafood meals. In order to digest fish and other small invertebrates, their digestive tracts have to be a little extra.
46. Worm body plans factor into their internal anatomy, with regard to removal of waste products from the digestive process. Just like any other organism that metabolizes proteins, there are toxins that must be dealt with.
47. Because of the restrictive **mesothelium** between segments, fluids build up in each segment, there are tradeoffs. While this allows the pressure to build up for **peristaltic locomotion**, it still restricts fluid flow between segments.
48. This means that a classical **excretory system** is not a great design. Kidneys and plumbing really won't fit all the way through the animal. Alternately, annelids filter soluble waste products from each segment.
49. Pairs of tiny organs called **metanephridia** filter the blood and secrete urine from openings at each segment.
50. Speaking of blood, let's go back to the front of the worm again and examine the **circulatory** and **respiratory systems** used by segmented worms....at least those that have them.
51. Segmented worms are usually large enough to need some help above what simple diffusion can provide.
52. They often use oxygen-carrying pigments. Some types have red **hemoglobin** while others use a green pigment called **giant hemoglobin**, which is molecularly similar (also iron-based), but is forest green in color.
53. The front few anterior segments of **Oligochaetes** and most **Polychaetes** contain two lateral blood vessels with five pairs of muscular rings. Lateral vessels connect the two vertically-oriented blood vessels.
54. These form ten little crude pumping **hearts** that push the fluid through a ladder-like system of blood vessels.
55. Additionally fluid pressure from the peristaltic movements of the worm ensure that their **closed circulatory system** manages to push the fluid throughout the body of the worm in a complete circuit.
56. **Leeches** use two lateral blood vessels, but the interior of their bodies is not nearly as divided into distinct septa as those of earthworms. They can't rely on as much internal pressure to keep squishing the blood through the vessels.
57. Instead, their **hearts** are spread out vertically down each blood vessel, almost independently of one another. These little pumping muscles provide pumping pressure in places that the wall of the body cannot.
58. **Respiratory** strategies differ between the types of segmented worms. Diffusion is the primary source of oxygen for all segmented worms, but some of them are fat enough that they need some additional help.
59. Bristle worms often make use of extensions of the skin called **parapodia** that extend into thin little filaments. These are solely for the purpose of gaining surface area for oxygen to diffuse into capillary beds beneath them.
60. **Parapodia** extend into the bristle-like **setae** that can also be used like gill filaments in some species.
61. Since leeches are usually big fat tubs of goo that live in stanky anoxic swamp mud, they also need some help. Many types of leeches extend the epithelium layer into their body cavity to form **respiratory sacs** that act like crude lungs.
62. So what about the love lives of worms? Inquiring minds want to know. The love lives of these slimy boogers actually provide some evolutionary clues that may explain how invertebrates might have originally diverged.
63. Since life began in the ocean, the assumption is that marine polychaetes probably provide the best clues about how everything began for the annelids. They also have the most diverse type of reproductive strategies.

64. Like the more primitive roundworms, many marine polychaetes have **separate sexes**, which is more atypical for **lophotrochozoans** than **hermaphroditism**.
65. Furthermore, there are some mollusk-like things about the way that some of these marine bristle worms reproduce. Some species of polychaetes have a larval stage called a **trochophore**.
66. **Trochophores** are shaped like a toy top. They swim through the plankton using two lines of cilia along their midsection, along with a tuft of cilia at the top of the body. Oysters and other shellfish have similar larvae.
67. However, some marine polychaetes have evolved past this point, enclosing their larvae in egg cases that remain at the bottom. This prevents their offspring from mostly being decimated by filter-feeding.
68. Some polychaetes use external fertilization and broadcast their sperm and eggs into the water, other species use internal fertilization and direct male-female mating, while others are sequential or permanent **hermaphrodites**.
69. There are even polychaetes that seem to only develop sex organs when they need them and other species that reproduce once and die. They are among the most reproductively diverse and confusing groups of animals known.
70. In sum, if you think some species of marine worm reproduces in a certain way, they probably do. Scientists haven't even figured out a rhyme or reason WHY or HOW some species within the SAME classifications reproduce.
71. Almost all earthworms and leeches are lifelong **hermaphrodites**, though some leeches start out as male and change sexes as they age. Evolutionarily speaking, hermaphroditism makes sense for, since it doubles offspring numbers.
72. Worms and leeches are seen as food by most of nature. They are protein spaghetti for birds, lizards, turtles, fish, and even some lady named Carol that I once met, who bakes them into chocolate chip cookies. I did not take one.
73. Therefore, doubling their reproductive rate makes sense. Earthworms and leeches typically line up in opposite directions, match up the **sperm ducts** and **oviducts** and exchange sperm. These are stored in the **spermathecae**.
74. From there, the eggs are fertilized in the ovary and the eggs are encased in a mucus-laden **egg cocoon** produced by the **clitellum**, a collar-shaped gland that interrupts the worm's segments about a third of the way back.
75. The egg-coccoon is laid into the soil or mud, and from there, offspring hatch and resemble miniature adults.
76. Now that we've covered the anatomical layout of annelids, let's take a look at how they are divided into classifications. Anatomy plays a large role in these subdivisions.
77. Given their reproductive diversity and origin within the ocean, **polychaetes** are usually thought to be the most ancient group of annelids. Their classification is still up in the air.
78. **Class Polychaeta** is problematic to many taxonomists, who consider it to be paraphyletic, since the huge number of differences in their reproductive abilities, habits, and lifestyles, suggests different origins.
79. There are around a dozen families and orders of **basal polychaetes** that aren't much like the other members of the group and that no one really knows what to do with. They all seem like ancient, weird evolutionary dead ends.
80. For instance, the two examples shown below are basal polychaetes. They have some commonalities with the internal anatomy of other annelids, but they also share some characterstics of other groups of worms.
81. No one really knows what to do with them and only about five people in the entire world really care, so we will move on from them. Unless you are a starfish or a crab, they aren't your problem.

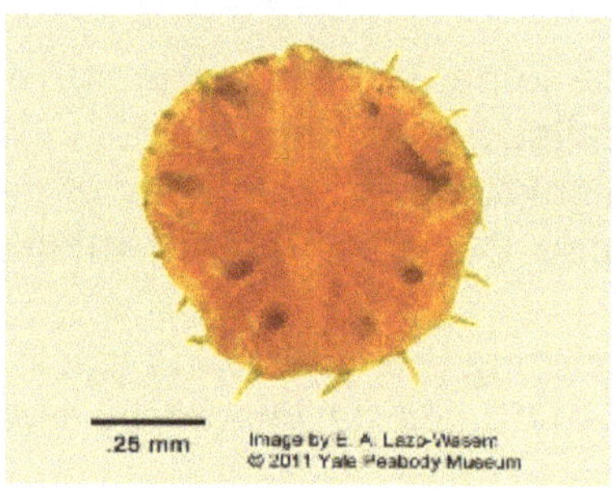

FAMILY MYZOSTOMIDAE
PARASITES OF STARFISH AND OTHER ECHINODERMS

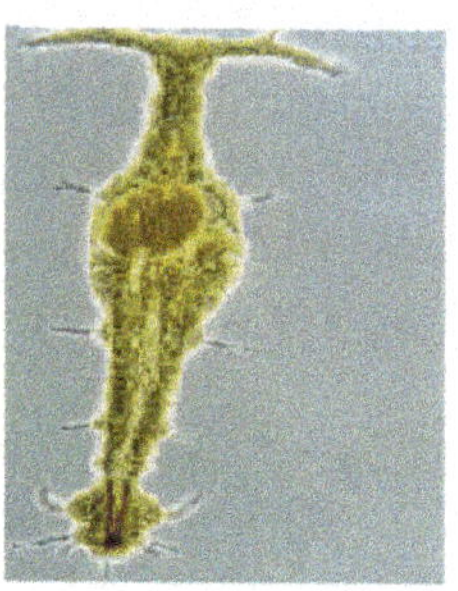

FAMILY HISTRIOBDELLIDAE
PARASITES OF CRUSTACEAN GILLS

A SELECTION OF REALLY STUPID LAWSUITS

*A woman visited Wildwater Kingdom (PA) on Halloween. She did not expect employees to be dressed in monster costumes and ran from them in terror, injuring herself. She sued....of course she did.
*A man who looks sort of like a very short Michael Jordan sued MJ and Nike $416 million each for defamation and emotional trauma for looking like him.
*A man sued Kroger and Dillon Foods for $7 million after he developed lung problems from his habit of huffing the fumes from microwave popcorn.

82. Polychaetes run the gamut of evolutionary designs. Fireworms and predatory Eunicid worms are predators. The former patrol the reefs looking for victims, while the latter prefer to ambush unsuspecting victims as they pass.

83. The most horrifying of the Eunicid worms is from Australia, is as big as a garden hose, and grows to 15 feet long. It's basically a worm snake. It ambushes fish the size of bream and drags them to a watery grave.

84. Other polychaetes are more peaceful citizens of Neptune's realm. A number of different orders of polychaetes use their bristles to filter plankton and edible trash out of the water. Others cruise along looking for delicious garbage.

85. The diagram below certainly only scratches the surface of the number of different diverse orders of marine polychaetes. However, it does impart the relative diversity of lifestyles and body designs.

ORDER AMPHINOMIDAE
SEA MICE AND FIREWORMS. HAVE VENOMOUS BRISTLES. PREDATORS OF CORALS, ANEMONES, CRABS.

ORDER EUNICIDAE
PREDATORY MARINEWORMS DIVIDED FRONT SEGMENTS WITH ANTENNAE, PALPS, COMPOUND EYES, JAWS.

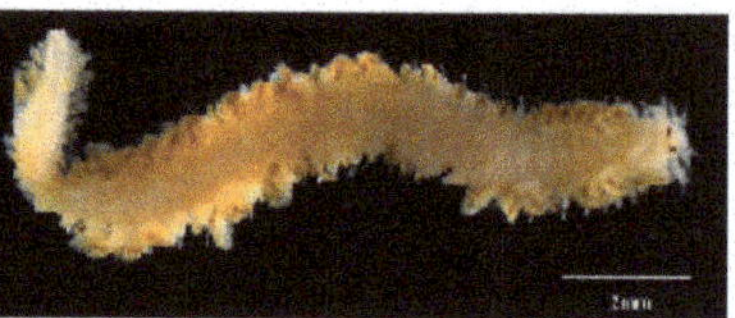

ORDER PHYLLOCIDIDAE
BENTHIC SCAVENGERS AND PREDATORS OF SMALL ANIMALS. HAVE 1-2 PAIRS OF EYES & SMALL ANTENNAE. LIVE IN BURROWS.

ORDER CHAETOPTERIDAE
LIVE IN MUCUS-LINED BURROWS AND FILTER FEED TRASH OUT OF THE WATER.

ORDER POGONOPHORA
GIANT TUBEWORMS. LIVE IN SUPERHEATED WATER NEAR VOLCANIC VENTS AND HAVE SYMBIOTIC ARCHAEBACTERIA THAT LIVE IN GUT AND PROVIDE NUTRITION.

ORDER SABELLIDA
CHRISTMAS-TREE AND FEATHER DUSTER WORMS. LIVE IN BURROWS AND PROTRUDE TO FILTER FEED.

86. **Polychaetes** are considered to be less evolved than the remaining annelids because of their reproductive inconsistencies, their separate sexes, the absence of a fixed number of segments, and several other issues.

87. The **Oligochaetes**, by comparison, are far more predictable. No oligochaetes have separate **trochophore** juvenile stages, but they hatch from eggs and start out as miniature versions of adults. All are **hermaphrodites**.
88. Most species of oligochaetes have a genetically fixed number of segments and defined reproductive organs.
89. All oligochaetes (and segmented worms more advanced than themselves) have a **clitellum**, which is a collar-like interruption to the segments, where reproductive organs are located.
90. Morphologically speaking, oligochaetes have a lot more similarities among themselves than polychaetes.
91. There are around 7,000 species of earthworms, and another 2,000 native to freshwater, marine, or groundwater habitats. In spite of differences in size and color, they all pretty much have similar body forms.
92. The oligochaetes are divided into **Order Haplotaxida**, **Order Lumbriculida**, and **Order Moniligastrida.** Differences in segmentation and the location of the **clitellum** and **gonopores** are the bases for the divisions into orders.
93. It would be difficult for an amateur to classify an earthworm into orders. Correction...while it might not be THAT difficult with some sort of taxonomic guide, it is not likely that an amateur would actually BOTHER to do so.
94. After all, how many people do you know that are interested in taking a closer look at a worm's doo-dads?
95. The ecology of earthworms in the soil is interesting, in that different species claim different **niches** in the soil.
96. Epigeic worm species remain on the surface, endogeic worms make a system of lateral burrows, with anecic worms tunnel deep into the sub-soil. All three types are important to the mixing and microbiota of healthy soil.
97. The diagram on the next page depicts worms from all three classifications. The top-dwelling earthworm in the diagram (the red worm) is a member of Order Lumbriculida, while the deeper worms are members of Haplotaxida.
98. The giant blue earthworm on the right is a member of Moniligastrida. Those species tend to only be found in Asia.

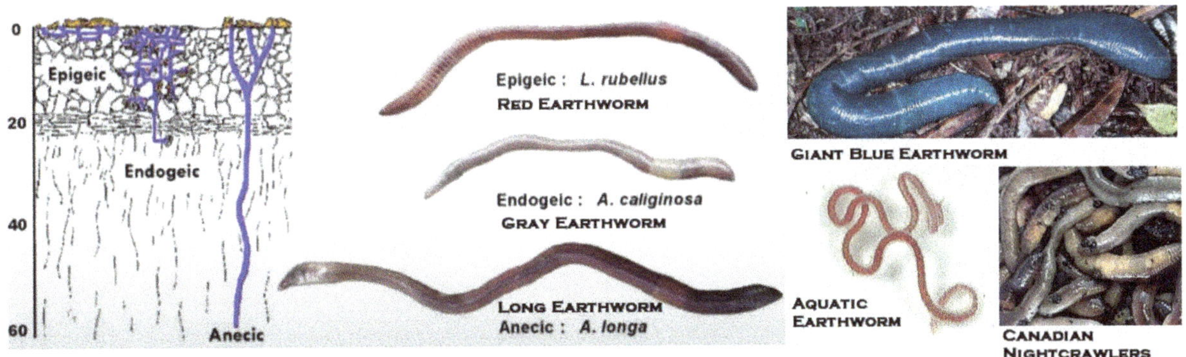

99. Now we move on to three orders of annelids that have evolved to become parasitic. A few anatomical differences evolved progressively among these groups. Among these is a far less restriction among septa between segments.
100. **Order Acanthobdellida** contains a single species of leech-like worm that parasitizes the gills of fish. It is not a true leech. In spite of having jaw-like mouthparts like a leech and being a blood feeder, it lacks a sucker on the tail.

101. **Order Branchiobdellida** is a group of **ectoparasites** that mostly prey on crustaceans. They DO have a sucker on their tail like a leech, but they have several unique anatomical features that differ from leeches.
102. For instance, they have de-evolved the front two segments at the head, have tentacles around the mouth, and have reduced their total body segmentation to only 15 segments. Leeches have far more segments than this.
103. The pictures below show these obscure annelids.

ORDER ACANTHOBDELLIA
FISH PARASITE

ORDER BRANCHIOBDELLINA
CRUSTACEAN PARASITES

A CONTINUED SELECTION OF MORE REALLY STUPID LAWSUITS

*Robert Lee Brock sued Robert Lee Brock for $5 million as a consequence of Robert Lee Brock causing Robert Lee Brock to imbibe alcoholic beverages, resulting in his own arrest for public drunkenness. Since has incarcerated and had no income, he asked the state to pay the damages to Robert Lee Brock. Somehow, the suit made it to court.

* A prisoner sued the state of Michigan because the prison food he was being served was causing him hardships due to excessive flatulence.

*A woman allowed her son to run loose in a furniture store as she shopped. Later, she tripped over her own spoiled brat and broke her ankle. She sued the furniture store for allowing the situation to occur.

104. **Order Hirudinea** contains the true leeches. Leeches have a fully developed sucker on their tail, air sacs for breathing that sit adjacent to their lateral blood vessels, and either biting mouth parts or a distendible pharynx.
105. Some leeches are blood-feeding parasites, while others have de-evolved this lifestyle and become aquatic predators of invertebrates and other small animals.
106. The pictures below detail several families of leeches and provide pictures of representative species.

JAWED LEECHES THAT LACK A PROBOSCIS

SUB-ORDER EROPBDELLIFORMES

AQUATIC INVERTEBRATE PREDATORS. NO LONGER SUCK BLOOD.

SUB-ORDER HIRUDINIFORMES

BLOOD-SUCKING ECTOPARASITES WITH ANESTHETIC GLANDS & ANTICOAGULANTS.

LEECHES WITH A SUCKING PROBOSCIS

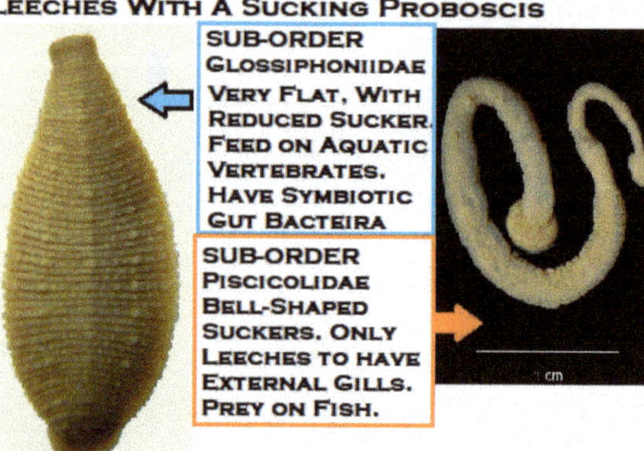

SUB-ORDER GLOSSIPHONIIDAE
VERY FLAT, WITH REDUCED SUCKER. FEED ON AQUATIC VERTEBRATES. HAVE SYMBIOTIC GUT BACTEIRA

SUB-ORDER PISCICOLIDAE
BELL-SHAPED SUCKERS. ONLY LEECHES TO HAVE EXTERNAL GILLS. PREY ON FISH.

F) Phylum Echiura: Spoon Worms

1. Phylum Echiura includes spoon worms, which are considered to be close cousins of Annelids, while some biologists even classify them within the group.
2. Spoonworms have a proboscis organ that cannot be retracted into the body. They use it like an elephant's trunk to scoop food from the bottom into their mouths. They range in size from an inch to several feet long.

3. True coelomates like the annelids, they have concentric segments of muscular bands around the body. However, there are a few anatomical proboscis differences between spoon worms and annelids.
4. Unlike annelids, most of their body is not covered with bristle-like setae.
5. In addition to nephridial organs, spoonworms also have a pair of ciliated diverticulae that filter their body fluids for waste and expel the waste from the anus. This is probably to account for their large size.
6. Likewise, spoonworms use their anus to breathe. They oxygenated water in through the anus and expel it like a bellows. Likewise, they can also use diffusion through the proboscis and sin to get oxygen.
7. Also due to their larger and fatter sausage-like bodies, their intestines are coiled many times to get enough nutrition, unlike the long straight intestines of most annelids.
8. All spoon worms are marine and almost all live in either burrows or tubes and filter the sediment for food with their spoons. The tube-dwelling species create a case of mucus and sediment around themselves.
9. A picture of a spoonworm follows the next section over their cousins, the peanut worms.

H) Phylum Sipunculata: Peanut Worms

1. **Phylum Sipunculata** includes the peanut worms. Like the proboscis worms, some taxonomists also place them among the annelids. However, unlike annelids, they have no discernible **segmentation**.
2. **Peanut worms**, unlike proboscis worms CAN retract their proboscis back into a ciliated mouth. The mouth, itself, has about two dozen ciliated **tentacles** that are used to help it filter through trash it would enjoy eating.
3. Most peanut worms are detritus feeders like the proboscis worms, but a few of them are capable of filter feeding plankton out of the water with highly modified tentacles that they wave around.
4. Because they have a large surface area, the tentacles also double in their function, also serving as organs of oxygenation for the body fluids, much like a bunch of feathery gills.
5. Their bodies change from a tapering worm-shape when the proboscis is extended into a peanut-shape when the proboscis is drawn back into their heads.
6. Peanut worms have **chemoreceptors** on the tips of the tentacles, capable of tasting the water, and they also have light-senstive cells that help them sense general shapes, shadows, predators, and prey.
7. The digestive system of sipunculates is also coiled, rather than like the linear tract of true annelids.
8. Some peanut worms are burrowers, but others also live in the carcasses of large fish and whales, in tunnels under coral heads, in empty shells, under masses of seaweed, in rock crevices, and in split-level neighborhood homes.
9. Most peanut worms reproduce sexually and mate in large swarms. Their larval stages are **trochophores**. However, some peanut worms are **parthenogenetic** and these species are entirely female with self-fertilizing eggs.

IN HONOR OF PEANUT WORMS.... FACTS ABOUT PEANUTS!

1) THERE ARE NEARLY 1500 PEANUTS IN A 32 OZ. JAR OF PEANUT BUTTER
2) NGUBA WAS THE CONGOLESE WORD FOR PEANUTS WHERE THEY CAME FROM.
3) NGUBA BECAME 'GOOBER' IN THE COLONIAL SOUTH WHERE THEY WERE GROWN.
4) PEANUTS ARE LEGUMES, NOT NUTS. THEY ARE RELATED TO PEAS AND BEANS.
5) ABOUT 2% OF KIDS ARE ALLERGIC TO PEANUTS, THE MOST COMMON FOOD ALLERGY.
6) A 32 OUNCE JAR OF PEANUT BUTTER IS LEGALLY ALLOWED TO HAVE 273 BUG PARTS.
7) JIMMY CARTER WAS A GOOBER-EATING PEANUT FARMER BEFORE BEING PRESIDENT.

10. The picture at right shows a peanut worm, while the picture on the left shows the aforementioned spoonworm.

SPOONWORM

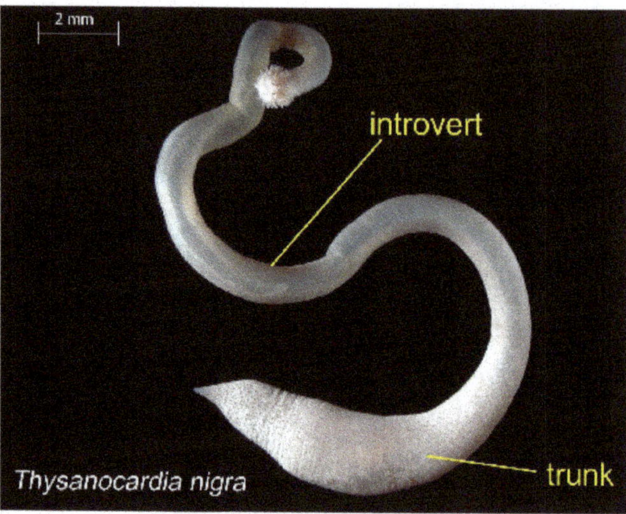

PEANUT WORM

I) Phylum Mollusca: Snails, Chitons, Bivalves, and Cephalopods

1. **Phylum Mollusca** includes lunged and gilled snails of all types, limpets, chitons, bivalves, and cephalopods. In spite of a few unifying characteristics that unify them in classification, they are a highly diverse lot.
2. In many ways, mollusks appear to be the natural evolutionary progression past the segmented worms. They are soft, muscular, and covered in mucus. The more primitive members are still **hermaphrodites.**
3. Like some of the polychaete worms, the larval stage of some mollusks is a planktonic **trochophore**. However, not all mollusks fit this bill, contributing another layer of mystery to just who evolved from who and how.
4. Like all **lophotrochozoans**, mollusks have a soft muscular body that is supported hydrostatically by fluid pressure within the tissues. In at least one life stage, all mollusks also have tentacles surrounding the mouth.
5. Mollusks are the largest and most evolutionarily successful group of lophotrochozoans, with more than 84,000 known species, and second in ubiquity only to the **arthropods** among invertebrates.
6. Let's start by describing what all mollusks DO have in common, before diverging into discussions about the various taxa included under the wide umbrella of the phylum.
7. The **mantle** is an organ common to all mollusks. It is a muscular membrane that forms a protective covering around the **visceral mass** (organs). In some mollusks, cells in the mantle secrete a **shell**, while it is naked in others.
8. The mantle forms the **coelom** in the mollusk body. Among mollusks with **open circulatory systems**, this open pocket forms the **hemocoel**, which is a reservoir where blood and interstitial fluids collect.
9. The mantle typically continues well past the body cavity, with flaps wrapping back inward on both sides to form ravioli-like pockets for the respiratory organs.
10. There, the gills or lungs sit inside this pouch, oxygenating the fluids of the **hemocoel**, before the heart picks them back up and sprays them back over the rest of the organs or diverts them through vessels.
11. In **gastropods** (snails), **bivalves** (shellfish), and several other taxa of mollusks, **epithelial cells** on the outer margin of the mantle secrete protective layered shells composed of calcium carbonate and proteins.

12. Another commonality in most mollusks, other than bivalves, is the presence of a scraping mouthpart called the **radula**. The radula is made of **chitin** and is usually ridged or toothed.
13. In snails, limpets, and chitins, the radula is something like a file or a paint-scraper. It is used to dislodge algae from surfaces when they feed. In the **cephalopods**, the radula has evolved into a parrot-like beak that can crack bone.
14. Another organ common to all members of the phylum is the presence of a massive muscular **foot**. The foot varies in appearance among its component classes, based on its evolved functional purpose.
15. In snails, limpets, and chitons, the foot functions like a giant suction cup. It is used for clinging to surfaces as they feed, especially where currents or pounding waves might dislodge them or smash them into the rocks.
16. In bivalves, the foot is often lengthened into a finger-like appendage used for digging burrows. In the case of the geoduck clam, the foot is a foot-long whopper. Typically, bivalve feet are delicious battered and fried.
17. The foot bears little resemblance to its original form in the **cephalopods**, since it is divided into arms and tentacles used for manipulating objects with impressive control. Octopi can unscrew jars and paint pictures with theirs.
18. Compared to most invertebrates, most mollusks (but not all) have impressively large brains. One anatomical quirk is that the molluscan brain surrounds the esophagus, with the digestive tract passing through the **olfactory lobes.**
19. Like the segmented worms, the **nerve cords** then diverge laterally into two paths down both sides of the body, with the exception of the oddball bivalves, where they take three paths.
20. At this point of discussion, it is more useful to discuss each individual taxa within the phylum, since the anatomical, reproductive, and behavioral differences between groups are profound.
21. **Class Gastropoda** includes all marine and freshwater snails, gilled land snails, sea slugs, and terrestrial slugs. All of its members either have a single spiraling shell secreted by the mantle or it has devolved into a scale-like patch.
22. Snails date back 500 million years. There are at least 700 families of snails comprising around 70,000 species.
23. With so much diversity in form, it is difficult to make sweeping generalizations about the anatomy of all snails, as there is almost sure to be an exception to almost every organ system in some species.
24. Snails have been reclassified multiple times from the morphological similarities used to group them into **sub-classes** to a **clade system** based on anatomical layout, to a newer **clade system** based on molecular biology.
25. Most snail shells grow from the **mantle** in a concentric spiral, with the visceral mass beneath them also laid out in something of a spiral pattern in order to fit under the protective shell.
26. Starting at the head, the mouth of the snail is tipped with a toothed **radula** used for scraping algae. However, some species like cone shell snails have a **harpoon** organ that shoots a venom-tipped dart into prey animals.
27. Two pairs of **tentacles** act as tactile and **olfactory** receptors that let them dig and taste their way around to decide just what disgusting squishy and putrid substance might be something that they would like to eat.
28. Surrounding the mouth is a spongy **digestive gland** that secretes enzymes into the food as it enters the esophagus and stomach. This is where God's little practical joke on snails begins.
29. The digestive tract takes a horseshoe-shaped U-turn into a long intestine that passes through the visceral mass, allowing absorption of nutrients into the fluids in the **hemocoel**, before making its way back to **mantle cavity**.
30. There, snails effectively poop on top of their own heads, since their anus exits the shell above their tentacles.

31. The digestive tract passes under an **open circulatory system**, where a one or two chambered **heart** picks up **hemolymph** and trickles it over organs through open-ended blood vessels that function like a sprinkler system.
32. While major organs do have vessels, they all terminate in open ends at some point.
33. From there, the blood pools and collects in a pouch under the heart called a **hemocoel**, where the heart picks it back up again for redistribution. Their blood carries oxygen with copper-based **hemocyanin** pigments.
34. Along with shell characteristics, the **respiratory system** design is one of the characteristics used to diverge snails into sub-classes in the classical system. There are also some other anatomical differences in the viscera.
35. For the purposes of anatomical layout and ease of understanding, we will go with the anatomical clade system of classification that splits snails into groups based on their internal anatomy.
36. The diagram that follows shows the internal anatomy of snails from each group.

Sub-Class	Respiratory System	Other Visceral Differences	Usual Types of Snails in this Group
Caenogastropoda	Siphon leads into a large feather-like gill on the side of the heart.	Single-Chambered Heart Kidneys sit toward back of the shell.	Marine snails such as cone shells, murexes, moon snails, and cowries.
Archaegastropoda	Paired gills on either side of the heart sitting above the hemocoel.	Two-Chambered Heart Kidneys descend from the Hemocoel.	Limpets, turbinate snails, sea snails, nerites, cave snails, abalone.
Pulmonogastropoda	Single lung that opens to the side of the shell for oxygenation.	Single chambered heart with kidney in middle of viscera.	Land Snails, freshwater snails, terrestrial Slugs

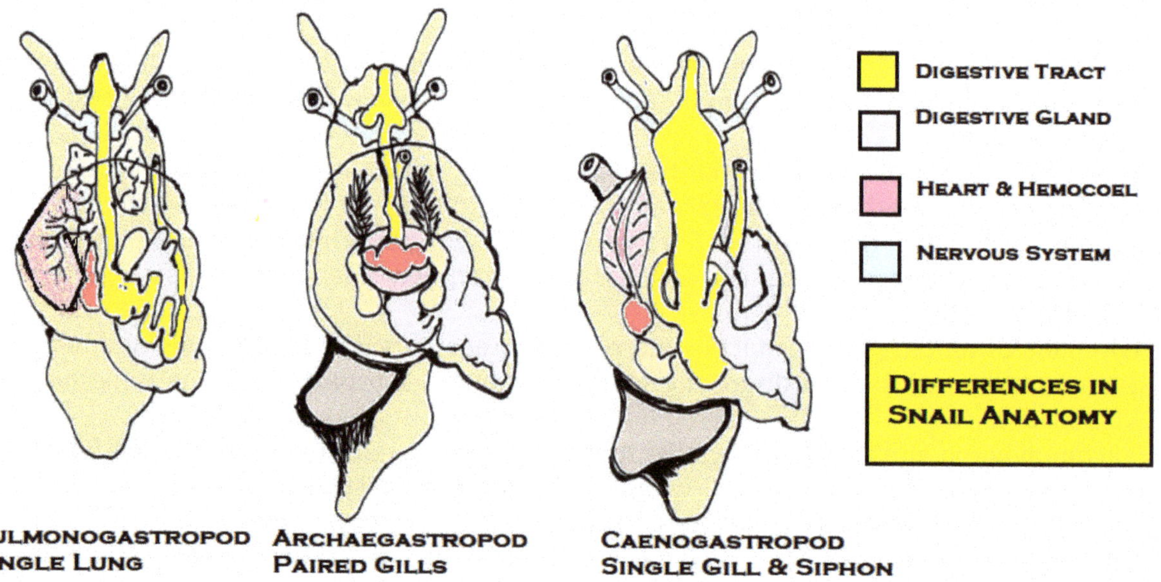

37. Adjoining the hemocoel and heart in snails are the **nephridia** or **kidneys**. They are important in excreting waste, but also play a role in **osmoregulation** of the tissues, relative to the outside environment.
38. These organs are particularly important in marine species, since salinity can fluctuate.
39. It is important to remember that the system that actually classifies snails into sub-taxa is archaic and has been replaced by a newer system of **clades** that takes molecular data and evolution into account.
40. For instance, there are lunged and gilled snails in the modern system that are more closely related to one another than they are to other snails that have convergently and independently evolved similar anatomy.
41. So, in spite of differences in placement, all gastropods have several common digestive tract features.
42. All snails have a U-shaped digestive tract that begins behind the **radula** in the mouth, follows the **pharynx** into the stomach and turns through an **intestine.**
43. A spiraling **digestive gland** sits under the curve of the shell and empties digestive enzymes into the intestine.
44. From there, the intestine moves back up to the anterior end of the shell and terminates in the anus.
45. The **nervous system** of gastropod mollusks is heavily focused on the senses.
46. Tactile information and chemical detection are particularly important to snails, since they Zamboni themselves along surfaces, slowly tasting things and feeling around for food.
47. Snails have **mechanoreceptors** that send messages about spatial position back to a center in the brain that integrates these messages. **Statoliths** inside the snail's head help it to distinguish up from down.
48. Likewise, an **olfactory lobe** of the brain also analyzes odors and tastes that are sent back to this point from hundreds of **chemoreceptors** that are located at the tips of four **tentacles.**
49. Vision quality varies among different classes and orders of gastropods. Some have simple **ocelli** that basically are just light detectors, while others have complex eyes with **lenses** and optic nerves, reminiscent of cephalopod eyes.
50. Snails have both a **peripheral nervous system** that extends to sensory and tactile nerves, while the **central nervous system** sends major bundles of **ganglia** to the **foot**, **mantle cavity**, gills or lungs, and viscera.
51. Reproductive strategy and anatomy varies greatly among orders of snails.
52. As a general rule, terrestrial and freshwater snails tend to be **hermaphroditic**. Some marine snails are regular or sequential hermaphrodites, but many groups have evolved separate sexes.
53. Hermaphroditic snails align their **genital pores** when mating.
54. All of their reproductive organs are internal, but the **penis** emerges from one snail, enters the others' **vagina**, and sends a **love dart** full of packets of sperm known as **spermatophores** into the reproductive tract of the other.
55. Once the love dart enters the **hermaphroditic duct**, it is stored in a compartment called the **spermotheca.**
56. From there, the sperm packet is digested inside of a **bursal canal**, releasing the sperm to swim to a pouch-like female compartment where fertilization of the eggs can occur.
57. **Nidamental glands** put a covering on the eggs after **albumen glands** nourish them with yolk.
58. This rigor morale is necessary on land, since sperm have no way of swimming to the egg without some sort of mechanism allowing **internal fertilization**. Hermaphroditism also doubles reproductive chances.

59. While a few **dioecious** snails (separate sexes) do use **external fertilization**, it is much more common for them to use internal fertilization like the hermaphroditic species, but each snail has one set of organs or the other.
60. There is variability among these snails as well, as some species are **sequential hermaphrodites** that have a single set of gonads known as **ovotestes** that can produce either type of gamete in response to different hormones.
61. Most of these snails begin life as males and transform into females as they become larger and more able to provide nourishment to a clutch of eggs.
62. The diagram below shows how the reproductive system of hermaphroditic snails is laid out. Dioecious snails have similar organs, but they only have one set.

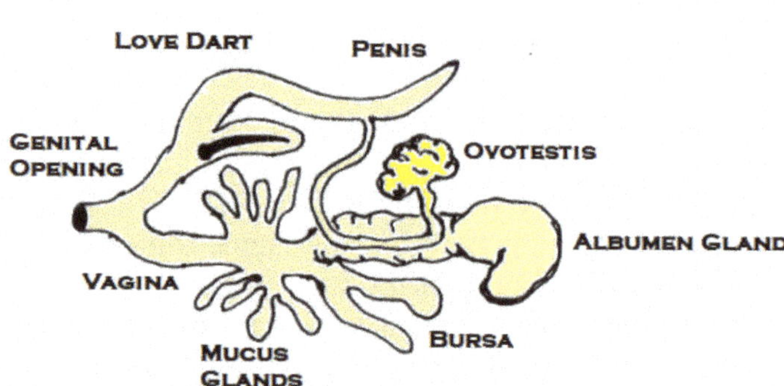

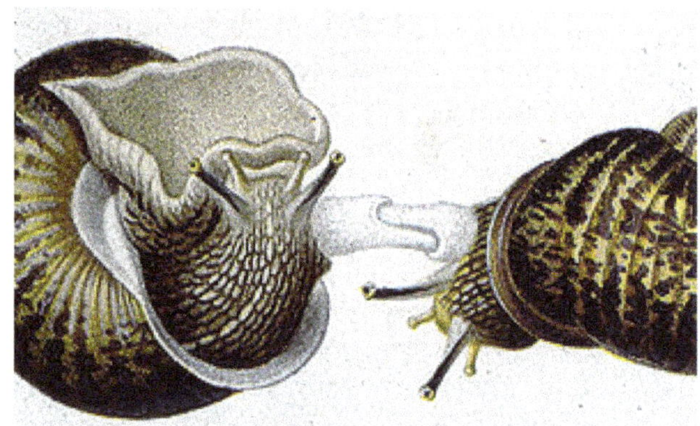

63. While it is beyond the scope of this text to dive deeply into snail taxonomy, the diagram below gives a few examples from representative gastropod orders and a few details pertaining to their classification.

PANPULMONATA: USUALLY TERRESTRIAL OR FRESHWATER, HERMAPHRODITIC. LUNGS COMMON.

LUCIDELLA SNAIL

GIANT AFRICAN LAND SNAIL

ASSASSIN SNAIL

GIANT GARDEN SLUG

EUOPISTHOBRANCHIA: SEA SLUGS AND A FEW SNAIL SPECIES WITH A FOOD-GRINDING GIZZARD

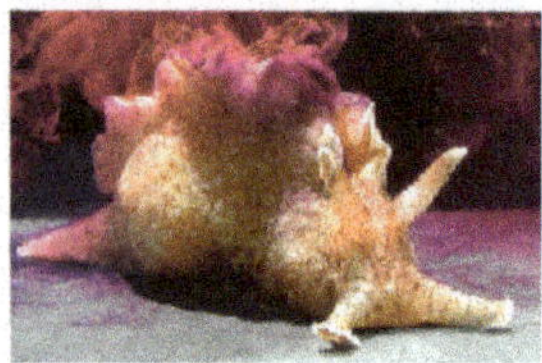
SEA HARE SLUG

ELYSIA SEA SLUG

YELLOW STRIPED NUDIBRANCH

CHROMODORIS NUDIBRANCH

NUDIPLEURA: SEA SLUGS WITH EXPOSED GILLS OUTSIDE THE BODY

CAENOGASTROPODA: MOSTLY MARINE AND AQUATIC SNAILS WITH A SIPHON AND SINGLE GILL.

COMMON WHELK

MITRE SNAIL

QUEEN CONCH

PERIWINKLE SNAIL

APPLE SNAIL

NERITOMORPHA: DIVERSE GROUPING OF ALL SHAPES. RADULA WITH MANY TEETH.

FINGERNAIL LIMPET

FLAMINGO TONGUE SNAIL

LINED NERITE SNAIL

KEYHOLE LIMPET

HELICINA SNAIL

VETIGASTROPODA: SHELLS HAVE PERPENDICULAR STRIATIONS

COLLISTOMA SNAIL

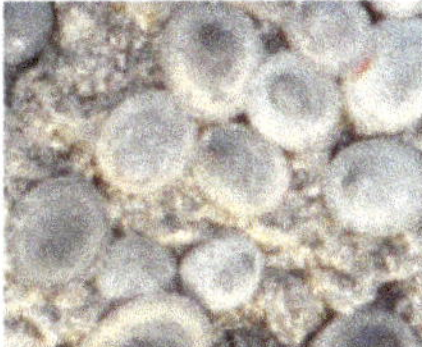
VENT LIMPET

TURBO GRAZER SNAIL

BLUE TROCHOID SNAIL

WINGED LIMPET

PATELLOGASTROPODA: TRUE LIMPETS WITH GILLS. FALSE LIMPETS HAVE LUNGS.

64. Most, but not all, land snails with lungs belong to **Order Panpulmonata**, as do their slug brethren.
65. Sea slugs aren't quite as easy to classify, as some have exposed gills, while others do not.
66. Members of **Order Euopisthobranchia** lack external gills and grind their food in a bird-like gizzard, while nudibranchs in **Order Nudipleura** have exposed gills and do not have a gizzard.
67. While there are hundreds upon hundreds of familiar sea shell animals (snails) like conchs, cowries, and whelks, the great majority of these belong either to **Order Caenogastropoda**, having a siphon and single large gill.
68. Limpets and false limpets are both really snails, with the difference being in whether they have lungs or gills.
69. While limpets seem to be their own entity but are not, there is another group of singe-shelled suction-cup shaped mollusks that do belong to their own unique class. These are the **chitons** of **Class Polyplachophora.**
70. **Chitons** have 8 overlapping calcified plates that form a plate-like dorsal shell. Each is called an **aragonite valve.**
71. By flexing the plates and leveraging their muscles, they can gain traction across the bottom and move. They can also roll up into a ball like a roly-poly to protect themselves from predators.
72. The **mantle** of the chiton forms the plates and extends under the plates in a skirt-like **girdle** that forms a suction-cup like border to the foot muscle.

73. If you turn a chiton over, you will see two grooves that run parallel lengthwise down the body. These are called **mantle cavities.** They feed a flow of water across a long line of **gill filaments** on each side.
74. The internal layout of a chiton is quite different than a gastropod snail.
75. While they do have chitin-based scraping **radulae** like snails**,** they have an additional organ called a **subradulary organ** that functions like a tongue. It is a chemosensor, tasting and smelling surfaces for edible algae.
76. Chitons have a bizarre system of vision, wherein crystallized portions of the edges of the shell form light-sensing **ocelli** that can be shaped into crude lenses that can give them information about the relative shape of objects.
77. Interestingly, chitons get by completely on clusters of **ganglia** throughout the body and they do not have a centralized **cerebral ganglion**. They simply have a ventral **nerve cord** that radiates nerves to different organs.
78. So in case you're wondering, the insinuation is true. Chitons do not have a brain.
79. The circulatory system of chitons includes a tube-shaped **heart** that is located at the far posterior of the body and pushes blood anteriorly over the organs with a different open circulatory design.
80. The digestive system has a large **stomach** that sits on top of the **digestive gland** and terminates into a long coiling **intestine**. The **kidneys** empty into the intestine and out of the anus.
81. A large internal **gonad** sits in front and under the heart on the dorsal surface of the chiton. It leads to ducts that terminate in a **gonopore** in front of the anus. Chitons are separate sexes and usually use **external fertilization**.
82. The diagram below shows several species of chitons and a generalized diagram of the internal anatomy.
83. While there are several different orders of chitons, the distinctions in taxonomy are subtle enough to be nearly meaningless to a non-expert of chitins.
84. In other words, 349,999,985 of the 350 million people in America probably don't care.

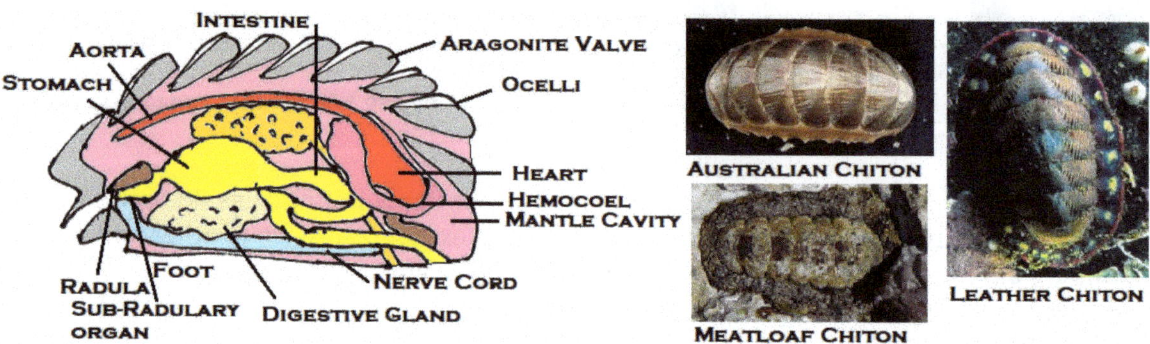

85. Now let's move on to the other major group of animals sought out by shell collectors.
86. With that, we move on to a group of mollusks that, while having anatomical similarities in some regard, are laid out completely differently than the single-shelled gastropods. **Class Bivalvia** includes shellfish with two hinged shells.
87. In the common vernacular, **Class Bivalvia** includes numerous types of shellfish, including clams, razor clams, mussels, oysters, scallops, geoducks, shipworms, cockleshells, and numerous other obscure members.
88. Bivalves have two shells secreted by a **mantle membrane**, a large powerful **foot muscle**, **siphon** organs that pump water over their gills for respiration and filter feeding, an **open circulatory system**, and no head.
89. The **mantle** forms an epithelial pouch that lines the shell, surrounding the organs in a bag, and using special glands to secrete two shells composed of calcium carbonate and proteins.

90. Since bivalves have no head to start our anatomical journey, we will start at the **incurrent siphon**, which pulls water into the shell of the bivalve, carrying whatever food particles, pheromones, or chemical signals it may carry.
91. The water is filtered through the **gills**, oxygenating the countercurrent blood vessels that run perpendicular to the water. Additionally, the gill filaments trap food particles like algae and plankton from the water with **cilia**.
92. Some bivalves have various mucus-secreting organs and glands in front of the stomach or on the gills, since particles stick better to snot. This snot is readily slurped up by connoisseurs of raw oysters on the half-shell.
93. From there, an organ called a **palp** is used like a tongue to remove the food particles. They pass down the **esophagus** to a gut, where an enzyme-secreting liver-like **midgut gland** empties into the pouch.
94. A long winding **intestine** makes an S-shape or a coil as it passes through the **mantle cavity**.
95. From there, the **anus** empties waste into the path of the **excurrent siphon**, which sprays excretions into the water.
96. The **heart** sits in a **hemocoel**, usually protected by the thickened hinge of the shell, known as the **umbo**. It has two **atria** that serve as return sinks from each gill. From there a **ventricle** pushes the blood into an **aortic bulb.**
97. The aortic bulb builds pressure in the hemolymph, since blood vessels narrow behind it, allowing pressurized hemolymph to be diverted down open-ended blood vessels that bathe each major organ.
98. Paired **kidneys** are composed of many units of filtering **nephrons** and located beneath the intestines. It filters the **hemolymph** in the mantle cavity and empties nitrogenous wastes from a **bladder** and out of the excurrent siphon.
99. Bivalves are, almost inarguably, the dumbest of all mollusks by a landslide. Since all they do is sit around and suck up garbage, they don't need a massively large **brain**, so they don't have one.
100. Instead, a **cerebral ganglion** sits atop of the viscera, controlling the senses.
101. Nerves for **mechanoreceptors** and **chemoreceptors** emanate from the ganglion in pairs, allowing shellfish to maintain their position, taste the water, and sense currents and chemical information.
102. Some species of mollusks have an organ called an **osphradium** on the underside of the shell that has concentrated nerves that are used to taste the water or detect particles.
103. Dozens of individual nerves radiate from this ganglion, **terminating** in either crude **photoreceptors** or true **eyes** of various complexity. In more primitive mollusks, photosensors only allow them to detect light in shadows.
104. In bivalves with simple eyes, such as some clams, these are just light-detecting **photosensor cells** covered with a **lens**. In scallops, the eyes have **retinas** and mirrored membranes that produce true images.
105. We would be amiss in talking about mussels if we didn't talk about their **muscles**. There are three muscles of varying importance found in bivalves, though some have de-evolved one of the adductors.
106. The **foot**, as previously mentioned, is massive compared to the size of the animal. It is particularly large in clams and mussels, since it is used for digging burrows and helping the animal push off the bottom to change direction.
107. The foot, itself, is controlled by a pair of muscles called **pedal protractors** and **retractors**. It is only found in bivalves like clams that can extend their foot. These muscles are vestigial or absent in other shellfish like oysters.
108. In the geoduck clam, the foot outweighs the entire rest of the animal and can be more than a foot long.
109. The **posterior adductor muscle** and **anterior adductor muscle** control the opening and closing of the shell and work as antagonists to the **adductor ligament** to push and pull water through the **siphons**.
110. While the adductors are large in scallops (and the part that gets sautéed in lemon butter), they are reduced in other bivalves like oysters, which have completely devolved the anterior adductor muscle.

111. Some bivalves like flame scallops have tufted muscle-controlled organs called **byssus threads** that are used to adhere to surfaces, make transfers of sperm during reproduction, or augment water filtration.
112. While a few bivalves are hermaphrodites, most are separate sexes and most use **external fertilization**.
113. The **gonads** are found either near or connected to the kidneys near the **excurrent siphon**.
114. Both sexes of most bivalves release their gametes into the water column, with sperm and eggs joining in fertilization in the water column. Release is cued by day length, water temperature, and/or pheromones.
115. Once the fertilized egg begins to divide, it floats in the plankton and becomes a ciliated larva known as a **trochophore**. After a few days, this undergoes metamorphosis into a different larval form called a **veliger**.
116. Trochophores are shaped like a spinning top, have several bands of cilia, and mostly feed on diatoms.
117. Veligers retain cilia for a long time, eventually developing their adult organ systems in stages and developing a shell as their mantle grows and gains secretion capabilities. Veligers grow larger and larger over time.
118. **Veliger larvae** are still microscopic or very small and remain in the **zooplankton** at considerable risk of being filter fed long before they can pass through several more veliger stages to maturation.
119. Freshwater mussels often use a bizarre form of **internal fertilization**, wherein only the male releases sperm into the water, where it is filtered by female bivalves. From there, the sperm fertilize ripe eggs.
120. Once these larvae begin to grow their hinged shells, they are released from the female when they are still microscopic in size. These larvae are called **glochidia** and are more akin to the veliger stage of saltwater relatives.
121. From there, they attach themselves to the gills of freshwater fish and live parasitically until they mature to a certain size and drop off into the sediment.
122. Pocketbook mussels use a similar strategy, but instead of broadcast-releasing all of their glochidia, they release a pouch-like pocket that resembles a worm. Unsuspecting fish bite into them, releasing the glochidia to their gills.
123. The diagram below shows the general anatomical layout of a bivalve and their larval stages.

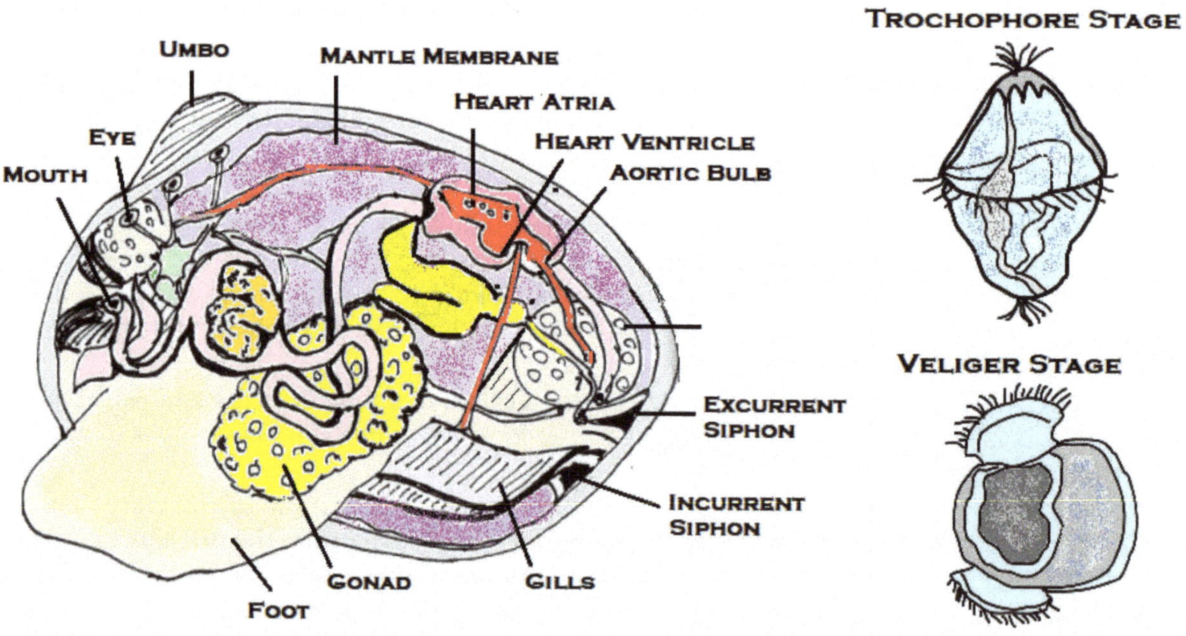

124. Much like the gastropods, the classification of bivalves is under debate and no single system of taxonomy has been agreed upon. We will keep try to thread the needle

125. Such differences as the location of adductor muscles, how the shell is hinged, the presence or absence of adductors or byssal threads, the plumbing of the siphons, the appearance of various larval stages and DNA and other molecular differences are all used to classify bivalves under different systems.

126. The diagrams on the next page show representative members of some of the major orders of bivalves and account for the subtle differences that make different types of shellfish what they are.

127. So here we are with some trapped white space, which is taboo in the publishing world....We'll fill this spot with some random trivia. Snails make the list, we'll go with some find lophotrochozoan dining.

DELICIOUS LOPHOTROCHOZOAN RECIPE

LEMON-BUTTER SCALLOPS
1 LB. FRESH SCALLOPS
3 TBSP SALTED BUTTER
1 LEMON, SECTIONED
6 CLOVES GARLIC, MINCED
1 SMALL BUNCH OF PARSLEY, CHOPPED
FRESH GROUND BLACK PEPPER
COARSE SEA SALT

MELT BUTTER ON MEDIUM HEAT. ADD SALT & PARSLEY. WHEN BUBBLING, QUICKLY TURN HEAT (SHOULD TAKE LESS THAN 30 SECONDS). DROP HEAT DOWN TO LOW TO FINISH. SQUEEZE LEMON OVER SCALLOPS AND ADD GARLIC TO BUTTER. SEASON WITH PEPPER AND MORE SALT. EAT THEM.

ADD MICROGREENS IF YOU WANT IT TO LOOK EXTRA SPIFFY.

WARNING: SCALLOPS ARE ONE OF THE EASIEST THINGS TO OVERCOOK EVER. IF YOU DO, THEY WILL BE LIKE EATING RUBBER BANDS.

ORDERS CARDITIDA, PHOLADOMYIDA, MYIDA, LUCINDA, VENERIDA, AND A FEW OTHERS: MARINE AND FRESHWATER CLAMS. DIFFERENCES IN HABITAT (MARINE OR FRESHWATER), SHELL STRUCTURE AND POSITIONING OF ORGANS ACCOUNT FOR BEING PLACED INTO DIFFERENT ORDERS. CLAMS LACK BYSSAL THREADS.

CARDIDA CLAM

CHESTNUT CLAM

MEDITERRANEAN CLAM

PACIFIC GIANT GLAM

ORDERS UNIONIDAE AND MYTILIDAE: FRESHWATER & SALTWATER MUSSELS, RESPECTIVELY. HAVE BYSSAL THREADS, HINGE, AND DIFFERENT ADDUCTOR MUSCLE ANATOMY FROM CLAMS.

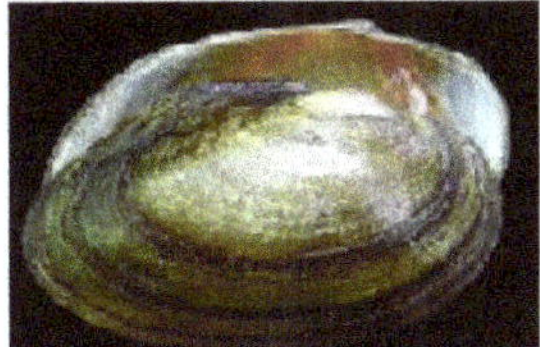

GIANT FLOATER

ZEBRA MUSSEL

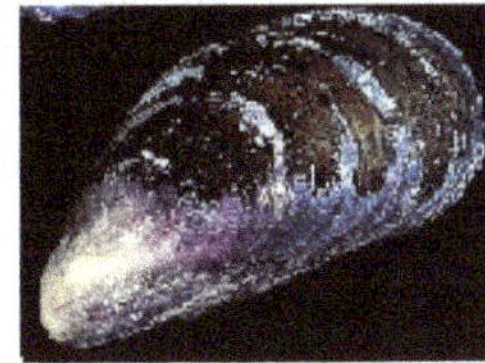

BLUE MUSSEL

FANSHELL MUSSEL

ORDER ARCIDA: OYSTERS. OYSTERS DO NOT HAVE AN EXTENDABLE FOOT AND THEY LACK AN ANTERIOR ADDUCTOR MUSCLE.

ORDER PECTINIDA: SCALLOPS. SCALLOPS HAVE THE ABILITY TO SWIM BY CLAPPING THEIR SHELLS TOGETHER WITH ADDUCTOR MUSCLES. SCALLOPS HAVE ADVANCED EYES.

EASTERN OYSTER

PACIFIC ROCK OYSTER

WEATHERVANE SCALLOP

KING SCALLOP

OTHER BIVALVE ORDERS AND REPRESENTATIVES

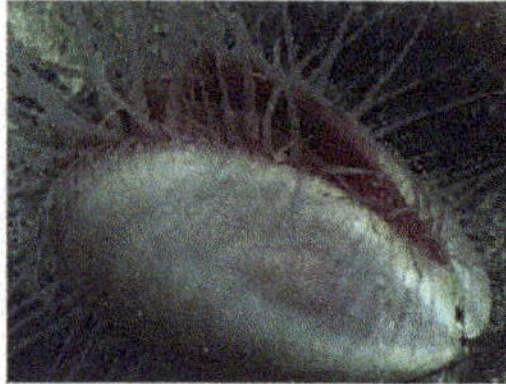
ORDER LIMIDA
FLAME SCALLOPS

ORDER PTERIIDA
PEN SHELLS

ORDER ARCIDA
ARK SHELLS

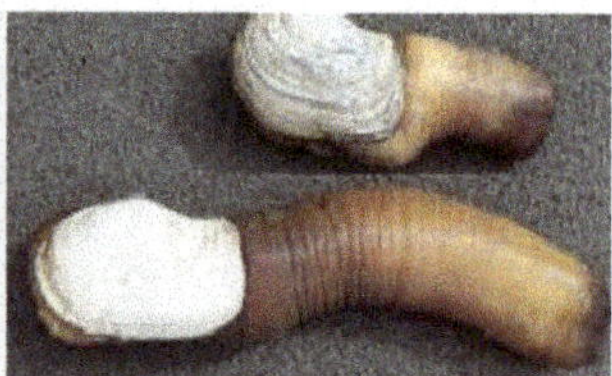
ORDER MYOIDA
GEODUCKS & SHIPWORMS

128. Now we get to the kings of the mollusks, and arguably, the kings of all invertebrates, the **cephalopods**.
129. **Class Cephalopoda** is almost shocking in its degree of evolutionary advancement its members show, as compared to other orders of mollusks.
130. The circulatory systems, digestive systems, nervous systems and degree of intelligence shown by cephalopods are quantum leaps in design over analogous structures found among bivalves, gastropods, or chitons.
131. The cephalopods include several orders of squid, vampire squid, nautilus, argonauts, octopi, and cuttlefish.
132. Like all mollusks, cephalopods have a muscular **mantle** that envelops the viscera. In the case of more primitive and ancient cephalopods like argonauts and chambered nautilus, it secretes a shell.
133. However, more evolved cephalopods have only internal remnants of a vestigial shell.
134. Squid have a cartilaginous pen-shaped shell remnant called a **gladius** that forms a spine-like rod behind the organs. Octopi have discarded shells altogether.
135. Externally, the layout of cephalopod external anatomy is vastly different from that of their molluscan relatives.
136. The **foot** has evolved into separate **arms** and **tentacles**. Arms are shorter and used to manipulate objects, while tentacles are longer and primarily used to slap and grab prey. Both are covered in **suckers**. These suckers are tipped with chitnous teeth in many types of cephalopods.
137. The number of arms and tentacles varies by the order of cephalopod.
138. In the the case of octopi and argonauts, there are 8 arms and no tentacles. Squid, vampire squid, and cuttlefish have 8 arms and a pair of predatory tentacles. The primitive chambered nautilus has more than 90 small tentacles.
139. Pigment-filled **chromatophores** of several colors mottle the skin of cephalopods, allowing them to camouflage themselves against surfaces, mimic predators, and communicate intentions and emotions to other individuals.
140. A thick layer of mantle muscle surrounds the **mantle cavity**, terminating in **siphon retractor muscles** in all cephalopods, and in additional **funnel retractor muscles** that control the opening and closing of the skirts of squid.

141. The agility and mobility of cephalopods can be attributed to layered muscle rings. A center layer of longitudinal muscle or collagen is surrounded by angled layers of muscle fibers, giving the animal mobility in all directions.
142. All cephalopods have a powerful muscular **siphon** that is the exit duct for the reproductive gametes, wastes, and defensive ink clouds. Additionally, it is used to suck oxygenated water over the **gills** and to jet propel the animal.
143. The siphon sits on the posterior surface of the cephalopod. The orientation of the body of the cephalopod literally turns 'normal' on its head. Essentially, the head is at the bottom of the animal in the middle of its appendages, while the organs sit at the top of the animal. Let's begin at the bottom.
144. A beak-like serrated **radula** sits in the middle of the arms and tentacles, leading into a heavy muscular **buccal bulb** capable of crushing prey into smithereens before they are slurped up the **esophagus**.
145. The gut of cephalopods is the shape of a horseshoe, with the mouth on the bottom of one of the arms, the cecum at the top curve, and the anus on the other arm of the horseshoe, adjoining the siphon.
146. The **esophagus** leads to the **stomach**, which is duct-fed by a gigantic **midgut gland** that functionally qualifies as a **liver**, given the breadth and diversity of enzymes it produces. The liver sits directly atop the brain.
147. Most of the digestion actually occurs where the stomach gives way to a blind-ended **cecum** pouch that slowly steeps the slurry of food and enzymes and liquefies it for absorption in the long **intestine**.
148. The intestine descends toward the **siphon**. Right above the anus, a glandular **ink sac** pulls pigment from waste and concentrates it into a viscous ink that is used like a James Bond smokescreen against predators.
149. The cells of the ink sac mostly secrete a mixture of melanin and mucus to make the cloud.
150. Unlike most of the relatives, cephalopods have a highly efficient **closed circulatory system**. A **systemic heart** pumps oxygenated blood through the **ascending** and **descending aortae**.
151. Much like advanced vertebrate animals, these arteries diverge into smaller arteries that supply each organ.
152. A pair of **gill hearts** pump deoxygenated blood through the capillaries of two feather-like **gills**. Countercurrent flow of water currents are pumped by the siphon across these capillary beds, oxygenating them.
153. From there, the blood returns to the systemic heart for redistribution.
154. The blood, itself, is **hemocyanin** based. Hemocyanin has copper atoms chelated by protein domains. It is clear when deoxygenated and the color of blue raspberry Kool-Aid when oxygenated.
155. The **nephridia**, also called **kidneys** by some, are a pair of spongy tubular organs that sit in the cleft between the systemic heart and gill heart, filtering the blood and pumping them into the **vena cava.**
156. Several sac-like projects exit the vena cava, inflating and deflating with the motion of the siphon. They open to a pore-like opening. Every time the cephalopod sucks water in and expels it, waste is expelled through the pore.
157. While these are major advances in anatomy that show some evolutionary convergence with much more advanced vertebrate animals, it is the quantum leap of the **nervous system** that is most impressive.
158. The **brain** not only has very large **olfactory bulbs** and **optic bulbs** that are used to gather information about their environment, but they also have the ability to make associations, plan, and think.
159. Octopi are often problematic pets in saltwater aquariums, because they figure out how to escape their tanks.
160. They cannot be kept with any other fish or crustaceans, because they can plan an attack and eat prey larger than themselves. Octopi can also open jars to remove food, count objects, and recognize their keepers.
161. Cephalopods also protect their brain in a hard cartilage structure called a **cranium** that functionally resembles the skull of vertebrate animals. However, it sits atop the buccal bulb and walls off the visceral cavity of the mantle.
162. The **eyes** of cephalopods, with the exception of the primitive chambered nautilus, have **lenses** and **retinas** much like a vertebrate eye, polarizing light onto the optic nerve, processing into detailed counter-shaded images.

163. Chambered nautilus are still relatively unevolved, and their eyes function like a pinhole camera.
164. In spite of being capable of camouflaging themselves in impressive fashion, cephalopods do not have color vision. Unlike the tri-colored cone cells of vertebrates, they only have a single type of **photoreceptor cells**.
165. The vision center of the brain, however, integrates message from visual cues to nerves that control the **chromatophores** in the skin, allowing them to match the contrast, shading, and patterns behind them.
166. These chromatophores are used to produce numerous patterns that visually communicate mating intent to the opposite sex and to competitors of the same sex during spawning.
167. All cephalopods are **dioecious**. Males typically fight viciously over females. Once they've obtained a mate, they wrap themselves around them in a bear hug and interlock their arms, facing mouth-to-mouth.
168. Unless they are octopi, the male releases multiple **spermatophore** packets out of the **seminal receptacle**, through the **penis**, and out the **siphon**. From there, the male uses special modified arm tips called **heterocycli** to transfer the sperm packets to the arms and mantle of the female.
169. Male octopi use their penis to directly transfer spermatophores via **internal fertilization**.
170. Depending on the species, some females will mate with only one dominant male or with multiple males.
171. There are even species of cephalopods where males attempt to dislodge the spematophores of competitors or they pose as other females and either transfer their spermatophores to another mistaken male, who then inadvertently passes these on to the next female he mates with.
172. Once mating has occurred, the female takes up sperm packets and stores them, releasing a sperm-attracting compound to attract the sperm to the **oviducts** when the eggs are ripe.
173. Once fertilized, a pair of **nidamental glands** secretes a protective case around the eggs and links these cases together into a **clutch**, which are then expelled from the siphon and attached to a surface.
174. Most cephalopods are **semelparous**, expending so much energy in reproduction that they essentially starve themselves to exhaustion and die. It is a cruel twist of fate that such advanced animals only live a few years.
175. The diagram below shows the generalized anatomy of a female squid.

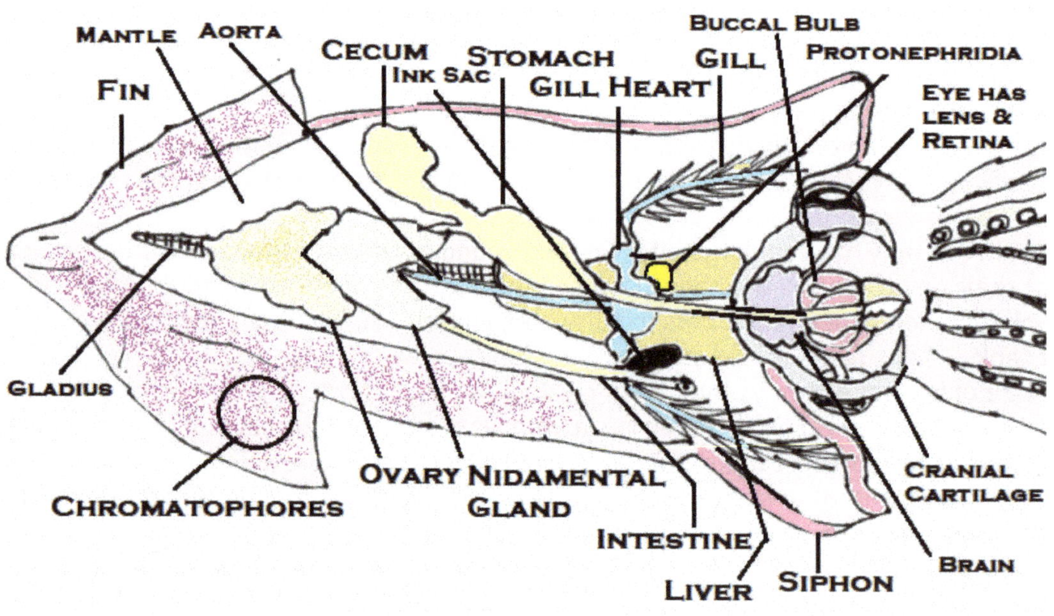

176. It is impossible to generalize reproduction across all types of cephalopods, because there are so many differences in reproductive behaviors and anatomy.

177. Let's now take a brief look at how cephalopods are classified. The diagram below lists the major classes of cephalopods and gives a description of the criteria that serve to place them in their respective taxa.

Order Nautilidae
Chambered Nautilus

True shells with air-filled chambers for buoyancy. Pinhole camera eyes. 90 or more tentacles.

Order Argonautidae
Argonaut Octopus

Pelagic octopi. Males are tiny. Females float with false shell made of egg case.

Order Vampiromorphidae
Vampire Squid

Not a true squid. Have 8 arms like connected with a membrane. Ear-like mantle fins. Deep sea scavengers.

Order Octopoda
Octopus

Benthic ambush predators with 8 arms. Tentacles absent. Beak has venom gland. Highly intelligent.

Order Sepioloda
Bobtail Squid

8 arms and 2 tentacles with suckers. Skin has bioluminescent bacteria symbiote. Rounded mantle.

Order Sepiida
Cuttlefish

8 Arms, 2 tentacles. Most advanced chromatophore system of any cephalopod. Mantle secretes calcified cuttlebone.

Order Idiosepius
Pygmy Squid

Tiny (2 cm or less) ambush predators. Secrete glue-like substance to stick to seaweed and wait. Inject venom into prey (shrimp).

Order Myopsida
Myopsid Squid

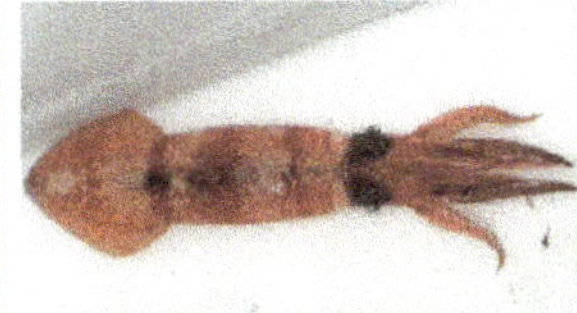

8 Arms, 2 Tentacles. Pelagic predators. Eyes are covered with clear membrane and lack lids. Simple suckers (no teeth). 2 pair of nidamental glands in females .

Order Spirulada
Ram's Horn Squid

Very rare deep sea squid with light organs. Coiled buoyant internal shell. Tentacles & arms can fully retract.

Order Bathyteuthoidea
Bathypelagic Squid

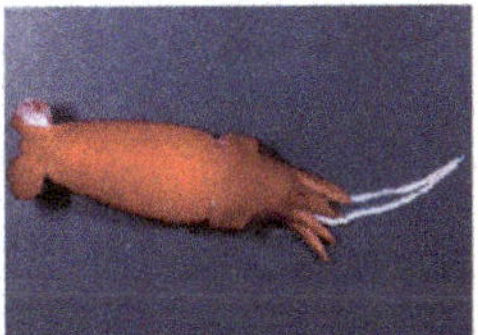

Deep ocean pelagic predators. Lack corneal membrane over eye. Females have 2 oviducts. Musculature differs from Myopsids.

J) The Lophophorate Clade: The Misfits

1. The **lophophorate clade** is a group of lophophorate phyla that don't fit into any other large classification.
2. These animals seem to have shared a common ancestor, but they are no longer close relatives to anything other than themselves. Most of these were evolutionary experiments that really didn't go anywhere, but they have managed to hang on in their early forms.
3. All of these animals have soft bodies lacking shells, as well as tentacles and ciliated feeding structures.
4. Rather than cover each of these relatively obscure phyla separately, we will highlight the major anatomical characteristics of each phyla, give an example or two, and wrap up.
5. Lets begin with **Phylum Brachiopoda,** known commonly as brachiopods or lamp shells.
6. Superficially, lamp shells look like bivalve mollusks, but if opened, it is abundantly clear that the shell is a case of coincidental convergent evolution. Internally, brachiopods look nothing like a bivalve.
7. Brachiopods have shells on the top and bottom, rather than the left and right like bivalves. This would not be obvious unless the shell is opened and the orientation of the body inside is examined.

8. The top shell is called the **pedicle valve**, while the lower shell is called the **brachial valve.** Their fit is used to sub-classify brachiopods into two classes of brachiopods called **articulate** and **inarticulate.**
9. Articulate brachiopods have toothed edges that interlock at the shell hinge, while inarticulate brachiopods do not.
10. Brachiopods are burrowers that open their shells at the door of their homes, catching sinking and flowing food particles. They remain anchored in their burrows with a foot-like **pedicle**. This organ is made of connective tissues in inarticulate brachiopods and it is an extension of the coelom in articulate species.
11. A set of **shell abductor muscles** opens and closes the shell. There are muscle fibers for emergencies that can snap the shells closed quickly, and slow fibers that operate the shell normally. Some can dig with this mechanism.
12. The shells of brachiopods are laid down in 3 alternating layers of calcified minerals and proteins.
13. A **mantle membrane** lines the shell and encloses all of the internal organs in the back part of the shell near the hinge. However, **mantle lobes** keep going to the front of the shell and make a balloon-like space.
14. Inside the enclosure is their **lophophore**, which is a crown of cilia-covered **tentacles**. The lophophore is a horseshoe shape in most brachiopods, but can be coiled many times in larger species.
15. The lophophore keeps its shape with a combination of fluid pressure and cartilage supports.
16. Its job is to trap food particles from the water. The lophophore uses mucus to trap particles and then sweeps them into the mouth with the cilia covering its surface. It is also the primary respiratory and excretory organ.
17. Brachiopods feed by passing filtered water through funnel-like structures called **chetae** that direct food toward the mouth. The **pharynx** and **gullet** are next. Both secrete digestive enzymes and sweep the food with cilia.
18. The stomach is next, which absorbs most of the nutrients, before giving way to a very short **intestine** that finishes the digestion process.
19. Wastes are filtered out by diffusion and leave through the surfaces of the lophophore filaments.
20. There is an **open circulatory system** with a small **heart** that sends oxygen-carrying **hemerythrin** pigments and nutrients over the organs inside the coelom. The body wall of the coelem also flexes and sweeps materials with its cilia, keeping nutrients and oxygen distributed.
21. The diagram below shows the general anatomical layout of a brachiopod.

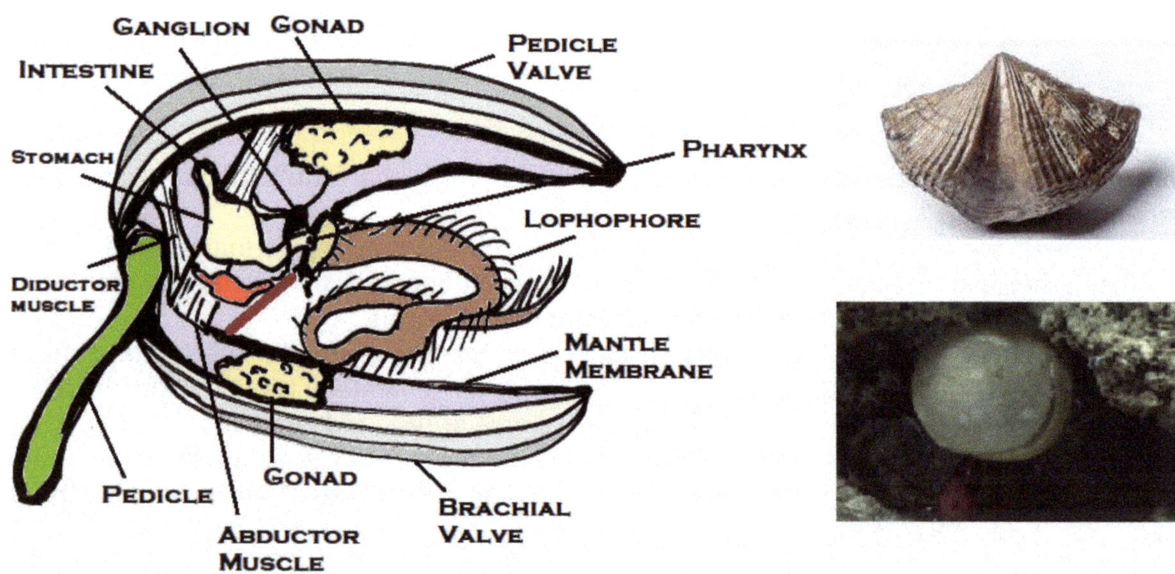

22. The nervous system of brachiopods is very simple. Articulate brachiopods have an upper and lower pair of **ganglia**, while inarticulate brachiopods only have the lower ganglia. These branch into sensory nerves.
23. The sensory nerves innervate the lophophore and its surrounding muscles, allowing them to contract the organ, sense chemicals and tactile cues, and to sense gravity via the use of **statocysts** in nearby balance organs.
24. Brachiopods tend to be separate sexes. Each shell has a pair of **gonads** that release either eggs or sperm for **external fertilization**, though females of some species have a **brood pouch** and release planktonic larvae.
25. Both types of larvae look like miniature versions of adults and sink to the bottom once their shell becomes too heavy for them to keep themselves suspended in the plankton.
26. The anatomy of a brachiopod is shown below, along with a picture of the real thing.
27. Now we move on to the animal group that, more than any other, probably leaves more junior biologists scratching their heads as to what in the devil they just found. News crews also like them.
28. **Phylum Bryozoa** is the **bryozoans** which frequently wash up onto beaches as 'mysterious blobs' that can be several feet across. Invariably, someone with knowledge of biology calls the news station and tells them it's not a mystery.
29. Almost all bryozoans are **colonial**, meaning that hundreds or thousands of tiny animals live together. While they are much more complex anatomically, they use the same concept as corals, establishing large growths together.
30. All **bryozoaons** produce a colonial **cystid** which is a matrix secreted together by the epidermises of all of the animals in the colony. Many species make soft, gelatinous, protein matrices, but others calcify theirs.
31. The epidermis is the outer layer of each animal's **body wall**. Underneath it, consecutively, are bands of tough connective tissue, muscle layers, and the lining of the **coelem** that holds the organs.
32. There are different types of **zooids** in the bryozoan colony that work collaboratively. Most zooids are **autozooids**. These are joined by protective **avicularia**, where a snapping beak-like structure replaces the lophophore.
33. **Autozoids** feed and pass nutrients on to the autozoids, which fend off small animals that would try to feed on them. They are dependent upon feeding autozooids to remain alive.
34. Like brachiopods, **autozoids** have a **lophophore**. However, it is shaped like a crown of cilia that funnels food into the mouth. From there, filtered nutrients enter a guitar-shaped digestive tract.
35. The first stop is the **pharynx**, followed by a muscular **gizzard** that grinds the food and forces it into the **stomach**. The **intestine** absorbs nutrients. It bends upward and back toward the mouth, so waste can be expelled.
36. The anus cannot be located at the bottom of the animal, because that is where it is anchored to the colony.
37. Since they are so small and they can pump water back and forth into their **coelem** with **retractor muscles**, bryozoans lack any type of circulatory, respiratory, or excretory systems.
38. **Heterozoids** contain gonads and are **hermaphroditic**, though many species tend to pass through cycles of male and female gamete production, making them, functionally, one sex at a time.
39. **External fertilization** is the mode of reproduction. Bryozoan larvae are ciliated, have a protective chitin shell, and remain in the plankton until they begin to grow into larger colonies and settle out.
40. Some species start to look like floating trees, because they produce **kenozooids** that are essentially hollow body cavities that lengthen and extend into branches, providing room for more autozooids to spread out.

41. Like the **avicularia**, they rely on feeding autozooids to keep them alive.
42. The anatomy of a bryozoan animal is shown below.

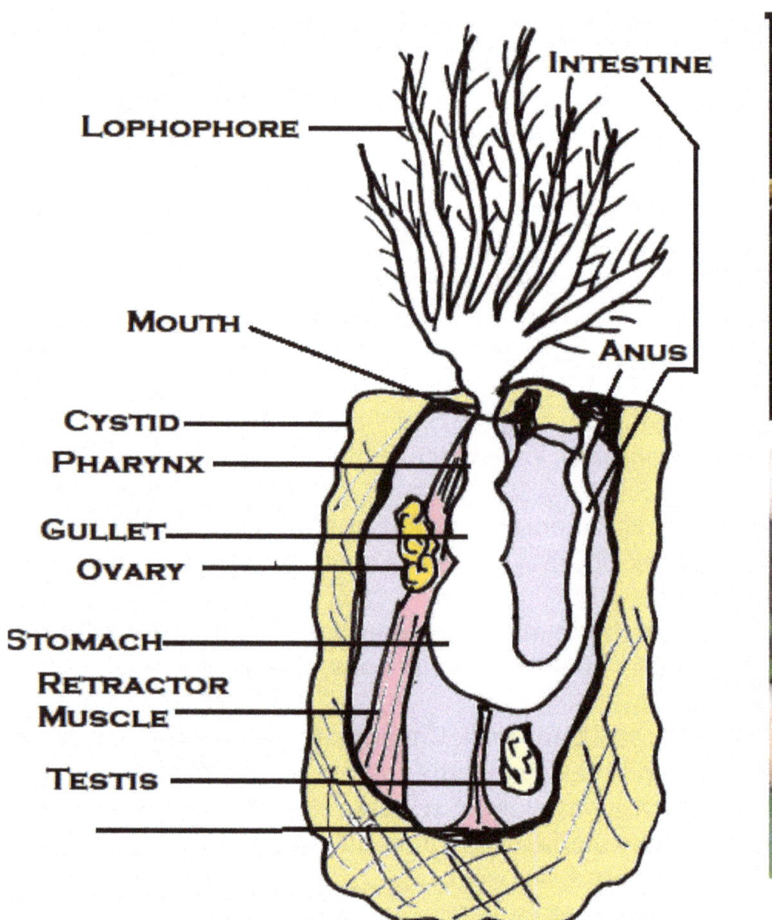

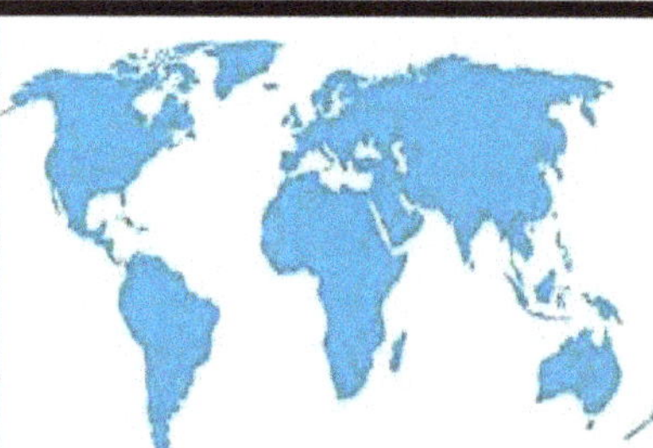

GEOGRAPHY TRIVIA STUDY BREAK (ANSWER PG. 119)

1) NAME THE 5 'STANS' THAT USED TO BE PART OF THE U.S.S.R.
2) WHAT 2 SOUTH AMERICAN COUNTRIES ARE LANDLOCKED?
3) NAME THE 2 ISLANDS THAT ARE DIVIDED INTO 2 COUNTRIES.
4) WHAT IS THE NORTHERNMOST COUNTRY WITH PENGUINS?
5) WHAT COUNTRY HAS 22 CITIES OF 10 MILLION OR MORE PEOPLE?
6) WHAT AFRICAN COUNTRIES SHARE NAMES WITH RIFT LAKES?

PART B: DEUTEROSTOME ANIMALS

A Comprehensive Guide to Echinoderms, Hemichordates, Urochordates, and Chordate Vertebrate Animals

OUTLINE TABLE OF CONTENTS

Deuterostome Animals

SECTION 1: Deuterostome Characteristics & Primitive Deuterostome Phyla

A) General Characteristics of Deuterostomes

1. From a young age, most people are taught that the correct way to sub-divide and classify animals is between vertebrates and invertebrates. This is only crudely correct.
2. In reality, what truly delineates animals into their most general division is what happens with the geometry and orientation of the developing **embryo**.
3. **Protostomes**, as we saw in the previous chapter, use the **blastopore** to develop their mouth. The anus (if present), forms later from the **gastroceol**.
4. **Deuterostome** animals have the opposite developmental pattern, forming their anus from the blastopore and adding the mouth later from the gastrocoel.
5. In other words, protostomes develop mouth-first and deuterostomes develop butt-end first.
6. Given that most children learn about vertebrates and invertebrates in elementary school, it is kind of understandable why they aren't correctly taught the differences between heads and butts at that age.
7. Additionally, the embryonic cells of **deuterostomes** show **radial cleavage**, rather than **spiral cleavage**. This means that the cells are neatly stacked atop one another, rather than staggered like a brick wall.
8. In deuterostomes, multiple births from identical twin clones are possible, because the radial cleavage allows the embryo to split neatly down an even plane before cells have had a chance to **differentiate**.
9. Before differentiation, cell fates have not been determined, so all genes in the genome remain potentially active. Therefore, two new blastulae form and resume division as if they were a single sphere all along.
10. Differences in gene switching between the embryos also accounts for the slight phenotypic differences that occur even in identical twins, along with differences in environmental cues that influence these patterns.
11. As compared to most phyla of protostomes, the average deuterostomes (with the exception of **echinoderms**) are much more anatomically complex and advanced than the majority of protostome phyla.
12. Let's take a look at how the embryos differ in their developmental patterns. The diagram below conveys this.

THE PREFIX 'DEUTERO' MEANS 2ND IN LATIN. THEREFORE, DEUTEROSTOMES EVOLVED 2ND AFTER THE PROTOSTOMES. THEREFORE, DEUTERONOMY IS THE 2ND BOOK OF THE BIBLE. NOW LET'S LOOK AT SOME OTHER FAMOUS SECONDS RELEGATED TO THE DUSTBIN OF HISTORY.

*ALFRED WALLACE FINISHED 2ND TO CHARLES DARWIN ON THE THEORY OF EVOLUTION
*THE BUFFALO BILLS HAVE FINISHED 2ND (LOST) IN ALL 4 SUPERBOWLS THEY PLAYED
*LINUS PAULING WAS 2ND PLACE BEHIND WATSON & CRICK'S DISCOVERY OF DNA STRUCTURE
*TENZING NORGAY WAS THE 2ND PERSON BEHIND SIR EDMUND HILLARY TO SUMMIT EVEREST
*ALFRED LANDON FINISHED 2ND TO FDR OR HE WOULD HAVE BEEN PRESIDENT DURING WW2

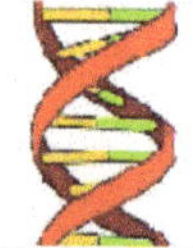

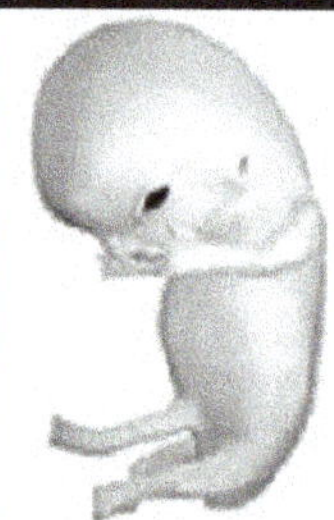

THINGS YOU MAY NOT KNOW ABOUT FETUSES

1) THEIR SENSE OF TASTE IS DEVELOPED AROUND 8 WEEKS OLD.
2) BABIES TASTE FOOD FLAVORS FROM MOM IN AMNIOTIC FLUID.
3) NORMAL HUMAN GESTATION CAN LAST FROM 37 TO 42 WEEKS.
4) BABIES SHOW EMOTIONS AND CRY INSIDE THE WOMB.
5) AFRICAN ELEPHANTS CAN BE PREGNANT FOR UP TO 22 MONTHS.
6) POSSUMS GIVE BIRTH INTO THEIR POUCHES AFTER JUST 2 WEEKS.
7) A WOMAN FROM MALI GAVE BIRTH TO NONTUPLETS IN 2021.
8) BY 14 WEEKS, THE GENDER OF THE FETUS IS DETERMINED.

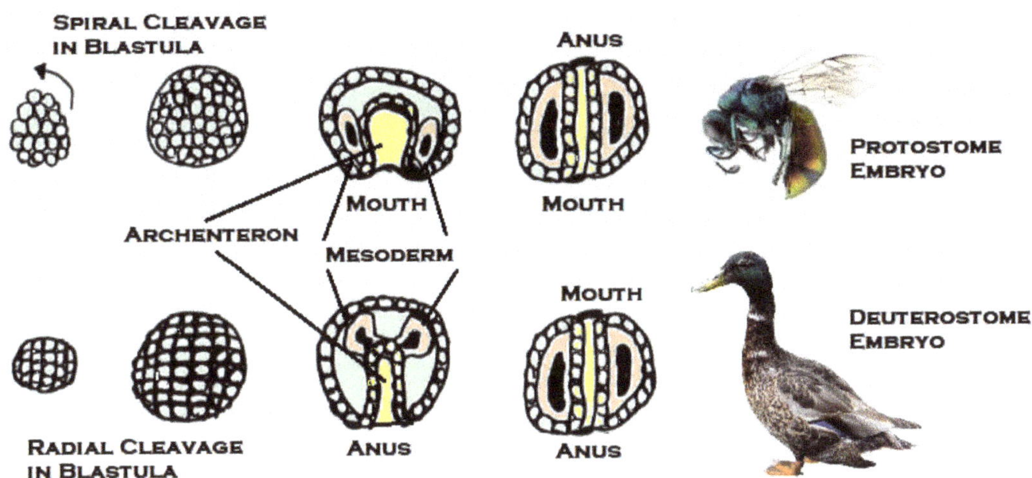

13. First, there is a difference at the earliest stages of cell division. Mitosis goes in a spiraling, staggered pattern in protostomes, while it happens in a regular geometric stacking pattern in deuterostomes.
14. Next, there is a difference in how the **mesoderm** develops. The middle layer of tissue emerges from different ends of the **archenteron**, which is the early tube-like gut in a developing embryo.
15. In protostomes, the mesoderm begins developing from the endoderm next to the **blastocoel**. It is eventually pushed to both sides of the spherical embryo by the growing **archenteron**, forming a **coelem** in the middle.
16. In deuterostomes, the mesoderm forms from pockets of endoderm at the distal end of the embryo. It does not form next to the blastocoel, because this will be the anus, not the mouth, in a deuterostome.
17. The pockets of tissue eventually break away and form a layer of muscle and connective tissue. This growing donut-shaped pocket is hollow in the middle, forming the coelom.
18. In mammals, for instance, this is why there are muscles around organs (such as the stomach and intestines), an empty space, and then a muscular lining to the gut cavity behind the ribs and abdomen.
19. Eventually the growing **archenteron** reaches the distal end of the embryo, opening into a mouth.
20. This embryonic pattern holds true from the most primitive deuterostomes to the most advanced. A lot of people argue that 'most advanced' means us, but I have my doubts, given the evidence in the section below.
21. It might be time to give a competent dolphin the chance to be president.
22. Anyway, sea urchins are studied by embryologists, because their eggs are large, numerous, easily obtainable, and they share nearly identical-looking early developmental stages with us.
23. There are three major clades of deuterostomes that seem to have diverged long ago.
24. These are **Phylum Echinodermata** (starfish, sea urchins, sea cucumbers, and others), **Phylum Hemichordata** (acorn worms), and **Phylum Chordata** (cephalochordate lancets, urochordate sea squirts, and vertebrates).
25. With that, let's begin our journey through the deuterostome zoo.

GEOGRAPHY TRIVIA STUDY BREAK ANSWERS

1) Turkmenistan, Uzbekistan, Kazakhstan, Kyrgyzstan,Tajikstan
2) Bolivia, Paraguay
3) Hispaniola (Haiti, Dominican), New Guinea (Indonesia, Papua)
4) China
5) Malawi and Tangankyika (Former Country)

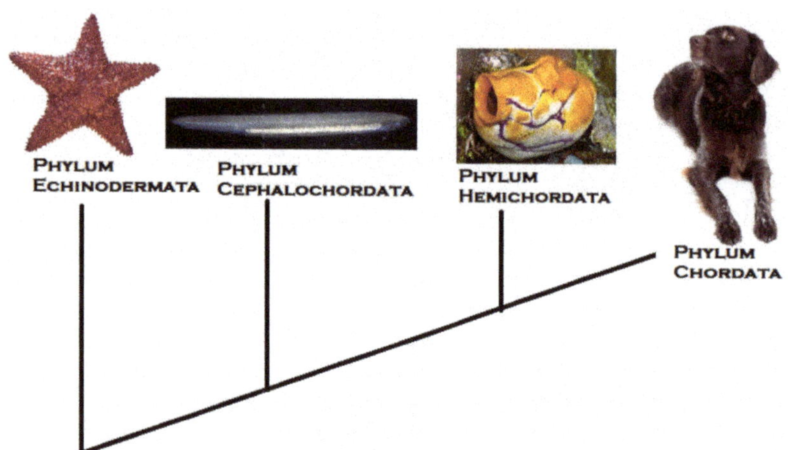

A Quote To Give Reason to Doubt the Superiority of Human Intelligence

"Whenever I watch television and see all those starving kids, I can't help but cry....I mean I'd love to be skinny like that, but not with all those flies and death and stuff........"

Five Time Grammy Winner and Artist of the Year, Mariah Carey

B) Phylum Echinoderma

1. **Echinoderms** are a group of spiny-skinned, soft-bodied deuterostomes that include starfish, brittle stars, sea urchins, sea cucumbers, crinoids, sand dollars, sea lilies, and briny dumplings.
2. **Echinoderms** have **radial symmetry** as adults, though this seems to be a case of evolutionary reversion to a much simpler body form, because they have ciliated planktonic larvae with **bilateral symmetry**.
3. Echinoderm larvae grow faster on the left side as they develop, eventually absorbing the right side completely. From there, the remaining side of the body divides into five, six, (or multiples of these) parts around a midpoint.
4. Echinoderm means 'spiny skin' due to the presence of calcified plates that form a protective covering over their epidermis. There is a mesh-like protein layer called the **stereom** running through the skin that binds together hundreds of calcified **ossicles** like chain mail armor.
5. **Ossicles** can take many forms among different types of echinoderms. In starfish, they are nodules, in sea cucumbers they are flat plates, but in sea urchins, they protrude as a corona of protective spines.
6. There are a wide variety of different colors of echinoderms, as the skin is full of pigment cells that can combine melanin, carotenes, and other pigments, producing a wide variety of different colors.
7. Many echinoderms produce protective mucus, toxins, or both in the skin, since they move slowly and can't do a whole lot to actively defend themselves.
8. Another mesh-like layer found in the skin of echinoderms is called **catch connective tissue**. When relaxed, the animal has a soft squishy texture, but when flexed like a muscle, it becomes stiff.
9. This allows starfish or sea cucumbers to hold their ground, grabbing onto rocks or anchoring themselves in a crevice if a predator tries to pull them out.
10. Additionally, hydraulically-controlled **tube feet** protrude from underside of each leg like dozens or hundreds of little suction cups. These can be used to hold onto the bottom or grab prey as it passes.
11. Internally, the tube feet are connected to bulb-like **ampullae** that are used to squeeze or extract fluid into the tube feet like a turkey baster bulb, deflating or inflating them as needed.
12. The ampullae branch off of **radial canals** that bisect each arm. The radial canals are positioned like

spokes on a wheel hub, joining a circular **central canal** that forms the **water vascular system** of the animal.

13. Internally, echinoderms are rather unimpressive in their complexity. Mostly they look like a big tub of goo.
14. The **digestive system** begins with the **mouth** in the center underside of the animal. It follows a short **esophagus** into a **cardiac stomach** and a second **pyloric stomach** that branches off into each arm or segment.
15. The cardiac stomach, in many types of echinoderms, can be distended out of the body to pick up food, while the pyloric stomach does the lion's share of the digesting and absorbing, sending materials to each segment.
16. Different classes of echinoderms vary in the length and presence or absence of the intestine and anus.
17. Starfish and sea urchins have a short **intestine** that terminates in an anus on top of the body in the 'bullseye' between all five legs. Sea cucumbers and crinoids have a long coiling intestine. Brittle stars have devolved the intestine and anus altogether, making use of a **gastrovascular cavity** like much more primitive animals.
18. Large identical **digestive glands** take up a large amount of space on the superior surface of each arm or segment, emptying digestive enzymes into the tube-like lobe of the pyloric stomach.
19. There is no true circulatory or respiratory system in an echinoderm, because all the squish-squashing of fluids through the hydraulic vascular system takes care of the distribution of oxygen and nutrients.
20. Early in their development, the **coelem** of echinoderms divides into three lobes. The gut, the gonads, and the canal system are each suspended in their own sub-compartment full of fluids.
21. The division around the ring canal and arms is called the **haemocoel**, the **gastrocoel** surrounds the gut, and the **protocoel** surrounds the gonads. Each is full of oxygenated fluid with circulating immune cells.
22. Patrick the starfish was fairly accurate in the notion of the relative stupidity of echinoderms, because they have no brain. The nervous system consists of a **nerve net** of mostly reflex nerves, with **ganglion** in each arm.
23. Given their relative simplicity, echinoderms can undergo **dedifferentiation** in damaged tissues, allowing them to revert cells back to something like stem cells, which can then re-differentiate into whatever organ is needed.
24. Each segment of echinoderms also has a pair of gigantic **gonads** that produce copious amounts of gametes. Most echinoderm species are distinctly male or female, and all use **external fertilization**.
25. Eggs and sperm are usually released according to tides and the phase of the moon. The gametes find one another in the plankton and form ciliated larvae. These then develop left-centric, absorbing the right side of the body, and finally cloning this side into (usually five) identical segments.
26. Female echinoderms of some starfish species brood the eggs by storing them in their pyloric stomach or holding them under their arms until they hatch. However, most echinoderm parents are deadbeat **R-strategists** who just let their eggs go and hope someone survives.
27. Echinoderms also rely heavily on **fragmentation** as adults and **budding** as larvae.
28. Ancient Mediterranean fishermen found out the hard way about fragmentation.
29. After getting starfish continually snagged in their nets, they started cutting them into little pieces. This backfired tremendously until someone figured out why they kept multiplying instead of dying.
30. Echinoderm larvae are also capable of budding and cloning themselves, thereby increasing their populations in the very stage where filter-feeders usually take out most of the population of any given plankton.
31. The diagram below shows the general anatomical layout of a starfish.

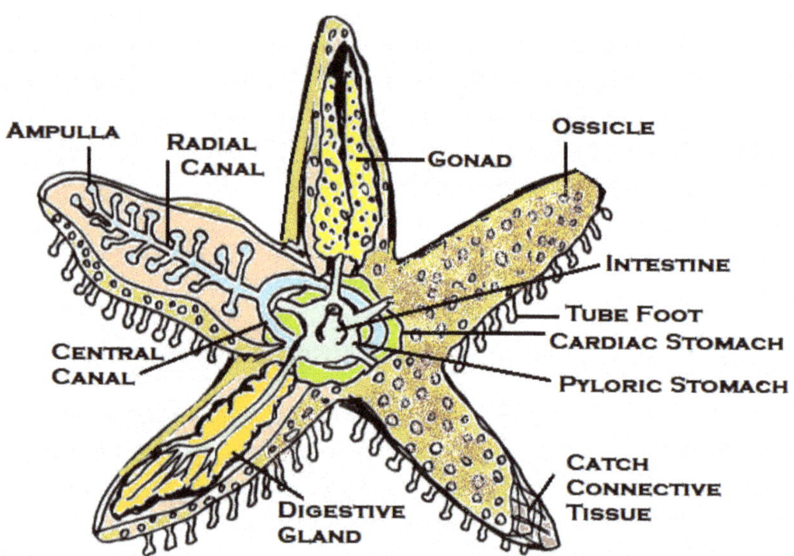

Starfish are quite dumb, so in the spirit of that sentiment, here are some 'You're So Dumb….' insults to fill some page space. You never know when you might need them.

You're so Dumb…..

You picked your nose & lost 10 IQ points.
You install light bulbs with a hammer.
You bought a solar-powered flashlight.
You called 911 to ask the dispatcher out.
You lit a match to check on a gas leak.
You drove through a drive-in window.
You think a good practical joke is to tell everyone on the plane you have a bomb.
You got fired from the bank for stealing suckers and pens.
You went to the produce aisle to try to find some Fruit-of-the Loom.

32. Now let's take a look at how Phylum Echinodermata is divided into classes.
33. There are five major groups of echinoderms, each with major anatomical differences.

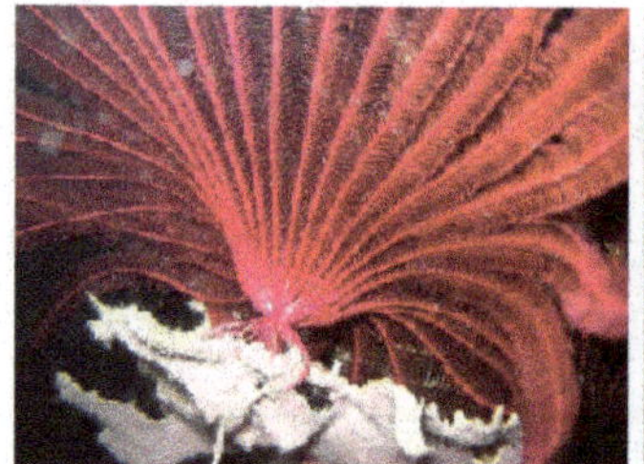

Class Crinoidea: Sea Lilies, Feather Stars
*Ligament covered with ossicles anchors animal to bottom. Free swimming forms have vestigial stalks.
*Suspension feeders that filter plankton.
*Ancient group that dates to 480 mya.

Class Holothuroidea: Sea Cucumbers
*Ossicles are beneath skin and usually very tiny in size, some species armored.
*Giant gonad running length of body
*Expel sticky threads from anus when threatened by predators.
*Tube feet modified into tentacle ring around mouth; used for feeding.

Class Echnioidea: Sea Urchins
Symmetrical globular test made of five parts. Spiny ossicles that protrude. Tiny tube feet. Intestine is long and coiled. Larvae have arms.

Class Ophiuroidea: Brittle Stars
Central disc distinct from arms & has all organs.

Class Asteroidea:True Starfish
Central disc is not distinct from arms. Gonads and digestive tract extend to arms.

C) Phylum Hemichordata

1. **Phylum Hemichordata** includes **acorn worms** and some strange and obscure animals called **pterobranchs**, which live in coral-like colonies. Acorn worms live in burrows in the ocean.
2. Both groups are suspension feeders, eating trash in the sand and plankton.
3. Acorn worms are segmented into a pre-oral lobe (the acorn), a collar, and a trunk. They share many characteristics with true chordates, including a **coelom, pharyngeal gill slits**, and a **dorsal nerve cord**.
4. Acorn worms, being worms, are also **bilaterally symmetrical**. They have a definite head (the acorn) which has a ring of cilia around the mouth for filtering food from the sand and from the surrounding water.
5. The **collar** or **mesosome** segment has a hollow support rod derived from the gut called the **stomochord**, but the other segments do not. This is why they are called **hemichordates**.
6. However, unlike true chordates, the stomochord is not made of cartilage or derived from the mesoderm. Instead, it is a pouch emerging anteriorly from the mouth. The term 'hemichordate' is a misnomer.
7. However, DNA and ribosomal RNA do suggest that this group is the half-way point between the true chordates and the echinoderms, though they are closer to the echinoderms.
8. Acorn worms, as noted, filter feed trash and plankton out of the water. The mouth sits in the collar segment and brushes food particles down the digestive tract by using waving cilia.
9. From there, water pressure inside the **pharynx** from gill slits, along with more cilia, drag the food particles down the **esophagus** and then onto a long **intestine**. There are no digestive glands or accessory organs.
10. A cluster of excretory cells called a **glomerulus** sits atop the **stomochord** in the proboscis and acts like a kidney, filtering out nitrogenous waste and pushing it through the digestive tract to make an exit.
11. The respiratory system functions much like that of a fish, with open **gill slits** and the mouth circulating water across a pair of large open-ended blood vessels called the **dorsal vessel** and **ventral vessel.**
12. The **heart** is not directly connected to the blood vessels, but pulsates blood over the organs in the **mesentery cavity** by flexing and squishing fluids around, which enter and exit the vessel ends for redistribution.
13. The **nervous system** consists of a **dorsal nerve cord** with a cluster of **ganglion** on the anterior end that seems to coordinate muscular movements and ciliary beating. It creates a wishbone shape with a **ventral nerve cord.**
14. Acorn worms don't have eyes, nor do they have a lateral line. They may have tasting **chemoreceptors**, but the only definitive sense that we know they have is tactile. There are nerve-endings throughout for touch reception.
15. Acorn worms have two different sexes. Their **testes** or **ovaries** are paired and lie directly behind the pharynx in front of the gut. They have **oviducts** or **sperm ducts** that open behind the gill slits.
16. The females lay big blobs of eggs inside a sticky secretion. Males then follow tactile and biochemical cues to the eggs and use **external fertilization**.
17. The larvae resemble those of starfish and other echinoderms, with bands of concentric cilia to help them swim. This is one of the primary reasons that they are considered to be an evolutionary link between groups.

English Teacher Special: Trivia Study Break

1) What do you call the part of speech is the term for a double vowel, such as in FOOD, JOINT, FUEL, GOURD, etc.
2) The Rooster goes 'Cock-a-Doodle-Doo' is an example of what literary device used to portray sounds?
3) What is the preposition in this sentence? 'I threw a bundt cake into the politician's face'
4) What literary device is used for emphasis in the phrase 'So far, so good, so what?

(Answer pg. 126)

18. The diagrams below show a real acorn worm along with acorn worm anatomy.

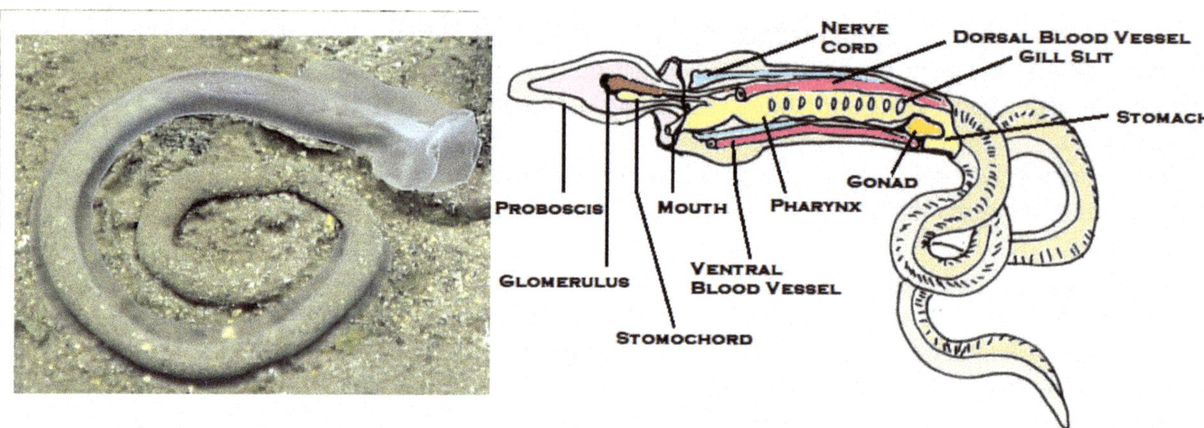

19. **Pterobranchs** have similar anatomy to acorn worms, albeit differently shaped.

20. They live in colonies and can asexually reproduce by **budding**. Additionally, the larvae resemble **planula**, so they are classified separately from acorn worms for those reasons. Very little else is known about them.

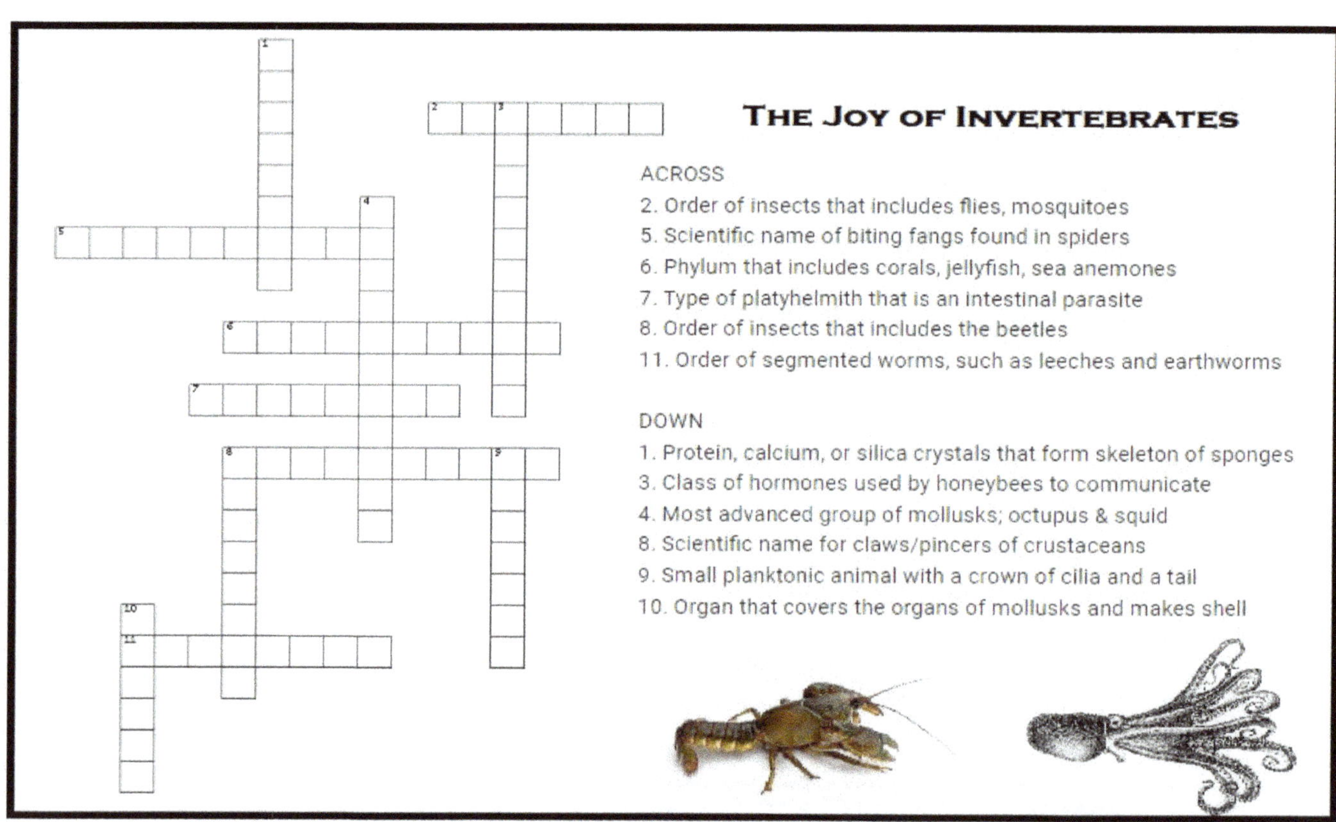

SECTION 2: Chordate Characteristics and Primitive Chordate Phyla

A) Chordate Characteristics

1. Chordates are **deuterostome coelomates** with **bilateral symmetry** and **cephalization** in most. Genetically, according to ribosomal RNA and DNA evidence, they share a lineage with echinoderms and hemichordates.
2. All chordates have a cartilage **notochord** that forms a rigid support rod down their dorsal surface, protecting a **dorsal neural tube.** In most vertebrates, the notochord calcifies into bony **vertebrae** over a **spinal cord.**
3. The spinal cord gives way to a **brain** in the anterior head region. The brain ranges in complexity, but is generally much larger, relative to the size of the body, than it is in the majority of protostomes.
4. All chordates, at some point in their life cycle, have **pharyngeal gill slits** along the side of the neck or trunk.
5. These remain present in their full number in more primitive members, such as jawless fish, but they are re-absorbed into the embryo and closed off in advanced terrestrial vertebrates like humans.
6. Speaking of necks, **segmentation** exists in vertebrates, but it can be quite hard to tell that there are head, thoracic, and abdominal segments, because these are fused in many chordates.
7. Likewise, all chordates, whether only in the embryo phase, or for life, have a post-anal **tail**. The abdomen leading up to the tail also has chevron-shaped segmented muscle fibers known as **myomeres**.
8. These are obvious in a salmon filet, but less so in the 'six pack' abs of a human.
9. Chordates are anatomically advanced, with a number of complex organ systems. This is partially due to increased body volume and greater need for circulation and distribution of materials.
10. All chordates have a **closed circulatory system** with pumping heart that distributes nutrients, oxygen, immune cells, antibodies, dissolved gases, and other materials to all of the organ systems.
11. With the exception of sea squirts, and to a partial degree, lancelets, chordates have an **endoskeleton**.
12. In jawless fish, cartilagous fish, and a few primitive bony fish, portions are made of cartilage. In higher vertebrates, the skeleton ossifies into bone.
13. As in all embryos, the **ectoderm, mesoderm,** and **endoderm** give rise to the various organ systems.
14. The ectoderm layer develops into the skin, but also into the nerves. A ridge called the **neural crest** folds inward as the embryo develops, creating a tunnel where the spinal cord and brain will form from the cells in the pocket.
15. The mesoderm gives rise to the circulatory system, the muscles, the blood, endoskeleton, fat, and kidneys.
16. The endoderm will develop into the rest of the internal viscera. The gill slits and respiratory tissue, along with the digestive system and gonads develop from the innermost layer of embryonic cells.
17. All chordates have complete respiratory, circulatory, digestive, endocrine, immune, reproductive, and nervous systems, reflective of their degree of complexity.
18. There are the three sub-phyla of chordates. These are **urochordata** (sea squirts), **cephalochordates** (lancelets), and **vertebrata** (vertebrates), which dominates the species representation of the group.

B) Sub-Phylum Urochordata: Tunicates

1. **Phylum Urochordata** contains the tunicates, also known as sea squirts.
2. At first glance, sea squirts appear to be brightly colored sponges, as their feeding strategy and **sessile** lifestyle is similar to what sponges do. However, sea squirts are very anatomically complex, with

complete organ systems.

3. They are considered to be **chordates** because they have free-swimming fish-like larvae with a **notochord** and crude eyes. As adults, both structures disappear and they settle in for a lifetime of couch potato-ism.
4. The **pharyngeal gill slits** are present and obvious in the larval stage and they develop into a basket-shaped filter-feeding structure called a **pharyngeal basket**, which is perorated by openings called **stigmata**.
5. An groove-like organ lined with cilia, known as an **endostyle**, secretes mucus into the net to help trap food.
6. Starting at the top of the animal, there is all kinds of weirdness. Since they are filter feeders, they siphon water in through a flexible **buccal siphon** that jets water through the pharyngeal basket like a giant colander.
7. Since sea squirts are deuterostomes with a true coelom, they have an innervated muscular mesoderm called a **mantle** that is capable of flexing the buccal siphon. It also expels water from the **atrial siphon**.
8. So, like a sponge, they have an inflow of water carrying food particles, and an outflow causing suction.
9. The mantle is covered by a **tunic**, which is a weird leathery shell-like organ that is made of a combination of proteins and a carbohydrate called **tunicin** that is closer in composition to cellulose than anything else.
10. The **mesentery** forms a fibrous net-like matrix of connective tissue that supports the pharyngeal basket and siphon openings, maintaining shape and preventing collapse.
11. The pharyngeal basket brings plankton, algae, and other assorted trash to the 'apex' of the net, where it is funnel into a mouth, through an **esophagus** and on to a **stomach** and **intestine**. A **pyloric gland** secretes digestive enzymes into the digestive tract to help break down the food for absorption.
12. The anus emerges from the **atrial siphon**, where waste is expelled. There are cells that secrete ammonia near the atrial siphon, but there are no obvious kidneys or glomeruli, because waste diffuses out easily.
13. Food is readily absorbed into the bloodstream of tunicates, because the **heart** pumps fluids through a closed loop of blood vessels, with a bed of **mesentery**-like vessels attaching to the gut.
14. Sea squirts may not be rocket scientists, but they do have a **brain** and dorsal nerve cord. They also possess a **neural gland** that seems to be the precursor to the vertebrate **pituitary gland**.
15. Tucked under the digestive tract are a pair of **gonads**. Sea squirts are **hermaphrodites** that release sperm into the water. It is taken up through the **atrial siphon** of a different individual.
16. Fertilized eggs are brooded inside the body cavity until they hatch. From there, small larvae are released out of the atrial siphon and into the water column.
17. As the fish-shaped larvae grow, their pharyngeal baskets enlarge, the eyes and notochord shrink to nothing, and the atrial siphon starts on the inside of the body cavity and eventually opens to the outside.
18. Essentially, the sea squirt loses its rigid shape and re-orients itself 90 degrees onto its side for sessile life.
19. It is worth noting that there are some types of sea squirts that remain in the water column as suspension feeders for their adult lives.
20. The anatomical layout of a typical tunicate is shown below, along with pictures of two species.

English Teacher Special Trivia Answers

1) Diphthongs are double vowels
2) Onomatopoeia refers to imitated noises
3) Into...specifies WHERE you threw the bundt cake
4) Anaphora uses repeated words (such as SO)

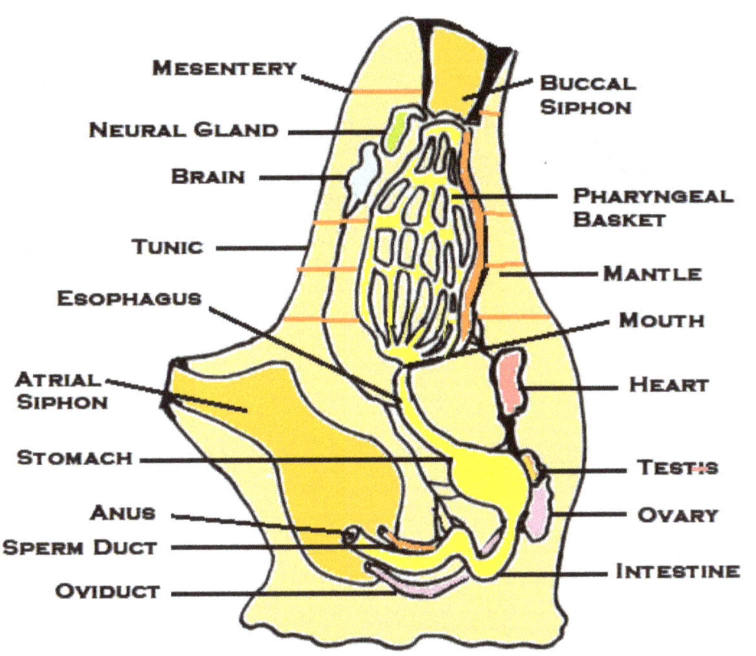

Sea Vase

Golden Tunicate

C) Sub-Phylum Cephalochordata: Lancelets

1. **Cephalochordates** (lancelets) look like very primitive fish and share several rudimentary parts of their anatomy with fish. They are burrowing marine animals that usually get no bigger than the size of a pencil.
2. Lancelets are fairly obvious ancestors of lampreys, the most primitive fish. They are basically the fish equivalent of a student starting a class project that they didn't bother to finish, but they tried to dress it up and turn it in anyway. They are there just to take their 'C-' and be done with it.
3. DNA evidence has since confirmed that lancelets are almost certainly the ancestors of modern fish.
4. Lancelets have open **pharyngeal gill slits** and both a **cartilage notochord** and **neural tube** on the dorsal surface.
5. Unlike more advanced vertebrates, the **notochord** is one solid piece, rather than divided into discs.
6. Lancelets have obvious muscular segments (**somites**) in their abdomen and a **muscular post-anal tail.**
7. Their heavily **tentacled mouth** is used like a net, thrust out of their burrows in the sand, trapping food particles that float past in their mucus. The gill slits open and create suction to pull water in.
8. These gill slits are located on the sides of a tunicate-like **pharyngeal basket**, which traps the particles and funnels them into the digestive tract. Their gut contains a **cecum** that sits in front of the **intestine**.
9. After enzymes in the cecum slowly digest the slurry of plankton and garbage, it makes its way through the intestine for absorption into the bloodstream.
10. Speaking of a bloodstream, the circulatory system of lancelets is very crude. There is no heart, and basically there is just a loop of vessels that carry fluids through the body cavity and organs as the animal flexes.
11. There is no functional respiratory system either, since lancelets are usually about the size of a match stick.
12. Lancelets are plenty small to do gas exchange by diffusion. Since all they do is sit in a burrow, they are so inactive that they don't burn a lot of fuel or have a fast metabolism.
13. Lancelets do have a **brain** that is divided into rudimentary **ventricles** like those of higher vertebrates.

14. Lancelets have a primitive **frontal eye**. Its cells seem to have a genetic link with parts of the eye in higher vertebrates. There is a pinhole-like opening on top of the head called a **neuropore** that opens into the eye.
15. There are **pigment cup cells** that bear similarity to **rods** and **cones**, along with other cells that bear similarities to those in the **retina** of higher vertebrates.
16. In front of the eye is a pointed **rostrum** that forms the anterior-most surface. It is used for digging.
17. The diagram below shows the anatomical layout of a lancelet, along with a specimen.

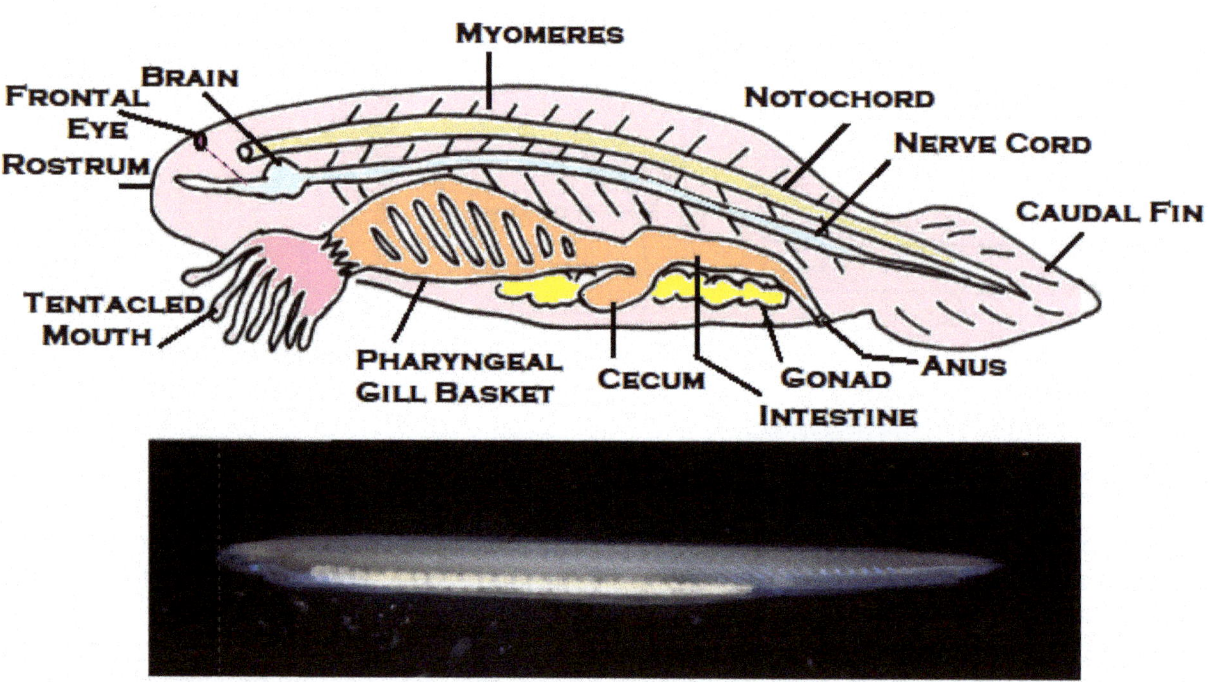

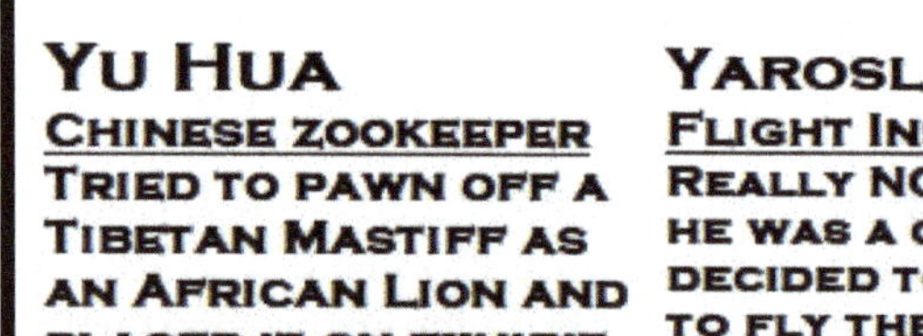

A NOD TO THE UNQUALIFIED....

IN HONOR OF LANCELETS....WHO JUST AREN'T QUITE GOOD ENOUGH TO BE FISH....

YU HUA

CHINESE ZOOKEEPER

TRIED TO PAWN OFF A TIBETAN MASTIFF AS AN AFRICAN LION AND PLACED IT ON EXHIBIT

YAROSLAV KUDRINSKY

FLIGHT INSTRUCTOR

REALLY NOT A FLIGHT INSTRUCTOR, HE WAS A COMMERCIAL PILOT WHO DECIDED TO ALLOW HIS CHILDREN TO FLY THE PLANE. PREDICTABLY THEY CRASHED INTO A MOUNTAIN.

VLADIMIR PUTIN

MILITARY STRATEGIST

DECIDED TO BRING UKRAINE BACK TO THE OLD USSR LIKE THE GOOD OLD DAYS WHEN HE WAS KGB. SO FAR HE HAS LOST 100 BILLION DOLLARS AND 204,000 TROOPS AND COUNTING.

SECTION 3: Sub-Phylum Vertebrata

A) Vertebrate Characteristics

1. **Sub-Phylum Vertebrata** includes animals with vertebrae. With the exception of the cartilage discs of jawless fish, cartilaginous fish, and a few primitive groups of bony fish, these vertebrae are fully calcified into bone.
2. The ancestral origin of the vertebrae, of course, is the **notochord**, which is present in early embryos before segmenting into **vertebral discs** that give the adult organism much greater flexibility, mobility, and control.
3. The vertebrae, themselves, have bony **processes** that stick out to protect the nerve cord.
4. **Ossification** of cartilage into bone thematically repeats itself throughout the skeleton of most vertebrates.
5. Rigid bone allows muscles to have fulcrum points for greater force and protects the animal from damage.
6. **Vertebrates** all show **cephalization** and have a **brain** divided into **ventricles** that have specialized functions.
7. As animals ascend the evolutionary tree, the brain-to-body ratio grows progressively larger, along with the size of the **cerebral cortex**, which is the processing center of the brain that allows higher thought.
8. Compared to invertebrate phyla, vertebrates have an extremely large head and brain, as well as a **cranium**, which is protective cartilage or bone. The **cranium** sits atop the **vertebral column.**
9. All of these nerves **differentiate** early on in the embryo phase from **neural crest cells**.
10. **Neural crests** are common to all vertebrate embryos, and don't just become the brain and spinal cord, but also develop into the jaws, facial muscles, and cranium.
11. Some of these nerves develop into **cranial nerves**, which innervate the **sense organs** and fine motor movements in the head. Taste, hearing, vision, and smell are controlled by these.
12. As the spinal cord descends, the **central nervous system** branches off into the **peripheral nervous system**, via paired **spinal nerves** that innervate the limbs and internal organs.
13. The **nervous systems** of vertebrates are the most advanced in the animal kingdom. Not only is the brain divided into ventricles, there is an increasingly large **cerebrum** as vertebrates rise through the evolutionary tree.
14. The cerebrum makes associations, calculations, analyses, and is responsible for higher thought processes.
15. The table below summarizes some of the major components of the vertebrate nervous system.

GEOGRAPHY TEACHER STUDY BREAK QUIZ

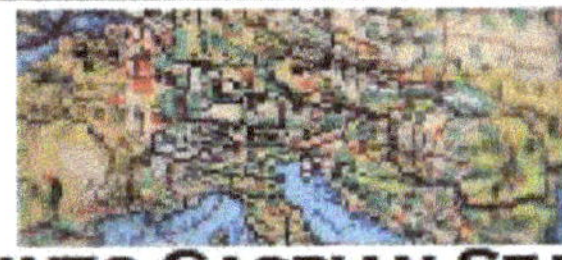

'VERTEBRATE' STARTS WITH 'V' AND SO DO THESE PLACES.

ANSWERS ON PAGE 145

1) LONGEST RIVER IN EUROPE. STARTS IN RUSSIA AND EMPTIES INTO CASPIAN SEA.
2) WEST AFRICAN RIVER THAT FLOWS THROUGH GHANA TO THE ATLANTIC OCEAN.
3) HOME OF U.S. PRESIDENTS WASHINGTON, JEFFERSON, MADISON, AND MONROE.
4) Y-SHAPED ARCHIPELAGO NATION THAT IS 2,200 MILES EAST OF AUSTRALIA.
5) ONE OF MANY SOUTH AMERICAN COUNTRIES LIBERATED BY SIMON BOLIVAR.

Vertebrate Body System & Major Function	Component Organs	Functions
Nervous System **Sensing, Processing, and Reacting to Stimuli, Maintaining Homeostasis**	**Forebrain**	Contains the cerebral cortex (thought and association), along with the thalamus (sensory signals) and hypothalamus (numerous functions).
	Midbrain	Contains colliculi, tegmentum, peduncles. Cranial nerves emerge from here. Responsible for senses, motor control, sleep, etc.
	Hindbrain	Medulla oblongata, pons, cerebellum. Responsible for numerous homeostatic functions, balance, movement, and body temperature.
	Cranial Nerves	Innervate the senses and motor control of the head and face. Vision, hearing, swallowing, talking, and other senses are under its control.
	Spinal Cord	Afferent and efferent nerves meet in reflex arcs here, as brain is connective to peripheral nervous system here.
	Spinal Nerves	Innervate the organs and limbs (peripheral nervous system). Branch off of spinal cord in lateral pairs.

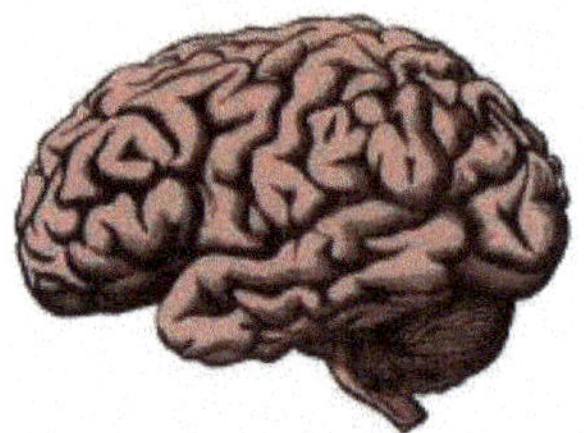
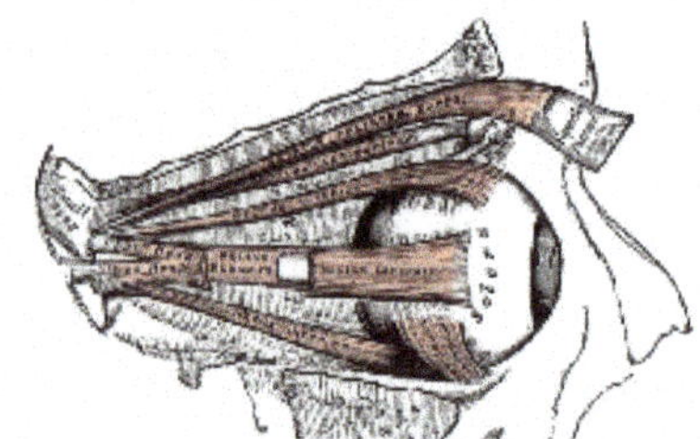
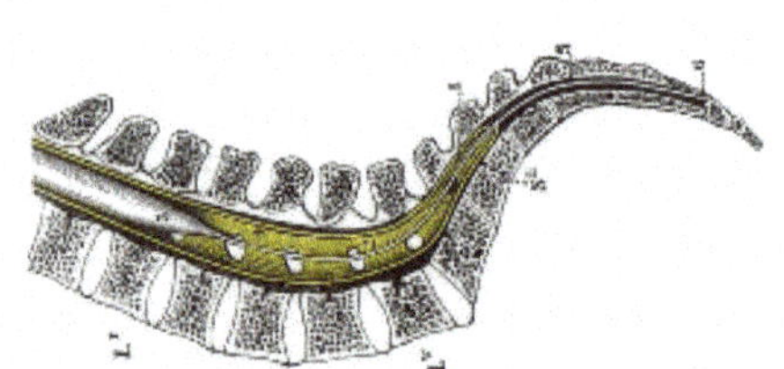

16. In addition to the major advances in the spinal cord and brain, vertebrates all have numerous distinctly advanced organ systems.

17. One hallmark of vertebrate animals is the **endocrine system**, which is a set of functionally interconnected glands that secrete signal hormones at various targets, causing cellular changes in response to stimuli.

18. The table below summarizes some of the major endocrine organs in vertebrates.

Vertebrate Body System & Major Function	Component Organs	Functions
Endocrine **Homeostasis via Hormone Signaling**	**Pituitary Gland**	Master Control Gland; Growth into Adult Form
	Pineal Gland	Regulation of Circadian Rhythms
	Thyroid Gland	Regulation of Metabolic Rate
	Parathyroid Gland	Regulation of Calcium Levels of Blood, Bones
	Pancreas	Manufactures Hormones that Regulate Digestion & Metabolism
	Adrenal Glands	Manufactures epinephrine & norepinephrine; Flight or fight

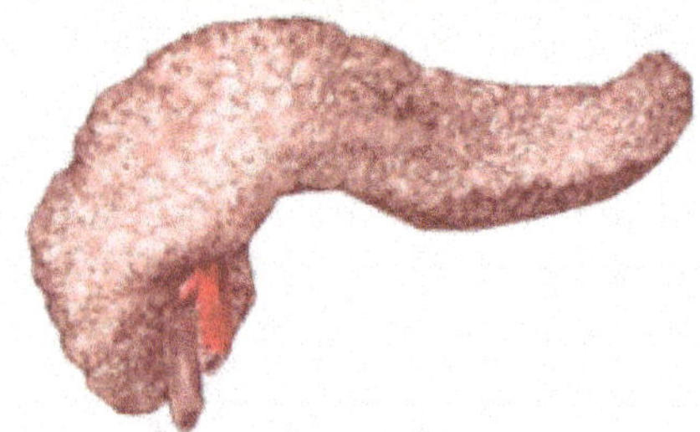
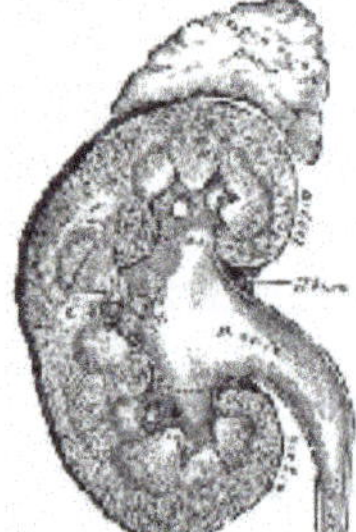
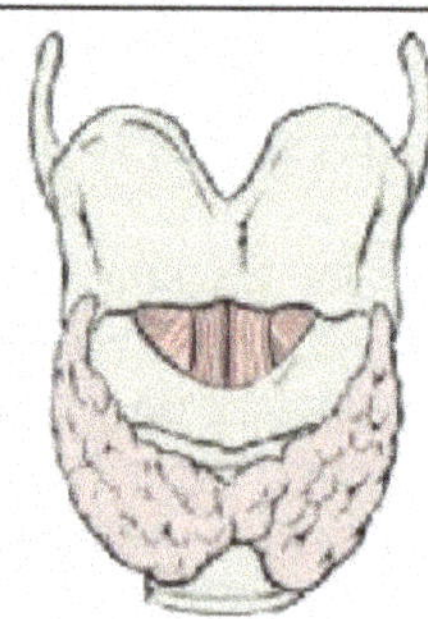

19. As many of the organ systems are, the beginning of one system can give way to the start of the next. Endocrine control is a big part of the digestive process in vertebrates. All vertebrates have a complex **digestive system**.
20. Unlike protostome invertebrates, who show a variety of designs between and within phyla and classes, all vertebrates have the full complement of differentiated digestive organs, each with distinct functions.
21. In the case of the **liver** and **pancreas**, a single organ can have dozens or hundreds of roles in metabolism.
22. The digestive system articulates with the **circulatory system**, since the blood and lymph provide a direct highway for nutrients to be distributed to cells.
23. As the **small intestine** takes up nutrients, they are absorbed into the bloodstream by a bed of blood vessels known as the **mesentery**. Fats are taken up by **lacteal vessels** in the intestine, encased in LDL and HDL particles in the **lymphatic vessels**, and funneled back into the blood.
24. The table below summarizes some of the major organs of the digestive system.

Digestive Digestion & Extraction of Nutrients from Food	Mouth & Teeth	Pulverization of food to increase surface area for digestion
	Esophagus	Peristaltic motion to push food into the stomach
	Stomach	Crude digestion of food via pepsin, HCl, and peristalsis
	Small Intestine	Majority of digestion and absorption of food via enzymatic action
	Pancreas	Secretion of digestive enzymes into small intestine
	Liver	Production off bile; storage of macronutrients
	Gallbladder	Storage and secretion of bile into small intestine
	Large Intestine	Re-absorption of water and nutrients; passage of waste

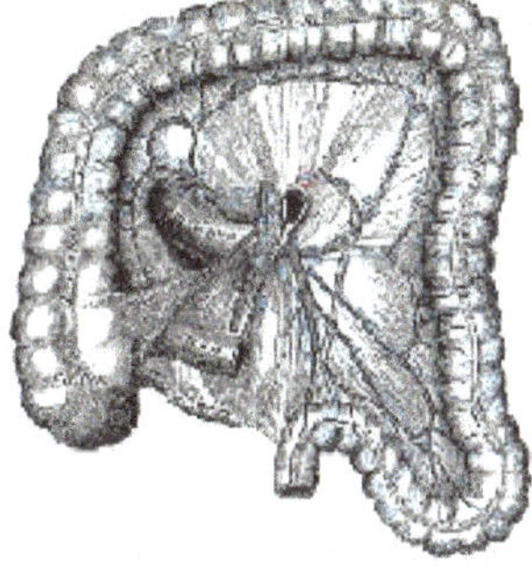

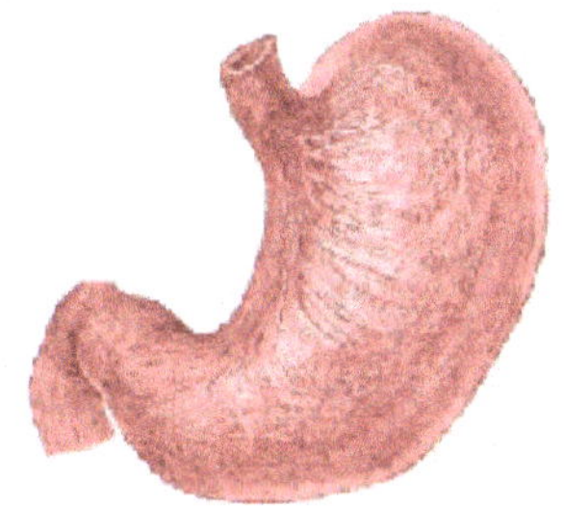

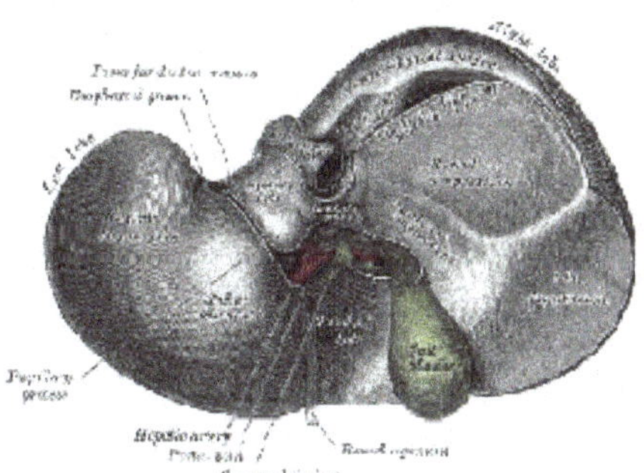

25. The **circulatory system** of all vertebrates relies on a pumping heart to distribute blood and oxygen to the tissues.
26. As vertebrates grow larger and more voluminous in size, and metabolism speeds up in **endothermic** (warm-blooded) animals, the heart must be increasingly larger and more efficient.
27. Fish only need a two-chambered heart, with deoxygenated blood cycling through the **gills** and on to the body.
28. Amphibians, with the development of **lungs**, require separate **atria** to receive oxygenated blood back from the lungs and deoxygenated blood back from the body. The only have a single **ventricle** that pumps mixed blood.
29. However, since amphibians have huge mouths and lots of moist skin, they get away with this, as much oxygen can diffuse through these moist membranes.
30. However, diffusion works poorly across the scaly skin of reptiles. They developed a **septum** to segregate oxygenated and deoxygenated blood. Smaller reptilians have a partially divided three-chambered heart.

31. However, crocodilians are too massive to get away with mixing their blood, so they have a fully developed septum and a four-chambered heart.
32. The table below summarizes some of the major circulatory system organs found in vertebrates.

Circulatory Distribution of Nutrients & Gas Exchange with Cells	Arteries	Distribution of oxygenated blood to tissues from heart
	Veins	Return of deoxygenated blood to heart from tissues
	Capillaries	Distribution of materials to-and-from tissues and cells
	Heart	Circulation of blood through body tisses
	Lymphatics	Absorption and distribution of lipids; highway for immune cells
	Red Blood Cells	Distribution of oxygen through body tissues
	White Blood Cells	Immunity against invaders; See immune system

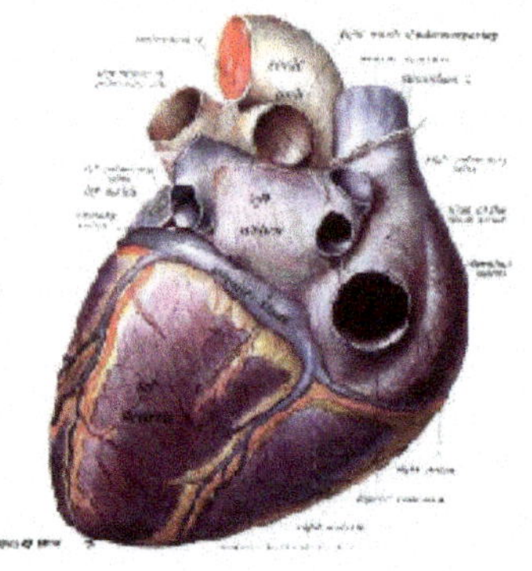

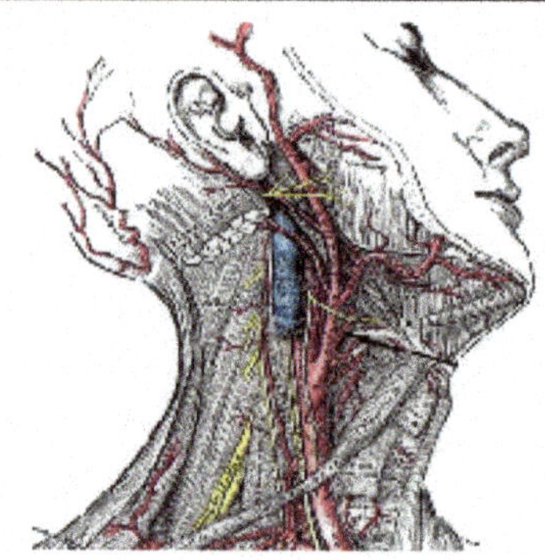

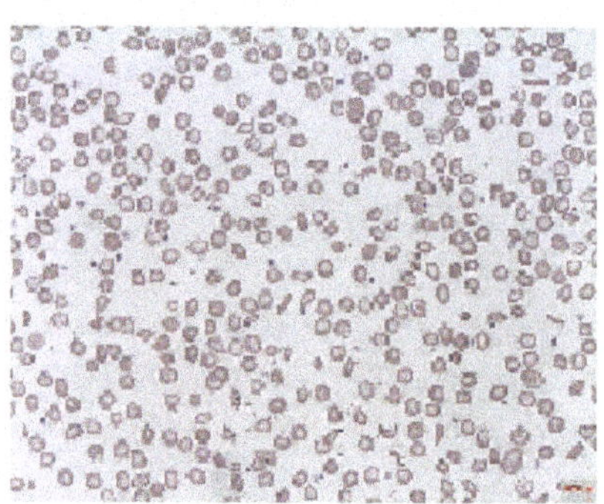

33. Because birds and mammals are **endotherms**, their metabolism runs several times faster than cold-blooded animals, so they require more oxygen for a higher rate of metabolism. Only a four-chambered heart will do.
34. The **respiratory system** is intimately connected with the circulatory system, due to the fact that gas exchange relies directly on transfer of oxygen and carbon dioxide across blood vessels.
35. Whether this occurs through **lungs** or **gills**, the mechanism is the same. Oxygen diffuses into the vessel due to higher partial pressure outside, while carbon dioxide diffuses out, due to higher partial pressure inside.
36. The table below summarizes some of the major parts of the vertebrate respiratory system.

Respiratory Gas Exchange	Gills	Gas exchange through filaments perpendicular to water flow
	Gill Rakers / Arches	Keeps blood vessels of gills expanded for maximum surface area
	Swim Bladder	Exchanges gases from blood. Flotation in fish. Evolved into lungs.
	Lungs / Alveoli	Gas exchange with air, via capillaries in moistened epithelium
	Bronchi / Bronchioles	Distribution of inhaled and exhaled gases to and from lung tissues
	Pharynx / Larynx	Flow of air through mouth. Allow vocalization in land vertebrates

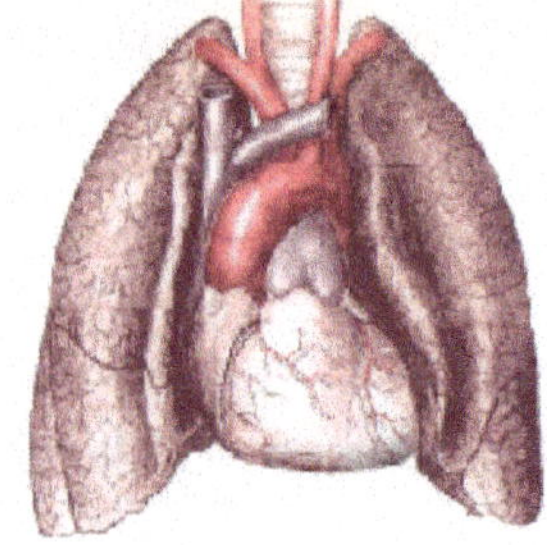

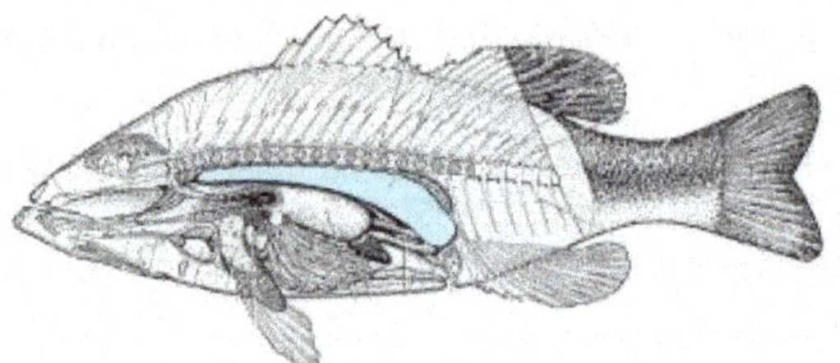

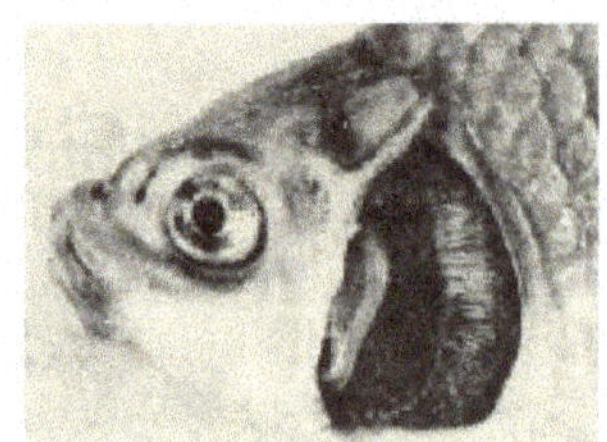

37. Another system almost completely interconnected with the circulatory system is the **immune system**. While **erythrocytes** (red blood cells) carry oxygen, **leukocytes** (white blood cells) protect against invaders.

38. It is beyond the scope of this chapter to cover the complete array of different types of white blood cells and their roles, but there are dozens of sub-types. Some manufacture **antibodies**, others use **endocytosis** to swallow up invaders, while others secrete various cytotoxins that help destroy invaders.

39. **Lymph nodes**, the **thymus**, and the **spleen**, along with bone marrow, all generate new immune cells and empty them into circulation. In birds, an additional organ known as the **bursa** serves in this role.

40. The table below summarizes some of the major components of the vertebrate immune system.

Immune Defends Host's Cells From Being Attacked by Invading Germs	Thymus	Manufactures T-cells in response to invaders
	Spleen	Filters blood and controls numbers of RBC and WBC released
	Lymph Nodes	Generate new immune cells, especially B-cells. Trap invaders.
	Bone Marrow	Stem cells inside marrow mature into various types of blood cell
	T-Cells	Neutralize invaders with antibodies on their surface
	B-Cells	Release antibodies that seek out and neutralize invaders
	Phagocytic Cells	Various classes of cells that endocytose invaders
	Cytotoxic Cells	Various groups of cells that secrete substances the kill invaders

41. Eventually that same blood requires filtration. Metabolic toxins, chemical remnants of dispatched pathogens, excess salts, and other waste must be removed. This is the role of the **excretory system**.

42. While the **liver** does generate the majority of this waste as urea, as amino acids are deaminated, it is the role of the **kidneys** to remove the waste by filtering the blood and pushing out the filtrate as urine.

43. The major components of the excretory system of vertebrates are summarized below.

Excretory	Kidneys	Filter salt ions, nitrogenous wastes, and toxins from blood
Removes Nitrogenous Wastes and Toxins from Metabolism	Bladder	Stores liquid waste for removal from body
	Integument	Skin also removes various wastes from sweat glands, secretions
	Gills	In fish, excess salt ions or ammonia can be pumped out of gills.

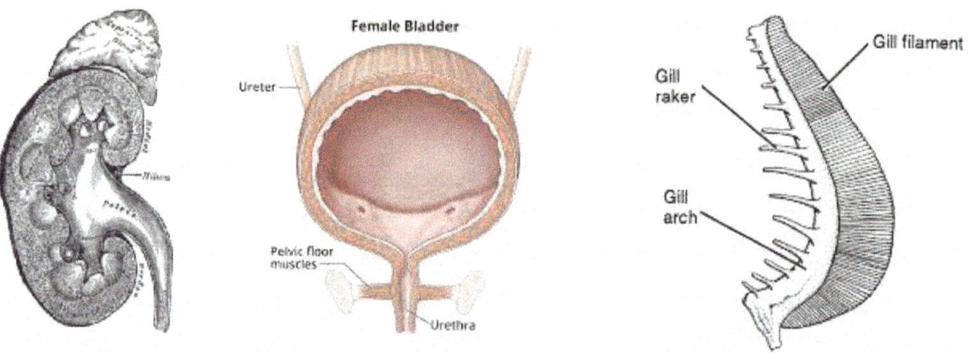

44. Often the excretory system is plumbed with common openings to the **reproductive tract**.

45. By-and-large, most vertebrates are **dioecious**, having separate sexes. There are some exceptions, with some fish like angelfish and wrasses showing **sequential hermaphroditism**, as they change sexes with age.

46. A few vertebrate species, seemingly at random, are all female and **parthenogenetic**, with self-fertilizing eggs. For example, some species of silverside fish and whiptail lizards reproduce this way.

47. The majority of vertebrates perform **spermatogenesis** in the **testes** via **meiosis** and **oogenesis** in the **ovaries**, with fertilized **zygotes** progressing through predictable stages of embryo development.

48. **External fertilization** is mostly restricted to fish and a few amphibians, though a few fish use modified fins like a **penis** to perform **internal fertilization**. Direct transfer closer to the egg increases the odds of fertilization.

49. Reptiles and mammals use **hemipenes** or a **penis**, respectively, for this purpose, and birds join **cloacal openings.**

50. Once sperm has been transferred through the female **vagina** and into the **uterus**, the fate of the embryo depends on the level of evolutionary advancement and adaptation of the vertebrate.

51. Most fish and amphibians are **oviparous**, laying masses of jelly-like eggs that they often abandon, though some do brood a nest or protect their young. Most reptiles are also **oviparous**, but they add a shell, significantly more nourishment, and a watery **amnion** to the egg, which frees them from being tied to a water source.

52. Some species of fish and reptiles, such as dogfish or garter snakes are **ovoviviparous**, allowing the eggs to hatch internally in the mother. The live young are born at a much larger size, upping the odds of survival.

53. Birds are strictly **oviparous**, but for different reasons. Birds cannot afford to become pregnant, because it would leave females vulnerable to predators when they became too fat to fly.

54. Unlike lower oviparous vertebrates, birds have numerous protective parental behaviors and invest a lot in raising the offspring to adulthood.

55. With the exception of oviparous monotremes like the platypus, all mammals are **viviparous**, giving birth to live young that are nourished by the mother.

56. In the case of **marsupials**, this is mostly via the mother's milk inside the pouch, whereas **placental mammals** nourish the young with the **placenta** inside the uterus and later with milk as the young develop.

57. Some of the major reproductive organs found in vertebrates are summarized below.

Reproductive **Procreation of Species**	Testes & Vas Deferens	Produce sperm via meiosis and export it from body
	Prostate Gland	Provides secretions that nourish sperm and help it survive to egg
	Penis	Delivers sperm to vagina, if present
	Ovaries & Fallopian Tubes	Produce ova via meiosis and export them to uterus
	Uterus & Vagina	Route for delivery of sperm. In viviparous animals, nourishes egg
	Shell Glands	In oviparous animals, secretes protective shell over egg
	Cloaca	In egg-laying animals, a utility body opening for reproduction

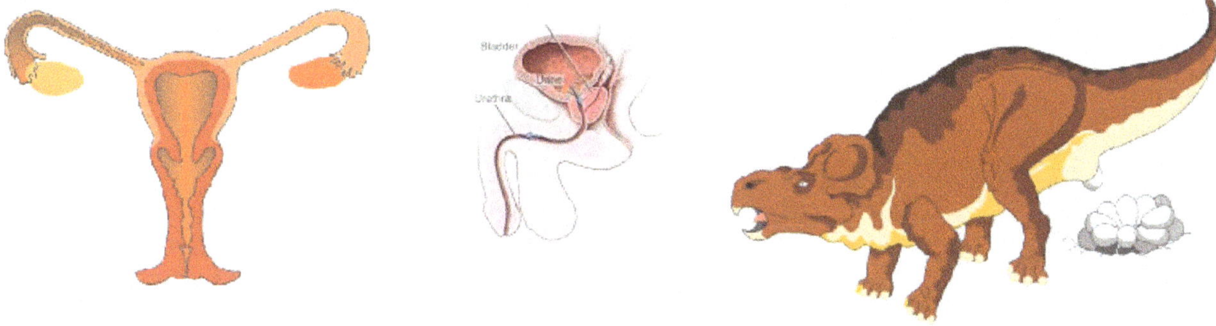

58. Another strictly mammalian feature is **hair**, which is produced by the **follicles** of the **integument**. The same cells produce **scales** in fish and reptiles and **feathers** in birds.

59. Dove-tailing back to the very concept of what makes animals distinctly vertebrate in character, is the **vertebrae** themselves, which are part of the musculoskeletal system.

60. In general, the musculoskeletal system of vertebrates is reflective of their bilateral symmetry, with limbs and muscles occurring in symmetrical pairs, innervated by symmetrical spinal nerves.

61. The musculoskeletal system is also one of the most fluid of the vertebrate systems, as it has evolved in dramatically different directions, according to ecological niche and environmental pressures.

62. It is this system that has allowed wahoo to swim 70 miles per hour through the ocean, tree frogs to clear jumps nearly 100 times their body length, lions to take down wildebeests, and peregrine falcons to fly at 180 mph.

63. Some of the major components of the vertebrate integument are summarized below.

Integumentary **Lining and Protection of Body Surfaces; Homeostasis**	Epidermis	Layer of tissue that provides external protective layer over body
	Dermis	Base layer of tissue that connects skin to muscle and fat
	Sweat Glands	When present, provides homeostatic cooling mechanism
	Sebaceous Glands	Oil glands or preen glands that seal in moisture
	Follicles	Produce keratinous scales, hair, or feathers for protection

HAIR
EPIDERMIS
DERMIS
BLOOD VESSELS
HAIR FOLLICLE
SWEAT GLAND

64. The final table summarizes some of the major component of the vertebrate musculoskeletal system.
65. It is beyond the scope of this short section to go into the exhaustive detail required to really study every system. This will be done in later chapters. Specific modifications and adaptations to distinct systems will be mentioned as we progress through the taxonomy of the vertebrate phylum.
66. We now move on to working our way through the many different taxa of vertebrate animals.

Musculoskeletal **Mechanical support and movement of body**	Skeletal Muscles	Used for mechanical movement of limbs and body
	Smooth Muscles	Used primarily for involuntary movements, such as digestion
	Cardiac Muscles	Used in involuntary contraction of heart muscle
	Bones	Used for leverage, support, and to manufacture immune cells
	Ligaments	Used to connect bone to bone at articulation points
	Tendons	Used to connect muscles to bone and transfer force

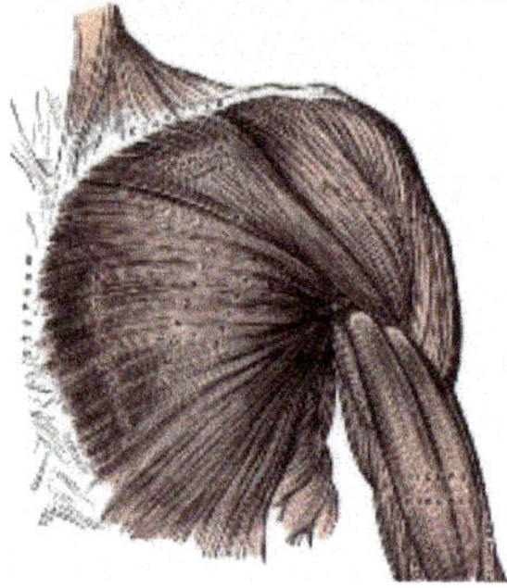

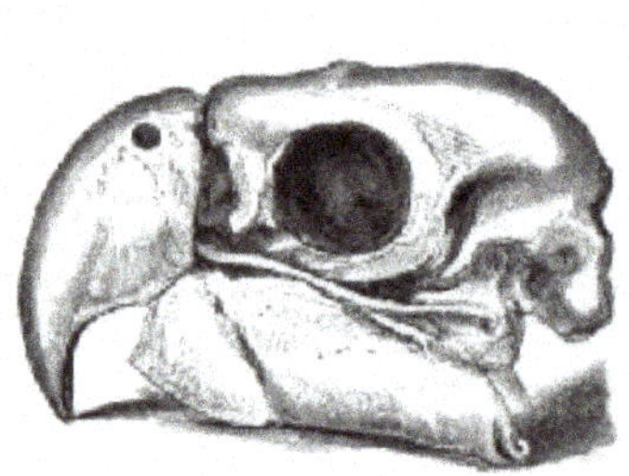

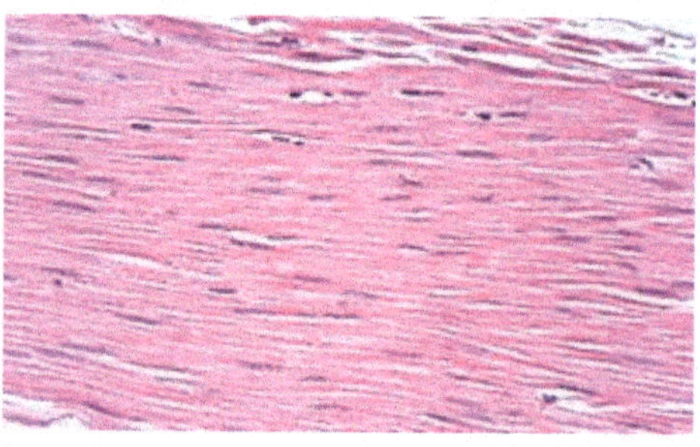

B) Class Agnatha: Jawless Fishes

1. **Class Agnatha** includes the jawless fishes. They are represented by the more primitive hagfish of **Order Myxiniformes** and the slightly more advanced lampreys of **Order Petromyzontiformes.**
2. **Agnathans** have a flexible **cartilage skeleton** (though they do have vertebral discs), a single paddle-like **caudal fin**, and **open pharyngeal gill slits**. The absence of a lower jaw gives this group their name.
3. In spite of lacking a lower jaw and having a cartilage skeleton, lampreys do have a plate of **bony teeth** with dentin and enamel. These make spiraling concentric rows leading into the oral cavity.
4. Hagfish have a **cranium** made of **cartilage**, but they have a simple **notochord** that is not divided into **vertebrae**.
5. Lampreys have the cranium AND they have a cartilage notochord divided into vertebrae.
6. The **brains** of agnathans are divided into **ventricles** and continue into a **dorsal nerve cord**. While have eye spots that are simple light detectors, lampreys have fully functional vertebrate **eyes** as adults.
7. Both groups of jawless fish have a single nostril in the top of their head that leads to an **olfactory sac**.
8. Hagfish have copious tactile **tentacles** around their mouth, which has two rows of false teeth made of keratin plates. These are used to crush their food to smithereens as they tear off chunks of rotten meat.
9. Just about everything about hagfish is disgusting. In addition to living inside of dead sharks and dolphins and eating their way out, they have hundreds of **slime glands** that can produce gallons of slime in short order.
10. The presence of open **pharyngeal gill slits** in agnathans is a throwback to the suspension feeding design of lancelets, but only certain lampreys use the gills to assist with feeding. They are mostly used for respiration.
11. Blood vessels are plumbed past the gill slits in parallel fashion, allowing the maximum surface area contact between the flowing blood and the oxygenated water flowing past.

12. Doxygenated blood enters the **atrium** of the **heart** via the **vena cava**, where it drains to the **ventricle**. The ventricle pumps the blood through the **ventral aorta** and **dorsal aorta**, which pass the gills, picking up oxygen.
13. In fish, each major organ has its own arterial blood supply. For instance, the **gastric artery** supplies the **stomach**, the **renal artery** supplies the **kidneys**, and the **hepatic artery** supplies the **liver**.
14. Fish only have a single loop, so deoxygenated blood makes a circuit and returns to the gill arches.
15. Lampreys and hagfish have the standard vertebrate digestive system, with accessory organs. The main tube of the digestive tract proceeds from **pharynx** to **espophagus** to **stomach,** then on to an **intestine.**
16. A **liver** produces **bile** and other secretions and enzymes that help with emulsification and digestion, while a **pancreas** produces proteases and carbohydrate-digesting enzymes.
17. Reproductively, almost nothing is known about hagfish, except that they lay eggs in sticky masses. Some species are separate sexes, while others are hermaphroditic. To date, no one has ever seen a pair mating.
18. If one would have to guess, they probably have their tender moments inside the carcass of a dead rotting whale at the bottom of the ocean, since that's what they like to eat.
19. Considering that this happens in 40-degree water half-a-mile deep, this probably explains the lack of volunteers to interrupt the private moments of hagfish lovers.
20. Lampreys are nest builders, wherein the female lays eggs in a pile of pebbles, and the male uses **external fertilization** when he finds the nest.
21. Though some live as full-time freshwater scavengers, the majority of lamprey species are **anadromous**. They mate and spawn in freshwater rivers and creeks, returning to the sea as they grow into adults.
22. The ocean has larger fish, such as the sharks or salmon that they tend to parasitize for their blood.
23. While modern agnathans are garbage feeders or blood-sucking parasites, it wasn't always that way.
24. Jawless **ostracoderms** existed in pre-historic oceans before cartilaginous fish evolved the lower jaw and outcompeted them in all predatory niches. Numerous ocean temperature changes didn't help them either.
25. Ostracoderms such as **astrapsids** and **placodonts** had armored plates on their body and disc-like mouths. Presumably, they fed like rays, picking up mollusks and arthropods off the bottom for meals.
26. The diagram below shows hagfish and lamprey specimens, a placoderm fossil, and general internal anatomy.

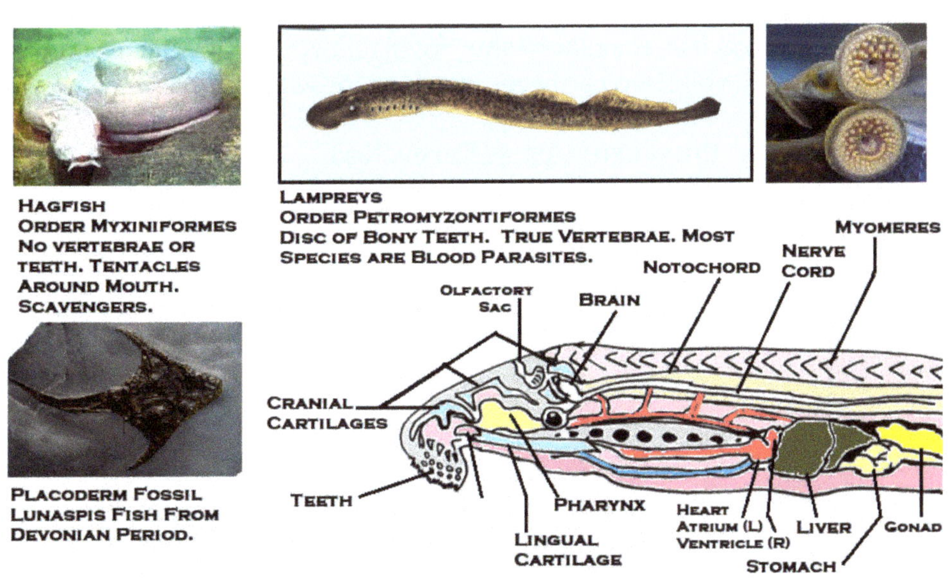

C) Class Chondrichthyes: Cartilaginous Fish

1. **Class Chondrichthyes**, the cartilaginous fish are a quantum leap in evolution over the jawless fish. When they appeared on the scene about 400 million years ago, it spelled doom for most jawless fish.
2. **Class Chondrichthyes** includes primitive chimaera ratfish, and numerous types of rays, skates, and sharks.
3. The development of a lower jaw from the **gill arches** was a devastating competitive blow. The presence of a lower jaw opened up a huge number of predatory niches unavailable to more primitive jawless fish.
4. The ability to bite down on prey indirectly allowed massive increases in speed. Sharks, for instance, could afford to streamline their bodies like rockets, rather than having to rely on serpentine twisting motion to attack.
5. Not only did this allow pelagic species to hit their prey like a sledgehammer at high speed, it opened up the entire water column for hunting.
6. Even species that remained benthic ambush predators, like rays, could still crush their prey between mouth plates and dispatch them quickly, rather than needing to 'cookie cutter' them to death.
7. Unsurprisingly, this ability to move up the food chain also allowed cartilaginous fish the freedom of opportunities to make a lot of additional evolutionary adjustments.
8. Shockingly, most cartilaginous fish have a **cartilage skeleton** with separate **vertebrae** and well-defined **cranial cartilage** plates in the skull. Their **gill arches** are also rigid cartilage, keeping them open for water flow.
9. Cartilaginous fish retain **open pharyngeal gill slits** from the embryo stage. The **gill filaments** are positioned under these open slits at perpendicular angles to the direction of water flow for maximal surface area.
10. Sharks lack an **operculum** (bony flap) above their gills like more advanced fish, nor do they have the accessory muscles that can open and close this flap to oxygenate the lungs while they sit passively.
11. Rigid **gill cartilages** provide the support to keep the filaments spread out for respiration.
12. These cartilages are also bent forward and evolved to form the lower jaw. It is still possible to see this cartilage modify into its fate as a lower jaw in the early stages of all vertebrate embryos.
13. Jawless fish like lampreys and hagfish have a radiator-grill type arrangement of open gill slits between the gill cartilages that suspend the gill filaments.
14. In the earliest cartilaginous fish, the **placodonts**, fossils show that the first gill arch moved forward to create a crude lower jaw, while two cartilages migrated forward in modern cartilaginous fish, further reinforcing the jaw.
15. The diagram below shows this progression as fish evolved.

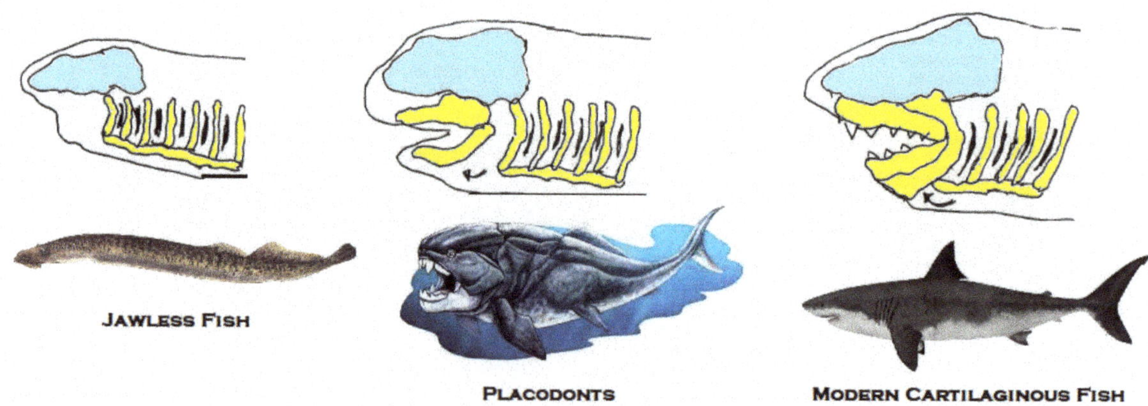

16. Since they can't flex their gills, harks and rays must stay in constant motion or sit in a flowing current to keep their gills oxygenated. This is called **ram ventilation**. It puts them at a distinct disadvantage to bony fish.
17. The body of cartilaginous fish evolved rapidly to accommodate predatory behavior. Instead of the puny single tail fin of lampreys and hagfish, cartilaginous fish developed several sets of fleshy **paired fins**.
18. **Pectoral fins** and **pelvic fins** provide thrust and crude rudder-like control at the front of the body, **anal fins** do the same at the rear of the body. The **dorsal fin** and **caudal fin** slice through the water and provide balance.
19. Unlike the more advanced bony fish, none of these fins are retractable, due to the absence of rays and spines. This means that sharks and rays must make a huge arc like an aircraft carrier to make a turn.
20. While a mako shark may be able to slam into a clueless fish at 70 mph, if a speedy prey fish like a mackerel sees it coming, it can turn on a dime and avoid the rush. Rays and skates are also limited to one good ambush shot.
21. For this reason, some cartilaginous fish, particularly large ones, changed tactics and remained or returned to **suspension feeding**. Remember...the earliest gills, such as the pharyngeal basket of lancelets, were originally used as dual-purpose feeding and respiratory organs. The blueprints are still there in the genes.
22. Support for this idea comes from the fact that many large sharks STILL ARE **suspension feeders**, such as whale sharks, Greenland sharks, megamouth sharks, and basking sharks.
23. Plankton might not taste as good, but there's always a lot of it, and you don't have to chase it down. This is really the only way to sustain massive behemoths like whale sharks and manta rays. There just isn't enough fish.
24. While their skeleton is very much cartilage, sharks and rays DO have bony jaws. Cartilage doesn't tend to work too well when you're trying to crush a sea lion with a bite. They also sell well in trashy Florida tourist traps.
25. Cartilaginous fish have plates or teeth made of **dentin** protein and **enamel**, just like any other tooth. The center of teeth also have a living **pulp cavity**. They are **deciduous** and grow in rows, constantly growing and replacing.
26. They are larger, but mostly identical in structure to the sand-papery scales that cover the body.
27. Unlike true teeth, these teeth and scales are embedded in the flesh and not the jawbone. They are constantly shed and replaced because of the abuse that they take from biting down on bone or getting in fights.
28. Cartilaginous fish evolved in numerous other ways to augment the roles within their niches.
29. Another adaptation that needed to happen for effective **predation** was flotation. Since the swim bladder had not yet evolved, cartilaginous fish had to find another way.
30. Sharks, rays, and skates have a massive **oily liver**, which is so full of fat that they float rather easily.
31. The evolution of the digestive system was not merely limited to the liver. This needed to happen because of the massive amounts of protein and fat that predators need to process to get nutrition.
32. In addition to the bile-secreting liver, the **pancreas** of cartilaginous fish is a large lobed gland under the main tube of the gut. It churns out a concoction of lipases, proteases, and other digestive enzymes.
33. While they have a true **stomach**, cartilaginous fish did not make it to the evolutionary point of having long coiled intestines. However, the same idea showed itself in the form of **spiral valves**.
34. The inside surface of the intestines is covered with corkscrew-shaped membranes that increase the amount of available surface area to extract nutrients from the food.
35. The **circulatory system** of cartilaginous fish is **closed** with a **2 chambered-heart**.
36. Blood flow begins its journey from the capillaries of **gill filaments** through a **pulmonary vein** into the **atria** of the heart. A small chamber called an **auricle** helps with any overflow or backflow.

37. From there, a more muscular **ventricle** squeezes the blood through the **aorta**, which splits into the various arteries that supply the organs, such as the **hepatic** (liver), **gatric** (stomach), **carotids** (brain), and so on.
38. Deoxgenated blood travels through **veins** and eventually arrives back in the **capillaries** of the gill filaments, where the entire loop begins again.

YOUR ODDS OF BEING KILLED BY WEIRD RANDOM THINGS (Shark Attack Included)

Shark Attack	1 in 3,748,067	Lightning Bolt	1 in 138,393
Falling Tree You Didn't Cut	1 in 233,750	Dog Attack	1 in 86,781
Choking on Your Food	1 in 2,535	Crashing Jetliner	1 in 137,500
Allergic Reaction	1 in 44,192	Angry Hippo	1 in 92,500
Vending Machine Falls on You	1 in 140,000	Hit by Meteorite	1 in 250,000
Taken Out by Serial Killer	1 in 256,410	Crashing Elevator (Wahh!)	1 in 134,000
Electrocuting Yourself	1 in 14,705	Slipping on Banana Peel	1 in 15,000,000,000

39. The diagram below shows the digestive and circulatory systems of a typical cartilaginous fish.

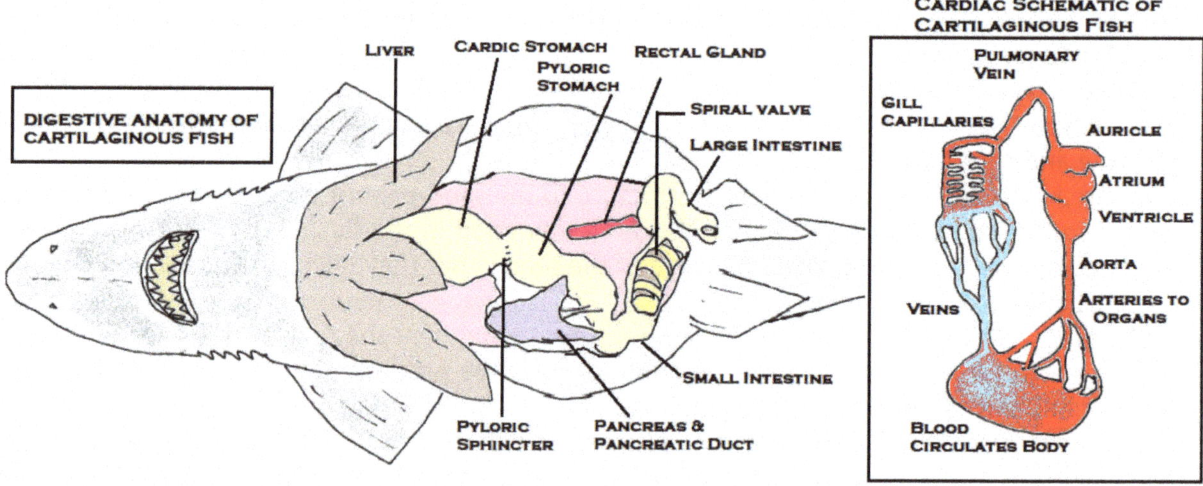

40. The **excretory systems** of cartilaginous fish are unique in the animal kingdom, in that they take advantage of the fact that osmosis does not depend on WHAT is dissolved, but how MUCH is dissolved.
41. The **kidneys** of cartilaginous fish detoxify ammonia into **urea** and then purposely release the urea back into the bloodstream to counterbalance the molarity of the salt concentration in the surrounding water.
42. Additionally, there are specialized regulatory cells in the gills that block the loss of urea to the surrounding water and a **rectal gland** that concentrates salts from the urine and expels them out of the anus.

43. Many sharks have impressive **osmoregulatory** ability if given time. For instance, bull sharks can live in full strength seawater, but they can go many miles into freshwater rivers.
44. One directionally-challenged bull shark found 15 miles North of St. Louis once. Apparently GPS didn't work.
45. In addition to having exceptional homeostatic ability, cartilaginous fish also have some sensory superpowers.
46. Cartilaginous fish have **lateral lines** down the sides of their bodies, which are basically innervated pits filled with ciliated cells. Much like the way hearing works, vibrations in the water stimulate nerve endings.
47. When the ciliated hairs are moved, this causes **ion channel proteins** to open, starting a cascade of sodium channels that depolarize the length of the nerve all the way to the brain.
48. A thrashing swimmer who fell off their surf board can then be found. From there, additional senses help.
49. Under the nose of the shark, the **ampullae of Lorenzi** detect electric fields given off by the nervous system of their prey. This is how sharks and rays can easily find food at night in muddy water. They 'see' the electricity.
50. Cartilaginous fish also have some anatomical advances that are far beyond jawless fish. It could even be argued that some of these advances are more impressive than bony fish.
51. The **olfactory organs** of cartilaginous fish are massive and each innervate to a pair of **olfactory bulbs** behind them, which send nerve impulses down the **olfactory tracts** to the middle of the cerebrum.
52. From there, the shark can decide what the smell is and whether he wants to eat it. Much like you smelling fresh baked brownies, the great white shark can smell some fresh Kevin the surfer and let himself have a cheat treat.
53. Cartilaginous fish have a relatively small **forebrain**, as compared to other vertebrates, but it is considerably larger in size than almost all protostome invertebrates could ever hope for. While they are relatively unintelligent, sharks are still capable of learning and remembering behaviors, foods, and dangers.
54. The **midbrain** and **hindbrain** of cartilaginous fish are relatively large, as compared to the forebrain.
55. Their larger sizes are a necessity, given the importance of feeding and movement to their lifestyle. They need precision control of homeostatic functions and the ability to respond quickly to stimuli.
56. The diagram below shows the parts of the brain and some of the sensory organs of chondrichthyes.

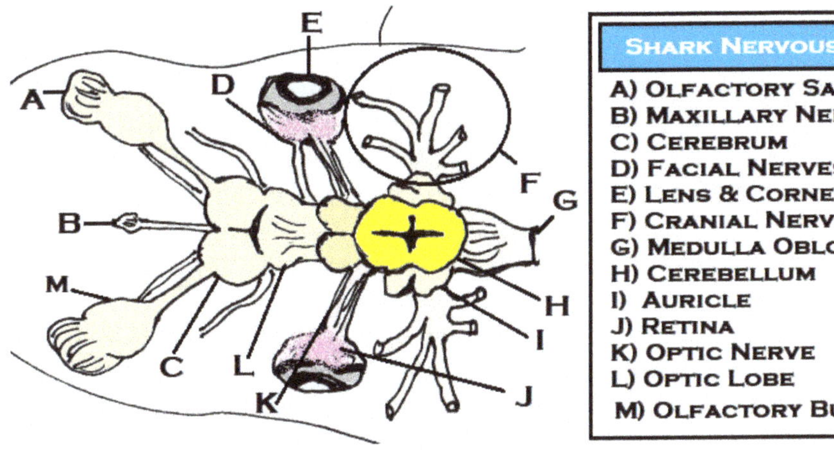

Some Obscure Phobias

Ablutophobia: Fear of taking a shower or bath.

Omphalophobia: Fear of seeing belly buttons.

Genuphobia: Fear of seeing people's knees.

Lachanophobia: Fear of vegetables and produce.

Pupaphobia: Fear of creepy puppets.

57. The **reproductive system** of the chondrichthyes bears some surprises, in terms of strategy.

58. While more advanced bony fish tend to be deadbeat parent **R-strategists** that crank out as many eggs and larvae as possible, with the hope that ANYONE survives, this is not the case with chondrichthyes.
59. All cartilaginous fish are either **oviparous** or **ovoviviparous**, but they are much closer to **K-strategists** on the continuum of reproductive strategy. They have fewer, larger, and more well-protected offspring.
60. Cartilaginous fish stake their bets on a decently larger percentage of their offspring surviving. Even if this number is only a few percent, it is still a far cry from the estimated 1 in 100,000 bass that ever see adulthood.
61. Male sharks and rays have internal **testes**. Their **sperm ducts** exit the body at the base of a pair of **clasper fins** that are used like a **penis** to deliver sperm through the **cloaca** of the female and into the **vagina**.
62. From there, the **vagina** opens up into two lateral **uterine horns**. These are tipped with **oviducal glands** that produce mucus and proteins that can form egg cases.
63. In between the two sides of the uterus, an **oviduct** traces its way back to either one or two **ovaries**, depending on the type of cartilaginous fish. The ovary fills the eggs with large quantities of rich yolk.
64. The diagram below shows the reproductive tracts of a shark.

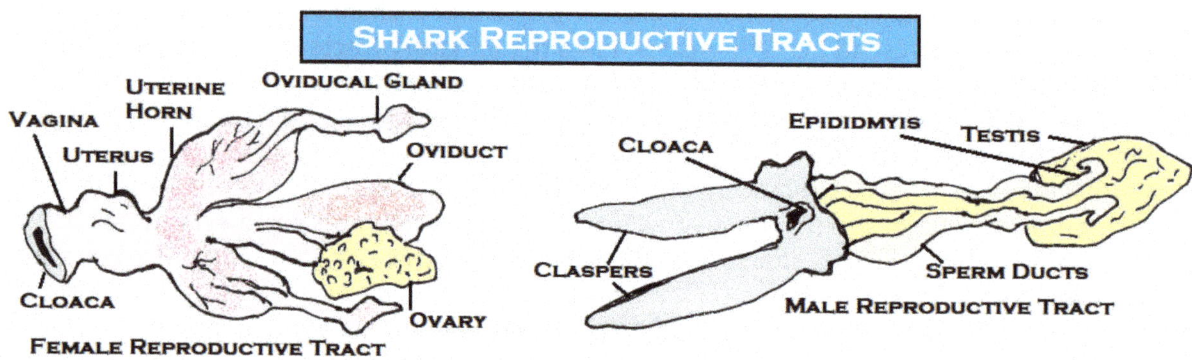

65. In **oviparous** chondrichthyes like skates, eggs are laid in cases that resemble pockets of ravioli. Even when laid, the eggs are much larger than those of bony fish and the embryos are much further developed.
66. **Ovoviviparous** members of the group, like rays and dogfish, allow the eggs to hatch inside of the uterus, giving live birth to **pups** that are exponentially larger than the juveniles of bony fish.
67. Both strategies hedge the bet that survival of larger offspring should have much better odds.
68. This is not without its drawbacks, thanks to people. Since sharks have fewer offspring that take longer to mature, this means that their populations can be devastated with relative ease.
69. Thanks to shark-finning, trophy fishing, long-lining, and stupid people who think 'Jaws' could really happen, most large shark species are either threatened or endangered.
70. By one estimate, there are less than 5,000 full-sized adult great white sharks left in the WORLD and there probably were NEVER more than a few hundred thousand. Why? Simple mathematics.
71. If you walk back the food chain and realize that a 2,000 pound great white shark is an apex predator, it becomes clear that just one animal needs access to 20,000 pounds of large fish at any given time to feed itself.
72. Keep going back down the food chain all the way to the planktonic steps and it becomes apparent that one shark needs thousands of tons of plankton and hundreds of square miles of territory to feed itself.

73. With general characteristics of the group covered, let's move on to how the chondrichthyes are classified.
74. In spite of being an ancient group of fish and losing most of their claim to evolutionary dominance to bony fish, cartilaginous fish still make up 13 orders of fish comprising nearly 1000 living species.
75. There are two living **sub-classes** of cartilaginous fish. The **Holocephali** are the more ancient group and comprise ratfish and chimeras, while sharks, rays, and skates belong to the more evolved **Elasmobranchs**.
76. Chimeras and ratfish have small beak-like mouths, a single gut without a distinct stomach or intestine, a protective spine in front of their **dorsal fin**, and they lack a fully developed **caudal fin**.
77. Rather than trying to successively detail each group through the text, the next page depicts some of the major order of cartilaginous fish, along with a brief description.
78. In the meantime, please enjoy a word from our sponsors and please seek their products out at any vendor that sells these fine and sophisticated goods.

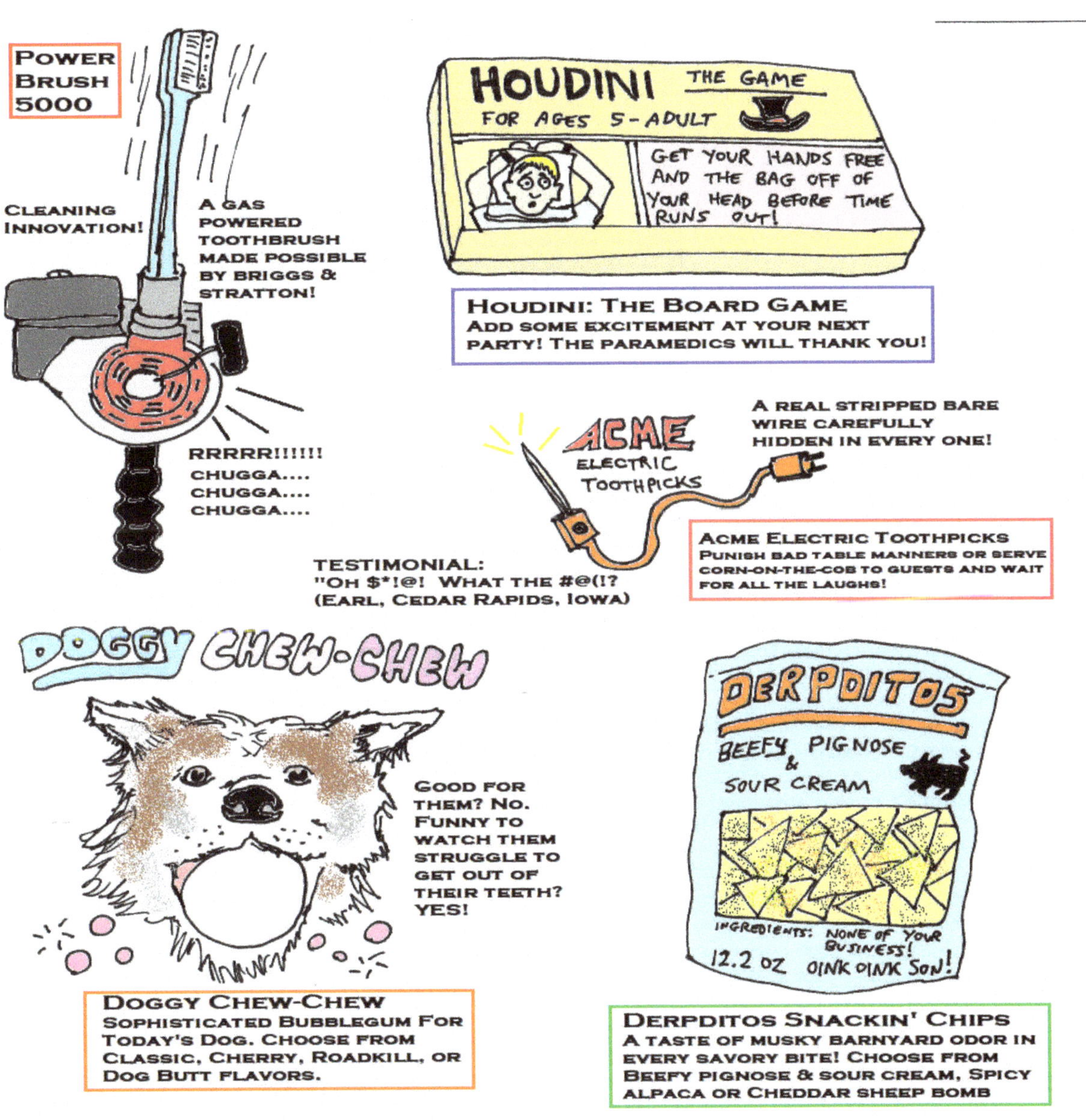

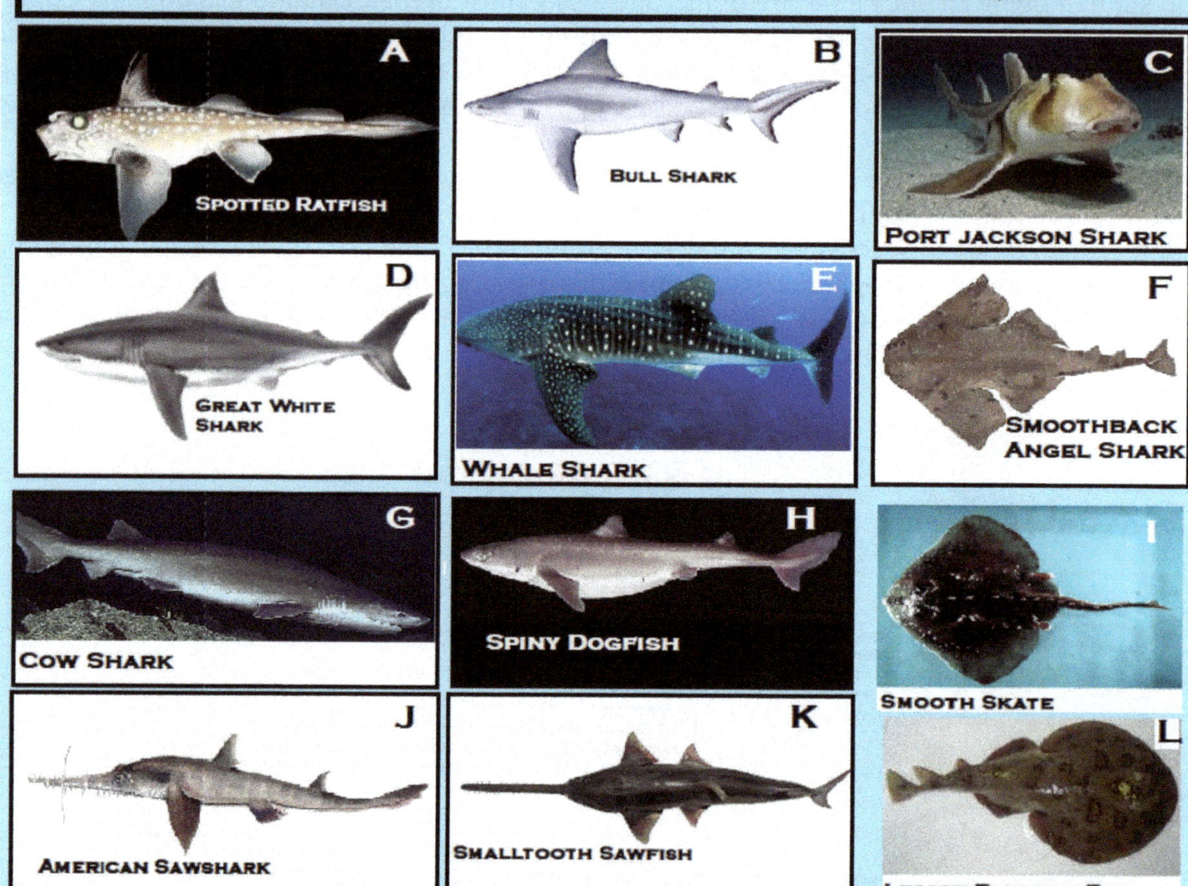

A) Subclass Holocephali; Order Chimaeriformes (Ratfish and Chimeras). Spine on dorsal fin. Continuous gut without chambers. Rat-like caudal fin.

B) Subclass Elasmobranchi; Order Carchariniformes (Catsharks, Hammerheads, Hound Sharks, Requiem Sharks) Eyelids, 2 dorsal fins, anal fin, 5 gill slits.

C) Subclass Elasmobranchi; Order Heterodontiformes (Horn & Bullhead Sharks) No rostral cartilage or eyelids. Nose flaps. 2 spiny dorsal fins. Small size.

D) Subclass Elasmobranchi; Lamniformes (Mackeral sharks, Thresher sharks, Sand, Goblin, and Megamouth sharks) 5 gill slits, 2 dorsal fins, large mouth.

E) Subclass Elasmobranchi; Order Orectolobiformes (Bamboo, Whale, Carpet, Nurse Sharks) Short wide mouth with barbels. Spiracles for respiration. Camo.

F) Subclass Elasmobranchi; Order Squatiniformes (Angel sharks) Flat head and torso. Cylindrical tail. Extensible jaws with needle-like teeth. Ovoviviparous.

G) Subclass Elasmobranchi; Order Hexanchiformes (Frilled Sharks) Resemble prehistoric shark fossils. 7 Gills, Single Dorsal fin. Eel-like body. No eyelids.

H) Subclass Elasmobranchi; Order Squaliformes (Dogfish, Gulper, Sleeper, and and Lantern Sharks) Cat-like nocturnal eyes, 2 dorsal fins, highly variable.

I) Subclass Elasmobranchi; Order Rajiformes (Skates) Laterally flat, gigantic dorsal fins, Gill slits on ventral surface, spiracles. Oviparous with egg cases.

J) Subclass Elasmobranchi; Order Pristiophoriformes (Saw Sharks) Protruding teeth used to slay prey. 6 Gills, barbels around mouth, ovoviviparous. Rare.

K) Subclass Elasmobranchi; Order Rhinopristiformes (Sawfish, Banjofish, Guitarfish, Drumsetfish) Shovel-shaped rostrum with teeth. Ovoviviparous.

L) Subclass Elasmobranchi; Order Torpediniformes (Electric rays, Torpedo rays) Pancake-shaped body with electric organs behind pectoral fins. Shark-like tail.

D) Class Osteichthyes: Bony Fish

1. **Class Osteichthyes** (bony fish) have a number of advances over the cartilaginous fish, the most obvious, which is a **bony skeleton** and **bony scales**. Additionally, they have true **bony teeth**.
2. **Bony fish** have a bony flap called an **operculum** over their gills that protect them. They also have muscular attachments that allow them to voluntarily control water flow through the operculum as they breathe.
3. This allowed many more species of benthic and sedentary bony fish to evolve.
4. The **spiracles**, the openings that allow water flow into the pharyngeal cavity of cartilaginous fish, are still present in some of the less-evolved types of bony fish, but they are largely vestigial or devolved in advanced **teleosts**.
5. The **gills,** themselves, are attached to cartilaginous **gill rakers** in rows. As in the gills of more primitive relatives, the gills of bony fish work on the simple principle of countercurrent flow.
6. The **afferent blood vessels** carry deoxygentated blood from the body through the gill filaments, which are set at right angles to water flow. This maximizes water contact, so that the **efferent blood vessels** can use their entire lateral surfaces for the diffusion of oxygen headed into the blood and back to the body.
7. All these larger gill vessels are subdivided into thousands of little capillary beds, maximizing surface area.
8. Unlike jawless or cartilaginous fish, most bony fish have a **swim bladder**, which is supplies by a bed of blood vessels known as the **rete mirabile**. Blood gases are exchanged with the swim bladder there.
9. Since gases have different partial pressures at different depths, the swim bladder inflates or deflates, allowing the fish to maintain its position in the water column. This gives more precise control than the oily liver of sharks.
10. The swim bladder, itself, played a major role in the evolutionary history of vertebrates. While there is not a perfectly direct evolutionary trend, many of the groups of bony fish considered to be more ancient and primitive, have a swim bladder that is connected to the pharynx by a tube called the **ductus pneumonsus.**
11. While most fish are **physoclistus**, meaning that they have no connection between the throat and swim bladder, **physostomous** fish are able to directly gulp air into their swim bladder and augment their blood oxygenation.
12. Many types of primitive bony fish, such as lungfish, bichirs, and gar can gulp air. Some more advanced bony fish, such as the catfish and the eels can also do this, which allows them to survive in poorly oxygenated water.
13. Unsurprisingly, the school of thought in evolutionary biology, is that **lungs** evolved from the swim bladder.
14. The **circulatory system** of all fish (not just bony fish) consists of a **two-chambered heart** on a continuous circulatory loop that runs through the gills and body, without a detour to the **rete mirabile.**

15. The diagram below shows a schematic of the circulatory and respiratory systems in a bony fish.

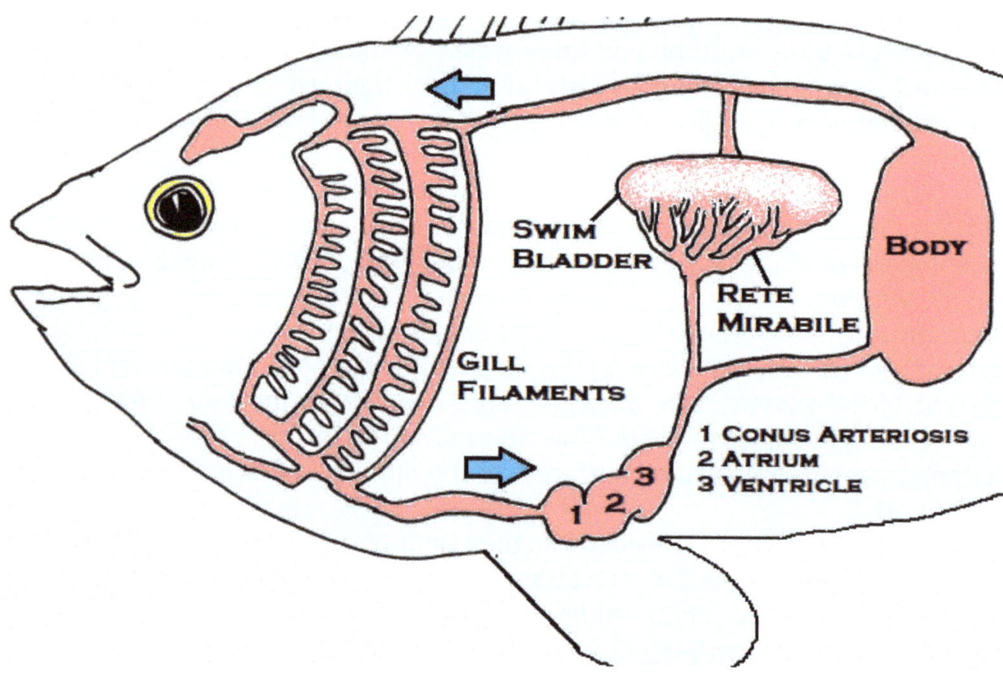

16. Blood cycles from the body back to the heart through the **ventral aorta** into an overflow bag called the **conus arteriosis**, which corresponds to the auricles of more advanced vertebrates.

17. From there, the blood falls into the **atrium**, and is pushed through to the more muscular **ventricle.**

18. A **pacemaker node** is present between the two chambers, similar to the **sinoatrial node** found in the top of the heart in mammals. As the heart beats, it pushes the blood through the **dorsal aorta**.

19. The **rete mirabile** is positioned along this route as a sort of bypass, with blood re-entering the dorsal aorta after passing through this route. From there, major **arteries** branch off and provide blood supply to the organs.

20. Many of these vessels are ubiquitous to all vertebrates, such as the **hepatic artery** (liver), **renal arteries** (kidneys), **gastric artery** (stomach), and **celiac artery** (body cavity).

21. More specific to fish, each fin has a major blood supply named after its location (such as the **caudal arteries** and **veins**) and each muscle segment in the body wall is supplied by vessels that branch regularly from the vertebrae.

22. While there are a few major differences in the internal anatomy of bony fish and cartilaginous fish, we will concentrate on those differences, rather than repeating much of the same information from the prior section.

23. The digestive system of bony fish differs from those of cartilaginous fish in a couple of regards.

24. First, relative to body size, the **liver** is smaller, since it doesn't have to store oil to be responsible for buoyancy.

25. Second, bony fish attain their digestive surface area differently than sharks or rays. The **stomach** is subdivided on its posterior end into blind-ended fingers called **pyloric cecae**. **Gastric glands** line these.

26. In some fish that eat a large amount of vegetable matter, such as pacu, catfish, and mullet, these can be extremely large. They couple this with coiled **intestines** to get maximal surface area for digestion.

27. Many of these aforementioned fish have gut microbes that allow them to power through cellulose and ferment their food like a cow. A large **mesentery** surrounds the coiled intestines, transporting nutrients into the blood.
28. Internally, the reproductive systems of bony fish are notably reduced from those of cartilaginous fish, due to their heavy reliance of **R-strategism**, rather than **K-strategism**.
29. With some notable exceptions, almost all bony fish are **oviparous egg-layers** with **external fertilization**. This makes large oviducts and uterus-like organs unnecessary in the females of most bony fish species.
30. However, due to the much larger volume of eggs and sperm needed to maximize reproductive rates, the **testes** and **ovaries** of both genders usually take up large volumes inside the body cavity by comparison to sharks.
31. There are a few types of fish that are **ovoviviparous live-bearers**, such as guppies, mollies, and silversides. Some would consider male seahorses to also be **ovoviviparous**, since they protect the eggs in a pouch.
32. The males of these species sometimes have modified **anal fins**, which are used to deliver sperm like a penis.
33. While also not technically ovoviviparity, many cichlids are mouthbrooders, holding the eggs in the mouth, until they hatch. The effect is the same....larger juveniles that have a higher likelihood of escaping predators.
34. Some fish, such as minnows, certain catfish, and sunfish, also build and protect stone nests, but this type of life strategy tends to be the exception and not the rule, and evolved for specific environmental circumstances.
35. By-and-large, most fish simply do not employ internal fertilization, nor do they have live birth or care for young.
36. Rather, the female lays zillions of eggs, a male she may or may not ever meet, fertilizes these externally, and then everyone goes their separate ways.
37. It's no wonder, then, that it is estimated that only 1 of every 100,000 largemouth bass lives to be 10 pounds.
38. Most baby fish get consumed as part of the plankton or as tiny juveniles before they ever make it to reproductive age. An even smaller portion of these live to the equivalent of old geezers of the fish world.
39. The external anatomy of bony fish is obviously different from that of cartilaginous fish. At this point, it is useful to make the distinction among the largest evolutionary divergence of the **osteichthyes**.
40. Bony fish are sub-divided into the **Sarcopterygii** (lobe-finned fishes) and the **Actinopterygii** (ray-finned fishes).
41. Both groups of fish have most of the same types of fins in the same general anatomical locations, but they differ in the position of various limb bones and the absence, presence, number, and position of **rays** and **spines**.
42. Both groups of fish have much greater lateral mobility and the ability to make tight maneuvers while swimming, because they can extend and retract fins, flex and relax them, and use them like sails as they swim.
43. In general, most fish have between one and three **dorsal fins** along the back, a **caudal fin** that serves as a tail, and **pectoral**, **pelvic**, and **anal fins** bordering those regions of the ventral body surface.

44. The diagram below shows the general layout of the fins on the body of a bony fish.

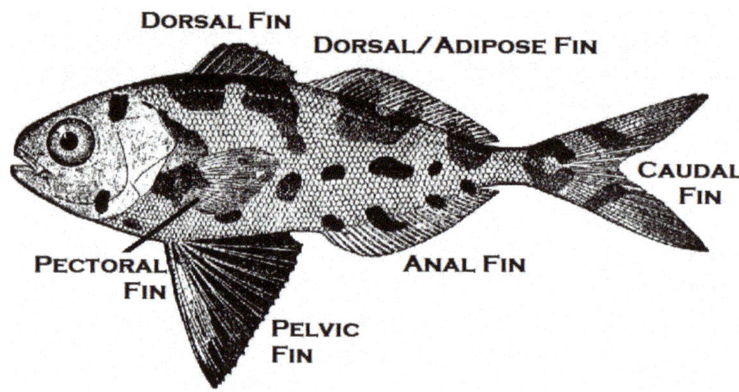

45. At this point, to understand the anatomical nuances that effectively sub-classify bony fish, it is useful to discuss the evolutionary history and phylogenetic tree of bony fish.

46. As mentioned, the most ancient evolutionary split occurs between the lobe-finned and ray-finned fish.

47. Due to differences in the expression patterns of **homeobox genes** in their embryonic development, these two fish taxa do not have the same set of adult bones at the fin base.

48. For instance, lobe-finned fish retain a **humerus** in their pectoral fins, while this bone is a crescent-shaped **caracoid bone** that fuses with the **scapula** (shoulder) in ray-finned fish.

49. You will also notice dramatically different shapes and positions for the **ulna**, **radius**, and **carpals** of fins.

50. The diagram below shows the difference in the layout of the fin bones of the two groups.

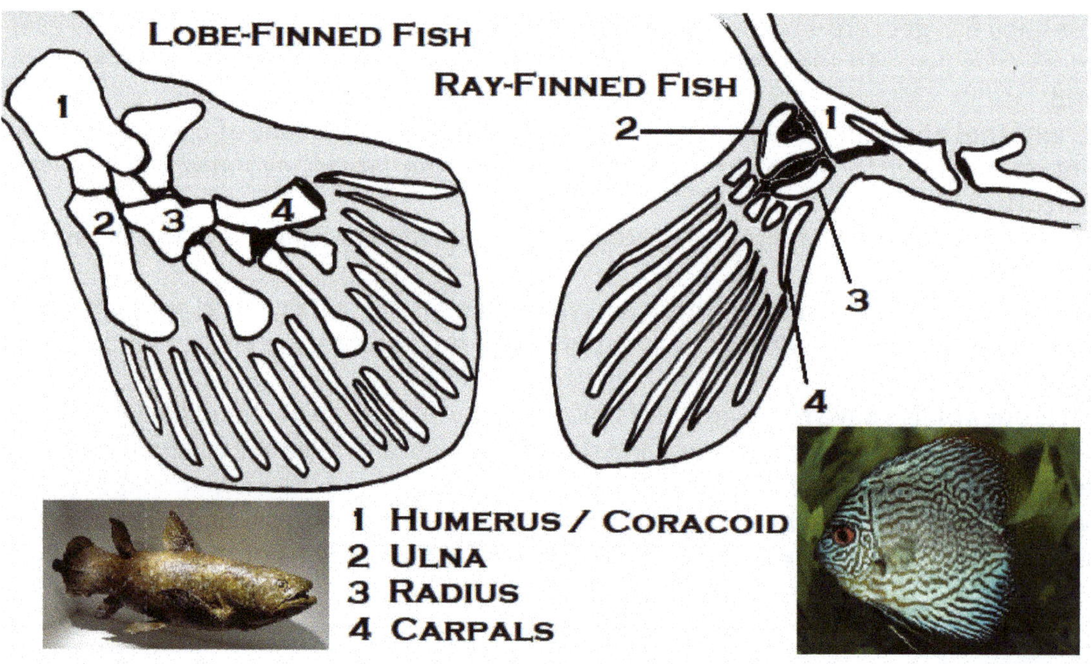

51. Now let's take a look at the evolution of the **Sarcopterygii** (lobe-finned fishes). There are two extinct groups and two extant primitive groups of lobe-finned fish. A fifth group are no longer recognizable as fish.
52. The now-extinct **Order Onychodontiformes** are the most ancient group of lobe-finned fish. Like sharks, they had **spiracles** for water flow in their skull. Their teeth were primitive and tusk-like.
53. Members of **Order Dipnoi** (lungfish) are still alive and well, albeit only in the Southern hemisphere across South America, Africa, and Australia. They also have **spiracles** opening into the pharyngeal cavity.
54. Lungfish are **physoclistus**, in that their swim bladders have a duct that also opens up in the pharyngeal cavity, allowing them to gulp air and survive living in mud puddles and stagnant ponds until better days arrive.
55. Lungfish have primitive bony scales called **cosmoid scales** that are mostly made of bone and function like a suit of chain mail. No other extant type of fish have them, though they do appear in other extinct fish fossils.
56. All members of **Order Porolepimorpha** are also extinct. Their skull anatomy and fin positions differ from members of **Order Coelocanthimorpha**, but both members are thought to have given rise to the **tetrapods**.
57. **Coelocanths** were discovered to be alive and well in the 1930's off the East coast of Africa, it was about as shocking as going to your deer stand and watching a triceratops come stomping through the woods.
58. Coelocanth fossils date back more than 300 million years and were assumed gone with the dinosaurs.
59. **Amphibians** were the first **tetrapods** to crawl out of the ocean onto land and start eating insects. In the old days, some evolutionary biologists thought that **porolepimorph fish** evolved into salamanders and caecilians, while **coelocanths** evolved toward frogs.
60. Since we don't have the DNA of any porolepimorphs, scientists are stuck comparing coelocanths to amphibians. Their DNA is closer to tetrapods than that of any other fish in existence.
61. DNA comparisons with caecilians and salamanders have also led most taxonomists to reject the old theory about separate ancestral lineages for frogs and the rest of the amphibians.
62. The diagram below shows the putative evolutionary history of the **Order Sarcoptyerygii** and pictures of their members, along with short descriptions about their distinct characteristics.

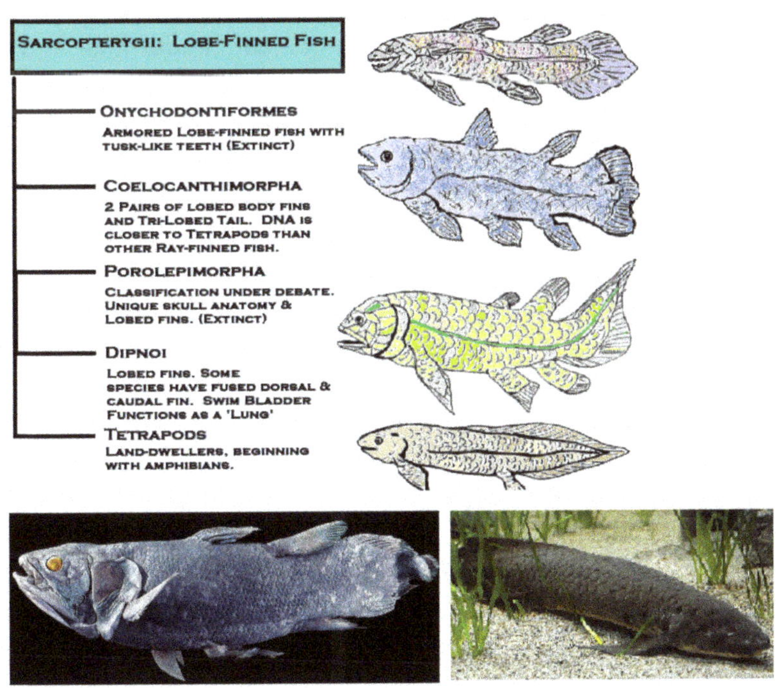

63. The ray-finned fishes of **Class Actinoptergyii** make up the overwhelming majority of living fish species.

64. While ray-finned fishes diverged from lobe-finned fishes a long time ago, that doesn't meant that their evolutionary diversion from cartilaginous fish had been completely worked out at that point.

65. Primitive ray-finned fish still retain many characteristics that are reminiscent of cartilaginous fish.

66. For instance, some species have vestigial spiracles, partially cartilaginous skeletons, heterocercal (shark-like) tail fins, bony scutes or ganoid scales, and ampullae of Lorenzini.

67. The schematic below shows the evolutionary divergence of the ray-finned fishes.

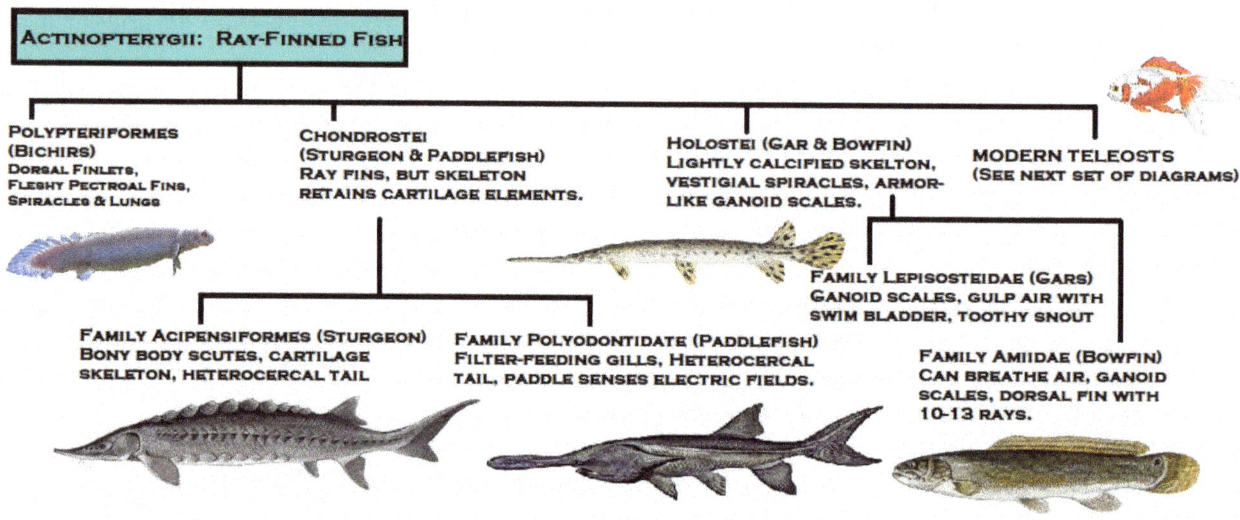

68. **Order Polypteriformes** include a group of fish known as bichirs or ropefish. They are primitive eel-shaped fish with fleshy pectoral fins, spiracles, and **physoclistus** swim bladders.

69. **Order Chondrostei** includes sturgeons and paddlefish. Both groups of fins have distinctly shark-like traits, with only partially calcified skeletons, heterocercal caudal fins, and electric field organs in their barbels or paddles.

70. **Order Holostei** includes gar and bowfin. Both fish have primitive bony **ganoid scales** and vestigial spiracles. Both also have physoclistus swim bladders and partially calcified bones.

71. While it may seem like we've covered a large number of bony fish groups to this point, this would be misleading. Well over 95% of the living species of fish actually belong to **Order Teleostii**, the modern bony fish.

72. **Teleosts** have fins with rays and spines, a fully calcified skeleton, usually have **physostomus** swim bladders that do not connect to the pharynx, and have completely discarded spiracles and most other primitive traits.

73. As we have done so far with the other groups of fish, we will work our way through the teleosts, starting with the least evolved and concluding with the groups of fish with the most derived characteristics.

74. The first major divergence in teleosts occurs between **Superorders Elopomorpha** and **Osteoglossomorpha**.

75. These groups have major fundamental differences in the appearance and development of the larval stage.

76. Members of **Superorder Elopomorpha** develop from leaf-shaped **leptocephalus** larvae that are laterally compressed and resembled leaves, since the **myomeres** of their developing abdomen look like ribs.

77. The way that the yolk sac is absorbed, the gut develops, and the bones of the skull develop differ fundamentally between the groups. Leptocephali also metamorphosize into a second stage of life, known as **glass eels**.
78. Surprisingly, some fish, such as tarpon, develop through these stages, but bear no resemblance to eels as adults.
79. **Order Anguilliformes** includes such well-known members as the catadromous conger eel, which migrates to freshwater to reproduce and back to the ocean in their adult stage.
80. Additionally, moray eels, a favorite of scuba divers, belong to this group. Morays have a distinctive second pair of jaws at the back of their throat, making them particularly nasty ambush predators.
81. The taxonomy of **Superorder Elopomorpha** is shown in the diagram below.

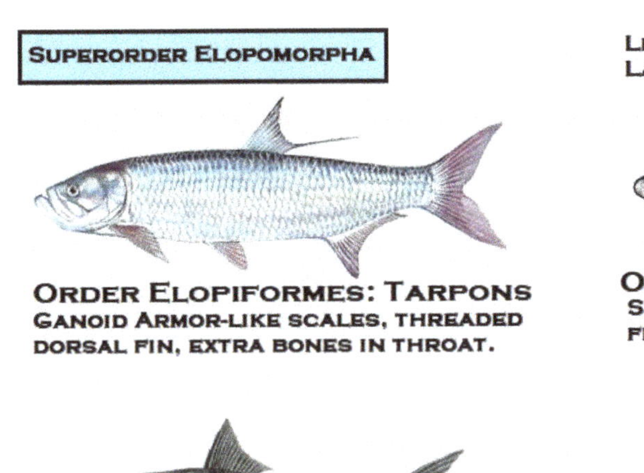

ORDER ELOPIFORMES: TARPONS
GANOID ARMOR-LIKE SCALES, THREADED DORSAL FIN, EXTRA BONES IN THROAT.

ORDER ALBULIFORMES: BONEFISH & LADYFISH
BONY SCALES, INFERIOR MOUTH, PHYSOCLISTUS SWIM BLADDER

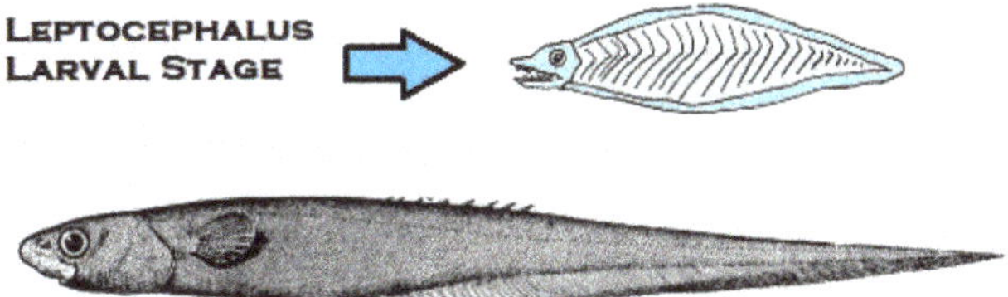

ORDER NOTACANTHIFORMES: SPINY EELS
SESSILE DEEP SEA SCAVENGERS AND MOLLUSK FEEDERS. ANAL FIN FUSED WITH CAUDAL FIN.

ORDER ANGUILLIFORMES: TRUE EELS
METAMORPHIC LARVAL STAGES. SOME SPECIES MIGRATE TO FRESHWATER TO REPRODUCE.

82. **Order Osteoglossomorpha** includes the next group of bony fish considered to be the next order of relatively primitive fishes that evolved a long time ago. They are colloquially called bony tongues.
83. Bony-tongued fish have teeth or bony plates growing directly from their tongue. The bones in their skull, gill arches, and caudal fin are laid out differently than more evolved fish, and resemble those of many extinct taxa.
84. Additionally, the intestines and cecal pouches of bony-tongued fish are on the left of their stomachs, while they are on the right of the stomach in all fish of more advanced taxa.
85. The mooneyes of **Order Hiodontidae** look like herring or shad, superficially because of convergent evolution, but they have bony tongues and the number and shape of skull and gill raker bones characteristic of this group.
86. The **Order Osteoglossidae** contains several sub-orders that have distinctly different traits. In spite of their commonalities in internal anatomy, each group has some distinctive things about them.
87. **Suborder Osteoglossidei** includes armored Amazonian giants, such as the arowana and arapaima, as well as freshwater butterflyfish, which are kept in South American themed freshwater aquariums.
88. **Suborder Notopteroidei** contains elephant fishes and African knifefishes. Both use organs to detect the electric fields coming off of prey animals or predators. Knifefish can also generate weak electric currents.
89. The organ is in the nose of elephant fish and under the lateral line of knifefish.

90. The diagram below shows the major orders of fish that belong to **Order Osteoglossomorpha.**

SUPERORDER OSTEOGLOSSOMORPHA

ORDER OSTEOGLOSSIDAE: AROWANAS, ARAPAIMAS, KNIFEFISH, ELEPHANT FISH. TYPICAL BONY TONGUE ANATOMY WITH DIGESTIVE TRACT LAID OUT OPPOSTITELY OF MOST BONY FISH.

ORDER HIODONTIDAE: MOONEYES SUPERFICIALLY RESEMBLE HERRING. TYPICAL BONY-TONGUE INTERNAL ANATOMY

ORDER OSTEOGLOSSIDAE

SUBORDER NOTOPTEROIDEI
A) PETER'S ELEPHANTFISH
B) CLOWN KNIFEFISH

SUBORDER OSTEOGLOSSODEI
C) ARAPAIMA

91. The remaining bony fish are all members of **Superorder Clupeocephala**.

92. Without getting into minutiae, this implies that the bones of the skull form a shield-like structure that is a distinctly different shape than the the skulls of Elopiformes or Osteoglossiformes.

93. **Superorder Clupeocephala** is then divided into two clades known as **Otocephala** and **Eutelostii**. Otocephalans have a canal that links the swim bladder and eardrum in the skull, while euteleosts do not.

94. One of the largest orders that belong to **Clade Otocephala** is the **Order Clupeiformes**. These include most fish that are characteristically noted for being greasy and smelly and ending up in cans with hot sauce or mustard.

95. The herrings, anchovies, sardines, and shad are all clupeiformes. They lack a **lateral line**, have a gas duct from the swim bladder to the gut, and have **gill rakers** adapted for straining plankton out of the water.

96. Members of the obscure **Order Alepocephalae** are known as slickheads, since thy lack scales on the head. They live deep in the ocean, are planktivores, and have lateral lines.

97. The milkfish belong to **Order Gonorhynciformes**. Their first three vertebrae are fused into structures that resemble inner-ear bones that magnify noises from the swim bladder into the eardrum.

98. Milkfish get their name because they secrete a gooey white substance full of alarm pheromones if a predator chases them. Then all the milkfish panics and run around like someone yelled 'fire!' in a crowded theater.

99. The **Cypriniformes** are a very large order of fish that includes minnows, carp, suckers, and loaches. There are more than 4,000 known living species, making them the largest order in **Clade Otocephala**.

100. The cypriniformes have distinctive traits not found in many other groups of fish. They have a second dorsal fin called an **adipose fin.** They also have **pharyngeal teeth** on the roof of their mouth instead of lining the jawbone.

101. Additionally, they have a special loose-fitting bone called the kinethmoid that allows them to poke their lips way out in a sucking motion. Most of the fish in this group like to suck algae off of rocks, so this helps them do so.

102. Like milkfish, cypriniformes also release alarm pheromones if they see predators. This explains why minnows are such a pain in the butt to catch when you are bass fishing. Grab one and the rest of them all panic.

103. Members of the **Order Characiformes** seem to fill many of the same niches in the Southern hemisphere as cyrpiniformes do in the Northern hemisphere. This group includes tetras, tigerfish, piranhas, and pacu.

104. Characins have inner ear bones like milkfish, an adipose fin like cypriniformes, and their own distinct dentition. Many characins have large conical or serrated teeth that can slice prey (piranhas) or crush nuts and fruit (pacu).

105. The **Order Gymnotiformes** includes another group of knifefishes (no close relationship to African knifefishes) and the electric eels. Both have electrical organs anal fins that they undulate like eels.

106. Electric eels are not really eels at all, based on fundamental differences in anatomy. They are just evil eel-shaped fish that enjoy wallowing around in mud and lighting up anything that touches them like a Christmas tree.

107. The **Order Siluriformes** includes around 3,000 species of catfish. They are the second largest group in **Clade Otocephala** and have a large diversity of sizes, shapes, habitats, and ecological niches.

108. However, all catfish have barbels around the mouth impregnated with taste buds and an adipose fin behind their dorsal fin. Most species have a thick flat skull with cross-shaped bones for extra support.

109. While catfish may use their swim bladders to breathe in oxygen, they are usually smaller, relative to their body size than most other fish, because most catfish species are **benthic** scavengers that live on the bottom.

110. The diagram below shows representatives of the major orders found in **Clade Otocephali.**

CLADE OTOCEPHALI

ORDER CLUPEIFORMES: HERRING, ANCHOVIES, SARDINES. SOFT CTENOID SCALES, LATERAL LINE ABSENT, PLANKTIVOROUS.

ORDER ALEPOCEPHALI: SLICKHEADS. NO SCALES ON HEAD, LATERAL LINE, PLANKTIVOROUS.

ORDER GONORHYNCHIFORMES: MILKFISH. MILKY ALARM PHEROMONE SECRETIONS, VERTEBRATE FUSED TO FORM SOUND-MAGNIFYING EAR BONES.

ORDER CYPRINIFORMES: CARP, MINNOWS, SUCKERS. PHARYNGEAL TEETH, ALARM PHEROMONES, MOUTH BONES MODIFIED FOR GRAZING.

ORDER CHARACIFORMES: PACU, TETRAS, PIRANHAS, TIGERFISH. EAR BONES, TEETH ROOTED IN JAWBONE.

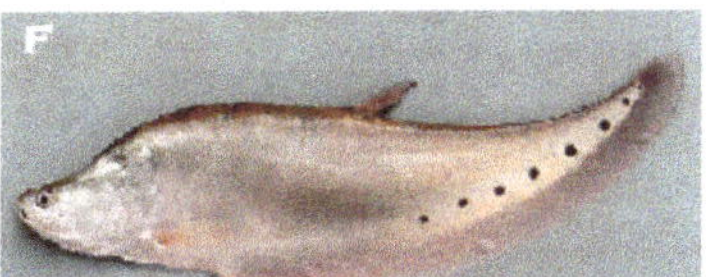

ORDER GYMNOTIFORMES: KNIFEFISH AND ELECTRIC EELS. ELONGATED ANAL FIN FUSED WITH CAUDAL FIN, ELECTRIC ORGANS.

ORDER SILURIFORMES: CATFISH. BARBELS COVERED WITH TASTE BUDS, ADIPOSE FIN, FLATTENED SKULL BONES.

111. The largest group of bony fish, by far, is **Clade Euteleost** (also called **Infraclass Teleostii)**.

112. Euteleosts have embyros with yolk sacs that develop in specific stages. Typically, as soon as the yolk is gone, they began feeding. Euteleosts have a floating **premaxillary bone** that is flexible, toothed, and used to grab food.

113. Euteleosts are further divided into **Infraclass Protocanthopterygii** and **Infraclass Neoteleostii**.

114. Members of **Protocanthopterygii** have two dozen or more vertebrae, arc-shaped bones under the pectoral fins, a toothed tongue, and an adipose fin. They usually can't protrude their lower jaw when they feed.

115. Ocean smelts and barrel eyes belong to **Order Argentiformes**. Ocean smelts look sort of like sardines, but with a forked tail and have internal anatomy characteristic of the infraclass.

116. Barreleyes are freakish looking fish with globular clear membranes around their eyes, making their brains visible. The clear membrane is there in order to funnel more light into their eyes, since they live in deep water.

117. **Order Galaxiiformes** includes a handful of mostly Australian species of scaleless stream-dwelling fish. They serve sort of the same ecological niche as darters do in North American streams.

118. **Order Esociformes** includes a family of ferocious freshwater predators, the pikes, pickerels, muskellunges, as well as a group of seemingly unrelated fish known as mudminnows, that have similar skeletal structures.

119. Both families of fish have elongated bodies with the dorsal fin set way back next to the caudal fin.

120. The **Order Salmoniformes** is one of the leading groups of fish to end up on dinner tables. Mostly cold water fish, they have a high body fat content to keep their cell membranes fluid. Their metabolic enzymes are also adapted to live at colder water temperatures than many groups of fish, and are sensitive to warm waters.

121. Combined with the soft ctenoid scales on their body, as well as predictable migrations and life histories, they are highly desired by fishermen. Salmon and trout frequently get themselves grilled and covered with sauces.

122. The diagram below shows the major fish orders that comprise **Infraclass Protocanthopterygii.**

INFRACLASS PROTOCANTHOPTERYGII

ORDER ARGENTIFORMES: SMELTS AND BARREL EYES. PLANKTIVORES THAT USUALLY LACK TEETH. SWIM BLADDER OFTEN ABSENT. ADIPOSE FIN.

ORDER GALAXIIFORMES: GALAXIDS. SMALL FRESHWATER STREAM FISH FROM AUSTRALIA. LACK SCALES. NO ADIPOSE FIN, DORSAL FIN FAR BACK.

A) RAINBOW SMELT C) NORTHERN PIKE
B) GOLLUM GALAXIAS D) BROOK TROUT

ORDER ESOCIFORMES: PIKES, PICKEREL, MUSKELLUNGE, MUDMINNOWS. ELONGATED NASAL BONES, TOOTHLESS MAXILLARY PLATE

ORDER SALMONIFORMES: TROUT, CHAR, SALMON, WHITEFISH, TAIMEN. CTENOID SCALES, ADIPOSE FINS, OFTEN ANADROMOUS. OILY FLESH AND ROE. ADAPTED FOR COLD WATER.

123. **Infraclass Neoteleostii** is grouped largely by skull and jawbone anatomy and by DNA evidence. It can be sub-divided into more than a dozen orders, each with distinctly different anatomical characteristics.
124. There are a number of families, classes, infraclasses, clades, and other taxonomic levels between Infraclass Neoteleostii and the numerous orders under its umbrella. However, the anatomical and molecular reasons for these groupings are not very meaningful to novices or useful for a cursory examination.
125. Instead, we will focus on the distinct characteristics that are used to classify fish into orders of neoteleosts.
126. To avoid confusion, we will divide the examination into two different groups. The first group will include those taxa that do not have hollow needle-like spines in their fins. These comprise many sub-taxa of various names.
127. After this, we will focus on members of **Clade Acanthomorpha**, those fish that DO have needle-like spines in their fins. This group includes between 50% and 60% of all living species of bony fish.
128. Let's begin with those that didn't make it into the needle fin club.
129. **Order Stomiiformes** includes a number of soft-bodied deep sea fish that are adapted to live in dark abyssal zones under incredible pressures. Their bodies are usually rubbery, fatty, and flexible.
130. Viperfish, dragonfish, and bristlemouths all belong to this group. Most fish in this group have vampire-like teeth connected to jaws with highly flexible ligaments. They can often eat prey as big as themselves.
131. Since they make their residence in the dark, cold abyss, this serves a useful purpose, as they don't know how many months away it might be until their next meal. Many are **bioluminescent** to attract their prey.
132. **Order Osmeriformes** include the true smelts, which superficially resemble members of Order Argentiformes. However, the skeletal architecture of their skull bones is very different, and they often spawn in freshwater.
133. **Order Ateleopodidae** is an obscure group of fish known as jellynoses. They have devolved much of their bony skeleton and have a large bulbous cartilage nose. They have a long anal fin and a pelvic fin reduced to one spine.
134. Lizardfish, dorkfish, and grinnerfish belong to the largest taxon of euteleosts outside of Acanthomorpha.
135. Together, they comprise **Order Aulopiformes.** They bones of their gill arches are a distinctly different shape and arrangement from other fish, their swim bladder is often vestigial, and their pelvic fins are far back on the body.
136. Additionally, some types of lizardfish are hermaphrodites, which is rare in the vertebrate world.
137. The diagram below shows the major orders of neoteleosts who are not part of the 'in group' with spiny fins.

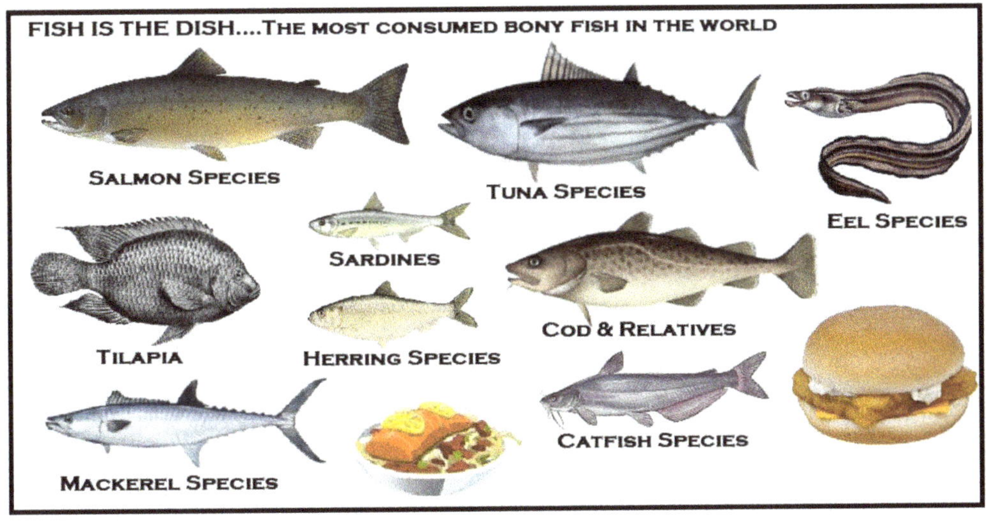

138. If fish played 'Magic the Gathering', these groups would be sitting around a table in the dorm with 12-sided dice, while the rest of the teleosts were tailgating at a football game.

NON-ACANTHOMORPHAN EUTELEOSTS

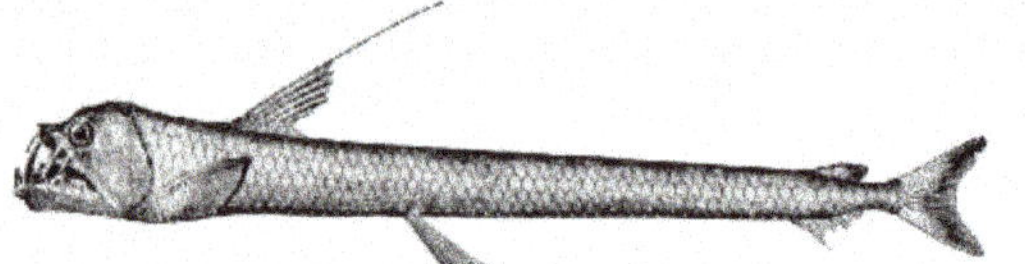

ORDER STOMIIFORMES: DRAGONFISH, VIPERFISH, BRISTLEMOUTHS. SOFT BODIES ADAPTED TO DEEP OCEAN PRESSURES. OFTEN BIOLUMINESCENT. NEEDLE TEETH, HUGE GAPE.

ORDER ATELEOPODIDAE: JELLYNOSES, TADPOLE FISH. SKELETON MOSTLY DEVOLVED TO CARTILAGE WITH LARGE NASAL CARTILAGE. LONG ANAL FIN.

ORDER OSMERIFORMES: TRUE SMELTS. INFERIOR JAW, ADIPOSE FINS, SILVERY COLORING. MANY SPECIES ANADROMOUS

ORDER AULOPIFORMES: LIZARDFISH AND GRINNERFISH. UNIQUE GILL ARCH STRUCTURE, VESTIGIAL SWIM BLADDER. ADIPOSE FIN. SOME SPECIES ARE HERMAPHRODITIC.

139. Now we tackle the larger group of fish, the true **Acanthomorphans**. Even this group is split into two superorders. The first is **Superorder Paracanthopterygii**, while the second is simply **Acanthopterygii**.

140. The major distinction between these two superorders has to do with anatomical differences in the jaw muscles.

141. Let's begin by looking at the orders that comprise **Superorder Paracanthopterygii.** Despite being classified as an outlier that doesn't fully fit anatomically with the rest of the group, we will include **Order Lampriformes** for ease.

142. **Order Lampriformes** includes the opahs, oarfish, and ribbonfish. Typically, when one of these guys washed up on shore, someone thinks that they've found a real life sea monster of some sort.

143. Oarfish have bright red tassled dorsal fins and can be nearly 20 feet long, resembling Chinese dragons.

144. Opahs, which have huge disc-like bodies that can be as big as a kitchen table, were recently discovered to be able to shunt blood into their muscles in such a way that they are warm-blooded, allowing them to swim faster.

145. Members of the order have a huge number of vertebrate, sometimes nearly 100. They typically are brightly pigmented, with red shades being common. They lack true spines in their somewhat floppy fins.

146. **Order Percopsiformes** includes blind cave fish, pirate perch, and trout perches. They have trout-like ctenoid scales and elongated bodies with the dorsal and anal fins positioned almost in front of the dorsal fin.

147. Dories and lookdowns make up the **Order Zeiformes**. Most fish in this group are as flat as pancakes and disc-shaped, with a few large spines in all of their fins.

148. John Dory filets, for whatever reason, are the gourmet rage right now with folks like Gordon Ramsay. Not sure exactly what there is to eat on something as thick as a few pieces of paper.

149. Tubeyes are a single species of truly obscure deep ocean fish. They aren't very big, have long streaming tail rays and eyes like binoculars to gather light as they feed for plankton. They belong to **Order Stylephoriformes.**

150. **Order Gadiformes** is comprised of cod, haddock, pollock, and other desirable food fish with flaky white meat. There are three fins on both surfaces of the body (dorsal and ventral) and many have barbels around the mouth.

151. The major groups of the **Superorder Paracanthopterygii** are pictured below.

SUPERORDER PARACANTHOPTERYGII

A

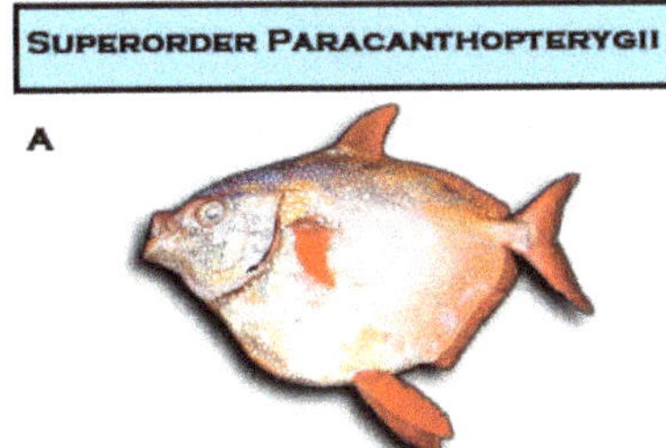

ORDER LAPIRIFORMES: OARFISH, OPAHS, RIBBONFISH. VERY LARGE NUMBER OF VERTEBRAE. NO TRUE SPINES IN FINS. BRIGHT COLORS, ODD BODY SHAPES.

ORDER PERCOPSIFORMES: TROUT PERCH, PIRATE PERCH, CAVEFISH. DORSAL FIN AND PELVIC FIN FAR BACK ON BODY. CTENOID SCALES. FINS HAVE A FEW SPINES, BUT MOSTLY RAYS.

ORDER ZEIFORMES: DORIES, LOOKDOWNS, OREOFISH. FLAT COMPRESSED BODIES WITH SPINY FINS AND AN EXTENDABLE MOUTH.

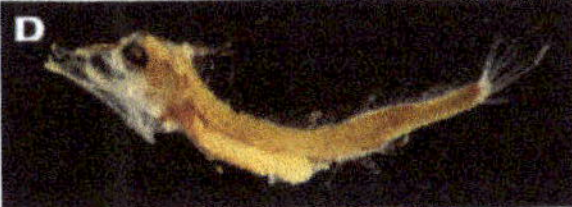

ORDER STYLEPHORIFORMES: TUBE EYES AND THREADFINS. DEEP OCEAN ABYSSAL SPECIES THAT FEEDS ON PLANKTON. TAILFIN RAYS STREAM BEHIND BODY. TUBULAR EYES TO LET IN MORE LIGHT.

E

ORDER GADIFORMES: COD, HADDOCK, POLLOCK. SPINELESS FINS. TWO DORSAL FINS, ADIPOSE FIN ON BACK. PELVIC FIN AND TWO ANAL FINS ON VENTRAL SIDE.

A) BIGEYE PACIFIC OPAH
B) BLIND CAVE FISH
C) SILVERY JOHN DORY
D) TUBE EYE THREADTAIL
E) ATLANTIC COD

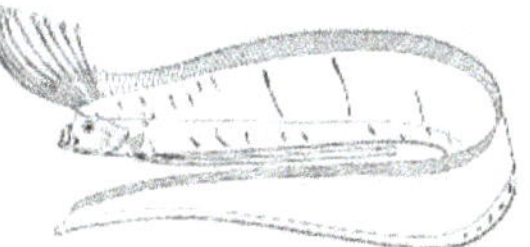

152. Even at this point, we still haven't accounted for nearly half of the bony fish species in existence.

153. **Superorder Acanthopterygii** includes a few minor orders and one gigantic order known as **Perciformes** that includes 150 different families and over 10,000 species of fish.

154. Obviously, we are going to have to change tactics in their coverage when we get there to prevent carrying this chapter on to the length of a novel. Let's begin by covering NON-Perciform orders of Acanthopterygii.

155. Due to differing numbers of spines in their dorsal fin and various other anatomical curiosities that don't quite fit the Perciformes, each of these four groups below were placed into different orders.

NON-PERCIFORM ACANTHOPTERYGIIANS

ORDER POLYMIXIFORMES: BEARDFISH. DEEP WATER FISH WITH PAIR OF TACTILE BARBELS.

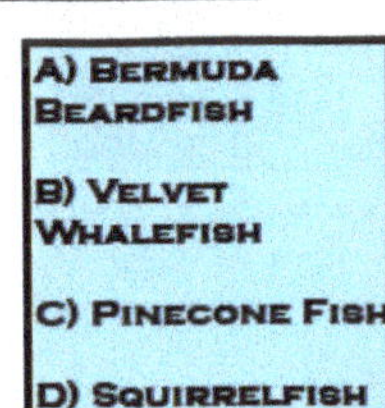
A) BERMUDA BEARDFISH
B) VELVET WHALEFISH
C) PINECONE FISH
D) SQUIRRELFISH

ORDER TRACHICHTHYOFORMES: PINECONE FISH, SLIMEHEADS. SCUTE-LIKE BODY SCALES, SPINY DORSAL FIN. BIOLUMINESCENT.

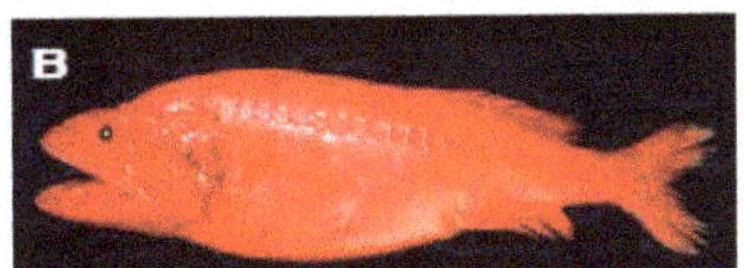

ORDER BERCYIFORMES: WHALEFISH, ROUGHIES, FLASHLIGHT FISH. LIVE DEEP ON CONTINENTAL SHELVES. LARGE NUMBER OF DORSAL FIN RAYS. SOME BIOLUMINESCENT.

ORDER HOLOCENTRIFORMES: SQUIRRELFISH, SOLDIERFISH. LARGE EYES FOR NOCTURNAL LIFESTYLE. SPINY GILLS, VENOM IN DORSAL SPINES.

156. We now get to the gargantuan **Superorder Perciformes**. All perciform fish have 17 dorsal spines in the front of their dorsal fins, followed by a series of soft rays. Their pelvic fins have one spine and several soft rays.

157. The scales of perciform fish are typically small and either **cycloid** or **ctenoid**.

158. Since we are not going to be extending this chapter by another 50 pages or so, we are going to present a selection of some of the most prominent families in the same graphic form with short descriptions.

159. The selections below represent species from some of the most well-known or biologically common groups.

160. Keep in mind, that in spite of the huge diversity of ecological niches, body morphologies, habits, and sizes, that all of the fish in the prior diagram (and the following diagram), are more closely related to one another than they are to any of the previously discussed taxa of bony fish.

161. Everything from a tiny goby to a half-ton swordfish to a rug-sized halibut or brightly colored cichlid are more closely related to one another than any of the members of Perciformes is to trout, catfish, or cod.

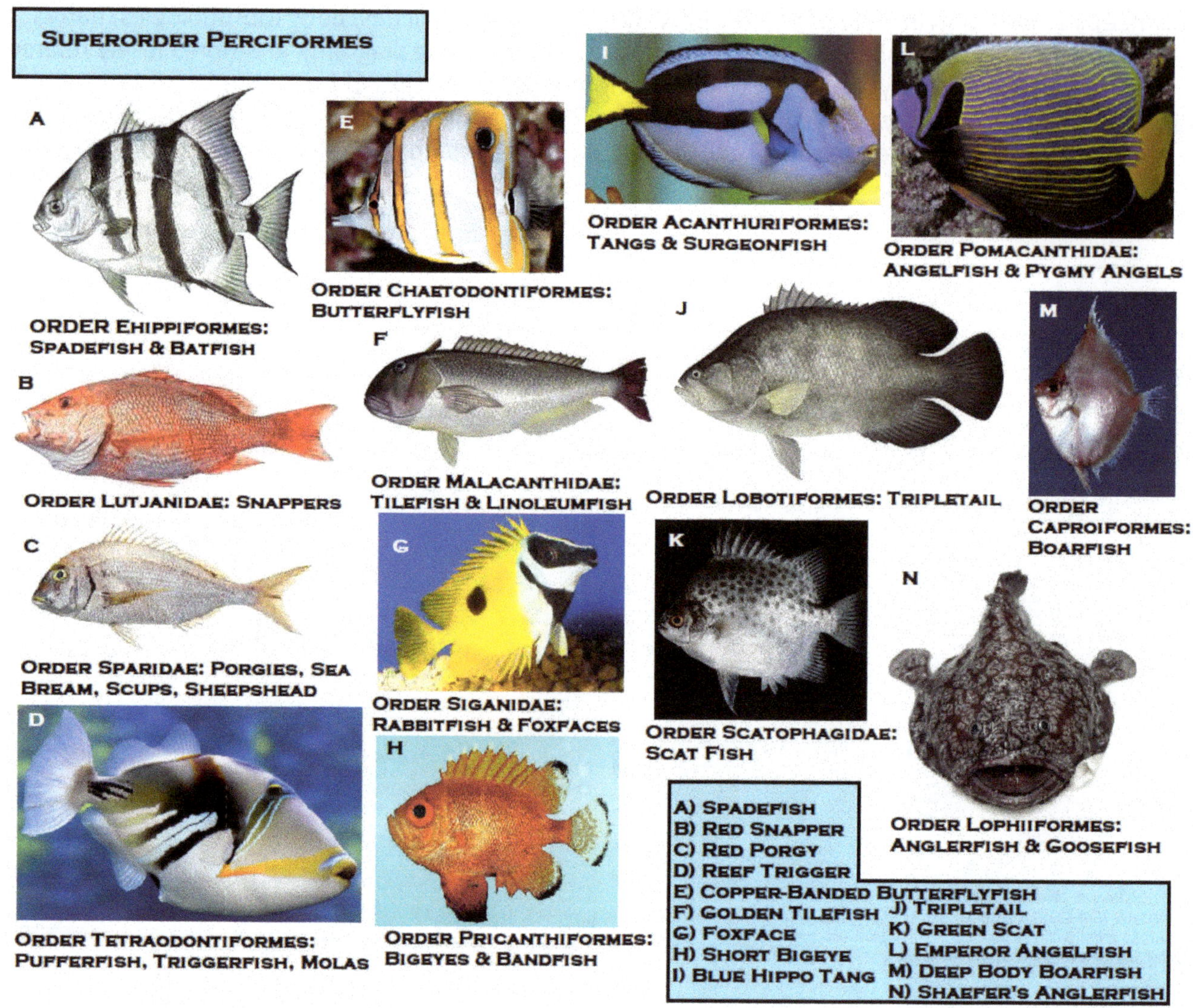

E) Class Amphibia: Amphibians

1. Without going onto an entire rabbit trail involving millions of years of natural history, there was a time when vertebrates only occupied the water and were completely absent from land. Enter amphibians.
2. The absence of vertebrates on land, along with a growing diversity of invertebrates, especially insects, created a huge set of open ecological niches. Eventually, fish evolved to take advantage of this set of circumstances.
3. The first amphibians trace their ancestry to lobe-finned fish about 370 million years ago in the fossil records.
4. In addition to the extra fin bones that could evolve into joints and propel them onto land, their **physoclistous swim bladders** opened to the outside, and were able to add surface area to evolve into true lungs.
5. In the early days, it is presumed that bony fish in shallow swampy areas, eventually evolved larger muscles and thicker bones around their pelvic an pectoral fins, allowing them to push themselves out of the water.
6. They could then ambush prey that showed up to feed or drink at the side of the water.

7. There are still some clear and present indications that fish and amphibians share a common ancestry.
8. First, the bones in the occipital area of the skull are similar. Amphibian teeth and fish teeth also have similar conical structures. The skins of both vertebrates are impregnated with mucus glands to seal in moisture.
9. As amphibians evolved, several features were essential in order to allow for life on land.
10. First and foremost, they had to solve the problem of breathing air. Maximizing surface area became essential.
11. As a result, amphibians had to retain a moist mucus-covered **skin** that promoted diffusion of gases directly into sub-surface capillaries. Likewise, the size of the mouth became exaggerated to do the same.
12. Toads have added **warts** to the skin to help contribute more surface area. Additionally, many frogs and toads also secrete toxins from the skin, since thin, permeable skin leaves them vulnerable to predators.
13. Caecilians are the lone type of amphibian with any type of scales, but these seem to have re-evolved and they bear no real similarity to fish scales. Instead of flat scales, they have concentric rings around the body.
14. Most amphibians, with the exception of cave dwellers, have pigmentation in their skin to protect them from UV and also to serve as warning coloration or as camouflage against surfaces.
15. The epidermal tissue of the skin bears similarity in cellular structure and vascularity to the endodermal tissue inside **lungs**. Along with the pulmonary blood supply, pleural tissues evolved from the **swim bladder** and the network of vessels of the **rete mirabile** of fish.
16. In more primitive amphibians, such as salamanders and caecilians, lungs are simply two lobes of hot dog shaped capillary beds. While there is some superficial folding, they have far less surface area than mammalian lungs.
17. Lunged salamanders have two simple lungs, while caecilians have a **tracheal lung** that runs along the trachea, which offsets the disadvantage of a smaller left lung, which is reduced to fit inside a tube-shaped body.
18. In addition to needing lungs to pull in enough oxygen, amphibians also had to evolve a way to circulate thir blood more effectively than the simple design of a two-chambered fish heart.
19. As a result, amphibians have a **three-chambered heart** with separate loops for the blood supply of the body and for the **pulmonary vessels**. The **right atrium** receives deoxygenated blood from the **vena cava** of the body, while the **left atrium** receives oxygenated blood back from the **pulmonary veins**.
20. Unfortunately for amphibians, both sources of blood mix in a single **ventricle**, making circulation much less efficient than it could be. While blood is pumped in two different directions, it is of mixed **oxygenation**.
21. Two sets of **pulmonary arteries** from the **ventricle** of the heart pump blood to the lobes of the lungs, while the **aorta** delivers oxygenated blood back to the tissues of the body.
22. Blood pumped through the aorta then needs additional help becoming fully oxygenated as it passes through capillaries under the skin and the mucus membranes of the mouth.
23. Obviously, the juvenile stages of amphibians do not rely on lungs, but instead, retain **gills** like those of fish. Several classifications of salamanders retain gills as adults and lead aquatic lifestyles, such as mudpuppies.
24. Additionally, there are also terrestrial lungless salamanders that get away with relying on gas exchange through moist skin and mucus membranes of the mouth. They are restricted to moist areas and very fragile.

25. The diagrams below show the designs of amphibian lungs and the three chambered heart.

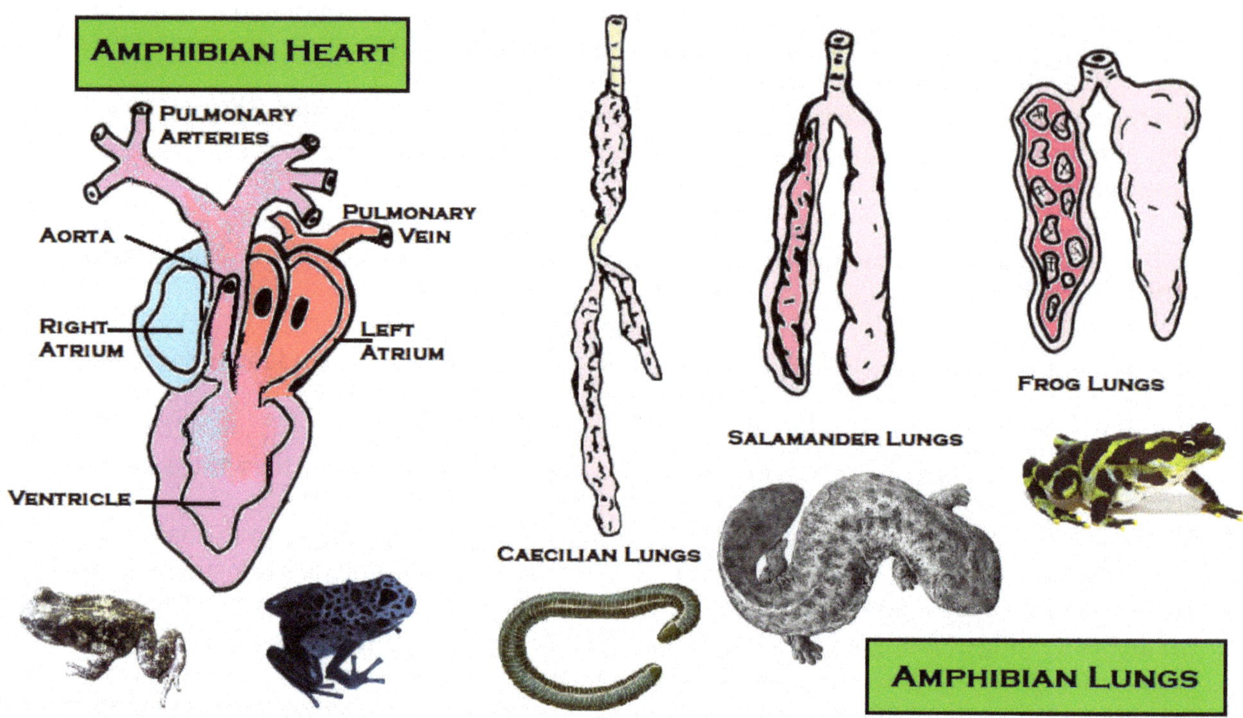

26. Beyond oxygenating their tissues, amphibians had to solve other problems brought about by terrestrial life.

27. Locomotion on land is a much different prospect than getting around in water. **In water, you flex your abdomen, wiggle your fins, and let inertia take over.** Air doesn't really push back, so more force is needed.

28. Amphibians had to make a lot of adjustments to their musculoskeletal system in order to move on land.

29. It was critical that they developed **paired limbs** with much greater musculature and thicker calcified bones.

30. Pectoral and pelvic fins gave way to two pairs of legs, as **homeotic genes** in the vertebrate limb gene cluster changed their switching and gene transcription patterns to cause limb bones to develop.

31. With the exceptions of caecilians and certain types of salamanders, most amphibians have four sets of carpals, metacarpals, and finger phalanges in their front limbs.

32. The back legs of most have five sets of tarsals, metatarsals and toe phalanges in their back legs.

33. These limbs are supported and moved by a much greater degree of musculature in the pectoral and pelvic girdles than is necessary in fish. A number of characteristic vertebrate muscles had to evolve for this purpose.

34. For instance, in frogs and most salamanders, the front legs receive tremendous leverage from the **pectoralis** muscles in the front and the **latissimus dorsi** down the lateral surfaces of their bodies.

35. The abdominal muscles of salamanders are segmented, somewhat like fish, but frogs have also had to develop the more characteristic 'six pack' **rectus abdominus** also seen in mammals, in order to effectively jump.

36. Both types of amphibians have similar types of leg muscles, though in frogs, the **gracilis** and **triceps femoris** muscles of the thighs and **gastrocnemius** muscles of the calves are gigantic for leaping.
37. Physics created another problem on land for amphibians, in the aspect of sound transmission.
38. Sound travels much more poorly in air than vibrations do in water. All larval amphibians retain a fish-like **lateral line** system, as do aquatic adult salamanders, but these organs just don't cut it on land.
39. Instead, terrestrial amphians had to develop another way to sense and transmit sound. Instead, the eardrum or **tympanum** evolved in amphibians, with a **stapes** or stirrup bone, to strike it and amplify vibrations.
40. As opposed to its appearance in mammals, the eardrum is fully visible on the lateral sides of the heads.
41. Likewise, **vocal cords** evolved in frogs, mostly so that they could locate mates and claim territorial rights.
42. Coming out of water presented challenges for vision. In addition to having adapt the lenses in their eyes for different refractive indices in air, their eyeballs also don't stay moist without help.
43. While not present in some aquatic amphibians, all terrestrial species had to evolve **eyelids** and a **nictitating membrane** to keep their eyes protected from drying out.
44. Air has a different refractive index than water, so the **lens** of the eye also had to evolve to a more convex shape.
45. Amphibians made a pretty good first effort to get themselves onto land with reduced competition for resources, but we all know that amphibians don't rule the world. There are definite weaknesses in their design.
46. Where they mostly went wrong (besides the whole wet skin thing and pathetically tiny lungs) is that they didn't evolve a system for fully moving their reproduction onto land.
47. All **amphibian larvae** (tadpoles) have **pharyngeal gills** and they must grow and develop underwater. Most are **suspension feeders** and scavengers or feed on insect larvae, though some are predatory.
48. The eggs of amphibians resemble fish eggs, as they have a jelly-like consistency and lack any sort of protective shell. The yolk and embryo are nearly exposed. This forces them to be laid in a wet environment.
49. Most amphibians make bubble nests underwater or in puddles, though some have made special adaptations to allow them to carry their larvae with them.
50. For instance, the **Surinam toad** moves its fertilized eggs onto its back and grows a second skin over them like a blister. The fluid between the layers of skin is the 'pond'.
51. **Darwin's frog** males keep a clutch of larvae in a moist sac next to their vocal cords, and juvenile frogs emerge from their mouth when they are born.
52. The tadpoles live in pits on the mother's back and hop out when they grow up.
53. The **Darwin frog** swallows its eggs and the tadpoles grow up in a fluid-filled sac on top of its vocal cords. The juvenile frogs then hop out of the parent's mouth when they are ready.
54. However, the great majority of amphibians must still find a pond.
55. Some amphibians haven't progressed all the way from their fish ancestry and exhibit **paedomorphosis**, meaning that they retain juvenile characteristics and must live underwater even as adults.
56. There are many gilled salamanders, such as the **axoltotl** (mudpuppy) that are completely aquatic. Some frogs, such as the **African clawed frog**, also spend their entire lives underwater.

57. The diagram below points out some of the major anatomical and developmental features of various amphibians.

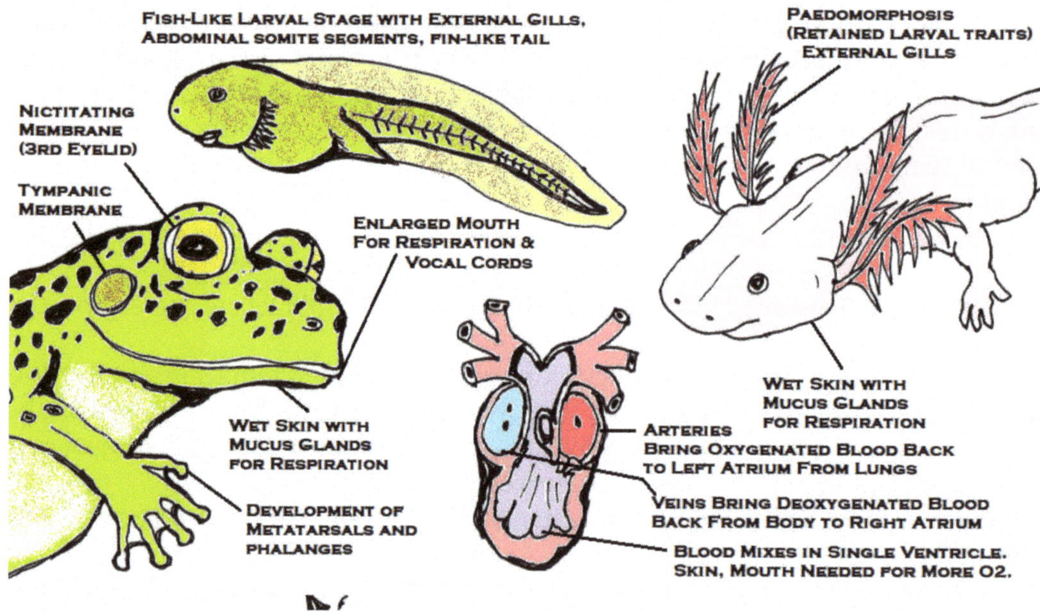

58. **Amphibians** are subdivided into three classifications. **Urodela** includes the salamanders, mudpuppies, and newts. **Anura** includes the frogs and toads. **Apoda** is the caecilians.

59. **Order Urodela** includes 10 families of salamanders. There is some variability in body morphology, but in general, most salamanders have elongated lizard-like bodies with blunt snouts and a long tail.

60. Many salamanders have a **prehensile tail** that can be used to hold onto rocks in current or assist them in mating. Usually they are spatula-like and laterally flat. Some newts also have fin-like projections on their tails.

61. Most salamanders have four limbs, but some, such as sirens, lack back legs. Interestingly, they can regenerate lost limbs and tails, as these genes never switch off during development like they do in most vertebrates.

62. Part of salamander classification is based on the number of limbs they possess, as well as the number of toes on the front and hind feet. Additionally, their respiratory systems also serve as a taxonomic criteria.

63. Salamander **lungs**, if present, are rudimentary and hot-dog shaped pouches. Wet skin is absolutely critical to their respiration. To keep it moist and keep diffusion going, **mucus glands** constantly bathe the skin.

64. Some salamander species have additional glands that make toxins for protection or sexual pheromones.

65. Some types of salamanders retain the gills from their larval stage for life, such as axolotls, sirens, and mudpuppies. These species are restricted to living underwater.

66. Some types of salamanders have **internal pharyngeal gills** that are oxygenated by opening and closing the mouth, while others have **external gills** that are flexed and controlled by pectoral muscles.

67. There are also **lungless salamanders** that rely entirely on their skin and large mouths for respiratory diffusion. Their bodies are usually long and worm-like, since too much volume creates oxygenation problems.

68. Almost all salamanders are ambush predators that lie in wait for insects, worms, fish, small animals, and Doritos.

69. As such, their senses are adapted for this lifestyle. They have **color vision**, a **vomeronasal organ** that can sense chemicals in the water (such as minnow pheromones), and a **tympanic membrane** that acts as an eardrum.

70. All larval salamanders have a **lateral line** like a fish, which detects vibrations in the water, which is retained in adults of species that spend most of their lives underwater.

71. Salamanders have ridge-like small teeth along their maxilla and mandible, but many also have **pharyngeal teeth** on their top palate for crushing bug shells and crawfish.

72. Their digestive systems, like their fish ancestors, consists of a stomach, small, and large intestine, as well as the accessory digestive organs (liver and pancreas).

73. Salamanders are the most primitive animals with **three-chambered hearts**. The **right atrium** receives blood back from the body, via the **vena cava**, while the **left atrium** receives oxygenated blood back from the lungs.

74. Since there is only one **ventricle**, this means that the blood mixes, and there is a heavy reliance on the moist membranes of the skin and mouth to fully oxygenated it as it travels.

75. Reproductively, salamanders find each other **by pheromone** cues or appearances in species that are **sexually dimorphic**. However, in such a busy day-and-age, some salamanders have come to rely on dating apps.

76. Salamander mating is not terribly exciting. Males deposit a package of sperm called a **spermatophore** on the ground or on a rock underwater. From there, the male dances around and tries to get the female to pick it up.

77. Once she does, it goes into her **cloaca**, where it is stored in a pouch called the **spermathecal** and saved for later. Eventually, the sperm are released at the right time, where they fertilize the eggs.

78. Generally speaking, the number of eggs laid is inversely proportional to the size of the eggs. Underwater species lay more small eggs, while fully terrestrial species lay fewer. A few species are **ovoviviparous** and give live birth.

79. **Order Urodela** is, as you might expect, yet another classification that biologists keep arguing about without consensus. However, most taxonomists split them into three sub-orders.

80. These are the **Crytpobranchoidea** (giant salamanders), the **Salamandroidea (**typical salamanders), and the **Sirenidae** (sirens). Skull structure, foot anatomy, reproductive, and reproductive differences drive the split.

81. The diagram below shows some representative species of a few of the 10 extant families of salamanders, along with a note about why each group is classified together.

A) FAMILY CRYPTOBRANCHIDAE (JAPANESE GIANT SALAMANDER) GILL SLITS, NO EYELIDS, SKIN FOLDS, GIANT
B) FAMILY SIRENIDAE (LESSER SIREN) EXTERNAL GILLS, CARTILAGE FRONT LIMBS, NO BACK LEGS
C) FAMILY AMBYOSTOMATIDAE (TIGER SALAMANDER) NOCTURNAL BURROWERS, FULLY DEVELOPED LUNGS
D) FAMILY PROTEIDAE (OLM) BLIND CAVE DWELLER, STRONG SENSE OF SMELL, EXTERNAL GILLS, UNPIGMENTED
E) FAMILY SALAMANDRIDAE (CALIFORNIA NEWT) 4 FRONT TOES, 5 BACK TOES, POISON GLANDS IN SKIN, LUNGS
F) FAMILY PLETHODONTIDAE (WESTERN SLIMY SALAMANDER) NO LUNGS, PROJECTILE TONGUE, TERRESTRIAL
G) FAMILY AMPHIUMIDAE (CONGO EEL) VESTIGIAL LEGS, PHARYNGEAL GILLS, LACK EYELIDS OR TONGUE
H) FAMILY PROTEIDAE (AXOLOTL) EXTERNAL GILLS, NO MAXILLARY BONE IN UPPER JAW, LIVE UNDERWATER

82. **Order Anura** includes frogs and toads. Their origin and evolution is still under debate, but it appears that they are a separate branch of amphibians than salamanders that evolved in different areas of the world.
83. While they share distant common ancestors, fossils seem to indicate that **salamanders** evolved in what is now East Asia, while frogs mostly evolved in what is now Africa and India.
84. However, they evolved in these regions before the Pangea split into continents, so both are circumglobal.
85. Both groups of amphibians had to solve the problem of terrestrial existence. Both groups arrived at similar or identical solutions, but each evolved distinct characteristics independent of the other.
86. Frogs did a better job of adapting to land, as evidenced by a larger number of species and wider distribution. There is no salamander answer to **toads**, which have found ways to survive in some very dry places.
87. Frogs developed eyes with a **nictitating membrane**, along with lenses that adapted to the different refractive index of light in air. Species that move back-and-forth, like bullfrogs, have lenses that split the difference.
88. Frogs developed **tympanic membranes** for detecting sound in the air, along with **vocal cords** for communicating with other members of their species, lessening the need for pheromones and close proximity to one another.
89. This allowed individual frogs to spread out and use more resources, yet still find one another for mating.
90. There are many similar anatomical features in frogs and salamanders, but since they seem to have evolved apart from one another, there are also major differences.
91. As compared to salamanders, almost all frogs lack any **tail**, the muscles of the back legs and pectoral region are enlarged for hopping, and their **metatarsals** and **phalanges** are lengthened and webbed.
92. Many other parts of their musculoskeletal system are also adapted for jumping and swimming.
93. Leverage from the back legs starts at the **pelvic girdle**. The joints of the **sacrum** and the **ileum** are loose and free to rotate as they transfer force. Frogs have a single thick bone in the calf, rather than a **tibia** and **fibula**.
94. This strong bone provides a level to transfer force from the gigantic **gastrocnemius** in the calf.
95. Likewise, the **fibula** is thick and stubby, providing another strong lever powered by the **triceps femoris**, **semitendonosus,** and **gracilis major**. Collectively, these are eaten with remoulade sauce in Cajun restaurants.
96. In the front, the **pectoralis**, **deltoid**, and **latissimus dorsi** muscles of a frog would make any bodybuilder jealous, transmitting large amounts of force to the front legs, and providing shock absorbers for landing.
97. Most arboreal frogs, like tree frogs, have **toe pads** that act like suction cups, catching them when they jump from leaf to leaf in the canopy. Some digging species, like **spadefoot toads** have shovel-like toe tips.
98. Frog skin is often camouflaged and spotted, but other species make no attempt to hide themselves. **Poison dart frogs** advertise their extreme toxicity with bright color. However, ALL frogs produce skin toxins of varied degree.
99. Hobbyists have learned this the hard way when they kept separate frog species together, only to find that one (or both) species have killed the other when the toxins of the opposite species were absorbed through the skin.
100. Most of these toxins are derived from prey insects and concentrated in glands in the skin.
101. While it makes them vulnerable to absorbing toxins (and why pollutants are wiping out many species), frogs need the extra surface area the wet skin provides in order to get enough oxygen from respiration.

102. This is because their lungs just aren't big enough to do the job when they are active. They are forced to rely on diffusion through the skin and their gigantic mouths to supplement their blood oxygen levels.

103. Besides being useful for grabbing prey nearly as large as themselves, the mouth is also critical to the respiration of the **lungs**, since frogs lack **ribs**. It acts like a bellows to force large amounts of air in and out.

104. The **three-chambered heart** also doesn't help, since it mixes outgoing oxygenated blood from the lungs with incoming deoxygenated blood from the body in the **ventricle**.

105. **Toads** managed to partially improve upon the designs of the skin and the lungs. The skin is impregnated with **mucus glands** that cover it with wet snot, while the lungs show the rudimentary beginnings of **alveolar** divisions.

106. Internally, the digestive system is pretty similar to that of the aforementioned salamanders.

107. Like salamanders, the **large intestine** terminates in a **cloaca**, which also contains openings for the excretory and reproductive systems, providing exits for urine, sperm, and eggs.

108. The **excretory system** of frogs functions like that of fish during tadpolehood, creating ammonia in the urine like fish. However, as the kidneys and liver mature, they metabolize ammonia into the much less toxic **urea**.

109. The love lives of frogs are a little bit different than salamanders. Rather than dropping off sperm packets, male frogs and toads use **internal fertilization** to directly transfer **sperm** into the **cloacal duct** of females.

110. Male frogs may also hold onto their partners for several days, mating many times. She is captive during this time, as the males grow enlarged **thumb pads** that give them an iron grip on their partner.

111. This is because in many species, such as leopard frogs, numerous males will try to jockey for position and knock other males off and take over. It's like a big game of king-of-the-hill until mating season ends.

112. Leopard frogs are **R-strategists** and try to mate as much as possible in a short spawn, flooding the environment with too many tadpoles for predators to consume. However, other frogs tend somewhere closer to **K-strategism**, with mating times being transient and ongoing, particularly in the tropics.

113. There is a wide degree of variability in mating habits and reproductive behavior in frogs. While most females lay jelly-like nests of eggs underwater, there are numerous strategies for getting the tadpoles to adulthood.

114. Amazonian tree frogs may lay their bubble nests in the cup-like center of a bromeliad plant, which floods in the rainforest, while strawberry frogs lay the eggs on land and pee on them to keep them moist.

115. There are dozens of other innovative ways that frog species help their tadpoles get to maturity, with some species providing parental care, with pouched frogs developing a marsupial-like pocket to protect them.

116. Frog taxonomy is complex. Their classification system is derived from fossil records, the shape of their pelvic girdle, the feet, reproductive characteristics, and a large number of chromosomal and genetic markers.

HOMAGE TO FROGS: KERMIT'S MUPPET TRIVIA ANSWERS ON PAGE 174

1) NAME KERMIT'S NEPHEW WHO WAS CHANGING FROM A TADPOLE.
2) WHO ARE THE TWO OLD GUYS IN THE BALCONY THAT MAKE FUN OF THE GUESTS AND ALL OF THE TALENT ACTS ON 'THE MUPPET SHOW'?
3) WHAT MUPPET HAD REAL HUMAN HANDS TO CONTROL FLYING COOKWARE?
4) WHAT IS MISS PIGGY'S FULL NAME THAT HASN'T BEEN USED SINCE THE 70'S?
5) WHAT SONG BECAME A HIT ON THE CHARTS AFTER IT WAS USED IN A MUPPETS SKIT WHERE TWO PINK ALIENS AND A BURNOUT HIPPIE CHARACTER SING?

117. For this reason, there is not a quick or easy explanation of why many of the families are distinct from one another. The diagram below shows representatives of ten of the extant 29 families of frogs.

118. The third group of amphibians, unknown to many, are the reclusive **caecilians** of **Order Gymnophiona**.

119. Caecilians are snake-like amphibians that seem to have diverged off of the main ancestral lineage of amphibians before frogs and salamanders split off, but since so few fossils exist, it is hard to know for sure.

120. All caecilians are found in the tropics of South America, Africa, India, or Southeast Asia, mostly in rainforests. As far as we know, earthworms are their favorite food, but they also eat insects, small animals, and Teddy grahams.

121. Most caecilians spend the majority of their lives burrowing underground or living under rocks in streams. Most are small nocturnal predators that make it a point not to be seen, so their obscurity is understandable.

122. Caecilians have several primitive features. They lack legs, have eyes that are little more than light receptors, have fused skull bones for burrowing, and use snake-like wriggling movements.

123. The skin of caecilians, like other amphibians, has **toxin glands** and **mucus glands**. However, concentric **calcified scales** are unique to the group. In addition to acting like protective armor, they help in burrowing.

124. Most caecilians have strong jaws lined with ridge-like teeth that can crush small animals or deliver a nasty bite to a predator. Some have **venom glands** that bathe the teeth in enzymes that digest the cells of their prey.

125. It is not surprising that caecilians would have **tentacles** above the nostrils, since they spend most of their time in the dark. These are full of **olfactory tissue**, and serve a dual purpose of feeling and smelling their way around.

126. Their internal anatomy is similar to that of frogs. They have a three-chambered heart, a similar layout to their digestive systems. Most species have primitive lungs, though some do not.

127. In an interesting case of **convergent evolution**, the left lung of caecilians is also **vestigial**, like those of snakes. Since both are long wiener-shaped animals, neither can fit two expanded lungs into the width of the body.
128. Given enough time, one would also expect that the left lungs of wiener dogs would also become vestigial.
129. Male caecilians have a penis-like **phallodium** organ which is used to transfer sperm into the female's cloaca.
130. Some female caecilians are **oviparous** and guard a clutch of eggs. In most species, the tadpole finishes developing in the egg and emerges as a juvenile that looks like a miniature adult.
131. However, most species of caecilians are **viviparous**. The larval caecilians hatch inside the female and continue on feeding on specialized nutrient-filled cells inside the oviducts.
132. Both systems of reproduction allow larger offspring with better chances of survival.
133. There are 10 known families of caecilians, with the primary means of classification being related to reproductive behaviors and habits, as well as scale structure and genetic differences.
134. The diagram below shows representatives from two of these families, each with different life histories.

GABOON CAECILIAN
FAMILY DERMOPHIIDAE
VIVAPAROUS; GIVE LIVE BIRTH TO YOUNG

YELLOW BANDED CAECILIAN
FAMILY ICTHYOPHIIDAE
OVIPAROUS; GUARD NEST OF LARVAE

CAECILIAN SPECIES

F) Class Reptilia: Reptile Evolution and Prehistoric Taxa

1. **Reptiles** continued with many of the designs that made amphibians successful on land and made numereous evolutionary improvements to move into numerous open terrestrial niches.
2. They were highly successful, dominating terrestrial life for around 250 million years, with much of that timespan consisting of the Triassic and Jurassic dinosaur ages. However, they were, by no means, the only reptiles.
3. The first reptiles were unremarkable lizard-like animals known as **Hylomonus.** There is still debate over whether their features fully qualified them as reptiles, so they are known as **basal amniotes**.
4. However, the one huge innovation that Hylomonus made was the **amniotic egg**.
5. Reproduction was the Achilles heel of amphibians for a long time, as they were forced to re-enter the water or otherwise make inconvenient arrangements to keep their eggs moist and their babies from suffocating.

6. **Basal amniotes** solved this problem by re-designing the egg, so as to put the pond INSIDE the egg.
7. **Amniotic eggs**, starting with the outside, have a leathery **shell** to prevent dessication. In reptiles, this is composed of a layer of fibrous proteins. Small pore spaces allow the embryo to breathe.
8. Inside the shell is a double membrane, giving way to thick layers of **albumen** (egg white) that give protein reserves to the developing embryo. A tether called the **chalaza** suspends the yolk and embryo to the shell.
9. Inside of the egg white is the **yolk sac**, which contains fatty nutrient-rich yolk to give energy to the embryo.
10. A sac called the **vitelline membrane** around the yolk keeps growing in a fertilized egg and wraps up the embryo inside of a sac called the **chorion**. The yolk sac, itself, provides a pipeline of nutrients near the embryo's belly.
11. The **amnion** is a second fluid-filled sac that grows around the embryo, essentially putting it inside of a pond. The **amnion** has been retained even in **viviparous** animals like mammals. Hence, the water breaks during delivery.
12. Finally, another membrane called the **allantois** forms from the **ectoderm** of the embryo. It grows into a sac full of blood vessels that are used for gas exchange and evacuation of wastes. It became the **placenta** in mammals.
13. The diagram below shows the part of an amniotic egg. Shelled eggs with an amnion are considered so important to terrestrial life that most biologists don't think land would have been settled without them.

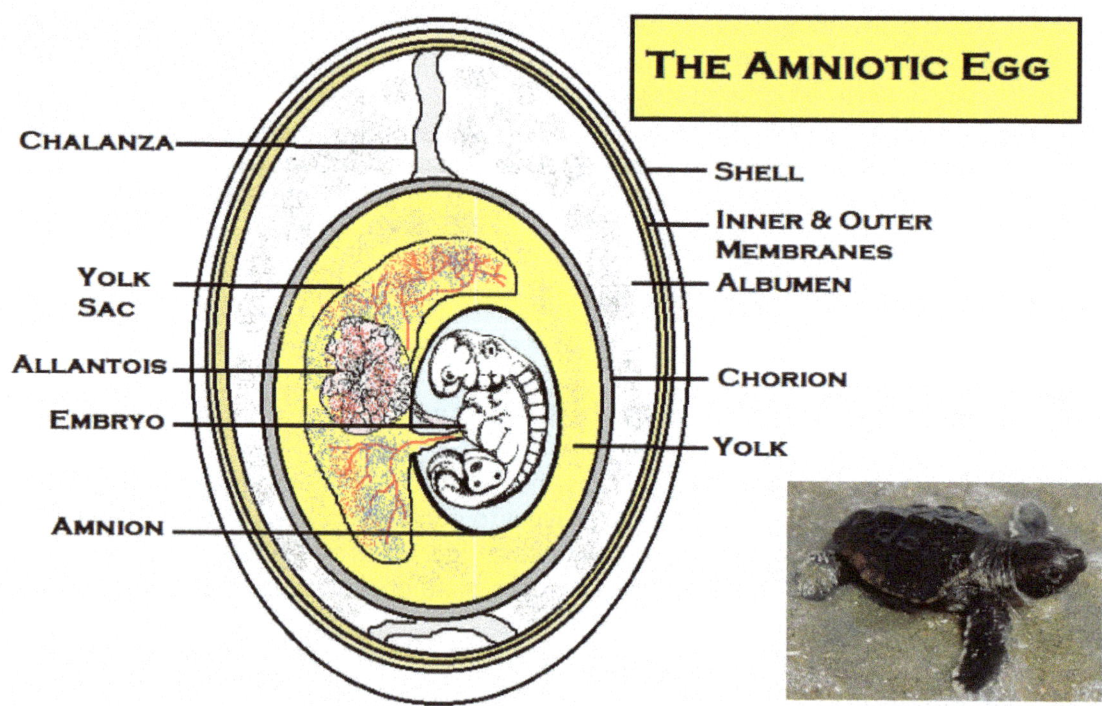

14. The modern **Class Reptilia** includes lizards, crocodilians, snakes, amphisbeneans, tuatauras, and turtles.
15. The biggest group of reptiles ever to exist, the dinosaurs, are extinct, though there are compelling arguments that birds should be included with dinosaurs and grouped with reptiles.

16. Reptiles took some major steps in expanding onto terrestrial niches, by adding a lot of features that emancipated them from water.
17. The **amniotic egg** was revolutionary for terrestrial life, but by no means was it fully sufficient to keep moving further away from water. Reptiles made numerous adjustments to their bodies as well.
18. Reptiles adapted an armor of **keratin scales** that greatly reduce the amount of moisture lost from the skin. There are several different shapes of reptile scales, but all are derived from layers of the **epidermis.**
19. The **lungs** had to expand dramatically to compensate for the loss of a moist external respiratory surface. To do this, reptile lungs evolved chambers called **alveoli**, which dramatically increased their surface area.
20. While most reptiles retain a **3-chambered heart**, the unrestricted mixing of oxygenated and deoxygenated blood in the **ventricle** could not be allowed to the extreme of amphibians.
21. Instead, a muscular **septum** evolved to partially divide the ventricle. **Crocodilians**, due to their gigantic size, must have a fully divided heart, and are the most primitive animals alive today with a **4-chambered heart**
22. Reptile **kidneys** changed the make-up of their nitrogenous wastes from ammonia and urea to **uric acid**, which is a solid white paste that is excreted through the **cloaca** along with feces.
23. While some water may be lost in the process of producing waste, it is dramatically less than with liquid urine.
24. Reptiles also further spread out their **pectoral girdle** and **pelvic girdle** to facilitate running and climbing. Nail beds also evolved and grew **claws**, which aided in climbing, predation, and self-defense.
25. Reptile **teeth** grew from the ridge-like plates in the mouths of amphibians and became large and conical. Like all vertebrates with teeth, they have a living **pulp cavity**, a protein layer called **dentin**, and a calcified enamel layer.
26. Reptile reproduction, in addition to the amniotic egg, also became independent of water.
27. Reptiles use **internal fertilization**. With the exception of turtles, male reptiles have a pair of **hemipenes** used to inseminate the female through the **cloaca**. Turtles simply mate cloaca to cloaca.
28. Reptiles also lay their nests away from water. Many of them have also evolved to tend to these nests, thus assuring a higher survival rate of their offspring.
29. While there are many more specific adaptations to terrestrial life, we will save the details of those for each particular taxa we discuss. Now let's delve further into the evolutionary history of reptiles.
30. As mentioned before, the first amniote in the fossil record was a lizard-like creature named Hyolomonus. Along with other similar creatures, these arose about 318 million years ago in the Carboniferous Era.
31. It is not certain whether they were advanced amphibians, primitive reptiles, or somewhere in-between.
32. However, as time went on, they fully evolved into many other primitive reptiles that would go on to become the **Sauropsids**, to which all modern reptiles belong.
33. About 250 million years ago, the **Synapsids** diverged from this main group and went in a different evolutionary dirction. So what is the difference between the two? Mostly skull anatomy.
34. **Synapsids** have an opening in their skull behind the eye socket (your temples), where jaw muscles can articulate. Additionally, **canine teeth** evolved in this group. The **mandible** also became a single tooth-bearing bone.
35. **Sauropsids** (with the exception of extinct **anapsids** and possibly modern turtles) have two skull openings for muscle articulations behind the eye. They lack canine teeth, and multiple bones in the jaw grow teeth.
36. There are also other differences. **Synapsids** have a **palate** on the roof of their mouth separating the sinuses from the mouth, while **sauropsids** do not.

37. **Synapsids** are the obvious ancestors of mammals (the only surviving synapsids) , because even in fossil records, there are structures that look like a dermis under the skin, follicles for hair, and primitive mammary glands. I
38. **Sauropsids** have thinner skin, simple scales, and no mammary glands.
39. Finally, it appears that many synapsids were **endotherms**, based on the presence of certain tissues.
40. The diagram below notes some of the major differences in synapsids and sauropsids.

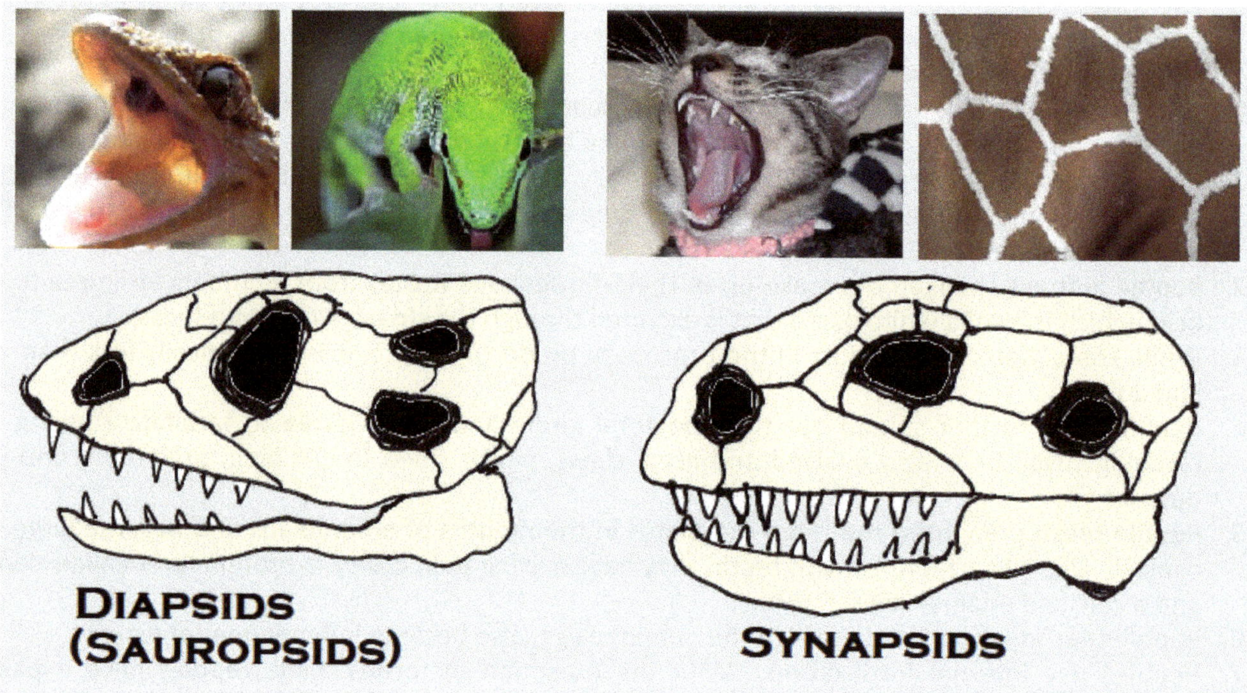

41. We will now concentrate on how Sauropsids diverged, as they are the ancestors of all modern reptiles.
42. The first evolutionary split occurred when the Sauropsids split to become two clades called **Parareptilia** and **Eureptilia** (which contains all modern reptiles).
43. Most members of both **Eureptilia** and **Parareptilia** were, or are, **diapsids**, with two openings behind the eye for jaw musculature. However, the size and arrangement of the skull bones differ significantly.
44. **Parareptilians** often had a triangular apron at the back of the skull formed by three pairs of bones called the postparietal, tabular, and subtemporalis. This is not the case in modern reptiles.
45. Some members of the parareptilian clade had **anapsid** skulls, wherein the cranial bones fused and closed off all the openings, in order to create an armor-like helmet.
46. Due to members with these anatomical similarities, for a very long time, **turtles** were thought to have evolved from the parareptilian lineage. However, DNA evidence has since debunked this theory.
47. With the exception of **mesosaurs**, almost all members of this clade had short, thick, boxy skulls.
48. Long pointy uniform teeth were the common type of dentition, though there was great variability in these too.
49. The vertebrae of parareptilians were very thick and boxy, as compared to eureptilians. Additionally, the shoulder blades and pelvic girdle around the hips are shaped differently in parareptilians.
50. Finally, a conspicuous feature of parareptilians, is that their hind limbs and front limbs were usually small, stubby, and of similar size. Overall, except for mesosaurs, their bodies were more tank-like.

51. Since we are discussing modern reptilians, we will move on from the parareptilians with the diagram below, which gives a brief phylogenetic summary of their taxa. All have been extinct for many eons.

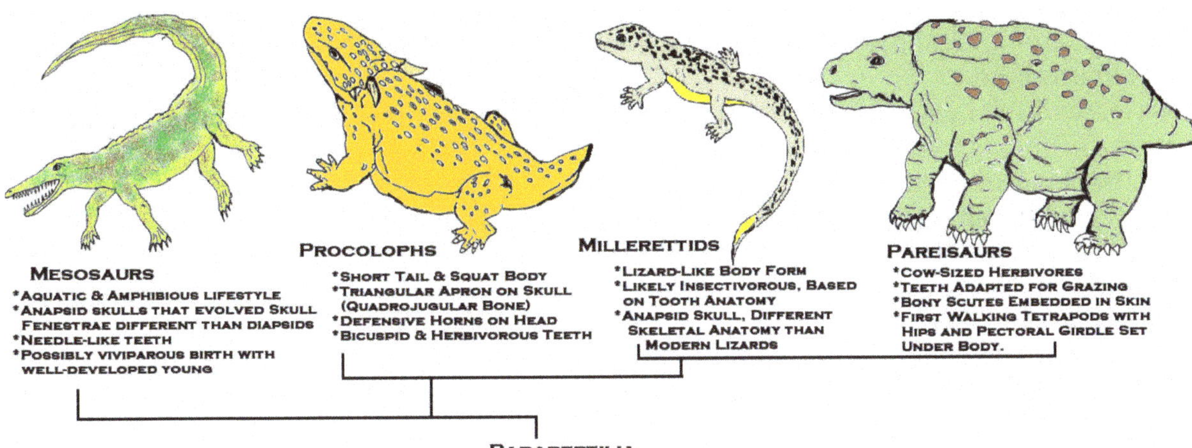

52. Now let's work our way through some of the major taxonomic splits of the **Eureptilians** that led to the evolution of the modern groups of reptiles and birds still in existence.

53. **Eureptilians**, as compared to **Parareptilians** have greatly reduced the size of the bones at the back of the skull. Additionally, they tend to have narrower vertebrae, much larger back legs, and a pelvic girdle with bones shaped so that they are specialized for running and climbing.

54. With the exception of two early groups, the **Captorhinids** and the **Paleothyrii**, all Eureptilians are **diapsids**, with two openings in the skull behind the eye orbital for jaw muscle attachments.

55. Both of the aforementioned groups had triangular skulls that more closely resembled those of large extinct amphibians, than they did to the remaining diapsid reptiles.

56. While the actual puzzle pieces of the cranial bone structure were like those of diapsids, they lacked the **fenestrae** (openings in the skull), like the remaining members of Eureptilia.

57. Both groups are illustrated below, with a few facts about the putative lifestyles of each.

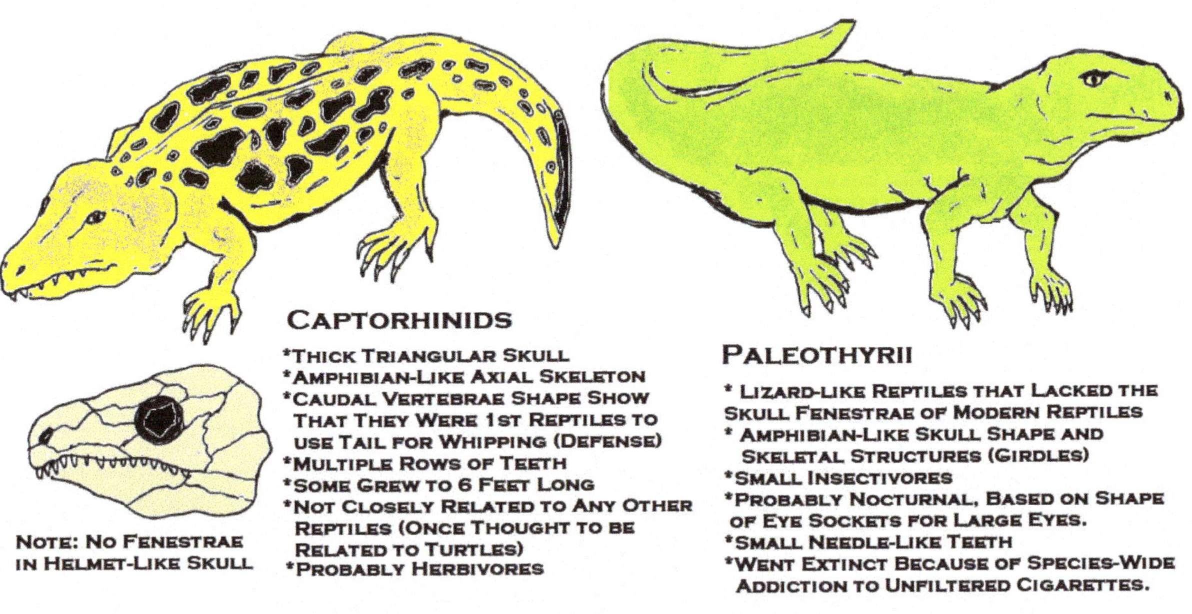

58. Now let's move on to the true **diapsid** reptiles. The first known diapsids in the fossil record belong to the group
Aerioscelidia. To an untrained observer, these ancient reptiles looked pretty much like lizards.
59. Again, the differences come down to the way the puzzle pieces of the cranium fit together (which were different). Additionally, they lacked some of the cartilages around the windpipe and sinuses that lizards have.
60. **Aerioscelidis** sit by themselves phylogenetically. They have two skull openings, but most of the other characteristics in their bone structures were more primitive than than all other diapsids.
61. The **Neodiapsids** include a group of reptiles known as **Claudiosaurs** that are considered to be the most primitive among the group, due to differences in their facial bones and sinuses.
62. Additionally, **Claudiosaurus** is thought to have been at least partially aquatic, because of a very small sternum and narrow leg bones. This makes it seem like the skeleton wasn't up to the job of full-time terrestrial life.
63. The remaining Neodiapsids are all members of clade **Sauria**, which includes all modern reptiles, as well as many extinct groups like the dinosaurs. They all share about two dozen common skeletal features.
64. The heads of all **Saurid** reptiles have external nostrils, lack canine teeth, have muscular connections on the dorsal side of the head, a lateral quadrate bone in the skull, and a number of other common bone positions.
65. Saurids also are the first group of reptiles to completely discard some of the lingering skeletal characteristics, such as forked ribs and to de-evolve the **cleithrum** bone, which holds up the gill arches in fish.
66. And now a word from a few more of our sponsors. A section this long isn't cheap, ya know?

67. **Sauria** also has distinct limb traits. They lack a fifth metatarsal bone in the feet, have a much more developed radius in the front limbs, have short thumbs, and typically have long fourth metatarsal bones.
68. Of course most of these traits count for snakes, since they evolved away their limbs.

HOMAGE TO FROGS: KERMIT'S MUPPET TRIVIA ANSWERS		
1) ROBIN	2) STATLER & WALDORF	3) SWEDISH CHEF
4) PIGULIA LEE	5) MANAH-MANAH (DOOT-DOO-DUH-DOO-DOO!)	

69. Before moving on to the next subdivision of phylogeny, let's review where we are so far with the diagram below.

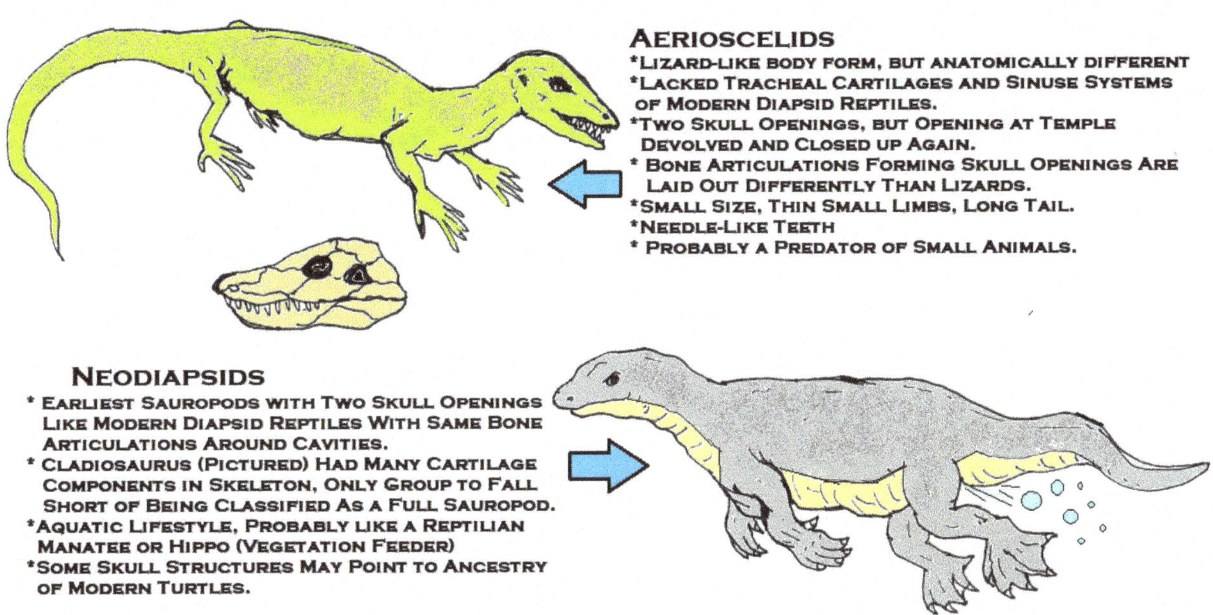

70. **Sauria** then diverges into two clades of **sauropods** known as **Lepidosauromorpha** and **Archosauromorpha**.
71. The former includes modern lizards, snakes, amphisbaenians, and tuatauras.
72. The latter split a second time and diverged into two further groups. The first clade of **Archosauromorphs** gave rise to crocodilians and birds, while turtles evolved from the second.
73. Let's look at **Lepidosauromorpha** first and begin discussing extant reptiles as we walk through the taxa.
74. **Lepidosauromorpha** have hip bones that cause them to walk and run in large rotations around the socket. As a result, the muscles in their trunk and their tail undulate like a swimming fish.
75. Snakes, though they have devolved their legs and most of their hips, are members of lepidosauromorpha, and consequently, have the familiar serpentine slither.
76. In spite of having legs, lizards also slither their body muscles in similar fashion while they walk.
77. The **pectoral girdle** also contributes to this motion, as the **coracoid processes** of the **scapula** (shoulder blade) can rotate around their articulation points on the **sternum** (breast bone).
78. **Lepidosauromorph** teeth are also fused to the jaw bones, glued in place by mineralization between the two.
79. From what researchers can tell, all members of this group of reptiles were always **ectotherms** (cold-blooded) and needed to bask in order to maintain a body temperature and run their metabolism effectively.
80. Lepidosauromorphs are subdivided into one extinct order and family known as **Kuhneosauridae** and into the extant order **Lepidosaura**, which includes modern tuatauras, lizards, snakes, and amphisbeneans.
81. Let's start with the extinct members of **Kuhneosauridae**. Imagine a reptilian bat, sugar glider, or toy balsa wood plane, and you can envision these reptiles. They were basically like flying lizards.
82. Thanks to super-elongated ribs, they had wings between their front and back legs, allowing them to jump out of trees and glide over to the next branch. Their vertebrae were also designed for cushioned impacts.

83. Like other **diapsids**, there were two additional skull openings for jaw muscles. The eye sockets were large, possibly meaning that they had large eyes and sharp vision like some sort of lizard hawk.
84. While no one can be certain, some say that Kuhneosaurs became extinct because they were the reptilian equivalent of drones, which are highly annoying like selfie sticks and fidget spinners.
85. Over time, there is a significant probability that they were eventually all blown out of the sky with 12 gauges by angry neighbors who became weary of them spying on them through their windows.
86. The diagram below shows the appearance of a Khuneosaur, along with its cranial anatomy.

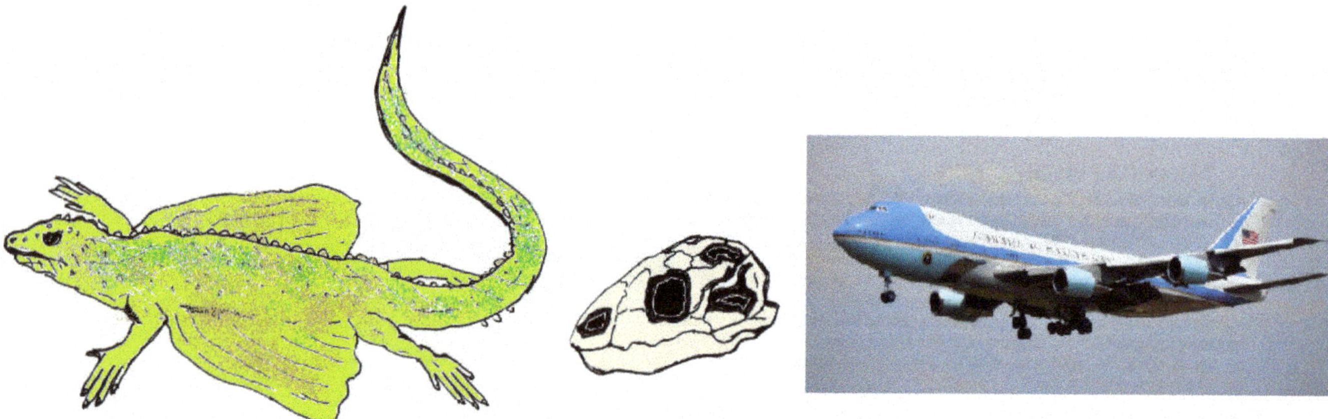

87. Now let's turn our attention to extant groups of reptiles.

G) Class Reptilia: Extant Reptile Taxa

1. Now we finally move on to the extant groups of **Lepidosaurs**. It includes two orders of reptiles.
2. **Order Rhynocephalia** includes two living species of tuataras and many extinct relatives. The **Order Squamata** contains thousands of species of living and extinct lizards, amphisbeneans and snakes.
3. Two species of tuataras, native to New Zealand, are all that remain of **Order Rhynocephalia**.
4. Originally, they were classified as lizards, due to their highly similar appearances, but a closer look revealed major differences in their skeletal anatomy that more closely resembled extinct fossils.
5. The first major differences can be found in the skull. Tuataras, unlike lizards, do not have external ear canals. They have unrooted teeth that are also found on the roof of the mouth. The cheekbones do not attach to the same bones at the base of the skull, and one of the two diapsid skull openings is mostly enclosed with bone.
6. Unlike lizards, tuataras also retain rib-like bones along the belly, which are more akin to fish and salamander anatomy than to other modern reptiles.
7. Male tuataras mate by pressing the cloacal opening to the female's **cloaca**, while male lizards have a pair of **hemipenes** that penetrate the cloaca. The only other reptiles that still use this mating system are turtles.

8. A tuatara is pictured below, along with a diagram of some of the distinctive skull features.

9. The **Order Squamata** includes nearly 11,000 existing species of lizards, snakes, and amphisbeneans and many more that have come and gone over the last couple of hundred million years.

10. All squamates have several common skeletal and anatomical features.

11. The skull of all members of this group have movable **quadrate bones** that can unhinge from the rest of the jaw, allowing them to stretch their mouths to a huge gape to swallow eggs and live prey larger than their girth.

12. Unlike tuataras, they lack the extra set of rib-like bones along their abdomens. However, they have a large, but variable, number of vertebrae that articulate into ribs. Some snakes have more than 100.

13. **Squamates** are named for the thick keratinized scales that cover their bodies. Some species, such as horned frogs and thorny devil lizards, take this to the extreme and have evolved spiky armor.

14. Reproductively, all male squamates have **paired hemipenes** that engorge with blood and extend out of a pouch when they mate with females. They use **internal fertilization** and insert them into the female cloacal opening.

15. While most squamates are **oviparous**, laying leathery eggs in nests, some species have evolved **ovoviparity**, wherein they let the eggs hatch inside the uterus and consume the egg yolk before birth.

16. This strategy, used by garter snakes, boas, and several other squamate families, results in larger young being born. Larger offspring means a greater likelihood of survival to adulthood, as they are better developed.

17. Now let's delve into the major taxa under the **Order Squamata**. We begin with the lizards.

18. There are several clades of lizards under Order Squamata. These sub-divide further into 16 families. Differences in skeletal anatomy, musculature, and reproductive strategies are used in classification schemes.

19. However, the basic gross anatomy of most lizards is very similar across all taxa.

20. Externally, lizards tend to have short necks (with the exception of the monitor family), they have muscular torsos, four legs set out to the sides of their body for running, and long tails.

21. In some families, such as chameleons, the tail is prehensile, but in most, it is used for balance and leverage.

22. Like all squamates, their skin is covered in keratin scales. Camouflaged patterns are common, as is the tendency for scales to pile up to create horns and spiky protective outgrowths, such as in thorny devil lizards.
23. Some types of lizards, such as anoles and geckos, have specialized scales that resemble suction cups on the soles of their feet, allowing them to use Van der Waal forces to climb walls and branches.
24. Lizards have a tongue that extends out of the mouth. In geckos, this is short and stubby, while in chameleons, it is rooted in the front and able to be distended almost the length of the body to trap insects.
25. Monitors and skinks have **olfactory sensors** in the tongue, allowing them to taste chemicals in the air and zero in on a prey animal or sun-bloated roadkill baking on the asphalt.
26. Additionally, many families of lizards actively use the **vomeronasal organ** inside their sinuses to detect **pheromones** from other individuals. Males use these cues to mate with females and fight other suitors.
27. Some lizards, such as tegus and monitors, have teeth socketed in the lower jaw, while others like agamas have teeth that form in ridges on top of the jaw, rather than being implanted in sockets.
28. A few lizards, particularly the Gila monster and beaded lizard, are **venomous.** Recently, it has been discovered that some members of the monitor family, particularly the Komodo dragon, also secrete toxic saliva.
29. They have **salivary glands** that have become specially adapted to secrete cell-destroying enzymes. Unlike snakes, they must gnaw on their intended target and rely on venom to seep into the cuts.
30. Lizard eyes are fully adapted for terrestrial life, with the **lenses** fully adapting to the refractive index of air. Additionally, the **pineal gland** at the top of the brain is buried under a clear scale that serves as a 'third eye'.
31. This **parietal eye** comes into play as a light sensor. Since all lizards are **ectotherms**, this allows them to gauge when the sun is at is highest points, and to bask, so they can **thermoregulate** their body temperatures.
32. Internally, lizards mostly represent an improvement over the amphibian design in several body systems.
33. Lizards have a **three-chambered heart** like amphibians. However, the **ventricle** is mostly divided with a muscular **septum**, which does a much better job of keeping oxygenated and deoxygenated blood from mixing.
34. Lizard lungs are much larger and contain **alveoli** to dramatically increase the surface area for gas exchange. This compensates for the fact that their skin is scaly and ineffective for respiratory exchange.
35. The **kidneys** of lizards are adapted to secrete **uric acid paste** and to retain most of the water in their nitrogenous wastes. By avoiding the production of liquid urine, they retain more water and can even live in deserts.
36. Reproduction is by **internal fertilization**, as male lizards have a pair of **hemipenes** that are used to transfer sperm into the **cloacal opening** of females.
37. Most lizards are **oviparous** and lay eggs covered with mostly a leathery keratin shell.
38. However, unlike amphibians, they have full **amniotic eggs** that enclose a 'pond' inside the egg to allow the embryo to develop independently of a water body.
39. Some families, such as glass lizards are **viviparous**, as the eggs attach to a **placenta-like** structure inside the female that continues to nourish the embryos after they have exhausted the supply of yolk in the egg.
40. This strategy allows larger, more-developed offspring at birth, protecting them from smaller predators and giving them greater survival abilities at the start of their lives.

41. The diagram below shows the anatomical layout of a typical male agamid lizard.

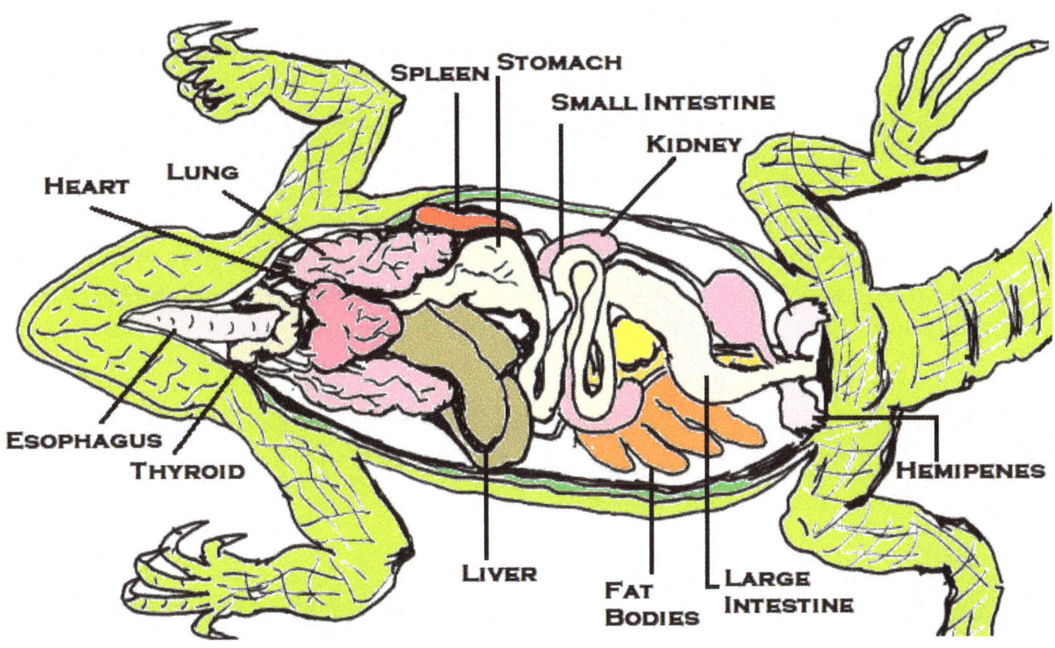

42. Various features in skull anatomy and musculature, along with differences in the feet, tail, and leg musculature are used in the taxonomic classification of lizards into families.
43. Let's go over a few of the most basic traits used in that classification scheme.
44. **Family Gekkonidae** (geckos) lack eyelids, have vocal cords, and are mostly carnivorous. Their skin is scaleless and many gecko species also have toe pad scales used to climb surfaces.
45. Gila monsters and beaded lizards belong to **Family Helodermatadae**. They are one of two families of lizards that have venom glands under the jaw. These lizards are adapted to deserts, with heavy scales and stout, fat bodies.
46. Chameleons are in the namesake **Family Chameleonidae**. They have turreted eyes that can rotate, prehensile tails, **zygodactyl feet** for gripping branches, and numerous **chromatophores** for camouflaging their skin.
47. Anoles, sometimes falsely called chameleons, due to the fact that they can also change their skin color, instead belong to **Family Polychrotidae**. Males have larged colored **dewlaps** to attract **sexually dimorphic** females.
48. Horned lizards are heavily armored with stout, flat bodies and stubby legs. **Camouflaged against desert rocks, these members of Family Phyrosomatidae thermoregulate by basking or hiding under rocks.**
49. **Family Varanidae** includes gigantic and foul-tempered monitor lizards. Build for predation, these old world lizards have long claws, an elongated body, and jaws with heavy bite force. Some species are also venomous.
50. The large **tegus** of **Family Telidae** superficially resemble monitors, but their bodies are heavier, their temperaments are much more docile, and they are also omnivorous. They are new world lizards.
51. Glass lizards belong to the **Family Pyogopodidae**. In addition to looking a lot like snakes and having vestigial little limbs (if they have them), these burrowers easily break off their tails if grabbed by a predator.
52. **Family Lacertidae** contains the most 'lizardy' of the lizards. Everything about most species is phenotypically what you would consider an 'average lizard'. Most are relatively small fast insectivores with long tails.

53. Iguanas and chuckwallas belong to **Family Iguanidae**. Unlike most lizards, some members are strictly herbivorous. They have a spiny crest along the back, sharp claws, and a long tail for balancing in trees.
54. **Family Scincidae** consists of numerous skink species distributed worldwide. They have small stubby legs, almost no neck, and a breakaway tail. Most are burrowers that run with a swift serpentine motion.
55. The basilisks of **Family Corytophanidae** look like little dragons. These omnivores have fin-like crests on their heads and backs and long skinny bodies and tails designed for swift running, even on the surface of water.
56. The plated lizards of **Family Gerrhosauridae** are stout-bodied little insectivores that have armor-like concentric rings of scales around their bodies. They have short tails, stout bodies, and an omnivorous diet.
57. The wrongly-named night lizards of **Family Xantusiidae** are **viviparous**, giving live birth to young that are larger and more developed, allowing them to survive predation at a higher rate.
58. The diagram below shows representatives of each of these families.

A) FAMILY GEKKONIDAE; LEOPARD GECKO
B) FAMILY HELODERMATIDAE; GILA MONSTER
C) FAMILY CHAMELEONIDAE; PANTHER CHAMELEON
D) FAMILY POLYCHROTIDAE; GREEN ANOLE
E) FAMILY PHYNOSOMATIDAE; GREATER SHORT HORNED LIZARD
F) FAMILY VARANIDAE; KOMODO DRAGON
G) FAMILY TELIDAE; ARGENTINE BLACK AND WHITE TEGU
H) FAMILY PYOGOPODIDAE; WESTERN GLASS LIZARD
I) FAMILY LACERTIDAE; IBIZA WALL LIZARD
J) FAMILY IGUANIDAE; FIJI IGUANA
K) FAMILY SCINCIDAE; WESTERN SKINK
L) FAMILY CORYTOPHANIDAE; GREEN BASILISK
M)FAMILY GERRHOSAURIDAE; SUDAN PLATED LIZARD
N) FAMILY XANTUSIIDAE; DESERT NIGHT LIZARD

59. **Snakes** belong to **Sub-Order Serpentes**, but remain classified within the squamates with lizards.
60. There are some fairly obvious links between lizards and snakes. Pythons, boas, and certain families of blind snakes have a **vestigial pelvic girdle** with remnants of leg bones.
61. Like lizards, snakes have **keratin scales**. However, unlike most lizards, snakes fully molt their skin in one contiguous piece and re-grow their epidermis throughout life as they grow larger.
62. It appears that most of the changes that occurred between snakes and lizards has to do with the regulation of **Hox genes** within the developmental **homeobox**.
63. Like lizards, snakes have all four sections of vertebrae, including cervical, thoracic, abdominal, and tail.
64. However, there appears to be a massive amount of repeat expression in the thoracic section of the body, giving snakes many more vertebrae and ribs than lizards.
65. Likewise, the Hox genes for limb development switched off at some point.
66. As snakes evolved to slithering lifestyles, mostly dependent upon ambush predation, they developed some unique adaptive physical features and behaviors.
67. Due to the muscular torso and flexible vertebrae, snakes have taken on a large variety of slithering styles. Some snakes undulate, while others move side-to-side.
68. Arboreal and cave snakes have developed ways to push off of surfaces to conserve energy and attack prey.
69. Many predatory snakes have **infrared sensing organs**, such as those found in rattlesnakes.
70. Additionally, the **Jacobson's organ** at the roof of the mouth has pronounced importance in snakes, extending into a forked tongue that can taste the air and sense chemical cues in the environment around it.
71. **Venom glands** developed in several families of predatory snakes. **Venom glands** are modified **salivary glands** that secrete a cocktail of cell-destroying enzymes, blood clotting factors, and neurotoxins.
72. The eyes of snakes have **cone cells**, indicating that they can see color. Some snakes, like mambas, have very sharp vision, while others, such as blind snakes, have very poor vision.
73. The **skull** of snakes has the same cranial bones of other vertebrates on its superior surface. Like all vertebrates, the crown of the skull is made of fused frontal, parietal, occipital, and temporal bones.
74. However, snakes gain their legendary ability to swallow large objects because of ligaments that loosely attach the jawbones to the skull, and to each other.
75. At the back of the skull on each sides, the **quadrate bones** articulate the top of the skull to the jaw. The **mandible** of the lower jaw is divided into two bones, with a flexible ligament bridging the middle.
76. This arrangement allows snakes to open their mouths to much wider circumferences than their own bodies, allowing an anaconda to swallow a large deer or for an everyday garter snake to eat a chicken egg.
77. To avoiding choking themselves during a meal, snakes can breathe and swallow independently, because the **esophagus** is located on top of the tongue, while the **trachea** opens into the airway underneath the tongue.
78. Internally, snakes are very much like lizards. They have similar three-chambered hearts and viscera.
79. However, unlike lizards, snakes have a **vestigial left lung** and a long sac-like enlarged right lung, allowing their respiratory system to fit in their tube-like bodies.
80. The **reproductive systems** of snakes are also lizard-like. The males possess a pair of **hemipenes** that retract into pouches when not in use. Like lizards, all snakes mate and use **internal fertilization**.
81. The reproductive strategies of different snake families varies greatly. For instance, a python is a python because they are **oviparous** egg layers. Boas, on the other hand, are fully **viviparous** and give live birth.
82. Many other snakes, such as garter snakes, also give live birth, but they employ a strategy of **ovoviviparity**, allowing the juveniles to feed of the yolk in the egg inside their bodies, increasing their size at birth.

83. Just think about it. Right now, in the attic above the very bed where you sleep, an entire nest of snakes has awakened from their winter hibernation to mate and lay eggs that will develop into even more snakes.
84. Eventually, while you sleep peacefully and unsuspectingly, the weight of the snakes on the air conditioning vent above your bed will become too much, the fasteners will give way, and an entire pile of slithering serpents will land on your face, awakening you in a pitch black room.
85. Now let's turn our attention to the sub-classification of snakes into families.
86. The most primitive groups of snakes are the thread snakes and blind snakes of **Family Leptotphlopidae** and a few other obscure families. All of them have distinctly blunt-ended bodies on both ends.
87. Most live underground in burrows, have poor eyesight or vestigial eyes, can't disarticulate their jaws like more advanced snakes, and often have few or no teeth in their upper jaws, since they feed on earthworms.
88. **Family Uropeltidae** includes the pipesnakes and flat-tailed snakes. They are also more primitive than most other snakes. Like threadsnakes, their skulls are rigid and their jaws don't move much.
89. Thanks to their underground lifestyles, they lack orbital bones altogether, their eyes mostly don't work, and their scales have evolved to be smooth. Their paddle-like tails are used for digging.
90. The remaining snake families belong to the **Suborder Macrostomata**. A defining feature of these types of snakes is the presence of a flexible disarticulating jaw with functioning teeth, along with well-developed eyes.
91. The constrictors are considered the least-evolved of the 'modern snakes' because they retain **vestigial pelvic bones** and have spines next to their genital openings that appear to be the remnants of claws.
92. **Family Pythonidae** includes such well-known old world species as ball pythons, carpet pythons, and green tree pythons. All use **constriction** to suffocate their prey. Four pairs of backward facing teeth snake the animal as it is slowly swallowed by a distensible jaw. Pythons are **oviparous** and brood eggs in a nest.
93. **Family Boidae** includes boa constrictors, rubber boas, anacondas and many other species of new world snakes. Like pythons, they constrict their prey. However, they are **viviparous**, giving live birth to well-developed young.
94. The remaining modern families of snakes belong to **Suborder Caenophidia**, which have no pelvic girdles.
95. **Family Colubridae** is the largest of these families, including nearly 1,800 of the 3,900 known snake species. This family includes mostly nonvenomous snakes like corn snakes, rat snakes, kingsnakes, and garter snakes.
96. The main trait that is shared by most Colubrids is that they have similarly shaped skulls with rear-facing fangs.
97. It is thought that Colubrids eventually evolved to give rise to **Family Viperidae.** This gains corroboration from the fact that a few members of the family, such as boomslangs, have venom and their teeth have migrated up.
98. As opposed to their less harmful cousins, vipers have **hinged fangs** at the front of the mouth, **venom glands** that evolved from salivary glands, and heavy muscular bodies for wrestling with larger prey. They have thick, rough diamond-shaped raised scales that serve as a sort of armor when fighting prey or fending off predators.
99. **Vipers** are often nocturnal, as reflected by their vertical pupils and their tendency to rely heavily on their **infrared organs** and **Jacobson's organs** in detecting prey.
100. **Family Achrochordidae** includes a unique family of snakes called wart snakes. They have extremely baggy, tough skin, no defined belly scales, and eyes positioned at the rear of the head.
101. All of these are adaptations to an aquatic lifestyle, as fish and frogs comprise a large portion of their diet.
102. **Family Elapidae** includes around 360 species of highly-evolved, mostly deadly, venomous snakes. Cobras, kraits, sea snakes, basically every nasty snake in Australia (there are A LOT) and mambas all belong to this family.

103. In addition to **hemotoxins**, their venom also contains powerful **neurotoxins**. Some of these snakes, such as taipans, brown snakes, and tiger snakes, can kill an adult human in under an hour without treatment.

104. Most **Elapids** are slender, but with wiry muscular strength. They care lithe and nimble and can quickly get around prey. They use a pair of hollow fangs that fold into a groove in the jaw when their mouths close.

105. Some **Elapids** have evolved unique features, such as the modification of ribs into hoods in many types of cobras, the paddle-shaped tails of sea snakes, and various cocktails of highly complex venoms.

106. There are many more families of snakes, but many of these are restricted to a few species with peculiar traits that have resulted in their sub-division into a separate family. Most are **Caenophilids**.

107. The diagram on the next page gives some examples of snakes that belong to the aforementioned families.

SNAKE FAMILIES AND REPRESENTATIVE SPECIES

A) FAMILY PYTHONIDAE; GREEN TREE PYTHON
B) FAMILY COLUBRIDAE; EASTERN BANDED KINGSNAKE
C) FAMILY VIPERIDAE; EYELASH VIPER
D) FAMILY ELAPIDAE; YELLOW-BELLIED SEASNAKE
E) FAMILY VIPERIDAE; MOJAVE RATTLESNAKE
F) FAMILY ELAPIDAE; KING COBRA
G) FAMILY COLUBRIDAE; BUTLER'S GARTERSNAKE
H) FAMILY ARCHOCHORDIDAE; JAVAN WART SNAKE
I) FAMILY BOIDAE; GREEN ANACONDA
J) FAMILY LEPTOTYPHLOPIDAE; BRAHMINY BLIND SNAKE
K) FAMILY ELAPIDAE; BANDED KRAIT
L) FAMILY UROPELTIDAE; LARGE SHIELDTAIL SNAKE
M) FAMILY COLUBRIDAE; CORNSNAKE
N) FAMILY XENOPELTIDAE; SUNBEAM SNAKE

108. While snakes and lizards once shared a common ancestor with the next group we will discuss, this divergence seems to have occurred at least 150 million years ago. **Turtles** are not closely related to any other living reptiles.

109. **Turtles** are **anapsids**, meaning that they have no openings in their skulls, other than the eye orbitals and nostrils. There are no openings for jaw muscle articulations found in the **diapsid** and **synapsid** reptiles.

110. Jaw muscles are anchored at the articulation of the neck and skull. As a result, their bites tend to be restricted to a powerful downward snapping motion. They must shake their heads to tear off pieces of food.

111. Unlike other reptiles, they lack teeth. Instead, they grow **keratin** beaks for cutting their food.

112. Turtles also have **keratin scutes** covering their bony shells. These are periodically shed like fingernails. The upper shell of a turtle includes the ribs and is called the **carapace**, while the lower shell is the **plastron**.

113. With the exception of the surface scutes, all parts of a turtle's shell consist of living tissue, a fusion of bone and epidermal tissue. Muscles are articulated to the inside of the shell.

114. A high degree of evolutionary modification has occurred in the necks and limbs of turtles, concomitant with their ecological niches and lifestyles.

115. The most ancient evolutionary split divided the **Order Testudines** into the **Suborder Pleurodira** (side necked turtles) and the **Suborder Cryptodira** (hidden necked turtles).

116. **Side-necked turtles** have 8 neck vertebrae and long snake-like necks that must be coiled to partially fit into the shell. **Hidden-necked turtles** can simply extend and retract their necks straight out of the shell.

117. **Side-necked turtles** only occur in the Southern hemisphere. All are aquatic and use their necks to reach into crevices to snatch prey, such as small fish, crawfish, and shellfish.

118. **Hidden-necked turtles** comprise the rest of turtles in existence. They also diverged into several directions.

119. The most ancient of these evolutionary divisions was the evolution of the shell. Most turtles continued to evolve a hard bony shell, but members of **Superfamily Trionicha** became **soft-shelled turtles.**

120. In addition to having leathery shells with large amounts of collagen, soft-shelled turtles have pig-like noses.

121. Hard-shell turtles then evolved into three separate lineages, based on their shell morphology and structure.

122. These lineages are the pond turtles and land tortoises with typical shells (**Superfamily Testudinidae)**, armored snapping turtles (**Superfamily Chelydroidea**), and smooth-shelled sea turtles (**Superfamily Chelonioidea).**

123. Additionally, there is a large amount of divergence in the **feet** of turtles. Some groups of turtles, such as tortoises and terrapins, retain toes with claws and have stub-like feet. Other groups, such as pond turtles and snapping turtles have clawed toes with webbed feet, while sea turtles have evolved flippers.

124. Since all turtles are basically wearing a suit of armor, they had to make major modifications to the way the **lungs** inhale and exhale, since the shell can't expand or contract the lungs, like it can in most vertebrates with lungs.

125. Instead of being anchored to the body wall by the **pleural cavity**, the lungs are pushed and pulled by the **abdominal muscles**. These muscles pull down on the internal organs, allowing the lungs to expand.

126. Additionally, turtles have multiple lobes and chambers to increase the surface area of the lungs.

127. Some turtles even have chambered cloacal openings and 'breathe through their butt'. Oxygen diffuses into the bloodstream when water is sucked into these cloacal openings. It is then expelled back out and repeated.

128. Aquatic and sea turtles have a much higher capacity for **anaerobic respiration** than most other vertebrates, since they are cold-blooded and don't need a lot of energy to bury themselves up in the mud and sleep.
129. They deal with excess lactic acid with a super-powered blood buffer system that also pulls calcium carbonate out of the minerals out of the shell if more bicarbonate ions need to be generated to get rid of acid ions.
130. Turtles also have valves that allow blood to be shut off from non-critical vessels when they are trying to conserve oxygen. It is for these reasons that they get away with a simple **3-chambered heart** like other reptiles.
131. One advantage of the shunt system of the blood vessels and the huge body volume in turtles, is that they can **thermoregulate** more effectively than most reptiles.
132. Pond turtles and sea turtles **bask** in the heat of the day, carrying the warmed blood from the fringes of their shells or flippers to their cores. Thanks to layers of fat inside the shell, this heated blood stays warm for long periods of time, allowing them to swim and remain active in cold water.
133. This is not the only long-term survival specialty that turtles have mustered.
134. Another turtle talent is use of their **urinary bladders** to store huge amounts of water and minerals when these things aren't abundant. Yes, turtles can hold their tee-tee for an almost indefinite period of time when needed.
135. Turtle reproduction varies between species, but all turtles use **internal fertilization.** Male turtles of most species have an indented narrow scute next to their tail that interlocks with a convex round scute of a female.
136. Male turtles have a thick long tail to house the **penis** inside the **cloacal opening**, while females have skinnier shorter tails, since their **cloaca** opens into the **vagina**.
137. Males simply climb the female and line up their cloacal opening with the female's. In some species, the sperm is stored, while in others, it directly fertilizes the eggs. From there, the gravid female eventually lays a nest.
138. All female turtles are **oviparous**. While a few turtles are 'deadbeat' parents that lay their eggs and leave, many species of pond turtles build intricate nests out of vegetation, while mother sea turtles bury theirs in the sand.
139. Other than the Teenage Mutant Ninja Turtles, most people underestimate turtles as slow, unintelligent living rocks. However, turtles have a relatively high degree of intelligence for a reptile and recognize their owners.
140. Additionally, many turtles will still be here after we are dead and gone. For instance, Jonathan the Seychelles tortoise is still alive, aged 190 years. An Aldabra tortoise lived to be 255 years old.
141. Now let's take a look at some of the families that comprise **Order Testudines.**
142. As previously mentioned, the most primitive group of turtles are three families of **side-necked turtles**. These groups live exclusively in the Southern hemisphere, and are most common in Southeast Asia and Australia.
143. For example, the **Family Chelidae** includes snake-necked turtles. Their necks must fold sideways into the shell and they have a different scute pattern than hard-shelled turtles.
144. Additionally, they are the only group of turtles with sex chromosomes. Hard-shelled turtle sex is dependent upon temperature, indicating that temperature-based gender determination was not a trait of early reptiles.
145. **Tortoises** belong to the **Order Testudinidae**. Tortoises are terrestrial, have thick scutes that add rings as they age, raised scales, clawed feet, and a large body volume. As they age, they become nearly entirely herbivorous.
146. **Order Emydidae** includes **terrapins** and a large number of **pond turtle** species. They usually have keel-shaped **carapaces** with ridged scutes in the middle, and they have a hinge in the middle of their **plastron.**

147. Since they can bend their plastron between the bell and chest, they have increased mobility for swimming. Additionally, the shape of their neck vertebrae and placement of muscular attachments classified this group.

148. Most members of **Emydidae** have webbed feet with claws. Diamondback terrapins, red-eared sliders, Eastern box turtles, bog turtles, spotted turtles, and dozens of other types of pond turtles share this characteristic.

149. **Family Chelydridae** includes the infamous snapping turtles. In addition to have deeply ridges scutes along their back, they have long tails, a sharp beak, a worm-like lure under their tongue, and musk glands.

150. The heaviest freshwater turtle in the world, the alligator snapping turtle, belongs in to this group.

151. **Family Chelonidae** comprises seven species of **sea turtles.** Some have bony scutes, such as the Green Sea Turtle, while others like the Leatherback, have collagenous shells with rudder-like vertical ridges.

152. Sea turtles have made a couple of evolutionary tradeoffs, exchanging speed for armor. Their shells are reduced in size and tapered toward the tail. Sea turtles cannot retract their heads or flippers, due to this compromise.

153. The feet, as mentioned, have gradually changed to **flippers**, thanks to **Hox gene** modifications, though they have retained the claws at the tips. These flipper-like appendages allow sea turtles to swim up to 20 miles per hour.

154. **Mud turtles** and **musk turtles** belong to **Order Kinosternidae**. These are all small, aquatic turtles with the ability to emit huge quantities of foul-smelling musk from glands near the tail. They lay eggs in underground burrows.

155. The **Pig-nosed turtle** of **Order Carettochelyidae** is monotypic, with only a single living species from New Guinea. Unlike their hard-shelled relatives, they have a soft, leathery shell. They have flipper-like feet like sea turtles.

156. And now a word from another sponsor. Act now. These deals won't last. Call now. Operators are waiting.

157. The related **soft-shelled turtles** of **Order Trionychidae** have similarly rubbery textured pancake-like shells. They have nostrils that can poke up like snorkels, as well. However, rather than flippers, they have feet tipped with three clawed toes. They are among the most foul-tempered turtles in existence, and will gleefully bite you.

158. The diagram below page shows representatives from several orders of turtles.

A) FAMILY CHELONIDAE; GREEN SEA TURTLE
B) FAMILY TESTUDINIDAE; AFRICAN SPURRED TORTOISE
C) FAMILY CARETTOCHELYIDAE; PIG-NOSED TURTLE
D) FAMILY CHELYDRIDAE; ALLIGATOR SNAPPING TURTLE
E) FAMILY CHELIDAE; GEOFFREY'S SIDENECKED TURTLE
F) FAMILY KINOSTERNIDAE; SONORAN MUD TURTLE
G) FAMILY TESTUDINIDAE; ALDABRA GIANT TORTOISE
H) FAMILY EMYDIDAE; EASTERN BOX TURTLE
I) FAMILY CHELIDAE; MATA MATA
J) FAMILY EMYDIDAE; DIAMONDBACK TERRAPIN
K) FAMILY TRIONYCHIDAE: SMOOTH SOFTSHELL TURTLE

159. We now turn our attention to the last extant group of reptiles, the **crocodilians**. Crocodilians are distinctly different from the other extant groups of reptiles. They are only distantly related to the others.

160. In case you're wondering, dinosaurs have not been forgotten. We will get to them shortly. We're not there yet.

161. It appears that the group of reptiles that evolved into the dinosaurs and birds diverged from the same common ancestor as crocodilians about 200 million years ago. These were the **archosaurs**.

162. **Archosaurs** were large, lumbering reptiles with socketed teeth, two openings in the skull for muscle articulations, and heavy skeletons with numerous muscular attachment points. They were stupid, large beasts.

163. Modern **crocodilians** have retained these aforementioned traits, though it is not really correct to call them modern, since they are mostly unchanged over the last 100 million years.

164. Starting at the head, crocodilians are **diapsids**. They have two large openings behind the eyes that allow articulation of powerful **masseter** muscles, which close the jaw with the bite force of a freight train.

165. The eye sockets, eardrums, and nostrils have all migrated to the top of the head in crocodilians, allowing them to float along pretending to be an innocent log until they grab a zebra by the face and pull it to a watery grave.

166. **Crocodilians** have jaws that articulate between the **atlas** of the spine and the **occipital bone** of the skull.

167. Depending on the species of crocodilian, the **maxilla** and **mandible** have between 60 and 80 socketed peg-shaped teeth. The jaws can slam down with a bite force of nearly two tons per square inch.

168. Worse, they are constantly ornery, because they got all them teeth and no toothbrush.

169. You could say that alligators, caimans, and crocodiles are finely-tuned, athletic killing machines.

170. The ball joints of their arms and legs articulate at an angle that makes them hang much more vertically than most other quadrupeds. They function much better as oars in the water, than legs on land.

171. However, lest you get overconfident, you will NOT outrun a crocodile or alligator. Even if it looks awkward, they can still run your butt down at 30 miles per house, clamp down on your face, and drag you to your doom.

172. The **skin** of crocodilians makes great boots and handbags, because they grow **keratin** impregnated **scales** that are many layers deep. In between the scales in the cracks, there are softer proteins to allow the skin to flex.

173. The scales grow in ridges in regular patterns and contain tiny openings that lead to **mechanoreceptors**. The scales are also impregnated with **capillaries**, allowing the reptile to circulate heat to their cores during **basking**.

174. **Bony scutes** called **osteoderms** grow to reinforce the ridge-like rows of scales on top of their bodies and head.

175. While the top side of crocodilians are covered with these ridged bony scales, the belly is covered with large smooth scales, which help aid them in sliding smoothly into rivers or dragging themselves out onto mud.

176. **Crocodilians** have much more advanced circulatory systems than other reptiles, and more closely resemble the anatomical arrangement of birds, than they do lizards or snakes.

177. The **heart** is **four-chambered** with a complete **septum** to divide oxygenated blood and deoxygenated blood.

178. Deoxygenated blood returns to a crocodile heart through the **vena cava** from the body into the **right atrium.**

179. From there, it drops through the **bicuspid valve** into the **right ventricle**, where it is pumped to the **lungs** via the **pulmonary artery**. Once oxygenated, the blood returns through the **pulmonary vein** to the **left atrium**.

180. Finally, the **left ventricle** pumps the oxygenated blood through the **aorta** and on to smaller vessels that route their way to the organs of the body (such as the carotids, the hepatic artery, the gastric artery and so on).

181. **Crocodilians** are simply too big and have too much body volume to get away with a 3-chambered heart with mixed blood. Additionally, their armor-covered bodies provide no real secondary way for them to oxygenate.

182. Interestingly, the **lungs** of crocodilians are set up more like a bird's than those of other reptiles or mammals. Like birds, they have **air sacs** that fill and empty over several inhalations and exhalations, rather than using one inspiration to draw in a large breath, and one exhalation to expel carbon dioxide.

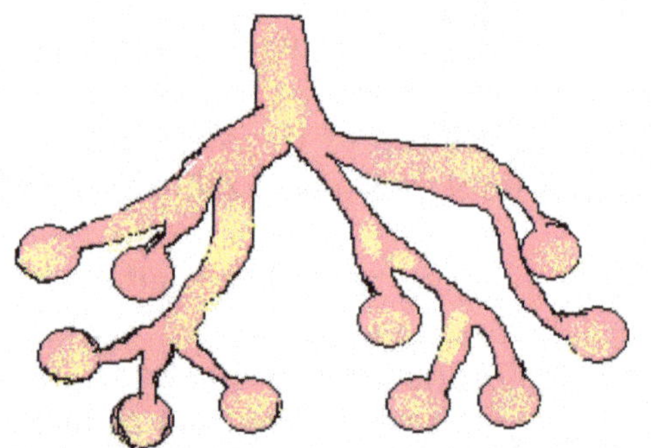

REPTILE LUNGS HAVE ALVEOLI FOR GREATER SURFACE AREA AND MORE GAS EXCHANGE

183. **Crocodilians** can stay underwater for extended periods, because they can close a valve on their **soft palate** that prevents them from inhaling water into their **trachea**. Since they are cold-blooded, they use far less oxygen than a similarly-sized mammal would, allowing them to stay submerged for 15 minutes or more.

184. Furthermore, there is an opening in the septum of crocodilian hearts that can close and force blood to skip the lungs and recirculate the body several times, extracting all the oxygen in the blood before needing to breathe.

185. When crocodilians want to drop down and sink, they clear their lungs. When it comes time to inhale, as they surface, they blow themselves up like a pool float, allowing them to stay on top of the water more easily.

186. Crocodilians are bird-like in another regard. They have a muscular **gizzard** between their **esophagus** and **stomach**, which helps to pulverize chunks of food.

187. Additionally, they have tooth-like projections inside the stomach called **gastroliths** that grind up food with the action of **peristalsis**. Their stomachs are also among the most acidic known in nature.

188. Therefore, the bloated rotting carcass of a dead antelope becomes short work.

189. Even bones and horns disintegrate as they spend enough time in the Sarlac-like stomach. Food also passes very slowly, since crocodilians are **ectotherms**. A single meal may be digested over months of basking.

190. Like other vertebrates, crocodilians have **kidneys**, but they are oddballs in one regard. Their **ureters** directly exit the **cloacal opening** without any stop for a **bladder**. Like birds, they pretty much let it rip if it's time to pee.

191. Several species of crocodiles, particularly those that live in estuaries and other saltwater habitats, have glands in their tongue that excrete excess salt and help them regulate their blood osmolarity.

192. Crocodilian reproduction, like all reptiles, is by **internal fertilization**. Unlike lizards and snakes (and more like turtles), male crocodilians have a single penis, rather than two hemipenes.

193. Crocodilians have mating displays, with much the same purpose as birds. Both try to impress each other by swimming around, rubbing on each other, buying each other cheap gifts from Target, dining out at pretentious restaurants, and making each other mix tapes.

194. The penis emerges from the cloacal opening during mating. After **fertilization**, female crocodilians lay a clutch of eggs in a **nest** that is comprised of rotting vegetation and grass. Like bird nests, they are hemispherical.

195. Unlike the majority of vertebrates, gender is not determined by gender chromosomes in crocodilians. Eggs at the top of the nest in the cooler section will develop as females. Eggs buried deeper in warm, rotting compost will develop as male. Gator farms purposely raise eggs at cooler temperatures to get the more docile females.

196. Crocodilians have **calcified eggs** that are much more similar to bird eggs than to the eggs of other reptiles.

197. Unlike other reptiles, crocodilians also raise their hatchlings like chicks, guarding them from other predators, scooping them up into their mouths if threats emerge, and depositing them back in the nest.

198. Some baby crocodilians stay with their mothers for as much as two years. Eventually, they get sent out of the nest because they won't do their laundry, sleep until noon, and take their parents for granted.

199. Now let's look at the small taxa of crocodilians. Since there are only 23 extant species, it is a small cohort.

200. There are only 3 families of crocodilians. These are the **alligators**, **gavials**, and true **crocodiles**.

201. **Family Alligatoridae** includes the American and Chinese alligators, as well as several species of **caimans**.

202. Both alligator species live in semi-tropical areas, with Northern temperate ranges that see frost. As a result, they are thicker bodied and may go into **torpor** in winter.

203. **Alligators** have wider body proportions, a rounded U-shaped snout with a wide head, and teeth that fit into the mouth when closed. They are much less aggressive in temperament than crocodiles and favor fresh water.

204. **Caimans** also favor freshwater, are particularly common in Central and South America, and are much more aggressive and agile. They have differences in scale armor patterns and skull structure, as compared to gators.

205. **Caimans** also have a mouth full of sharp needle-like teeth, as opposed to the fatter peg-like teeth of gators.

206. The **gavial** and **false gavial** of **Family Gavialidae** have long, skinny snouts with jacked-up teeth that project out in every direction. They use this beak-like snout to snag fish and amphibians. They don't eat large prey animals.

207. **Gavials** have a bulbous nose with a lot of mechanoreceptors to detect splashing fish. They get huge, growing up to 20 feet. **False gharials** have a tapered snout that is skinny at the tip. They are smaller, only getting to 13 feet.

208. There are 14 species of **true crocodiles**. As compared to gators and caimans, their snouts are much more triangular and narrower at the tip, their teeth protrude with the mouth closed, and they are more aggressive.

209. There is a great degree of evolutionary variability in crocodiles, due to their evolution in different types of tropical and sub-tropical habitats. For instance, **Nile crocodiles** are well adapted as river ambush predators, whereas the **American crocodile** and **Indian Mugger crocodile** are adapted to live in salty estuaries.

210. There is also a great degree of variability in size. There are crocodiles that grow only a few feet long, such as **Morelet's crocodile** and **Pygmy crocodiles**, whereas the **Australian Saltwater Crocodile** can grow to 20 feet.

211. The diagrams below show a sampling of the different types of extant crocodilians.

CROCODILIAN FAMILIES AND SPECIES

A) FAMILY ALLIGATORIDAE; AMERICAN ALLIGATOR
B) FAMILY CROCODYLIDAE; NILE CROCODILE
C) FAMILY ALLIGATORIDAE; SPECTACLED CAIMAN
D) FAMILY ALLIGATORIDAE; CUVIER'S DWARF CAIMAN
E) FAMILY CROCODYLIDAE; MUGGER CROCODILE
F) FAMILY CROCODYLIDAE; OSBORN'S DWARF CROCODILE
G) FAMILY GAVIALIDAE; INDIAN GAVIAL

H) Class Reptilia to Class Aves: The Link Between Dinosaurs and Birds

1. To understand the link between reptiles and birds, it is essential to cover how birds evolved from dinosaurs.
2. There are simply too many taxa of dinosaurs to cover in an overview section, so we will stick to some of the major distinguishing characters that arose during major evolutionary splits in the lineage.
3. No other vertebrate group has dominated the terrestrial earth the way that the dinosaurs did. Their diversity and the length of their reign are unrivaled. We would need an entire textbook to unpack it all.
4. For those reasons, we will stick to the basics here.
5. The aforementioned **crocodilians** and the rising line of reptiles that would eventually become the **dinosaurs** appear to trace to a common ancestor, the **archosaurs**, about 250 million years ago.
6. From there, the **archosaurs** diverged into the dinosaurs, and went in another direction to become the **pterosaurs**. That's right, **pterodactyls** were NOT dinosaurs.
7. **Archosaurs** had skull openings for muscular articulations in front of the eye orbit and behind it next to the mandible, making them **diapsids**. These same skull openings are found in dinosaurs and birds.
8. Like most dinosaurs, archosaurs had **socketed teeth**. These have since devolved in birds.
9. The **femurs** of archosaurs developed extra attachment points called **trochanters** on the ball joints, allowing many more muscular attachments and heavier, more muscular legs with more leverage.
10. Based on the layout and proportions of fossils, it is presumed that their lungs expanded greatly to accommodate the increased oxygen needs of their large bodies, and this led to the **air sacs** of modern birds.
11. As compared to **dinosaurs** and modern **birds**, it appears that **archosaurs** had far less lateral mobility because their ankle bones were tightly fixed to the base of their **tibia**, giving them a lumbering, oafy gait.
12. The diagram below summarizes some of the distinct anatomical traits of **Archosaur** skeletons.
13. Since it is well beyond the scope of this chapter to cover all of the different classifications of dinosaurs that ever existed over a 200 million year period, we will simply summarize some of the major orders, clades, and families of dinosaurs that exhibited major phenotypic changes as they evolved.
14. There were two major clades of dinosaurs. The **Ornothischian dinosaurs** are also called the 'bird-hipped' dinosaurs, while the **Saurischian dinosaurs** are colloquially called the 'lizard-hipped dinosaurs'.
15. So, it is major anatomical differences in the **pelvic girdles** of dinosaurs that provides the characters for the most fundamental phylogenetic split in their classification. There are also a few other distinguishing traits.
16. The hip bones of **Ornothischian dinosaurs** were clearly adapted for quadrupedal life. The Ornithischial **ilium** bone is angled back toward the tail, sitting atop the **ischium** and **pubis**, which both also point toward the tail.
17. Many of the Ornithischian dinosaurs were **sauropods**, which had long necks, tank-like bodies, elephant-like feet, and very long tails. Brontosaurs, diplodocus, and Argentinosaurs are well-known examples of these.
18. The openings between the bones create an angle for a pair of back legs that are fairly straight and inflexible.
19. Another Ornithischian feature consistent with this, is the fact that some dinosaurs belonging to this group had calcified tendons connecting their rear abdominal muscles to the pelvic girdle.
20. This is strongly indicative that none of these dinosaurs ever intended (or could) stand on their hind legs. Dinosaurs like the stegosaurus and triceratops belong to this group.

21. The skull of Ornithischian dinosaurs also has several differences, relative to the Saurischian dinosaurs. A triangular **premaxillary bone** sits in front of the mandible, allowing them to clip leaves and scoop food.
22. Ornithischians also had an eyebrow-like **palpebral bone** above the eye socket that provided extra protection.
23. These dinosaurs had a very small opening for muscular articulations under the eye at the front of the face. All of this is consistent with the idea that most members of this group were herbivorous grazers.
24. **Saurischian dinosaurs** had a much different shape to their pelvises. The saurischian ilium was shaped like a wedge and angled toward the front of the body.
25. May Saurischians were **therapods**, which walked on huge hind legs, a massive tail for balancing themselves, and had tiny front arms with prehensile claws.
26. The **ischium** and pubis **diverge** from this articulation to form a Y-like wishbone shape. This design allowed much greater flexibility at the hip sockets, and provided space for a pair of very large back legs.
27. This hip arrangement is consistent with the idea that many saurischian dinosaurs were bipedal predators that ran after their victims on their hind legs, such as the Velociraptors that ate Newman in Jurassic Park.
28. **Saurischian dinosaurs** had large openings in front of their eyes called **fenestrae** that allowed large, powerful biting muscles to articulate. They lacked a **premaxillary bone** and had pointed teeth.
29. Additionally, rather than long legs with flat feet, the front legs of saurischian dinosaurs were often comically small, yet tipped with clawed hands that were capable of gripping objects.
30. The diagram below depicts a few of these major anatomical differences.

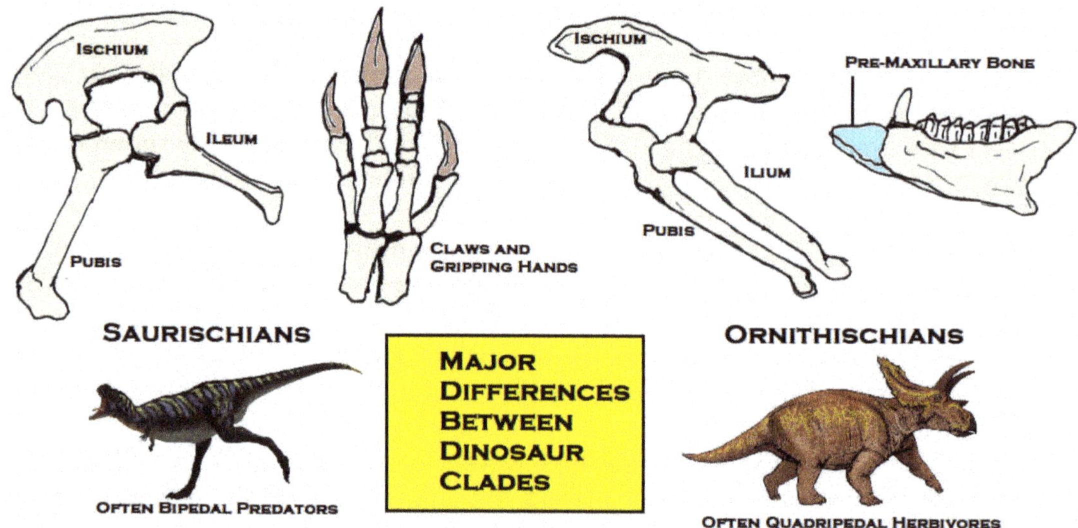

31. It is important to keep in mind just how many eras of natural history and how many species and taxa of dinosaurs we are talking about before citing specific examples.
32. Unlike extant species that represent a relatively small slice of time, we are talking about all the possible families of dinosaurs that existed over eons that spanned a whopping 150 million year period.

33. The summary below details some characteristics of the most noteworthy families of Saurischians.

PICTURE	SPECIMEN	DESCRIPTION
A	Staurikosaurus	Primitive early Saurischian dinosaur (200 mya) that only had 2 vertebrae joining the pelvis to the spine. Bipedal predator that ran down its prey. Might have had distensible jaw.
B	Saltasaurus	Had armored osteoderm plates up and down its spine. Hippo-like body form with spatula shaped teeth. Herbivorous grazer. Walked on all fours, but could raise up on hind legs.
C	Brontosaurus	Gigantic sauropod dinosaur with crane-like neck and massive body. Could be 70 feet long. Limb bones extremely sturdy and pubis and ischia fused to handle massive weight
D	Caudipteryx	Beak-like snout with teeth. Turkey-sized bipedal dinosaur that likely had feathers and might have been an endotherm. Stiff short tail. Claw-like hands. Probably omnivorous.

E	Shunosaurus	About 30 feet long, with a heavy herbivorous body. Tail had a club with osteoderms to slap predators. Long neck, jaws, thick maxilla, and teeth show that it was a grazer.
F	Diplodocus	Very long necks with 80 vertebrae. Heavy body and teeth designed for herbivory. Had keratin-like long scales along back like iguana. Among largest dinosaurs ever (100+ feet).
G	Camarasuarus	Odd box-shaped skull with very large nares and many openings for muscular attachments. Deep-set grinding teeth. Long neck, strong heavy limbs, hollow vertebrae, large body.
H	Archaeopteryx	Bird-like chicken-sized dinosaur with toothed beak-like snout, feathers, and a long bony tail. Wishbone in chest, backward facing first toe. Could be ancestor of modern birds.
I	Coelophysis	Bipedal carnivore with lithe body, long limbs, claws. Appeared to be a very fast runner, based on narrow hips, hinged ankles, and a tail that could be 'locked' straight by vertebrae.
J	Tyrannosaurus	One of the latest groups of dinosaurs to evolve. Massive hind legs and tail, small front limbs with gripping claws. Powerful jaws with ripping teeth. A giant 40 foot long predator.
K	Spinosaurus	Piscivorous dinosaur with needle-like teeth and crocodile-like skull. Spine-like vertebrae that could be raised to unfold a fin-like 'sail' that was probably used for thermoregulation.
L	Allosaurus	Large light skull with serrated teeth for carnivory. Jaw could articulate in a wide range. Hollow areas near vertebrae and large ribs seem to imply its lungs had air sacs.
M	Pelecanimimus	Ostrich-sized bird-like dinosaur with long toothed beak and crest on head. Large sternum with muscular articulations and other anatomical features indicate relation to birds.

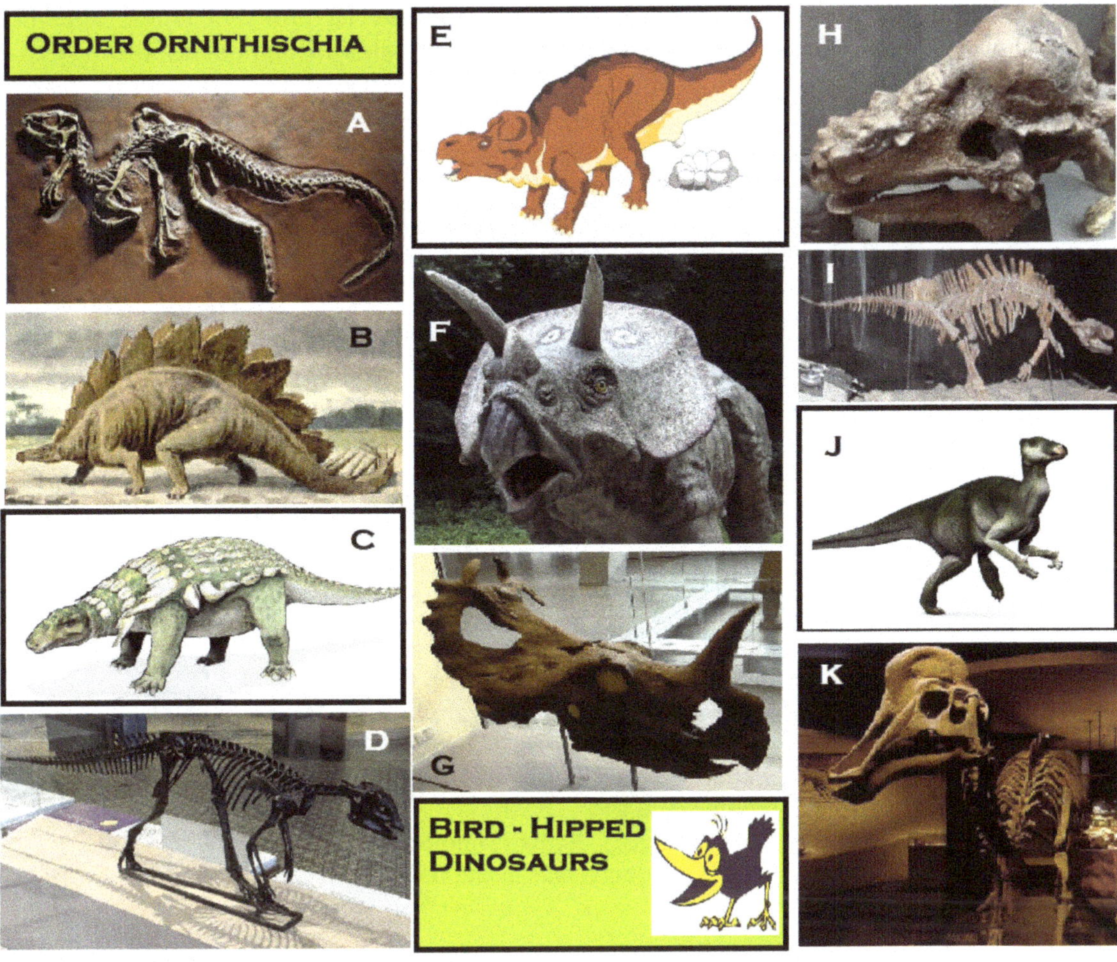

PICTURE	SPECIMEN	DESCRIPTION
A	Heterodontosaurus	Small bipedal dinosaurs. Omnivorous with tusks. Spine appears to show it had Porcupine-Like Bristles. Muscular forelimbs with 3 fingers. Ankles & Tibula Fused.
B	Stegosaurus	Armored plates along back had secondary function in thermoregulation. Large pectoral girdle with powerful muscle attachments. Small head. Herbivore. Hoof-like feet.
C	Ankylosaurus	Flat helmet-like skull covered with armor-like osteoderms that extended onto torso. Elephant-Sized with heavy body. Tail had a defensive club with armored spikes. Herbivore.
D	Polocanthus	Rhinoceros-sized herbivore with deeply curved hip bones and long back legs for a quadraped. Small head. Had armored plates of various sizes behind head on shoulders.
E	Protoceratops	Skull with armored plates formed by squamosal and parietal bones that extended down to cheeks. Cow-sized grazing herbivore with Beak-Like Mouth. Flat wide feet.
F	Triceratops	Armored Skull with frill and 3 horns derived from orbital and rostral bones. Beak-like mouth. Extremely thick hip bones and vertebrae. Slow-Moving Tank-Like Herbivore.
G	Centrosaurus	Another frilled, beaked herbivorous grazing dinosaur that was about the size of an elephant. Had two smaller horns in center of frill and numerous small horns around edge.
H	Iguanodon	Lizard-Like body shape. Long front legs and back legs. Walked on all fours, but could stand on back feet. Long tail Front of skull had no teeth, herbivorous teeth in back.
I	Rhabdodontisaurus	Shearing teeth with ridges in middle for stripping leaves. Small front legs and large backlegs with extra muscle attachments on femurs and pelvis. Long tail for balance.
J	Hadrosaurus	Built similarly to Rhabdodontisaurus, but with much longer front legs and anatomical differences in hip bones that are better evolved. Probably omnivorous.
K	Lambeosaurus	Large cranial crest and duck-like bill formed by maxilla. Had fifth digit on front foot that could be used like a thumb. Huge eye sockets indicate they probably had sharp vision.

34. It is generally agreed that birds evolved from therapod **Saurischian** dinosaurs. Specifically, birds seem to have evolved from a clade of dinosaurs called **Aviales**, which included the **Archaeopteryx** mentioned above.
35. Archaeopteryx clearly had feathers, based on imprints on fossils records, and it also shared other anatomical similarities to birds, with a beak-like snout, long scaled back legs, and a plume-like tail for counterbalance.
36. However, since the 1970s, more and more bird-like dinosaur fossils have been discovered that seem to have more congruous avian traits than archaeopteryx.
37. For instance, various bones from fossilized **Deinonychus** skeleton more closely resemble those of modern birds.
38. Muddying the water, there are also other lineages of flying dinosaurs, that while not likely to be direct ancestors to birds, cannot be altogether ruled out. These include the **Dromaesaurids** and the **Ornitholestes**.
39. Currently, there is not a clear-cut evolutionary path through the fossil lineage to modern birds. However, the anatomical and fossil evidence does suggest that birds most likely trace back to some group of **Aviales.**
40. With that established, let's move on to the modern birds, the last extant group of dinosaurs.

What beverage is enjoyed by carnivorous dinosaurs? Tea Rex
What happened when the dinosaur crashed his car? A Tyrannosaurus Wreck
Where did velociraptors buy their groceries? At the Dino-Store
When unruly dinosaurs got out of line, who restored order? The Tricera-Cops
What was underneath dinosaur toilets? The Dino-Sewers
Why did the Brontosaurus see a dermatologist? He had Dino-Sores
Why couldn't other dinosaurs tell if a pterodactyl was in the bathroom? Their 'P' was silent.

I) Class Aves: Modern Birds

1. Modern birds are **endothermic** diapsids that still share many common features with **Archosaurian** reptiles, such as scaled legs, amniotic eggs, parental nesting behaviors, air sacs in their lungs, and a four-chambered heart.
2. Scientifically-speaking, birds are the last remaining therapod dinosaurs. KFC serves dead fried dinosaur chunks, duck hunters are actually shooting dinosaurs out of the sky, and penguins are just big, fat greasy dinosaurs.
3. Let's start with the most obvious avian anatomical traits. Birds evolved **feathers** from scales, as both are derived from **keratin** and the same type of scale-generating cells in the epidermis.
4. Feathers, themselves, are necessitated by the evolution of **flight** and the evolution of **endothermy**.
5. **Feathers**, consequently, come in two basic types geared toward these aforementioned purposes.
6. **Contour feathers** form rigid panels that interlock to produce lift and surface area along the wings and tail.
7. **Down feathers** are soft and fluffy, trapping air to produce an insulating boundary layer next to the skin. Oil-secreting **preen glands** in the skin aid this function by secreting a layer of bird grease that locks out moisture.
8. Therefore, even geese flying in the same space as commercial airliners don't freeze before they get themselves sucked into jet engines. Yes, even today, dinosaurs still kill people. They just cause plane crashes instead.....

9. Some birds also secrete other substances onto their feathers, other than oil. For instance, some birds secrete antimicrobial compounds to hinder bacterial or fungal infections.
10. Others crush ants and other toxic insects and rub them on their feathers to combat mites and parasites.
11. There are numerous avian adaptations to flight other than feathers. Staying aloft requires a lot of aeronautical bioengineering. Drag, pitch, yaw, and lift are all necessary forces that have to be handled to fly.
12. First and foremost, the musculoskeletal system of birds is optimized for flight. With the exception of flightless birds, who devolved the trait, birds have **hollow bones** with **pneumatic cavities.** For strength, they are buttressed by hundreds of calcified deposits that form cross-braces.
13. The **sternum** is curved outward and continues into an enlarged **ferculum** (wishbone), which is capable of making numerous large articulations with the gigantic **pectoralis muscles** used for flapping the wings to take off.
14. The **humerus**, **ulna**, and **radius** are all lengthened and articulate to equally enlarged arm muscles, such as the **biceps, tensor brevis,** and **pronator muscles** of the forearm on the front of the wing, while the back of the wing boasts equally large **triceps**, **tensor posterius**, and forearm **extensors**. All are used in flight.
15. The **carpals** of the hand are reduced and, with the except of hoatzin chicks, who are born with claws, all modern birds have lost their **phalanges** to the dustbin of evolutionary advances.
16. The wings of birds are truly an engineering marvel of nature. Perhaps mankind should feel considerable conviction in knowing that the disassembled remnants of these miraculous biomachines can often be found simmering in pools of dumpster juice on hot July days in the alley behind Popeye's.
17. The diagram below shows some of the major muscles involved in flight in birds.

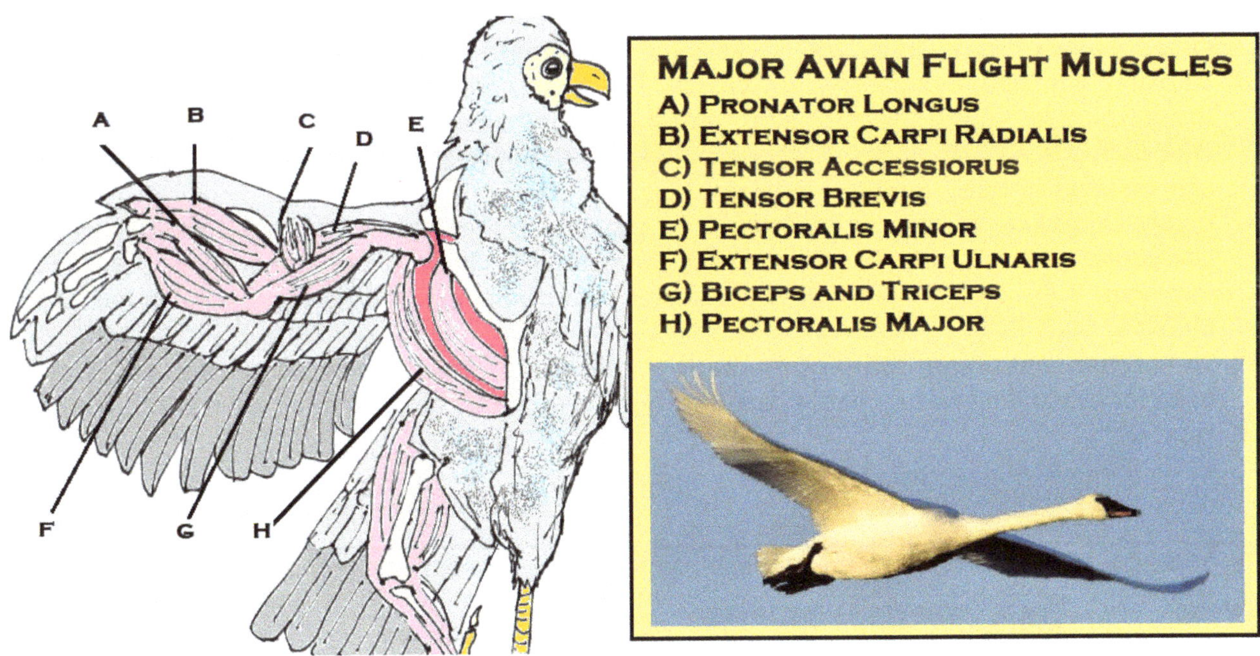

18. In addition to the musculoskeletal adaptations birds have made, their internal anatomy is also reflective of their need to cut weight. For instance, birds lack a **bladder** and produce solid **uric acid** as nitrogenous waste.
19. A bladder full of pee would do nothing for a bird, other than produce drag and extra weight. Birds are no different than most reptiles, in this regard, albeit for a different reason.

20. Many reptiles produce solid uric acid to conserve water, while birds make it for aerodynamic reasons.

21. The excretory system also only has a single **kidney**, allowing them to cut the weight of another organ.

22. The digestive system of birds differs, like that of mammals, begins with a **pharynx** and an **esophagus**, but this gives way to a compartmentalized digestive chamber that differs from mammalian stomachs.

23. The **crop** is the first chamber along the alimentary canal after the esophagus. It is simply a storage bag. This allows birds to binge eat and save back the nutrition for later. It has no digestive function.

24. The **proventriculus** and **gizzard** comprise two distinct parts of the **stomach**. The proventriculus, or foregut, secretes digestive enzymes and mixes incoming food with peristaltic contractions.

25. Behind it, the **gizzard**, or hindgut, is highly muscular. It uses sand, grit, and pebbles that the bird has intentionally swallowed. Like a grist mill, it crushes incoming foot into a paste, grinding it against the rocks.

26. Birds also secrete flakes of **keratin** from parts of the stomach lining, providing further grit for grinding food.

27. From there, the food slurry enters the **duodenum** of the **small intestine**, where the **gall bladder** secretes fat emulsifying bile salts, and the **pancreas** secretes various digestive enzymes in through the **pancreatic duct**.

28. As the food moves along the next two segments, the **jejunum**, and the **ileum**, nutrients are released from food macromolecules and are picked up by the blood vessels of the **mesentery** and absorbed into the bloodstream.

29. The **large intestine**, unlike those of mammals, is a very short tube with a pair of **cecal pouches** emerging backward off of the main tube like in a Y-shape. It reabsorbs water and nutrients from waste.

30. In some birds, the cecal pouches also host symbiotic bacteria that further break down food and release some of the vitamins and energy sources back into the gut of the bird.

31. The large intestine terminates at the **cloaca**. Peristaltic contractions force poo out of the bird in an uncontrollable manner. Birds have no control over their bowels. They can be having a conversation with each other one moment, and the next there is a loud squirting noise, which acts as an awkward conversation stopper.

32. It goes something like this...."Hey Kathy! How are you?' 'Fine Denise! How are the fledglings?' 'Well you know....trying to get that whole 'flying' thing down.' 'Oh yes! I remember those days...PFFTT!!! Pap! Pap!'....Silence..... 'Well look at the time, I better be going....I forgot that Katelyn has Campfire Chicks tonight.....'

33. The **rectum** and **ureter** both exit the body at the **cloaca**, which is a multi-purpose single opening used for evacuating waste, mating, and for laying eggs. Birds have no anus or urethra....they have a cloaca.

In Honor of Birds: A collection of things named for our avian friends

Bands	Sports Franchises	Vehicles	People
The Byrds	Atlanta Falcons	Ford Thunderbird	Ladybird Johnson
The Eagles	Philadelphia Eagles	Pontiac Sunbird	AJ Hawk
The Yardbirds	Seattle Seahawks	Plymouth Roadrunner	Brian Cardinal
Black Crowes	Arizona Cardinals	Pontiac Firebird	Larry Bird
Flock of Seagulls	Baltimore Orioles	Ford Falcon	Robin Leach
Jimmie's Chicken Shack	Toronto Blue Jays	Buick Skylark	Robin Williams
Fabulous Thunderbirds	St. Louis Cardinals	AMC Eagle	Russell Crowe
	Atlanta Hawks	Chrysler Turkey	Dan Quayle

34. The diagram below shows the basic parts of the avian digestive system.

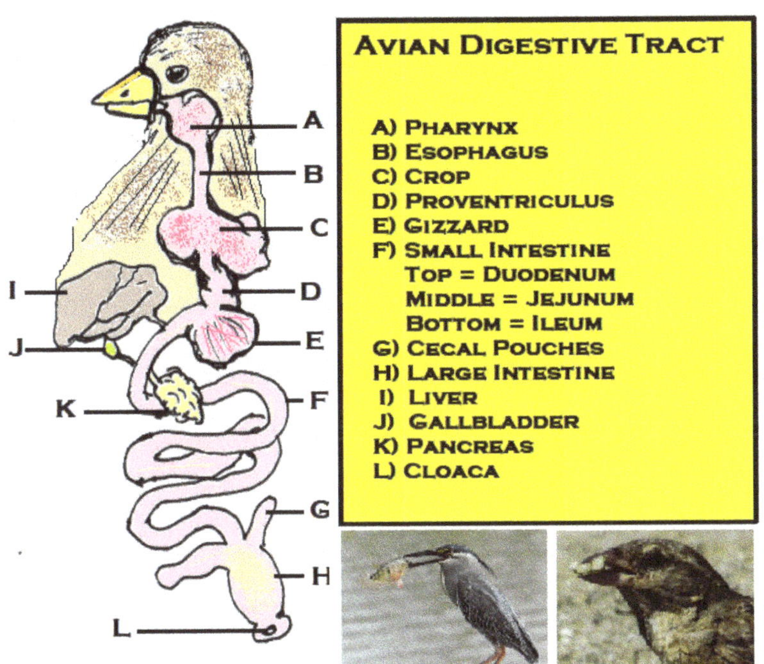

Birds in Popular Culture Quiz

1) List all bird-related NFL mascots.

2) List all bird-related MLB mascots.

3) Name 5 national restaurant chains that primarily sell dead fried birds.

4) Name the MLB pitcher who killed a pigeon mid-flight with a fastball.

5) Name 5 cartoon characters who identify as birds.

6) What is Harvey Birdman's profession.

7) What is the most popular bird-related song of all time and who is it by?

35. Bird reproduction is also necessarily **oviparous**. Female birds already gain the weight from eggs in various stages of **ovulation**. The last thing they need for getting off the ground is a womb full of chicks.

36. Therefore, birds are restricted to **oviparity**, which also requires a heavy investment in resource gathering, parent behaviors, and guardianship over a nest of developing fledglings.

37. Even their reproductive acts are taken into consideration, with regard to aerodynamics.

38. A few of the more primitive extant bird orders, such as kiwis, waterfowl, and poultry have retained a **penis** for copulation. More advanced orders of birds have devolved a penis, as it creates drag during flight. Th

39. When present, bird penises inflate with lymph, not blood, and they retract into a pocket the **cloaca** when they aren't in use. In female birds, a similar pouch inside the cloaca is used for sperm storage. Broods of chicks may have multiple paternities, and in some cases, sperm from different males compete to fertilize their eggs.

40. Keeping with the them of aerodynamic weight reduction, in most orders, female birds only have a single **oviduct** leading to a single **ovary**. However, large flightless birds and a few other orders retain both ovaries.

41. The final obvious feature keeping birds airborne are their foil-like tailfeathers.

42. Birds flex the **caudofemoralis muscle** and **abdominal obliques** in order to twist the tail like a rudder to change directions or to fan their contour feathers for cruising and gliding.

43. Flight, as you would surmise, takes a tremendous amount of metabolic energy. Birds had to adapt to these requirements by becoming **endotherms** in order to supply these caloric and oxygen needs.

44. Feathers, as we already mentioned, act as insulators. They trap escaping metabolic heat like attic insulation, redirecting convection currents into air spaces between the feathers and body.

45. The process of **endothermy** is controlled at the cell level and by the brain and circulatory system.

46. Compared to similarly-sized reptiles, birds have many more **mitochondria** in each cell, particularly in muscles. More broken bonds for ATP generation means more excess heat, as metabolism is not perfectly efficient.

47. In turn, there is plenty of excess heat generated from ATP production of metabolism and from the movement of muscles. It is possible to trap this excess heat (or release it), by contracting or expanding blood vessels.
48. The **hypothalamus** of the brain accomplishes this by acting as the body's thermostat, sending signals to blood vessels to contract or expand as needed. Shivering and fluffing the plumage can assist this process.
49. Since more mitochondria means more cellular respiration, this means birds have a high oxygen requirement.
50. In order to facilitate this high oxygen demand, the **circulatory** and **respiratory systems** of birds adapted.
51. Birds, like crocodilians, have a **four-chambered heart** with separate pulmonary and systemic loops.
52. Deoxygenated blood from the body enters the **right atrium** of the heart via the **vena cava**. Blood drops through the **bicuspid valve** into the **right ventricle**, which pumps it back to the lungs through the **pulmonary artery**.
53. Oxygenated blood returns from the lungs via the **pulmonary veins** into the **left atrium**, falls through he **tricuspid valve** into the **left ventricle**, where it is then pumped back to the body by the **aorta.**
54. Bird **lungs** are adapted to both aerodynamic needs and to the high oxygen demand of bird metabolism.
55. Unlike mammalian lungs, birds have a highly complex system of **air sacs** connected to the lungs. They serve the dual purpose of keeping birds aerodynamic and ensuring a constant supply of fresh oxygenated air.
56. When birds **inhale**, most of the first breath enters the **posterior air sacs** and fills them. When they exhale, air rushes back from the posterior air sacs and oxygenates the capillaries of the lungs.
57. The bird's first exhalation clears the lungs, but pushes fresh oxygenated air out of the posterior air sacs and back into the lungs, ensuring that the **pulmonary vein** never fails to carry back blood from oxygenated capillaries.
58. From there, they inhale a second time, filling the lungs temporarily, before inflating the **intraclavicular air sac** that branches off the lungs under the collarbones at the front of their body under the chest.
59. The **intraclavicular air sac** connects to airspaces inside both **humerus** bones, filling the hollow centers of the wing bones with air, creating even more lift for birds in flight.
60. The **posterior air sacs** serve the dual purpose of maintaining the large volume of the bird's torso without adding weight. Essentially, the main body of the bird is an air-filled balloon surrounding the organs.
61. The second exhalation clears the lungs completely of carbon dioxide, but in short order, the bird inhales again.
62. Bird lungs don't look the same as mammalian lungs at the tissue level. While mammals (and many reptiles) have thousands of globe-shaped **alveoli** to increase surface area for oxygen exchange, birds do not.
63. Instead, birds have tube-shaped **parabronchi** that form sort of a radiator grill, set at right angles between the **bronchioles** of the lungs and the **air sac** tunnels. Each long tube is lined with beds of **capillaries**.
64. Birds lack a **diaphragm**, so the expansion and contraction of their lungs and air sacs are controlled by the **intercostal muscles** of the ribs, as well as the **internal oblique muscles** of the abdomen.
65. When these muscles are contracted, the tip of the **sternum** is pushed down, expanding the volume of the chest cavity during inhalation. When they are relaxed, the sternum rises again, pushing air out of the lungs.

66. The respiratory system of birds also plays an essential role in **vocalizations**. An organ called the **syrinx** sits at the nexus of the location where the **trachea** branches into the **bronchi**.

Now offering curbside takeout meals!!

67. The diagrams below show the general layout of the avian **circulorespiratory system**.

This is an empty white space where a graphic wouldn't fit. I could go on rambling about obscure facts about birds, but at the moment, I am sad. Mike Leach, one of the greatest college football coaches ever, the architect of the air raid offense an numerous upsets, just passed away. In memoriam, here are some of his quotes.

1) There's a reason they only serve candy corn once a year. It's AWFUL! I completely HATE candy corn. Sprees in a box though....OUTSTANDING!
2) Somebody just said in passing, 'I hate cats'. Someone really hates cats, but I've never really figured that one out. But give credit to cats.....for the ability to generate that much animosity.
3) If you get into a fight, don't take your helmet off here. We aren't looking for dumb players. We want SMART players.
4) Not taking anything away from them....North Texas played fine, but if we could actually tackle someone, it might make a difference.
5) After a loss: Our players had their fat little girlfriends telling them what they want to hear, telling them how great they are.
6) I keep a Viking Axe by my bed for self-defense.

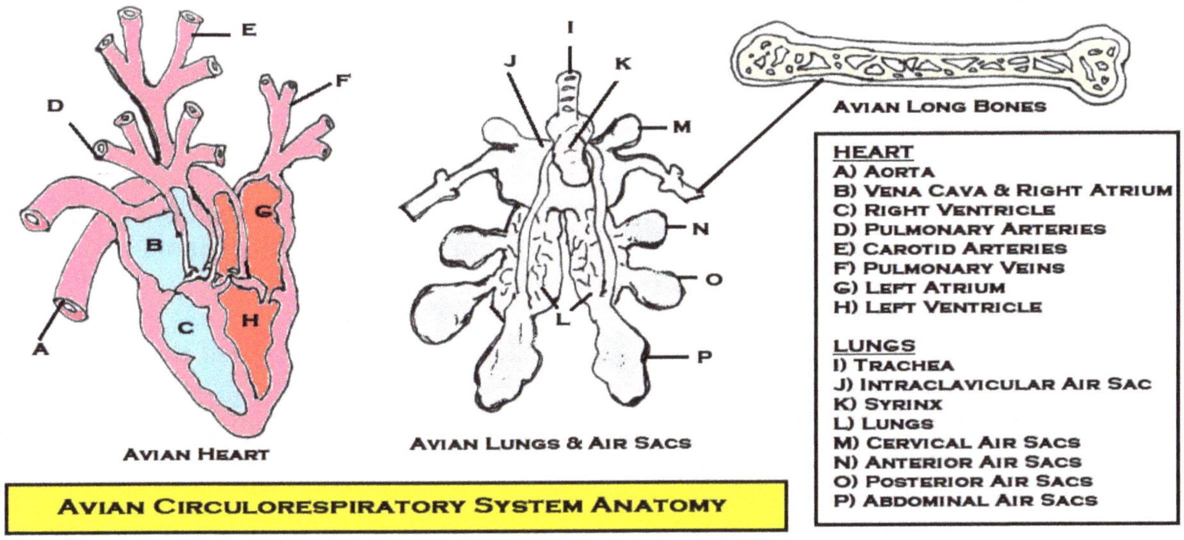

AVIAN CIRCULORESPIRATORY SYSTEM ANATOMY

68. The **syrinx** is a muscular organ that can contract and expand the bronchi. If it constricts them enough and air is forced over this gap, it produces the characteristic bird call of that particular species.

69. Vocalizations are highly dependent upon the length of the neck and the structure of the **larynx** above, explaining the great diversity of noises generated both within and between species. Species like cranes and geese with very long necks make distinct honks, while short-necked birds like canaries can only generate cheeps.

70. The vocalizations, themselves, are a product of complex behavioral characteristics, themselves a product of brains that integrate a wide range of instinctive, associative, and reasoned behaviors.

71. It was formerly thought that instinct was the largest factor that determined and regulated bird behavior. Since that time, this has been found not to be true, but there are certain behaviors that are so hardwired that they are nearly impossible to change. **Imprinting** of offspring to parents is one such example (more shortly).

72. The diagram below details the major sections of a bird's brain and describes their functions.

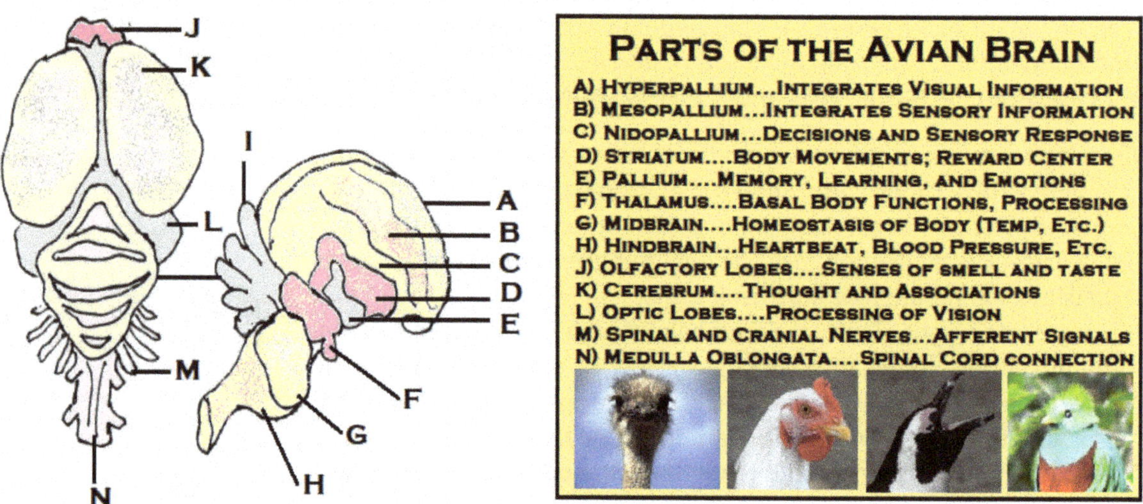

73. Bird vision, as you might expect, is usually better than our own. Peregrine falcons routinely spot rabbits from a mile up in the air and ambush them. Zooming hummingbirds can identify a heliconia flower and stop on a dime.

74. In addition to having red, blue, and green **cone cells** in their eyes, imparting full color vision, most birds also have UV-sensitive cones and can see things that we can't.

75. Many seemingly drab flowers or plumages come alive into an array of colors when seen through a UV filter.

76. Many birds have flexible **lenses** in their eye that can be bent to see at the correct refractive index underwater, such as cormorants. All birds also have a protective **nictitating membrane** or '3rd eyelid' for protection.

77. Like mammalian eyeballs, birds have a fluid-filled **vitreous humor** in the middle of the eye between the retina and the lens. However, they have an additional structure called the **pecten oculi** that looks like a radiator grill.

78. The **pecten oculi** is a brush-like capillary bed that brings nutrients and ions to the inner parts of the eye.

79. Depending on the order of birds, the **field of vision** varies, mostly due to evolutionary adaptations and lifestyles. For instance, eagles have a near panoramic vision, while owls have **binocular vision**.

80. While most birds have very acute vision, their other senses aren't quite as good. In most species of birds, the range of **hearing** is between about 1,000 and 4,000 Hertz. Their hearing within this range is very good.

81. However, humans have much greater sensitivity and ability to hear sounds toward the **infrasonic** and **ultrasonic** ranges. Most types of birds cannot effectively pick up noises of very low or very high frequencies.

82. Additionally, the inner ear of birds has a curved, but not spiral **cochlea** like mammals, meaning that there is less overall surface area for the hair cells that vibrate in response to sound.

83. The cranium of birds does not have a large volume, limiting the amount of space for sinuses and **olfactory cells**, so most birds don't have a particularly strong sense of smell.

84. It doesn't help that the nostrils emerge from the beak, which is made of **keratin** like a fingernail. This basically makes it impossible for birds to have an external nose. Birds with noses.....the stuff of nightmares....

85. One can also assume that birds don't have a very strong sense of taste, because a large portion of tasting is olfaction. We also know this because we can observe buzzards neck deep in the intestines of a sun-bloated pronghorn baking on the asphalt of route 66 somewhere in New Mexico.

86. Birds have a complex system of behaviors that depend upon virtually all of the heretofore mentioned anatomy and physiology we have discussed so far.

87. Rather than consider each individual behavior in narrative form, the tables on the next two pages summarize some of the major innate bird behaviors that characterize numerous members of **Class Aves**.

Bird Behavior	**Descriptive Factors**	**Examples**
Courtship & Sexual Selection	Most species of birds have intricate mating dances and calls. Sometimes gifts and tokens are presented to females, or nests are inspected. The great majority of birds use plumage coloration and arrangements as a mode of sexual selection. Females seek the fittest males for mating.	*Male peacock tail feather displays. *Bowerbirds build intricate nests and the best builders win the mates. *Birds-of-paradise have highly rehearsed and intricate mating dances to display their plumage.
Communication	Most birds have a 'language' of multiple calls that includes caws, squeaks, whistles, chirps, honks, songs, and so on. There are calls for predator warnings, territorial disputes, courtship, and so on. Additionally, many birds use body positioning and feather displays to convey messages.	*Mockingbirds copy the songs of other birds and animals to make their territory seem highly populated and reduce competition for resources. *White bellbirds find each other in the rainforest with a 125 dB amplified call.
Flocking	Birds spontaneously fly in formations, wherein they space themselves evenly, while making autonomous decisions about their spacing and position in flight. Birds flock to confuse predators, reduce their individual odds of being attacked, and to have many more pairs of eyes to spot them. Also associated with migration.	*Red winged blackbirds can form flocks of many millions of individuals. *Passenger pigeon extinction was accelerated by the fact that they formed gigantic flocks that made it possible to shoot several birds out of the sky with one shotgun shell.

Imprinting	Birds show filial imprinting due to hard-wired instinctive behaviors influenced by the limbic system. This causes both parent and offspring to form unbreakable social bonds at hatch and shortly thereafter. Chicks also sexually imprint on their own species, based on early observations. These behaviors are generally irreversible.	*Juvenile waterfowl, such as geese, ducks, and swans, will form single file lines behind their mother at all times. *Orphaned condor chicks must be reared with condor hand puppets, or they will later want to mate with humans, rather than condors.
Migration	Birds make seasonal flights, moving toward food, mating grounds, warmer temperatures, water, or other resources. Genetic programming, the pineal gland, and parental cues all prompt the move. Day length seems to be the main trigger. Most birds use the position of the sun and stars and possibly earth's magnetic field to navigate. Birds typically binge eat and put on fat before a long journey. They can sleep during flight.	*Arctic terns have the longest migration of any animal, breeding in Spring in the Arctic and flying back to the Antarctic for the Southern Hemisphere Summer. *Ruby-throated hummingbirds feed on trumpet vine in the Eastern USA in Summer and return to tropical America during the winter.
Nesting & Parenting	Highly variable between bird species, in terms of materials, size, length of brood period, and so on. Arctic birds make scrapes (dugouts), large birds like ospreys and flamingos make mounds, some birds burrow into hills (burrowing owls), hornbills nest in tree cavities, while most gather leaves, twigs, and other materials to build cup nests. In most species, both parents work around the clock to gather food and feed fledglings. Parental duties vary between species. While most birds are monogamous, some males have multiple nests.	*Penguins build stone nests and female incubates egg. After hatch, male penguin protects chicks under belly fold, while females feed. *Swifts and hummingbirds glue their small compact nests together with sticky saliva that sets into a mold. *African malleefowl males make a house-sized compost mound. Females lay eggs in warm spot and promptly leave when chicks hatch.
Preening	On the roost, most birds spend a lot of time distributing bird grease over their feathers, which is secreted by the preen glands. This waterproofs the feathers, keeps them warm, and secondary secretions provide protections against microbes and parasites. Secondarily, it is a social bonding activity that may be part of courtship rituals.	*Bohemian waxwings produce oils with sunscreen properties, which keeps UV from degrading their feathers or sunburning the bird. *Mated pairs of albatrosses preen each others' hard-to-reach areas, strengthening their bonds.
Roosting	Roosting is typically triggered by light levels, but may also be influenced by weather and predators. Birds lower their metabolic rates, usually tuck their heads under their wings, and sleep. Some birds may go into torpor (semi-hibernation) in order to conserve energy. Location of roost and position of body depends upon bird species.	*Hummingbirds would starve on the roost if they did not lower their metabolic rate dramatically. *Songbirds like robins and orioles lock their leg tendons when on the perch, preventing them from falling out of the tree during their sleep.

The Cassowary: A Bird that Behaves Like Axl Rose

Few birds carry the risk of a lethal confrontation, but the cassowary is not concerned with proper etiquette. With razor-sharp spurs on their feet, a cassowary can deliver a kick with a force of 1000 PSI. Over 200 people are injured by cassowaries each year. Cassowaries will attack you if you corner them, mess with their chicks, get in the way of a food source, or play music with auto-tune, such as the Black-Eyed Peas. They strongly dislike dogs, loud childen, and raw onions in potato salad.

Answers to Bird Trivia

1) Atlanta Falcons, Arizona Cardinals, Baltimore Ravens, Philadelphia Eagles, Seattle Seahawks
2) Baltimore Orioles, St. Louis Cardinals, Toronto Blue Jays
3) Bojangles, Chic-Fil-A, Church's , Kentucky Fried Chicken, Jollibee, Mrs. Winner's, Popeye's, Raising Cane's, Zaxby's
4) Randy Johnson, the Big Unit
5) Blu, Daffy Duck , Donald Duck, Foghorn Leghorn, Heckyl and Jeckyl, Iago, Roadrunner, Tweety, Superchicken, Woody, Zazu
6) Attorney-at-Law
7) Free Bird by Lynyrd Skynyrd

88. Birds are a great study subject for evolutionary biologists. As Darwin described in his famous evolutionary studies on finches, birds often make great case studies in **adaptation**, where form fits function.
89. In many cases, it is possible for a layperson to just look at certain birds and understand what their **ecological niche** must be. For instance, it is no mystery what pelicans are going to try to do in order to get a meal.
90. The **beaks** and **feet** of birds are usually adapted for feeding and foraging, while their wings, tails, and concomitant contour feathers are adapted to their particular style of flight.
91. As Darwin described with the Galapagos finches, as birds became isolated in certain environments, **natural selection** eliminated poor morphology and continue to shape surviving individuals to better adaptations.
92. Additionally, **sexual selection**, predation, competition, and climatological factors caused evolutionary changes in plumage, wingspan, vocalizations, and overall size of various birds.
93. The diagram below details some of these lifestyle-specific beaks and feet.

94. There are 41 different orders of birds in 248 families across the world, comprising nearly 11,000 known species.
95. Obviously, it is beyond the scope of this text to cover each of these in detail. For this reason, the diagrams below show representatives and short descriptions for representatives from about half of these orders.
96. You will notice that, more often than not, the bills and feet of these specimens comprise two of the major morphological factors that were used to classify them into their respective orders.

97. Let's begin with the **Infraclass Palaeognathae**, which includes mostly flightless birds. This group is considered to be more primitive than other birds because of differences in skull and pelvis anatomy.

98. As opposed to most groups of flying birds, the bones of flightless birds are much denser, their reproductive tracts have two ovaries, and the bones in the skull make a distinct ridge in the beak.

99. It would be incorrect to surmise that all flightless birds are extremely close relatives. From DNA evidence, it appears that flightlessness evolved on several different occasions, due to similar environmental niches.

100. The orders of birds shown below belong to **Infraclass Palaeognathae**. A representative of each is shown, along with facts about each specific order.

INFRACLASS PALAEOGNATHA

BIRD ORDERS

A) ORDER STRUTHIONIFORMES
OSTRICHES HAVE UNIQUE LEG BONE ANATOMY. SOLID BONES, LONG NECKS, 200-300 LBS.

B) ORDER REIHIFORMES
RHEAS ARE CLOSEST RELATIVES TO OSTRICHES. FOUND IN SOUTH AMERICA INSTEAD OF AFRICA.

C) ORDER APTERYGIFORMES
KIWIS HAVE VESTIGIAL WINGS, FOOTBALL-SIZED BODIES, ARE NOCTURNAL. NEW ZEALAND.

D) ORDER CASUARIIFORMES
CASSOWARIES HAVE CRESTS, WATTLES, LEG SPURS FOR FIGHTING. HIGH PARENTAL CARE.

E) ORDER CASUARIIFORMES
EMUS ARE TALLER AND THINNER, ADAPTED TO GRASSLANDS INSTEAD OF FORESTS.

F) ORDER TINAMIFORMES
TINAMOUS STILL FLY, BUT DNA, ANATOMY SUGGEST RELATION TO OSTRICHES AND RHEAS.

101. Most modern birds belong to the **Infraclass Neognatha**. Unlike most flightless birds, the **metacarpal bones** of their hands are fused, the third finger forms the tip of the wing, and different jaw and skull anatomy.

102. One of the major evolutionary losses is the the **vomer bone** that forms the main support of a snout or nose. While most flightless birds retain a ridge in the beak, due to the presence of this bone, it is absent in Neognaths.

103. Additionally, the females of most Neognaths (but not all), have only a single ovary, cutting weight for flight.

104. **Infraclass Neognatha** further splits into fowl birds, **Class Galloanserae**, and modern birds, **Class Neoaves**.

105. Let's consider the Galloanserae first. Most members of this group retain webbing between the **tarsal bones** of the back feet. As compared to other birds, they are highly **fecund**, reproducing constantly and developing very quickly. It is no wonder, given their capacity to reproduce, that most commercially important birds are fowl.

106. **Order Galliformes** and **Order Anseriformes** are classified under the Galloanserae umbrella as fowl birds. The latter are poultry birds, such as chickens, pheasants, and turkeys. The latter are waterfowl like ducks and geese.

107. The graphic at the top of the next page shows the two orders of fowl birds and gives some facts about them.

Recipe for Bawwssse Southern Fried Chicken

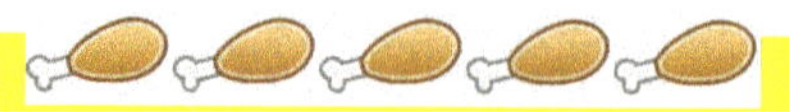

1) Mix 2 cups of buttermilk, ½ cup of dill pickle brine, 1 tbsp dill, 1 tbsp kosher salt, 1 tsbsp dry mustard, 1 beaten egg, 1 tsp cayenne pepper, 2 tsp garlic powder, 2 tsp kosher salt, 1 tsp marjoram, and 2 tbsp black pepper.

2) Soak 3-4 pounds of boneless chicken under the brine overnight in a sealed Tupperware container.

3) The next day, use a deep fryer or skillet to heat enough blended vegetable oil to cover your chicken.

4) Get a pair of tongs. Dredge your chicken in the following breading mix: 2 cups of all-purpose flour, 1 tsp baking powder, 1 tbsp salt, 1 tbsp black pepper, 2 tbsp dill weed, ½ tsp cayenne pepper, 1 tsp white pepper.

5) Flour mix should stick to chicken evenly. Shake off excess lumps of flour, reapply brine, and dredge again if necessary coating hasn't stuck. Slide your chicken directly into the hot oil with the tongs.

6) Cook until chicken starts to rise up in oil and turn appropriate color of golden brown on surface. Allow at least 7-10 minutes for meat in center to finish cooking. Finish in 375 F oven, if center is still pink. Enjoy!

108. **Superorder Neoaves** comprises around 95% of living bird species. While there are large differences between taxa within the same group, they all have some commonalities not shared by the aforementioned groups.

109. **Neoaves**, unlike their more primitive brethren, have lost or reduced many of the skullbones that were reptilian holdovers. With the exception of penguins and a few other oddballs, all neoaves are capable of flight.

110. Additionally, neoaves tend to have streamlined bodies and hollow bones necessary for flight. Female neoavians tend to have a single ovary, while males mate directly through the cloaca, rather than using a penis.

111. **Superorder Neoaves** can be subdivided into several clades that each include a number of bird orders. All of these divisions are primarily informed by DNA and molecular evidence that suggests common ancestry.

112. Some of the specific morphology and genetic evidence used to delineate these classifications is beyond the scope of this text. We will cover these orders in the most commonly accepted order of evolved complexity.

113. In the summaries below, any derived traits that are considered more advanced than the prior group will be mentioned. With that said, let's get real. Do you care what shape the orbital bone of the skull is in some obscure group of birds or do you really want to know how rRNA differs between woodpeckers and turkeys?

114. If you answered 'Yes!' to the question above, get an ornithology book and some binoculars, go to Banana Republic and get a pretentious-looking 'adventurer' outfit and leave me alone.

Neoavian Bird Orders

A) Order Phoenocopteriformes (Flamingos) Scooping Bill, Lockable leg Tendons for Wading & Sleeping, Plankton Feeders

B) Order Podicipediformes (Grebes) Intricate mating dances, nests float on water, spear-like bill for piscivory. Poor fliers.

C) Order Charadriiformes (Gulls, sandpipers, plovers, auks, etc.) Shorebirds adapted for scavenging, digging, or piscivory.

D) Order Gruiformes (Cranes, Rails, Limpkins, Gallinules, Bitterns) Long tibial bones adapted for wading. Spear-like bill for fishing. Both sexes usually drably colored. Short tail feathers.

E) Order Columbiformes (Doves, Pigeons, Dodos) Very large air sacs and pectoral muscles combine with wedge-shaped wings for explosive lift and speed. Females feed chicks with 'crop milk'.

F) Order Musophagiformes (Turacos) Fourth toe can be rotated back and forth to grip branches. Very noisy birds with lots of different calls. Build stick nests in trees. Chicks well-developed.

G) Order Cuculiformes (Cuckoos, Roadrunners) Long tibial bones and tarsals for hopping, perching, running. Many species of cuckoos are brood parasites, dropping eggs in other birds' nests.

H) Order Otidiformes (Bustards) Some species can top 40 pounds, making them largest of flying birds. Males twice as large as females. Throat sacs inflated in courtship. Omnivorous.

I) Order Ophisticomiformes (Hoatzins) Some think it is closest ancestor to Archaeopteryx. Chicks retain claws on wings. Adults have crests. Has a fermentive gut that makes them stink.

NEOAVIAN BIRD ORDERS

A) ORDER CAPRIMULGIFORMES (NIGHTJARS, WHIPPOORWILLS) VERY SHORT BILL DESIGNED FOR GULPING INSECTS, LONG WING FEATHERS, SHORT SQUAT BODIES & LEGS. ABLE TO HIBERNATE AND GO INTO TORPOR AT NIGHT.

B) ORDER PODARGIFORMES (FROGMOUTHS) HUGE WIDE FROG-LIKE MOUTH FOR EATING LARGE INSECTS, FROGS, MICE, SNAILS. SHORT WING FEATHERS, POOR FLIERS. CAMOUFLAGED WITH DRAB COLORS. NOCTURNAL.

C) ORDER APODIFORMES (HUMMINGBIRDS & SWIFTS) SMALL FEET, VESTIGIAL WALKING MUSCLES. HUMMINGBIRDS HAVE FASTEST WINGBEAT OF ALL AVES, LONG BILL FOR NECTAR FEEDING & ARE MIGRATORY. SWIFTS FLY AT HIGH SPEEDS.

D) ORDER PHAETHONTIFORMES (TROPICBIRDS) LARGE WHITE BIRDS WITH METER WIDE WINGSPANS, KITE-LIKE TAIL FEATHERS. MARINE AMBUSH HUNTERS THAT DIVE BOMB FISH. NEST ON BARE GROUND IN PAIRS, WITH MALES FEEDING OFFSPRING.

E) ORDER GAVIIFORMES (LOONS) DIVING AQUATIC BIRDS WITH WEBBED FEET. BILL IS DAGGER-LIKE AND USED TO STAB FISH, FROGS. BOTH SEXES LOOK IDENTICAL.

F) ORDER PROCELLARIFORMES (ALBATROSSES, PETRELS) MARINE BIRDS THAT FLY GREAT DISTANCES WORLDWIDE. TUBE-SHAPED BEAKS ENDING IN POINT. STRONG SENSE OF SMELL USED TO AID MIGRATION. LAY SINGLE EGGS IN NESTING COLONIES.

G) ORDER SPHENISCIFORMES (PENGUINS) WINGS REDUCED TO POWERFUL FLIPPERS. ADAPTED FOR DIVING PISCIVORY, WITH COUNTERSHADING, FLIPPERED FEET, AND THICK LAYER OF BLUBBER AND OILY DOWN FEATHERS. HOLD EGGS ATOP FEET.

H) ORDER CICONIIFORMES (STORKS) LARGE LONG-LEGGED BIRDS WITH VERY LARGE WINGSPANS DESIGNED TO FLY IN THERMAL UPDRAFTS. BEAKS TEND TO BE POINTED BUT VARY BY DIET OF SPECIES. BUILD GIGANTIC 2-3 METER-WIDE NESTS.

I) ORDER PELECANIFORMES (PELICANS, HERONS, IBISES) FOUR WEBBED TOES WITH LONG MIDDLE TOE WITH NAIL FOR PREENING. NOSTRILS ARE VESTIGIAL, DUE TO ADAPTATION OF BILL FOR FEEDING ON LARGE ITEMS, SUCH AS IN PELICANS.

NEOAVIAN BIRD ORDERS

A) ORDER CATHARTIFORMES (NEW WORLD VULTURES, CONDORS) SCAVENGERS WITH DECOMPOSING BACTERIA IN GUT, STRONG SENSE OF SMELL. FEATHERLESS HEADS COMMON. CAN ONLY HISS (NO SYRINX). HUGE WINGSPAN FOR SOARING.

B) ORDER ACCIPTRIOFORMES (HAWKS, EAGLES, KITES, OLD WORLD VULTURES) OPPOSABLE HIND CLAWS TIPPED WITH RAZOR-SHARP TALONS. HOOKED BILL FOR TEARING FLESH. MONOGAMOUS PAIRING WITH LONG JUVENILE STAGE.

C) ORDER STRIGIFORMES (OWLS) LARGE BOXY HEAD ATOP 14 NECK VERTEBRAE THAT CAN ROTATE WIDE RADIUS TO COMPENSATE FOR FIXED BINOCULAR VISION. NOCTURAL PREDATORS WITH SHARP TALONS AND BEAK. FLY SILENTLY.

D) ORDER TROGONIFORMES (QUETZALS AND TROGONS) BRILLIANT PLUMAGE AND LONG FLOWING TAIL FEATHERS. UNIQUE AMONG BIRDS IN THAT 1ST TWO TOES POINT BACKWARD AND TOES 3 AND 4 FACE FORWARD. FOREST OMNIVORES.

E) ORDER BUCEROTIFORMES (HORNBILLS AND HOOPOES) LONG DOWNWARD CURVED BILLS THAT FUNCTION LIKE A FEEDING SCOOP. HORNBILLS HAVE CRESTS ON UPPER MANDIBLE TO AMPLIFY CALLS. OMNIVORES. NEST IN ARBOREAL HOLES.

F) ORDER CORACIIFORMES (KINGFISHERS, BEE EATERS, MOTMOTS) HAVE 3 TOES THAT FACE FORWARD ON FEET AND POINTED BILLS USED FOR SPEARING PREY. PLUMAGE USUALLY COLORFUL BLUE OR GREEN. SLAM OR DROP PREY TO KILL.

G) ORDER PICIFORMES (WOODPECKERS, TOUCANS, TOUCANETS, HONEYGUIDES) HAVE 2 FORWARD AND 2 BACKWARD POINTED TOES. LACK DOWN FEATHERS. HEAD OF WOODPECKERS HAS SPONGY BONES AS SHOCK ABSORBERS. TOUCANS HAVE CURVED BILLS CAPABLE OF SCOOPING LARGE QUANTITIES OF FRUIT.

H) ORDER FALCONIFORMES (FALCONS, CARACARAS) CONVERGENT EVOLUTION TO ACCIPTRIOFORMES (HAWKS & ALLIES) WITH CARNIVOROUS BILL, TALONS. MOST TAKE OVER NESTS AND DON'T BUILD THEM, UNLIKE THE OTHER RAPTORS.

I) ORDER PSITACIIFORMES (PARROTS, MACAWS, COCKATOOS, PARAKEETS) FEET HAVE 2 TOES FORWARD AND 2 TOES BACKWARD. SHARP BILL FOR PEELING FRUIT AND SEEDS. LARGEST RELATIVE BRAIN SIZE AMONG BIRDS. MONOGAMOUS.

J) ORDER PASSERIFORMES (SONGBIRDS) HUGE VARIETY OF COMMUNICATION VIA SONGS AND OTHER SOUNDS. BORN HIGHLY UNDEVELOPED. COLORFUL PLUMAGE.

J) Class Mammalia: Monotremes, Marsupials, and Placentals

1. **Class Mammalia** comprises the most advanced group of vertebrates in numerous evolutionary regards.
2. In spite of some specifically poor representatives of mammals (Adolf Hitler, Rosie O'Donnell, Gucci Mane, Joe Biden, or Harry Stiles), our own human species is included in this group, since we are primates.
3. Members of **Class Mammalia** have a number of highly advanced features. Arguably, the development and expansion of the **cerebral cortex** is the most important of these.
4. The cerebral cortex is involved in making associations, logical reasoning, abstract thinking, and higher thought. It is responsible for granting mammals much greater intelligence than most other vertebrates.
5. **Endothermy** (warm-bloodedness) is another fundamental mammalian trait. The **hypothalamus** of the brain controls blood vessels circumference, constricting or opening them to retain or release muscular heat.
6. The mammalian brain is complex, with dozens of regions with varied functions. The diagram below shows the major lobes and components of the brain, including the **cerebral cortex**, **limbic system**, and **brain stem.**

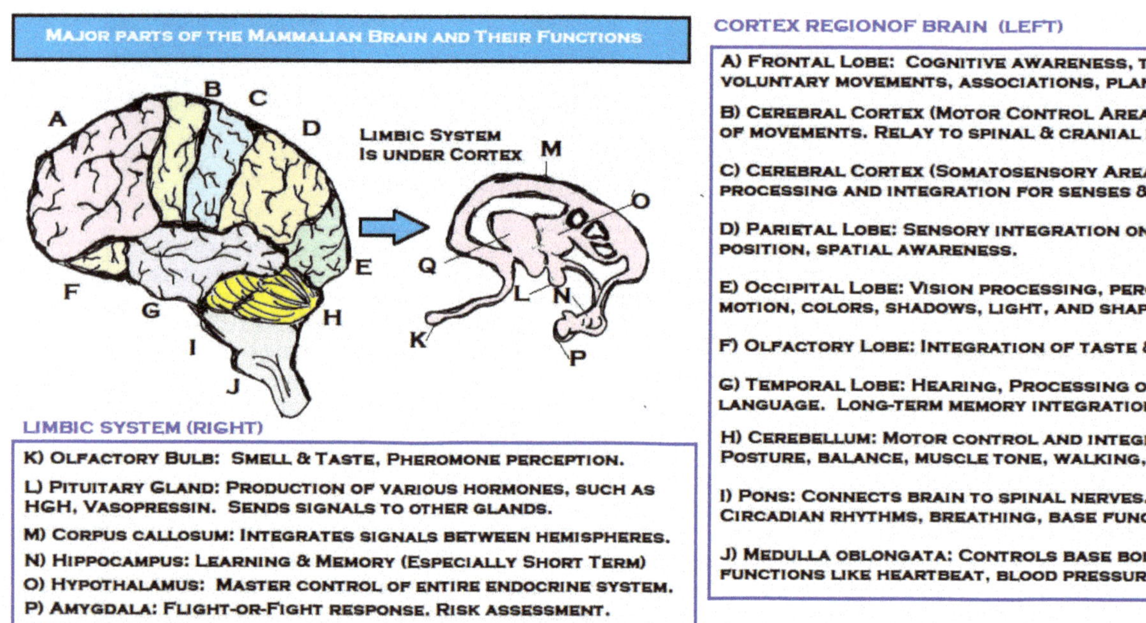

7. **Hair** acts as an insulator material, helping to retain more of this heat. Mammals developed hair by modifying **scales**, as both are composed of **keratin**. Some mammals, such as armadillos, retain some scaly features.
8. **Mammary glands**, the namesake organs of mammals, are actually modified **sweat glands** that produce **colostrum** and **milk** to nourish their offspring. This is in line with the fact that most mammals are **K-strategists**.
9. As you may remember, the name of the game with **K-strategists** is to maintain a population as close to the **carrying capacity** as possible. This requires a lot of parental care to ensure survival. Milk is a part of this.

10. Mammals also have a number of other features that evolved independently of any other vertebrates.
11. One obvious such feature is **differentiated teeth**. Mammals are the only group of vertebrates that have specific types of teeth. **Incisors, canines, pre-molars,** and **molars** are specific only to mammals.
12. Furthermore, the continued specialization and evolution of these teeth plays a major role in the classification scheme of mammals. The dentition of horses and lions varies dramatically, reflective of their dietary needs.
13. The structure of the teeth, themselves, is also more advanced than for many lower vertebrates.
14. At the center of the tooth is a living **pulp cavity** with blood vessels and nerves. Outside of this is a tough protein layer called **dentin**. Finally, the teeth are crowned with a very hard layer of **enamel**.
15. The mammalian jaw articulates to a skull bone below the ear called the **squamosal bone**. In other vertebrates, the jaw joint articulates to the **quadrate bone** further back toward the neck. Mammals lack this bone.
16. The **eardrum** of mammals differs from other vertebrates, such as reptiles, in that its **tympanic membrane** is inside the skull, rather than close to the surface.
17. Only mammals have the inner ear bones that vibrate to contact the oval window of the ear drum. These bones are known as the **malleus, incus,** and **stapes** (hammer, anvil, and stirrup in common vernacular).
18. The skull of mammals sit atop the **atlas** and **axis** vertebral bones. The **occipital condyles** are knobs on the sides of the skull that fit into the vertebral grooves.
19. The axis and atlas are the first two of between 6 and 9 **cervical vertebrae** in the neck. In most cases, these are followed by 12 **thoracic vertebrae**, and either 7 or 8 heavier **lumbar vertebrae**.
20. The diagram on the next page illustrates the most prominent bones in the mammalian skull and the four major types of **differentiated teeth**. Due to divergent evolution, the shapes and appearances of these bones and teeth can look wildly different between different orders of mammals.

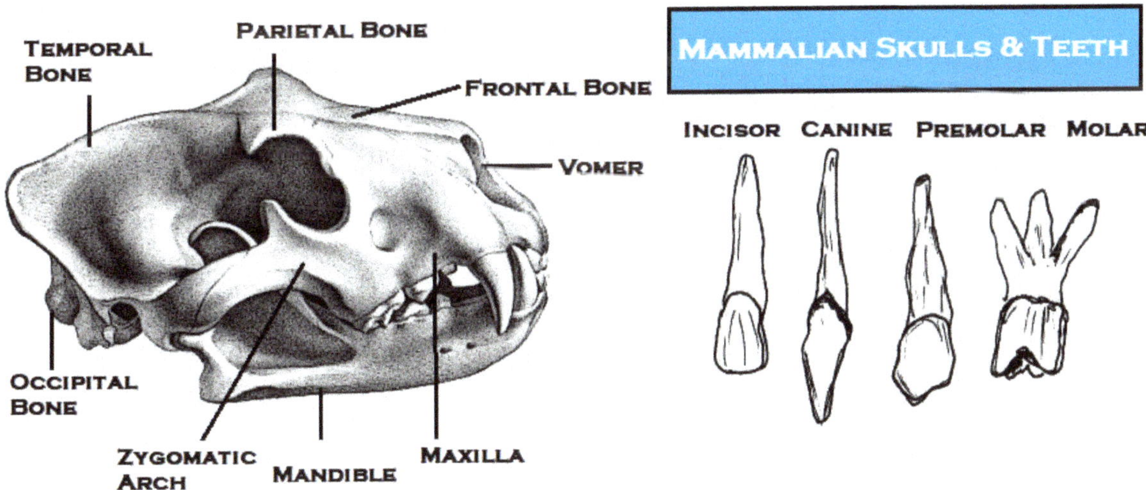

21. As in birds, the mammalian **hypothalamus** acts as a thermostat, sending signals to blood vessels to contract or expand as needed. **Endothermy** significantly raises energy demand, so oxygen demand rises correspondingly.
22. Many mammals, especially those that don't make their living running at high speed (such as manatees, rats, elephants, and online gamers) have large amounts of mitochondria-rich **slow-twitch muscle**.
23. This type of muscle is aerobic, and consequently, requires lots of oxygen to run its metabolic processes.

24. In order to facilitate this high oxygen demand, the **circulatory** and **respiratory systems** of mammals adapted.
25. Unlike many large lizards, mammals can't get away with a three-chambered heart. Mammals have **four-chambered hearts** with separate pulmonary and systemic loops to ensure adequate blood oxygenation.
26. Their circulatory loop is much like that of birds.
27. Deoxygenated blood from the body enters the **right atrium** of the heart via the **vena cava**. Blood drops through the **bicuspid valve** into the **right ventricle**, which pumps it back to the lungs through the **pulmonary artery**.
28. Oxygenated blood returns from the lungs via the **pulmonary veins** into the **left atrium**, falls through he **tricuspid valve** into the **left ventricle**, where it is then pumped back to the body by the **aorta.**
29. The **respiratory system** of mammals simply expands on the design seen in more advanced reptiles.
30. Mammalian lungs take up a larger portion of their thoracic cavity and have branched out into **bronchi**, **bronchioles**, and into small clusters of grape-like globular **alveoli**, whose membranes are full of **capillaries**.
31. Underneath the lungs, is the **diaphragm muscle**, which, when flexed, pulls downward, expanding the chest cavity and forcing air into the lungs. When relaxed, volume decreases and air is expelled out of the lungs.
32. While the diaphragm is partially under **autonomic control** (involuntary), the **intercostal muscles** between the ribs are voluntarily controlled to a greater degree, providing more control over inhalation and exhalation.

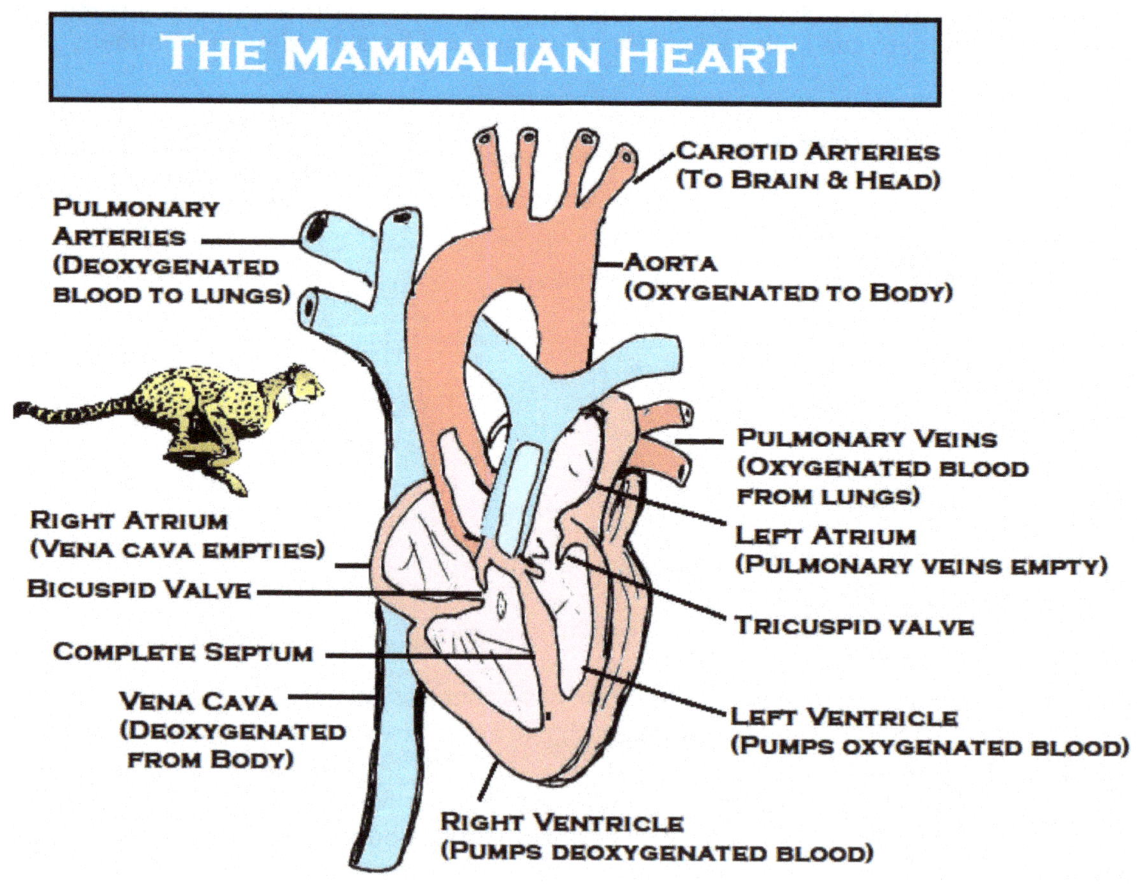

33. The mammalian digestive system consists of mostly the same basic organs along the alimentary canal.
34. However, there is a high degree of evolutionarily derived differences, based on adaptations to dietary needs.
35. Swallowed food passes the **pharynx**, enters the **esophagus**, and from there enters the first digestive chamber, which is the **stomach** in most mammals. However, **ruminants** have modified this chamber for **fermentation**.
36. When Bessie the cow or Carol the camel swallow fresh hay, it enters the **rumen** first. The rumen is full of symbiotic bacteria and protozoans that break down the cellulose and sugars in grass.
37. Extending off the front of the rumen is the **reticulum.** Any large pieces of food that get swallowed are trapped there and burped up again. When cows, antelope, llamas, et al chew their cud, this is where it comes from.
38. The contents of the reticulum are also what angry camels or llamas spit in your face if you annoy them. It isn't really spit. It's actually partially digested green paste mixed with snot. It also reeks like a cow pie.
39. The back of the rumen is called the **omasum**. It is used like a coffee filter. Its folds only allows finely ground paste and small particles to make it to the **abomasum**, which is the true digestive stomach.
40. All mammals have the same basic parts of the small intestine. The **duodenum** is connected to enzyme-producing digestive organs via ducts. It is the main chamber where macromolecule breakdown occurs.
41. The **bile duct** from the **gall bladder** (if present), enters this chamber. Bile is actually produced by the **liver** via breakdown of old red blood cells. In mammals that have one, excess bile is stored in the gall bladder.
42. There are many mammals, however, who do not. Almost no ruminants have one, nor do rhinos, elephants, or whales. In most cases, this is because their diet is not high enough in fats to necessitate the need for one.
43. Bile **emulsifies** fats like soap, breaking it into smaller droplets for easier digestion.
44. The **pancreatic duct** also squirts digestive enzymes into the small intestine from the **pancreas.** These enzymes include carbohydrate digesting enzymes, lipases, proteases, and nucleases.
45. As food makes its way through the **jejunum**, digestion continues, but digested products start to make their way into the blood vessels of the **mesentery**, which is a huge bed of blood vessels on the posterior surface.
46. Many of these digested macromolecules go directly to the liver through the **hepatic portal vein**. For instance, sugars (under the direction of insulin), cholesterol, and iron are all stored in the liver.
47. Fats enter lymphatic vessels called **lacteals**, where they are transported through the lymphatic system and enclosed in **LDL** or **HDL particles**, making them soluble in the bloodstream, before they enter at the **lymphatic duct** under the collarbones.
48. The **ileum** is the final segment of the small intestine, which does with a large portion of this nutrient absorption.
49. The **large intestine** consists of the **ascending, transverse, descending,** and **sigmoid colon**. These segments have two primary functions. They reabsorbs water and nutrients, while housing symbiotic bacteria that extract the last salvageable molecules from the gut contents, before sending it out the **rectum** and **anus** as waste.
50. These symbiotic bacteria are also important to the health of mammals, as they take up residence and repel harmful pathogenic bacteria by outcompeting them.
51. Some mammals have a well-developed **cecum** that extends off of the ascending colon. Humans know this chamber better as an **appendix**. However, the cecum is critical to the digestion of fibers in many mammals.

52. For instance, horses and rhinos rely solely on the cecum as a fermentative pouch, since they lack the four chambered stomach of ruminants. Likewise, rabbits and many leaf-eating monkeys rely heavily upon one.
53. While the aforementioned features are often used as criteria for taxonomic classification, there are two organ systems in mammals that form most of the basis for their separation into orders and families.
54. The **reproductive system**, along with its concomitant behaviors and life strategies, is the basis of the classification of mammals into 3 infraclasses. These are the **monotremes**, **marsupials**, and **placentals**.
55. We will save the discussion of each reproductive system and strategy for the discussion of each taxa.
56. Likewise, the **musculoskeletal system** is highly evolved and modified according to the lifestyle and needs of different groups of mammals.
57. While the great majority of bones and muscles are common to all mammals, the shapes and dimensions are not.
58. For instance, all **phalanges** are not equal. If you're a human, you have a gripping hand with an opposable thumb. If you're a bat, they are elongated and form the scaffolding for your wings. If you're a leopard, they are modified into paws for bounding, leaping, and swatting prey.
59. We will save specific details of the musculoskeletal systems as well. We will discuss these anatomical adaptations along with the group as we cover them. Now let's begin our journey through **Class Mammalia**.
60. The most primitive group of ancestral mammals are in **Order Monotrema**. There are only five living species in this order. One of these is the duck-billed platypus, while the other four are species of echidnas.
61. All living monotremes are remnants of a past time, only found in Australia and New Guinea, since competition from highly evolved **placental mammals** mostly never arrived. However, **marsupials** did mostly push them out.
62. **Monotremes** are **oviparous**, laying leathery eggs in nests, much like reptiles.
63. Their reproductive tract is also very reptilian, with two **uterine horns** that terminate into a **cloacal canal** and **cloaca**. Like reptiles, the intestines and bladder both empty out of this single opening/

And now....Some real fortune cookie messages authored by disgruntled employees, actually found by people

One day you will die in an Arby's in Columbus, Ohio.	**When you squeeze an orange, orange juice will come out.**
You resemble a muppet, so people won't take you seriously.	**You couldn't be any less interesting, but it's cute the you try.**
Enjoy yourself.....while you still can.	**No snowflake in an avalanche ever feels responsible.**
Your pets are planning to eat you.	**Your mom's diet is not working. She's a fat hog.**

64. The diagram below shows the layout of the monotreme reproductive tract.

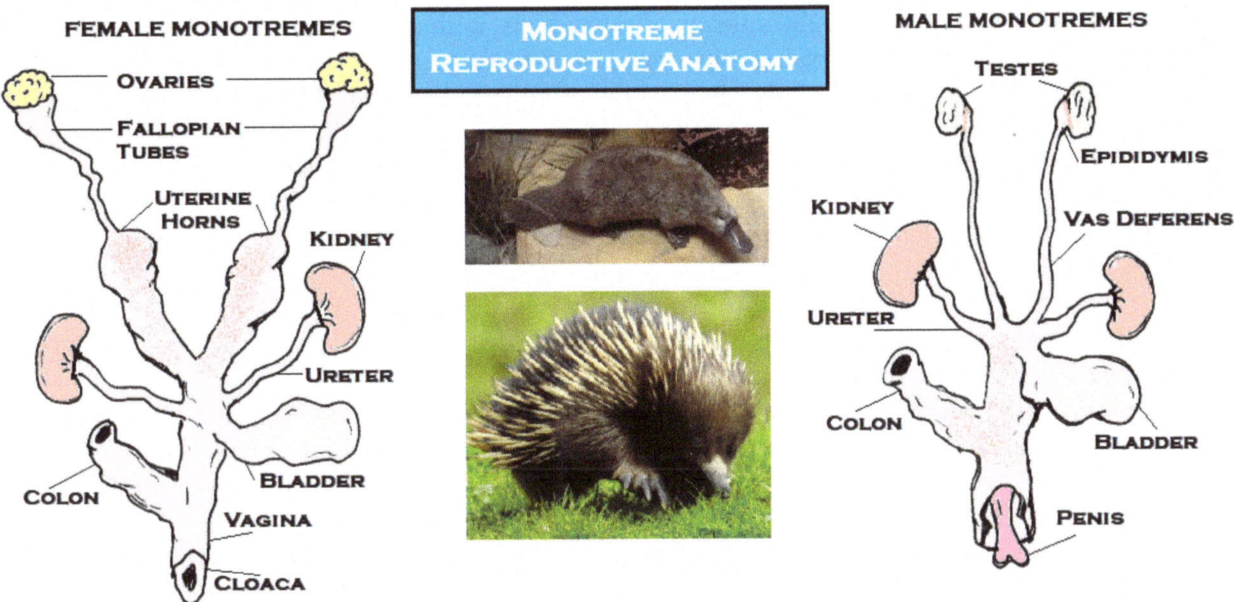

65. Interestingly, monotremes are toothless and have beak-like snouts. However, they are soft and pliable and not keratinous like a bird's beak. Both are capable of sensing electric fields with special **electrolocation organs**.
66. Genetically, monotremes appear to have veered onto a completely different course from other mammals, as they have five pairs of sex chromosomes.
67. Unlike other mammals, male platypuses are XZ, while females are XX on the determining pair.
68. Now let's look at the two extant families.
69. **Family Tachyglossidae** are the echidnas, also called spiny anteaters. In a case of convergent evolution, they have developed many traits of true anteaters, with a long skinny snout, sticky tongue, and digging claws.
70. Likewise, echidnas are armored with quills and dense fur to repel predators and insect bites.
71. Platypuses of **Family Ornithorhynchidae** have similarly dense fur, but have adapted to riparian live, with webbed feet, and an otter-like tail. They feed on fish, mollusks, and crustaceans.
72. Interestingly, male platypuses have venomous spines in their back legs to repel predators that might try to drag them out of the water and roast them on the barbie with a bloomin' onion.

ORDER MONOTREMA

A) FAMILY TACHYGLOSSIDAE (ECHIDNAS) ONLY TERRESTRIAL EGG-LAYING MAMMALS STILL IN EXISTENCE. COVERED WITH QUILLS, SHARP CLAWS, STICKY TONGUE, NO TEETH. INSECTIVOROUS.

B) FAMILY ORNITHORHYNCHIDAE (PLATYPUS) RIPARIAN EGG-LAYERS. MALES HAVE VENOMOUS SPINES ON BACK LEGS. LEATHERY 'DUCK BILL' AND CLAWS. PISCIVOROUS DIET.

73. Members of **Infraclass Marsupiala** dominate the mammalian fauna of Australia, New Guinea, and New Caledonia, since they evolved in isolation, free from competition from **placental mammals.**

74. Worldwide, there are around 330 species of marsupials, with more than 230 of these in Australasia.

75. Marsupials are **viviparous**, giving birth to live offspring, albeit extremely underdeveloped in comparison to placental mammals. Everything about the layout and function of the reproductive tract is different.

76. Marsupials have two **ovaries** and **oviducts** that give way to two **uterine horns** of narrow diameter.

77. Instead of a **placenta**, the developing embryo is nourished by a **yolk sac** from the egg as it undergoes early development. Since this food source quickly runs out, it is forced to migrate into the pouch, where it is born.

78. After the baby moves from the uterus, it makes itself down one of two **lateral vaginas** that form a pretzel-shaped reproductive canal with the **cervix**. From there, the baby exits the **urogenital opening** into the **pouch.**

79. Once inside the pouch, they attach to a nipple and finish developing via the nourishment in their mother's milk.

80. Unlike monotremes, marsupials have separate openings for the anus and reproductive tract.

81. Only female marsupials have pouches. Interestingly, in male marsupials, the **penis** is behind the **scrotal sac** and **testes** because the loop including the **prostrate gland** and **Cowper's glands** is in reverse of that in placentals.

82. The diagram below shows the reproductive tracts of both marsupial genders.

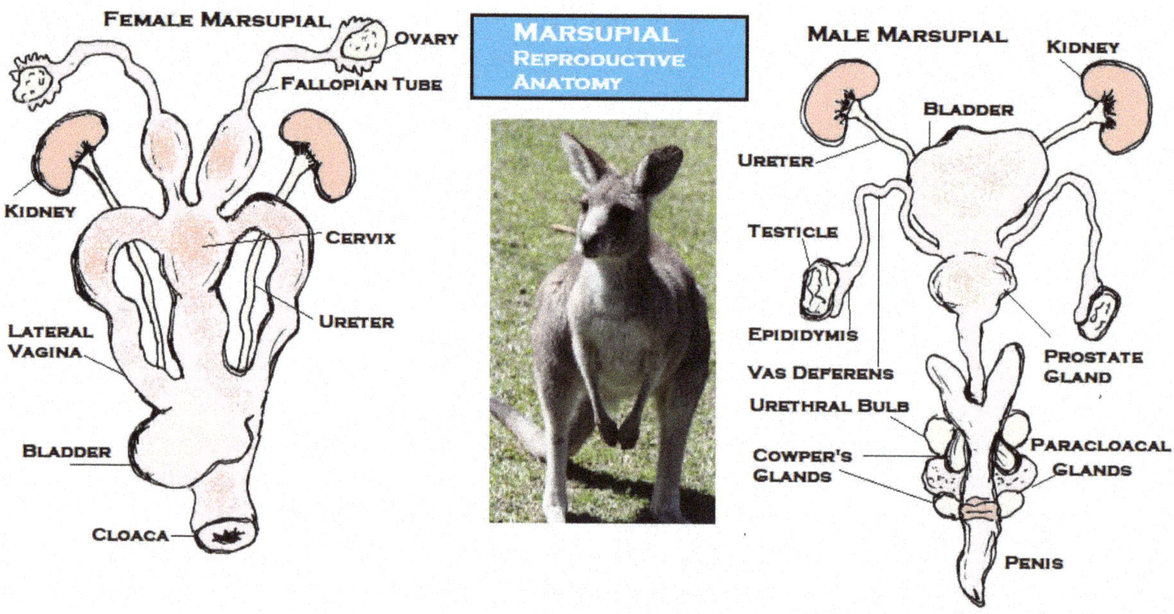

83. There are three orders of marsupials in existence. These are the more ancient **Order Didelphimorpha** (possum-like marsupials), the **Order Paucituberculata** (shrew possums) and the more evolved **Order Australidelphia** (Australian marsupials such as kangaroos and koalas).

84. The more primitive members of **Order Didelphimorpha** are found worldwide and tend to have cat-like bodies, long snouts, a sagittal crest on their skull, small brains with reptilian features, and 50 teeth in their jaw.

85. Their teeth get larger toward the back of the mouth. They have small front **incisors**, they have large **canines** that are often used in defense or predation, and they have very large **tricuspid molars** in the back for gnawing.

86. Internally, their digestive tract has a **cecum**, which is sometimes necessary, since most possums are omnivores that will literally eat anything, including fermenting trash out of the bottom of a dumpster in July.
87. Possums have several reptilian traits, including scales on the tail, a flat-footed gait, a small **cerebrum** in the brain lacking **sulci** (hence less surface area for though), and a forked penis in males, resembling reptile hemipenes.
88. Additionally, they have a lower body temperature than most mammals (which makes them immune to rabies) and they seem to have no sense of self-preservation. The greatest ambition of most possums is the dream of hearing a loud 'thud', while ending up smeared across four lanes of asphalt by the tires of a passing 18-wheeler.
89. The **Order Paucituberculata** includes the shrew possums. They are rat-sized South American possums that differ from true possums, in that they have hairy tails and completely different dentition from true possums.
90. Unlike true possums, they have two huge lower incisors used to prey on insects and small animals. They also have far fewer teeth than true possums, a three-chambered stomach, and corkscrew-shaped penises in males.
91. Many scientists think shrew possums are the evolutionary link to the rest of marsupials and that they resemble the earliest possums to evolve. The most compelling piece of evidence is the complete absence of a **pouch.**
92. Unlike the great majority of marsupials, they keep their underdeveloped young in a burrow as they grow up.
93. **Superorder Australidelphia** contains a large number of divergent species of marsupials. Their diversity is due to the **adaptive radiation** that the first marsupials underwent, filing each absent ecological niche as they colonized.
94. It is hard to generalize very many common morphological features, due to their widely different evolutionary patterns, as DNA sequencing provides most of the evidence of common ancestry.
95. However, it can be generalized that most members of **Australidelphia** have higher degrees of intelligence and brain development, different dentition, and highly evolved musculoskeletal systems, as compared to possums.
96. The diagram below depicts members of all classifications of marsupials.

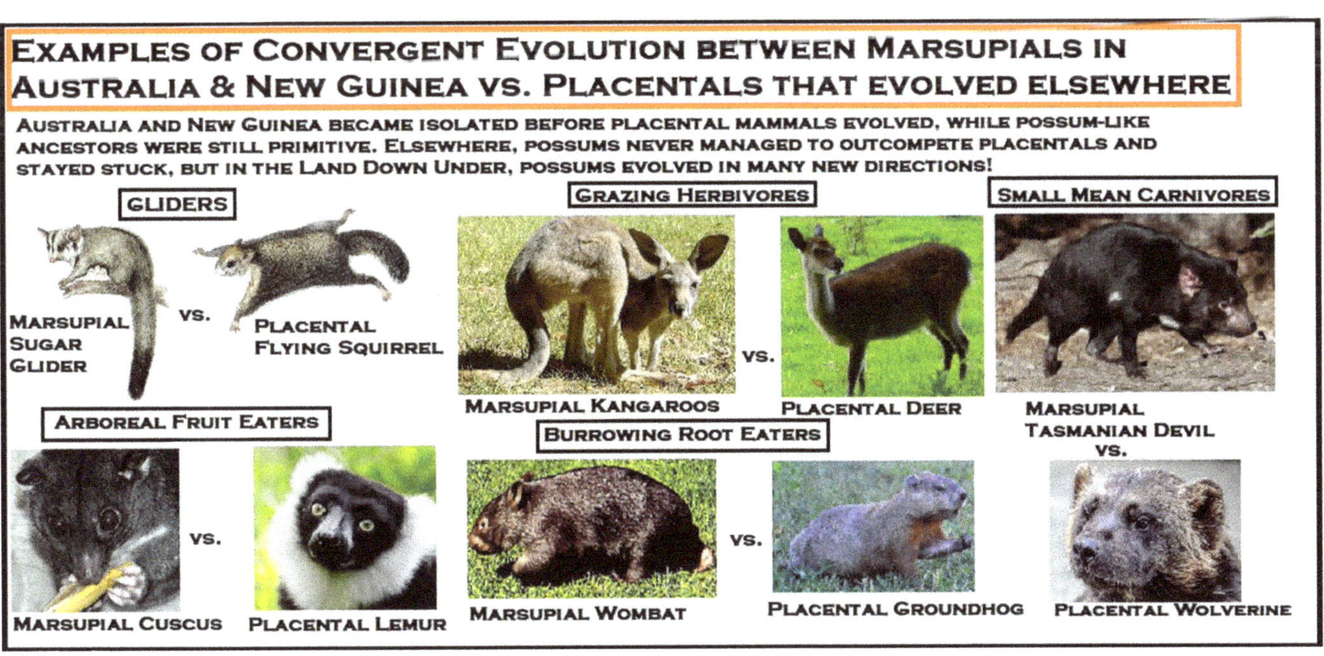

Infraclass Marsupiala (Selected Representatitves)

A) Order Didelphimorpha; Family Didelphidae (Virginia Possum) Primitive brain, low body temperature, flat walking gait, scaled tail, forked penis in males.

B) Superorder Australidelphia; Order Dasyuromorphia (Numbat) Mongoose-like striped body. Not closely related to any other marsupials (DNA). Termite eaters with an extra tooth between molars and pre-molars and sticky tongue.

C) Superorder Australidelphia; Order Dasyuromorphia (Tasmanian Devil) Burrow dwelling wolverine-like predator. Prehensile thumb-like front claw. Bite is more powerful than any other mammal. Highly evolved ability to regulate body temp.

D) Order Paucituberculta; Family Caenolestidae (Dusky Caenolestid) Native to deep Amazon forests. Primitive insectivorous ancestral marsupials that lack a pouch. Young raised in burrows. Dentition and furry tail differ from possums.

E) Superorder Australidelphia; Order Diprotodontia (Koala) Niche-dependent consumer of Eucalyptus leaves. Vestigial tail, two opposable claws on front feet, ridges on hands to stay in tree. Pouches have sphincters to hold young in.

F) Superorder Australidelphia; Order Diprodontia (Wombat) Groundhog-like burrowing herbivores that consume roots and grasses. Backward-facing pouch to avoid dropping baby when burrowing. Mark territory with cube-shaped poop.

97. So both aforementioned groups of blokes (monotremes and marsupials) come from the land down under.

98. Let's pause for a second and review the Australian National Anthem, which was recorded by Men-At-Work in 1982. It may not be the 'official' national anthem, but we all know the truth. Your quiz is on the next page

QUIZ: DO YOU COME FROM THE LAND DOWN UNDER?

1) **Referred to as a 'Kombi' in the song, what type of transportation is this (also seen in the video)?**
2) **What did the strange lady do for the singer?**
3) **Where did the singer buy bread from the man who was 6 foot 4 and full of muscles?**
4) **What did the smiling muscled man give to the singer after he asked him if he speaks his language?**
5) **Repeated several times, why does the singer warn the listener to take cover?**
6) **Where was the singer when he accused a man of trying to tempt him?**
7) **Why couldn't the singer be tempted?**
8) **In the song, Australian women are said to do what, while men do what?**

99. We now move on to the kings of the mammalian dominion, the **placental mammals**. Placental mammals have distinct advantages of marsupials in their reproduction, their intelligence, and their physical adaptations.

100. Placental mammals have **long gestations**, allowing time for offspring to develop to a much greater degree. Additionally, they are able to deal with multiple births more easily, since they aren't limited by pouch room.

101. This is all possible because the **placenta** replaces the **yolk sac** in these mammals. The placenta provides a constant pipeline of nutrients to the developing fetus, via the mother's bloodstream.

102. Due to this major advantage, marsupials in the Americas and Asia were not able to compete with placentals for any advanced ecological niches. Only possums and shrew possums exist on these continents.

103. In Australia, kangaroos developed in the niche that deer (placentals) won in the other locations, groundhogs took the niche of wombats, flying squirrels replaced sugar gliders, cats took the niche of quolls, and so on.

104. There are other major anatomical differences between **marsupials** and **placentals** as well.

105. Almost all marsupials have a set of V-shaped **epipubic bones** that are completely absent in placentals. These are stick-like bones that extend from a joint on the **pubis**. They are intended to support a pouch with a baby.

106. The ankle bones of **placental mammals** are better-designed to support their weight, forming a grooved joint with the ends of the **tibia** and **fibula** that is absent in marsupials.

107. As a general rule, most placental mammals (but not in all cases) would win a battle of wits with a typical marsupial. Unilaterally, the most intelligent orders of mammals with the largest brains are placentals.

108. All placental mammals belong to **Infraclass Eutheria**. From there, they are subdivided into three different **clades** that group orders together with putative ancestral and DNA connections. Additionally, there are a number of ungrouped orders that do not share such close evolutionary connections.

109. **Clade Afrotheria** includes elephants, hyraxes, aardvarks, manatees, elephant shrews, tenrecs, and others.

110. **Clade Xenarthia** includes sloths, armadillos, and anteaters

111. **Clade Boreoeutheria** includes primates, hares, rabbits, hedgehogs, shrews, and others.

112. Bats, rodents, carnivores, even-toed hoofed animals, odd-toed hoofed animals, pangolins, pinnipeds, and whales do not belong to a clade. Their evolutionary histories are considered too distant to other groups.

113. Let's now begin our journey through the different orders of **placental mammals** by looking at examples of **Afrotherian mammals**. We begin with the clade **Afroinsectivora**, which contains three extant orders.

114. All members of **Afroinsectivora** have at least some dietary component consisting of insects, as the name would imply, and they all have long flexible snouts and unusual dentition. Tenrecs, elephant shrews, and aardvarks belong to this clade. The diagram below depicts these representatives.

AFROTHERIAN PLACENTAL MAMMAL CLADE AFROINSECTIVORA

A) FAMILY TENRECIDAE (LOWLAND STREAKED TENREC) SMALL OMNIVOROUS NOCTURNAL MAMMALS WITH POOR EYESIGHT, HIGHLY SENSITIVE WHISKERS AND HEARING. PRIMITIVE IN THAT THEY HAVE A CLOACAL OPENING LIKE REPTILES. LOW BODY TEMPERATURE & INTERNAL TESTES.

B) FAMILY ORYPTEROPODIDAE (AARDVARK) ONLY EXTANT MEMBER OF FAMILY. LONG TUBULAR SNOUT. MOLARS ARE ONLY TEETH AND LACK ENAMEL. LARGE EARS TO RADIATE HEAT. CURVED THIGH BONES FOR LEVERAGE. CLAWS FOR DIGGING FOR TERMITES AND ANTS. RELEASE MUSK DURING MATING SEASON. SOLITARY OTHER THAN DURING BREEDING.

C) FAMILY MACROSCELIDEA (GIANT ELEPHANT SHREW) LONG PROBING SNOUTED INSECTIVORES WITH GRINDING TEETH IN THEIR CHEEK FOR EXOSKELETONS. TRUNK CAN BE FLEXED TO GRAB FOOD. LONG LEGS AND EXTREMELY FAST RUNNERS. ONLY ASSOCIATE FOR BREEDING.

115. Now we move on to the other clade of Afrotherians. Elephants, manatees dugongs, and hyraxes all belong to **Clade Paenungulata**. Visual inspection of these wildly different animals might make you think the taxonomists that organized these into a group were on the sauce. However, DNA evidence suggests common ancestry.

116. Elephants and hyraxes share similarities between the anatomy of their respective tusks and front teeth. They have similarly shaped toenails and foot pads as well.

117. Additionally, males of both groups have internal testicles and females have similar placental anatomy and very long gestation periods. Their nipples are under their front legs, rather than on the belly.

118. Sirenians, like manatees, also have similar toenails, both have pachyderm skin with bristles, and their bone structures suggest that they once had hoofed ancestors....the same ancestors as the other groups.

119. Speaking of manatees, most people aren't aware that their offspring are actually not called calves. The proper name for a sub-adult individual is 'boyatee'. Another name for adult manatees is 'BAM! What did I hit?'

120. The diagrams below depict families belonging to **Clade Paenungulata.**

AFROTHERIAN PLACENTAL MAMMALS

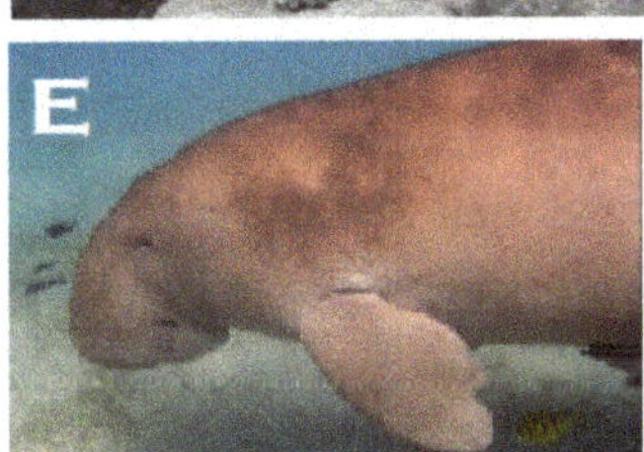

A) FAMILY ELEPHANTIDAE (AFRICAN FOREST ELEPHANT) TRUNK HAS 150,000 MUSCLES THAT GIVE FINE MOTOR CONTROL OR INCREDIBLE POWER. EARS ACT AS RADIATORS. EXTREMELY LARGE & HEAVY MUSCULOSKELETAL SYSTEM. LIVE IN MATRIARCHAL FAMILY SOCIETIES WITH HIGHLY ORGANIZED SOCIAL STRUCTURES.

B) FAMILY ELEPHANTIDAE (INDIAN ELEPHANT) EARS AND TUSKS ARE SMALLER THAN AFRICAN RELATIVES. TEMPERAMENT IS CALMER. DIGEST FOOD BY CECAL FERMENTATION. LEG BONES ARE SOLID, RATHER THAN HAVE MEDULLARY CAVITY. CONNECTIVE TISSUES AROUND LUNGS PROVIDE SUPPORT AGAINST WEIGHT.

C) FAMILY PROCAVIIDAE (ROCK HYRAX) TRUNK-LIKE SNOUT MUSCLES, TRUNK-LIKE FRONT TEETH, FOOT PADS, CRESCENT TOENAILS RESEMBLE ELEPHANTS. OMNIVOROUS DIET OF PLANTS, EGGS, INSECTS, FRUIT. LIVE IN FAMILY GROUPS IN ROCK CREVICES. FEMALE HAS 8 MONTH GESTATION AND LONG-TERM CARE.

D) FAMILY TRICECHIDAE (WEST INDIAN MANATEE) VESTIGIAL PELVIS WITH A FEW REMNANT INTERNAL BONES. FRONT LEGS MODIFIED INTO FLIPPERS. FERMENTIVE GUT FOR HERBIVOROUS DIET. PAYCHDERM SKIN. HIGH PARENTAL CARE.

E) FAMILY DUGONGIDAE (DUGONG) HORSESHOE-SHAPED UPPER LIP USED LIKE A VACUUM CLEANER ATTACHMENT TO FORAGE FOR SEA GRASS. POOR EYESIGHT, FLIPPERS ARE MORE FULLY FORMED THAN IN MANATEES. MALES HAVE TUSKS.

LAND DOWN UNDER QUIZ ANSWERS

1: VW Van

2: Took him in and made him breakfast

3: Brussels, Belgium

4: A Vegemite Sandwich

5: Presumably a storm is on the way. "Can't you hear the thunder?"

6: Bombay, India

7: Because he comes from a land of plenty. He probably has what he needs.

8) Women glow and the men plunder.

121. Now we move on to the bizarre **Clade Xenarthra**. This group includes the anteaters, tree sloths, and armadillos.

122. While fossil records and DNA systematics say that the members of this group are distant relatives, superficial inspection doesn't make this obvious. No one ever looked up in a tree and mistook a sloth for an armadillo.

123. However, the members of this group share a number of strange anatomical features that don't match up with other mammals. The **vertebral processes** of **Xenarthrans** have jointed articulations, making the spine flexible.

124. Additionally, female members of this group don't have a distinct **uterus** and vagina, like most placental mammals do. It is one continuous structure. Male xenarthrans have internal **testicles**.

125. The testes are internal, due to the fact that they have some of the lowest body temperatures of all mammals. This accounts for their slow metabolism, and the fact that sloths spend almost 90% of their existence sleeping.

126. While anteaters lack them altogether, the teeth of the other **Xenarthrans** are not rooted and lack enamel. Instead, a layer of calcified connective tissue called **cementum** protects the **dentin** layer.

127. Armadillos have a reduced number of peg-like teeth, while sloths lack any canines and incisors, using the molars in the back of their mouths to grind leaves very, very slowly.

128. Xenarthrans were formerly grouped with pangolins and aardvarks, due to their absence or reduction of teeth, until it became obvious via DNA analysis, the other animals were unrelated cases of convergent evolution.

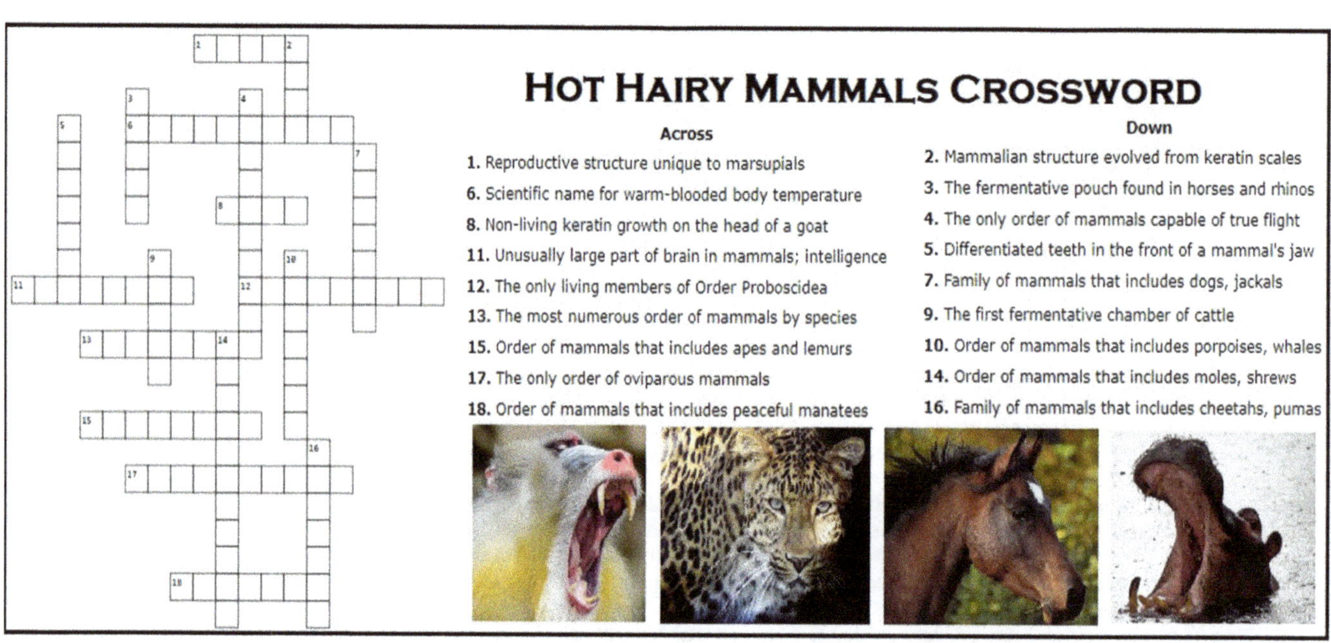

129. The diagram below depicts several members of this clade and describes their characteristics.

Xenarthran Placental Mammals

A) Family Chlamyphoridae (Pink Fairy Armadillo) Fluffy white hair on ventral surface of body. Thin, flexible nail-like keratin plates are used to regulate body temperature and roll into protective ball. Extremely fast burrower.

B) Family Chlamyphoridae (Six-Banded Armadillo) Six rows of keratin scales with bristle-like hairs in-between. Wedge-like plates on tympanic bone behind ears. Omnivorous insect eaters and scavengers. Scent glands between plates.

C) Family Dasypodidae (Nine-Banded Armadillo) Nine rows of keratin scales with bristle-like hairs in between. Tympanic bone shaped differently, teeth smaller than other family of armadillos. Wedge-like claws for digging ants & termites.

D) Family Bradypodidae (Brown Throated Sloth) Three sets of blade-like claws for hanging from trees. No incisors or canines. Digestive tract lacks cecum or gall bladder, but have 4-chambered fermentive stomach that is VERY slow.

E) Family Cholopolidae (Linnaeus's Two Toed Sloth) Two sets of blade-like claws Heavier-bodied, longer arms than three-toed sloths. Teeth reduced to only 5 pairs. DNA shows convergent evolution with 2-toed sloths, not close relation.

F) Family Myrmecophagidae (Giant Anteater). Toothless nozzle-like snout lacks teeth, but has long sticky tongue for trapping ants. Tongue is attached to sternum, allowing it to flick ants 3 times per second. Walks on front knuckles.

130. The next stop on our journey through mammals is our own putative home. Primates belong to a largest clade of mammals known as **Boreoeutherians**, along with shrews, rodents, flying lemurs, rabbits, hedgehogs, and moles.

131. About now, you may be asking yourself how any of these animals could possibly be that closely related to us. It isn't so much that they are still close relatives, it's that the males have a **scrotum** with external testes.

132. Yes, you read that right. Tracing back through the fossil records, a common ancestor to all these groups can be found about 70 million years back. Likewise, DNA analysis shows these groups to be more closely related to one another than to mammals in other outgroups.

133. Many (but not all) members of **Magnorder Boreoeutheria** have opposable thumbs for gripping, a large brain to body ratio, and color binocular vision. They retain a **cecum**, but none have compartmentalized digestion.
134. With that said, 70 million years is a long time for your morphological features to diverge and evolve into something very different than what was there in the beginning.
135. It appears that the first major evolutionary split of the **Boreoeutherians** divided the group up into two smaller clades known as **Clade Glires** and **Clade Euarchonta**, with most members of the former group adapted for terrestrial life and the ancient members of the latter adapted for life in the trees.
136. There are certainly many exceptions to the ground/tree rule in BOTH clades, but these exceptions are cases of later evolutionary strategy changes to fill open ecological niches (for instance, tree squirrels).
137. **Clade Glires** includes the **Order Lagomorpha** (rabbits, pikas, and hares) and **Order Rodentia**.
138. **Clade Euarchonta** includes **Order Primates** (monkeys, apes, hominids, and others), **Order Dermoptera** (flying lemurs), and **Order Scadentia** (tree shrews).
139. Let's begin in Clade Glires with the Order Lagomorpha. Rabbits, hares, and pikas all have acute hearing, tend to burrow, and are generally prolific reproducers. They have several unique features that distinguish them from their closest relatives in **Order Rodentia**.
140. Rabbit skulls have a distinct difference from rodents, in that the bone in the back of the eye socket, the **post-orbital process** is solidly fused to the rest of the cranium and to the cheekbones.
141. Rabbits, hares, and pikas all have four incisors, whereas rodents have a single pair of continuously growing incisors used for gnawing. Lagomorphs are herbivores with a fermentive gut, rather than omnivores.
142. The foot pads of rodents are bare, whereas, lagomorph feet are furry, assisting them in being stealth.
143. The diagram below depicts several members of Order Lagomorpha.

144. Now we move on to **Order Rodentia**, a sister taxa to the lagamorphs that share a common ancestry.
145. As previously mentioned, the dentition or rodents is distinctly different from that of lagomorphs, in that they have only two pairs of orange-colored continuously growing **incisors** used in gnawing.

146. The **masseter muscles** of the cheeks are enlarged, allowing them to generate considerable cutting and rasping force. Hence, beavers can drop gigantic trees, dam up streams, and flood expensive lake homes.

147. Most rodents have plump short torsos and short powerful limbs. Many have claws used for burrowing. All rodents have opposable thumbs on their front feet and bare foot pads used for gripping.

148. Several groups of rodents have extra lateral skin folds that are unique to the order.

149. Hamsters, chipmunks, and squirrels have such folds extending as **cheek pouches** along the neck, which they use in gathering and storing food. Flying squirrels have extra skin on the torso between the limbs for gliding.

150. Most rodents are moderately or highly intelligent and have a relatively large brain-to-body ratio, which is somewhat of a paradox, since their brains lack **sulci** and are not deeply folded like many mammals.

151. Rats, for instance, are capable of learning by classical and operant conditioning, remembering associations between stimuli, and some experiments have suggested that they are also self-aware.

152. Beyond some of these general commonalities, rodents are a highly evolved taxa of mammals, with considerably different adaptations and morphology between families.

153. The first major branch of **Order Rodentia** belong to **Suborder Hystricomorpha**. These rodents have a very large opening for muscular articulations beneath the eye orbit that extends between the cheeks and jaw.

154. This allows a wide range of motion for powerful scissor-like incisors. Members of this group are shown below.

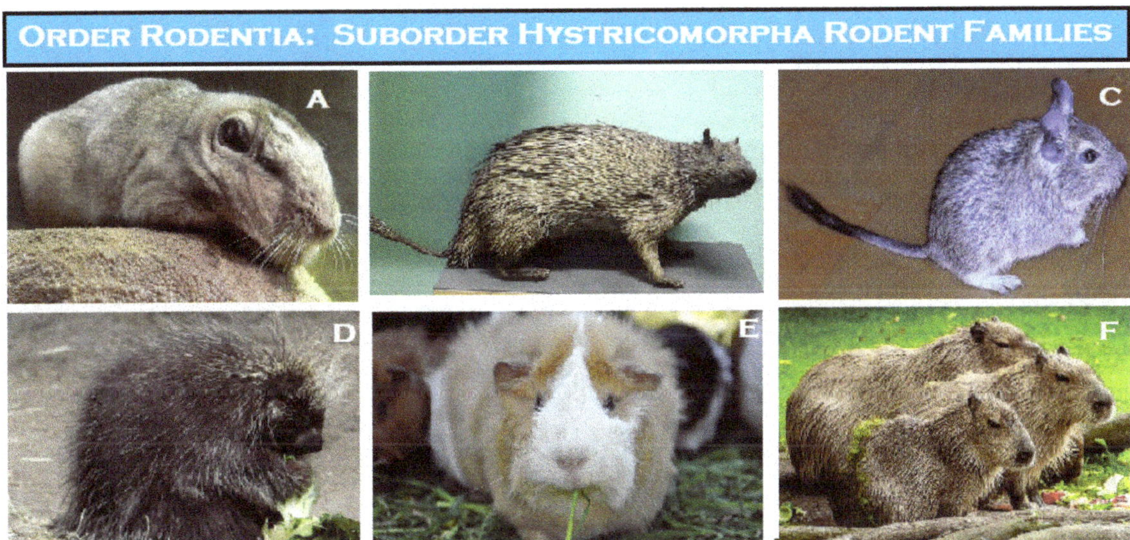

A) FAMILY CTENDACTYLIDAE (NORTH AFRICAN GUNDI) SHORT-BODIED STOCKY ROCK DWELLERS WITH SHORT TAILS, FOUR TOES ON FEET, BRISTLES BETWEEN BACK TOES. TEETH LACK ORANGE ENAMEL. LIVE IN COLONIES AND SOUND ALARM CALLS AT PREDATORS. EAT SUCCULENT PLANTS.

B) FAMILY HYSTRICIDAE (ASIAN BRUSHTAIL PORCUPINE) SMALL ELONGATED BODIES WITH SHORT SHARP QUILLS AND A TAIL THAT ENDS IN A 'BRUSH' MADE OF QUILLS. LIVE IN BURROWING SOCIAL GROUPS. MOSTLY FEED ON ROOTS, BUDS, FRUIT, BUT WILL ALSO EAT INSECTS AND EGGS.

C) FAMILY OCTODONTIDAE (MOUNTAIN DEGU) SMALL SOUTH AMERICAN RODENTS WITH LONG BUSHY TAIL USED FOR BALANCE WHEN CLIMBING. COUNTERSHADED WITH GRAY OR BROWN FUR ON BACK AND WHITE ON BELLY. HERBIVORES THAT FEED ON BARK, LEAVES, AND CACTI.

D) FAMILY ERITHOZONTIDAE (NORTH AMERICAN PORCUPINE) HAVE TRUE MOLARS, CLAVICLES, AND LACK THUMBS ON FRONT FEET, WHICH DIFFERS FROM OLD WORLD PORCUPINES. LARGE, STOUT ARBOREAL RODENTS THAT EAT FRUIT, NUTS, FLOWERS, SEEDS. QUILLS INTERSPERSED IN HAIR.

E) FAMILY CAVIIDAE (DOMESTIC GUINEA PIG) VESTIGIAL SHORT TAIL. HAVE CHEEK POUCHES FOR FOOD STORAGE. SHORT, STOUT BODY. COLONIAL MOUNTAIN-DWELLERS THAT FEED ON SEEDS, GRASS, GREENS. SHELTER IN CREVICES, BUT DON'T BURROW. LARGE RANGE OF VOCALIZATIONS.

G) FAMILY CAVIIDAE (CAPYBARA) LARGEST RODENT THAT CAN ATTAIN 150 POUNDS. AQUATIC IN NATURE, FEEDING ON REEDS, AQUATIC VEGETATION. LIVE IN LARGE FAMILY GROUPS, COMMUNICATE WITH WHISTLES, CLICKS. FRONT FEET HAVE 3 TOES, BACK FEET HAVE 4 TOES.

155. The next sub-order of rodents are those with squirrel-like characteristics. **Order Sciuromorpha** includes rodents where there is a distinct separation between the **masseter muscle** and the cheekbone arches.

156. Many members of this order also have **cheek pouches** and have mostly evolved in two directions. Arboreal members of the group have long tails for balance, while the rest are short-tailed burrowers.

157. Another feature is that many of its members like to commit suicide by chewing on electrical transformers and exploding in a shower of sparks, before landing on the pavement as a steaming barbecued squirrel.

158. Which is all poetic justice for those little punks. Squirrels are not your friends. When they aren't trying to chew their way into your attic, barking at you to blow your cover on hunting trips, or stealing from bird feeders, they spend a lot of their time plotting to kill you or take over the world.

159. The diagram below shows members of several different families of squirrel-like rodents.

ORDER RODENTIA: SUBORDER SCIUROMORPHA RODENT FAMILIES

A) FAMILY APLONTIDAE (MOUNTAIN BEAVER) PRIMITIVE SKULL AND MUSCLE STRUCTURE. MUCH SHORTER MASSETER MUSCLE THAN ALL OTHER RODENTS. ARE NOT BEAVERS, IN SPITE OF NAME. LIVE NEAR WATER, BUT DO NOT BUILD DAMS. EAT MOSTLY FERNS AND CAN CLIMB TREES.

B) FAMILY SCIURIDAE (RED SQUIRREL) ARBOREAL NEST-BUILDERS THAT EAT SEEDS AND NUTS. CHEEK POUCHES USED FOR FORAGING AND STORAGE FOR LATER. MATE DURING WINTER ACCORDING TO SOCIAL HIERARCHIES, HAVE 3 KITS IN NEST THAT EMERGE DURING SPRING.

C) FAMILY MARMOTINI (EASTERN CHIPMUNK) A SMALL GROUND SQUIRREL THAT CAN CLIMB TREES BUT PREFERS TO HIDE IN BURROWS. USES CHEEK POUCHES TO TRANSFER DIRT OUT AS THEY DIG. ONLY SOCIALIZE DURING MATING. FORAGES FOR NUTS, BUDS, FRUIT, FLOWER BULBS, INSECTS.

D) FAMILY MARMOTINI (YELLOW-BELLIED MARMOT) A SOCIAL COLONIAL GROUND SQUIRREL THAT CAN GET CAT-SIZED. DIG BURROWS UNDER ROCKY GROUND, DUE TO CONSTANT FEAR OF RAPTORS. DIURNAL GRAZERS OF GRASS, WEEDS, SEEDS, EGGS. HIBERNATE FOR MORE THAN HALF OF LIVES.

E) FAMILY SCIURIDAE (SOUTHERN FLYING SQUIRREL) SECRETIVE, NOCTURNAL, ONLY LEAVE TREE CAVITIES TO FORAGE FOR LICHENS, NUTS, BERRIES, INSECTS. MEMBRANE BETWEEN LEGS CALLED PATAGIUM IS USED LIKE A HANG-GLIDER. USE TAIL AND OUTSTRETCHED LEGS LIKE PARACHUTES.

F) FAMILY GLIRIDAE (FAT DORMOUSE) MOUSE-LIKE APPEARANCE, BUT TAIL IS FURRY AND JAW IS BUILT LIKE A SQUIRREL. MOST HAVE NO PREMOLARS IN JAW. FOSSILS INDICATE THAT THEY ARE ONE OF OLDEST TYPES OF RODENTS. GORGE IN SUMMER AND SPEND 6 MONTHS HIBERNATING.

160. As you have probably surmised by being alive, rodents are QUITE successful in evolving and filling ecological species. There are A LOT of them. Forrest Gump and Bubba could have a LONG listing session.

161. 'Field mice, dormice, cotton rats, Norway rats, black rats, muskrats, chipmunks, beavers, nutrias, capybaras, fried mice, boiled mice, mouse Creole, popcorn mice, mouse scampi.....3 days later....'And that's about it.....'

162. Rodents make up nearly 50% of all living mammal species. This is the nice way of saying, there's MORE.

163. **Order Castorimorpha** contains the beavers and kangaroo rats. It is bizarre that these guys are related, but DNA fingerprints show that they clearly evolved from a common ancestor and are distantly related to other groups.

164. The front incisors are enlarged and extend past the lower incisors in both types of rodents, and the **masseter muscle** is rooted underneath and almost parallel to the **zygomatic arch** (cheek bones).

165. Both types of animals also use their front ever-growing front incisors as cutting tools.

166. In the case of beavers, they like to gnaw down aspen trees and flood people's lake subdivision homes. Kangaroo rats use their giant incisors as a weapon to fight off snakes and to attack grasshoppers and crickets for prey.

ORDER RODENTIA: SUBORDER CASTORIMORPHA RODENT FAMILIES

A) FAMILY HETEROMYIDAE (DESERT KANGAROO RAT) BIPEDAL RODENTS THAN CAN JUMP OFF OF BACK LEGS. NOCTURNAL DESERT BURROWERS THAT ARE OMNIVOROUS. LARGE PAIR OF INCISORS ARE USED TO DEFEND THEMSELVES AGAINST SNAKES. OMNIVOROUS. MAKE HIGH-PITCHED CRIES.

B) FAMILY GEOMYIDAE (MOUNTAIN POCKET GOPHER) SOLITARY BURROWERS THAT RARELY GO TO SURFACE. DIG NETWORK OF TUNNELS UNDERNEATH VEGETATION, WHICH THEY PULL INTO BURROW AND FEED ON ROOTS, SHOOTS. POOR VISION. CHEEK POUCHES EMPTIED INTO TUNNEL FOOD STASH.

C) FAMILY CASTORIDAE (NORTH AMERICAN BEAVER) HEAVY-BODIED DAM-BUILDERS THAT LIVE IN MONOGAMOUS PAIRS WITH YOUNG. DAMS USUALLY HAVE UNDERWATER ENTRANCE. EAT REEDS, BARK, VEGETATION. TAIL STORES FAT. ANAL GLANDS MAKE VANILLA-SCENTED MUSK (CASTOREUM).

CIVICS TEACHER CONSTITUTIONAL STUDY BREAK QUIZ

1) WHICH AMENDMENT WAS THE ONLY ONE EVER REPEALED?
2) WHAT ARE THE MINIMUM AGES FOR A U.S. REPRESENTATIVE AND A SENATOR?
3) WHAT MAJORITY VOTE IS REQUIRED TO TERMINATE A U.S. REPRESENTATIVE?
4) FROM WHICH ARTICLE DOES THE U.S. PRESIDENT DERIVE HIS POWERS?
5) WHY DO MOST PEOPLE HATE THE 16TH AMENDMENT?

ANSWERS PG. 233

167. Now we arrive at **Order Muroidea**, which account for the largest number of mammals of any order, by a long shot. While rodents are 50% of all known mammal species, rats and mice account for about 40% on their own.

168. To be bluntly honest, only an expert could distinguish between hundreds of species of small brown vermin.

169. To be even more honest, unless said experts work for a pest control company, they should probably re-evaluate the true value of their life's work.....but then again, in a confessed moment of self-awareness, I'm the one sitting here writing this book full of obscure biology facts.

170. Yes, you are about 800 pages into a book that consists of information that is mostly only likely to be directly profitable if it helps you win a free plate of nachos some day on trivia night at Pootie's Bar and Grill

171. Real wisdom posits that it is easier to avoid personal responsibility and self-reflection, so I'm going to keep going and we'll both pretend that an expansive knowledge of rodents will help you find true love and make millions.

172. Members of **Order Muroidea** have incisors that overlap with a narrow margin. Their pork-chop shaped masseter muscles sit completely underneath the cheekbones.

173. Mice and rats also use an enlarged **temporalis muscle** to tear and masticate food. In a sense, all the rodents in this group have a 'fivehead' that extends all the way from their ears to their eyes.

174. The diagram below shows representatives of **Order Muroidea**.

ORDER RODENTIA: SUBORDER MUROIDEA RODENT FAMILIES

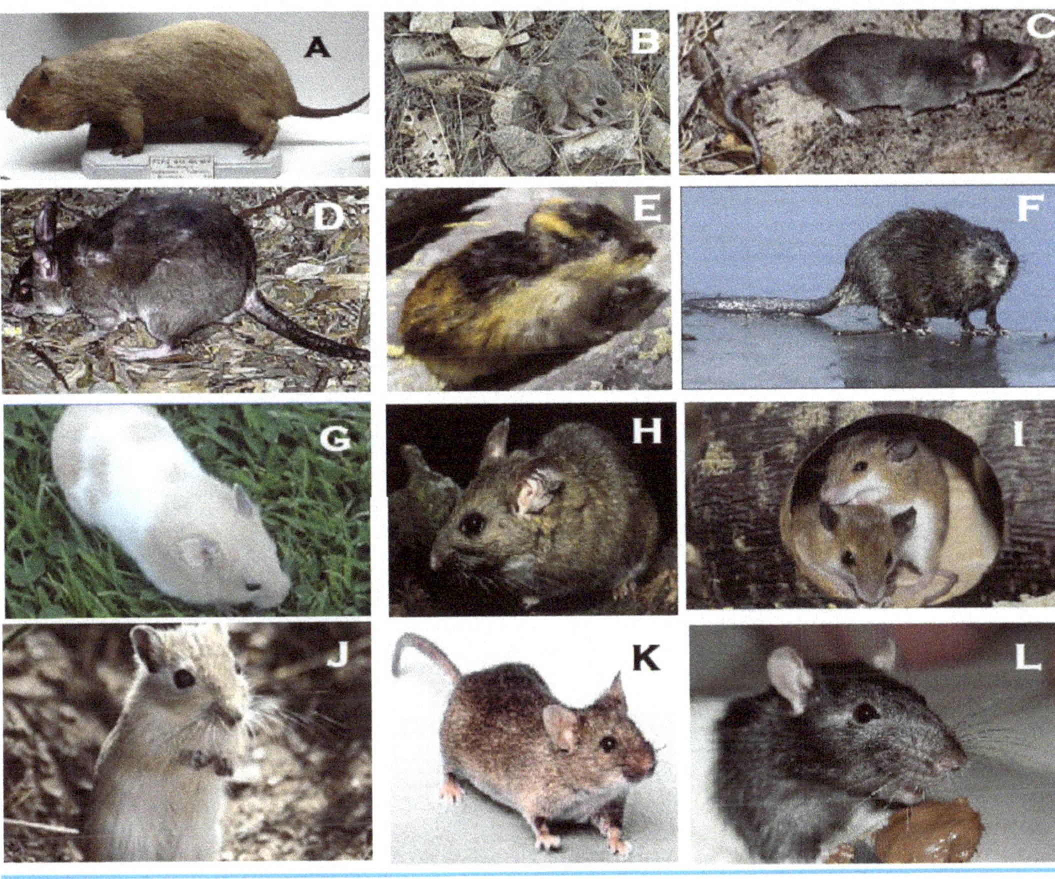

A) FAMILY RHIZOMYINAE (LARGE BAMBOO RAT) NOCTURNAL BURROWERS THAT EAT ROOTS AND RHIZOMES (ESPECIALLY BAMBOO). LACK CHEEK POUCHES. PLUMP BODY.

B) FAMILY CALOMYSCIDAE (AZERBAIJANI MOUSE-LIKE HAMSTER) SHARE A COMMON ANCESTOR WITH HAMSTERS, BUT LACK CHEEK POUCHES, SCENT GLANDS. LONG TAIL.

C) FAMILY CRICETOMYINAE (LONG-TAILED POUCHED RAT) NOCTURNAL BURROWERS WITH EXTREMELY SENSITIVE OLFACTION, LONG TAILS, MASSIVE CHEEK POUCHES.

D) FAMILY NESOMYINAE (MALAGASY GIANT RAT) UNUSUAL RODENT, IN THAT THEY ARE MONOGAMOUS AND ONLY HAVE 1-2 OFFSPRING PER YEAR. NOCTURNAL FORAGERS.

E) FAMILY ARVICOLINAE (NORWAY LEMMING) TEETH ARE UNIQUE IN THAT MOLARS ARE TRIANGLE-SHAPED. SHORT TAILS. DO NOT ACTUALLY COMMIT MASS SUICIDE.

F) FAMILY ARVICOLINAE (MUSKRAT) CHUNKY AQUATIC RODENTS THAT FEED ON ROOTS AND REEDS. BURROW INTO SIDES OF RIVER BANKS. SCALY TAIL. MUSK GLANDS.

G) FAMILY CRICETIDAE (SYRIAN HAMSTER) GIGANTIC CHEEK POUCHES, VESTIGIAL TAIL, STOUT BODY. FERMENT FIBROUS FOOD IN CECUM. MUSK MARK TERRITORIES.

H) FAMILY CRICETIDAE (RIPARIAN WOODRAT) BUILD MASSIVE NESTS IN CREVICES, INCLUDING HOUSES. STORE FOOD IN NEST, ALONG WITH OTHER RANDOM OBJECTS.

I) FAMILY MURIDAE (AFRICAN PYGMY MOUSE) EXTREMELY FECUND. CAN BREED AT 2 MONTHS OF AGE, HAVE 100'S OF YOUNG OVER LIFESPAN. DOMESTICATED AS PETS.

J) FAMILY MURIDAE (MONGOLIAN GERBIL) NATIVE TO NORTH ASIAN STEPPES, LIVE IN PATRIARCHAL GROUPS, WITH DOMINANT MALE AND FEMALES MATING. KEPT AS PETS.

K) FAMILY MURIDAE (HOUSE MOUSE) GLOBAL RESIDENT OF CITIES, HOMES. SPECIES HAS BEEN DOMESTICATED FOR MEDICAL RESEARCH, PETS. OMNIVOROUS NESTERS.

L) FAMILY MURIDAE (NORWAY RAT) HIGHLY ADAPTABLE GLOBAL RESIDENT OF HOMES, SEWERS, ETC. HIGHLY INTELLIGENT. DISEASE VECTOR FOR BUBONIC PLAGUE FLEAS.

175. The final group of rodents belong to **Order Dipodoidea**. All members of the group have kangaroo-like back legs capable of propelling them long distances through the air.
176. Additionally, rodents in this group have a large gap between the gnawing incisors in the front of their mouth and the premolars in the back. Their jaw muscles, again, are also uniquely positioned among its members.
177. Most of these rodents live in colder climates, many live in deserts, and long hibernations are the norm.
178. Additionally, many species have ears like radar dishes that funnel distant sounds and radiate heat to keep cool.
179. The diagram below shows examples of families within Order Dipodoidea.

ORDER RODENTIA: SUBORDER DIPODOIDEA RODENT FAMILIES

A) FAMILY SMINTHIDAE (CHINESE BIRCH MOUSE) BURROWERS THAT EMERGE TO FEED ON SHOOTS, BUDS, BERRIES. PREHENSILE TAIL. LEAP FROM TREE-TO-TREE.

B) FAMILY ZAPODIDAE (OREGON JUMPING MOUSE)TWO INCISORS, NO CANINES, ONLY ONE PREMOLAR. LIVE IN MARSHES. DOUBLE WEIGHT FOR HIBERNATION.

C) FAMILY ALLACTIGINAE (FOUR-TOED JERBOA) MASSIVE TARSALS FOR LEAPING LIKE A KANGAROO. FLAT MOLARS FOR DIET OF GRASS & SEEDS. NOCTURAL.

180. As we continue our journey through **Magnorder Boreoeutheria**, we arrive at **Clade Euarchota** , which includes tree shrews and primates. These groups share a putative common ancestor with rodents and rabbits.
181. The presence of opposable thumbs is common to most groups, but so far, the only link between the groups is shared DNA sequences and similar locations of transposable elements in their genomes.
182. **Order Scadentia** includes the tree shrews, which are distinctly different from the mole-like ground shrews presented to you as cat gifts. Tree shrews superficially resemble squirrels, but they are anatomically different.
183. Tree shrews, unlike squirrels or other rodents, have **binocular vision**. Their eye orbitals are positioned on their skull to give them a 180 degree complete panoramic view, which aids in arboreal life.
184. Also like **primates**, they have a very high brain-to-body ratio and are more intelligent than rodents.
185. Also unlike rodents, they have unspecialized **molars** lacking cusps and a different **incisor** arrangement.
186. Tree shrews are omnivorous and work together in family groups to gather food.
187. **Order Dermatoptera** is another mammalian order that is in no-man's land. An evolutionary stopover, it includes the flying lemurs, which have a membrane between their arms and legs, which is used for gliding between trees.

188. They superficially resemble lemurs, but are not. They have several distinctive features that separate them from true primates. The most obvious is a row of comb-like **incisors** with dozens of tines used for grooming.

189. Unlike primates, their incisors are double-rooted in the **maxillary bone.**

190. Additionally, they also have webbing between their toes that prevents them from climbing effectively, they use their flying membranes as a pouch to carry their babies, and they lack opposable thumbs.

191. Otherwise, anatomically and genetically, there are a number of similarities to true primates. The second diagram below shows the Sunda colugo, one of two extant species of this obscure group.

192. The first diagram below shows a Northern tree shrew, which is a typical member of **Order Scadentia**. There are two other families of tree shrews, which are rather obscure, that have smooth tails and tufts on their tails.

ORDER SCADENTIA: TREE SHREWS

FAMILY TUPAIIDAE (NORTHERN TREE SHREW) DNA ANALYSIS SHOWS THEM TO BE CLOSER TO PRIMATES THAN TO RODENTS. WIDELY VARY THEIR BODY TEMPERATURE FROM DAY (ACTIVE) AND NIGHT (INACTIVE). USED BY GENETICISTS TO STUDY EVOLUTION. OMNIVORES THAT LIVE IN FAMILY GROUPS IN TREE TOPS.

ORDER DERMOPTERA: FLYING LEMURS

FAMILY CYNOCEPHALUS (SUNDA COLUGO) HAVE MOST EFFECTIVE GLIDING ABILITY OF ANY MAMMAL. CAN COVER OVER 200 FEET IN A SINGLE GLIDE. GET TO END OF BRANCHES BY HOPPING. FEED ON FLOWERS, NECTAR, FRUITS, LEAVES, AND BUDS AT NIGHT. SOLITARY AND RARELY SEEN. ONE OF TWO LIVING SPECIES. EVOLUTIONARY RELIC.

193. **Order Primates**, in regard to intelligence and intellectual capacity, is the most evolved group of mammals.

194. **Primates** can be divided into two suborders. **Suborder Strepsirrhini** contains the lemurs and lorises, while tarsiers, new world monkeys, old world monkeys, and apes belong to **Suborder Haplorhini**.

195. **Suborder Strepsirrhini** is restricted to the island of Madagascar. Much like the adaptive radiation that occurred in Australian marsupials as a result of early isolation of primitive ancestors, the same happened there.

196. Early primate ancestors diverged in two different directions when Madagascar became isolated from mainland Africa. On the continent, monkeys and apes evolved. Prosimians and lemurs evolved on Madagascar.

197. While it isn't always an accurate way to describe them, the **Strepsirrhinids** often have moist noses like a dog, whereas monkeys and other simians have dry noses. However, this is far from the best distinction to note.

198. Lemurs and lorises have smaller brain-to-body ratios, have larger olfactory bulbs in their brains, communicate with pheromones, have incisors modified for grooming their fur, and have a reflective membrane in their eye called a **tapetum lucidum**, since they are almost all nocturnal.

199. Additionally, the lower jaw of lemurs and lorises is divided into two distinct halves, while members of the **Order Haplorhini** have a full mandible. Additionally, the two groups have differently shaped ankle and leg bones.

200. Finally, lemurs and lorises have two **uterine horns** that each develop a **placenta**, whereas tarsiers, monkeys, and apes have a single apple-shaped uterus and placenta.

201. We will get to that all in a minute. By now you've probably guessed....another word from our sponsors.

CIVICS TEACHER CONSTITUTIONAL STUDY BREAK QUIZ ANSWERS

1) THE 18TH AMENDMENT FOR PROHIBITION OF ALCOHOL WAS REPEALED BY THE 21ST AMENDMENT.
2) U.S. REPRESENTATIVES MUST BE 25 OR OLDER; U.S. SENATORS MUST BE 30 OR OLDER.
3) A 2/3RD MAJORITY IS REQUIRED TO VOTE SOMEONE OUT OF CONGRESS FOR BEING A CROOK.
4) EXECUTIVE POWERS COME FROM ARTICLE II.
5) THE 16TH AMENDMENT ESTABLISHED THE INCOME TAX.

THE VIDEOGAME OF THE YEAR! EVERYONE IS RAVING ABOUT 'THE SKYRIM OF SCHOOL BUS DRIVING'! GET YOUR COPY NOW FOR XBOXX OR BS5. LIMITED QUANTITIES!

PLAY AS FRIENDLY PROTAGONIST MR. BOWERS, WHO OFTEN HAS CANDY, LIFE ADVICE AND PROTECTIVE WEAPONRY TO GIVE OUT TO THE KIDS.

FOLLOW ALL TRAFFICE LAWS AND DRIVE THE SPEED LIMIT TO SCHOOL! DON'T FORGET TO PUT ON YOUR FLASHING LIGHTS AND MAKE CARS STOP!

HAVE LOADS OF FUN SHUSHING YOUR KIDS AT RAILROAD CROSSINGS, MAKING THREATS TO ASSIGN SEATS, AND FILING DISCIPLINE REPORTS ON THE KIDS IN THE BACK WHO KEEP MOONING CARS.

THREATEN TO 'STOP THIS BUS RIGHT NOW!' AND MEAN IT. PULL OVER AND WAIT AN HOUR IF YOU LIKE!

DON'T HIT THE COWS, TRACTORS, CARS, TRUCKS, TRASHCANS, FIRE HYDRANTS, ELDERLY PEDESTRIANS, MAILBOXES OR LIONS AS YOU DRIVE TO SCHOOL.

WITH THE HELP OF STUDENTS DENNIS, BO, AND JACK, FIGHT OFF THE SCHOOL BUS CREEPER WHO KEEPS TRYING TO PUNCH HIS WAY ONTO YOUR BUS!

202. The diagram below shows representatives of several families of Strrepirrhinid primates.

HAIRY HEROES: FAMOUS NON-HUMAN PRIMATES IN HISTORY

KOKO THE GORILLA
FOREVER CHANGED THE WAY THE WORLD VIEWED GORILLAS. HAD AN IQ THAT MIGHT HAVE BEEN AS HIGH AS 95, KNEW MORE THAN 2000 WORDS IN SIGN LANGUAGE, HAD A PET CAT, AND ADORED MR. ROGERS.

KEN ALLEN THE ORANGUTAN
THE GREATEST ESCAPE ARTIST IN ZOO HISTORY, HE MANAGED TO GET OUT OF HIS EXHIBIT AT SAN DIEGO ZOO NINE TIMES! HE LIKED TO TOUR THE ZOO WHEN HE DID ESCAPE, LOOKING AT OTHER ANIMALS....EXCEPT THE TIME HE STARTED THROWING ROCKS AT ANOTHER ORANGUTAN HE DIDN'T LIKE.

ALBERT THE RHESUS MONKEY
ALBERT WAS A PIONEER IN SPACE EXPLORATION, AS HE WAS THE FIRST PRIMATE IN SPACE, LAUNCHED FROM WHITE SANDS, NEW MEXICO ABOARD A V-2 ROCKET. SADLY, THE FIRST ASTRONAUT IN HISTORY SUFFOCATED AND DID NOT MAKE IT BACK ALIVE.

JOVIAN THE SIFAKA LEMUR
THE OFFICIAL SPOKESLEMUR FOR DUKE UNIVERSITY LEMUR CENTER, HE HAD HIS OWN TV SHOW, COMPLETE WITH VOICEOVERS FROM A PROFESSIONAL PUPPETEER

BINX THE CAPUCHIN MONKEY
HUGE HOLLYWOOD STAR WHO HAD ROLES IN 'GEORGE OF THE 'JUNGLE' & ACE VENTURA FILMS.

Suborder Strepsirrhini Families

A) Family Lemuridae (Ring-Tailed Lemur) Cat-like body, diurnal omnivore. Scent-marking and complex communications. Can do math and use tools. Moves on ground with running hops.

B) Family Indridae (Diademed Sifaka) Live in small groups that establish a fixed scent-marked territory. Stubby hairless black face. Extremely large thumbs form a U-shape hand.

C) Family Cheirogaleidae (Goodman's Mouse Lemur) Females mate with multiple males and employ sperm competition, unlike most mammals. Tiny, secretive, omnivorous, and Nocturnal.

D) Family Lorisidae (Gray Slender Loris) Large binocular eyes for night vision. Omnivores. Long, skinny limbs & vestigial tail. Produce toxins from elbow glands to discourage predators.

E) Family Galagidae (Northern Greater Galago) A large bush baby that hops from tree-to-tree eating insects and fruit. Use scent to mark territories, which overlap for males & females.

F) Family Lepilemuridea (Red-Tailed Sportive Lemur) Nocturnal and Arboreal. Hop on back legs on ground. Solitary folivores. Cecum is enlarged to ferment leaves. Furry face, short snout.

203. Now we move on to the larger group of primates in **Suborder Haplorhini**. These are the 'dry nosed' primates.

204. I guess this implies that monkeys and people don't walk around cluelessly with snot dripping out of their nose. This is apparently the biggest qualification to be the most evolved group of animals on earth.

205. With the exception of tarsiers, all members of Haplorhini have apple-shaped uteruses, tend to have single births, and take exceptional care of their offspring, which stay with their mothers for an extended time period.

206. The high brain-to-body ratio makes Haplorhine primates capable of a great deal of learning and association, allowing for complex social structures, arithmetic abilities, and conceptualizations of tools and bartering.

207. **Opposable thumbs** and **binocular vision** are also hallmarks of this group, as both are adaptations to the trees.

208. The diagram below gives a quick survey of the many types of Haplorhinid primates. It does not do justice to the variety and diversity of this advanced group of mammals.

209. We now exit the **Boloeutherian** mammals and move on to **Magnorder Laurasiatheria**. This essentially groups
210. together the other orders of mammals that evolved from a common ancestor on the Laurasian supercontinent.
211. However, this is not without controversy, as there are certain anatomical features and DNA sequences that imply that primates and shrews might have shared a common ancestor in the past. Some scientists still group the shrews, moles, and kin in Magnorder Boloeutheria.
212. **Magnorder Lautasiatheria** is further subdivided into **Order Eulipothypia** and **Order Scrotifera**.
213. Moles, shrews, solenodons, and hedgehogs all belong to **Order Eulipothyphia**. Their distinctive features include tube-shaped furry bodies, sharp digging claws, limited (and sometimes vestigial) eyesight, and distinctive teeth.
214. However, as is the case in most modern taxonomic classifications, similarities to the their DNA sequences provide the majority of the evidence that they once shared a common ancestor.
215. DNA evidence also may suggest that the insectivores and primates may have shared a common ancestor as well.
216. The diagram below shows a few representatives of this group of insectivores.

ORDER EULIPOTHYPHIA: INSECTIVORES

A) FAMILY SORICIDAE (SOUTHERN SHORT-TAILED SHREW) BURROWERS WITH STRONG SENSES OF SMELL AND TOUCH & VERY POOR VISION. EXTREMELY HIGH METABOLIC RATE REQUIRES THEM TO EAT THEIR WEIGHT IN INSECTS & WORMS EACH DAY. SMALL TEETH.

B) FAMILY TALPIDAE (EASTERN MOLE) EXTREMELY LONG AND POWERFUL CLAWS WITH EXTRA THUMB ON EACH PAW. HEMOGLOBIN IS SPECIALLY ADAPTED TO DEAL WITH A BUILD-UP OF CO2 IN BURROWS. SOLITARY ANIMALS THAT EAT MOSTLY EARTHWORMS.

C) FAMILY ARENACIDAE (EUROPEAN HEDGEHOG) COVERED WITH PORCUPINE-LIKE BRISTLES AND CAPABLE OF ROLLING INTO A BALL TO DETER PREDATORS. IMMUNE TO MANY SNAKE VENOMS. NOCTURNAL OMNIVORES THAT ESPECIALLY LIKE INSECT LARVAE.

217. The remaining groups of mammals all belong to **Clade Scrotifera**. As the name implies, these are all mammals whose male representatives have external scrotums with free-hanging testes.
218. Generally speaking, the testes need to hang outside the body, because the animals in this group have a relatively high metabolic rate that generates too much heat for proper development of viable sperm cells.

219. There is controversy surrounding this grouping, because DNA doesn't always seem to point to common ancestry, and there are also quite a number of unrelated mammals (like us) who also have scrotums.

220. Whatever the case may be, we will cover the remaining animals under this taxonomic umbrella.

221. **Order Chiroptera** is the most highly distributed and numerous (in terms of species) of the scrotiferans.

222. The **phalanges** and **metacarpals** are highly elongated in bats, while the **carpals** are reduced to tiny proportions. The remaining arm bones are stubby and articulate to powerful shoulder and chest muscles.

223. The **radius** of the forearm provides the thrust for flight. Their **femurs** are angled out of the hips at nearly a right angle, thereby allowing the legs to push the trailing edge of the wings along.

224. Additionally, their **tibia** and **fibula** are fused and the claws of the feet are angled in like spaghetti server tools, so that they can grab onto a roost when they shape-shift and need to hide from vampire hunters.

225. The skull anatomy and dentition of bats vary greatly, depending on whether the species are insectivores or whether they consume fruit, nectar, blood, or small animals.

226. **Sonar echolocation**, and its requisite folded amplifying noses and radar dish ears, is an adaptation found in insectivorous species, but not in fruit bats, since fruits generally don't fly unless they are thrown.

227. There are nearly 1500 species of bats known, which make them the second most numerous mammals behind rodents. They are found almost everywhere on earth, other than extreme deserts and tundra.

228. Bats have so successfully occupied the niche for mammalian flight, that we cannot possibly cover each family in a sensible amount of space, so here are some representatives of the most noteworthy families.

Bats: A Decidedly Mixed Bag of Creatures

It's hard to know what to make of bats as a collective whole. They've been responsible for bringing untold misery to the human race through their filthy little mouths, yet the also remove another untold source of misery by eating mosquitoes. I'll let you decide.

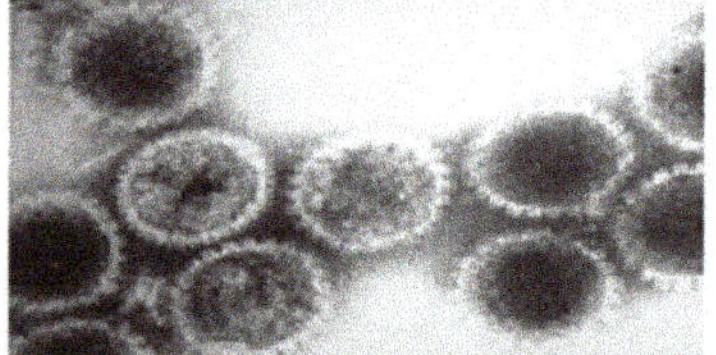

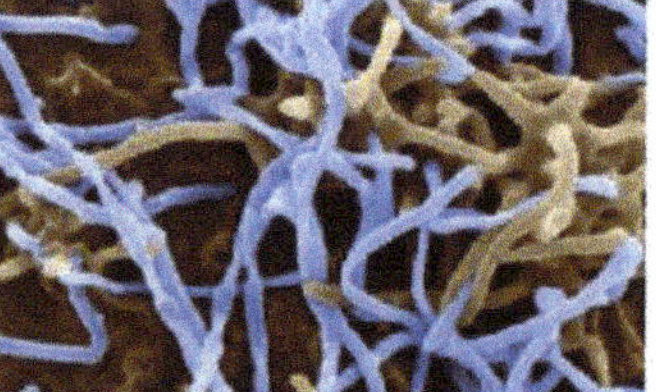

Rabies Vectors Bats are carriers of rabies, which is 100% fatal to humans, but not to bats. While bats do not carry as much rabies as people think, they can bite painlessly as victims sleep. 100,000 people per year still die in Africa and India.

Ebola Vectors In 2014, they finally figured out that fruit bats were the natural host for Ebola virus. Thanks to their migration across Africa (and ending up in stew pots) that year, about 20,000 people died.

Unholy Creatures of the Night How much more evidence do we all really need? It's common knowledge that vampires shape shift into bats to gain easy access to the attics of homes, where they emerge after midnight to suck the blood of unsuspecting homeowners. Adding insult to injury, some also steal Amazon packages off the porch.

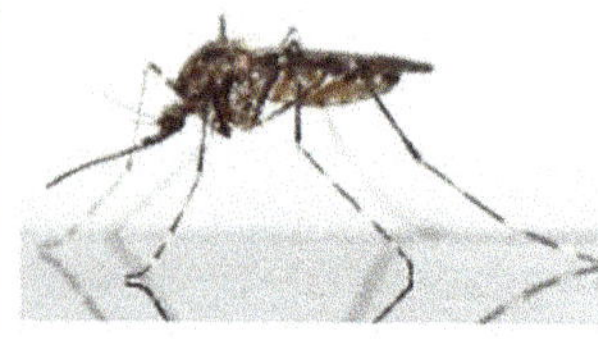

Mosquito Assassins One small insectivorous bat can catch and eat 5,000 to 10,000 small insects per night. That's thousands of mosquitoes that can't spread malaria to the typical 250 million people per year or dengue fever to 400 million!

Order Chiroptera: Bat Families

A) Family Pteropodidae (Ryuku Flying Fox) Wingspan of more than 4 feet. Roosts in tropical dry forests and consumes figs, nectar, other fruits. Important pollinator of banyan trees. Do not use echolocation. Nocturnal.

B) Family Megadermatidae (Greater False Vampire Bat) Large leaf-shaped nose and big ears for echolocation. Lack a tail completely. Insectivores that roost in caves. Initially were mistaken for vampire bats, hence name.

C) Family Phyllostomidae (California Leaf-Nosed Bat) Short wings with wide span built for short bursts of speed. Excellent echolocation. One of most agile and quick bat species. Roosts hanging with one dominant foot.

D) Family Myzopodidae (Madagascar Sucker-Footed Bat) Suction cup-like appendages on wrists and ankles for sticking themselves to broad leaves of Traveler's Tree to roost. Eat Insects. Named by Mr. T who first got one.

E) Family Rhinolophoidea (Bumblebee Bat) At 1.5 inches, is one of smallest mammals on earth. Big pig-like nose, large ears, reduced eyes. Only active 1-2 hours per day eating flies and moths. Roost and sleep most of their life.

F) Family Molossidae (Broad-Eared Freetailed Bat) Long tail with a ring of cartilage that can retract or extend the tail like a rudder in flight. Eat beetles and moths at night. Roost in large groups in crevices & caves.

G) Family Phyllostomidae (Vampire Bat) Feed exclusively on blood. Lack echoreceptors, but have thermoreceptors on nose instead to locate blood under skin. Parasitize larger animals. Front teeth evolved to cut skin.

H) Family Vespertilionidae (Virginia Big-Eared Bat) Long ears half as long as torso of bat. Females are capable of storing sperm during hibernation & inducing pregnancy later. Nocturnal insectivores. Colonies of thousands.

I) Family Vespertilionidae (Common Pipistrelle) Very small bats weigh less than an ounce. Emit high-pitched shrieks in echolocation. Males sing to attract females. Pregnant females roost together. Feed around streams.

J) Family Vespertilioniidae (Rufous Mouse-Eared Bat) Unusually long-lived bats that lack telomeres on chromosomes. Consume insects, but also fish for small minnows over water. Ears and face superficially resemble mice.

K) Family Vespertilioniidae (Javan Big-Thumbed Bamboo Bat) As namesake implies, has sizeable pads on paws. Extremely large external ears. Hunt insects and nest in bamboo thickets. Sometimes hitch-hike instead of flying.

229. **Order Pholidotaphora** includes the pangolins, which used to be classified with anteaters, armadillos, and sloths, until molecular evidence showed that they aren't closely related at all.

230. In the past, it was assumed that the similar shape of their snouts, reduced teeth, sticky tongue, and claws pointed toward common ancestry with anteaters and armadillos. Turns out, it was **convergent evolution.**

231. In fact, pangolins share a common ancestor with the group of animals that evolved into carnivores.

232. Pangolins are nocturnal burrowers that are covered in armor-like scales made of keratin. When threatened, they can roll into a ball and kick their claws out at the threat. They also can spray a skunk-like musk.

233. Pangolin tongues are also rooted under their sternum, rather than in hyoid bone in the neck. This lets them extend it deep into termite mounds. They have devolved teeth, since they are not necessary.

234. Since they lack teeth, pangolins eat rocks like birds, and use a specialized compartment in their stomach as a **gizzard** to grind up the insects they eat, since their chitin exoskeletons aren't very digestible.

235. Pangolins live alone, only interacting during mating season. When baby pangolins are born, their scales are soft and white, hardening up as they age.

236. The diagram below shows two representative pangolin species.

ORDER PHOLIDOTAPHORA: PANGOLINS

A) FAMILY MANIDAE (CHINESE PANGOLIN) CAT-SIZED PANGOLIN WITH NARROW SNOUT. MALE PANGOLINS ALLOW FEMALES AND OFFSPRING TO SHARE BURROW TO NURSE. A VICTIM OF POACHING FOR CHINESE MEDICINE. POPULATIONS IN SHARP DECLINE.

B) FAMILY MANIDAE (GROUND PANGOLIN) LARGER PANGOLIN THE SIZE OF A SMALL DOG. SCALE COLOR VARIES BETWEEN INDIVIDUALS. CLAWS ARE SO LONG THEY MUST BE TUCKED TO WALK ON FRONT LEGS. BABIES RIDE ON MOTHER'S TAIL. BURROWERS.

AUTOMOTIVE TEACHER STUDY BREAK QUIZ

ANSWERS ON PAGE 251.

LET'S SEE IF YOU KNOW HOW TO FIX A CAR OR IF YOU GET YOURSELF STRANDED...

1) WHAT ARE THE TWO MOST COMMON PARTS THAT FAIL, CAUSING A RADIATOR TO OVERHEAT?
2) WHAT DOES THE TERM 'TUNE UP' REALLY MEAN? WHAT TOOLS DO YOU NEED TO DO ONE?
3) WHAT DO THE NUMBERS IN TIRE SIZE MEAN, SUCH AS 235/75/R16?
4) HOW DO YOU KNOW WHEN IT IS TIME TO CHANGE YOUR BRAKE PADS?
5) YOUR CAR STARTS, BUT CHUGS AS YOU GAIN SPEED BEFORE SHUTTING OFF. WHAT'S THE ISSUE?

237. Now we arrive at, arguably, the group with the coolest mammals, the **Order Carnivora**. This group includes the lions, tigers, bears, skunks, weasels, wolverines, hyenas, and badgers that we all know and love.

238. Carnivores have exceptionally long **canine teeth**, sharp cutting **incisors**, heavy **zygomatic** cheek bone arches, **sagittal crests**, and large **masseter** and facial muscles for ripping and tearing meat.

239. Most carnivores have five toes on the front feet (with one being a dewclaw), while most have four toes on the hind feet, though some have five. Seals and sea lions, of course, have feet modified into **flippers**.

240. **Order Carnivora** can be sub-divided into **Suborder Feliformia** (cat-like carnivores) and **Suborder Caniformia** (dog-like carnivores), based on differences in dentition, skull anatomy, torso musculature, and claws.

241. **Feliformia** includes the obvious cats, hyenas, mongooses, civets, genets, and binturongs.

242. All feliform carnivores have spheres on the underside of the skull called **bullae** that completely surround the structures of the inner ear. As compared to caniform carnivores, they have shorter snouts and fewer **molars**.

243. While there are certainly many exceptions (such as cheetahs and mongooses), the majority of feliforms have **retractable claws**. Their body morphology tends to be stouter, shorter, and more muscular than canids.

244. Most felids have tails that extend to nearly the length of their body, especially in species that climb, giving them an appendage for balancing on limbs. This complements the shorter, more powerful legs and shoulders.

245. While not always the case (such as in lions, the majority of feliforms are solitary hunters who stalk their prey.

246. The next page details representatives of the families of **Order Feliformia**.

ANIMALS ENDANGERED FOR THE DUMBEST REASONS

PANGOLINS
OVER THE LAST 20 YEARS, THEY'VE BECOME THE MOST ILLEGALLY TRAFFICKED MAMMAL IN THE WORLD? WHY YOU ASK? ALL 8 SPECIES ARE ENDANGERED BECAUSE THEIR SCALES, WHICH ARE KERATIN LIKE FINGERNAILS, ARE USED FOR THEIR 'MAGICAL POWERS' IN CHINESE MEDICINE.

SEA TURTLES
6 OF THE 7 SPECIES ARE ENDANGERED BECAUSE OF CONDOS, EARRINGS, AND SUNGLASSES FRAMES. IN MANY COUNTRIES, THEY ALSO DROWN IN FISHING TRAWL NETS.

CONDORS
WHILE NOT SOLELY RESPONSIBLE, JOHNNY CASH CERTAINLY DIDN'T HELP. HE THREW A LIT CIGARETTE OUT OF HIS CAR, STARTING A FOREST FIRE THAT COOKED 49 BIRDS IN A BURNING RING OF FIRE, SETTING BACK THE CONSERVATION PROGRAM DECADES AS THE FLAMES GOT HIGHER.

RHINOS
ALL 5 SPECIES OF RHINOS ARE ALSO ENDANGERED, MOSTLY FOR THE SAME STUPID REASON AS PANGOLINS. THEIR HORNS ARE ALSO KERATIN AND ALSO USED FOR 'MAGICAL POWERS' AS AN APHRODISIAC.

STEPHEN ISLAND WREN OK...THIS ONE IS ACTUALLY EXTINCT. A CAT NAMED MR. TIBBLES OWNED BY A LIGHTHOUSE KEEPER ATE THE ENTIRE POPULATION IN 1894.

Order Carnivora: Suborder Feliforma (Cat-Like)

A) Family Hyeanidae (Spotted Hyena) Competitive matriarchal social structure. Females are large and external genitalia are indistinguishable from males. Scavengers and opportunistic hunters.
B) Family Hyaenidae (Aardwolf) Desert insectivores with sticky tongues. Raid termite mounds for most of their food. Have 5 toes on front feet, whereas other hyenas have 4. Striped coat.
C) Family Herpestidae (Banded Mongoose) Show convergent evolution in many ways to weasels (Caniform carnivores). Long torsos, short legs with claws, pointed snout. Fierce little predators.
D) Family Herpestidae (Meerkat) Burrowers with a complex hive-like social hierarchy. Can close ears to avoid entry of dirt as they dig with large claws. Can adjust metabolism to temperature.
E) Family Eupleridae (Fossa) Evolved independently and convergently to cats on Madagascar. Body is cat-like, but snout is mongoose-like. Fierce predator of lemurs and birds. Mark with scent glands.
F) Family Viverridae (Binturong) Unique, heavy-bodied climber that walks flat-footed. Omnivores that eat almost anything. Shake long bushy tails to communicate. Urine mark with butter scent.
G) Family Viverridae (Linsang) Closest living relative to true cats. Long skinny cat-like body, but snout is elongated. Nocturnal predator of small animals. Spots and stripes provide camouflage.
H) Family Viverridae (African civet) Convergent evolution to raccoons, in eye rings and in diet of trash, eggs, insects, fruit. Nocturnal. Spotted coat provides camouflage. Large skull crest.
I) Family Felidae (Cheetah) Fastest living terrestrial animal can sprint 70 mph for short distances. Unique among cats in that claws are non-retractable. Enlarged heart, lungs. Streamlined body.
J) Family Felidae (Pallas's Cat) Native to rocky steppes. Well camouflaged. Flat heat, bushy tail that can be wrapped for insulation. Solitary hunters of marmots and smaller rodents. Reclusive.
K) Family Felidae (Cougar) Not a true big cat, due to inability to roar. Highly adaptable to numerous habitats, as it can be found in deserts, rainforests, taiga, and temerate forests. Apex predator.
L) Family Felidae (Fishing Cat) Layered fur that traps air, well-adapted for diving after fish. Also has webbed feet for swimming. Threatened by draining of wetlands for human populations.
M) Family Felidae (African Lion) Unique among cats in living in social prides. Hunt cooperatively, due to difficulty of stalking large, fast prey in grasslands. Mane is secondary sex characteristic.
N) Family Felidae (Bengal tiger) Striped pattern provides camouflage in flooded grasslands. Solitary hunters of antelope, deer, hogs. Territories of males will overlap with several females.
O) Family Felidae (Snow Leopard) Not a true leopard, but a relative of the tiger adapted for montane life. Padded paws and long, insulated tail for scampering ability over rocks. Reclusive.
P) Family Felidae (Canada Lynx) Padded paws allow for silent stalking of snowshoe hares. Tail is reduced in length. Ears are tufted. Subject of long ongoing study of predator-prey cycle.

Order Carnivora: Suborder Feliforma (Cat-Like)

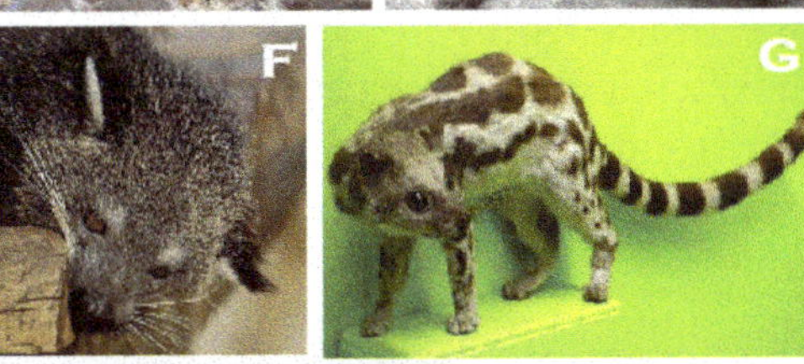

A) Family Hyeanidae (Spotted Hyena) Competitive matriarchal social structure. Females are large and external genitalia are indistinguishable from males. Scavengers and opportunistic hunters.
B) Family Hyaenidae (Aardwolf) Desert insectivores with sticky tongues. Raid termite mounds for most of their food. Have 5 toes on front feet, whereas other hyenas have 4. Striped coat.
C) Family Herpestidae (Banded Mongoose) Show convergent evolution in many ways to weasels (Caniform carnivores). Long torsos, short legs with claws, pointed snout. Fierce little predators.
D) Family Herpestidae (Meerkat) Burrowers with a complex hive-like social hierarchy. Can close ears to avoid entry of dirt as they dig with large claws. Can adjust metabolism to temperature.
E) Family Eupleridae (Fossa) Evolved independently and convergently to cats on Madagascar. Body is cat-like, but snout is mongoose-like. Fierce predator of lemurs and birds. Mark with scent glands.
F) Family Viverridae (Binturong) Unique, heavy-bodied climber that walks flat-footed. Omnivores that eat almost anything. Shake long bushy tails to communicate. Urine mark with butter scent.
G) Family Viverridae (Linsang) Closest living relative to true cats. Long skinny cat-like body, but snout is elongated. Nocturnal predator of small animals. Spots and stripes provide camouflage.
H) Family Viverridae (African civet) Convergent evolution to raccoons, in eye rings and in diet of trash, eggs, insects, fruit. Nocturnal. Spotted coat provides camouflage. Large skull crest.
I) Family Felidae (Cheetah) Fastest living terrestrial animal can sprint 70 mph for short distances. Unique among cats in that claws are non-retractable. Enlarged heart, lungs. Streamlined body.
J) Family Felidae (Pallas's Cat) Native to rocky steppes. Well camouflaged. Flat heat, bushy tail that can be wrapped for insulation. Solitary hunters of marmots and smaller rodents. Reclusive.
K) Family Felidae (Cougar) Not a true big cat, due to inability to roar. Highly adaptable to numerous habitats, as it can be found in deserts, rainforests, taiga, and temerate forests. Apex predator.
L) Family Felidae (Fishing Cat) Layered fur that traps air, well-adapted for diving after fish. Also has webbed feet for swimming. Threatened by draining of wetlands for human populations.
M) Family Felidae (African Lion) Unique among cats in living in social prides. Hunt cooperatively, due to difficulty of stalking large, fast prey in grasslands. Mane is secondary sex characteristic.
N) Family Felidae (Bengal tiger) Striped pattern provides camouflage in flooded grasslands. Solitary hunters of antelope, deer, hogs. Territories of males will overlap with several females.
O) Family Felidae (Snow Leopard) Not a true leopard, but a relative of the tiger adapted for montane life. Padded paws and long, insulated tail for scampering ability over rocks. Reclusive.
P) Family Felidae (Canada Lynx) Padded paws allow for silent stalking of snowshoe hares. Tail is reduced in length. Ears are tufted. Subject of long ongoing study of predator-prey cycle.

247. The **Suborder Caniformia** includes dogs, bears, foxes, weasels, wolverines, badgers, and otters.

248. As compared to the skulls of Suborder Feliformia, the caniforms typically have larger and more powerful jaws with more molars, while the underside of the skull does NOT form a round bulla around the ear canal.

249. Dog-like carnivores also tend to walk on the pads of their feet, rather than on their tiptoes. With some exceptions like certain foxes, not very many species in Order Caniformia have retractable claws.

250. Male caniforms lack Cowper's glands, while male feliforms have them. While all carnivores have a **penile bone** that supports the male organ, it is considerably longer in caniforms.

251. Additionally, many male cat-like carnivores have nail-like keratin barbs on their penis to ensure that they impregnate females, while dog-like carnivores do not.

252. Members of Caniformia trend toward being omnivorous, rather than strictly carnivorous. A few members, such as the panda, are not even omnivorous. Consequently, the gut is longer in dog-like carnivores than in cats.

253. A smattering number of Caniform representatives are shown on the next page. Meanwhile, please enjoy another sections of ads from our sponsors. We tried Gucci, Rolex, and Rolls Royce, but not one called back.

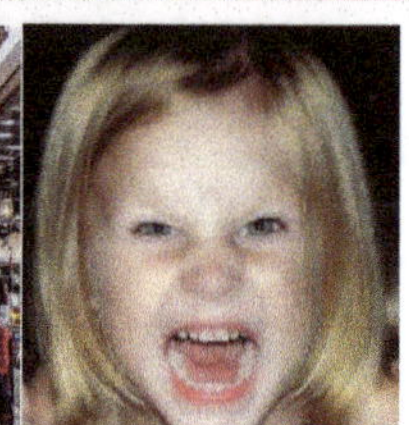

ORDER CARNIVORA: SUBORDER CANIFORMA (DOG-LIKE)

A B C D E F G H I J K L M N O P Q R

A) FAMILY CANIDAE (TIMBER WOLF) LIVE IN FAMILY PACKS WITH A SOCIAL HIERARCHY CONTROLLED BY ALPHA WOLVES. HOWL TO RALLY PACK AND POSITION DURING HUNTS. PRIMARILY HUNT DEER.

B) FAMILY CANIDAE (AFRICAN PAINTED DOG) FUSED MIDDLE TOE PADS, LACK BACK SET OF MOLARS IN OTHER DOGS. COLORFUL MOTTLED COAT. PREMOLARS ARE KNIFE-SHAPED. MALES STAY WITH BIRTH PACK.

C) FAMILY CANIDAE (GOLDEN JACKAL) LIVE IN MONOGAMOUS PAIRS AND MARK TERRITORY WITH POOP AND URINE. MAY HUNT COOPERATIVELY, BUT DON'T FORM PERMANENT PACKS. SCAVENGERS & OPPORTUNISTS

D) FAMILY CANIDAE (BUSH DOG) AMAZONIAN DOGS ABOUT THE SIZE OF A WEINER DOG. PRE-MOLARS ARE KNIFE-LIKE, TOES ARE WEBBED, LEGS SHORT. DNA INDICATES VERY DISTANT RELATIONSHIP WITH WOLVES.

E) FAMILY CANIDAE (RED FOX) AS COMPARED TO OTHER CANIDS, SKULL IS NARROWER, BONE STRUCTURE IS LIGHTER. COMMUNICATE WITH CRIES. MATED PAIRS ESTABLISH DENS WITH OFFSPRING. MUSK GLANDS.

F) FAMILY CANIDAE (RACCOON DOG) IN SPITE OF RACCOON-LIKE APPEARANCE, ARE MORE RELATED TO FOXES. CAN CLIMB TREES EASILY. ONLY DOGS THAT HIBERNATE. OMNIVORES. MONOGAMOUS PAIRS.

G) FAMILY CANIDAE (GRAY FOX) SMALLER AND SLENDER COMPARED TO RED FOXES. CAN CLIMB TREES AND JUMP BETWEEN BRANCHES LIKE A CAT. MAKE THEIR DENS IN HOLLOW TREES. OMNIVOROUS DIET.

H) FAMILY URSIDAE (AMERICAN BLACK BEAR) STOCKY BEAR WITH WIDE FACE & SHORT SNOUT. SENSE OF SMELL IS 7 TIMES STRONGER THAN BLOODHOUND. PREFER DEEP MOUNTAINOUS WOODS. TERRITORIAL.

I) FAMILY URSIDAE (GIANT PANDA) DIVERGED FROM OTHER BEARS 30 MILLION YEARS AGO. RETAINS CARNIVOUS DIGESTIVE TRACT, BUT EATS BAMBOO SHOOTS (HIGH IN STARCH/PROTEIN). GIANT MOLARS.

J) FAMILY URSIDAE (POLAR BEAR) ONE OF TWO SPECIES OF BROWN BEARS. BODY ADAPTED FOR TUNDRA AND COLD OCEAN WITH THICK BLUBBER, CLEAR FUR, BLACK SKIN. AGGRESSIVE HUNTERS OF SEALS.

K) FAMILY PROCYONIDAE (COMMON RACCOON) HAVE OPPOSABLE THUMBS THEY USE TO FORAGE FOR FOOD. MASK ENHANCES NIGHT VISION BY ABSORBING GLARE. HIGHLY INTELLIGENT. VICIOUS IF CORNERED.

L) FAMILY PROCYONIDAE (RED PANDA) NOT A CLOSE RELATIVE OF GIANT PANDA, BUT ALSO HAS WRIST BONES MODIFIED INTO FALSE GRIPPING THUMB. HIMALAYAN OMNIVORE OF BAMBOO, INSECTS, EGGS.

M) FAMILY MEPHITIDAE (STRIPED SKUNK) STOUT BODY WITH SHORT LIMBS. WALK IN A PLANTIGRADE WADDLE. ANAL GLANDS PRODUCE FOUL-SMELLING OIL TO DETER PREDATORS. EATS INSECTS & BERRIES.

N) FAMILY MUSTELIDAE (WOLVERINE) SQUAT, HEAVY ANIMAL WITH BEAR-LIKE CLAWS THAT ARE USED FOR CLIMBING. PELT IS FULL OF OIL GLANDS THAT DETER MOISTURE. SCAVENGE MASSIVE AMOUNTS OF FOOD.

O) FAMILY MUSTELIDAE (EURASIAN OTTER) BROWN AND TAUPE COUNTERSHADED FUR. OIL GLANDS IN SKIN LOCK OUT MOISTURE. CARNIVORES WITH TREMENDOUS STRENGTH FOR SIZE. MATE UNDERWATER.

P) FAMILY MUSTELIDAE (BLACK-FOOTED FERRET) ADAPTED FOR BURROWING WITH LONG, LITHE BODY, SHORT WHISKERS, SMALL EARS, SHARP CLAWS. PREY ON PRARIE DOGS. SOLITARY & TERRITORIAL.

Q) FAMILY MUSTELIDAE (HONEY BADGER) POUND-FOR-POUND THE NASTIEST ANIMAL IN NATURE. IMMUNE TO MANY VENOMS, AS THEY RAID BEEHIVES, EAT COBRAS. LIONS AVOID THEM. POWERFUL DIGGING CLAWS.

R) FAMILY MUSTELIDAE (AMERICAN MINK) EAT FISH, FROGS, EGGS, CRUSTACEANS. HOME RANGE IS ALMOST ALWAYS NEAR A STREAM OR RIVER. FARMED COMMERCIALLY FOR SOFT PELT. CAN CARRY COVID.

254. It turns out that there are even more members of **Order Carnivora**. Formerly classified as their own distinct order, **Sub-Order Pinnipedia** includes sea lions, seals, and walruses.

255. Shared DNA sequences, combined with morphological and fossil evidence, point directly to common ancestry between seals and ancient mustelids. One group took to terrestrial life, while the other to water.

256. Due to their aquatic and marine lifestyles, selection pressures drastically changed the pinniped body from their caniform relatives. Their bodies became streamlined, their limbs morphed into flippers, and their necks lengthened. Additionally, their heads rounded, their snouts shortened, and their eyes enlarged.

257. Pinnipeds reduced or eliminated their external ears, evolved breasts and testicles that can be pulled into body pouches, and reduced the number of teeth in their mouths for their piscivorous diets.

258. Certain seals, such as elephant seals and sea lions, are **sexually dimorphic**, with males growing many times larger than females. Elephant seal males develop elephant-like noses used for honking at other competitors.

259. Some of their physiological changes are also impressive. Many marine seals have specialized cartilaginous rings in their lungs that can force enough air out of their nostrils to collapse the **lungs** for diving.

260. Seals are able to completely shut their nostrils and the cartilage flaps in their **pharynx** to keep water out of the trachea as they dive. Since their lungs are empty, during deep dives, blood gases enter the lungs.

261. The ability of seals to draw air out of the blood prevents them from getting 'the bends' decompression sickness.

262. Seals have huge blood vessel networks throughout their muscles that give them significantly more blood supply than a similarly sized terrestrial carnivore. Additionally, they have much more **hemoglobin** in their blood, more **myoglobin** in their muscles, and more red blood cells overall.

263. Seals have dense furry coats with oil glands that trap air pockets. Along with thick layers of blubber, they essentially have their own wet suits, preventing hypothermia in even the coldest Artic or Antarctic waters.

264. The diagram below shows several representative pinnipeds.

265. But first....a word from the first option in self-defense.

Order Carnivora: Clade Pinnipedia (Seals & Allies)

A) Family Phocidae (Hooded Seal) Leopard fur pattern. Males have secondary sex trait of inflatable sac on forehead and in nostrils. Can dive to 600 m for fish, krill, squid.

B) Family Phocidae (Caspian Seal) Evolved from ringed seals in Arctic after becoming landlocked. Migrate North to South on brackish Caspian eating herring. Monogamous.

C) Family Phocidae (Grey Seal) Large Northern Atlantic seal weighing up to 800 lbs. Dive to 70 m for eels, rays, etc. Live in large colonies. Clap flippers to communicate.

D) Family Phocidae (Leopard Seal) Mostly solitary seals that live on ice floes. Male call is one of loudest in nature (170 dB) in breeding season. Prey on penguins, seal pups, fish.

E) Family Phocidae (Southern Elephant Seal) Up to 11,000 lbs. Largest terrestrial carnivores on earth. Males have huge snouts. Rarely come on land except to mate.

F) Family Phocidae (Hawaiian Monk Seal) Feeds off of coral reef animals, such as fish, lobsters, squid. Lay on sand beaches and shed fur and top layer of epidermis yearly.

G) Family Otariidae (Galapagos Sea Lion) Like other members of its family, has external pinna on ears. Live in large social groups. May hunt cooperatively, herd and trap fish.

H) Family Otariidae (New Zealand Fur Seal) Dives deeper and longer than any other seal up to 1000 feet deep. Communicate with barks. Preyed upon by killer whales & sharks.

I) Family Odobenidae (Pacific Walrus) Can weigh 2 tons or more. Enlarged canine tusks are used to break holes in ice, lift selves out. Whiskers. Throat air sac for buoyancy.

266. Now we follow the other lineage that the **Scrotiferan clade** evolved into, known as **Clade Euungulata**, better known as the hoofed animals or ungulates. The ungulates can then be further divided into two primary groups.

267. The even-toed hoofed mammals belong to **Order Artiodactyla**, which includes pigs, deer, antelope, camels, giraffes, hippos, cattle, and several other families. This is also the lineage that whales evolved from.

268. **Order Perrisodactyla** include the odd-toed hoofed animals, which are horses, donkeys, rhinos, and tapirs.

269. Let's begin with **Order Artiodactyla**, which is a diverse group of more than 200 hoofed animals. Besides an even number of toes, this group of ungulates also sports a distinctive four-chambered fermentive gut.

270. The chambers of the stomach include the **rumen, reticulum, omasum,** and **abomasum.**

271. The **rumen** is the 'brew tank' of the digestive tract. It takes in massive quantities of plant material that have been chewed, burped up, and re-chewed and acts as a fermentation vat for microbes to break down cellulose.

272. The **reticulum** filters out trash that the animal needs to regurgitate and reject.

273. The **omasum** squeezes out water and dissolved nutrients before sending the contents to the **abomasum** behind it, which is like a true stomach. The abomasum releases digestive juices and acid to continue food breakdown.

274. In addition to these distinct digestive features, the skeletal system of artiodactyls is usually well-adapted for quadrupedal running. The leg bones (tibia, fibula, humerus, ulna, and radius) are all elongated.

275. Even-toed ungulates also lack a **clavicle** (collar bone), making their front legs looser and more flexible for long strides. Additionally, their **scapulae** (shoulder blades) are also flat and flexible.

276. Many even-toed ungulates have also developed defenses against the many predators that want to turn them into a meal. **Antlers** and **horns** are common adaptations, as are defensive **tusks** and powerful kicks.

277. The diagrams below show a number of noteworthy members of this taxa.

278. But first, a word from one of our most respected sponsors……

A) Family Camelidae (Bactrian Camel) Native to Gobi desert. Have two humps full of fat, thick wooly coat. Migratory, following water. Adaptable diet.

B) Family Camelidae (Llama) Migrated to South America from ancestors in Western USA. No hump. High levels of hemoglobin in blood for altitude.

C) Family Tayasuiidae (Collared Peccary) Related to pigs, but very short tail, small ears, presence of scent glands near tail differ. Omnivorous.

D) Family Suiidae (Red River Hog) Native to Central African rainforests. A wide range of calls & grunts. Omnivorous consumers of herbs, eggs, grubs.

E) Family Suiidae (Russian Wild Boar) Males have 'razorback' hackles of bristles on back. Aggressive tusked omnivores. Invasive species in USA.

F) Family Hippopotamidae (Hippopotamus) Live in family groups in territories in rivers. Aggressively defend area with tusks. Sweat gives skin a pink hue.

G) Family Tragulidae (Lesser Mouse Deer) One of smallest hoofed animals. Lack antlers. Elongated canines used to fight in rut. Feet have 4 toes.

H) Family Antelocapridae (Pronghorn) Branched bony horns covered in keratin. Can run up to 55 mph. Lungs, trachea, heart adapted to keep up.

I) Family Giraffidae (Okapi) Unknown to science until 1900. Diverged from giraffes and went to forests. Stripes resemble filtered sunlight in forest.

J) Family Giraffidae (Masai Giraffe) Weigh up to 3000 lb. Only 7 vertebrae of massive size make up neck. Ossicone horns used for fighting during rut.

K) Family Cervidae (Red Deer) Widespread from Europe into Western Asia. Stags can weigh 500 pounds or more, have manes, shed antlers each year.

L) Family Cervidae (Fallow Deer) Retain spots throughout their life. Males have shovel-like antlers, keep harems. Grass makes up largest part of diet.

M) Family Cervidae (Reindeer) Found circumglobally in Arctic. Have been domesticated and herded for centuries in Scandinavia. Diet of lichens,moss.

N) Family Cervidae (Reeves's Muntjac) Less than 40 pounds. Consume a wide variety of plant materials. Males have short straight antlers and tusks.

O) Family Cervidae (Moose) Largest deer. Males may weigh 1500 lb. Males grow blade-like antlers that are shed. Snout adapted for grazing in water.

Order Artiodactyla: Odd-Toed Ungulates

A) Family Moschidae (Siberian Musk Deer) Grow elongated tusks instead of antlers. Mark territory with musk and circular brush piles. Eat lichens.

B) Family Bovidae (Amerian Bison) Hump-like fat pad behind head to absorb shock from butting rivals. Nomadic grazers. Short horns. Poor vision.

C) Family Bovidae (Cape Buffalo) Curved horns used to gore lions. Bulls may weight nearly a ton. Exceptionally aggressive in defending the herd.

D) Family Bovidae (Yak) Long dense fur for living near Himalayas. Do not moo, but make squeaking noises. Domesticated long ago for meat, milk, and fur.

E) Family Bovidae (Water Buffalo) Weigh 700 lbs. to a ton. Submerge bodies to regulate body temperatures. Feed on aquatic vegetation. Domesticated.

F) Family Bovidae (Greater Kudu) Very large antelope with spiral horns and white markings. Take cover in bush during day. Graze at dusk and dawn.

G) Family Bovidae (Black-Fronted Duiker) Very small, elusive forest antelope that are mostly solitary. Have preorbital glands that secrete pheromones.

H) Family Bovidae (Thomson's Gazelle) A small antelope of around 50 lbs. May gather in herds of 100,000 to graze in rainy season. Favorite Cheetah prey.

I) Family Bovidae (Bohor Reedbuck) Deer-sized antelope that feeds on reeds, grasses in swamps. Copious oil glands that waterproof fur with grease.

J) Family Bovidae (Dall Sheep) Native to mountains of Canada and Alaska. Rams have curved horns, ewes straight. Headbutting maintains social order.

K) Family Bovidae (Iberian Ibex) Males have long curving horns, female small. Divide into male and female groups, except during breeding. Sure-footed.

L) Family Bovidae (Rocky Mountain Goat) Beard, short tails and horns. Have padded flexible hooves with dewclaws to maintain grip. Eat lichens, mosses.

M) Family Bovidae (Musk Oxen) In spite of cow-like appearance, more related to goats and sheep. Exceptionally thick fur to withstand Arctic blizzards.

N) Family Bovidae (Blue Wildebeest) Graze on short grasses and migrate with rainy season in herds of thousands. Cow-like body form, humped shoulders.

O) Family Bovidae (Gemsbok Oryx) Large desert antelope with saber-like horns nearly 3 feet long. Black markings on face deflect sun from eyes.

279. So now we arrive at a point where the evolutionary history of the next group of animals might make some people scratch their heads and conclude that the biologists who classified whales are stupid or crazy.

280. Yes, that's right, whales of **Infraorder Cetecea** were determined to have evolved from even-toed ungulates.

281. Since whales no longer have hooves, or even legs, other anatomical features and DNA provide the evidence.

282. The closest living relatives of whales are hippos. They share similar joint anatomy to hippos, both male hippos and whales have internal testicles, and both have thick blubber and tough hairless gray skin.

283. Whales, in spite of being largely carnivorous or planktivorous, retain a chambered gut like other Artiodactyls.

284. Whales are, obviously, some off the most evolved mammals of all. As their ancestors returned to the water, multiple limb bones became **vestigial** and their bodies became streamlined for aquatic locomotion.

285. The bones, themselves, are impregnated with much more **cartilage** than terrestrial animals, giving them flexibility for turning underwater.

286. The **cervical vertebrae** are fused, preventing the whale from turning their head, but maintaining a torpedo shape for efficient swimming. The flippers articulate at the **thoracic vertebrae**, as there are no clavicles.

287. The **humerus**, **radius**, and **ulna** are extremely compact and stubby and sit at the base off the **flippers**. The **carpals** and **metacarpals** are also reduced, while the **phalanges** make up most of the length of the flippers.

288. The **pelvic girdle** is vestigial, with the remnants of hips and leg bones confined to the inside of the body.

289. Whales have special physiology. A sperm whale may dive 5,000 feet deep or more. The only way this is possible is because there are major evolutionary modifications to the circulatory and respiratory systems.

290. Unlike land animals, whales can clear almost the entire volume of their **lungs** and completely replace the spent CO_2 laden air with fresh oxygenated air when they emerge to breathe from their **blowholes**.

291. The blowholes, themselves, evolved from the **nostrils** of land animals, as their canals pass through the same bones as terrestrial animals with snouts. However, the bones of the face migrated back on the head.

292. Whales have a tremendous amount of **myoglobin** in their muscles and **hemoglobin** in their blood, allowing them to carry many times more oxygen than a terrestrial mammal. Their hearts are also massive.

293. **Echolocation** is another major adaptation of whales, as they are able to communicate with their pod and to bounce sound off of schools of fish to determine their presence. Their **cochleas** in their ears are well-adapted to hear **infrasonic frequencies.** They are able to distinguish objects from prey, these senses are so strong.

294. **Toothed whales** are more primitive than **baleen whales**. Carnivorous whales like dolphins, orcas, and sperm whales have peg-like teeth, while baleen whales have brush-like sheets for plankton filtration.

295. Would you believe Nicholas Sparks bought a sponsorship? I'm told the book & movie both drop next month.

BEST ZOOS IN THE UNITED STATES FOR ANIMAL LOVERS

NOW THAT WE'RE ABOUT TO SAY GOODBYE, YOU SHOULD GO SEE SOME REAL ANIMALS FOR YOURSELF. IN NO PARTICULAR ORDER, THESE ARE THE ZOOS CONSIDERED TO BE THE BEST ON THE PLANET AND WHY THEY HAVE THEIR REPUTATIONS.

SAN DIEGO ZOO & WILD ANIMAL PARK	3700 SPECIES OF ANIMALS, 660 PLANTS. ENDANGERED ANIMAL BREEDING & GENETICS. KOALAS, PANDAS, PYGMY HIPPOS, RHINOS.
HENRY DOORLY ZOO & AQUARIUM OMAHA	LARGEST INDOOR DESERT & RAINFOREST EXHIBITS. 962 SPECIES. RED PANDAS, BUSH ELEPHANTS, 1.2 MILLION GALLON AQUARIUM.
BRONX ZOO NEW YORK	OUTSTANDING REPTILE HOUSE WITH GHARIALS, GIANT RIVER TURTLES, DART FROGS. MAJOR BREEDING PROGRAMS FOR SNOW LEOPARDS, OKAPIS, GIRAFFES, MORE.
CINCINNATI ZOO	ONE OF MOST SUCCESSFUL ZOOS FOR BREEDING PROGRAMS AND GENETICS. BREEDING FOR LOWLAND GORILLAS, CHEETAHS, GIRAFFES. LAST ZOO TO HAVE SUMATRAN RHINOS.

296. The diagram below depicts a few representatives of **Infraorder Cetecea**.

A) Order Monodontidae (Narwhal) have tusk derived from canine tooth used to detect vibrations from prey. Unlike most whales, no dorsal fin, jointed neck.

B) Family Phocoenidae (Harbor Porpoise) small whale less than 6 feet long. Females larger than males. Triangle-shaped dorsal fin. Eat schooling fish.

C) Family Phocoendiae (Bottlenose Dolphin) comparable to human in brain to body ratio. Highly intelligent: self-awareness, use tools, sonar language.

D) Family Phocoenidae (Killer Whale) a very large dolphin. Several races with different behaviors (Level of Agression) and diets (Fish or Sea Lions)

E) Family Phocoenidae (Atlantic Spotted Dolphin) Relative of Bottlenose Dolphins that can hybridize with them. Hunt squid cooperatively at night.

F) Family PHocoenidae (Pink Amazon River Dolphin) Long nose and prominent sonar melon needed in muddy waters. Highly social. Wedge-shaped dorsal fin.

G) Family Physeteridae (Sperm Whale) Head has very large melon full of waxy liquid for sonar echoes. About 40 Feet. Can dive more than a mile for squid.

H) Family Balaenopteridae (Humpback Whale) can be 50 feet long, 40 tons. Use baleen plates in mouth to strain krill, plankton, small fish. Leap frequently.

I) Family Balaenopteridae (Blue Whale) Largest living animal. Can be nearly 100 feet long, 200 tons. Solitary krill eaters. Can live to 100 years or more.

J) Family Balaenopteridae (Northern Minke Whale) One of smallest baleen whales. Grows to about 25 feet. Hunted for food in Scandinavian countries.

297. **Order Perissodactyla** is the last mammalian order we will cover. This classification includes rhinos, tapirs, donkeys and horses. From there, this chapter will ride off into the sunset like a happy cowboy story.
298. Members of Order Perissodactyla include the **equines**, which walk on a single modified hoof, as well as the **odd-toed ungulates**, who use three toes to bear their weight (as in rhinos).
299. The **tibia** of the back legs, and the **ulna** and **radius** of the front legs are centered directly over the middle (3rd) toe of each foot, providing support like the legs of a table.
300. Some other unique things about their bone structure include the restricted rotation of their ankle bones (hooves cannot turn laterally), short thick **humerus** and **femur** bones, and the absence of **clavicles**.
301. The skull of Perissodactyls has an enlarged **mandible** (lower jaw) bone that articulates at the very base of the **temporalis** of the skull. This results in a huge mouth that can process large amounts of hay in each bite.
302. The teeth, themselves, have a very large gap called a **diastema** between the front **incisors** and the **premolars** and **molars** at the back of the jaw. The shape and size of the back teeth depends on the diet of the animal.
303. Horses and donkeys have flat, fused plate-like back teeth that can handle the high silica content of grass, while the teeth of rhinos and tapirs are more cone-like, since they eat other types of vegetation and fruits.
304. The digestive system of Perissodactyls also varies dramatically from that of Artiodactyls (cattle and allies).
305. Rather than having four distinctive chambers in the stomach, there is a single enlarged **cecum** on the small intestine for the fermentation of cellulose in grass. This is much less efficient in extracting nutrition.
306. The reason for this is two-fold. First, there are not nearly as many different (or varied) microbes in the single pouch. Additionally, the surface-area-to-volume ratio is much smaller.
307. This is the reason that horses colic easily if they eat too much sweet feed. The single chamber can become easily overloaded and swell with gas and twist over the rest of the intestines, resulting in a life-threatening condition that a vet has to fix.
308. Horse manure is also the compost of choice for gardens, because many of the nutrients that the horse meant to digest pass right on through. This benefits your growing garden, as the nutrients are released to your veggies.
309. All members of Order Perissodactyla are herbivorous grazers. Most form herds. Additionally, parenting is a strong suit among them, as offspring remain with their mothers much longer than many other mammals.
310. **Gestation** in the odd-toed ungulates surpasses or rivals that of humans, with mares being pregnant for 10 to 11 months, while female rhinos may be pregnant for as long as 15 to 16 months.
311. This all ensures the birth off a well-developed baby that is locomotive within a half hour of their birth. The infant mortality rate is relatively low, and some members of this order can live to be more than 50 years old.
312. If you are looking for a group of mammals that had a large part in shaping human history, this group would not be a bad choice. Virtually every army in the old world relied on horses in their campaigns, while farmers and citizens depended upon them for transportation and work. Also...who doesn't owe tapirs a debt of gratitude?

313. The diagram on the next page shows some representatives of **Order Perissodactyla**.

314. Happy trails until next chapter. Having made most of the mane points, the author is going to hoof it out of here for now. We'll say 'hay' again then.

Alright this is the last bit of trapped white space in this chapter. I bet you thought another advertisement was going to be in this slot. Well, you're wrong. Let's make a list of all the other things you were wrong about, shall we?

YOU THOUGHT	REALITY
Americans landed on the moon in 1969	Merv Griffin produced the entire thing on a movie set. It was ACTORS!
The Titanic was a real ship that sank in 1912	The titanic is just a MOVIE. Come on! A ship that big could never sink
Falling objects eventually reach a terminal velocity because air resistance counters gravity at that point.	A penny dropped from the Empire State Building will embed 25 feet into the sidewalk and can easily kill you just from the shockwave it produces.
Pop rocks and CO2 filled snapping candy are harmless fun that all kids should enjoy.	The kid who played in a bunch of 1980's sitcoms died because he ate a bunch of packs of pop rocks and sodas and his stomach exploded.
People should work hard and be kind to others.	True strength is the ability to be rude, entitled, & selfish with no shame.

ORDER PERISSODACTYLA (ODD-TOED UNGULATES)

A) Suborder Hippomorpha (Przewalski's wild Horse) Stocky short Mongolian wild horse that diverged from Equus horses long ago. Breeding programs to prevent extinction.

B) Suborder Hippomorpha (Somali Wild Ass) Native to desert scrublands of African horn, but critically endangered. Seem to move in-and-out of family groups regularly.

C) Suborder Hippomorpha (Grant's Zebra) Black and white camouflage breaks up outline on savanna against lions. To borrow one, you'll have to ask Grant. He owns them.

D) Suborder Hippomorpha (Cape Mountain Zebra) Thinner and smaller than plains zebras. Stripes are also thinner and more numerous. Form breeding and bachelor social groups.

E) Suborder Ceratomorpha (Malaysian Tapir) Distensible, flexible elephant-like nose that can grip foliage during feeding. Solitary underbrush grazers. Eaten by leopards.

F) Suborder Ceratomorpha (Brazilian Tapir) Foals have white spots that fade into brown coat as tapir matures. Graze on palm nuts and aquatic foliage. Good swimmers.

G) Suborder Ceratomorpha (Black Rhinoceros) Triangular front lip with two horns. Can weigh up to 3 tons. Mud baths & thick skin protect against acacia thorns and parasites.

H) Suborder Ceratomorpha (White Rhinoceros) Square front lip with two larger horns. Can weigh 4 tons. Northern subspecies is functionally extinct; only 2 females alive.

I) Suborder Ceratomorpha (Indian One-Horned Rhinoceros) Unlike African species, has just one horn. Armor-like plates cover quadrants of body. Native to Himalayan foothills.

AUTHORS NOTES AND ACKNOWLEDGMENTS

When I was a kid, I was obsessed with animals and had numerous pets, bug collections, and could think of no place I would rather go than the zoo. While I did not grow up to be the keeper of the San Diego Zoo that I swore I would be, I've had a pretty good consolation prize teaching various honors, AP, and college biology courses over the years. It all started out with a plan to become a biology professor at a major research university....that is until I realized that I was clumsy and terrible at lab work and that I would rather not move all over the country living on Ramen noodles until I finally found a faculty position at middle age after several post-docs. I thoroughly enjoyed teaching during graduate school, so that's what I thought I would do for a little while until I figured out my career in academia. A couple of decades later, that IS what I do. It's been a fun ride. I've been a biology teacher, chemistry teacher, adjunct professor, football coach, academic team coach, AP coordinator and reader, principal, greenhouse curator, hall monitor, disciplinarian, pseudo dad at school, amateur cartoonist, and about a thousand other things in a profession that almost never gives you the same day twice.

After numerous iterations of AP biology and Dual Enrollment College Equivalency biology through multiple local colleges, I've accumulated a massive treasure trove of my own note system. It is in outline form, lettered and numbered, so that students can make a quick reference without having to scan an entire chapter of text. I've included illustrations, pictures, cartoons, and random side columns for the express purpose of holding the interest of teens and twenty-somethings. I try to use vernacular that they understand. Over the years, I've gotten such positive feedback from my students that I made the decision to publish all of these study guides into a set of biology reference books. It is my hope that you, the reader, find these books convenient, entertaining, and easier to read than your text. There are boldfaced words that refer to key vocabulary words or make reference to biological classification names that can be easily referenced online. I have tried my best to translate biology into plain English. It is immaterial to me if I sell 10 copies or thousands of these guides. If I help just one more biology student somewhere to gain an understanding of the topic and reach their academic goals, it was worth it.

I owe a debt of gratitude to so many people over the years that I can't name them all. I am going to attempt to name some of you.....and if I leave you out here, you are not exempt from my gratitude. Thank you so much to....

Jesus Christ, my wife Debbie, my parents Ronnie and Babs, my sister Karen, my son Ben, my daughter-in-law McKinley, all of my former biology students including (but not limited to.......Sydney Clouatre, Seth White, Joey Dunn, Aaron Ekback, Hayden Mills, Britney Greer, Kris Clark, Jaron Lehman, Callie and Avery Rades, Ben Moore, Lorena Magana, Will McConnell, Curtis Ledford, Alyssa Speck, Abby Pate, Kristen Quick, Ahmed Metwally, Nissa White, Dhriti Patel, Josie Poston, the Dairy Queen gang, Jayden Taylor, Bazya Smith, Liam King, Laura Kate Gleaton, and so, so many more, Dave Harvey, Sandy Steele, George Sanders, Gary Gibson, Latonja Turner, Tim Sansbury, Chris Dutton, Erin Potterf, Ed and Sue Pottorf, Charles Good, Rahim Kapadia, all of the members of my coaching fraternity, all of the long-lost brothers in my college fraternity, all friends past and present, and so many more. All of you have provided a piece of this long and ever-evolving puzzle.

GLOSSARY AND INDEX

TERM	DEFINITION
Abdomen	The rear segment of an animal. In vertebrates, many of the digestive organs are in the abdomen. In many invertebrates, tail muscles, respiratory organs, and gonads are here.
Abdominal Plates	Chitin exoskeletal plates that protect the ventral surface of abdomen in some insects.
Abomasum	In ruminant members of Order Artiodactyla, the fourth fermentive stomach chamber that receives food from the omasum and sends it on the small intestine.
Acariformes (Mites)	Order of arachnids that includes the blood-sucking trombid mites and the chewing sarcoptid mange mites. Hard abdominal plates protect a complex divided gut.
Accipitriformes	Order of birds of prey that includes hawks, eagles, and kites. Features include acute vision, curved beak for predation and ripping flesh, talons on zygodactyl feet, wide wings span, thick flight feathers.
Achelta (Spiny Lobsters)	Classification of crustaceans colloquially called lobsters, but lack distinctive cheliped claws. Instead, have large prominent antennae that are used like chopsticks.
Actinopterygii (Ray-Finned Fish)	Class that includes most living species of bony fish. Fish in this taxa have sail-like fins supported by rays and (often) bony spines), allowing them to be raised and lowered.
Acoelomate	Triploblastic animals (flatworms) that develop with the endoderm, mesoderm, and ectoderm sandwiched together with no space between muscles and organs. The design of the body restricts lateral movement and worm has to undulate to move.
Adaptation	An evolutionary change made by a species in response to environmental pressures. Note that evolutionary adaptations are not voluntary or in a single generation.
Adipose Fin	Small fin found between the dorsal fin(s) and caudal fins of certain groups of fish, such as salmonids and catfish. It is fleshy and lacks rays and spines.
Adductor Muscles (Bivalves)	Located on the posterior and anterior edges of the shell, these are two powerful muscles used to close the hinge. They act as antagonists to the adductor ligament. The adductor muscles are consumed in scallop seafood dishes.
Adductor Ligament (Bivalves)	Rooted at the edge of the shell at the hinge, this is a ligament that opens the shell when flexed and is used to push water through the siphons.
Aerioscelid	Group of early primitive reptiles that superficially resembled lizards, but had triangular amphibian-like skulls with no fenestrae, needle-like teeth, and long whip-like tails.
Afferent Blood Vessel	Blood vessels that bring blood into the organ in question. For instance, the pulmonary vein is afferent to the heart, bringing in oxygenated blood to pump.
Afrotheria	Clade of mammals that includes elephants, hyraxes, aardvarks, shrews, tenrecs, and manatees. Similarities in snout structure and bones of the feet are used as classifiers.

Agnatha (Jawless Fish)	Most primitive class of vertebrates, the jawless fish have bony jaws, but cartilage in their skulls and vertebrae. They lack paired fins and have open gill slits.
Air Sac	Any of several pairs of epithelial sacs (intraclavicular, anterior, posterior, abdominal) found extending off the lungs of birds, adding volume to the chest cavity to aid flight. Birds require two full inhalations and exhalations to fill or clear both the lungs and sacs.
Albumen	Nutritive storage protein founds in eggs that aids the development of an embryo. Most commonly known as 'egg white', it is found in all amniotic eggs.
Allantois	An embryonic membrane derived from the endoderm that sits underneath the chorion. Its function is to collect wastes and to exchange oxygen and carbon dioxide.
Alveoli	Spherical sacs that extend off the epithelial tissues of a lung, dramatically increasing the surface area available for gas exchange to the capillaries. While amphibians have some division of lung tissue, these are first seen in earnest in reptiles.
Ambylpgyi (Whip Spiders)	Order of arachnids with extremely long legs and spike-lined pedipalps that they flick to impale prey. Lack tail of whip scorpions. Females build nests and protect their young.
Amnion	A liquid-filled sac that encloses a developing embryo in reptiles, birds, & mammals, effectively serving as a self-contained pond and allowing vertebrates to settle land.
Amniotic Egg	An egg that has a 'self-contained pond' in the sense that the embryo is bathed in amniotic fluid inside of the amnion, allowing the parent organism (reptile, bird, or monotreme) to reproduce away from a water body.
Amoebocyte (Sponges)	Protozoan-like cells embedded in the matrix of sponges. These cells perform the majority of the biological functions in sponges, such as endocytosis of food and generation of gametes.
Amoebocyte (Invertebrates)	Blob-like cells capable of phagocytosis that swim around the hemolymph serve as a crude immune system for certain types of invertebrates, such as velvet worms.
Amphibian (Frogs, Newts, etc.)	A class or vertebrates that includes frogs, salamanders, newts, caecilians, and more. Characterized by development of lungs, vocal cords, paired appendages, and other terrestrial adaptations. Members are still restricted to need for aquatic reproduction.
Amphipoda (Amphipods)	Order of crustaceans that includes segmented, flattened members that lack a distinct carapace, Includes sowbugs and many scavenging and parasitic marine members.
Ampullae of Lorenzini	Organs located in the snout of cartilaginous fish and some primitive bony fish, such as sturgeon that detect electric fields coming from prey and other objects. They appear as a pit-like openings that are lined with ciliated nerves.
Anacostraca (Fairy Shrimp)	Fairy shrimp. Residents of salt lakes, tide pools, and transient habitats. Have two pairs of antennae, helmet-like exoskeleton with 20 segments, 11 pairs of legs. Small size.
Anadromous	Type of fish that spends the majority of their adulthood in the ocean, but returns to the freshwater stream of their juvenile stage to spawn. Example: Coho salmon.
Anaerobic Respiration	Any system of metabolism that operates without the need for oxygen as a final electron acceptor. Usually, this refers to some for of fermentation, wherein glycolysis runs and produces 2 ATP and pyruvate and NADH are converted to a waste product.
Anal Fins	Fins found in front of the anal vent in most cartilaginous and bony fish. They are used like a rudder in swimming, and sometimes modified for copulation in male fish.

Anal Pore	In comb jellyfish, a small canal that exits the gastrovascular cavity to release waste. In protozoans, a region on the cell, where waste vesicles are evacuated.
Anapsid (Turtles)	Ancient clade of reptiles that includes modern turtles, wherein the helmet-like skull lacks any openings for muscular attachments. Only the eye sockets have openings.
Annelida (Segmented Worms)	Order of lophotrochozoan invertebrates that have distinct ring-like segments that inflate under hydraulic pressure of the body wall. True coelomates, they have a closed circulatory system, a divided gut, and are hermaphroditic. Ex: earthworms, leeches.
Anseriformes	Order of birds that includes ducks, geese, swans, waterfowl. Features include rounded toothed bill, oily feathers, prolific preen glands, mating dances, bright plumage, corkscrew penis in males.
Antennae	Tactile organs located on the head of many invertebrates, especially insects and crustaceans that are used for feeling surfaces, judging distances, and picking up chemical cues in taste receptors. They also get FM radio.
Antennules	Smaller pair of tactile sensors located near the mouth at the anterior end of a crustacean. Emerge as a smaller pair of appendages underneath the antennae.
Antibody	A fork-shaped soluble protein that circulates the blood, sticking to antigen proteins on the surface of invading organisms or viruses. Produced by B-cells in large quantities.
Anticoagulants	Compounds, usually proteins, found in saliva of blood-eating organisms and venomous snakes that interfere with clotting reaction of blood. Allows parasites (ticks.leeches, etc.) to continue feeding or venom to take greater effect.
Antler	Found in members of Family Cervidae (deer), these are bony growths that emerge from the skull, nourished by velvety tissue as they grow. Unlike horns, they are shed yearly.
Anthozoa	Class of cnidarians that includes the true corals. Most are colonial polyps in the adult stage. Some feed on plankton or small animals, ambushing them with tentacles, while others feed symbiotically from the zooxanthellae inside their tissues. Some do both.
Anura (Frogs)	Order of amphibians that includes frogs and toads. Characterized by aquatic tadpole life stage, 3-chambered heart, respiratory exchange through skin, vocal cords.
Anus	Muscular opening at the posterior end of the alimentary canal that originates as the first opening of the deuterostome embryo. Muscular sphincter eliminates waste.
Aorta	Largest artery in the body of vertebrates. Carries oxygenated blood directly from the pumping of the left ventricle of the heart to the major organs of the body.
Apoda (Caecilians)	Order of Amphibians that includes the snake-like caecilians. Characterized by legless segmented bodies, burrowing behaviors, 3-chambered heart, aquatic larval stage.
Apodiformes	Order of birds that includes the hummingbirds and swifts. Features include very high metabolism, long bill in hummingbirds for nectar feeding, insectivorous beak in swifts. Rapid flight, cannot walk.
Appendix	Vestigial extension that branches off of the ascending colon as a remnant of the cecum (fermentative pouch) in mammals that have devolved this need, such as humans.
Apterygiformes	Order of birds that includes kiwis. Vestigial wings, fur-like feathers, long bill, very large eggs.
Arachnida	Class of arthropods that characteristically have 8 legs, 8 eyes, book lungs, chelicerae, pedipalps, and an open circulatory system. Includes spiders, scorpions, mites, etc.

Araneae	Order of arthropods that includes the true spiders. Have spinnerets and silk glands, book lungs, venom glands behind chelicerae, and sucking stomach with digestive cecae
Archenteron	The tunnel-like alimentary canal that forms in the developing embryo. In true coelomates, it connects the blastopore and gastrocoel to make the digestive tract.
Archeopteryx	A member of the bird-like clade of dinosaurs called the Aviales, it is regarded as the possible ancestral link between reptiles and modern birds. Fossils are feathered.
Archosauromorpha	Group of ancient reptiles that gave rise to two lineages of modern reptiles, with the first group becoming crocodilians and birds and the second becoming the turtles.
Artery	Blood vessels that have a thick smooth muscle wall outside of the internal epithelial tissue to withstand the higher systolic blood pressure requisite of them in carrying the efferent blood away to the body or lungs when the heart pumps.
Arthropod	Advanced coelomate ecdysozoans that have molted exoskeletons, jointed appendages, metamorphosis, and advanced reflexes. Includes arachnids, insects, crustaceans, more.
Artiodactyla	Order of mammals that includes hoofed mammals with four-chambered guts, such as cattle, deer, giraffes, pigs, hippopotamuses, antelope, peccaries, and pronghorns.
Astacidae (True Lobsters)	Classification of crustaceans that includes true lobsters, which are characterized by large pinching chelipeds that are used for defense, predation, and object manipulation.
Asymmetry	An organism, especially an animal, that develops in a random pattern, making it impossible to divide into any symmetrical half. Sponges are a primary example.
Asexual Reproduction	Reproduction that produces exact genetic clones of the parent. Includes binary fission in single-celled organisms and budding and fragmentation by mitosis.
Atlas	The hoop-shaped first cervical vertebrae, whose articulations support the skull.
Atrial Siphon	Attached to the innervated mantle membrane, it is the organ that sea squirts use to expel water as they filter feed.
Atrium / Atria	The muscular chamber(s) at the top of the heart that receive blood from afferent vessels. In fish, this is a single chamber. In other vertebrates, the right atrium receives deoxygenated blood from the vena cava, while the right receives oxygenated blood back from the pulmonary vein. The pacemaker node controls release to ventricles.
Auricles (Comb Jellyfish)	Lobe-shaped structures toward the opening of the gastrovascular cavity that are used to funnel water into the feeding structures, so plankton can be filtered.
Autonomic Nervous System	Part of the peripheral nervous system, this subdivision of the nervous system includes all involuntary homeostatic processes, such as heart rate, digestion, and respiration.
Autozooids	In Bryozoans, these are the members of the colony that have a lophophore and digestive tract. They feed other members of the colony that lack these structures.
Aves	Class of vertebrates that includes the modern birds. Characterized by feathers, keratin beak, endothermy, oviparity, air sacs in chest cavity, and many common behaviors.
Aviales	The clade of dinosaurs that gave rise to modern birds via one evolutionary path. Had beak-like snouts, clawed feet, feathers, and some had wing-like membranes.
Avicularia	A beak-like structure that replaces lophophores in some Bryozoan colony members. Used to protect other autozooids

Axis	In vertebrates, the second vertebrae that interlocks with the atlas. It has a projection that articulates with the skull to form a pivot point. Neck muscles articulate to axis.
Axon	Branch-like structures that are triggered by stimuli or receive electrical signals or neurotransmitters from other nerves, causing the nerve to depolarize and fire off.
B-Cell	A type of lymphocyte produced in the bone marrow that is responsible for humoral immunity. They produce antibodies and participate in inflammation process with other white blood cells. Abundant in lymph nodes and the spleen.
Baleen	Brush-like keratin bristles found in the mouth of filter-feeding whales for straining plankton, krill, and other foods from the water. Baleen replaces devolved teeth.
Basal Amniote	Small lizard-like reptiles, such as Hylomonus, that evolved the first amniotic eggs, allowing their embryos to become independent of water with a 'pond in an egg'.
Basking	Behavior found in many ectotherms, especially reptiles, wherein solar energy or ambient heat from convection is used to raise the body temperature to increase the metabolic rate for digestion and activities requiring blood flow to the muscles.
Biceps	Large two-headed skeletal muscle that articulates at the elbow and shoulder joints. Used in lifting in bipedal animals and running, swatting, and jumping in quadrupeds.
Bicuspid Valve	Heart valve located between the right atrium and the pulmonary artery that prevents the backflow of deoxygenated blood in mammals and birds.
Bilateral Symmetry	An organism, especially an animal, that can be divided into two equal and symmetrical halves down a midline. Example: right and left side of body in humans
Bile	A substance produced in the liver from the breakdown of membrane lipids during the breakdown of red blood cells. Bile salts are the end-product. Stored in the gallbladder, hey have a soapy texture used in the emulsification of fats in the intestine.
Bile Duct	Duct that empties into the duodenal section of the small intestine, originating at the gallbladder. Bile salts are squirted through it during the digestive process.
Binocular Vision	Evolved type of vision characterized by forward-facing eyes, sacrificing width of field-of-view for acuity and improved depth perception. Present in primates, dogs, owls, etc.
Biodiversity	Refers to relative richness in number of species per given area of habitat in ecology.
Bioluminescence	The ability to generate light from biochemical enzymatic reactions in living cells. Various systems for the production of light exist, such as the breakdown of luciferin in lightning bugs or the generation of light by green fluorescent protein in jellyfish.
Biomagnification	The tendency of lipid-soluble chemicals to become more-and-more concentrated as they are consumed and passed up the food chain. For instance, mercury in large fish.
Biomass	Refers to total amount of living tissue per given area of habitat in ecology.
Biramous Appendages	Refers to legs or other appendages that end in two forked tips. For instance, the claws, legs, and swimmerets of a lobster are all biramous.
Bivalve / Bivalvia (Shellfish)	Class of mollusks better known as 'shellfish' with two hinged shells around a mantle and gut cavity. No head. Have incurrent and excurrent siphons for moving water to filter feed. Have a muscular foot for digging and burrowing. Clams, scallops, mussels, etc.

Bladder	Organ that acts as a storage sac for the collection of urine from the kidneys and for evacuation of nitrogenous wastes. Sphincter relaxation releases urine.
Blastula	A hollow ball of cells that forms during the development of an embryo, as the zygote enlarges and increased the surface area to volume ratio.
Blastocoel	The hollow space inside the blastula.
Blastoderm	The layer of cells that makes up the outer part of the blastula.
Blastopore	The opening in the developing gastrula that will become the mouth in protostomes and will develop into the anus in deuterostomes.
Blattoidea (Cockroaches)	Order of insects that includes the cockroaches. Characterized by symbiotic microbes in gut, scavenging of wide range of foods, membranous wings, and colonial behavior.
Blood	Complex mixture of fluids that contains plasma, antibodies, hemoglobin-rich red blood cells for gas exchange, and numerous classes of germ-fighting leukocytes (white cells). A connective tissue that is part of circulatory, respiratory, immune, and endocrine systems.
Blowhole	In whales, the respiratory openings at the top of the head. As whales evolved from mesonychids, the nasal openings migrated upward and fused together.
Body Wall	Refers to the inner layer of mesoderm muscles inside the coelom (body cavity) that face the organs. Sometimes used as for leverage points in hydrostatic invertebrates.
Book Gills	Found under the tail in horseshoe crabs, they are multiple feathery membranous respiratory organs that stack in sheets like the pages of a book, ensuring that there is enough surface area for the oxygen demand of the large body volume.
Book Lungs	The respiratory system of arachnids, who must have several layers of moistened epithelial sheets to exchange gases quickly enough for their large body mass. Found in the abdominal segments, opening to spiracles on the underside.
Boreoeutheria	Clade of animals that includes primates, rodents, hedgehogs, shrews, and rabbits. Characterized by common bone structures, large cranial capacity relative to body size.
Brachial Valve	The lower shell of a Brachiopod (lampshell). Used like a castanet with upper shell.
Brachiopoda (Lamp Shells)	Order of lophotrochozoans that bear a superficial resemblance to bivalves, but have unique internal anatomy, including coiled lophophore and pedicle shell ligament.
Bronchi and Bronchioles	Bronchi branch from the trachea to each lung, diverging into smaller branched airways called bronchioles. They are composed of smooth muscle, cartilage, and an epithelium.
Brood Pouch	Convergently evolved structures of various tissue types used by a variety of animals (crustaceans, brachiopods, marsupials) to protect eggs or offspring next to the body.
Bryozoan	Order of soft-bodied lophotrochozoan animals that live in large marine colonies. Roles of members (zooids) vary and their anatomy reflects this accordingly.
Brain	Master organ of central nervous system. It controls basal body functions, locomotion, sensory information, emotions, information processing, thought, and decision-making.
Buccal Siphon	In tunicates (sea squirts), this tube-like organ sucks water in, allowing plankton to be strained out by the pharyngeal basket below.

Bucerotiformes	Order of birds that includes hoopoes and hornbills. Features include large curved bills, with bony plate for amplifying calls in hornbills. Nesting in hollowed-tree cavities, with male bringing food.
Budding	Form of asexual reproduction, where miniature clones of a parent are generated from mitotic division of undifferentiated cells. Common in simple invertebrates like corals.
Bullae	Characteristic of feline skulls, these are spherical walls in the cranium that completely surround the inner ear structures, differentiating felid carnivores from canids.
Bursa	Immune organ that serves a similar function to the thymus of mammals in juvenile birds. Divided into many different folds, it is rooted at the cloacal opening.
Byssus Threads	Threadlike muscular organs found in some bivalves, such as mussels and bivalves that are extended from shell and used to adhere to surfaces and transfer sperm to females.
Caenophidia (Snakes)	The Suborder of snakes that contains most living species. They are distinguished from the Suborder Macrostomata by the complete lack of a pelvic girdle (devolved).
Calcarea (Hard Sponges)	Class of sponges that incorporate calcified limestone into their matrix, providing a degree of protection against consumption by reef animals.
Canine Teeth	In mammals, conical differentiated teeth positioned between the incisors and the premolars at the corners of the jaw. Used for puncturing and holding prey or fighting.
Capillaries	Smallest of the blood vessels, they are essentially tunnels made of a unicellular layer of epithelial tissue, which allows for quick and easy diffusion of nutrients and oxygen into the surrounding tissues that they pass.
Caracoid Bone	In ray-finned fishes, a curving bone inside the body wall that articulates perpendicularly with the ulna and radius at the base of the fins. Muscles that move fins articulate here.
Carapace	Hard protective external shell covering the thorax and abdomen. In ecdysozoan invertebrates, this is usually made of chitin. In vertebrates, such as turtles, it is a combination of keratin in the integument, along with bone.
Carnivora	Order of mammals with dentition and digestive systems designed for carnivory, claws, and musculoskeletal systems designed for predation. Includes cats, dogs, bears, weasels, hyenas, raccoons, otters, foxes, jackals, binturongs, wolves, and others.
Cardiac Stomach	In echinoderms (such as starfish), it is the central digestive organ in the center of the animal, connecting to multiple tunnel-like pyloric stomachs in the center of each arm.
Caridea (True Shrimp)	A suborder of crustaceans that are distinguished by the ability to pump water over the gills with the walking legs, a jointed muscular abdomen, a rostrum, and long antennae.
Carotid Arteries	The efferent vessels that send a blood supply the head, branching directly off of the aorta. The brain is dependent upon the carotids as the origins of blood supply.
Carpals	The main long bones of the front hands or appendages in vertebrates. Their shape, size, and proportion may be modified for evolutionary needs.
Carrying Capacity	In ecology, the maximum number of individuals of a species that an environment can support indefinitely. Can vary yearly with food supply, predators, etc. Symbolized as K.
Cartilage	Connective tissue that is essentially loose chondrocytes embedded in a secreted matrix of glycoproteins and connective tissues. Texture is increasingly harder and more fibrous from hyaline (ex: ears) to elastic (ex: knee) to fibrous (ex: vertebral discs).

Catadromous	Refers to fish that migrate from freshwater, where they spend most of their adulthood, into the ocean to spawn, where larvae grow up. Example: American eels.
Catch Connective Tissue	Mesh-like fibrous connective tissue that runs through the body cavity of echinoderms. When flexed, it allows the echinoderm to hold its body into a protective rigid shape.
Cathartiformes	Order of birds that includes new world vultures, condors, and buzzards. Carrion feeders with thick, armor-like flight feathers used in gliding, naked heads, powerful immune systems, talons on feet.
Caudal	Referring to the tail region, anatomically speaking.
Caudal Appendages	Set of brush-like appendages found near the tail region of priapulid worms. Used for burrowing and the removal of nitrogenous wastes via diffusion out of the tissues.
Caudal Fin	A fin or fin-like appendage located at the posterior of an animal, used for swimming.
Caudofemoralis	A large powerful muscle in the tail of birds that, when flexed, allows them to control the angle and spread of their tail feathers, aiding in changing direction during flight.
Cecum / Cecae	Blind-ended digestive pouches used to gain surface are for extraction of extra nutrients. Often filled with fermentative mutualistic microbes, as in rabbits.
Central Canal	Flexed and relaxed, it is an organ in echinoderms that serves as the central point of hydraulic pressure and locomotion, branching into the ampullae that end in tube feet.
Celiac Blood Vessels	The set of arteries and veins that serve as a junction point in carrying blood supply to the organs inside the body cavity.
Cementum	Calcified connective tissue (replacing enamel) that covers the dentin in teeth of mammals of Order Xenarthra, such as sloths and armadillos.
Central Nervous System	The subdivision of the nervous system that consists of the brain and spinal cord. The brain controls all bodily functions and integrates and processes all information, while the spinal cord is a relay to the peripheral nervous system
Cephalization	Presence of a definite head at the anterior end of bilaterally symmetrical animals.
Cephalochordata (Lancelets)	A subphylum of chordates that includes only lancelets. While they have fish-like somites, a notochord and a neural tube, they lack the complete cranium of vertebrates.
Cephalopoda (Octopus, Squid)	Class of mollusks that includes chambered nautilus, squid, vampire squid, and octopi. As compared to other mollusks, brain and eyes are very advanced, circulatory system is fully closed, and mantle membrane is internal in most species. Foot divided into tentacles with gripping suckers.
Cephalothorax	A body segment that is a fused combination of a head and thorax. Found in many crustaceans (such as a lobster) and some arachnids (such as spiders)
Cerebral Ganglion	A cluster of nerve bodies found in the head of many invertebrates that functions as a primitive brain, controlling body movements, reflexes, and secreting certain hormones.
Cerebellum	Located behind the fourth ventricle of the brain, when bisected, its nerves are branched. Functions in muscle control, movement, spatial awareness, and balance.
Cerebrum	Encompassing two hemispheres in the anterior part of the brain and the first two ventricles, it has multiple functions, including integration of sensory information, speech, intelligence, memory, problem-solving, higher thought, and emotions.

Cestodes (Tapeworms)	Class of flatworms that live parasitically in the intestinal cavities of vertebrates. They have devolved almost all organs, including eyes and digestive system and are essentially chains of cloned segments, each containing hermaphroditic gonads.
Cetecea	Order of mammals that includes toothed whales and baleen whales. Features include loss of leg bones, modification of arm bones into flippers, nostril fusion into blowhole, and presence of baleen plates in mouths of larger filter-feeding species.
Chaetognatha (Arrow Worms)	Phylum of marine worms that have keratin jaws, compound eyes, paired fins on the body, and relatively few organ systems. Hermaphroditic. Often found in the plankton.
Chalaza	Tether-like membrane inside of amniotic eggs that suspends the yolk and the embryo.
Cheek Pouches	In rodents, a long extension of the buccal cavity that extends laterally down both sides of the body, allowing gathering and temporary storage of multiple food items.
Chelicerates	One of the two major clades of arthropods. Mouthparts are designed for puncturing and biting and may or may not be attached to venom glands. Example:
Chelicerae	Biting mouthparts found in arachnids, such as spiders and scorpions.
Chelipeds	The modified first pair of appendages that serve as claws in most crustaceans. Muscular segments covered with a hard chitin shell. Delicious with butter. Used for grabbing food, pinching predators during self-defense, manipulating the substrate.
Chemoreceptors	Nerve cells that sense chemical changes in the environment. They are covered with membrane protein receptors attached to signaling pathways that trigger a response.
Chemosensory Organs	Any organ that is innervated with chemoreceptors, whose function is to detect changes in surrounding environmental chemistry. For example, taste buds and sinuses.
Chilopoda (Centipedes)	Class of arthropod invertebrates that includes the centipedes. Have dozens of legs and segments, venomous chelicerae, and internal anatomy similar to that of insects.
Chitin	Fibrous, insoluble glycoprotein of various chemical formulations that is used as a base compound for protective shells or stalks in animals (such as crustaceans and hydroids). Coincidental different chitin compounds are found in fungal cell walls.
Chiroptera	Order of mammals that includes bats and flying foxes. Features include modification of carpals and phalanges into wings, sonar in insectivorous species, roosting behaviors.
Chlorogonen Cells	Clusters of cells found in each segment of annelids that perform liver-like functions, such as producing digestive enzymes and storing fat and glycogen.
Choanocytes (Collar Cells)	Flagellated cells at the mouth of a sponge that generate water flow current for filter feeding by whipping and pulling water into the osculum (mouth-like opening).
Chondrichthyes	Class that includes the cartilaginous fish (sharks, rays, skates, ratfish). As compared to agnathans, they have evolved a lower jaw, paired fins, an oil liver for buoyancy, intestinal spiral valve, and many other features. However, they retain primitive open gills and their reproduction is much slower and more limited than most bony fish.
Chondrostei	Order of bony fish whose only extant members are sturgeon and paddlefish. They retain cartilage components in their skeleton, heterocercal tails, and ampullae of Lorenzini, much like their cartilaginous fish ancestors.
Chordata (Chordates)	Phylum of animals who have a dorsal notochord, develop a neural tube and nerve cord, a complex digestive system, closed circulatory system, pharyngeal gill slits, and a tail.

Chorion	The outer membrane that surrounds the amnion and embryo in an amniotic egg. With the allantois, it exchanges blood gases and nutrients from the shell. In placental mammals, its tissues develop into the placenta that will nourish the growing fetus.
Chromatophore	A pigmented cell located in the epithelial membrane of many animals. Connected to autonomic nerves, they can be stimulated to flex or relax in patterns or in unison, thereby changing the color of the animal for camouflage or communication.
Chrysalis	Typically refers to the chitin-shelled obtate larval stage in butterfly metamorphosis.
Cigautera Toxin	Neurotoxin produced by dinoflagellates, especially those in coral, that concentrates in large predatory fish by biomagnification after they feed on smaller coral eating fish.
Cilia	Hair-like extensions of the cytoskeleton made from microtubules. One cell can have hundreds. They are common where microscopic materials need to be 'swept' along. For example, cilia in the fallopian tubes push the egg toward the uterus.
Ciliate	A phylum of protozoans that swim using hair-like microtubule projections like oars.
Circulatory System	Body system responsible for distributing oxygen, nutrients, and immune cells to meet needs of all cells in other organ systems. Varies in complexity, based upon the degree of evolution of the animal. Absent in small invertebrates capable of using diffusion.
Clade	In the modern system of evolutionary taxonomy, it is a group of organisms grouped together by characters that imply that they have all evolved from a common ancestor.
Cladocera (Daphnia)	Order of crustaceans that includes the water fleas (daphnia). Small, transparent members of aquatic and marine zooplankton with a single fused carapace. Many species are all female; generate egg clutches by parthenogenesis. One compound eye.
Claspers	Modified anal fins found in male members of the Chondrichthyes. Used like a pair of penises to transfer sperm into the cloacal openings of females.
Class	Order of taxonomic classification that is more specific than class and inclusive of orders and all subordinate classifications (family, genus, and species).
Clavicle	The collar bone found in some mammals. Articulates to scapula and sternum.
Cleavage	Mitosis during development that divides a zygote in half multiple times to create a blastula. Increases surface-area-to-volume ratio to adjust to increased metabolism.
Clitellum	Specialized collar-like segment found in segmented worms. The oviducts and sperm ducts emerge here and worms line up their clitella in opposed directions to mate.
Cloaca	Multi-function body opening found in most vertebrates, such as birds and reptiles, where the intestine, urinary tract, and reproductive ducts all empty.
Closed Circulatory System	An advanced circulatory system, wherein blood remains completely enclosed in a complex circuit of arteries, veins, and capillaries without direct contact with most organs. Nutrients and gases traverse from the bloodstream to tissues by diffusion.
Clutch	Refers to the entire cluster of eggs ovulated by an oviparous female animal in one reproductive event. Many female animals carry the clutch (such as copepods) under the abdomen or protect it by building nests (such as sea turtles and birds).
Cnidarian	Phylum of soft-bodied marine animals that have two tissue layers, no true organs, usually two life stages (polyp & medusa), and tentacles tipped with stinging cells.

Cndiocyte	Cells located along the surface of cnidarian tentacles. The produce venom and contain the barbed harpoon-like nematocyst organelles that fire venom into the target.
Coarctate Pupae	Refers to insects that develop like nested Russian dolls inside the previous exoskeletal molt, before splitting this outer shell and emerging as a larger instar. Example: cicadas.
Cochlea	The spiral inner cavity of the inner ear, which contains the Organ of Corti. Lined with ciliated hair cells, they respond to the vibration of otoliths, producing heard noises.
Cocoon	Typically refers to the silk-covered obtate larval stage in the metamorphosis of moths. However, caddisflies and some other insects also create structures called cocoons.
Coelomate	Animal body design that incorporates a true body cavity, allowing organs to move with flexibility while being tethered in place by muscles of the mesoderm. Segmented worms and almost all other more advanced animals make use of this design.
Collagen	Fibrous, rubbery connective tissue protein that is used to fill gaps and provide support in the tissues of animals.
Colloblast	Feeding structures used by comb jellies to trap plankton in filter-feeding. They are comb-like structures located on the tentacles that secrete a glue-like substance.
Colon	Segment of the large intestine (ascending, transverse, descending, or sigmoid). Involved in the reclamation of water and nutrients from food, as well as microbial production of beneficial nutrients. Peristalsis passes food remnants on to rectum.
Colonial Animal	Refers to mostly sessile animals (bot not always), wherein all members of the group contribute to building a protective home. Examples are corals, hydroids, bryozoans.
Colonial Protozoans	Groups of single-celled eukaryote protozoans that form a matrix around themselves and live cooperatively in colonies. Sponges appear to have evolved from these.
Colostrum	The protein-rich substance secreted by the mammary glands as the first batch of milk. Extremely nutrient dense, full of antibodies, and lower in fat than conventional milk.
Columbiformes	Order of birds that includes pigeons, doves, dodos. Extremely large pectoral muscles for fast flight, small head, rounded and streamlined body, short tail, extremely accurate migratory abilities.
Complete Metamorphosis	Series of life stages, wherein juvenile stages and instars have distinctly different anatomy and appearances than the mature adult stage. Example: caterpillar vs. moth.
Compound Eye	Found in many invertebrates, multiple lens facets and optic nerves integrate back to a processing center to integrate a single image, as opposed to single lens design of vertebrates.
Cone Cells	Photoreceptor cells located in the retina of the eye that are responsible for the detection of color vision. Contain retinol pigment, which responds photochemically to light, causing nerve impulses to be sent to the vision center of the brain.
Contour Feather	Rigid keratin-rich feathers found on the outermost surface of birds. They overlap in layers and have a thick center calamus for support. Responsible for keeping the body an aerodynamic shape to stay in flight.
Conus Arteriosus (Fish)	A muscular sac at the apex of the heart that assists fish in pumping oxygenated blood. It is located posterior to the ventricle and helps push the blood into the body tissues.

Convergent Evolution	Pattern of evolution, wherein genetically unrelated (or distantly related) organisms develop and evolve similar morphology, due to similar environments or needs.
Copepoda (Copepods)	Order of crustaceans known as copepods. Most numerous animals on earth as pat of zooplankton. Have a single compound eye, long horn-like antennae, and a tapered body with a
Copepodite	Sub-adult life stages of copepods that occur between the naupliar stages of metamorphosis and the final adult form.
Coral Bleaching	Phenomenon that occurs when rising water temperatures, silt, pH shifts, or some other irritant causes symbiotic algae to leave their coral hosts, resulting in slow starvation for the polyps, death of the local reef, and major damage to ecosystem.
Coronal Cilia	The crown-like ring of cilia that surrounds the vase shaped mouth of rotifers. They whip in unison, drawing plankton into the mouth.
Cosmoid Scale	Prehistoric type of fish scales that are only found in a handful of surviving species like lungfish. Have a layer of dentin-like substance sandwiched between two layers of bone. Overlap and provide an armor-like covering over the body.
Countercurrent Flow	The respiratory system used by fish, wherein the openings of the gills funnel incoming water at a perpendicular orientation to the gill vessels, ensuring that the maximum amount of blood (lateral side of vessel) is available for diffusion of gases.
Courtship	Behaviors that are used by members of the opposite sex to attract potential mates. Particularly prevalent in birds, with plumage, dances, and calls dictating success.
Cowper's Glands	Also known as the bulbourethral glands, they neutralize acidic fluids in the urethra to allow sperm to travel without damage.
Coxal Glands	Excretory organs found in many arthropods, which are often located at the base of each leg. They filter and excrete nitrogenous wastes from protein digestion.
Cranial Cartilage (Chondrichthyes)	In cartilaginous fish, the cranium is composed of plates of cartilage that do not ossify into bone. Cranium consists of the chondrocranium, palatoquadrate, basal plate, etc.
Cranial Nerves	A set of 12 pairs of nerves that emerge from the forebrain, midbrain, or brainstem. Most of them control sensory functions (olfaction, vision, etc.) or reflexes and movements of the head, face, and neck area (oculomotor, trigeminal, etc.).
Cranium	The part of the vertebrate skull that forms a protective enclosure around the brain. Cartilage in Agnathans and Chondrichthyes, ossified into bone in other vertebrates.
Crepuscular	A species whose Circadian rhythms may fluctuate seasonally or environmentally, meaning that at times that species is active in daytime or during the night.
Crocodilia	Most advanced order of living reptiles that includes alligators, crocodiles, caimans, and gavials. Advances over other reptiles include 4-chambered heart, nesting and nurturing behaviors by mothers, and much larger body size.
Crop	Organ between the esophagus or pharynx and stomach of many animals that acts like a blender jar, regulating the amount of crudely processed food entering for digestion, ensuring that all food is processed efficiently. Found in earthworms, birds, and others.
Crossing Over (Meiosis)	A mechanism of genetic recombination that occurs during Prophase I of Meiosis I. Pieces of paired homologous chromosomes break and switch places, generating recombinant chromosomes with novel combinations of genes in eggs and sperm.

Crustacea (Crustaceans)	Class of arthropods, (such as crabs, daphnia, amphipods) characterized by chitinous exoskeleton, jointed appendages, such as antennae, walking legs, swimmerets, and gills and the ability to osmoregulate. Anatomy varies markedly between orders.
Cuculiformes	Order of birds that includes cuckoos and roadrunners. Angular wings, long tail, downward pointed top bill, three forward toes, one backward. Cuckoos lay eggs in other birds' nests (ectoparasites)
Cryptodira	Suborder of turtles that are called 'hidden necked' turtles colloquially. Includes the large majority of extant turtles that can draw their necks into their shells.
Ctentophore (Comb Jellies)	Comb jellies. Phylum of soft-bodied marine animals with two tissue layers, no true organs. Have rows of ciliated combs that are used for filter-feeding plankton.
Cubozoa (Box Jellyfish)	Class of cnidarians known as box jellies that spend the majority of their lives as pelagic opportunistic predators. Highly venomous. Body morphology differs from true jellies.
Cuticle	Layer of hard connective tissue, usually keratin, that surrounds the integument and provides protection for ecdysozoan invertebrates, such as insects and crustaceans.
Cystid	Non-living protein matrix secreted by bryozoans that glues the colony together.
Cysts (Parasitic worms)	Dormant embryos or larvae covered by a hard casing, often as a result of misdirection in the bloodstream to muscle tissues. When ideal conditions of a host gut return, cysts begin to develop and ultimately become an adult worm infestation.
Deciduous Teeth	Refers to teeth that are shed and replaced and intended to be temporary. Humans have one set of deciduous differentiated teeth, whereas many animals, such as sharks, have continual rows of deciduous undifferentiated teeth being replaced for wear.
Deltoid	Large spherical muscle atop the shoulder that has a large degree of control over the movement of the front shoulder joint.
Demoptera (Earwings)	Order of insects that includes the earwings. Characterized by two claw-like appendages at end of segmented abdomen and reduced wings. Scavengers of rotting vegetation.
Demospongae (Soft Sponges)	Class of sponges that have soft matrices made from spongin and other soft proteins. The type of sponges used traditionally for natural cleaning sponges.
Dendrite	Extensions of nerve cell membranes and cytoplasm that form synapses with the axons of efferent neurons, receiving signals or neurotransmitters that pass the impulse.
Dendrobrachiata (Prawns)	Suborder of crustaceans that have many anatomical similarities to shrimp, but differ in that the females release their eggs into the plankton, rather than carrying a clutch.
Dentin	Layer of teeth underneath the enamel that covers and protects the pulp cavity. It is composed of apatite and other minerals mixed with collagen and other proteins.
Dermis	A guy in accounting that smells vaguely of corn chips and unwashed socks that he has re-worn for several weeks. He wears clip-on ties and still collects Pokemon cards as a middle-aged adult man.
Detritivore	An organism that feeds on detritus (dead organic matter). A scavenger. Along with decomposers, they help return nutrients to the soil for uptake by producers. Ex: vulture
Deuterostome	Animals whose embryos develop the posterior end first, with the first opening in the gastrula becoming an anus. Includes echinoderms and chordate animals

Dewlap	Flap of skin that hangs from the neck of many animals, with varied functions. May be used in thermoregulation (lizards) or a colored secondary sex characteristic (turkeys).
Diaphragm Muscle	Found only in mammals, when flexed, it pushes downward and increases the volume of the chest cavity, causing a pressure differential that forces air to enter the lungs. When relaxed, the chest volume decreases, causing exhalation.
Diapsid	A clade of reptiles that has two openings in the skull for muscular attachments, in addition to the eye sockets. Includes all modern reptiles other than turtles.
Diastema	Space between the canine teeth and incisors found in certain animals, especially herbivores. This allows large quantities of plants to be stored in the cheeks at once, with the animal gnawing it down and swallowing small bits like a blender.
Differentiated Teeth	Found only in mammals, it refers to the phenomenon of teeth evolving into incisors, canines, pre-molars, molars, and other specialized types. All differentiated teeth have a living pulp cavity with protective dentin and enamel layers on the outside.
Digestive Gland	An organ found in the thorax of arthropods and, through convergent evolution, also in many mollusks and some other phyla, that secretes digestive enzymes through a duct into the alimentary canal during digestion. Similar in function to a liver and pancreas.
Digestive Tube	The primary digestive structure in spiders, which takes in liquified remnants of prey. Ducts from the digestive gland deliver enzymes into the compartment.
Dioecious	A species that has separate male and female sexes with only one distinct set of reproductive organs per individual. Applies to most vertebrates and ecdysozoans.
Diploblastic Animal	Animals that have only two tissue layers (the ectoderm and the endoderm). Contain a layer of jelly-like mesoglea between these. Includes cnidarians and ctenophores.
Diploid	A cell, such as the adult somatic cells of animals, that contains two copies of each distinct chromosome per cell nucleus, allowing for genetic variation.
Diplopoda (Millipedes)	Order of arthropods that includes the millipedes. Characterized by dozens to hundreds of legs and segments. Scavengers in leaf litter. Internal anatomy similar to insects.
Dipnoi (Lungfish)	Order of fish that includes the lungfish. Covered with armor-like cosmoid scales. They are physoclistus, with spiracles opening into a duct in the pharyngeal cavity that connects to the swim bladder, which they can use like a primitive lung.
Diptera (Flies and allies)	Order of insects characterized by one pair of true membranous wings and mouthparts specialized for sucking or scavenging. Includes flies, midges, mosquitoes, and gnats.
Differentiated Cells/Tissues	In multi-celled organisms, cells derived from stem cells or meristems that have turned genes on or off and/or developed according to different environmental cues resulting in them having different appearances and functions.
Digestive Gland	Various iterations of this organ are found in many different invertebrates. Typically, a spongy soft gland that sits atop the stomach or intestine, excreting various catabolic digestive enzymes through connected ducts, aiding in the digestion of food.
Digestive Tract	The alimentary canal that is derived from part of the endoderm in embryo. Functions in extracting and absorbing nutrients from food. Complexity depends on animal.
Dinoflagellates	Phylum of maroon-colored algae that are common in ocean plankton, but also as symbiotic residents of corals as zooxanthellae. Many species generate toxins and bioluminescence, providing a degree of protection to corals, in addition to sugars.

Dioecious Plant	Plants, such as pine trees, wherein separate male and female reproductive structures (i.e. seed cones and pollen cones) are located at distinctly different locations on the same supportive sporophyte plant.
Directional Plane	In anatomy, used to refer to the location and direction of various structures. Examples: medial is toward the middle, sagittal is down the center, etc.
Diurnal	A species whose Circadian rhythms cause it to be instinctively active during daylight.
Divergence	In evolutionary terms, this occurs when a related group of organisms shares a common ancestor. Due to isolation in new environments or division of resources, the group evolves in two different directions, becoming increasingly different in traits.
Diverticulae	A pair of coiled, ciliated organs near the posterior of spoonworms that filter waste.
Domain	Largest and most general biological classification based on cell structure. Eukaryotes (true nucleus) are large, complex cells with multiple organelles. Eubacteria and archaebacteria are prokaryotic domains without true nuclei, yet have major differences in biochemical composition and ribosome structure between them.
Dominant Gene	In diploid organisms, if present, will control the expression of a physical phenotype over the recessive gene. For instance, purple flowers are dominant to white in peas.
Dorsal Fin	The fin that emerges from the dorsal surface of fish. Used like a rudder in swimming.
Dorsal Nerve Cord	Found in chordate deuterostome animals, it is located on the dorsal surface (and protected by vertebrae in the vertebrates). It connects the brain to spinal nerves that control various body structures and returns signals from those organs for integration.
Down Feather	Bird feathers that are located underneath the contour feathers. Their filaments are wispy, thin, and soft. They insulate the bird and are particularly important in chicks.
Drone	Male hymenopterans, which often have a single set of chromosomes, and serve no other purpose, but to mate with the queen.
Ductus Arteriosus	A short duct that partially divides the pulmonary and systemic circulatory loops in fish.
Ductus Pneumosus	A tube-like organ that connects the swim bladder to the mouth in physoclistus fish that are capable of using the swim bladder like a lung.
Duodenum	The first segment of the small intestine after the pyloric sphincter. It possesses glands that neutralize the stomach acid. Bile and pancreatic ducts enter this portion of the small intestine and the fine digestion process begins here, with some absorption.
Ecdysozoan	One of the major two clades of complex triploblastic invertebrates. Characterized by jointed appendages and a protective cuticle around the body. Example: arthropods.
Ecdysteroids	Hormones produced by the brain of insects that control stages of the molt cycle.
Echinodermata (Starfish & Allies)	Phylum of deuterostome invertebrates that possess radial symmetry, ring canals and tube feet, spiny skin, and the ability to reproduce by fragmentation.
Echiura (Spoonworms)	Phylum of lophotrochozoan invertebrates that share some anatomical similarities to segmented worms, yet have a unique proboscis organ used for feeding and diverticulae at the posterior end for filtering waste.

Echolocation	A communicative ability used by bats, whales, some birds, and a few other animals. A noise originating with the animal is bounced off of surrounding objects and picked back up by audioreceptors. The brain integrates the noises to determine objects' positions.
Ectoderm	The outer tissue layer in a developing embryo that becomes the skin, epidermal tissue, and the nervous system. Folds into neural crest to close the brain and spine.
Ectotherm(ic)	Colloquially called 'cold blooded' animals, includes all invertebrates and most vertebrates other than birds and mammals. They must alter their body temperature by changing their location in the environment with behaviors, such as basking.
Ectoparasite	A parasite that derives benefits from its host without entering its body cavity. Dermal parasites are usually blood feeders (ticks, lampreys, lice), while some ectoparasites simply steal resources from the host, such as cowbirds abandoning babies for other songbirds to raise the chick in their stead.
Efferent Blood Vessel	Blood vessels that carry blood away from the heart and toward the body or the lungs. For instance, the aorta and pulmonary arteries are efferent vessels.
Egg Cocoon	System of reproduction used by segmented worms and ribbon worms, wherein a mass of eggs in covered with a thick mucus coating, which forms a protective shell until conditions are optimal for emergence of offspring.
Ejaculatory Ducts	Openings in the body of male invertebrates, particularly crustaceans, that allow the passage of semen or sperm packets to exit the reproductive tract and pass to a female.
Embryoblast	The side of a developing embryo that will become the organism.
Emulsification	In the digestive system, the process that is used to homogenize fats and lipids into the digestive slurry. Amphoteric bile salts and peristaltic contractions break up droplets.
Enamel	The hard apatite (calcium phosphate) layer that is deposited above the dentin layer on the outer biting surface of vertebrate teeth.
Endocrine System	System of glands that export their hormonal products into the bloodstream or body fluids. Most endocrine glands produce steroid-based hormones to signal other cells far away from the source. Examples: adrenal glands, thyroid gland, pituitary gland.
Endocytosis	Uptake of materials by active transport that are too large to be taken up by membrane proteins or diffusion. The cell they enter must reorganize the cytoskeleton and take up a vesicle or form a vacuole to import large materials, such as fats, into the cell.
Endoderm	Cells in the layer of the developing embryo that are fated to become the future digestive system and the reproductive system.
Endoparasite	A parasite that enters a host and lives directly off of nutrition inside their body. The liver is a popular site, due to its store of glycogen, as is the small intestine for its slurry of digested food. Examples: tapeworms, roundworms, botfly larvae.
Endoskeleton	System of body support in vertebrates, wherein muscles articulate to bones and cartilage derived from the mesoderm layer of the embryo. Provides fulcrum system for muscle movements, protection, and immune functions. Examples: bones in human skeleton.
Endostyle	A ciliated groove-like organ found in tunicates (sea squirts) that secretes mucus and traps plankton, directing food sources into the pharyngeal basket.

Endotherm(ic)	A vertebrate organism that is capable of maintaining an internal body temperature independent of the surrounding environment. Colloquially called 'warm blooded'. The hypothalamus of the brain controls blood vessel diameter, allowing it to trap or release metabolic heat generated by muscle contractions. Example: people, birds, horses.
Eosinophil	A specialized type of leukocyte that mediates allergic responses and responds to parasitic infections. They secrete cytotoxic chemicals and activate mast cells.
Ephemoroptera (Mayflies)	Order of insects characterized by an aquatic larval stage with pronged gills at the tip of the abdomen and a very brief flying adult stage that mates and dies. The mayflies.
Ephyra	Juvenile life stage of jellyfish that breaks off of the tip of the scyphistoma, swims off, and transforms into the adult medusa stage.
Epidermis	Outermost layer of the integument, colloquially known as the skin or mucus membranes. Serves protective and thermoregulatory functions, sensory functions as site of many nerve endings, secretes various substances, and anchors hair or feathers.
Epipubic Bones	A pair of V-shaped bones only found in the pubic region of marsupials and absent in placentals and monotremes. They function as mechanical supports for the pouch.
Erythrocyte	Red blood cells. Each one contains some 300 million molecules of oxygen-carrying hemoglobin, a porphyrin protein. They lack a nucleus and usually live about 3 months.
Esophagus	Component of digestive tract that links the pharynx to the stomach, carrying a bolus of chewed food or liquids into the digestive tract.
Estivation	A survival strategy used by a handful of mammals native to very hot, dry places, such as brushtail possums. As in hibernation, metabolic rate falls and there is dormant sleep.
Eumetozoan	'True animals' in the sense that there are definite tissues and organs with specific functions that coordinate in a multi-celled animal. All animals EXCEPT sponges.
Euphausiaceae (Krill)	Order of shrimp-like crustaceans that have multiple legs and swimmerets and similar body features, but differ in that females release their egg clutches to the plankton.
Eureptilia	One of two clades of ancient reptiles that evolved from the sauropods. Most had diapsid triangular skulls with axial amphibian-like skeletons.
Eutheria	The infraclass that includes all placental mammals. All members of this group grow a placenta from the chorion of the egg and carry a pregnancy through a gestation.
Exarate Pupae	Juvenile stages of certain insects, wherein the general segmented body form of the insect remains mostly intact, pupae can move in some capacity, and remaining appendages can be extended. Ex: beetle grubs.
Excretory Pore	The opening that releases urine and nitrogenous wastes from the body in many invertebrates. In crustaceans, ducts under the antennae connected to green glands.
Excretory System	Body system designed for the filtration and removal of nitrogenous wastes from protein digestion and maintaining osmotic balance of salts in body fluids. Functions may be done by specialized cells in simple invertebrates, while complex animals have kidneys.
Exoskeleton	A hard outer cuticle found in ecdysozoan invertebrates that protects the internal organs of the bearer. Also forms first-class lever attachments with muscles, allowing animals with an exoskeleton to generate much greater force than those with endoskeletons.

External Fertilization	System of sexual reproduction common in many invertebrates and fish in marine or aquatic environments. Sperm and eggs meet for fertilization outside body of parents.
Falconiformes	Order of birds of prey that includes falcons. Features include curved bill, talons, thick flight feathers, many features similar to eagles and hawks, but skull structure differs, more similar to parrots.
Fangs	Long pointed teeth used in prey acquisition or self-defense. Undifferentiated in snakes they may be hollow with a duct to a venom gland. Mammalian fangs are modified canine teeth. Some fish also possess conical fangs, such as anglerfish.
Fecundity	Refer to the reproductive capacity of a species. The capacity is the result of the number of eggs or sperm generated in each event, the frequency of estrus and mating, and also the lifespan of the organism.
Femur	The largest long bone in the body, which is located in the thigh. Articulates with quadriceps muscles and forms a ball and socket joint with the pelvic girdle.
Fenestrae	Openings in bones that usually serve as natural points for muscle articulations or for nerves or blood vessels to pass.
Ferculum	The wishbone of birds, which articulates with the sternum and scapula, providing a buttressed support for the gigantic pectoral muscles required for flight.
Fertilization	The union of a sperm to an egg to create a zygote. In this process, the antigens of the sperm trigger receptors on the egg, which depolarizes to block other sperm. From there, division of the zygote by cleavage begins as it proceeds to the blastula stage.
Filter Feeding	Ancient strategy for obtaining nutrients in marine and aquatic animals that involves the movement of plankton and food particles over a straining organ of some type (such as a gill or lophophore) that allows passive collective of nutrition.
Flame Cells	Ciliated filtration structures that function in the removal of nitrogenous waste from flatworms and a few other primitive invertebrates. Essentially function like kidneys.
Follice (Integument)	A cluster of cells located deep in the epidermal layer that form a globular pit, producing a column of keratin-rich cells that die off at the surface
Follicle (Ovarian)	A pocket-shaped sac that emerges from ovarian tissue, surrounding a developing egg-secreting hormones that control the ovulation process as the egg matures.
Foot	The muscular organ common to members of class Mollusca. It is used for digging in bivalves, gliding locomotion in gastropods, and divided into tentacles in cephalopods.
Forcipucles	Pair of pinching mandibles found in centipedes, which are envenomated through ducts by glands located at their base. Used in predation and defense.
Forebrain	Contains the structures in the anterior and superior parts of the brain, including the cerebral cortex, the limbic system, the thalamus, hypothalamus, and hippocampus. Unlike the brainstem, it is involved in thought, association, and memory.
Fragmentation	Form of mitotic asexual reproduction, wherein cut pieces of a parent organism generate new clones from the fragments. Example: Each arm of a starfish can generate a clone.
Frontal Eye	A primitive light-detecting organ found at the anterior end of cephalochordate lancelets. Useful in detecting shadows and movement, but not with acuity.

Funnel Retractor Muscle	Used to open and close the funnel of cephalopods, these muscles contract and relax to produce jet propulsion out of the siphon as squid and octopus swim.
Gallbladder	Located on the underside of the liver in many mammals, it is ducted pouch that allows bile to be stored and released into the duodenum of the small intestine.
Galliformes	Order of fowl birds that includes chickens, pheasants, turkeys, quail, peacocks, and others. Features include gourd-shaped bodies, pecking and scratching behaviors, social pecking order, wattled neck.
Gametes	Haploid reproductive cells. Sperm, eggs, or haploid spores (fungi and some algae).
Gastric Vessels	The gastric artery and gastric vein circulate the blood supply to-and-from the stomach.
Gastrocnemius	The large calf muscle that articulates to the tibia and fibula and to the knee joint.
Gastrolith	In crocodilians and other animals that lack sufficient grinding teeth, rocks and stones are swallowed to aid peristalsis in grinding up food and increasing surface area.
Gastropoda (Snails)	Class of mollusks characterized by scraping mouthparts (radula), tentacles, suction-cup like food, spiral organ mass under the mantle, and a single protective shell (snails).
Gastrovascular Cavity	Opening in the middle of the alimentary canal in primitive animals that have a mouth, but no anus, such as a flatworm. Digestion and extraction of nutrients occurs here.
Gastrozoid	A type of polyp in colonial hydroids that are primarily responsible for feeding.
Gastrula	Vase-like structure that forms in a developing embryo after the first opening forms from the invagination of the blastoderm layer of cells.
Ganoid Scale	Jointed rhombus-shaped scales that interlock like armor in certain primitive fish, such as gar, bichirs, sturgeon, and paddlefish. They are bony with a thin protein layer atop.
Gaviiformes	Order of birds that includes loons. Pointed triangular bill, diving piscivorous behavior, webbed feet.
Germ Layers	The three layers of tissues found in a developing embryo. The ectoderm, mesoderm, and endoderm all develop into different organ systems.
Gestation	In oviparous or ovoviviparous animals, refers to the length of time a mother carries a pregnancy. Indicative of how long it takes for embryos to develop to maturity.
Gill	A respiratory organ of marine and aquatic animals that typically involves the flow of blood vessels or hemolymph through thin membranes of epithelial tissue at countercurrent angles, allowing diffusion of oxygen into body fluids and removal of carbon dioxide. Many different designs of varying complexity exist in animal kingdom.
Gill Arches	The arch-shaped cartilaginous scaffolding in the gills of fish that provide a structural support to suspend the gill filaments for oxygenation. Located lateral to the pharynx.
Gill Filaments	Found in fish, amphibians, and numerous invertebrates (albeit dissimilar in design), they are capillary beds typically positioned at countercurrent perpendicular angles to water flow, allowing oxygen to diffuse from water into the bloodstream. Supported by gill arches in vertebrates. Invertebrate gill filaments vary in support and design.
Gill Heart	Located atop the gills of cephalopods, these are a pair of muscular pumping organs that force deoxygenated blood from somatic blood vessels into the gill filaments.

Gizzard	Muscular crushing organ in front of the stomach or intestine that pulverizes food particles, often with the assistance of sand or grit particles or chitinous teeth.
Gladius	Found in certain cephalopods, such as squid, the remnant of the shell manufactured by the mantle. It is a keratin or calcified pen-shaped rod atop the body behind the gonad.
Glochidia	Microscopic larval stage of many freshwater clams and mollusks. Two sides of shell are already evident, opening into a ciliated surface. Often attach to fish gills for water flow.
Glomerulus	Globular shaped cluster of capillaries and nerves that transport blood into the Bowman's capsule of the kidney nephron for filtration of wastes and toxins.
Gnathiferans	Lophotrochozoan animals that have chitin jaws inside a mouth ringed with tentacles or cilia. The group includes the rotifers and the arrow worms.
Gonads	Male and female reproductive organs. Catch-all term for ovaries and testes. Meiosis in these organs produces gametes (sperm or eggs).
Gonpores	Modified rear pair of legs found in male millipedes. Used for copulation like a penis.
Gonozoid	A type o f polyp in colonial hydroids that are primarily responsible for reproduction.
Green Glands	Kidney-like excretory organs found in head of crustaceans. Filter nitrogenous wastes.
Gullet	Enzyme-secreting digestive sac behind the pharynx in the digestive tract of lampshells.
Gymniophoma (Caecilians)	Order of amphibians that have snake-like bodies with absent or vestigial legs. They also have evolved concentric protective scales. Often blind due to burrowing lifestyle.
Haemocoel	A pouch-like chamber located in the body cavity of animals with open circulatory systems. Blood or hemolymph exits efferent vessels to this structure, where it is once again picked up by the heart and sprayed over the organs.
Hair	In mammals, the evolved remnants of scales made off keratin. Hair is manufactured by root bulb cells, is of various types, and is used for insulation and protection.
Haplodiploidy	Unique system of gender and caste determination found in honeybees and some hymenopterans, wherein the queen can hormonally control the genetic content of her eggs to produce drones, other queens, workers, and so on.
Haploid	A cell, such as a sperm, egg, or adult fungal hyphae that contains only one copy of each different chromosome in the nucleus.
Harpoon Organ	A venomous needle-like organ that emerges from the radula of certain snails, such as cone shells. Used in predation and defense, it is attached to a deeper venom sac.
Heart	Circulatory organ responsible for pumping and distributing blood, hemolymph, oxygen, immune cells, nutrients, and other components to all the tissues of an animal. Designs vary in complexity across the animal kingdom. In vertebrates, the heart evolved from two chambers to four chambers with separate somatic and pulmonary loops.
Hemerythrin	Oxygen-carrying pigment that is found in the muscle tissues and body fluids of some marine invertebrates. Consists of two protein chains and chelated iron atoms.
Hemichordata (Acorn Worms)	Phylum of marine deuterostome worms with unique anatomy. Have dorsal nerve cord, pharyngeal gill slits, and a supportive stomochord around the gut in collar segment.
Hemipenes	In male reptiles, these are dual copulation organs that emerge from vents during mating. They are inserted into the cloacal vent of female reptiles for sperm transfer.

Hemiptera (True Bugs)	Order of insects that includes true bugs such as aphids, stinkbugs, bedbugs, and cicadas. Sucking mouthparts, soft membranous wings and carapace, incomplete metamorphosis.
Hemocoel	Body cavity found in certain invertebrates, where internal organs float in fluid-filled sac.
Hemocyanin	Copper-based respiratory pigment found in certain invertebrates, such as horseshoe crabs and some mollusks. Copper chelates surrounding protein chains to form a pocket that holds oxygen. Circulates in the blood.
Hemoglobin	A porphyrin protein made of four peptide chains centered around iron atoms that pick up oxygen molecules. May allow as many as 30 times as much oxygen to saturate the blood as would happen by diffusion.
Hemolymph	Common among invertebrates with open circulatory systems, a yellowish or beige fluid that circulates through body cavities, allowing gases to diffuse, nutrients to pass, and primitive immune cells to circulate and attack invaders. No red blood cells present.
Hemotoxin	A toxin that targets body tissues. Various hemotoxins from different venomous animals may rupture red blood cells, cause clotting problems, or damage organs.
Hepatic Portal Vein	A short blood vessel in the celiac trunk that acts as a shunt, carrying nutrient-rich blood directly from the intestinal mesentery, pancreas, and gallbladder into the liver.
Hepatic Vessels	The hepatic artery and vein carry blood supply to-and-from the liver.
Hermaphrodite	An organism that has two functional reproductive tracts of the opposite sex. Presence of testes and ovaries in all individuals is an evolutionary strategy that increases chances for offspring. Common in many invertebrates, especially lophotrochozoans.
Heterocycli	Structures found on the tips of the arms in male cephalopods that are used to transfer sperm packets into the siphons of females.
Heterozooids	Hermaphroditic members of bryozoan colonies that contain ovaries and testes but lack digestive structures, necessitating that they be cared for by autozooid colony members.
Hexacorallia	Group of anthozoan cnidarians that includes hard corals, anemones, and certain types of polyps. Body of polyp is often symmetrical in multiples of six. Many generate colonial limestone skeletons and bud or fragment asexually to reproduce.
Hexactinellida (Glass Sponges)	Class of deep ocean sponges that incorporate silica into their matrices, thereby protecting the amoebocytes of the sponge against consumption and pressure.
Hibernation	State of mammalian dormancy controlled by the hypothalamus of the brain, wherein metabolism dramatically slows down, body temperature drops, and sleep ensues as an adaptation to avoid starvation or hypothermia during cold winter months.
Hindbrain	The lower portion of the brain containing the cerebellum, pons, and medulla oblongata. Primarily involved in reactionary and homeostatic activities. Spatial coordination, body position, body temperature, and heartbeat are controlled here.
Hindgut Gland	Found in various forms in different invertebrates, primarily responsible for the extraction of water and nutrients back from waste as it is passed out of the body.
Hirudinea (Leeches)	Class of segmented worms that are blood-feeding parasites. Have a sucker-like mouth with glands that produce blood-thinning compounds. Also have a posterior sucker on the tail to allow them to stick to hosts. Capable of stretching body dramatically.

Holocephali (Ratfish)	Primitive sub-class of cartilaginous fish that contains the ratfish. They are characterized by primitive vertebrae, cartilage skeletons, horn in front dorsal fin and whip-like tail.
Holostei	An infraclass of primitive bony fish that includes only bowfin and gars. Characterized by shark-like spiracles, partially cartilaginous skeletons, and armor-like scales.
Homeotic Genes	A group of genes that activate in a prescribed order for a prescribed length of time during embryo development, causing limbs, organs, and other parts to develop.
Horn	A pointed bony outgrowth that emerges from the cranium in certain members of Artiodactyla that is covered in a keratin sheath. Permanent structure, unlike antlers.
Horsehair Worms	Similar to roundworms, but they have de-evolved their gut and obtain nutrients by diffusion through the skin. Hosted in gut of insects like mantises and cockroaches.
Humerus	The long bone at the top of the arm that articulates to the scapula and to the ulna and radius toward the elbow. Like all long bones, has marrow in center and layer of apatite.
Hydrostatic Skeleton	A body support system common among simple invertebrates and lophotrochozoans, wherein body compartments or canals are filled with fluid like a water balloon to keep body shape. Especially common in marine animals, such as coral, worms, cephalopods.
Hymenoptera (Bees, ants)	Order of insects that is characterized by social hierarchies and hives, pheromonal communications, and stinging defenses. Includes bees, wasps, ants, and allies.
Hypostome	Serrated needle-like biting mouthparts found in ticks. Used to draw blood.
Hypothalamus	Located in the center of the limbic system in the midbrain, it is the master control center of homeostatic functions, sending hormonal signals to the endocrine system.
Hydrozoa	Class of cnidarians that includes hydroids, Portuguese man-of-war and other similar animals that spend the major of their life as colonial polyps that grow in colonies on stolons or branches derived from communally excreted chitin structures.
Ileum	Final segment of the small intestine, it absorbs nutrients, such as B-vitamins into the mesentery and takes up leftover bile salts, which are sent through the hepatic portal.
Imprinting	An avian behavior, wherein fledglings quickly associate their caretaker as their parent, triggering instincts for them to follow and emulate parental actions relentlessly.
Incisor Teeth	Mammalian teeth located at the front of the maxilla and mandible that are typically shovel-shaped or pointed for ripping and tearing. Enlarged and pointed in carnivores. Number and shape vary, depending on evolved diet of mammal.
Incomplete Metamorphosis	A series of life stages, wherein each juvenile stage or instar continues to resemble miniature versions of the adult body plan. Exoskeleton is molted to get larger. Found in insects, such as the true bugs, cockroaches, mantises, and in certain crustaceans.
Independent Assortment	In meiosis during metaphase I, each chromosome lines up at a random orientation in the middle of the cell to be pulled apart in anaphase for cell division in gamete formation. This generates random chromosome combinations in the offspring.
Independent Segregation	In meiosis, the concept that combinations of chromosomes form at random after telophase I and II, since chromosome pairs are separated after the cell divides.
Infrasonic Range	Range of sound waves less than 20 Hz, which only certain animals (large pachyderms, whales, some fish) are capable of detecting, though vibrations may be felt.

Insecta (Insects)	Class of arthropods characterized by six legs, paired antennae, paired wings, Malpighian tubules, open circulatory systems, metamorphosis, and molting. At least 32 orders exist.
Insectivora	Order of mammals that includes shrews, tenrecs, hedgehogs, and others. Needle-like teeth, five claws on each foot, tube-like nose, small ears, short carnivorous gut.
Instar	Any of a series of juvenile stages of molting insects. For example, in fruit flies, there are four stages (instars) of maggot larvae of increasing size and complexity.
Integumentary Layer	The outermost layer of body tissues (skin) that include the epithelial and the connective tissues that protect the body. In ecdysozoan invertebrates, a cuticle or exoskeleton exists. It is a soft tissue layer in lophotrochozoan invertebrates and most chordates.
Intercostal Muscles	Located between the ribs of mammals, these voluntary skeletal muscles greatly enhance inhalation and exhalation volumes by flexing during respiration.
Internal Fertilization	Common form of sexual reproduction, in which sperm is delivered directly into the reproductive tract of the female during mating. Eggs are still inside female tract.
Intestine	Tube-like organ in the alimentary canal that is responsible for the digestion and absorption of nutrients from food. May be a tube or have multiple compartments. Varying complexity, depending upon how evolved the animal is.
Invasive Species	An organism that explodes in population, disrupts the food chain, and may do damage to environment, when introduced to an area where it is non-indigenous. The consequences can be severe, due to lack of natural predators and competitors.
Ion Channel Proteins	A type of protein located in cell membranes that allows salt ions to enter or exit. Typically, they are donut-shaped, with the diameter and charge of protein designed to pull in a specific ion. Some are used in passive transport, others are attached to an ATP pump and are used to force ions against their gradient in active transport.
Ischium	One of the two wedge-shaped outer curved bones of the pelvic girdle that form the hips. They form a U-shape in the pelvis of females and a V-shape in males.
Isopoda (Isopods)	Order of crustaceans that have horizontally flattened pill-shaped segmented bodies with four mouthparts, chitin body plates, and a rounded tail. Scavengers or parasites.
Isoptera (Termites)	Order of insects that includes the termites. Characterized by soft unpigmented bodies, social colonies with castes, and symbiotic gut microbes that digest cellulose from wood.
Jacobson's Organ	A blind-ended sac in the sinuses that is part of the olfactory system in vertebrates. There are nerve endings for pheromones and other types of chemical that relay signals back to the hypothalamus through cranial nerves. Located directly above the palate.
Jejunum	The middle segment of the small intestine between the duodenum and ileum. Has a large role in absorbing monosaccharides, amino acids, nucleotides, and fatty acids.
Jugular Veins	These are the efferent veins in the neck that carry deoxygenated blood back from the head and back to the vena cava, so it can re-enter the heart.
K-Strategist	Organism with the reproductive strategy of maintaining its population near the carrying capacity of the environment. Typically have long lifespans, high survival rates, good degree of parental care. Examples: humans, dogs, eagles, crocodiles.
Kenozooids	In bryozoans, hollow tube-shaped zooids that aid in flotation of the colony.

Keratin	Hard, fibrous, hydrophobic protein used by animals for protective or insulator purposes. Hair, nails, and many animal shells and cuticles are built from keratin.
Kidney	Paired blood filtration organs found in vertebrates and some advanced invertebrates. Consists of thousands of tube-shaped nephrons consisting of cells with numerous ion-channel proteins that have differential permeability to various dissolved substances, extracting excess salts, toxins, and nitrogenous wastes to produce urine.
Kingdom	Second-largest classification in the Linnaean scheme. Very general base features are used to group organisms into kingdoms, such as animals, plants, fungi, etc. These include type of sexual reproduction, type of cell nucleus, multicellularity, etc.
Kingdom Animalia	A classification of eukaryotes that have these things in common: mobile at least in some life stage, no cell walls, lysosomes in cells, almost always diploid, reproduce sexually unless this trait has de-evolved to give way to budding.
Kinorynch	Known as mud dragons commonly, small worm-like members of Scalidophora that live as burrowing filter feeders in marine environments. Spines at each jointed cuticle.
Kuhneosauridae	Group of ancient diapsid reptiles that evolved in a different direction than modern tuataras, lizards, snakes, and crocodilians. Gliders with different bone structure.
Labia	The lip-like appendage that emerges from the mouth of segmented worms.
Lacteal(s)	Ducted lymphatic vessels located in the small intestine and the mesentery that take up lipids for encasement in LDLs and HDLs before they are shunted into the bloodstream.
Lagomorpha	Order of mammals that includes rabbits and hares. Features include fermentative cecum pouch in the gut, long ears, short tail, exaggerated quadriceps muscles for leaping.
Large Intestine	Organ that scavenges remaining nutrients and extracts water from the remnants of digested food passed from the small intestine. Many bacterial symbiotes reside here, aiding in production of certain vitamins and preventing pathogens from invading. Segments consist of the ascending, transverse, descending and sigmoid colon.
Larynx	Hollow muscular tube that is positioned between the pharynx at the back of the mouth and the bronchi of the lungs. Animals with vocalizations can force air through a set of vocal cords here, such as frogs, birds, and mammals.
Lateral Line	An organ located on the lateral surfaces of fish that consists of pit-like channels that open to a internal canal lined with ciliated cells that detect water movements.
Lateral Vaginas	In marsupials, the female reproductive tract opens from the cloaca into these two birth canals, which form a pretzel shape with the cervix, connecting to two uterine horns.
Latissimus Dorsi	Large sheet-like muscles under the front limbs, extending down the lateral surface of the torso. Used in running in quadrupeds and lifting in bipeds.
Lens	Convex surface structures of animal eyes that direct light to a focal point on the retina during the processing of images.
Lepidosauromorpha	Group of ancient reptiles that diverged from Kuhneosaurs and eventually evolved into modern lizards, snakes, tuataras. Hip bones evolved sockets that allow leg joints to rotate in large circumference, allowing undulation during running involving tail muscles.
Lepitodptera (Butterflies & Moths)	Order of insects that includes butterflies and moths. Two pairs of membranous wings covered in scales, complete metamorphosis, straw-like mouthparts, tactile antennae.

Leptocephalus Larvae	Leaf-shaped larval fish with large abdominal somites and poorly-defined caudal fin. Larval form is unique to Elopomorph fish, such as tarpon, moray eels, and bonefish.
Leukocyte	Generalized class of white blood cells that differentiate from bone marrow stem cells and progress into several different classes of immune cells with different functions. Includes monocytes, B and T lymphocytes, eosinophils, neutrophils, and basophils.
Limbic System	Central part of the brain that is involved in emotional response and behavior regulation. Includes the hypothalamus (hormonal control), amygdala (emotions), the thalamus (relay of information), and the hippocampus (memory formation).
Liver	Multi-functional organ of the digestive tract located on the right side (in vertebrates) that detoxifies metabolic byproducts, stores cholesterol, glycogen, and iron, processes amino acids for gluconeogenesis, and produces bile for fat emulsification.
Lophophorate	A clade of protostome invertebrates that have soft bodies, lack shells, tentacles, and brush-like feeding structures covered in cilia. Includes brachiopods and bryozoans.
Lophophore	A brush-like ciliated feeding organ used by brachiopods and bryozoans to trap plankton and food particles suspended in the water for feeding.
Lophotrochozoan	One of the two evolutionary splits that occurred in more advanced triploblastic invertebrate animals. Characteristics include tentacles around the mouth, soft bodies lacking cuticle, hermaphroditism common. Examples are mollusks, segmented worms.
Love Dart	Found in hermaphroditic gastropods, it is a sharp sword-like male reproductive structure made of sharp calcified tissues that is used to stab into the tissues of a mate, delivering sperm directly into the female reproductive tract.
Lung(s)	Respiratory organ(s) composed of epithelial mucus membranes, capillary beds, and smooth muscle. Essentially, they provide large amounts of extra surface area for the diffusion of oxygen into the bloodstream, in addition to the skin.
Lymph Node(s)	Numerous glands of fibrous spongy tissue rich in leukocytes. Located along lymphatic vessels in the neck, groin armpits, intestinal tract, and other locations. They filter and attack viruses, bacteria, infected cells, and other invaders. They manufacture B-cells.
Lymphatic Vessels	A part of fluid circulatory system that funnels interstitial fluid from tissues through a set of vessels and capillaries, terminating in ducts that re-enter the bloodstream. Also function in transport of lipid LDL and HDL particles and
Macrophage	Leukocytes of several classes that phagocytically engulf igerms and infected cells and digest them enzymatically via endocytosis. Some circulate blood, others in tissues.
Macrostomata (Snakes)	The Suborder of snakes that is distinguished from the Suborder Caenophidia, in that they retain some of the bones of the pelvis in vestigial form. Examples: boas, pythons.
Malpighian Tubules	Set of blind-ended pouch-like organs that emerge from the hindgut of insects and several other types of ecdysozoan invertebrates. Used to extract and salvage water and nutrients from waste before it leaves the body.
Mandible	Refers to various parts of the jaw, depending on the animal. In many arthropods, mandibles are hand-like mouthparts used to pick up, manipulate, or crush food. In vertebrates, it refers to the lower jaw or the beak.
Mandibulata	Clade of arthropods, such as insects, that primarily have segmented mouthparts evolved for the manipulation of their food or materials, rather than needle-like biting chelicerae.

Mammalia	Class of animals that are endothermic deutorostome chordate vertebrates. Other essential characteristics include four-chambered heart, large cerebral cortex, milk glands, oviparity (monotremes only) or viviparity, and differentiated teeth.
Mantle	A layer of dermal and muscular tissue that surrounds the visceral mass of organs in a mollusk. The epithelial layer secretes a shell in gastropods, bivalves, and may secrete a shell (nautilus) or internal support structures (squid, cuttlefish). Its extra surface area is also utilized in respiration and evacuation of waste from body tissues.
Mastax Pharynx	The muscular chewing pharynx of a rotifer.
Mantodea (Mantises)	Order of insects that includes praying mantises. Characterized by serrated front claws, biting mouthparts, stalk-like neck segment, large abdomen, production of egg clutches.
Marsupial Mammal	An order of mammals that evolved before placental mammals, utilizing a birthing system, wherein a crudely developed embryo crawls into a protective dermal pouch in the mother, attaches to a nipple, and continues to develop. Even juvenile marsupials return to the pouch. Major anatomical differences in reproductive tract vs. placentals.
Masseter	A large powerful facial muscle that articulates at the temporalis and the zygomatic arch. It attaches to the lower jaw and is one of the main muscles used in chewing food.
Matrix	A non-living network, membrane, or concrete-like substance in animals, wherein cells are embedded for their protection or to maintain the shape of the colony or tissue. Example: body of sponges, mesoglea of jellyfish, cartilage.
Maxilla	Refers to the upper jaw in vertebrates, or to associated mouthparts on the upper portion of the jaw in various invertebrates.
Maxillipeds	Hand-like mouthparts found on the upper jaw of invertebrates. Used to manipulate food or other materials or to catch prey.
Mechanoreceptors	Small sensory organs located in the integument that are sensitive to touch, pressure, changes in position, and vibrations. Typically, they are ciliated or encapsulated nerve endings that use signal transduction via ion channels to stimulate connected nerves.
Medulla Oblongata	Part of the hindbrain that acts as a relay connection between the brain and the spinal cord. Regulates basal metabolic functions, including heart rate, body temperature, respiratory rate, swallowing, sneezing, and coughing.
Medusa	The mobile, swimming life stage of cnidarians. Bell-shaped, the tentacles typically point down, sweeping the water for prey. Jellyfish and box jellyfish are medusae as adults.
Megalops	Planktonic juvenile stage of many decapod crustaceans, characterized by large compound eyes and notable development of appendages and carapace.
Meiosis	A 9-step series of cell divisions in the ovaries or testes that generate sperm or eggs. Diploid germ cells proceed through meiosis I, which shuffles the chromosomes and separates homologous pairs, and meiosis II, which generates four haploid gametes.
Mesenchyme	Cells at the center of a developing embryo that become the mesoderm tissue layer.
Mesenchyme Muscles	Simple ring-shaped muscle tissues found in cnidarians that aid them in swimming and capturing prey. Derived from the endoderm, they fail to fully form a mesoderm layer.
Mesentery	A large bed of blood vessels and lymphatic lacteal vessels that emerges from the peritoneum posterior to the digestive tract. Especially important in the absorption of nutrients from the wall of the small intestine during digestion.

Mesoderm	Layer of tissue in a developing embryo sandwiched between the endoderm and the ectoderm. Fated to become muscles, blood, bones, and connective tissues.
Mesoglea	Jelly-like protein matrix that provides cushioning and support in between the ectoderm and the endoderm of cnidarians like jellyfish and corals.
Mesosoma	The armored middle body segment of certain invertebrates, such as scorpions.
Mesosome	In acorn worms, a hollow segment derived from the digestive tract that contains the supportive stomochord. Basis for classification into hemichordate.
Mesothelium	Layer of muscular tissue that articulates between the body wall and organs of annelid worms, defining segments. Walls generate fluid pressure used in wiggling and support.
Metamorphosis	A series of distinctly different life stages that occur in invertebrates, with growth and changes following the molting of the exoskeleton.
Metanephridia	Nephron-like tubules found in each segment of annelids that function like miniature kidneys, removing salts and nitrogenous wastes from the interstitial fluids.
Metatarsal	Bones of the foot. Highly modified in length, shape among vertebrates as the result of evolutionary divergence to meet lifestyle needs of animal.
Microvilli	Microscopic projections that increase the surface area and absorptive capacity of cells in the gut epithelium. In humans, these extend from the inner walls of the intestine.
Midbrain	The part of the brain that acts as a relay system between hemispheres. Contains the structures of the limbic system, such as the hypothalamus and the thalamus.
Midgut Gland	Especially important in crustaceans, insects, mollusks, they are found in various form in many other invertebrates. Like the pancreas in vertebrates, its cells manufacture digestive enzymes that are dumped into the alimentary canal too breakdown food.
Migration	Seasonal movement of animals triggered by environmental cues and behavioral instincts. Occurs for multiple reasons, including avoidance of inclement weather conditions, pursuit of food and/or water, and movement to alternate courtship and mating grounds.
Milk	Nutritive fluid produced in the mammary glands of all mammals except monotremes. Contains high lipid content, sugars, proteins, and immune factors that nourish young.
Miracidia (Flatworms)	The ciliated larvae of flatworms that emerge from egg cysts in fecal matter. Typically, they crawl or swim to their next host, burrowing through the skin and entering the bloodstream, where they hitch a ride to the intestine or other target organ.
Mitochondria	Cellular organelle responsible for metabolizing food molecules. Glycolysis sends pyruvate into matrix to undergo Kreb's cycle, which in turn, sends its products to the intermembrane space to undergo the electron transport chain. Converts the energy in chemical bonds of food molecules into ATP, the energy currency of the cell.
Molar Teeth	The teeth at the back of the mammalian jaw that are primarily used for crushing and grinding. Typically have four or five knob-like cusps with a canal in the middle.
Mollusca (Mollusks)	Advanced group of triploblastic lophotrochozoans that have a mantle organ surrounding the organs, which usually generates a shell, as well as a muscular foot organ. Classes include gastropods (snails), bivalves (shellfish), cephalopods (octopus and squid).
Molting	Periodic shedding and re-growth of the exoskeleton in growing arthropods and/or during metamorphosis. Process is under control of brain hormones.

Monogenea (Gill Worms)	A group of hermaphroditic parasitic flatworms that live in the gills of fish. Some are oviparous egg layers with a free-swimming stage, others are viviparous, release larvae.
Monotreme Mammal	Group of primitive mammals that are oviparous, including duck-billed platypus and various types of echidna. Lay leathery reptile-like eggs. Also have leathery toothless snout, clawed feet, and a much lower internal body temperature than other mammals.
Mucus Glands	Found in the epidermis of amphibians, they secrete a gelatinous protein matrix of mucus that keeps the skin moist, allowing respiration to occur via diffusion through the skin.
Musculoskeletal System	In vertebrate chordates, the collection of bones, muscles, ligaments, tendons, and connective tissues that provide functional structure support to the body and coordinate movement under control of motor neurons.
Mutualism	Symbiotic relationship of mutual benefit between two species. For example, microbes in the gut of cattle receive nutrition and a home in exchange for extracting more nutrition for the cow and by outcompeting potential disease microbes that might try to attack.
Myoglobin	The oxygen-carrying pigment present in muscle tissues. Similar to hemoglobin, it contains a heme group with a surrounding single protein chain, rather than four.
Myomere(s)	Chevron-shaped blocked muscular segments that are found in the abdominal muscles of fish and early vertebrate embryos. Connective tissues between the myomeres allows the muscles to push off of each other and swim in undulating and serpentine motions.
Myriapoda	Order of arthropods that includes centipedes and millipedes. Body has numerous segments and legs, biting mouthparts. Internal anatomy bears resemblance to insects.
Mysida (Opossum Shrimp)	An order of crustaceans, wherein females develop a pouch-like organ that protects hatching eggs and developing larvae, releasing them only when highly developed.
Myxiniformes (Hagfish)	Most primitive order of vertebrates, these are jawless fish that lack a fully formed cranium, have cartilaginous vertebrae, open gill slits, and lack a lower jaw. Scavengers.
Nauplius	Refers to juvenile life stages that result during metamorphosis events in crustaceans.
Natural Selection	Evolutionary process commonly known as 'survival of the fittest', wherein the best adapted phenotypes survive at a higher rate, gradually changing the species over time.
Nematocyst	Found in the cnidocytes of cnidarians, they are modified Golgi bodies that deliver a dose of venom through a barb when their trigger-like cellular mechanism is touched.
Nematodes	Small soil-dwelling roundworms of Order Nematoda that typically parasitize the root tissues of plants. Important ecological function in turning the soil.
Nematoidea	Classification of ecdysozoans that lack appendages, but have cuticle, separate sexes. Roundworms and horsehair worms belong to this group.
Nematoda (Roundworms)	Phylum that includes roundworms. Most primitive group of animals with a one-way digestive tract. Ecdysozoans with cuticle around body and two sexes. Organs float in a false body cavity, the pseudocoelom. Mostly parasitic.
Nemerteans (Ribbon Worms)	Phylum of marine deuterostome invertebrate lophotrochozoans that have a long feeding proboscis organ that can be retracted into the body. Acoelomate body plan with a closed circulatory system, primitive kidney-like cells, and oviparous or viviparous reproduction.

Neodiapsid	Large clade of reptiles that includes cladiosaurs and all members of sauria that includes dinosaurs, modern reptiles, and other extinct taxa. Structure of diapsid skull, along with about two dozen skeletal features are used in this classification scheme.
Neoteleostii	Large grouping of bony fish that have pharyngeal muscles and teeth used in grinding food, as well as spiny dorsal fins. Includes perciforms, cod, and several other orders.
Nephron	Filtration unit of the kidneys that osmotically extracts salts and nitrogenous waste from the blood, returning water and essential minerals back into the cleaned blood. Consists of the bed of capillaries known as a glomerular, with loops of tubules of variable permeability. Vertebrate kidneys may have thousands to over a million of these units.
Nerve	Clusters of neurons that transmit neurotransmitters or afferent action potentials from their axons and receive efferent signals through their dendrites.
Nerve Net	Primitive sensory tissues found in cnidarians. The net-like mesh of nerves extends into the tentacles, firing off reflexes that contract their prey into the gastrovascular cavity.
Nervous System	Body system that receives stimuli, processes information, and formulates reactions and responses. Depending on complexity of animal, may include a central ganglion, reflex arcs, a brain, clusters of ganglia, a spinal cord, and cranial and spinal nerves.
Neural Crest	Cells found in the developing neural tube that migrate to various parts of the developing nervous system, giving rise to accessory cells and structures in the skull and spine. L
Neural Gland	Predecessor to the pituitary gland of more advanced chordates, it is a structure found in tunicates that provides hormonal regulation to its body systems.
Neural Tube	Embryonic structure that develops from the ectoderm layer of tissue as it folds into a ridge to create the predecessor of the brain and spinal cord. Folds in, fuses around the cranium and spinal column.
Neuropore	Pinhole-like opening into the neural eye in cephalochordate lancelets.
Neurotoxin	A toxin that disrupts the natural functions of the nervous system by blocking or opening potassium or sodium channels or by directly damaging nerve cells by demyelinating them or otherwise changing their structures. Found in the venom of many animals.
Neurotransmitter	Biochemical messenger molecule that are released in vesicles from the dendrite of one neuron to receptors on the axons of the next neuron in sequence. When receptors are triggered, they start a secondary messenger pathway that leads to an action potential.
Nictitating Membrane	Colloquially called the 'third eyelid', it is retractable clear membrane found in reptiles, birds, and mammals (though it is vestigial in many) that covers the cornea of the eye, moisturizing it and protecting it against damage. Articulates to front corner of eyelids.
Niche	The ecological roles and relationships incumbent upon a particular species in a given ecosystem. Example: squirrels are arboreal prey animals important in seed distribution.
Nidamental Gland	In cephalopods, glands found in females inferior to the ovary, which are responsible for encasing eggs inside of a protective membrane.
Nocturnal	A species whose Circadian rhythms cause it to be instinctively active during night.
Notochord	A long cartilage tube that develops superior to the gut and below the neural tube on the dorsal surface of chordates, providing support. Retained in lower chordates, it is replaced by the spinal cord and vertebrae as most vertebrates develop.

Notostraca (Tadpole Shrimp)	Order of crustaceans known as tadpole shrimp. They lack the nauplius juvenile stages of most other crustaceans and simply get larger until they attain tadpole-shaped adult form. They have a helmet-like carapace.
Nuchae	Clusters of ciliated feeler organs that are found on the head of annelid worms.
Nudipleura (Gilled Snails)	A clade of gastropods that includes nudibranchs and sea slugs. Characterized by the presence of branch-like exposed gills that are visible on the surface of the body.
Nymph	A juvenile invertebrate that resembles a miniature version of the adult form in invertebrates that use incomplete metamorphosis.
Oblique Muscles	Sheet-like lateral abdominal muscles that span the lateral surfaces of the torso between the ribs and the hips. Used in rotating the torso, running, pacing, and jumping.
Obtect Pupae	Type of pupal insect, wherein appendages are bound up inside exoskeleton and body may reorganize into a notably different morphology. Larvae are mostly immobile. Example: the cocoons and chrysalis of lepidopterans.
Ocelli	Primitive eye-like cells or organs that contain pigmented compounds for light detection and rudimentary vision. Innervated, so animal can respond to stimulus.
Occipital Bone	The bone at the posterior of the cranium that covers and protects the brainstem and provides articulation points for the muscles at the back of the neck.
Occipital Condyles	Two rounded hemispherical projections that extend from the occipital bone at the base of the skull and provide articulation points between the skull and cervical vertebrae.
Octocorallia	Group of anthozoan cnidarians that includes soft corals, sea pens, and gorgonians. Skeletal matrices are proteinaceous, rather than mineralized. Body forms are often found in multiples of 8.
Odonata (Dragonflies)	Order of insects that begins with predatory aquatic larval stage. Two pairs of membranous wings as flying adult predators of mosquitoes and other small insects.
Olfaction	Chemoreception better known as the sense of smell. Process works when odor molecules trigger olfactory receptors that relay information to the olfactory nerve.
Olfactory Sac	Found in jawless fish, the single nostril at the top of their heads leads to this chamber which is lined with olfactory receptors. Not part of sinuses, as in higher vertebrates.
Olfactory Lobe	Part of the forebrain found underneath the frontal lobe, it is innervated by the olfactory nerve and processes sense of smell. Sends signals to amygdala, cerebral cortex, and the hippocampus, which interpret meaning of odors and commits them to memory.
Oligochaete (Earthworms)	A subclass of annelids better known as earthworms. They have reduced sandpaper-like setae on their ventral surface, lack eyes, lay egg cocoons, are hermaphrodites, have a divided digestive tract to process leaf litter, and have a closed circulatory system.
Omasum	The third stomach chamber found in members of Order Artiodactylaa. It is folded many times into wrinkled membranes that resemble pages like a book. The extra surface area allows the animal to maximize absorption of water and nutrients from food.
Onychophora (Velvet Worms)	Velvet worms. Primitive ecdysozoan invertebrates with multiple body segments. Defend themselves and hunt prey with glands that shoot glue-like substance onto target.
Oogenesis	The process of egg production by the ovaries of female animals via meiosis.

Open Circulatory System	Common among advanced invertebrates. In this system, the heart has openings called ostia and/or open-ended vessels and functions as a sort of 'sprinkler system', distributing fluids over the organs, before it pools in the hemocoel and is redistributed again.
Operculum	A set of four cranial bones in teleost fish that form a bony protective flap over the gills. Since muscles articulate to the operculum, bony fish can open and close the flap to drive water over the gills and oxygenate them.
Ophistoma	Fused thorax and abdomen segment found in spider and some other arachnids, that houses circulatory and respiratory systems and the reproductive tract.
Opiolones (Harvestmen)	Class of arachnids that includes the daddy longlegs and harvestmen. Incapable of spinning webs, they are ambush predators with fused body segments and stink glands.
Opposable Thumbs	Found only in primates, many rodents, and a handful of other animals like pandas and koalas, it refers to thumbs that can be independently moved to allow gripping and manipulation of objects. The medial surface of the thumb faces the interior of the hand.
Optic Lobe	A pair of lobes located in a section of the midbrain that receive signals from the optic nerves that analyze and interpret visual stimulations.
Optic Nerve	Cluster of nerve bodies that receive stimuli from the retina and send afferent messages down this cranial nerve into the vision processing center of brain or cerebral ganglion.
Order	A Linnean classification taxa that is more specific than a phylum, but more general than a class. Inclusive of crude differences between members of the same phylum. Example: major differences in dentition and skull bones differ in orders of subphylum mammalia.
Organs	A group of tissues that work together to perform a common biological function. For instance, the stomach consists of smooth muscle, epithelial, endocrine, and nervous tissues that all contribute to the digestion of food.
Organ System	A group of organs that work together to perform common biological functions. For instance, the circulatory system consists of the heart, arteries, veins, etc. that are all responsible for contributing the circulation of oxygen, nutrients, and immune cells.
Orthoptera (Grasshoppers)	Order of insects that includes grasshoppers, kaytdids, and crickets. Characterized by incomplete metamorphosis, cutting mouthparts, and large spring-like back legs.
Osculum	The mouth-like opening in the center of many sponges, which is used to generate water flow to assist filter-feeding.
Osmoregulation	The maintenance of the correct osmotic ion concentrations in the tissues of an animal. Regulated by tissue and organs of varying complexity in different animals. For example, the gills and kidneys of fish exchange salt ions and ammonia with surrounding water.
Ossicle(s)	Calcified projections that form the basis of the 'spiny skin' moniker of the echinoderms. Formed of calcium carbonate. May be hard projections in starfish or spines in urchins.
Osteichthyes (Bony Fish)	The superclass of fish that includes all bony fish, including lobe-finned and ray-finned fish, primitive and advanced. Common features include partially or fully calcified bony skeletons, presence of an operculum, different scales, paired fins and nostrils.
Ostia	Openings on the surface of invertebrate hearts that use open circulation. These suction blood back into the heart from the hemocoel to be pumped out again over the organs.
Ostracoda (Seed Shrimp)	Order of Crustaceans known as seed shrimp, which have a fused single carapace without segments, two pairs of mouthparts, and a single simple eye. Planktonic or benthic.

Osteoderm	Refers to skin where the integument fuses to bony nodules to form armor. Found in various reptiles, such as crocodilians, snapping turtles, and some lizards.
Ostracoderm	An ancient armored jawless fish that was one of the ancestors of modern fish. Replaced by better-adapted members of Chondrichthyes with the evolution of the lower jaw.
Ova	Refers to mature, ripened egg cells that are capable of fertilization to form an embryo.
Ovaries	Reproductive organs of female animals. Germ cells in the ovaries divide by meiosis to produce genetically unique egg cells for fertilization and production of offspring.
Oviducts	Openings in female animals that provide a path for eggs or embryos to leave the ovary and exit the body for reproductive purposes.
Oviparous	Refers to animals that are true egg-layers in their life strategies. All nutrition for the developing embryo is contained inside a sealed egg that is external to the mother.
Ovoviviparous	Refers to animals that are livebearers, yet do not nourish the developing embryo with a placenta. Allows protection of eggs and increases chance of juvenile survival, by allowing them to hatch and develop to a larger size in the mother. Ex: dogfish sharks.
Ovipositor	An organ at the end of the abdomen of many female invertebrates that dispenses clusters of eggs into nests or onto surfaces.
Ovotestes	Found in certain hermaphroditic gastropods, these are gonads that can produce either eggs or sperm, depending on the hormonal cue that triggers the development process.
Ovulation	Process that produces ova inside the ovaries of female animals. Begins with meiotic divisions of germ-line cells that produce haploid cells. From there, hormonal regulation triggers maturation process inside of a protective follicle. Development differs with taxa.
Paedomorphosis	The retention of juvenile-like traits in adult animals, due to mutations or switching issues with homeotic genes. For example, barking and puppy-like skulls in miniature dogs.
Palate	The roof of the mouth. The soft palate is formed by epithelial tissues, while the hard palate formed by the palatine and maxillary bones. Only found in mammals, some turtles, and in crocodilians. Absent in birds, amphibians, fish, and most other reptiles.
Paleothyrii	Ancient Eureptilians with lizard-like bodies and nocturnal lifestyles that were among the last to have pelvic girdles and anapsid skulls with amphibian-like features
Palp	Tongue-like appendage used to remove filtered plankton from the gill filaments of bivalve and chiton mollusks, so that it can be swallowed and passed into the esophagus and digestive tract.
Palpebral Bone	Ridge-like protective bone above the eye orbits of Ornithischian dinosaurs.
Panarthropodia	Group of ecdysozoans that have jointed appendages in addition to cuticle around the body. Includes the arthropods, tardigrades, and velvet worms.
Panpulmonada (Land Snails)	Clade of snails that includes land snails and slugs. Primary characteristic is the presence of wet skin and a single lung, which is used instead of gills for respiration.
Pancreas	Gland located near the celiac trunk that is about the size and shape of a chicken finger. Produces a cocktail of digestive enzymes and hormones, including insulin for storage of carbohydrates in the liver and glucagon that triggers the release of sugars to blood.

Pancreatic Duct	Tube-like opening that releases digestive lipases, proteases, amylases, nucleases, and other enzymes into the duodenum during the digestive process.
Pantapoda (Sea Spiders)	Order of arthropods that includes the sea spiders. Unique anatomy includes sucking mouthparts that give way to gut compartments inside the legs. Small marine predators.
Paraphyletic	A taxonomic classification that includes members that may resemble one another morphologically, but in reality, might be grouped together because of convergent evolution, rather than genetic relatedness or recent common ancestry.
Parapodia	In oligochaetes, extensions of the epidermis that form leg-like or bristle like structures on each segment. Often used to gain surface area for respiration, for crawling, and may be envenomated with stinging glands.
Parareptilia	Extinct clade of reptiles that diverged from ancestors of the extant Eureptilia. Features included anapsid skulls with posterior triangular apron formed by three bones not found in modern reptiles. Included mesosaurs, procolophs, and several other taxa.
Parasitiformes	Order of arachnids that includes the bird mites and ticks. Suck the blood of their victims with needle-like hypostome mouthparts. Most have a hard chitin protective carapace.
Parasitism	A lifestyle strategy and ecological relationship, wherein one organism directly steals resources and lives off of a host organism, which receives negative consequences. Ectoparasites live on the surface (ticks, fleas), while endoparasites invade (tapeworms).
Parasympathetic Nervous System	Refers to the autonomic nervous system circuits that are in control when an organism is in a calm, resting state. Digestion proceeds normally, heart and respiration rates are lower, pupils are constricted, bladder is contracted, among other effects.
Parazoans	Animals that have no true tissues or organs. Sponges are the only group of animals to qualify. They resemble giant colonies of protozoans with no definite shape.
Parietal Eye	The so-called 'third eye' of lizards that is characterized by a semi-transparent scale on top of the skull that acts as a pinhole to the pineal gland, allowing the reptile to sense incoming light to trigger basking behaviors for thermoregulation.
Parthenogenesis	A system of asexual reproduction derived from sexual reproduction, wherein self-fertilization of eggs occurs. There are several different methods by which this happens, but most commonly, a second set of chromosomes generated in meiosis is retained.
Passeriformes	Order of birds that includes song birds like robins, orioles, mockingbirds. Features include syrinx adapted for singing multiple calls, migratory behavior, 3 forward toes.
Pecten Oculi	A brush-like capillary bed found in the eyes of birds that brings nutrients and nourishment to the functional structures of the eye.
Pectoral Fin	The fin located on the lateral surfaces behind the gill slits or opercula of fish. Used to propel the fish forward or flapped to maintain or steer their position in the water.
Pectoral Girdle	Includes the sternum, clavicle, and ribs of the chest cavity. Protects the heart and lungs, provides articulation points for shoulder muscles and the ball joint of the humerus.
Pectoralis	Large pair of chest muscles that articulate to the sternum and clavicles in mammals or the sternum and coracoid bone and fercula in birds. Used for pushing and running in mammals and reptiles, and enlarged disproportionately for flight in birds.
Pedicle Valve	The top shell of a lampshell brachiopod, which helps protect the lophophore.

Pedipalps	Hand-like facial appendages found in arachnids that are used to manipulate prey, food, web spinning, and other day-to-day tasks. They are above or to the side of chelicerae.
Pedunculata (Gooseneck Barnacles)	Order of crustaceans known as barnacles that live a sessile lifestyle attached to rocks, filter feeding plankton out of the water column by using bristled modified legs called cirri. Essentially stand on their head inside their carapace, anchored by peduncle organ.
Pelecaniformes	Order of birds that includes pelicans. Bill modified into pouch-like scoop for preying on fish. Webbed feet, gigantic wing span, feathers change color as juvenile birds mature.
Pelvic Fin	The fin located on the ventral surface under the gill slits or opercula of fish. Used to propel the fish forward or flapped to maintain or steer their position in the water.
Pelvic Girdle	The bones of the hips, including the ischium, ileum, and pubis. They form a supportive fulcrum point for the ball of the femur to rotate during running or jumping.
Penile Bone	While certain orders of mammals lack this bone, male mammals in most classification have this bone that stabilizes an erection for mating.
Penis	External male copulatory organ that is used to transfer sperm during internal fertilization. Most commonly associated with mammals, where it is made of spongy tissues that engorge with blood. Reptiles have similar hemipenes. Other male animals also have similar organs of different design via convergent evolution (Ex: ducks).
Perciformes	Order of bony fish that includes perch-like fish and is most numerous in terms of species. Classified into group by presence of spines in fins, position of caudal fins on the body, number of rays in other fins. Includes basses, grouper, angelfish, sunfish, many more.
Peripheral Nervous System	The portion of the nervous system that excludes the brain and spinal cord and includes all spinal and cranial nerves and smaller associated nerves of muscles and organs.
Peristalsis	Set of involuntary smooth muscle contractions that push food down the alimentary canal during digestive process. Found in esophagus, stomach, both intestines.
Peritoneum	The connective tissue membrane that attaches the muscles of the body wall to the organs in the body cavity of coelomate animals.
Perrisodactyla	Order of mammals that includes the even-toed hoofed animals with fermentative cecum in gut. Includes horses, donkeys, zebras, rhinoceroses, tapirs.
Petromyzontiformes (Lampreys)	Order of primitive fish that are among the least-developed vertebrate animals. Lack a lower jaw, have open skills, a single nostril, and mostly cartilaginous skeletons.
Phalanges	Bones, coded by homeotic developmental genes, that in humans make up the bones of the fingers and toes, and in other animals, are modified into various types of feet, such as bat wings, whale flippers, panther paws, and cow hooves.
Phallodium	A penis-like organ used by male caecilians to transfer sperm to the vent of females.
Pharyngeal Basket	A net-like feeding structure located in the throat of tunicates that is used for straining plankton and food particles out of the water during filter-feeding.
Pharyngeal Gill Slits	One of the major key features of chordate embryos, they are located on the external body surface between the throat and the pharynx. They are retained in lower vertebrates in gills or filter feeding structures, such as in lampreys, or highly modified into various components in terrestrial vertebrates.
Pharyngeal Teeth	Found in many types of fish, these are crushing teeth located at the top of the pharynx.

Pharynx	The throat cavity behind the mouth and in front of the gut in animals. Important in feeding in numerous types of primitive invertebrates.
Phasmotodea (Walking Sticks)	Order of insects that includes the walking sticks. Extremely long legs and carapaces that are camouflaged to look like vegetation. Sap eaters that produce toxic secretions.
Pheromone	A hormone manufactured by a different individual of a species, which diffuses through air or water before triggering the receptors of a different individual. Most common are sex pheromones, wherein an individual signals members of the opposite sex for mating.
Pholidota	Order of mammals that includes pangolins. Lack teeth, have a long sticky tongue, body covered in keratinized plates of armor, roll into a ball when threatened.
Photic Zone	The portion of a lake or ocean near the surface that sunlight is capable of penetrating, allowing photosynthetic algae and plants to support a food chain. At most, 100 meters.
Photoreceptor	Light-detecting clusters of cells that utilize isomeric pigments to detect photons and trigger neurons in the cerebral ganglion. Most just detect crude shadows and shapes.
Phylum	The level of Linnaean classification more specific than domain or kingdom, but more general than order. Different phyla have large anatomical and physiological differences between them. For instance, molds and mushrooms are different phyla of fungi.
Physoclistus Swim Bladder	Refers to fish that have no opening between the swim bladder and the digestive tract. These fish must fill and empty the swim bladder with blood gases and cannot gulp air.
Physostomous Swim Bladder	Refers to fish that have a canal that connects the swim bladder and digestive tract. These fish are capable of gulping air to fill and empty the swim bladder, as well as using gases from the blood. In some fish, this allowed the swim bladder to evolve into a crude lung (such as in lungfish) that further evolved into true lungs in amphibians.
Phytoplankton	Component of plankton that consists of producers, such as algae and cyanobacteria. Produces food for marine and aquatic ecosystems, especially for the zooplankton. Neither component of the plankton can swim against the current or tides.
Piciformes	Order of birds that includes woodpeckers, toucanets, and toucans. Bill pick-like in former and curved in latter two. Structure of neck bones, sternum, and torso similar in all. Often bright colors.
Pigment Cells (Arthropods)	Contain light-sensitive compounds that alter their structure when struck by light, triggering nerve impulses back to the vision center of the cerebral ganglion.
Pigment Cup Cells	Found in the crude frontal eye of cephalochordate lancelets, these light-detecting cells bear a resemblance to the rod and cone cells of higher vertebrates.
Pineal Gland	A gland located at the back of the limbic system in mammals and close to the surface of the skull in reptiles. Produces melatonin, regulating circadian rhythms and sleep cycle.
Pinnipeda	Order of mammals that includes seals, sea lions, and walruses. Limb bones modified into flippers, dense fur that traps boundary layer of air, carnivorous gut, social behaviors.
Pituitary Gland	A small gland that extends from the ventral surface of the hypothalamus. It is under control of the hypothalamus and releases a number of hormones that stimulate various body functions, sending out hormones that stimulate glands to produce their hormones.
Placenta	An organ found in viviparous female mammals that develops from the chorion and allantois of an egg and nourishes the embryo by growing umbilical vessels to the maternal blood supply inside the uterus.

Placental Mammal	As in the majority of mammals, a system of reproduction and development where the developing embryo implants into the wall of the uterus, wherein the placenta also grows and takes over nourishment duties from the egg. A much larger and more developed baby will emerge after a large degree of development occurs in the uterus.
Placoid Scale	The triangular toothlike scales present only in cartilaginous fish. Analogous to teeth, in that they have a pulp cavity and a layer of dentin-like protein. Collectively, have a sandpaper texture. Used for protection and streamlining.
Planktivore	Typically omnivorous, a marine or aquatic animal that usually filter-feeds on components found in the plankton, such as bacteria, algae, larval animals, copepods, and protozoans.
Planula	The ciliated free-swimming microscopic worm-like juvenile life stage of sponges.
Plastron	The bottom shell of turtles and tortoises. Made of shield-like bone and keratin.
Platyhelminthes (Flatworms)	Phylum of invertebrates that includes flatworms with acoelomate body plan. Most are parasites or scavengers. Its classes include tapeworms, flukes, and planarians.
Platytrochozoans	Lophotrochozoan animals that have soft bodies and tentacled or ciliated mouths at some life stage. They lack toothed chitin jaws. Includes the flatworms and the mollusks.
Plecoptera (Stoneflies)	Order of insects that have algal-feeding aquatic larval stage with two pronged tail fibers. Adults have long folded membranous wings and two long antennae and is short-lived.
Pleural Cavity	The chest cavity in the thorax that contains the heart and lungs (and air sacs in birds). Bounded by ribs. The diaphragm sits at the bottom of this cavity in mammals.
Pleurodira	Suborder of turtles found in the Southern hemisphere known as the side-necked turtles. As opposed to testudines, their snake-necks have 8 vertebrae and do not fully retract.
Pneumatic Cavities	Refers to the spaces in the hollow bones of birds. The shaft of the bones are buttressed, rather than solid, allowing birds to cut weight for flight aerodynamics.
Polychaete (Bristle Worms)	Class of segmented marine worms that have foot-like parapodia bearing setae (bristles) on each segment and biting mouthparts. Similar internal anatomy to earthworms.
Polyp	The sessile vase-like life stage of cnidarians. They have a muscular basal disc that acts like a suction cup to stick them to the bottom. The tentacles point upward and scour the water for food. Corals and anemones, in their familiar forms, are polyp stage animals.
Porifera (Sponges)	The most primitive phyla of animals. They lack true tissues, organs, or a true body cavity. Matrix of protozoan-like cells that live cooperatively in a matrix-like skeleton. Marine filter feeders that can be classified as soft, glass, or calcareous sponges.
Porocyte	Donut-shaped cells that form tube-like openings into the matrix of a sponge, allowing the flow of materials for filter-feeding.
Polyplacophora (Chitons)	Class of mollusks that have a mantle-generated series of 8 overlapping armor-like plates, a suction-cup like mantle girdle, and mantle cavities bearing gills.
Pons	The part of the hindbrain that bridges the thalamus and the medulla oblongata. Responsible for relaying sensory information from the body to the brain and carrying signals from the brain to the spinal cord for motor control
Potassium Channel	A type of ion-channel membrane protein that controls the passage of potassium across a membrane. Located in the membranes of most cells, they play a large role in the proper function of nerves, endocrine gland secretions, and keeping membrane potential.

Predation	Ecological relationship, wherein a heterotrophic larger predator (or pack of predators) kills and consumes the prey organism to derive energy.
Preen Gland	Found in birds and located at the base of the tail, these are large sebaceous glands that secrete oil. When preening, bird grease is spread over the feathers for waterproofing.
Prehensile	Refers to an appendage, usually a tail, that can be controlled for gripping objects.
Premaxillary Bone	Small bones found in front of the maxilla in certain vertebrates. In Ornithischian dinosaurs like triceratops, they formed the triangular beak-like leaf-cutting mouthpart.
Premolar Teeth	Differentiated mammalian teeth that are located between the canines and molars. Only have two cusps. Utilitarian function, capable of chewing and crushing, but also tearing.
Priapulid worm	A group of scalidophoran ecdysozoans that have concentric rings of cuticle and spines around the body. Scavengers that burrow in sand and can grow to banana size.
Primary Consumer	An herbivorous or omnivorous heterotrophic organism that feeds on primary producers, thereby transferring energy to the next trophic level of the food chain.
Primary Producer	An autotrophic organism that occupies a role at the base of the food chain, producing food, whose energy is ultimately distributed to all the consumers of the ecosystem. Photoautotrophs, such as plants and algae, are the most common types of producers.
Primary Productivity	Refers to the amount of photosynthesis per square meter per year. Measured in grams of carbon or kilocalories produced. Determines the size of a food web for an ecosystem.
Primates	Order of mammals that have a large cerebral cortex, thinking ability, binocular vision, and opposable thumbs. Includes apes, monkeys, lemurs, prosimians, and hominids.
Proboscis	In primitive invertebrates, such as priapulid worms and ribbon worms, an extensible and retractable organ that emerges from the head to aid in feeding and digging.
Proboscidea	Order of mammals that includes the three extant elephant species. Features include trunk with 100,000 muscles for manipulation of objects, tusks, fermentative gut, herding.
Proglottids	The segments of a tapeworm, that functionally can fragment and create a new tapeworm clone. Each segment has a pair of ovaries and testes and feeds by diffusion.
Propodium	A body segment that results from the fusion of the thorax and abdomen.
Prosoma	Another name for the cephalothorax of many invertebrates. Head and chest are fused.
Prostate Gland	Gland found in male mammals that creates the components of semen that keeps sperm nourished and protected en route to egg. Found only in mammals. Non-mammals have tube-like seminal vesicles instead.
Proteoglycans	Group of proteins used as 'packing foam' in between cells and in connective tissue. Rich in hydrophobic amino acids cross-linked to carbohydrate side chains.
Protocanthopterygii	One of the two infraclasses of teleost fish. Characteristics include numerous vertebrae, arc-shaped bones under pectoral fins, adipose fins, and glossal teeth. Includes smelts, pike, salmonids, and galaxiformes. Considered to be more primitive than neoteleosts.
Protonephridia	Primitive kidney-like organs that filter nitrogenous wastes in rotifers.
Protostome	Group of animals whose embryos develop mouth first from the opening of the gastrula. Includes most groups of invertebrates other than echinoderms.

Proventriculus	Stomach-like compartment in the gut of birds that secretes digestive enzymes and pushes food with peristalsis. It regulates passage of food into the gizzard for grinding.
Pseudocoelomate	Animal body design where the organs derived from the endoderm (guts, gonads) float freely in a space (pseudocoelom) inside the mesoderm (muscle layer). Allows 360 movement at the expense of vulnerability to damage.
Pseudoscorpiones	Order of arthropods that includes the pseudoscorpions. They have modified pincer-like pedipalps like a true scorpion, but lack a stinging tail and are capable of spinning webs.
Psittaciformes	Order of birds that includes parakeets, parrots, lorikeets, macaws. Muscular curved bill for cracking seeds and scooping fruit, bright plumage, zygodactyl feet, intelligent.
Pterobranch	Members of the phylum hemichordata that resemble colonies of filter-feeding worms. Benthic marine invertebrates that resemble acorn worms in anatomy.
Pterosaur	Order of extinct reptiles that included pterodactyls and others. Characteristics included winged flight, endothermy, fusions in spine and shoulder blades, and hollow bones.
Pubis	Pair of U-shaped bones at the bottom of the pelvic girdle that fuses with the ischium and ileum to form the pelvic girdle in most vertebrates other than fish.
Pulmonary Artery	The only artery in vertebrates that carries deoxygenated blood. It emerges from the right atrium and pumps deoxygenated blood into the respiratory surfaces of the lungs.
Pulmonary Vein	Large vein that returns oxygenated blood to the heart from the lungs in vertebrates with separate somatic and pulmonary loops. Empties into the left atrium for redistribution.
Pulp Cavity	Center living part of a mammalian tooth that contains blood supply, innervation, immune cells, and specialized cells that secrete the proteinaceous dentin layer above.
Pulmonary Blood Vessels	Refers to vasculature that routes to the lungs or gills from the heart. The circulatory loop that carries deoxygenated blood out and returns oxygenated blood into the heart.
Pyloric Cecae	Blind-ended pouches that branch from the stomach of many fish, increasing digestive surface area. Especially prominent in herbaceous and omnivorous fish like catfish.
Pyloric Gland	In tunicates, a gland that secretes digestive enzymes into the stomach.
Pyloric Sphincter	Ring of involuntary smooth muscle that regulates the passage of stomach contents into the duodenum. Triggered by lowering pH of stomach contents.
Pyloric Stomach	In echinoderms, digestive canals that extend into each body segment that branch off of the cardiac stomach in the middle of the body.
Quadrate Bone	Lateral skull bone found in most vertebrates. Forms part of the operculum in fish, skull crest in many amphibians and reptiles, and articulation points to spine in many others.
Queen	Reproductive female individuals in Hymenopteran colonies. Capable of hormonally controlling the sex and type of their offspring. Usually much larger and longer-lived than the other members of their colonies. Must replace themselves for hive to continue.
R-Strategist	An organism that attempts to maximize its reproductive rate to produce as many offspring as possible. Typically have short lifespans, low or no parental care, and very low juvenile survival rates. Examples include weeds, insects, fungal spores, larval fish.
Radial Cleavage	Developmental pattern of deuterostome embryos. Cells divide in such a way that they align vertically, allowing single embryo to split into clones and produce multiple births.

Radial Symmetry	An organism, especially an animal, that can be divided in multiple planes like slices of pizza, to form equal halves. Common in diploblastic animals (jellyfish).
Radius	Smaller interior bone of the forearm that articulates at the wrist below the metacarpals and at the elbow. Used for lifting in bipeds and running and jumping in quadrupeds.
Radula	The scraping keratinized tooth-like mouth parts of gastropods (snails) that are used to rasp food sources, such as algae, off of surfaces. Envenomated in some snails.
Ram Ventilation	The respiratory technique used by fishes with open gills, such as sharks, wherein the mouth is opened and a flow of moving water is forced over the gill arches.
Ray	The vertical bony or cartilaginous support structures that allow the fins of members of the Actinopterygii to be extended or folded during swimming.
Recessive Gene	In diploid organisms, must be present in two copies to be expressed in the physical phenotype. Usually the result of a mutation that destroyed the function of the wild type dominant gene. Example: white flowers (ww) don't produce pigments.
Rectal Gland	A gland located near the cloacal opening of members of class Chondrichthyes. Used in osmoregulation, it consists of filtration tubules that collect and secrete a hyper-concentrated solution of salt back into the water.
Rectum	The final segment of the large intestine, an extension of the sigmoid colon, which collects waste, extracts excess water, and sends nerve signals to the sphincter to evacuate when there is sufficient pressure on the walls.
Reflex Arc	A common afferent and efferent spinal nerve that integrate their signal and response at a spinal ganglion, bypassing the need for processing in the brain and allowing a very fast response to a critical stimulus. Example: tail flick in lobsters, pulling hand off of stove.
Renal Blood Vessels	The hepatic artery that carries oxygenated blood into the kidney, the hepatic vein that removes deoxygenated blood from the kidney, and all associated minor kidney vessels.
Reptilia (Reptiles)	Class of vertebrates that includes anapsid turtles and diapsid lizards, snakes, crocodilians, and amphisbaeneans. Characterized by scaly skin, ectothermic metabolism, heart partially or fully divided by septum, lung alveoli, and production of uric acid waste.
Respiratory System	System used for exchanging gases with environment. Respiratory organs combine epithelial and circulatory systems. Complexity and size depend on size of animal and degree of evolutionary advancement. Typically gills or lungs are present.
Reproductive System	Body system responsible for producing eggs or sperm via meiotic division in the ovaries or testes, producing hormones that coordinate the development of offspring and secondary sex characteristics, for the maturation process of gametes (such as ovulation of eggs) and, in some cases, for housing and/or nourishing the developing embryo.
Rete Mirabile	In fish, a complex network of blood vessels that regulate blood gas levels and adjust the level of inflation in the swim bladder to allow vertical changes of position in the water. Also regulates the passage of nutrients between efferent and afferent blood vessels.
Reticulum	The second chamber in the stomach of ruminants, it is basically a filtration system, sending small food particles on to the omasum for finer digestion, rejecting undigested larger particles, and trapping non-food items for later regurgitation.
Retina	Layer of pigmented photoreceptor cells and afferent bipolar and ganglion cells at the back of the eye that are sensitive to photon energy, passing on neurochemical signals to the brain through the optic nerve. Photoreceptors pass the signal to bipolar cells that send signals to the ganglion cells that stimulate the axons of the optic nerve.

Retractable Claws	Found only in members of Family Felidae (cats) and some members of Family Viveridae (civets and genets), the nail bed of the claw is rooted on the third toe bone. When the second toe bone is moved by a flexor tendon, a ligament pushes the third toe forward and extends the claw. When relaxed, the claw is retracted.
Retractor Muscle	In priapulid worms, the muscles that extend and retract the proboscis organ.
Rheiformes	Order of flightless birds that includes rheas. Show convergent evolution with similarity to ostriches.
Rhynocephalia	Order of reptiles whose only extant member is tuataras and other extinct species. Unique features include slower metabolism and lower body temperature than other reptiles, prominent third eye, spiny crest down back, skeletal features that fall somewhere between lizards and dinosaurs.
Rhyncocoel	A false body cavity found in ribbon worms that houses the extensible proboscis organ. Like flatworms, the rest of the organs are compressed in an acoelomate body plan.
Ricinulae (Tick Spiders)	Order of arachnids that can lock their abdomen and thorax together, have early instars with only six legs, and have more anatomical similarities to mites than true spiders.
Ring Canals	Found in jellyfish and echinoderms, fluids are pushed through these tube-like structures to move and change body shape. Anatomy is coincidental product of convergent evolution and different in origin. Tube-like in echinoderms and circular in jellyfish.
Rodentia	Largest order of mammals that includes rodents, such as rats, mice, squirrels, beavers, capybaras, agoutis, dormice, groundhogs, marmots, and others. Features include cheek pouches, continuously growing incisors, opposable thumbs in many, furry body.
Rods	Sensitive photoreceptor cells in the retina that have their primary function in nocturnal vision and peripheral vision. They detect black and white and are many times more sensitive than the cone cells associated with color vision.
Rotifera (Rotifers)	Phylum of lophotrochozoan invertebrates that are members of the plankton. Bodies are vase-shaped. They filter feed by whipping a ring of cilia around the head to draw in algae. Complex digestive and circulatory systems for tiny animal.
Rostrum	Horn-like appendage found between the antennae or in front of the head in various invertebrates, especially crustaceans. Used primarily as defense against predators.
Rumen	The front stomach compartment of a ruminant. Gigantic in size, it is involved in crude digestion of large food particles, acting as a fermentative vat. Cud is regurgitated from the rumen, allowing grass and herbaceous plants to be chewed again for surface area.
Ruminant	Members of the Order Artiodactyla (cattle, sheep, pigs, deer, etc.) that have a stomach divided into the rumen, omasum, abomasum, and reticulum, each with different roles in the process of fermentative digestion, which is aided by symbiotic gut flora.
Sacrum	Last segment of the vertebral column that is comprised of several vertebrae that undergo calcification and fuse together to support the spine. In many animals, the posterior surface articulates to the bones of the tail.
Sauropsid	The ancestral group of reptiles that diverged in a different direction than Synapsids, to which all modern reptiles belong. By comparison, they have thinner skin, simpler scale structure, no palate in the roof of the mouth, and lack mammary glands or viviparity.
Salivary Gland	Glands connected to the buccal cavity that secrete digestive enzymes that aid in the first steps of food breakdown and digestion. May also secrete venom or anticoagulants.

Sarcopterygii (Fleshy Finned Fish)	Class of bony fish that includes mostly extinct members, coelocanths, and lungfish. Pelvic and pectoral fins are fleshy, with ulna, radius, and carpals extending into the body of fins.
Sauria	Clade of Neodiapsid reptiles that includes dinosaurs and all modern reptiles. Skeletal commonalities, such as position of nares and skull bones and the orientation of the ribs.
Saurischian Dinosaur	Refers to dinosaurs with pelvic girdles angled and shaped for quadrupedal locomotion, like that of modern crocodilians and lizards. Examples include stegosaurus, diplodocus
Scale	A bony and/or keratinized outgrowth of the integument that emerge from follicles in the epidermis in reptiles, birds, and mammals, but grow from the dermis in fish. Primarily protective in function, bird feathers and mammalian hair are modified scales.
Scalidophora	Branch of ecdysozoan classification which includes kinorynchs and priapulid worms. Characterized by spines and cuticle that grows in concentric rings around the body.
Scapula	The shoulder blade bone that articulates with the humerus in a ball-and-socket joint and in a synovial joint with the clavicle. Protects upper rib cage, lungs, and heart.
Scolex	Grappling-hook shaped modified front segment of tapeworms that allows them to anchor themselves to the wall of the small intestine, where they absorb nutrients.
Scorpiones (True Scorpions)	Order of arachnids that have venom glands at top of stinging telson at end of abdomen, gigantic claw-like pedipalps, book lungs, and cerebral ganglion in middle of thorax.
Scrotum	In most mammals, the scrotum is a sac of skin that houses the testes outside of the body cavity, keeping them at the lower temperature required for sperm development.
Scute	A bony protective plate or scale that covers an epidermal surface. Example: dorsal scutes in sturgeon and snapping turtles.
Scyphozoa (Jellyfish)	Class of cnidarians that includes the true jellyfish, which spend the majority of their lives in the medusa stage as opportunistic predators in the pelagic zone of the ocean.
Scyphistoma	Juvenile polyp stage in jellyfish. Develops from the embryo in the water column and swims to the bottom, implanting itself to divide and begin a strobilus.
Segmentation	Appears in animals that have distinctly different sections of that develop according to homeotic genes. Advanced invertebrates and chordates typically have distinct head, thorax, and abdomens. Segments may be fused or sub-divided in many animals.
Semelparous	Refers to animals that breed once in their lifetime, usually consuming so many resources that it leads to their death. Examples include mayflies, many spiders, Pacific salmon.
Sequential Hermaphrodite	Organisms that start out life as one sex and hormonally change to the other (example male to female clownfish), due to various environmental cues and genetic controls.
Seminiferous Tubules	Tunnel-like ducts that carry sperm cells from their origin in the lining of the testes to the ejaculatory duct or penis for exit during fertilization.
Secondary Sex Characteristics	Body morphologies that vary between genders of a species that are designed to attract the opposite sex as a show of genetic fitness.
Separate Sexes	Species that have separate male and female genders with only one type o f reproductive tract and gamete formation per organism. Typically determined by sex chromosomes.

Septum	Muscular wall of the heart that divides the pulmonary loop from the somatic loop between the right and left ventricles. Partially present in reptilian 3-chambered hearts and fully formed in crocodilians, birds, and mammals to accommodate size, endothermy.
Sequential Hermaphrodite	The process of hormonally changing sexes during their lifetime, due to hormonal changes and environmental cues.
Serpentes	Suborder of diapsid reptiles that includes the snakes. Characterized by de-evolution of the limbs, vestigial left lung, elongated right lung, consecutive kidneys, and molting.
Sessile	Refers to (usually) a marine bottom-dwelling animal that remains motionless or moves only while rooted in place. Sessile animals rely on filter-feeding or ambush to meet their nutritional needs. Examples include barnacles, oysters, sponges.
Sessilia (Acorn Barnacles)	Order of filter-feeding sessile crustaceans. Use cement glands to glue themselves to a surface. Devolved gills and heart, as oxygen diffuses into their body with current. Use modified legs called cirri to trap plankton. Six armored plates protect the animal.
Setae	In segmented worms, the set of keratinized bristles that extend from the epithelium of the ventral surface. Primarily used for gripping and locomotion in most annelids, may be envenomated in marine bristle worm polychaetes.
Sexual Dimorphism	The common tendency among many animal species, for the two sexes to have distinctly different appearances. This may be due to sexual selection or biological functionality.
Sex Pheromones	Hormonal compounds generated by members of the opposite sex that can trigger receptors in cells of potential mates of same species and modify their behaviors.
Sexual Dimorphism	The biological phenomenon, in which members of the opposite sex have distinctly different anatomical features and organs. Secondary sexual characteristics common.
Sexual Reproduction	Reproductive strategy that involves combining randomly shuffled sets of chromosomes in the gametes (sperm and eggs) of two parental organisms, generating new combinations of traits that aid in genetic diversity and evolution of the species.
Sexual Selection	During the process of competition for mates, the opposite sex (usually females) decides on the suitability of the genes of a suitor, leading to long-term evolutionary changes. Example: female peacocks mate with males with the largest, brightest plumage.
Siphon	In mollusks, tube-shaped muscular organs that create water flow via efferent suction and afferent expulsion. Bivalves have incurrent and excurrent siphons, while cephalopods can reverse water flow in-and-out during jet propulsion.
Siphon Retractor Muscles	In cephalopods, the set of long longitudinal muscles responsible for flexing and relaxing the siphon during jet propulsion swimming.
Siphonoptera (Fleas)	Order of insects known as fleas. Biting mouthparts for blood-feeding, hinged powerful back legs that allow jumping distances of many body lengths. Notorious disease vectors.
Sipunculata (Peanut Worms)	Phylum of protostome lophotrochozoan worms that are unsegmented and characterized by a distensible proboscis that is used to gather food. Mouth is tentacled.
Sirenia	Order of mammals that includes manatees, dugongs, sea cows. Pelvic girdle vestigial, front limbs modified into flippers, fermentative digestive tract, bristles around mouth.
Small Intestine	Primary digestive organ that absorbs monosaccharides, amino acids, fatty acids, nucleotides, and other nutrients into the bloodstream in the adjoining mesentery and lacteal vessels. Consists of the duodenum, jejunum, and ileum segments.

Socketed Teeth	Teeth that are rooted in openings in the mandibular and maxillary bones of the jaw. Only mammals and crocodilians have teeth where the pulp cavity enters the bone.
Sodium Channel	A type of ion-channel membrane protein that maintains sodium levels and adjusts membrane potentials in numerous cells. Critical to proper nerve function, they open to allow the membrane to depolarize, sending an action potential.
Solfugidae (Camel Spiders)	Order of arachnids also known as Solfugids, characterized by large size, enormous biting pedipalps, straw-like pharynx, and adhesive glands. Camel spiders lack webs or venom.
Somite(s)	In vertebrate embryos, a series of segmented chevron-shaped tissues that give rise to abdominal muscles, vertebrae, ribs, and other tissues. Fish retain this segmented appearance in the lateral muscles of the abdomen.
Sperm Ducts	Openings in male animals that provide a means of exit for semen carrying sperm cells.
Spermatogenesis	The process of sperm production in the testes of male animals via meiosis.
Spermathecae	An organ found in many female arthropods that takes in, stores, and maintains sperm after mating, until it time-releases for fertilization when right environmental cues arrive.
Spermatophore	Sealed packets of sperm that are transferred from males to females in many invertebrates, such as arachnids. The female can then delay becoming gravid until she releases the sperm when the right conditions for offspring arise.
Sphenisciformes	Order of birds that includes penguins. Front limbs modified into flippers, webbed feet, blubber, oily feathers, rapid swimming and diving, shared nesting duties with male incubating eggs on feet.
Spinal Nerves	In humans, 31 paired nerves that are rooted in the spinal cord. The efferent ventral roots carry signals to organs and muscles from the brain, while the afferent dorsal roots relay information back to the nerve bodies in the spinal cord and on to the brain.
Spinnerets	Organs located in the abdomen of spiders, pseudoscorpions, and some mites that produce silk and extrude it into webs.
Spiracles	Openings in the body of invertebrates that lead to the respiratory tract. Often found on the abdominal segment. For instance, insects have spiracles that open to tracheal tubes.
Spiral Cleavage	Pattern of embryo development found in protostomes. Cells divide in such a way that they do not align vertically, making it impossible for an embryo to split into twins.
Spiral Valve	Found in the intestine of sharks and other cartilaginous fish, a corkscrew-shaped set of epithelial folds that increase the surface area for digestion, as opposed to the coiled intestinal design of more advanced vertebrates.
Spleen	Organ located on the left lateral side of vertebrates under the ribs. Has multiple immune functions, including production of B and T lymphocytes, filtration of cellular debris, removal of damaged and aging red blood cells, and multiple other immune functions.
Spongin	Soft protein used as the matrix housing amoebocytes in members of Demospongae.
Squamata	Order of reptiles that includes snakes, lizards, and amphisbaeneans. Traits include presence of hemipenes in males, shedding of skin, partially divided 3-chambered heart.
Stapes	The stirrup bone of the inner ear. In amphibians, it strikes the eardrum and amplifies vibrations, allowing sensitivity to quieter sounds. Evolved in amphibians.

Statocyst	Cells or organs that are used by many primitive invertebrates to keep their orientation and balance. Usually contain some sort of crystal or mineral deposit that contacts ciliated nerves that fire on contact, allowing animal to respond to stimulus.
Stem Cell	Animal cell that has not yet been fated to become any specific
Stereom	In echinoderms (such as sea urchins), a mesh-like protein matrix that runs throughout the integument and holds the spiny calcified ossicles in place on the surface of the skin.
Sternal Plates	Chitin exoskeletal plates that protect the ventral surface of certain insects.
Sternum	The breastbone where the ribs and clavicles articulate. Protects the heart and lung from damage and helps to form the front wall of the thoracic cavity.
Sterocecal Pouch	An organ found in arachnids that extracts excess water from waste, before moving it out.
Stigmata	Openings in the pharyngeal baskets of tunicates that allow a water flow carrying particles to enter the pharynx for filter feeding.
Stomach	Anterior digestive pouch after the esophagus, crop, or gizzard in animals with differentiated digestive organs. In vertebrates, it is involved in crude digestion, wherein acid, pepsin, and peristalsis break up the food bolus and increase its surface area.
Stomatopoda (Mantis Shrimp)	Order of crustaceans that have hinged front claws that can be snapped at supersonic speed to stab or stun prey. Have powerful photoreceptors in compound eyes. Fluted telson and uropods with large swimmerets on abdomen for rapid backward swimming.
Stomochord	In acorn worms, a hollow pouch derived from the gut that acts as a support rod for the body. Acorn worms are not true chordates because a true notochord is cartilage.
Strigiformes	Order of birds that includes owls. Features include nocturnal binocular vision, fixed eyes, panoramic neck rotation, talons on zygodactyl feet, thick insulator feathers, carnivorous diet.
Strobili (Cnidarians)	Structure that is characteristic of the juvenile life stage of jellyfish. A tree-like stack of polyps divides mitotically, developing as they move toward the tips of each branch.
Struthioniformes	Order of flightless birds that includes ostriches. Wings are used in running, but flightless. Bones solid, largest egg in animal kingdom, long neck for seeing over savanna, thick black or gray feathers.
Stylet	Straw-like mouth used by tardigrades (water bears) for feeding on plant juices.
Subradulary Organ	Found in gastropod mollusks, it is a chemosensory organ located inside the radula that functions like a tongue, tasting and smelling surfaces in the hunt for food.
Suspension Feeder	Refers to animals that feed on food particles suspended in the water. Inclusive of all filter feeders (whales, sponges, whale sharks, etc.), but also refers to zooplankton who feed directly on algae and food particles that are suspended alongside them.
Sweat Glands	Numerous small exocrine glands found in the integument that secrete water to the skin's surface for thermoregulation via evaporative cooling. Eocrine sweat glands are found on all skin surfaces, while apocrine sweat gland ducts are located in hair follicles.
Swim Bladder	In most bony fish, this organ fills with gases from the blood supplied by the rete mirabile and provides buoyancy and flotation. Later evolved into lung in amphibians.
Swimmerets	Paired leg-like biramous appendages found on each segment of the abdomen in many crustaceans. Used for swimming, holding onto surfaces. Often, the front pair are sexually dimorphic, as males have a rigid front pair used in transfer of sperm to female.

Symbiont	Refers to a symbiotic organism (usually mutualistic) that lives in or one a host.
Symmetry	Refers to the shape of an animal's body plan. Asymmetry, radial symmetry, and bilateral symmetry are the three possibilities. See these definitions for more on each.
Synapsid	Ancient class of reptiles that had a single set of skull openings for muscle articulations, other than the eye sockets. Included extinct therapsids and others. Mammals evolved from this group of reptiles and are the only living representatives.
Syrinx	The lower part of the larynx in birds, it is positioned in the chest cavity above the lungs. It connects to the tracheal tube and amplifies sound vibrations into distinctive calls.
Systemic Heart	In cephalopods, it is located centrally between the gill hearts in the center of the body cavity. Pumps oxygenated blood to organs through ascending and descending aortas.
T-Cell	Manufactured by the thymus, these lymphocytes have antibodies on their surface that target the antigens of invaders. Cytotoxic T-cells release compounds that destroy infected cells, while Helper T-cells send attack signals to other immune cells .
Tapetum Lucidum	The reflective inner membrane inside the eye that spans the surface between the lens and the retina. Especially prominent in nocturnal animals, it aids in vision in darkness.
Tardigrade (Water Bears)	Phylum of primitive ecdysozoans with segmented bodies, cuticle around body, and spiny foot-like appendages. Pseudocoelomates. Feed on plant juices with straw-like mouth.
Tarsal	The assemblage of bones that form that top of the foot, the ankle, and the heel in terrestrial vertebrates. Divergent evolution has rendered very different shapes and dimensions, concomitant with the ecological niche and function of the limb.
Teleost	The largest infraclass of ray-finned fishes, it includes all classes of bony fish that can fully move their upper and lower jaws, have an operculum, a full bone skeleton, and symmetrical tail fins. Most (but not all) also have a swim bladder.
Telson	A central tail segment that is used as a rudder and flipper in many marine and aquatic invertebrates (crawfish, lobsters, horseshoe crabs, etc.)
Temporalis	Large sheet-like muscle that articulates to the skull above the ear (on the surface of the temporal bone). Assists in chewing motion by controlling movement of the mandible.
Tensor Brevis	In birds, a large muscle in the front of the wing that articulates to the scapula, helping to control the flapping of the wings at the pivot point between the wings and torso.
Tensor Posterius	In birds, a muscle that connects the wing to the torso on the back lateral surface, keeping the wing rigidly flexed during flight.
Tentacles	Projection-like tissues or organs that are usually numerous and lengthy. Some tentacles are simple tissues that extend off of the epithelium (cnidarians), while others are complex modified organs with multiple tissues (cephalods).
Testudines (Turtles)	Order of reptiles that includes tortoises and turtles. Characterized by anapsid skull, carapace and plastron (upper and lower shells), clawed paddle-like feet, cloaca.
Tetraploid	An organism that has 4 copies of each chromosome per cell nucleus, retaining all chromosomes back to its grandparents. Much more common in plants, it does occur in some animals, such as tree frogs. During meiosis I, cells are tetraploid for a short time.
Tetrapod	Any terrestrial vertebrate animal that walks on four legs.

Urodela (Salamanders)	Order of amphibians that includes salamanders and newts. Characterized by tailed lizard-like quadrupedal bodies, large mouths, tube-shaped or absent lungs, moist skin.
Urogenital Organs	Organs that serve the dual purpose of allowing the exit of nitrogenous wastes from the excretory system and the entry or exit of gametes (sperm or eggs) for reproduction.
Uropods	Lateral tail segments used as swimming flippers in many types of crustaceans.
Uterus	Muscular female reproductive organ that provides protection for developing embryos. In ovoviviparous animals, it provides a place of refuge for live young. In viviparous animals, the embryo embeds into the placenta in the uterus during pregnancy.
Uterine Horns	Y-shaped dual lateral pouches that occur prominently in most vertebrates, allowing implantation from fertilized embryos on both sides. Reduced in primates like humans.
Tardigrades (Water Bears)	Phylum of pseudocoelomate invertebrates that bear similarities to arthropods in their segmentation and digestive systems. Microscopic in size. Feed on plant juices with a straw-like mouth called a stylet. Clawed appendages. Can go dormant for decades.
Trophoblast	The side of a developing embryo that is not fated to become the organism. It stores nutrients and contains the yolk sac and helps the embryoblast grow.
Uric Acid	Solid white paste produced by the excretory system of birds and reptiles. Alternative to soluble ammonia or urea allows water conservation in reptiles and flight in birds.
Vagina	Female genital opening that receives the penis during copulation. Lined with epithelial tissue, it terminates at the cervix, the entry to the uterus.
Vas Deferens	A tube that extends from the epididymis on the surface of the testes and into the sperm ducts or urethra and penis, providing a pathway for sperm to exit for reproduction.
Vein	Blood vessels that carry blood n the afferent direction away from the heart. Valves to prevent backflow. Have thinner layers of smooth muscle, as compared to arteries.
Veliger Larvae	The second juvenile stage of snails and bivalves. Have a foot-like organ used to swim called a velum, along with two shell-like lobes that are ciliated for movement.
Vena Cava	The largest afferent vein in the body of vertebrates. Carries deoxygenated blood back from body tissues and empties into the
Venom	Any of hundreds of different toxic compounds, such as hemotoxins or neurotoxins that are used for predation or defense by the bearer. Venoms are delivered directly into the bloodstream of the victim by various means, such as bites, stingers, or barbs.
Ventral Nerve Cord	Found in all invertebrates other than sponges and diploblastic animals, it connects the basal ganglion or brain with nerves that branch to organs and muscles of the body. Located on the belly, since most invertebrates have an opposite pattern of development.
Ventricle(s) of Brain	Four distinct fluid-filled sacs in the brain that develop from the neural tube. They secrete cerebrospinal fluid to keep the brain cushioned from impacts.
Ventricle(s) of Heart	The lower pumping chambers of the heart that have thick muscular walls and chordae tendinae. In fish, amphibians, and most reptiles, there is a single ventricle where blood mixes, while crocodilians, birds, and mammals have a right ventricle that pumps deoxygenated blood to the lungs and the right sends oxygenated blood to the aorta.

Vertebrata (Vertebrates)	Phylum of animals that includes fish, amphibians, reptiles, birds, and mammals. Features include a dorsal nerve cord protected by cartilaginous or bony vertebrae, an advanced nervous system, closed circulation, and accessory digestive organs.
Vertebral Disc	In vertebrates, discs of fibrous cartilage that articulate between each of the vertebrae as shock absorbers and for proper alignment of the spine. Centers are gelatinous.
Vertebral Process	The vertical projections that emerge from vertebral bones. They serve a protective function. Shape depends on location (cervical, thoracic, or lumbar).
Vestigial Structures	Anatomical features that have a bygone purpose and no longer serve a biological function. They are retained from earlier ancestors and have not yet devolved. Examples include wisdom teeth, appendix, leg bones in snakes, dewclaw in dogs.
Visceral Mass	The mass of organs in a mollusk that are surrounded by the mantle membrane. In gastropods, these are laid out in a spiral arrangement, in bivalves, it includes the brain.
Vitelline Membrane	The membrane that surrounds the egg yolk and prevents its disintegration. Nutrients and proteins can diffuse through the membrane for use by the growing embryo.
Vitreous Humor	Matrix of clear protein-rich liquid that fills the interior of the eyeball between the lens and the retina. Helps set the shape of the eye and allows proper focal length.
Viviaparou	Refers to reproductive system utilized mostly by vertebrate mammals, wherein the developing embryo implants itself into uterine wall and is nourished and maintained by the placenta. Increases survival by producing large, well-developed offspring.
Vocalization	The process of using sound to communicate, especially among terrestrial animals. Calls may be differentiated for courtship, territorial behavior, predator calls, care of young.
Vomer	In vertebrates, the vertical nasal bone that divides the nostrils. Highly variable in depth and size, depending on changes for need brought about by divergent evolution.
Walking Legs	Pairs of jointed appendages on the carapace of crustaceans that are used for crawling along the bottom. Gills are rooted at the base, allowing water current to flow with gait.
Water Vascular System	Most commonly seen in starfish and other echinoderms, it is a system of fluid-filled canals that can be hydraulically compressed to move the limbs. Also known as a hydrostatic skeleton, it maintains shape and supports the animal.
Worker	A caste of female Hymenopterans that are functionally sterile. They gather nectar, build hives, care for larvae and the queen, and typically are short-lived.
Xenarthia	Clade of mammals that includes sloths, armadillos, and anteaters. Common anatomical features include a sticky prehensile tongue, reduced dentition, and large claws.
Xiphosura (Horseshoe crabs)	Order of arthropods that includes horseshoe crabs. Characteristics include compound eyes, carapace with rudder-like tail, book gills, mouth in center of ten legs under body.
Yolk Sac	Rich in fat and protein, it is the food supply for a developing embryo.
Zoea	Early planktonic larval stage of many decapod crustaceans, wherein there are exaggerated rostral and dorsal spines on the carapace that keep the larvae afloat.
Zooplankton	Component of plankton that is comprised of heterotrophic larval animals, small invertebrates, protozoans, or larger animals that lack the ability to swim against the currents or tides. Many members feed on phytoplankton and on other members of zooplankton. A major food source for filter-feeding animals.

Zooxanthellae	Dinoflagellate algae that live inside the tissues of many corals symbiotically. In exchange for protection in a sunny area, the algae feed the corals a cut of the sugars they generate from photosynthesis and generate toxins that deter predators.
Zygodactyl	Common anatomical layout of bird's feet, where two toes face forward and two toes face backward, allowing for gripping and perching.
Zygote	A fertilized egg with a full set of genetic plans. Occurs after sperm penetrates egg and the egg begins to divide. First stage of life where most animals are diploid.
Zygomatic Arch	In vertebrates, the bones of the cheeks that articulate with the temporal and parietal bones of the skull. Variable in shape, due to divergent evolution based on needs.

www.ingramcontent.com/pod-product-compliance
Ingram Content Group UK Ltd.
Pitfield, Milton Keynes, MK11 3LW, UK
UKHW050145280726
14058UKWH00006B/844